心理学英語
［精選］文例集

高橋雅治
Masaharu Takahashi
デイビッド・シュワーブ
David W. Shwalb
バーバラ・シュワーブ
Barbara J. Shwalb
◀著▶

朝倉書店

まえがき

　2013年に『心理学のための英語論文の基本表現』という例文集をシュワーブ夫妻とともに出版した（高橋ら，2013）．そこでは，心理学論文でよく使われる410例の基本的な表現を掲載した．本書は，それら410例の表現に865例の表現を追加した拡大版である．

　質の高い英語論文を執筆するためには，英語表現をネイティブに近いレベルまで充実させる必要がある．そこで，まず第1章において，執筆の初心者が英語表現を充実させる方法を解説した．次に，第2章から第9章において，1275例の表現を著者注，要約，序文，方法，結果，考察，表，図という論文のセクションごとにまとめた．また，読者が必要な表現を見つけ出しやすいように，文章パターンを探すための索引をつけた．本書が若手研究者の論文執筆に役立つことを心から願っている．

　最近，自然科学分野における日本の論文出版数の停滞や低下が指摘されている（たとえば，村上と伊神，2017; Springer Nature, 2017）．それでは，人文社会科学の一分野である心理学の論文出版数はどうなっているのだろうか．これを明らかにするために，SCOPUSを用いて心理学のいくつかの研究分野における1970年代から2017年までの論文出版数の推移を調べた．その結果，今回分析したいくつかの分野では日本発の論文（所属機関が日本国内にある著者が1人以上含まれる論文）の出版数が増加傾向にあることが確認された．たとえば，著者の専門である学習心理学の主要な3誌（*Journal of the Experimental Analysis of Behavior, (Animal) Learning & Behavior, Learning and Motivation*）に掲載された日本発の論文について，出版数（3誌の論文数の合計）と占有率（3誌に掲載された全論文数に日本発の論文数が占める割合）を調べたところ，1968–1977年は3篇（占有率は0.24%），1978–1988年は22篇（2.56%），1988–1997年は26篇（3.06%），1998–2007年は32篇（3.34%），2008–2017年は35篇（3.38%）であった．心理学では論文出版数の絶対値が小さいことから，現時点で一般的な結論を導くことは時期尚早かもしれない．しかし，同様の増加傾向は心理学における最高峰の雑誌とされる *Journal of Experimental Psychology* の5誌でも確認できた．したがって，日本の心理学は，海外の知見を受容する段階から，国内の知見を海外に向けて発信する段階に移行しつつあるといえるかもしれない．

　思い起こせば，私が英語で論文を書こうと思い立ったのは院生時代に習った故戸田正直先生に感化されたからであった．戸田先生は若手の育成にとても熱心で，「これからは欧米の後塵を拝してばかりではいけない」ということをよくおっしゃっていた．

当時はその深い意味がよくわからず，知識や技術を生み出す国際競争で遅れをとってはいけない，そのためには独創的な研究をしなければならない，というようなニュアンスで捉えていた．しかし，グローバル化とナショナリズムが交錯する今日の混沌とした世界を見ていると，「後塵を拝さず」という考えはもっと遠いところを見据えていたのではないかと思う．そもそも心理学が属する人文社会科学という研究分野は，知識を作り出すという役割に加えて，人類の幸福につながる多元的な価値や意味を作り出すという役割も合わせ持っている（吉見，2016）．したがって，人文社会科学の分野で日本発の論文が増えるということは，大げさな言い方かもしれないが，あいまいさに耐えつつ長い間平和を維持してきた人々の価値や意味が，混迷するこの世界に少しずつ影響を与え始めることを意味しているように思われる．

　心理学分野における文例集の出版を全面的に支援していただいた朝倉書店に感謝する．本書を，これまでの研究を支えてくれた指導者，同僚，後輩，そして家族に捧げる．特に，自分のことよりも常に家族のことを優先してくれる妻玲子がいなければ，文例集の編纂という長い道のりを歩み切ることはできなかった．ここに感謝の意を表する．

2018 年 11 月
　北彩都ガーデンより冠雪の十勝岳連峰を眺めつつ

高橋　雅治

引用文献

村上昭義, 伊神正貫. (2017). 科学研究のベンチマーキング 2017. *NISTEP RESEARCH MATERIAL*, No.262, 文部科学省科学技術・学術政策研究所. doi: 10.15108/rm262
Springer Nature. (2017). Nature Index 2017 Japan, **543(7646)**, S1–S40.
高橋雅治, デイビッド・シュワーブ, バーバラ・シュワーブ. (2013). 心理学のための英語論文の基本表現. 朝倉書店.
吉見俊哉. (2016).「文系学部廃止」の衝撃. 集英社新書.

まえがき

　本書は，高橋先生との4冊目の共著である．私たちは最初の共著を1998年に出版し，その後も協力して心理学のグローバル化に貢献する努力を続けてきた．今回も本書の執筆に招いていただいたことに感謝する．本書を手に取ったあなたに始まる一人ひとりの読者を手助けすることで，心理学の国際化に寄与できることを心から願っている．

　私たちが日本の心理学に貢献したいと願うようになったのは，1970年代に遡る．その頃出会った日本の心理学者がロール・モデルとなり，日本とアメリカの心理学の間の架け橋になろうという気持ちを私たちに奮い起こさせてくれたのである．初めに，1977年に故祐宗省三先生（Shwalb & Sukemune, 1998）がデイビッドを広島大学大学院のゼミに招いてくれた．祐宗先生の並外れた国際的研究は，広島大学と武庫川女子大学において40年以上にわたり学生の良きお手本となった．私たちの次のロール・モデルは，東京大学と白百合女子大学で教鞭をとられた故東洋先生（Azuma, 2005）であった．東先生は博士論文のための東大訪問を手助けしてくださり，（その後25年務めた）発達心理学研究の英語要約の編集に招いてくださった．東先生は，他者への援助と謙虚さのお手本のような先生であった．また，日本総合愛育研究所におられ，その後青山学院大学の教授になられた故庄司順一先生（B. J. Shwalb, D. W. Shwalb, & Shoji, 1994）は，数名のお子さんの里親を務める臨床心理学者であり，心理学者は重要な研究を出版するだけでなく，個人レベルでも子供たちの人生を改善することができることを教えてくれた．さらに，私たちの30年間の協力者で，千葉大学におられた中澤潤先生（現植草学園大学・植草学園短期大学学長）は，彼の指導者である祐宗先生が示してくれた手本に従い，異なる世代の研究者と地球規模で協力して数多くの英語論文を出版してきた．最後に，中京大学の杉江修治先生（Sugie, Shwalb, & Shwalb, 2006）は，日本各地の数百にのぼる学校で教員の指導者をつとめてきた．彼は毎年日本中の学校を訪問して共同学習を伝授することにより，日本の教育をより人道的なものに変えてきた．

　思えば，私たちは合衆国の先生を手本として，心理学論文を書く方法を学んできた．故ハロルド・スティーブンソン（Harold Stevenson）教授は，忍耐と勤勉が長いキャリアを通して生産性を維持する鍵であることを教えてくれた．彼は，自分が学生や同僚に求めるのと同じ高さの基準を自らの業績に対して課していた．また，ミシガン大学でのバーバラの指導教員であったウィルバート・マッキーチ（Wilbert McKeachie）教授は，自らの卓越した業績よりもむしろまわりの人々を気づかうことにより，私たちに大きな影響を与えた．彼は今年97歳になるが，今でも毎日大学のオフィスに出勤して学生にアドバイスを与えている．さらに，マイケル・ラム（Michael Lamb）教授（D. W. Shwalb, B. J. Shwalb, & Lamb, 2013）は，心理学研究の知見が重要な社会問題の解決に役立つことを教えてくれた．法律が子供たちの人生に与える影響に関する彼の熟達した研究は，多くの国においてより良い家族関係の構築を促進してきた．

最後に，デイビッドのミシガン大学大学院での指導教員であり，現在はカリフォルニア大学アーバイン校の教授であるジャクリーン・エクルズ（Jacquelynne Eccles）教授は，教え子たちへの献身により，学者が生涯のロール・モデルになり得ることを示してくれた．彼女は，自分の業績よりも自分の教え子たちに誇りを持つことを常に切望している．日本と合衆国で出会ったこれら指導者は，学者としてだけではなく，ひとりの高潔な人格者として国際的な遺産を築き上げてきた．

　ここで強調したいのは，私たちの先生もまた「学者は自分よりも他人のことを考える良い人間になれる」という手本を受けついでいることである．私たちもこれらの先生から影響を受けて，仕事を通して恩を返さなければと思うようになった．みなさんも，他者に対するロール・モデルとなるような良き指導者を手本として欲しい．

　最後に，日本の心理学に対する朝倉書店の寄与に感謝する．

　本書を，生涯の最愛の友であり家族に対する愛情のお手本である，田中栄次郎氏とヨシ子夫人，故三宅正也氏と三代子夫人，そしてシュワーブ家にとって天福ともいえる友人である田中家と三宅家の四世代のご家族に捧げる．

2018 年 11 月
南ユタ州シーダー市にて赤色岩の山々を眺めつつ

デイビッド・W・シュワーブ，バーバラ・J・シュワーブ

引用文献

Azuma, H. (2005). Forward. In D. W. Shwalb, J. Nakazawa, & B. J. Shwalb, Eds., *Applied developmental psychology: Theory, practice, and research from Japan* (pp.xi–xvii). Charlotte: Information Age Publishing.

Shwalb, B. J., Shwalb, D. W., & Shoji, J. (1994). Structure and dimensions of maternal perceptions of Japanese infant temperament. *Developmental Psychology*, **30(2)**, 131–141.

Shwalb, D. W., Shwalb, B. J., & Lamb, M. E., Eds. (2013). *Fathers in cultural context*. New York: Routledge.

Shwalb, D. W., & Sukemune, S. (1998). Help seeking in the Japanese college classroom: Developmental, cultural and social-psychological influences. In S. Karabenick Ed., *Strategic help seeking: Implications for knowledge acquisition* (pp.141–170). Hillsdale: Erlbaum.

Sugie, S., Shwalb, D. W., & Shwalb, B. J. (2006). Respect in Japanese childhood, adolescence, and society. *New Directions for Child and Adolescent Development*, **114**, 39–52.

目　　次

1. 本書の使い方 ———————————————————————— 1
   1.1　本書の特徴 ———————————————————————— *1*
   1.2　英語表現を見つけ出す方法 ———————————————— *2*
   1.3　文章パターンの使い方 —————————————————— *3*
   1.4　質の高い英語論文を書くために —————————————— *3*
   　　1.4.1　表現のバリエーション　　*3*
   　　1.4.2　語句の書き換え　　*4*
   　　1.4.3　文章全体の書き換え　　*5*
   1.5　スムーズ・バリエーションとエレガント・バリエーション ——— *9*
   1.6　おわりに ———————————————————————— *10*

2. 著者注（Author Note） ———————————————————— 11
   2.1　所　属 ———————————————————————— *11*
   　　2.1.1　研究実施時の所属　　*11*
   　　2.1.2　所属の変更　　*12*
   2.2　謝　辞 ———————————————————————— *12*
   　　2.2.1　研究費　　*12*
   　　2.2.2　研究協力　　*13*
   　　2.2.3　コメント　　*15*
   2.3　特記事項 ———————————————————————— *16*
   　　2.3.1　イークォル・コントリビューション　　*16*
   　　2.3.2　未公刊論文　　*16*
   　　2.3.3　学会発表　　*17*
   　　2.3.4　利益相反　　*17*
   　　2.3.5　法律の遵守　　*18*
   2.4　連絡先 ———————————————————————— *18*

3. 要約（Abstract） —————————————————————— 19
   3.1　背　景 ———————————————————————— *19*
   3.2　目　的 ———————————————————————— *20*

- 3.3 方　法 ——————————————————— *21*
  - 3.3.1 参加者と心理検査　*21*
  - 3.3.2 実験内容　*22*
  - 3.3.3 メタ分析　*23*
- 3.4 結　果 ——————————————————— *24*
  - 3.4.1 具体的な結果　*24*
  - 3.4.2 結果と意味　*25*
  - 3.4.3 複数研究　*26*
- 3.5 考　察 ——————————————————— *27*
  - 3.5.1 予測・仮説・モデルとの一致　*27*
  - 3.5.2 結果の意味　*28*
  - 3.5.3 総　論　*29*

4. 序文（Introduction） ————————————————— *30*
  - 4.1 研究の背景 ——————————————————— *30*
    - 4.1.1 全体的な動向　*30*
    - 4.1.2 初期の研究　*31*
    - 4.1.3 多くの研究　*32*
    - 4.1.4 研究の増加　*33*
    - 4.1.5 長期にわたる研究　*34*
    - 4.1.6 概念・用語の定義　*35*
    - 4.1.7 先行研究による定義　*36*
    - 4.1.8 症候群・症状・障害の定義　*38*
    - 4.1.9 パラダイム　*39*
    - 4.1.10 アプローチ・取り組み方　*41*
    - 4.1.11 課　題　*42*
    - 4.1.12 測度・尺度　*43*
    - 4.1.13 変　数　*45*
  - 4.2 先行研究の知見 ——————————————————— *46*
    - 4.2.1 単独の知見　*46*
    - 4.2.2 逸話・事例・インタビューによる知見　*49*
    - 4.2.3 共通する知見　*50*
    - 4.2.4 研究グループによる知見　*53*
    - 4.2.5 一貫した知見　*55*
    - 4.2.6 一般的な知見　*56*

4.2.7　証拠・データ　*57*
　　4.2.8　知見の具体的な内容　*59*
　　4.2.9　知見の強調　*62*
　　4.2.10　最近の知見　*63*
　　4.2.11　追加的な知見　*64*
　　4.2.12　矛盾した知見　*66*
 4.3　先行研究の理論的・実践的な帰結 ──────────── *68*
　　4.3.1　示唆・意味　*68*
　　4.3.2　予測の支持　*71*
　　4.3.3　解釈・説明　*72*
　　4.3.4　結論　*74*
 4.4　理論・モデル・仮説 ────────────────── *75*
　　4.4.1　理論　*75*
　　4.4.2　モデル　*78*
　　4.4.3　等式　*80*
　　4.4.4　仮説　*80*
　　4.4.5　仮定　*81*
　　4.4.6　予測　*82*
　　4.4.7　理論・モデル・仮説との一致・不一致　*83*
 4.5　先行研究のトピック ────────────────── *84*
　　4.5.1　先行研究における重要なトピックを述べる　*84*
　　4.5.2　先行研究の中からテーマを絞る　*85*
　　4.5.3　先行研究から導かれる問題　*87*
　　4.5.4　数値データに基づく問題の重要性の指摘　*89*
　　4.5.5　障害の困難さに基づく重要性の強調　*90*
　　4.5.6　自分の意見　*91*
 4.6　先行研究の問題点 ─────────────────── *92*
　　4.6.1　先行研究が少ない　*92*
　　4.6.2　説明の矛盾・争点　*96*
　　4.6.3　先行研究の弱点　*97*
　　4.6.4　展開の必要性　*98*
 4.7　本研究のテーマ・関心・目的 ────────────── *101*
　　4.7.1　テーマ・関心　*101*
　　4.7.2　単独の目的　*102*
　　4.7.3　複数の目的　*107*

    4.7.4　目的と研究内容　*109*
    4.7.5　目的と理由　*110*
    4.7.6　一連実験の目的　*111*
    4.7.7　評論のテーマ・目的　*112*
  4.8　内容の予告 ─────────────────────── *114*
    4.8.1　仮説・予測　*114*
    4.8.2　具体的な内容　*117*
    4.8.3　研究計画の根拠　*119*
    4.8.4　先行研究をヒントにした　*120*
  4.9　一連の実験をつなぐ ─────────────────── *121*
    4.9.1　前の実験をまとめる　*121*
    4.9.2　次の実験につなげる　*122*

5. 方法（Method）──────────────────────── *124*
  5.1　参加者・被験体 ──────────────────── *124*
    5.1.1　学生の参加者　*124*
    5.1.2　社会人の参加者　*126*
    5.1.3　参加者の年齢・性別・男女の割合　*127*
    5.1.4　参加者の教育歴・収入・過去経験　*128*
    5.1.5　参加者の人種　*129*
    5.1.6　参加者の人口統計学的情報の収集　*130*
    5.1.7　募集方法　*131*
    5.1.8　参加者への報酬　*134*
    5.1.9　参加者の参加資格・スクリーニングと除外・参加拒否　*135*
    5.1.10　より大きいサンプルとの関係　*139*
    5.1.11　参加者のグループ分け　*141*
    5.1.12　参加者の匿名性と機密性　*142*
    5.1.13　事例研究の参加者　*142*
    5.1.14　被験体（動物）　*143*
  5.2　装　置 ────────────────────────── *146*
    5.2.1　実験装置　*146*
    5.2.2　コンピュータ　*148*
  5.3　材料・刺激・薬品・課題 ──────────────── *149*
    5.3.1　材　料　*149*
    5.3.2　刺　激　*151*

5.3.3 薬　品　*152*
 5.3.4 課　題　*153*
5.4 教　示 ──────────────────────────── *154*
 5.4.1 教示の内容　*154*
 5.4.2 教示の操作　*156*
 5.4.3 教示の呈示法　*157*
5.5 場　所 ──────────────────────────── *158*
5.6 データ ──────────────────────────── *159*
 5.6.1 反　応　*159*
 5.6.2 観察・報告　*160*
5.7 心理検査 ─────────────────────────── *161*
 5.7.1 内容・目的　*161*
 5.7.2 リッカート法　*166*
 5.7.3 標準化・下位尺度・複合尺度　*168*
 5.7.4 逆転項目　*171*
 5.7.5 試行後質問紙　*172*
 5.7.6 質問項目の具体的な内容　*172*
 5.7.7 テストバッテリー　*173*
 5.7.8 期間・回数・方法　*174*
 5.7.9 妥当性と信頼性　*175*
5.8 研究デザイン ───────────────────────── *178*
 5.8.1 独立変数と従属変数　*178*
 5.8.2 条件の設定　*180*
 5.8.3 デザイン　*181*
 5.8.4 条件への割り当て　*182*
 5.8.5 参加者のマッチング　*183*
5.9 具体的な手続き ──────────────────────── *185*
 5.9.1 先行研究の踏襲　*185*
 5.9.2 一連の研究の手続き　*186*
 5.9.3 研究の実施者　*187*
 5.9.4 キー押し　*187*
 5.9.5 評価テスト　*188*
 5.9.6 小論を書かせる　*189*
 5.9.7 内容分析　*189*
 5.9.8 得　点　*189*

5.9.9　基準の達成　*190*
　　5.9.10　ディブリーフィング（研究後の内容説明）　*190*
5.10　試行・ブロック・セッション ―――――――――――――――― *191*
　　5.10.1　試　行　*191*
　　5.10.2　ブロック　*192*
　　5.10.3　実験段階　*193*
　　5.10.4　セッション　*193*
　　5.10.5　順序の無作為化　*194*
　　5.10.6　カウンターバランス（相殺）　*195*
　　5.10.7　手続きや実験に要した時間　*197*
5.11　予備的研究 ――――――――――――――――――――――― *198*
5.12　観察者による符号化・点数化 ―――――――――――――――― *198*
　　5.12.1　符号化・点数化の方法　*198*
　　5.12.2　信頼性のチェック　*200*
　　5.12.3　評定者間の一致度　*200*
5.13　操作チェック ―――――――――――――――――――――― *201*
5.14　インタビュー ―――――――――――――――――――――― *202*
5.15　ウェブ調査 ――――――――――――――――――――――― *203*
5.16　倫理的ガイドラインの遵守 ――――――――――――――――― *204*
5.17　動物学習 ―――――――――――――――――――――――― *205*
　　5.17.1　訓練手続き　*205*
　　5.17.2　試行とセッション　*207*
5.18　薬物・神経科学 ――――――――――――――――――――― *209*
5.19　データの欠損 ―――――――――――――――――――――― *210*
5.20　統　計 ――――――――――――――――――――――――― *211*
　　5.20.1　記述統計　*211*
　　5.20.2　*t* 検定　*211*
　　5.20.3　相関と回帰　*212*
　　5.20.4　分散分析　*213*
5.21　メタ分析 ―――――――――――――――――――――――― *215*
　　5.21.1　文献検索とデータの抽出　*215*
　　5.21.2　統計量の計算　*216*
5.22　統計ソフトウェア ―――――――――――――――――――― *217*

6. 結果（Results） —— 219

6.1 参加者 —— 219
- 6.1.1 参加者の動向 　*219*
- 6.1.2 参加者の割合 　*220*

6.2 データの分析と結果の傾向 —— 221
- 6.2.1 分析の方針 　*221*
- 6.2.2 計算方法 　*222*
- 6.2.3 外れ値 　*222*
- 6.2.4 データの分割 　*223*
- 6.2.5 平均と標準偏差 　*223*
- 6.2.6 結果の傾向 　*224*
- 6.2.7 操作チェック 　*226*

6.3 統計的解析 —— 227
- 6.3.1 カイ二乗検定 　*227*
- 6.3.2 t 検定 　*228*
- 6.3.3 その他の検定 　*229*
- 6.3.4 有意差の有無 　*229*
- 6.3.5 有意差傾向（$p < .10$） 　*231*
- 6.3.6 分散分析の実施 　*233*
- 6.3.7 多変量分散分析の実施 　*235*
- 6.3.8 分散分析の主効果と交互作用 　*235*
- 6.3.9 多変量分散分析の主効果と交互作用 　*239*
- 6.3.10 分散分析の下位検定 　*240*
- 6.3.11 因子分析（探索的因子分析） 　*242*
- 6.3.12 因子分析（確証的因子分析） 　*244*
- 6.3.13 構造方程式モデリング（共分散構造分析） 　*245*
- 6.3.14 主成分分析 　*248*
- 6.3.15 相関と偏相関 　*248*
- 6.3.16 単回帰分析 　*251*
- 6.3.17 重回帰分析 　*251*
- 6.3.18 階層的重回帰分析 　*251*
- 6.3.19 階層的ロジスティック回帰分析 　*255*
- 6.3.20 媒介分析 　*255*
- 6.3.21 変数の制御 　*256*
- 6.3.22 成長曲線モデル 　*257*

  6.3.23　メタ分析と効果量　*257*
 6.4　表への言及 ──────────────────────── *259*
  6.4.1　人口統計学的なデータの表　*259*
  6.4.2　記述統計の表　*259*
  6.4.3　平均と標準偏差（標準誤差）の表　*260*
  6.4.4　相関係数の表　*261*
  6.4.5　結果の要約の表　*262*
  6.4.6　因子・パス係数・効果分解の表　*262*
  6.4.7　メタ分析の表　*264*
  6.4.8　表から示される結果　*264*
 6.5　図への言及 ──────────────────────── *266*
  6.5.1　グラフの内容　*266*
  6.5.2　図から示される結果　*266*
 6.6　付録への言及 ─────────────────────── *267*

7.　考察（Discussion） ─────────────────────── *268*
 7.1　目的・仮説・内容の再確認 ──────────────────── *268*
  7.1.1　目的の再確認　*268*
  7.1.2　仮説の再確認　*270*
  7.1.3　重要な手続きの再確認　*271*
 7.2　知見の再確認 ─────────────────────── *272*
  7.2.1　おもな知見　*272*
  7.2.2　重要な知見　*273*
  7.2.3　結果のまとめ　*275*
 7.3　仮説や予測との一致・不一致 ──────────────────── *276*
  7.3.1　仮説や予測との一致　*276*
  7.3.2　仮説や予測との不一致　*278*
 7.4　先行研究との一致・不一致 ───────────────────── *279*
  7.4.1　論点の再確認　*279*
  7.4.2　先行研究との一致　*280*
  7.4.3　先行研究の再現　*284*
  7.4.4　先行研究の拡張　*284*
  7.4.5　先行研究との不一致　*285*
 7.5　知見の意味 ──────────────────────── *286*
  7.5.1　示　唆　*286*

　　　　　　　　目　　次

7.5.2　理論的・実践的な帰結　*289*
7.6　知見の説明・原因・理由 ――――――――――――― *293*
　7.6.1　説　明　*293*
　7.6.2　原因・理由　*296*
　7.6.3　推　論　*298*
7.7　知見の重要性・貢献 ――――――――――――― *300*
　7.7.1　重要性　*300*
　7.7.2　貢　献　*301*
7.8　限界・短所・長所 ――――――――――――― *304*
　7.8.1　限界・短所　*304*
　7.8.2　長　所　*307*
7.9　今後の展開の可能性 ――――――――――――― *309*
　7.9.1　追試の必要性　*309*
　7.9.2　今後取り組むべき問題　*310*
　7.9.3　よりよい方法論の示唆　*313*
7.10　要約と結論 ――――――――――――― *316*
　7.10.1　全体の要約　*316*
　7.10.2　知見についての結論　*316*
　7.10.3　仮説・理論についての結論　*318*
　7.10.4　今回の研究の意義についての結論　*319*

8.　表の説明 ――――――――――――― *321*
　8.1　題　名 ――――――――――――― *321*
　8.2　一般注 ――――――――――――― *322*
　　8.2.1　データについての一般注　*322*
　　8.2.2　記号，略語についての一般注　*323*
　　8.2.3　データの見方についての一般注　*324*
　8.3　特定注と確率注 ――――――――――――― *324*
　　8.3.1　一部のデータについての特定注　*324*
　　8.3.2　一般注・特定注・確率注を含む注　*325*

9.　図の説明 ――――――――――――― *327*
　9.1　題　名 ――――――――――――― *327*
　　9.1.1　イラスト，写真の題名　*327*
　　9.1.2　グラフの題名　*329*

9.2 上下，または，左右のパネルの説明 ———————————— *331*
9.3 縦軸と横軸・凡例・略語・再掲の説明 ——————————— *332*

引用文献 ————————————————————————— *335*
索　引 —————————————————————————— *341*

1 本書の使い方

1.1 本書の特徴
1.2 英語表現を見つけ出す方法
1.3 文章パターンの使い方
1.4 質の高い英語論文を書くために
1.5 スムーズ・バリエーションと
　　エレガント・バリエーション
1.6 おわりに

1.1 本書の特徴

　本書は，心理学の論文で使われる1270例余りの英語表現を収録した英語表現集である．編纂にあたっては，実際の執筆に役立つ実践的な英語表現を集めること，および，同じ内容について複数の英語表現を収録することを心がけた．

　実践的な表現を選定するために，以下の方法を用いた．まず，収録すべき表現の概要を決め，それに沿って一流誌に掲載されている心理学論文の中から質の高い表現を選び出した．次に，それらを日本語に翻訳して整理し，論文を構成するセクションごとにまとめた．選定の過程でネイティブの視点から見て修正が必要であると判断された場合には，英語表現の一部を修正した．このような手法により，研究参加者の表現，心理テストの表現，分散分析や構造方程式モデリングの表現など，心理学分野の実践的な英語表現を数多く収録することができたと自負している．

　編纂においては，1つの内容について可能な限り多様な英語表現を集めることを心がけた．たとえば，4.2.1項には，先行研究の知見を述べる表現として evidence, demonstrate, report, reveal, indicate, argument などを用いた12例の表現を掲載した．また，7.4.2項には，「結果が先行研究と一致する」ということを述べる表現として，offer further corroboration of, corroborate, be in line with, be consistent with, correspond with, support などを用いた14例の表現を掲載した．

　このように多様な表現を収録した目的は，原稿のレベル・アップを目指す執筆者を手助けすることである．自分でも経験があることだが，執筆があまり得意ではない段階では，定型的な英語表現をつなぎ合わせただけのぎこちない原稿を投稿してしまうことが多い．実際，若手研究者の書いた論文を審査していると，研究内容は優れてい

るにもかかわらず，表現のバリエーションが貧弱で文章のつながりが不自然な原稿にしばしば出くわす．先行研究の知見を述べるために，"Author (Year) found that ..." という表現を繰り返し使っている原稿などはその一例である．もちろん，議論の正確さを重視する視点から見れば，少数の定型的な表現を多用した原稿になんら問題はない．だが，この例のように過去の知見に言及する表現が毎回決まりきったものである場合，審査者は先行研究についての議論が浅いという印象をもってしまう可能性が高い．なぜならば，先行研究の知見を英語で述べるための英語表現としては，「明確な証拠により例証した」，「それまでわからなかったことを解明した」，「新しいことを主張した」などのように，知見の追加がもつ意味合いを伝えるためのバリエーションが豊富に存在するからである．読者に論旨を正確に伝えるためには，議論の内容に応じてそれらのバリエーションを的確に使いこなす技能が必要となる．

後（1.4.1 項）にも述べるように，表現のバリエーションを充実させることは，質の高い論文を書くための第一歩である．執筆の初心者には，本書を活用して表現のバリエーションを使いこなす技能を身につけてほしい．

1.2　英語表現を見つけ出す方法

本書では，心理学の英語論文でよく使われる表現を内容ごとにまとめ，それらを論文を構成するセクション（著者注，要約，序文，方法，結果，考察，表，図）ごとに分類して示した．たとえば，研究参加者の情報を記述するさまざまな表現を，「年齢や性別の表現」，「募集方法の表現」，「報酬の表現」などのグループごとにまとめ，それらを「方法」のセクションの章に示した．したがって，目次をたどれば，探し求めている表現を見つけ出すことができるだろう．

もちろん，論文のセクションによる分類は絶対的なものではなく，実際の執筆では，たとえば「方法」のセクションで用いる表現を，「結果」のセクションで用いることもよくあることである．したがって，目当ての表現が見当たらない場合には，他のセクションの章も参照するとよい．

また，末尾には，日本語と英語の詳細な索引を設けた．これらの索引に掲載されているページをたどれば，頭に浮かんだ断片的なキーワードから目的の表現にたどり着くこともできるだろう．

なお目次や索引から目的の表現にたどり着いたら，ぜひともその表現の前後にある類似した表現もチェックしてほしい．なぜならば，最初にたどり着いた表現が最も適切であるとは限らないからである．複数の類似した表現が見つかったら，それらの中から適切な表現を選び出す作業が必要となる．そのヒントについては，1.4 節で解説する．

1.3 文章パターンの使い方

本書には，一流誌の論文から抽出した質の高い例文が掲載されている．だが，どんなに質の高い例文であっても，ただ眺めているだけでは，それを応用して独自の文章を書くことは難しい．そこで，本書では，複数の英語表現に共通して含まれる基本的な文章パターンを実際に使われた例文とペアで提示することにした．

文章パターンの表記では，表現すべき内容に応じて変えるべき部分を **X**, **Y**, **Z** などの変数として表した．その際，変数の部分に名詞や名詞句などが入る場合には単一のアルファベット（**X** など）を用い，文章や動詞句などが入る場合には 3 個のアルファベット（**XXX** など）を用いることにした．

たとえば，4.2.7 項には，次のような文章パターンが掲載されている．

Evidence that XXX comes from Y research.

XXX であることの証拠は，Y の研究から得られている．

このパターンでは，Y の部分に先行研究の研究対象を名詞や名詞句で挿入し，XXX の部分に先行研究から得られた知見を文章の形で挿入することができる．たとえば，Y の部分に「運動学習（motor learning）」という名詞句を，XXX の部分に「教示が学習の増強において重要な役割を果たす（instructions play an important role in enhancing learning）」という文章を挿入すれば，以下のような文章を生成することができる．

Evidence that instructions play an important role in enhancing learning comes from motor learning research.

教示が学習の増強において重要な役割を果たすということの証拠は，運動学習の研究から得られている．

文章パターンの運用方法を体得するためには，文章パターンと併記された実際の例文を詳細に見比べて，文章パターンがどのように使われているかを理解するとよい．このようにして文章パターンの使い方をあらかじめしっかりと身につけておき，執筆に際しては常に先行研究で使われていない独自の文章を生成するように心がければ，いわゆる剽窃の問題を回避することができるだろう．

1.4 質の高い英語論文を書くために

1.4.1 表現のバリエーション

質の高い英語論文を書くためには，質の高い英語論文を読むことが重要である．なぜならば，質の高い論文に触れることにより，新しいアイデアを論理的に構築するための思考力，および，構築したアイデアをわかりやすく伝えるための表現力が身につくからである．思考力と表現力はいわば車の両輪であり，どちらが欠けていても優れ

た論文を書くことはできない．

　本書には，一流の論文で使用されている質の高い英語表現が数多く収録されている．したがって，本書をうまく活用すれば，さまざまな表現の使い方を体得し，論文英語の表現力を高めてゆくことができる．実際，英語を第二言語として学ぶ学生を対象とするアカデミック・ライティングの分野では，表現のバリエーションを充実させることが質の高い文章を書くための第一歩であるとされている（Bailey, 2006; Carlock et al., 2010 など）．このことは，心理学にもあてはまる．すなわち，心理学分野の表現を充実させることは，質の高い心理学論文を執筆するための重要な基盤となる．以下では，本書を活用して心理学分野の英語表現を充実させ，体得した多様な表現を適切に使いわけるスキルを身につけるための道筋を示す．

1.4.2　語句の書き換え

　アカデミック・ライティングのトレーニングでは，多様な表現を身につけるための最初のステップとして，文章を構成する語句を同意表現（同意語または同意語に相当する表現）に書き換える方法が推奨されている．

　比較的アカデミックではない文章で使われる語句の場合，書き換えはそれほど難しくない．なぜならば，シソーラスなどで同意表現を見つけることができれば，簡単に書き換えが実行できるからである．だが，心理学で使われる専門的な表現については，残念ながら市販の辞書に同意表現が掲載されていることは少ない．そのため，心理学分野で書き換えを行うためには，個々の表現について同意表現をひとつひとつ身につけておかなければならない．

　たとえば，心理学では，「分散分析の結果からあることが示された」ことを表現するために indicate という動詞を使うことが多い．だが，本書には分散分析の表現が 35 例収録されており（5.20.4 項，および，6.3.6 〜 6.3.10 項），それらの表現を丹念にチェックすれば，分散分析の結果を述べるための動詞としては，indicate 以外にも confirm, find, reveal, show, yield などの同意表現があることがわかる．したがって，たとえば「1 要因の分散分析により有意な差異が見出された」ということを述べる場合，次のような同意表現があるといえる．

　A one-way ANOVA indicated [/confirmed /found /revealed /showed /yielded] significant X.
　1 要因の配置の分散分析は，有意な X を示した [/ 確認した / 見出した / 明らかにした / 表した / もたらした]．

　本書には，これ以外にも，心理学で使われる語句の同意表現が随所に掲載されている．執筆の初心者は，それらを参考にしながら第一稿で用いた語句をより適切な同意表現に書き換える訓練から始めるとよい．

1.4.3 文章全体の書き換え

アカデミック・ライティングにおいて表現のバリエーションを充実させるための第二のステップは，文章全体の書き換えである（Bailey, 2006; Carlock et al., 2010）．前述の語句の書き換えとは異なり，文章全体の書き換えには高い思考力に裏打ちされた高度な技能が要求される．だが，表現を文章レベルで書き換える技能は，（1）全体的なニュアンスを制御することが可能になる，（2）文章のつながりがスムーズで読みやすい段落を書くことが容易になる，（3）修辞的技法を活用した説得力のある議論を構築することが可能になる，などのメリットをもたらしてくれる．以下では，文章全体を適切に書き換える技能を身につける道筋を，これら3つのメリットに沿って解説する．

(1) ニュアンスの制御

文章全体を書き換えると，全体的なニュアンスが大きく変化する．たとえば，4.1.8項には，症候群などを定義する表現として，以下の文章パターンが収録されている（わかりやすさのために一部を簡略化して引用，以下同様）．

①This phenomenon has been called X.

この現象は，Xと呼ばれてきた．

②X is conceptualized as referring to Y.

Xとは，Yのことをさすものとして概念化されている．

③X describes Y.

Xとは，Yのことである．

④X is characterized by Y.

Xは，Yにより特徴づけられる．

⑤X is characterized by Y that may be accompanied by A, B and C.

Xは，A，B，Cを伴うかもしれないYにより特徴づけられる．

⑥X is a[n] Y disorder, characterized by Z.

XはYの障害であり，Zにより特徴づけられる．

⑦The term X has recently been coined in YYY.

Xという用語は，最近，YYYを行う際につくられた．

これらのバリエーションをひとつひとつ身につけることにより，全体的なニュアンスを制御することができるようになる．たとえば，①のようなcallを用いた表現は，単に症候群の名称を述べているだけであり，比較的ニュートラルなニュアンスしかもたない．だが，②や③のようなconceptualizeやdescribeを用いた表現は，症候群の概念化を強調するニュアンスをもった段落を構築する場合に用いることができる．また，④〜⑥に示したcharacterizeを用いた表現は，症候群のある特徴を強調する文脈を展開する場合に役立つ．さらに，対象とする概念が研究者にとって目新しいことを強調する場合には，⑦のようなcoinを用いた表現のほうが，ニュアンスがより的確に伝わる．

このように，実際の執筆では，段落に埋め込まれたときに伝えたいニュアンスが伝わるかどうかを考慮しながら，文章全体の書き換えの可能性を検討するとよい．

(2) スムーズな文章の構築

表現のバリエーションが充実すれば，文章同士がスムーズにつながっている段落を構成することができるようになる．たとえば，growing という表現を使って，「先行研究が増えている」という内容を述べる場合を考えてみよう．4.1.4 項には，先行研究が増加していることを示す以下のような文章パターンが掲載されている．

①A growing body of evidence suggests that XXX.
　XXX であることを示唆する証拠が増えている．
②There is growing evidence that XXX.
　XXX であるという証拠が次第に増えてきている．
③There is a growing body of literature which indicates that XXX.
　XXX ということを示す研究が次第に増えてきている．
④There is a growing interest in X within the Y field, with studies suggesting that ZZZ.
　Y の分野では X に対する興味が高まりつつあり，ZZZ ということを示唆する研究がある．
⑤The growing literature on X focuses on Y.
　X に関する文献は増えており，それらは Y に焦点を当てている．
⑥This growing body of research on X has identified a number of Y factors.
　X に関するこのような研究は増加しており，多くの Y 要因を同定してきた．

これらの中で，①〜④は，段落の最初で「あることを示す研究が増えている」ことを書き始める場合に用いられる表現である．一方，⑤と⑥は，段落内の先行する議論をまとめて「これまでの研究から，さまざまな知見が明らかにされてきている」というような文脈に適した表現である．

①〜④については，先行研究のもたらした科学的な証拠を基盤として現在増加しつつある研究内容についての議論を展開したいなら，evidence を用いた①や②が適切である．また，過去の文献の動向に焦点を当てた議論なら③が，研究者の興味という視点に基づいて議論を組み立てている場合には④を用いるとよい．

一方，⑤と⑥を比べると，増加しつつある先行研究の内容を概観した後で，1 つの要因に議論の的を絞ってゆくような段落で使うなら⑤が，それとは反対に，これから複数の要因に議論を広げてゆく段落で使うなら⑥がよいだろう．

このように，多様な表現を文脈に応じてうまく使いこなすことができれば，スムーズで読み取りやすい文章を構築することが可能となる．

(3) 修辞的技法の活用

修辞的技法（rhetoric）とは，巧みな表現を駆使することにより読者を説得する技法

のことである．科学では論理的な議論が重視されることを考えれば，科学論文に修辞的技法は必要ではないと思われるかもしれない．だが，実際のところ，科学論文では修辞的技法を駆使した巧みな議論がたびたび見受けられる．その一例として，研究の長所と短所について議論する場合を考える．たとえば，7.8.1 項には，自らの研究の限界や短所を述べるための複数の文章パターンが掲載されている．

①This sample of N participants is small and limited with regard to X as well as Y and Z.
N 名の参加者という今回のサンプルは数が少なく，かつ，X，Y，Z の点で限定されたものである．

②We also acknowledge that XXX.
我々は，XXX ということも認めなければならない．

③It is important to note that X and Y were confounded with one another.
X と Y が互いに混同されていることに注意することは重要である．

④The present results may be biased because XXX.
XXX なので，今回の結果には偏りがあるかもしれない．

⑤One limitation of the study was its reliance on X.
本研究の限界の 1 つは，X のみに依存したことであった．

⑥Several limitations to this X study should be noted.
今回の X 研究には，いくつかの限界があることに注意しなければならない．

⑦Several limitations require consideration concerning X.
X に関しては，いくつかの限界について考慮する必要がある．

⑧The current study has obvious limitations, such as X, Y, and Z.
今回の研究には，X，Y，Z のように，明らかな限界がある．

⑨When interpreting the results of X, readers should bear N caveats in mind.
X の結果を解釈する際には，N 個の重要な警告を心に留めておくべきである．

⑩Although the study has several strengths, including X, Y, and Z, it also has several limitations.
この研究は X，Y，Z などのいくつかの長所をもつが，いくつかの限界もある．

⑪Although the findings from this study add to the existing literature on X and Y, a number of limitations deserve mention. First, AAA. In addition, BBB. Third, CCC.
本研究から得られた知見は X と Y に関する既存の文献に寄与するけれども，多くの限界があることは言及に値する．第一に，AAA である．加えて，BBB である．第三に，CCC である．

⑫Because this was an exploratory study, conclusions and implications should be considered in light of its limitations.
今回は探索的な研究であり，結論と意味については，その限界を考慮しながら考察されるべきである．

一流雑誌に掲載された論文に，このように巧みな英語表現が数多く使われている事実に驚かれるかもしれない．だが，実際には，一流雑誌だからこそ修辞的な表現が必要になることが多い．なぜならば，競争の激しい一流雑誌への投稿では，論文が取り扱っているテーマについて著者と同じくらいかそれ以上に造詣の深い審査者を相手に，限られた紙面への掲載をめぐって粘り強い交渉を行わなければならないからである．そのような手持ちの駒を何もかも見通されているような相手との交渉では，研究の長所も短所もすべてオープンにして交渉を進めるほうがよい結果をもたらすことが多い．その一方で，審査者に研究の短所が多いという印象をもたれてしまうと，今度は掲載を拒否される確率が高くなる．いわゆる，バランスの問題である．したがって，原稿の中で自らの研究の長所や短所に触れる場合には，議論の戦略的な構築が重要となる．

　上記の例のどの表現を用いるべきかについては，どのような議論を構築するかにより異なる．たとえば，上記の①〜④は，研究に含まれる問題点を，研究全体の価値判断にまで議論を広げることなく，あくまで結果を解釈するための議論の一部としてさりげなく触れたい場面でよく使われる．

　一方，⑤〜⑨は，limitation や caveat という明示的な表現を使っており，短所を直接的に述べる段落の始まりに適した表現である．当然のことながら，これらの表現を使うにあたっては，報告する成果にかなりの自信があること，および，短所を述べる段落の前に，研究の長所についての主張を十分に積み上げた複数の議論が存在していることが大前提となる．万が一，長所についての議論を先行させずにこれらの表現を使用すると，原稿全体が自虐的に見えてしまう．

　また，⑩〜⑫は，研究設定の問題点や実証的データとしての不明瞭さなどから，研究成果に自信がない場合に適している．そのようなケースでは，「長所も多いけれども短所も多い」というような議論を積み上げつつ，受理の判定にぎりぎりで持ち込むような交渉になるので，⑩や⑪のようなフラットな表現が使いやすい．特に，「あくまで探索的で不備なデータだが，研究者のために掲載して残しておく価値があるのでは」というような低い姿勢で交渉に臨む戦略なら，⑫のような控えめな表現が適している．

　本書には，これ以外にも，先行研究の問題点や矛盾点を厳しく指摘して自らの研究の重要性を強調する場合（4.6節）や，知見の重要性や貢献について述べて論文が掲載に値することを主張する場合（7.7節）に有用な表現などが多数収録されている．当然のことながら，審査者全員が優れていると認めるような研究成果を投稿するのであれば，このような修辞的技法はほとんど必要とされない．だが，問題や限界は多いが後人のために文献として残しておきたいような成果をレベルの高い雑誌に投稿する場合には，修辞的技法を駆使した戦略的な交渉能力が必ずや必要となる．

1.5 スムーズ・バリエーションとエレガント・バリエーション

　これまでに述べてきたように，多様な表現を使い分ける技能を身につけておけば，スムーズで理解しやすい文章を書くことができる．本書では，文章をスムーズに展開するために必要なバリエーションを，「スムーズ・バリエーション（smooth variation）」と呼ぶことにする．

　だが，何ごとも過ぎたるは及ばざるがごとしであり，表現のバリエーションを過度に用いてはならないことに常に留意しなければならない．実際，若手研究者が書いた原稿には，行きすぎたバリエーションがときおり見受けられる．たとえば，「参加者」に言及する場合，最初に participants と表現しておきながら，後に students や men などに言い換えるケースなどである．科学論文では，表現が変われば違う内容を意味すると考えるのが一般的である．したがって，審査者は，これらの異なる表現が異なる参加者に言及しているととらえてしまうかもしれない．また，そのような誤解を免れたとしても，不必要なバリエーションは文脈を読み取りにくくし，審査者にストレスを感じさせることは確かであり，できる限り行わないことが好ましい．

　興味深いことに，英語の文体を研究する英語学の分野においても，過度のバリエーションに対する否定的な考え方が存在する．その最も典型的なものは，Fowler による「エレガント・バリエーション（elegant variation）」の概念であろう．Fowler は，1926 年に出版され現在でも使われ続けている英語用法辞典（Fowler, 2009）において，明瞭性を犠牲にして言い換えに熱中するのは二流の著者（second-rate writer）のすることであり，本人だけが優美と思い込んでいるというニュアンスを込めて，エレガントと皮肉っている（神崎, 2009）．逆に言えば，「曖昧さを回避できるならバリエーションに拘泥するよりも同一表現の反復や代名詞を用いるほうがよい」という考え方である．この考え方は，英語の文体についての議論において現在も主流として生き続けている（Greenbaum & Whitcut, 1988, p. 237; Partridge, 1994, p. 349）．

　ましてや，議論の明瞭性や正確性に重きをおく科学の分野では，「論文では，エレガント・バリエーションを避けるべきである」という認識が広く共有されている．たとえば，心理学や他の分野で用いられている執筆のガイドラインは，以下に示すように不必要なバリエーションを明示的に否定している．

- 「同意語の使用により意図せずに文意が微妙に変わってしまうかもしれない（"by using synonyms you may unintentionally suggest a subtle difference"）」（American Psychological Association, 2010）
- 「明瞭な一貫性のための最も重要なアドバイスは，重要な用語を繰り返して使うことである（"The best advice for clear continuity is to repeat key terms exactly"）」（Zeiger, 2000）

・「科学論文では，意味が明らかな場合のみ同意語を使う("use synonyms only if the meaning is plain")」(Booth, 1975)

したがって，表現のバリエーションを日々充実させると同時に，実際の執筆においては必要とされる最低限のバリエーションにとどめることを勧める．

1.6 おわりに

本章では，質の高い英語論文を書くために表現のバリエーションを充実させる道筋を示し，さらに，不必要なバリエーションは避けるべきであることを指摘した．これら2つのポイントを同時に実現することは，執筆の初心者にとって難度が高いかもしれない．だが，それをバランス良く実現できたときに，原稿は，論点が深く，論旨を読み取りやすく，かつ，説得力のある論文になっているにちがいない．若手研究者の健闘を心から期待している．

引用文献

American Psychological Association. (2010). *Publication manual of the American Psychological Association* (6th ed.). Washington, DC: Author.

Bailey, S. (2006). *Academic writing: A handbook for international students* (2nd ed.). London: Routledge.

Booth, V. (1975). Writing a scientific paper. *Biochemical Society Transaction*, **3(1)**, 1–26.

Carlock, J., Eberhart, M., Horst, J., & Menasche, L. (2010). *The ESL writer's handbook*. Ann Arbor: University of Michigan Press.

Fowler, H. W. (2009). *A dictionary of modern English usage*. Oxford: Oxford University Press.

Greenbaum, S., & Whitcut, J. (1988). *Longman guide to English usage*. London: Longman.

神崎高明. (2009). 小説の中のエレガント・バリエーション：英語の文体研究．商学論究, **57(2)**, 39–53.

Partridge, E. (1994). *Usage and abusage: A guide to good English*. London: Penguin Books.

Zeiger, M. (2000). *Essentials of writing biomedical research papers* (2nd ed.). New York: McGraw-Hill.

2
著者注（Author Note）

2.1　所　　属
2.2　謝　　辞
2.3　特記事項
2.4　連絡先

2.1　所　　属

2.1.1　研究実施時の所属

0001　1人の著者の1つの所属（大学）を述べる．
◆Author, Department, University [, City, Country].
著者，部署，大学 [, 市，国]
　　Robert D. Perkins, Stetson School of Business and Economics, Mercer University.　　(48)
　　（日本語省略）

　　（訳者注：米国外の大学の場合には市と国を記載するとよい）

0002　1人の著者の1つの所属（大学以外）を述べる．
◆Author, Organization, City, State [/Country].
著者，組織，市，州 [/ 国]
　　Neil S. Glickman, Westborough State Hospital, Westborough, Massachusetts.　　(17)
　　（日本語省略）

　　（訳者注：米国内の場合は州，米国外の場合は国を書く）

0003　1人の著者の2つの所属（大学）を述べる．
◆Author, Department, University [, City, Country], and Department, University [, City, Country].
著者，部署，大学 [, 市，国] と部署，大学 [, 市，国]
　　George W. Alpers, Department of Biological Psychology, Clinical Psychology, and Psychotherapy, University of Würzburg, Würzburg, Germany, and Department of Clinical and Biological Psychology, University of Eichstätt, Eichstätt, Germany.　　(1)
　　（日本語省略）

0004　2人の著者の同じ所属（大学）を述べる．
◆Author 1 and Author 2, Department, University [, City, Country].

著者1と著者2，部署，大学 [，市，国]
> Erica Hoy Kennedy and Dorothy M. Fragaszy, Department of Psychology, University of
> Georgia. (34)
> （日本語省略）

0005 3人以上の著者の所属（大学，大学以外，無所属）を述べる．

◆Author 1, Department, University [, City, Country]; Author 2, Organization, City, State [/Country]; Author 3, City, State [/Country].

著者1，部署，大学 [，市，国]（大学の場合）；著者2，組織，市，州 [/ 国]（大学以外の場合）；著者3，市，州 [/ 国]（無所属の場合）．

> Laura D. Kubzansky, Department of Society, Human Development, and Health, Harvard School of Public Health; Laurie T. Martin, the RAND Corporation, Arlington, VA; Stephen L. Buka, Brown University. (38)
> （日本語省略）

2.1.2 所属の変更

0006 現在の所属を述べる．

◆A is currently affiliated with X, City, State [/Country].

Aは，現在，州 [/ 国]，市にあるXに所属している．

> Heidi L. Warner is currently affiliated with Pine Rest Christian Mental Health, Urbandale, Iowa. (61)
> Heidi L. Warnerは，現在，アイオワ州アーバンデール市にあるパイン・レスト・クリスチャン・メンタルヘルスに所属している．

0007 現在の所属を簡潔に述べる．

◆A is now [/currently] at X [, City][, State /Country].

Aは，現在，[市][州 / 国にある] Xに所属している．

> Ashley Nunes is now at CSSI, Inc., Washington, DC. (47)
> Ashley Nunesは，現在，ワシントンD.C.にあるCSSI株式会社に所属している．

2.2 謝　　辞

2.2.1 研究費

0008 助成金による支援を述べる．

◆This research was [partially] supported by Grants [/grants] X from the Y.

この研究は，Yからの助成金Xによって [部分的に] 支援された．

> This research was supported by Grants R01 AG25667 and R01 AG25032 from the National Institute on Aging. (47)
> この研究は，国立加齢研究所からの助成金（R01 AG25667 と R01 AG25032）によって支援された．

0009 助成金による資金提供を述べる．

◆ This research was funded by a grant from the X (grant number).

本研究は，X からの助成金（助成金番号）を受けた．

> This research was funded by a grant from the National Institute of Alcohol Abuse and Alcoholism (NIH/NIAAA R01 AA 012547-06A2). (39)
> 本研究は，国立アルコール虐待アルコール中毒研究所からの助成金（NIH/NIAAA R01 AA 012547-06A2）を受けた．

0010 個人研究者への助成金について述べる．

◆ Funding for A has been provided by a grant from the X.

A は，X からの助成金により援助を受けた．

> Funding for Samuel Hannah has been provided by a grant from the National Sciences and Engineering Council. (24)
> Samuel Hannah は，全米科学技術会議からの助成金により援助を受けた．

2.2.2 研究協力

0011 多大なる助力と援助に感謝する．

◆ We would like to thank A and B of the X, C, and D, for their invaluable assistance and support of this project.

我々は，このプロジェクトにおいて計りしれないほどの援助と支援を頂いた，X の A と B，および，C と D に感謝する．

> We would like to thank Melissa Stephens and Annette Turner of the Missouri Gaming Commission, Kevin Mullally, and Judith C. Baer, for their invaluable assistance and support of this project. (46)
> 我々は，このプロジェクトにおいて計りしれないほどの援助と支援を頂いた，ミズーリ州賭博委員会の Melissa Stephens と Annette Turner，および，Kevin Mullally と Judith C. Baer に感謝する．

0012 原稿の準備における技術的な援助に感謝する．

◆ The author gratefully acknowledges the technical assistance of A in the preparation of this manuscript.

著者は，原稿の準備における A の技術的な援助に感謝の意を表する．

> The author gratefully acknowledges the technical assistance of Peggy M. Plant in the preparation of this manuscript. (30)

| 著者は，原稿の準備における Peggy M. Plant の技術的な援助に感謝の意を表する．

0013　実験の実施における援助，コメント，統計についての助言に感謝する．

◆We are grateful to A for assistance in conducting the experiment[s], to B for helpful comments on the work, and to C for statistical consultation.

我々は，実験の実施における援助を頂いた A，本研究に対する有益なコメントを頂いた B，そして，統計についての助言を頂いた C に感謝の意を表する．

> We are grateful to Mike Kinsella for assistance in conducting the two experiments, to Pavel Zahorik for helpful comments on the work, and to Nancy Collins for statistical consultation. (42)
> 我々は，2 つの実験の実施における援助を頂いた Mike Kinsella，本研究に対する有益なコメントを頂いた Pavel Zahorik，そして，統計についての助言を頂いた Nancy Collins に感謝の意を表する．

0014　データ収集における助力，技術的援助，後方支援に感謝する．

◆Special thanks are due to A and B for their help with data collection, C and D for technical assistance, and E and F for logistical assistance.

データ収集においてご助力を頂いた A と B，技術的な援助を頂いた C と D，後方支援を頂いた E と F に感謝の意を表する．

> Special thanks are due to Andrea Barkauski and Shanquin Yin for their help with data collection, Sharon Yeakel and Henry Zaccak for technical assistance, and Greg Myles and Kathy Fox for logistical assistance. (47)
> データ収集においてご助力を頂いた Andrea Barkauski と Shanquin Yin，技術的な援助を頂いた Sharon Yeakel と Henry Zaccak，後方支援を頂いた Greg Myles と Kathy Fox に感謝の意を表する．

(訳者注：logistical assistance とは，研究の準備や実行のための情報収集，物品の用意，切符の手配などの多岐にわたる後方支援のことである)

0015　データ収集における援助に感謝する．

◆The authors wish to acknowledge A for her [/his] valuable assistance with data collection.

著者らはデータ収集において価値ある援助を頂いた A に感謝の意を表する．

> The authors wish to acknowledge Kelly Kerr for her valuable assistance with data collection. (27)
> 著者らはデータ収集において価値ある援助を頂いた Kelly Kerr に感謝の意を表する．

0016　データの収集，転写，データ分析における援助に感謝する．

◆We express our appreciation to A, B, and C[,] for their assistance with data collection, transcription, and data analysis.

我々は，データ収集，転写，データ分析における援助を頂いた A, B, C に感謝の意

を表する.

> We express our appreciation to Carlos Baguer, Catherine Bitney, Jen Chau, Injae Choi, and Patricia Yoon, for their assistance with data collection, transcription, and data analysis. (8)
> 我々は，データ収集，転写，データ分析における援助を頂いた Carlos Baguer, Catherine Bitney, Jen Chau, Injae Choi, Patricia Yoon に感謝の意を表する.

0017 点数化と信頼性チェックにおける援助に感謝する.

◆We thank A, B, and C for their assistance in scoring X and conducting reliability checks.
我々は，X の点数化と信頼性チェックの実施における援助を頂いた A, B, C に感謝の意を表する.

> We thank Jessica Barr, Erin Ryan, and Andrea Wilson for their assistance in scoring the videotapes and conducting reliability checks. (49)
> 我々は，ビデオテープの点数化と信頼性チェックの実施における援助を頂いた Jessica Barr, Erin Ryan, Andrea Wilson に感謝の意を表する.

2.2.3 コメント

0018 有益なコメントに感謝する.

◆The authors thank A, B, and C for their helpful comments.
著者らは，有益なコメントを頂いた A, B, C に感謝する.

> The authors thank Jim Bettman, Amit Bhattacharjee, and Stephanie Finnel for their helpful comments. (35)
> 著者らは，有益なコメントを頂いた Jim Bettman, Amit Bhattacharjee, Stephanie Finnel に感謝する.

0019 有用な示唆と批判に感謝する.

◆We thank A, B, and C for their useful suggestions and criticism[s].
我々は，有用な示唆と批判を頂いた A, B, C に感謝する.

> We thank Seth Chin-Parker, Evan Heit, and Alan Neville for their useful suggestions and criticism. (24)
> 我々は，有用な示唆と批判を頂いた Seth Chin-Parker, Evan Heit, Alan Neville に感謝する.

0020 草稿へのコメントと示唆に感謝する.

◆We are grateful to A, B, and C for their comments and suggestions regarding drafts of this article.
我々は，本論文の草稿にコメントと示唆を頂いた A, B, C に感謝する.

> We are grateful to William Horrey, Walter Boot, and M. Kathryn Bleckley for their comments and suggestions regarding drafts of this article. (47)

我々は，本論文の草稿にコメントと示唆を頂いた William Horrey, Walter Boot, M. Kathryn Bleckley に感謝する．

0021 草稿に対する有益なコメントに感謝する．

◆We thank A and B for their helpful comments concerning [/on] [previous] drafts of this article.

我々は，本論文の [初期の] 草稿に有益なコメントを頂いた A と B に感謝する．

> We thank Drs. Melvin Lerner and Jim Olson for their helpful comments concerning previous drafts of this article. (6)
> 我々は，本論文の初期の草稿に有益なコメントを頂いた Melvin Lerner 博士と Jim Olson 博士に感謝する．

0022 初期原稿への洞察に満ちたコメントに感謝する．

◆We would like to thank A, B, and C for insightful comments on an earlier version of this article.

我々は，本論文の初期の原稿に対して洞察に満ちたコメントを頂いた A, B, C に感謝する．

> We would like to thank John Hummel, Stephan Lewandowsky, and Kenneth Malmberg for insightful comments on an earlier version of this article. (44)
> 我々は，本論文の初期の原稿に対して洞察に満ちたコメントを頂いた John Hummel, Stephan Lewandowsky, Kenneth Malmberg に感謝する．

2.3　特記事項

2.3.1　イークォル・コントリビューション

0023 2人の著者が等しく寄与している（イークォル・コントリビューションである）ことを述べる．

◆A and B contributed equally to this work.

A と B は，本研究に等しく寄与した．

> Matthew J. Huentelman and Dietrich A. Stephan contributed equally to this work. (31)
> Matthew J. Huentelman と Dietrich A. Stephan は，本研究に等しく寄与した．

2.3.2　未公刊論文

0024 論文が博士論文に基づいていることを述べる．

◆The research reported here formed part of A's doctoral thesis.

ここで報告される研究は，A の博士論文の一部であった．

> The research reported here formed part of Samuel Hannah's doctoral thesis. (24)

2.3 特記事項　　　　　　　　　　　　　　　　　　　　　　　　　　　　*17*

| ここで報告される研究は，Samuel Hannah の博士論文の一部であった．

0025 論文が他の原稿に基づいていることを述べる．
◆ This article is based in part on the data presented in X.
本論文は，X で発表されたデータに部分的に基づいている．

> This article is based in part on the data presented in the manuscript, "Racial/cultural identity and clients' constructions of race in the therapy relationship," by D. F. Chang, C. Bitney, and K. Feldman, 2009, Unpublished manuscript. (8)
> 本論文は，D. F. Chang, C. Bitney, K. Feldman（2009）の未発表の原稿である "Racial/cultural identity and clients' constructions of race in the therapy relationship" で発表されたデータに部分的に基づいている．

2.3.3 学会発表

0026 研究がすでに学会で発表されていることを述べる．
◆ This work was [/Portions of these data were] presented at the [Nth Annual /Biennial] X Conference [, City, State [/Country]].
この研究は [/ これらのデータの一部は]，[州 [/ 国] の市で開かれた] X 学会の第 N 回年次 [/ 隔年] 大会で発表された．

> This work was presented at the 12th Biennial Cognitive Aging Conference, Atlanta, GA. (7)
> この研究は，ジョージア州アトランタ市で開かれた認知老化学会の第 12 回隔年大会で発表された．

0027 予備的研究が学会で発表されたことを述べる．
◆ A preliminary version of this work was reported at the Nth Annual Meeting of the X in City, A B.
本研究の予備的な研究は，B 年 A 月に市で開かれた X の第 N 回年次大会において報告された．

> A preliminary version of this work was reported at the 40th Annual Meeting of the Psychonomic Society in Los Angeles, April 2000. (42)
> 本研究の予備的な研究は，2000 年 4 月にロサンゼルス市で開かれた心理科学協会の第 40 回年次大会において報告された．

2.3.4 利益相反

0028 利益相反がないことを述べる．
◆ I [/We] declare that we have no competing financial interests [/conflicts of interest].
私 [/ 我々] は，相反する金銭的利害関係 [/ 利益相反] がないことを宣言する．

> We declare that we have no competing financial interests. (31)

| 我々は，相反する金銭的利害関係がないことを宣言する．

2.3.5 法律の遵守
|0029| 法律を遵守していることを述べる．
◆All research complies with current X laws for Y.
すべての研究はYについてのXの現在の法律を遵守している．
> All research complies with current U.S. laws for the care and use of laboratory animals. (21)
> すべての研究は実験動物の管理と使用についての米国の現在の法律を遵守している．

2.4 連 絡 先

|0030| 連絡先を示す．
◆Correspondence concerning this article should be addressed to Name, Affiliation, Street Address. E-mail: Email Address
本論文についての連絡先は，「名前，所属，住所．電子メールアドレス」である．
> Correspondence concerning this article should be addressed to John T. Blaze, The University of Southern Mississippi, Room 224, Owings-McQuagge Box 5025, Hattiesburg, MS 39406-5025 USA. E-mail: john.blaze@usm.edu (3)
> （日本語省略）

|0031| 所属変更後の連絡先を示す．
◆Correspondence concerning this article should be addressed to Name, who is now at Affiliation, Street Address. E-mail: Email Address
本論文についての連絡先は「名前」であり，現在の所属先は，「所属，住所．電子メールアドレス」である．
> Correspondence concerning this article should be addressed to Erica Hoy Kennedy, who is now at the Department of Psychology, Frostburg State University, 101 Braddock Road, Frostburg, MD 21532. E-mail: ehkennedy@frostburg.edu (34)
> （日本語省略）

3 要約（Abstract）

3.1 背　景
3.2 目　的
3.3 方　法
3.4 結　果
3.5 考　察

3.1 背　景

0032 心理的障害の特徴をまとめる．

◆X is associated with A, B, and C, resulting in D.

X は，A, B, C と関連しており，結果として D をもたらす．

> Social anxiety disorder is associated with impairment in social and occupational functioning, significant personal distress, and a possible economic burden, resulting in a reduction in quality of life. (27)
> 社会不安障害は，社会的および職業的機能の障害，著しい個人的苦痛，起こりうる経済的負担と関連しており，結果として生活の質の低下をもたらす．

0033 先行研究を引用する．

◆Previous research has found X.

先行研究は，X を見出してきた．

> Previous research has found age-related deficits in a variety of cognitive processes. (47)
> 先行研究は，さまざまな認知的過程において年齢に関係する欠損を見出してきた．

0034 アイデアを対比させる．

◆On the one hand, XXX. On the other hand, YYY.

しかし，XXX である．その一方で，YYY である．

> On the one hand, research has highlighted intriguing discrepancies between the experience of symptoms and physiology during panic attacks. On the other hand, it has validated symptom reporting during therapeutic exposure to phobic situations. (1)
> しかし，これまでの研究は，パニック発作中の症状経験と生理的機能の間の興味深い乖離を強調してきている．その一方で，これまでの研究は，恐怖症の場面への治療的な曝露中に症状が報告されることを確認してきている．

0035　研究の必要性をまとめる.

◆Few studies have examined X.
Xを調べた研究はほとんどなかった.

> However, few studies have examined links between parent violence and outcomes among youth who are homeless. (22)
> しかしながら，親の暴力とその結果の間の関連をホームレスの若者で調べた研究はほとんどなかった.

3.2　目　的

0036　目的を，実験の内容とともに述べる.

◆The present study investigated the effects of X on Y.
本研究は，XがYに及ぼす効果を調べた.

> The present study investigated the effects of control of background sounds (type and loudness) on perceived intrusiveness of tinnitus and cognitive performance. (28)
> 本研究は，背景音（音のタイプと音の大きさ）の制御が，耳鳴りの侵入性の感覚と認知成績に及ぼす効果を調べた.

0037　目的を，概要とともに述べる.

◆The present X study demonstrates [/demonstrated] the influence of Y on Z.
今回のX研究は，YがZに及ぼす効果を例証する [/ 例証した].

> The present electroencephalographic study demonstrates the influence of emotional primes (angry, happy faces) on purchase decisions. (56)
> 今回の脳波研究は，情動プライム（怒った，または，うれしい顔）が購買意思決定に及ぼす効果を例証する.

0038　目的を，仮説とともに述べる.

◆In this study, we tested the validity of N assumptions about X: (a) YYY, and (b) ZZZ.
この研究で，我々はXについてのN個の仮説の妥当性を調べた．すなわち，(a) YYY，および (b) ZZZ という仮説である.

> In this study, we tested the validity of two popular assumptions about empathy: (a) empathy can be enhanced by oxytocin, a neuropeptide known to be crucial in affiliative behavior, and (b) individual differences in prosocial behavior are positively associated with empathic brain responses. (55)
> この研究で，我々は共感について普及している2つの仮説の妥当性を調べた．すなわち，(a) 共感は，親和的な行動において決定的な役割を果たすことが知られている神経ペプチドであるオキシトシンにより強められる，および，(b) 向社会的行動の個人差は，共感的な脳反応と正の関連を示す，という仮説である.

0039 目的を，用いたデータとともに述べる．

◆ Data from approximately N children in the X study were analyzed to examine Y.
X 研究の N 名の子供のデータが，Y を調べるために分析された．

> Data from approximately 14,000 children in the Early Childhood Longitudinal Survey—Kindergarten Cohort were analyzed to examine the associations between children's immigrant status and their academic trajectories from kindergarten to 3rd grade. (23)
> 幼児期縦断的調査—幼稚園コホート群の約 14000 名の子供のデータが，子供が移民であるか否かと，幼稚園から 3 年生までの学業成績の軌跡の間の関連を調べるために分析された．

0040 目的を，方法や意義とともに述べる．

◆ The current study contributes to the literature by exploring X in a sample of Y with Z.
本研究は Z をもつ Y のサンプルにおいて X を分析することにより，文献に寄与する．

> The current study contributes to the literature by exploring correlates of fathers' pediatric parenting stress in a sample of young children with Type 1 diabetes. (45)
> 本研究は，1 型糖尿病の子供のサンプルにおいて，小児科における父親の育児ストレスと相関する測度を探究することにより，文献に寄与する．

3.3 方　　法

3.3.1 参加者と心理検査

0041 参加者と測度を述べる．

◆ Participants completed measures of attitudes toward X.
参加者は，X に対する態度の測度に回答した．

> Participants completed measures of attitudes toward specific political issues. (9)
> 参加者は，特定の政治的問題に対する態度の測度に回答した．

0042 参加者と質問紙の開発をまとめて述べる．

◆ N psychology majors in a X class and M faculty members developed a Y questionnaire.
X の授業を受けている N 名の心理学専攻学生と M 名の教員が，Y 質問紙を開発した．

> Thirty psychology majors in a Tests and Measurements class and 49 faculty members developed a college-wide course ratings questionnaire. (53)
> 「検査と測定」の授業を受けている 30 名の心理学専攻学生と 49 名の教員が，大学全体にわたる科目評定尺度質問紙を開発した．

0043 参加者と質問紙をまとめて述べる．

◆ X completed Y questionnaires examining A, B, and C.
X が，A, B, C を検査する Y の質問紙に答えた．

Forty-three fathers of children 2–6 years old with Type 1 diabetes completed self-report questionnaires examining pediatric parenting stress, child behavior, participation in diabetes management tasks, and parental psychological resources. (45)
1型糖尿病のある2～6歳の子供の43名の父親が，小児科における育児ストレス，子供の行動，糖尿病管理課題への参加，親としての心理的な力量を検査する自己報告型の質問紙に答えた．

0044 子供の参加者と質問紙をまとめて述べる．

◆L Xth grade boys [/girls] and M Yth grade boys [/girls] completed N questionnaires about A and B.

L名のX年生の男子[/女子]とM名のY年生の男子[/女子]が，AとBについてのN つの質問紙に回答した．

Forty-two 5th grade boys and 42 8th grade boys first completed two questionnaires about cooperative/competitive and group/individualized activities. (54)
42名の5年生の男子と42名の8年生の男子が，まず，協力的/競争的，および，グループ/個別活動についての2つの質問紙に回答した．

3.3.2 実験内容

0045 刺激操作と測定内容を簡潔に述べる（論文英語では we や our を使うことは少ないことに注意）．

◆We varied the level of A in a B task and assessed its effect on C, using a measure of D.

我々は，B課題におけるAのレベルを変化させて，それがCに及ぼす効果をD測度を用いて評価した．

We varied the level of perceptual load on a letter-search task and assessed its effect on the conscious perception of a search-irrelevant shape stimulus appearing in the periphery, using a direct measure of awareness (present/absent reports). (43)
我々は，文字探索課題における知覚的負荷のレベルを変化させて，そのレベルが，周辺に呈示される探索とは無関連の形刺激の意識的な知覚に及ぼす効果を，意識の直接的測度（ある/なしの報告）を用いて評価した．

0046 組み合わせデザインをまとめて述べる．

◆The experimental design crossed instructions (1) to XXX and (2) YYY.

実験デザインは，(1) XXXを行うという教示と，(2) YYYを行うという教示を組み合わせたものであった．

The experimental design crossed instructions (1) to work individually or in a group and (2) to compete or do one's own best. (54)
実験デザインは，(1) 1人で，または，グループで作業をするという教示と，(2) 競争する，または，自分の最善を尽くすという教示を組み合わせたものであった．

3.3 方　　法　　　　　　　　　23

0047　訓練の詳細を簡潔に述べる．
◆For training, each X was placed in the center of the A for N min, and each time [that] the X entered the B, C were turned on.
訓練では，各 X が A の中央に N 分間置かれ，X が B に入るごとに C が呈示された．

> For training, each mouse was placed in the center of the plus-maze for 5 min, and each time that the mouse entered the aversive enclosed arm, a light and white noise were turned on. (21)
> 訓練では，各マウスが十字型迷路の中央に 5 分間置かれ，マウスが嫌悪的な閉鎖アームに入るごとに光とホワイトノイズが呈示された．

0048　実験群と統制群の処置をまとめて述べる．
◆During this X, half the rats [/participants] had access to Y; the remaining rats [/participants] did not receive Z.
この X の間，半分のラット [/ 参加者] は Y と接触した．残りのラット [/ 参加者] は Z を与えられなかった．

> During this phase, half the rats had access to a novel object on their initially unpaired side; the remaining rats did not receive objects. (49)
> この段階の間，半分のラットは，最初は対にされなかった側で，新奇な物体と接触した．残りのラットは，物体を与えられなかった．

3.3.3　メタ分析
0049　メタ分析の手続きをまとめて述べる．
◆N A, B, C, D X were identified. P, Q, R, S, and T were extracted.
A であり，B であり，C であり，D である N 個の X が同定された．P, Q, R, S, T が抽出された．

> Fifteen published, randomized, double-blind, placebo-controlled trials of selective serotonin reuptake inhibitors in social anxiety disorder were identified. Design, subject number, drug and dose, trial length, rating instruments, and baseline and end point data were extracted and then verified independently by a second investigator. (27)
> 社会不安障害における選択的セロトニン再取り込み阻害薬の治験の中で，出版され，無作為化され，二重盲検化され，偽薬コントロールがなされている 15 の治験が同定された．デザイン，被験者数，薬物と投与量，治験の長さ，評定法，ベースラインと終了時のデータが抽出され，その後，それらに誤りがないことを別の研究者が独立して確認した．

3.4 結　果

3.4.1 具体的な結果

0050 変数の関係をまとめる．

◆ There was a direct relationship between X and Y.

X と Y との間には直接的な関係があった．

> There was a direct relationship between the intensity of running and the severity of withdrawal symptoms. (33)
> ランニングの強度と離脱症状の重症度との間には直接的な関係があった．

0051 媒介変数をまとめる．

◆ X was [/Xs were] mediated by Y.

X は，Y により媒介されていた．

> These relationships were mediated by students' beliefs that confiding in a teacher may have unfavorable consequences. (58)
> これらの関係は，教師に打ち明けると好ましくない結果につながるかもしれない，という学生の信念により媒介されていた．

0052 使用したデータと結果をまとめて述べる．

◆ X indicated that YYY and that ZZZ.

X は，YYY ということ，および，ZZZ ということを示した．

> Feedback from the students indicated that this hands-on experience contributed to their satisfaction with the course and that it provided an opportunity to think critically about research. (53)
> 学生からのフィードバックは，この実地体験が科目に対する満足度に寄与し，さらに，研究について批判的に考える機会を提供したことを示した．

0053 投与量と結果をまとめて述べる．

◆ X (N–M g/kg) [dose-dependently /dose-independently] decreased Y, and increased Z.

X(N–M g/kg)は，[投与量依存的 / 投与量非依存的に] Y を減少させ，Z を増加させた．

> Ethanol (1.0–1.4 g/kg) dose-dependently decreased anxiety and learning, and increased locomotion. (21)
> エタノール(1.0–1.4 g/kg)は，投与量依存的に，不安と学習を減少させ，運動を増加させた．

0054 統計的分析の種類と結果をまとめて述べる．

◆ Confirmatory factor analyses demonstrated that the structure of X was explained best by Y.

確証的因子分析は，X の構造が，Y により最もよく説明されることを例証した．

3.4 結　　果

Confirmatory factor analyses demonstrated that the structure of political orientation was explained best by two moderately correlated dimensions. (9)
確証的因子分析は，政治的志向の構造が，中程度に相関する2つの次元により最もよく説明されることを例証した．

0055　メタ分析の結果を述べる．
◆ Effect sizes for the X ranged from N to M.
Xについての効果量は，NからMの範囲であった．

> Effect sizes for the Liebowitz Social Anxiety Scale ranged from 0.03 to 1.21. (27)
> リーボウィッツ社会不安尺度についての効果量は，0.03から1.21の範囲であった．

0056　回帰分析の結果を述べる．
◆ A, B, and C were significant predictors of X.
A, B, CはXの有意な予測変数であった．

> Self-esteem, relocation distance, and storm exposure were significant predictors of general psychological distress (GPD). (3)
> 自尊感情，移住した距離，嵐にさらされたことは，一般的心理的苦痛（GPD）の有意な予測変数であった．

3.4.2　結果と意味

0057　先行研究との一致を述べながら，結果をまとめる．
◆ Consistent with previous studies, A appears more effective than B for C, with improvements extending into D.
先行研究と一致して，AはCに対してBよりも効果的であり，改善はDにまで及ぶようである．

> Consistent with previous studies, selective serotonin reuptake inhibitors appear more effective than placebo for social anxiety disorder, with improvements extending into social and occupational functions. (27)
> 先行研究と一致して，選択的セロトニン再取り込み阻害薬は社会不安障害に対して偽薬よりも効果的であり，改善は社会的および職業的機能にまで及ぶようである．

0058　期待との一致を述べながら，結果をまとめる．
◆ As expected, XXX.
期待されたように，XXX．

> As expected, spiritual struggles with the divorce partially or fully mediated all but one of the links found between having appraised the divorce as a sacred loss or desecration and outcomes. (61)

期待されたように，離婚とのスピリチュアルな苦闘は，離婚を神聖さの喪失や神聖冒瀆であると評価したことと，その後の結果の間に見られる関連性の 1 つを除くすべてを，部分的あるいは完全に媒介していた．

0059 重要性を強調しながら，結果をまとめる．
◆ Importantly, XXX.
重要なことに，XXX．

> Importantly, left frontal asymmetry in response to stress exposure predicted increases in subsequent aggressive behavior, a finding that did not emerge in the no-stress condition. (60)
> 重要なことに，ストレスへの曝露に対する反応における左前頭の非対称性は，それに引き続いて起こる攻撃行動の増加を予測した．この知見は，ストレスのない条件では出現しなかった．

0060 結果と結論をまとめて述べる．
◆ Since XXX, we conclude[d] that YYY.
XXX ということから，我々は，YYY と結論する [/ した]．

> Since the neurological recovery from closed head injury (CHI) was correlated with the decrease of blood glutamate levels, we conclude that pyruvate blood glutamate scavenging activity contributes to the spectrum of its neuroprotective mechanisms. (64)
> 閉鎖性頭部外傷（CHI）からの神経学的な回復は血液中のグルタミン酸のレベルの減少と相関したことから，我々は，ピルビン酸の血液中のグルタミン酸塩の排除活動が神経保護機序の連続体に寄与すると結論する．

3.4.3 複数研究

0061 複数研究の結果をまとめる．
◆ N X experiments examining A and B indicated that YYY.
A と B を調べた N 個の X 実験から，YYY ということが示された．

> Three source recognition experiments examining receiver-operating characteristics and response deadline performance indicated that familiarity makes a greater contribution to source memory if source and item information are unitized during encoding. (12)
> 受信者動作特性と反応期限手続きにおける遂行行動を分析した 3 つの情報源再認の実験から，情報源情報と項目情報が符号化中にユニット化される場合には，熟知性が情報源の記憶により大きく寄与することが示された．

0062 複数研究で，後の結果が前の結果を確認したことを述べる．
◆ Experiment N confirmed X.
実験 N は X を確認した．

> Experiment 2 confirmed and extended these findings. (10)
> 実験 2 はこれらの知見を確認し，拡張した．

3.5 考　　察

3.5.1 予測・仮説・モデルとの一致

0063　結果が予測を支持することをまとめる．
◆These results empirically confirm X.
　これらの結果は，X を経験的に確認する．
> These results empirically confirm two unique aspects of anticipatory time perception in determining individuals' temporal discounting. (35)
> これらの結果は，個人の時間割引の決定における予期的時間知覚の 2 つの独特な側面を経験的に確認する．

0064　知見が仮説を支持することをまとめる．
◆These findings support the hypothesis that XXX.
　これらの知見は，XXX という仮説を支持する．
> These findings support the hypothesis that exercise-induced increases in endogenous opioid peptides act in a manner similar to chronic administration of opiate drugs. (33)
> これらの知見は，運動により誘発される内因性オピオイドペプチドの増加が，オピオイド薬物の慢性的な投与と類似した仕方で作用するという仮説を支持する．

0065　結果がモデルを支持し，測度を正当化することをまとめる．
◆These results support the X model of Y and validate the A as a measure of B.
　これらの結果は，Y についての X モデルを支持し，さらに，A が B についての測度として妥当であることを確認する．
> These results support the cognitive-tuning model of decision making and validate the N200 as a sensitive measure of the interplay of cognitive and affective aspects in decision making. (56)
> これらの結果は，意思決定についての認知的調整モデルを支持し，さらに，N200 が意思決定における認知的および感情的側面の相互作用に関する敏感な測度として妥当であることを確認する．

0066　結果が先行研究と矛盾することをまとめる．
◆This evidence suggests that[,] contrary to previous arguments, XXX.
　この証拠は，過去の議論とは反対に，XXX ということを示唆している．
> This evidence suggests that contrary to previous arguments, a member of a New World monkey species can solve an analogical problem. (34)
> この証拠は，過去の議論とは反対に，新世界ザル種の多くのメンバーが類推問題を解くことができることを示唆している．

3.5.2 結果の意味

0067 結果の具体的な意味をまとめる．

◆ These results suggest that XXX.
これらの結果は，XXX ということを示唆している．

> These results suggest that reflective normative feedback may offer a powerful new tool for female-targeted interventions. (39)
> これらの結果は，相手が自分に対してもっている規範のフィードバックが，女性をターゲットとする介入のための新しい強力な道具となるかもしれないことを示唆している．

0068 結果があることの重要性を示すことをまとめる．

◆ X results point to the importance of Y.
X の結果は，Y の重要性を示している．

> Simulation results point to the importance of school resources. (23)
> シミュレーションの結果は，学校資源の重要性を示している．

0069 知見が新しい測度を確立することをまとめる．

◆ These findings establish a new X measure of Y.
これらの知見は，Y についての新しい X 測度を確立する．

> These findings establish a new laboratory measure of a form of distractibility common to everyday life, and highlight load as an important determinant of such distractibility. (14)
> これらの知見は，日常生活に共通して見られる妨害性の形式についての新しい実験室測度を確立し，そのような妨害性の決定因としての負荷を強調する．

0070 結果の実践的な意味を列挙する．

◆ Implications for practice include X, Y, and Z.
実践的な意味としては，X, Y, Z が挙げられる．

> Implications for practice include the utility of new methodological tools and the efficacy of coaching for meeting leadership effectiveness. (48)
> 実践的な意味としては，新しい方法論的ツールの有用性，および会議における指導力の有効性に対してコーチングがもつ効力が挙げられる．

0071 評論の結果，問題の解決に経験的研究が必要であることをまとめる．

◆ X can be addressed with [/by] empirical research.
X は，経験的研究により取り組むことができる．

> All of these questions can be addressed with empirical research. (11)
> これらの問題は，すべて経験的研究により取り組むことができる．

3.5.3 総論

0072 特定のアイデアに的を絞ることを述べる．

◆Emphasis is placed on X.
X が強調される．

> Emphasis is placed on interventions that work at a sensorimotor or concrete operational level. (17)
> 感覚運動や具体的操作レベルで作用する介入が強調される．

0073 研究全体の意味についての長い議論をたった 1 文にまとめる．

◆Implications for X, Y[,] and Z are discussed.
X, Y, Z に対してもつ意味が論じられる．

> Implications for intervention, prevention and treatment are discussed. (46)
> 介入，予防，治療に対してもつ意味が論じられる．

0074 特定の知見の意味についての長い議論をたった 1 文にまとめる．

◆The implications of these findings for X are discussed.
これらの知見が，X に対してもつ意味が論じられる．

> These results suggest that given substantial experience, older adults may be quite capable of performing at high levels of proficiency on fast-paced demanding real-world tasks. The implications of these findings for global skilled labor shortages are discussed. (47)
> これらの結果は，しっかりとした経験があれば，ペースが速く要求水準が高い現実世界の課題において，高齢の成人が高いレベルの能力を十分に発揮することができるかもしれないことを示唆している．これらの知見が世界的な熟練労働の不足に対してもつ意味が論じられる．

4 序文 (Introduction)

4.1 研究の背景
4.2 先行研究の知見
4.3 先行研究の理論的・実践的な帰結
4.4 理論・モデル・仮説
4.5 先行研究のトピック
4.6 先行研究の問題点
4.7 本研究のテーマ・関心・目的
4.8 内容の予告
4.9 一連の実験をつなぐ

4.1 研究の背景

4.1.1 全体的な動向

0075 質的研究が調べてきたことを述べる.

◆ Qualitative research with X has explored Y.
X についての質的研究は，Y を調査してきた.

> Qualitative research with the homeless has explored hope and hopelessness. (41)
> ホームレスについての質的研究は，希望と絶望を調査してきた.

0076 心理学者がある要因を研究してきたことを，その理由とともに述べる.

◆ X psychologists have examined the factors that influence Y, as P develops over time.
P は時間経過とともに発達することから，X 心理学者は，Y に影響する要因を研究してきた.

> Developmental psychologists have examined the factors that influence the time frame in which children are able to comprehend analogies, as analogical reasoning develops over time. (34)
> 類推的推論が時間経過とともに発達することから，発達心理学者は，子供が類推を理解する時間的枠組みに影響する要因を研究してきた.

0077 これまでの努力の焦点について述べる.

◆ To date, X efforts have focused on Y.
　これまで，X のための努力は，Y に焦点を当ててきた．

> To date, nootropic drug discovery efforts have focused on the enhancement of cholinergic, glutaminergic, and serotonergic neurotransmission, and on phosphodiesterase inhibition. (31)
> これまで，向知性薬の発見のための努力は，コリン作動性，グルタミン作動性，セロトニン作動性の神経伝達，および，ホスホジエステラーゼの阻害を強めることに焦点を当ててきた．

0078 あるトピックに経験的に取り組むためにある手法を開発してきたことを述べる.

◆ To address this issue empirically, students [/researchers] of X have developed Y.
　この問題に経験的に取り組むために，X の研究者は Y を開発してきた．

> To address this issue empirically, students of animal learning have developed a behavioral assay for intentional, goal-directed action by devaluing the outcome following instrumental training. (37)
> この問題に経験的に取り組むために，動物学習の研究者は，道具的訓練後に結果の価値を低下させることによる意図的な目標志向的行為の行動的な分析法を開発してきた．

0079 もう 1 つの応用領域の動向について述べる.

◆ Another area of applied research that bears on the issue of X has examined Y.
　X の問題と関係する応用研究のもう 1 つの領域は，Y を研究してきた．

> Another area of applied research that bears on the issue of distraction has examined task interruptions. (14)
> 妨害の問題と関係する応用研究のもう 1 つの領域は，課題の割り込みを研究してきた．

0080 いくつかの先行研究の取り組みに言及する.

◆ Several studies have addressed X.
　いくつかの研究は X に取り組んできた．

> As reported above, several studies have addressed cognitive biases in anxiety disorders. (1)
> 先に述べたように，いくつかの研究は不安障害における認知的バイアスに取り組んできた．

4.1.2 初期の研究

0081 初期の研究の内容を述べる.

◆ In an early study, Author (Year) [, for example,] investigated X.
　初期の研究において，[たとえば] 著者（発表年）は，X を研究した．

> In an early study, Singer et al. (2004), for example, investigated empathy for pain when participants received pain themselves or witnessed their partners receiving pain. (55)

初期の研究において，たとえば Singer ら（2004）は，参加者自身が苦痛を受けた場合や，パートナーが苦痛を受けているのを目撃した場合の，苦痛への共感について研究した．

0082 初期の研究が提案したアイデアを述べる．

◆ In an early work, Author (Year) presented the idea that XXX.

初期の研究において，著者（発表年）は，XXX であるアイデアを提案した．

> In an early work, Meichenbaum (1977a) presented the idea that has been the foundation of much subsequent CBT. (17)
> 初期の研究において，Meichenbaum（1977a）は，後に続く多くの CBT の土台となるアイデアを提案した．

（訳者注：CBT; cognitive-behavioral therapy, 認知行動療法）

4.1.3 多くの研究

0083 多くの研究が調べてきたことを述べる．

◆ Many studies have examined X.

多くの研究が，X を調べてきた．

> Many studies have examined gender differences in psychological outcomes following disasters. (3)
> 多くの研究が，災害後の心理学的な結果変数における性差を調べてきた．

0084 多くの研究がある問題に系統的に取り組んできたことを述べる．

◆ X researchers have conducted a very large number of studies on Y, and systematically addressed Z.

X の研究者たちは，Y について非常に多くの研究を行い，Z に系統的に取り組んできた．

> Terror management researchers have conducted a very large number of studies on these points, and systematically addressed a wide range of criticisms. (11)
> 恐怖管理の研究者たちは，これらの問題について非常に多くの研究を行い，広範な批判に系統的に取り組んできた．

0085 多くの文献があるトピックに言及していることを述べる．

◆ The literature on X includes many references to Y.

X についての文献は，Y にたびたび言及している．

> The literature on psychiatric inpatient treatment of deaf people also includes many references to a cohort of deaf people who are low functioning, have severe language dysfluency, and have behavioral disorders but are not psychotic. (17)
> 難聴者の精神医学的な入院治療についての文献も，低機能で，失流暢で，行動障害をもつが精神病ではない難聴者のコホートについて，たびたび言及している．

（訳者注：コホートとは，同齢の集団のことである）

0086 かなり多くの文献が言及しているトピックを述べる．
◆ Throughout the literature on X, one finds references to Y.
X に関する文献の至るところで，Y への言及が見られる．

> Throughout the literature on mental health and deafness, one finds references to a cohort of deaf people with severe language, emotion, and behavioral problems. (17)
> 精神保健と聴覚障害に関する文献の至るところで，重度の言語，情動，および，行動問題をもつ難聴者のコホートへの言及が見られる．

（訳者注：コホートとは，同齢の集団のことである）

4.1.4 研究の増加

0087 あることを示唆する証拠が増えていることを述べる．
◆ A growing body of evidence suggests that X is an important factor.
X は重要な要因であることを示唆する証拠が増えている．

> A growing body of evidence suggests that proximity of the referent group is an important factor when evaluating peer influences on drinking behavior. (39)
> 飲酒に及ぼす同輩の効果を評価する場合に，準拠とされるグループの近接性が重要な要因であることを示唆する証拠が増えている．

0088 ある証拠が増えていることを述べる．
◆ There is [a] growing evidence that X activates Y.
X は Y を賦活するという証拠が次第に増えてきている．

> There is growing evidence that running and drug abuse activate overlapping neural systems. (33)
> ランニングと薬物中毒は，重複する神経系を活性化するという証拠が次第に増えてきている．

0089 あることを示す文献が次第に増えていることを述べる．
◆ There is a growing body of literature which indicates [/indicating] that X has beneficial effects on Y.
X が Y に有益な影響を及ぼすことを示す文献が次第に増えてきている．

> There is a growing body of literature indicating that exercise has beneficial effects on behavior and brain functioning. (33)
> 運動が行動と脳機能に有益な効果を及ぼすことを示す文献が次第に増えてきている．

0090 ある分野で興味が高まりつつある知見を要約する．
◆ There is [a] growing interest in X within the Y field, with studies suggesting that ZZZ.
Y の分野では X に対する興味が高まりつつあり，ZZZ ということを示唆する研究がある．

There is a growing interest in such ideas within the research field, with studies suggesting that the ability to accept tinnitus can be associated with better health among individuals with the condition. (28)
この研究分野ではそのような考えに対する興味が高まりつつあり，耳鳴りを受容する能力が，そのような条件をもつ人々における健康状態と関連していることを示唆する研究がある．

0091 あるトピックに関する文献が増えて，焦点が広がってきたことを述べる．
◆ The growing literature on X focuses on Y.
X に関する文献は増えており，それらは Y に焦点を当てている．

The growing literature on discrimination experienced by Asian Americans also focuses on a few group-specific phenomena. (32)
アジア系アメリカ人が経験する差別に関する文献は増えており，それらはグループに特有である少数の現象にも焦点を当てている．

0092 あるトピックの研究が増え，多くの要因を同定してきたことを述べる．
◆ This growing body of research on X has identified a number of Y factors.
X に関するこのような研究は増大しており，多くの Y 要因を同定してきた．

This growing body of research on predictors of pediatric parenting stress has identified a number of parent and child factors across psychosocial, medical, and demographic domains. (45)
小児科での育児ストレスの予測因子に関する研究は増大しており，心理社会的，医学的，および，人口統計学的領域にまたがる多くの親子要因を同定してきた．

4.1.5　長期にわたる研究

0093 何十年間に及ぶ先行研究について述べる．
◆ A large body of literature spanning more than N decades has investigated X.
N × 10 年以上にわたる膨大な研究が，X を調べてきた．

A large body of literature spanning more than two decades has investigated the role of frontal alpha activity with EEG. (60)
20 年以上にわたる膨大な研究が，EEG を用いて前頭におけるアルファ波活動を調べてきた．

（訳者注：EEG; electroencephalogram, 脳波）

0094 長い間論争を引き起こしている研究上の疑問を述べる．
◆ This question has intrigued psychologists for N decades and has led to a long-standing debate between X and Y.
この疑問は N × 10 年間にわたって心理学者の興味をひき，X と Y の間の長い論争を引き起こしてきた．

This question has intrigued psychologists for several decades and has led to a long-standing
debate between early and late selection views of attention. (43)
この疑問は数十年にわたって心理学者の興味をひき，注意の初期選択説と後期選択説を
巡る長い論争を引き起こしてきた．

4.1.6　概念・用語の定義

0095　定義を述べる．
◆ X refers to Y (Author, Year).
　X とは，Y のことである（著者，発表年）．

> Pediatric parenting stress refers to the stress experienced by parents of children with chronic
> illness (Streisand et al., 2001). (45)
> 小児科における育児ストレスとは，慢性疾患をもつ子供の親が経験するストレスのこと
> である（Streisand et al., 2001）．

0096　操作的定義を述べる．
◆ X is [often] operationalized as Y.
　X は，[しばしば] Y として操作的に定義される．

> Political orientation is often operationalized as a unidimensional left–right continuum. (9)
> 政治的志向は，しばしば左派 – 右派という 1 次元の連続体として操作的に定義される．

0097　心理学的な構成概念の定義を心理学史上の重要な理論と関係づける．
◆ The X construct has strong historical ties to Y, especially to Z.
　X という構成概念は，Y，特に，Z と歴史的に強く結びついている．

> The habit construct has strong historical ties to behaviorism, especially to Watson's (1913)
> and Skinner's (1938) radical behaviorism that famously eschewed cognitive and motivational
> mediators of behavior. (62)
> 習慣という構成概念は，行動主義，特に，行動の認知的および動機づけ理論的な媒介変
> 数を遠ざけたことで知られる Watson（1913）と Skinner（1938）の徹底的行動主義と歴
> 史的に強く結びついている．

0098　キーワードの定義を述べる．
◆ We use the term *X* to refer to Y.
　我々は，X という用語を，Y という意味で用いる．

> We use the term *spiritual struggles* to refer to spiritually based responses to stressors that result
> in heightened maladaptation. (61)
> 我々は，スピリチュアルな苦闘という用語を，より大きな不適応をもたらしてしまうよ
> うな，ストレス因子に対するスピリチュアリティに基づく反応という意味で用いる．

（訳者注：専門用語やキーワードはイタリック体を用いる）

`0099` キーワードの2通りの定義を述べる．

◆ The term *X* in this article refers to Y[,] or to Z.

本論文では，X という用語を，Y あるいは Z という意味で用いる．

> The term *activity* in this article refers to brain activity, or to decreased alpha. (60)
> 本論文では，活動性という用語を，脳の活動性，あるいは，アルファ波の減少という意味で用いる．

（訳者注：専門用語やキーワードはイタリック体を用いる）

`0100` キーワードの複数の定義を対比させながら述べる．

◆ We apply the term *A* to denote B[,] and the term *C* to denote D.

我々は，A という用語を B を意味するために，C という用語を D を意味するために用いる．

> We apply the term *race* to denote the former and the terms *race and/or ethnicity or race and/or ethnicity and/or culture* (REC) to denote the latter. (8)
> 我々は，人種という用語を前者を意味するために，人種や民族，あるいは，人種や民族や文化（REC）という用語を後者を意味するために用いる．

（訳者注：専門用語やキーワードはイタリック体を用いる）

`0101` キーワードの複数の定義を列挙しながら述べる．

◆ X1 is defined as Y1. X2 is indicated by Y2. X3 is seen in Y3. "X4" was coined in reference to Y4.

X1 は，Y1 と定義される．X2 は，Y2 のことである．X3 は，Y3 の中に見られる．「X4」は，Y4 を準拠として造り出された．

> Cooperativeness is defined as behavior or attitudes favoring shared goals. Competitiveness is indicated by a desire to outdo others or gain recognition. Individualism is seen in tendencies to challenge personal standards or to work alone. The fourth term, "interpersonalism," was coined in reference to the Japanese definition of self in terms of the relationships one has with others. (54)
> 協調性は，共有の目標を好む行動や態度と定義される．競争性は，他者に打ち勝ちたい，あるいは，認められたいという欲望のことである．個人主義は，行為規則に挑戦する，あるいは，1人で取り組むという傾向の中に見られる．4つ目の「間人主義」という用語は，他者との関係による自己についての日本語の定義を準拠として造り出された．

（訳者注：著者独自の定義の場合は " " をつける）

4.1.7 先行研究による定義

`0102` 先行研究に従って定義する（直接引用）．

◆ According to Author (Year, p. N), X can be defined as "Y."

著者（発表年，p. N）によれば，X は，「Y」と定義することができる．

4.1 研究の背景

According to Anderson (2000, p. 247), an analogy can be defined as "the process by which a problem solver maps the solution for one problem into a solution for another problem." (34)
Anderson（2000, p. 247）によれば，類推は，「問題解決者が1つの問題の解き方をもう1つの問題の解き方に写像する過程」と定義することができる.

0103 先行研究の定義を述べる（直接引用）.

◆ X has been defined as "Y" (Author, Year, p. N).
X は，「Y（著者，発表年，p. N）」と定義されてきた.

> Executive coaching has been defined as a process of "equipping executives with the tools, knowledge, and opportunities they need to develop themselves and become more effective" (Peterson & Hicks, 1996, p. 14). (48)
> 幹部社員コーチングとは，「自己を開発してさらに有能になるために必要な道具，知識，および，機会を経営者にもたせる（Peterson & Hicks, 1996, p.14）」過程と定義されてきた.

0104 先行研究の定義を述べる（直接引用）.

◆ As Author (Year) notes, X are "Y" (p. N).
著者（発表年）が述べているように，X は「Y（p. N）」である.

> As Lerner (1980) notes, immanent justice responses are "primitive in the sense that they treat an accidental association of a person's acts and a set of consequences as a sufficient basis for the assignment of blame" (p. 116). (6)
> Lerner（1980）が述べているように，内在的正義反応とは，「それらが，ある人の行為と結果集合間の偶発的な結びつきを，責任の割当てに対する十分な論拠として扱う，という意味において，原始的 (p.116)」である.

0105 先行研究における行動傾向の定義を述べる.

◆ X (Author, Year) has been defined as a tendency to YYY.
X（著者，発表年）は，YYY を行う傾向と定義されてきた.

> Highway hypnosis (HHy; "white-line fever" or "the vanishing hitchhiker"—Brunvand, 1981) has been defined as a tendency to become drowsy and suddenly fall asleep, sometimes into the REM stage, while driving an automobile (Sagberg, 1999). (15)
> 高速道路催眠（highway hypnosis, Hhy;「白線の熱病」あるいは「消えたヒッチハイカー」，Brunvand, 1981）は，自動車の運転中に眠気を催し突然眠ってしまい，ときには REM の段階にまで至ることもある傾向と定義されてきた（Sagberg, 1999）.

0106 理論における定義を述べる.

◆ In X theory, Author (Year) refers to Y as Z.
X 理論において，著者（発表年）は，Z のことを，Y と呼んでいる.

> In the Job Demands-Resources theory, Demerouti and colleagues (Demerouti, Bakker, Nachreiner, & Schaufeli, 2001) refer to job demands as those physical, psychological, and organizational aspects of the job that require sustained physical, emotional, and cognitive efforts. (52)

仕事の要求度‐資源理論において，Demerouti らのグループ（Demerouti, Bakker, Nachreiner, & Schaufeli, 2001）は，身体的，情動的，認知的努力を持続的に要求するような，仕事の身体的，心理的，組織的な側面のことを，仕事の要求度と呼んでいる．

4.1.8 症候群・症状・障害の定義

0107　現象の症状名を述べる．

◆ This phenomenon has been called X (Abbreviation for X).

この現象は，X（X の略語）と呼ばれてきた．

> This phenomenon has been called activity-based anorexia (ABA). (33)
> この現象は，活動性拒食症（ABA）と呼ばれてきた．

0108　症候群の定義を述べる．

◆ X is conceptualized as referring to Y.

X とは，Y のことをさすものとして概念化されている．

> Burnout is conceptualized as referring to individuals' feelings that they have depleted or exhausted their cognitive, physical, and emotional resources. (52)
> 燃え尽き症候群とは，認知的，身体的，情動的な資源を枯渇させた，あるいは，使い果たしたという個人の感覚をさすものとして概念化されている．

0109　臨床心理学的な概念の定義を述べる．

◆ X describes Y.

X とは，Y のことである．

> PTS describes an interrelated set of psychological reactions that occur after a traumatic event and produce intrusion, avoidance, and hyperarousal symptoms. (3)
> PTS とは，心的外傷を与える出来事の後に起こり，侵入，回避，過覚醒症状をもたらす心理的反応の相互関係的な集合のことである．

（訳者注：PTS; posttraumatic stress, 心的外傷後ストレス）

0110　障害の特徴を述べる．

◆ X is characterized by Y.

X は，Y により特徴づけられる．

> As a consequence, panic disorder with agoraphobia may develop. It is characterized by an avoidance of many situations in which having a panic attack could be dangerous or embarrassing. (1)
> 結果として，広場恐怖を伴うパニック障害が発症する．それは，パニック発作が起こると危険であるか困ってしまうような多くの場面の回避により特徴づけられる．

（訳者注：ここで，広場恐怖とは，用語から連想されるような広場そのものへの恐怖ではなく，見知らぬところで 1 人になることへの恐怖をさす）

0111　障害の特徴を，日常生活上の諸問題とともに述べる．

◆ X is characterized [primarily] by Y that may be accompanied by A, B and C.

Xは，[本来，] A, B, C を伴うかもしれない Y により特徴づけられる．

> Social anxiety disorder (social phobia) is characterized primarily by a fear of negative evaluation in social settings that may be accompanied by blushing, trembling and cognitive problems. (27)
> 社会不安障害（社会恐怖）は，本来，赤面，震え，認知的問題を伴うかもしれない，社会的環境における否定的な評価に対する恐怖により特徴づけられる．

0112 心理的障害を定義する．

◆ X is a[n] Y disorder, characterized by Z.

X は Y の障害であり，Z により特徴づけられる．

> Pathological gambling is an impulse control disorder, characterized by the inability to reduce or cease gambling, resulting in adverse social, psychological, financial, and legal consequences that include depression, suicide, divorce, unemployment, and homelessness. (46)
> 病的賭博は衝動性制御の障害であり，うつ，自殺，離婚，失業，ホームレスを含む社会的，心理的，財政的，法律的に不利な結果をもたらすような，賭博を減らすあるいは止める能力の欠如により特徴づけられる．

0113 障害を表す用語が新たに造られたことを述べる．

◆ The term X (Abbreviation of X) has recently been coined in YYY.

X（X の略語）という用語は，最近，YYY を行う際に造語された．

> The term fetal alcohol spectrum disorders (FASD) has recently been coined in establishing an inclusive diagnosis for all children influenced adversely by prenatal alcohol exposure. (40)
> 胎児アルコールスペクトル障害（FASD）という用語は，最近，胎児期のアルコールへの曝露により悪影響を与えられたすべての子供の包括的な診断を確立する際に造語された．

4.1.9 パラダイム

0114 実験室パラダイムを紹介する．

◆ To explore the mechanisms underlying the association between X and Y, researchers have used laboratory paradigms that ZZZ.

X と Y の間の結びつきの根底にある機序を探究するために，研究者は ZZZ という実験室パラダイムを用いてきた．

> To explore the mechanisms underlying the association between acute stress and dysregulated behaviors, researchers have used laboratory paradigms that induce aversive instigation and measure aggressive behavior. (60)
> 急性ストレスと調整不全行動の間の結びつきの根底にある機序を探究するために，研究者は，嫌悪的な煽動を誘発して攻撃行動を測定する，という実験パラダイムを用いてきた．

4. 序文 (Introduction)

0115 実験パラダイムの内容を述べる．

◆ In this paradigm, participants typically perform a[n] X task, for example, Y.
このパラダイムにおいて，参加者は，典型的には，たとえばYのようなX課題を行う．

> In this paradigm participants typically perform a visual search task, for example, search for a prespecified target letter. (14)
> このパラダイムにおいて，参加者は，典型的には，たとえば事前に指定された標的文字の探索のような視覚的探索課題を行う．

0116 原型となった実験パラダイムの内容を述べる．

◆ In the prototypical X experiment (e.g., Author, Year), Ps are trained to perform Q.
原型となったX実験（たとえば，著者，発表年）では，PはQを行うように訓練された．

> In the prototypical outcome devaluation experiment (e.g., Adams & Dickinson, 1981), animals are initially trained to perform an instrumental action to gain access to a particular outcome which is subsequently devalued. (37)
> 原型となった結果価値低下実験（たとえば，Adams & Dickinson, 1981）では，動物が最初に特定の結果を得るために道具的行為を行うように訓練され，その後，その結果の価値が低下させられる．

0117 実験パラダイムで参加者に呈示される材料を述べる．

◆ In the X paradigm, participants are presented with Y.
Xのパラダイムでは，参加者にYが呈示される．

> In the selectivity paradigm, participants are presented with lists of words, with each word in the list having a distinct value ranging from 1 point to 12 points. (7)
> 選択性のパラダイムでは，参加者に単語のリストが呈示され，そのリスト中の各単語には，1点から12点までの異なる値がつけられている．

0118 あるパラダイムが，本来とは異なるテーマを説明するために用いられてきたことを述べる．

◆ The X paradigm can also serve as a model of Y.
Xのパラダイムは，Yのモデルとしても役立ってきた．

> The ABA paradigm can also serve as a model of drug abuse. (33)
> ABAのパラダイムは，薬物中毒のモデルとしても役立ってきた．
>
> （訳者注：ABA; activity-based anorexia, 活動性拒食症）

0119 別のパラダイムを用いて情報を集める試みを述べる．

◆ Another research tradition tried to gather information about X by means of Y.
もう1つの研究の様式は，Xについての情報をYを用いて集めようとした．

> Another research tradition tried to gather information about the person's self-concept by means of cognitive measures, such as memory scores or response latencies. (13)
> もう1つの研究の様式は，人間の自己概念についての情報を記憶得点や反応潜時などの認知的測度を用いて集めようとした．

4.1.10 アプローチ・取り組み方

0120 アプローチの具体的な内容を述べる．

◆ In X approaches, P is instigated through Q.
　Xのアプローチでは，PはQを通して生起させられる．

> In classic behavior modification approaches, behavior change is instigated largely through manipulations of environmental contingencies. (62)
> 古典的な行動修正のアプローチでは，主に環境随伴性の操作を通して行動変容が生起させられる．

0121 アプローチの手法を述べる．

◆ One X approach is to evaluate P.
　1つのXアプローチは，Pを評価することである．

> One assessment approach is to evaluate the physiological changes that accompany panic attacks in the laboratory. (1)
> 1つの評価アプローチは，パニック発作に伴う生理学的な変化を実験室内で評価することである．

0122 アプローチの根拠を述べる．

◆ The rationale for using a[n] X approach is that Ps have too often relied on Q.
　Xのアプローチを採用する理論的根拠は，PはQに頼ることがこれまでに多すぎたことである．

> The rationale for using a subjective approach to social class is that psychologists have too often relied on a sociological approach to understand an individual level experience. (41)
> 社会的階層に対する主観的アプローチを採用することの理論的根拠は，心理学者が個人レベルの経験を理解するために社会学的アプローチに頼ることがこれまでに多すぎたことである．

0123 理論を支持するための取り組み方を述べる．

◆ Evidence in support of X theory has been obtained in many studies using both Y (e.g., Author, Year) and Z methods (e.g., Author, Year).
　X理論を支持する証拠は，Yの方法（たとえば，著者，発表年），および，Zの方法（たとえば，著者，発表年）の両方を用いた多くの研究において得られてきた．

> Evidence in support of Load Theory has been obtained in many studies using both behavioral (e.g., Cartwright-Finch & Lavie, 2006; Lavie, 1995; Lavie & Cox, 1997) and neuro-imaging methods (e.g., Bishop, Jenkins, & Lawrence, 2006; Pinsk, Doniger, & Kastner, 2004; Rees, Frith, & Lavie, 1997). (14)
> 負荷理論を支持する証拠は，行動的方法（たとえば，Cartwright-Finch & Lavie, 2006; Lavie, 1995; Lavie & Cox, 1997），および，神経イメージング的方法（たとえば，Bishop, Jenkins, & Lawrence, 2006; Pinsk, Doniger, & Kastner, 2004; Rees, Frith, & Lavie, 1997）の両方を用いた多くの研究において得られてきた．

42　　　　　　　　　　　　4．序文（Introduction）

0124　縦断的アプローチで用いられる大規模コホート群について述べる．
◆ The X, collected by Y, consists of a cohort of Z who entered P in Q.
　X は，Y により集められ，Q 年に P に入学した Z のコホートから成っている．

> The ECLS-K, collected by the U.S. Department of Education's National Center for Educational Statistics, consists of a nationally representative cohort of children (with a multistage probability sample design) who entered kindergarten in the fall of 1998 and who are being followed longitudinally.　(23)
> ECLS-K は，米国教育省の全米教育統計センターにより集められ，1998 年の秋に幼稚園に入学し，縦断的に追跡され続けている，国を代表する子供のコホート（多段階確率標本デザインによる）から成っている．

（訳者注：ECLS-K; Early Childhood Longitudinal Survey—Kindergarten Cohort, 幼児期縦断的調査—幼稚園コホート群：コホートとは，同齢の集団のことである）

4.1.11　課　題

0125　課題において参加者にあることが要求されたことを述べる．
◆ In their study, Xs were required to perform Y.
　彼らの研究では，X が，Y を行うように要求された．

> In their study, players of varying age and experience levels were required to perform a series of tasks deemed either relevant or irrelevant to the game.　(47)
> 彼らの研究では，さまざまな年齢と経験レベルのプレーヤーが，ゲームに関係がある，あるいは，関係がないと思われる一連の課題を行うように要求された．

0126　課題において参加者に反応を行うことが要求されたことを述べる．
◆ In a typical X task, participants make Y responses between different target stimuli.
　典型的な X 課題では，参加者は異なる標的刺激間の Y 反応を行う．

> In a typical flanker task, participants make speeded choice responses between different target stimuli.　(14)
> 典型的なフランカー課題では，参加者は異なる標的刺激間の選択反応を急いで行う．

0127　課題がある装置を用いることを，その開発者とともに述べる．
◆ Developed by Author (Year), the X task uses Y.
　X 課題は，著者（発表年）により開発され，Y を用いる．

> Developed by Silva and Frussa-Filho (1997), the PMDAT uses an elevated plus-maze consisting of two opposing, open arms and two opposing, enclosed arms.　(21)
> PMDAT は，Silva と Frussa-Filho（1997）により開発され，反対方向に伸びる 2 本の開放アームと，反対方向に伸びる 2 本の閉鎖アームから成る，高架式の十字型迷路を用いる．

（訳者注：PMDAT; plus-maze discriminative avoidance task, 十字型迷路弁別回避課題）

4.1.12 測度・尺度

0128 初期の測度を紹介する.

◆ Among the first attempts to assess A and B were C measures like D (Abbreviation for test; Author, Year).

AとBを評価する初期の試みの中には，D検査（検査の略語；著者，発表年）のようなC測度がある.

> Among the first attempts to assess implicit self-esteem and self-concept were projective measures like the Thematic Apperception Test (TAT; Murray, 1943). (13)
> 潜在的な自尊心と自己概念を評価する初期の試みの中には，絵画統覚テスト（TAT; Murray, 1943）のような投影法がある.

0129 尺度があることを測定するために用いられてきたことを述べる.

◆ The X scale has been used as a[n] Y scale to measure Z.

X尺度は，Zを測定するためのY尺度として用いられてきた.

> The CGI-I scale has been used as a clinical rating scale to measure treatment response in clinical trials involving several psychiatric disorders. (26)
> CGI-I尺度は，いくつかの精神障害を含む臨床治験における治療への反応を測定するための臨床評定尺度として用いられてきた.

（訳者注：CGI-I scale; Clinical Global Impression-Improvement scale, 臨床全般印象改善尺度）

0130 先行研究がある測度を使って患者を評価したことを述べる.

◆ Author (Year) assessed L patients with A (ages M–N years) with B and C, and later asked P to QQQ.

著者（発表年）は，AのあるL名の患者（年齢はM〜N歳）を，BとCを用いて評価し，その後，PにQQQを行うことを求めた.

> Margraf and colleagues assessed 27 patients with panic attacks (ages 18–60 years) with clinical interviews and standardized questionnaires and later asked them to keep a diary for 6 days (Margraf et al., 1987). (1)
> Margrafらのグループは，パニック発作のある27名の患者（年齢は18〜60歳）を，臨床面接と標準化された質問紙を用いて評価し，その後，6日間日記をつけることを患者に求めた（Margraf et al., 1987）.

0131 質問紙を用いた測度研究の一例を紹介する.

◆ In one study, X completed Y.

ある研究では，XがYに回答した.

> In one study, patients with different degrees of agoraphobic avoidance completed a questionnaire. (1)
> ある研究では，異なる程度の広場恐怖型の回避症状をもつ患者が，質問紙に回答した.

4. 序文 (Introduction)

0132 測度の計算方法について述べる．

◆A[n] X measure of Y is computed as Z.

YのX測度は，Zとして計算される．

> An IAT measure of implicit self-esteem is computed as the difference in mean categorization latency when self and pleasant share the same response key (self pleasant). (13)
> 潜在的な自尊心のIAT測度は，自己と快適さが同じ反応キーを共有している場合に分類にかかる平均反応潜時の差として計算される．

（訳者注：IAT; Implicit Association Test, 潜在的連合テスト）

0133 ある指数が測度として有用であることを述べる．

◆X provides a useful measure of Y.

XはYについての有用な測度を提供する．

> Thus, the selectivity index provides a useful measure of memory efficiency. (7)
> それゆえ，選択性指標は，記憶効率についての有用な測度を提供する．

0134 最近，新たな測度が導入されたことを述べる．

◆Recently, a new measurement tool for assessing X was introduced: the Y (Abbreviation for Y; Author, Year).

最近，Xを評価するための新しい測定手段が取り入れられた．すなわち，Yである（Yの略語；著者，発表年）．

> Recently, a promising new measurement tool for assessing implicit processes was introduced: the Implicit Association Test (IAT; Greenwald, McGhee, & Schwartz, 1998). (13)
> 最近，潜在的過程を評価するための新しい有望な測定手段が取り入れられた．すなわち，潜在的連合テスト（IAT; Greenwald, McGhee, & Schwartz, 1998）である．

（訳者注：研究論文では，recent や recently を，「2～3年前」という意味で用いることが多い）

0135 尺度が妥当であることを述べる．

◆The [sub]scales show (a) convergent validity because XXX, (b) discriminant validity in that YYY, and (c) convergent and discriminant validity in that ZZZ.

この[下位]尺度は，(a) XXXなので収束的妥当性があり，(b) YYYという点で弁別的妥当性があり，(c) ZZZという点で収束的妥当性と弁別的妥当性がある．

> The subscales also show (a) convergent validity because they correlate highly with the corresponding Profile of Mood States, (b) discriminant validity in that the subscales of the PANAS-X are less highly intercorrelated than POMS counterparts, and (c) convergent and discriminant validity in that well-acquainted peers' ratings correlate with self ratings. (25)
> また，この下位尺度は，(a) 対応する気分プロフィール検査（POMS）と高い相関を示すので収束的妥当性があり，(b) PANAS-Xの下位尺度はPOMS内のこれらに相当する尺度と比べて相互の相関がより小さいので弁別的妥当性があり，(c) 本人をよく知る同輩による評定が自己による評定と相関するので収束的妥当性と弁別的妥当性がある．

（訳者注：PANAS-X; Positive and Negative Affect Scales—Expanded Form, ポジティブ感情・ネガティブ感情尺度—拡張版）

4.1.13 変 数

0136 結果変数を列挙して紹介する．
◆ Two of the common outcomes measured in X research are A and B.
　X の研究において共通に測定されてきた結果変数として，A と B がある．
> Two of the common psychological outcomes measured in disaster research are general psychological distress (GPD) and posttraumatic stress (PTS). (3)
> 災害研究において測定されてきた共通の心理学的な結果変数として，一般的心理的苦痛（GPD），および，心的外傷後ストレス（PTS）がある．

0137 独立変数と従属変数についての最近の知見を紹介する．
◆ Recent studies of X have investigated the effects of Y on Z.
　X についての最近の研究は，Z が Y に及ぼす効果を調べてきている．
> Recent studies of amnesic patients have also investigated the effects of unitization on associative recognition. (12)
> 健忘症患者についての最近の研究もまた，ユニット化が連合再認に及ぼす効果を調べてきている．

0138 ある分野の研究における重要な変数を紹介する．
◆ X has been an important variable in research on Y.
　X は，Y についての研究における重要な変数であった．
> Students' sense of community has been an important variable in educational research on school climate. (58)
> 学生のコミュニティ意識は，学校風土についての教育学的研究における重要な変数であった．

0139 広く研究されてきた変数を紹介する．
◆ The two [/three] most widely studied X have been A [, B,] and C.
　最も広く研究されてきた 2 [/3] つの X は，A [と B] と C であった．
> The two most widely studied ideological beliefs have been right-wing authoritarianism and social dominance orientation. (9)
> 最も広く研究されてきたイデオロギーに関する 2 つの信念は，右派権威主義と社会的優位性志向であった．

0140 多数の研究が変数間の関連を報告してきたことを述べる．
◆ A large body of research has found evidence of an association between X and Y.
　膨大な数の研究が，X と Y の間に関連があるという証拠を見出してきた．
> A large body of research has found evidence of an association between hostility and coronary heart disease. (38)
> 膨大な数の研究が，敵意と冠状動脈性心疾患の間に関連があるという証拠を見出してきた．

0141　ある変数が多種多様な変数と相関することを述べる．

◆X has shown a consistent pattern of correlations with a diverse array of psychological variables, including A, B, and C.

Xは，A, B, Cを含む多種多様な心理学的変数と相関するという一貫したパターンを示してきた．

> Moreover, this axis has shown a consistent pattern of correlations with a diverse array of psychological variables, including perceptions of instability, uncertainty avoidance, and openness to experience. (9)
> さらに，この軸は，不安定性の認識，不確実性の回避，経験に対する寛大さを含む多種多様な心理学的変数と相関するという一貫したパターンを示してきた．

0142　多くの研究が，変数間に関連があることを例証してきたことを述べる．

◆Numerous studies have demonstrated a significant association between X and Y.

多くの研究が，XとYの間に有意な関連があることを例証してきている．

> Numerous studies have demonstrated a significant association between multiple indicators of health and measures of personality, using both larger dimensions like the Big Five personality traits, as well as more specific personality traits like optimism. (38)
> 多くの研究が，ビッグファイブ性格特性のようなより大きな次元や，楽観性のようなより特異的な性格特性を用いて，複数の健康指標と性格測度の間に有意な関連があることを例証してきている．

4.2　先行研究の知見

4.2.1　単独の知見

0143　先行研究が見出した知見を述べる（**found** を使いすぎないように注意）．

◆Author (Year) found that P was unrelated to Q.

著者（発表年）は，PはQと無関係であることを見出した．

> Charness (1981) found that the effectiveness of search for chess moves was unrelated to age among expert players. (47)
> Charness (1981) は，チェスのエキスパート選手では，詰め手の探索の有効性が年齢と無関係であることを見出した．

0144　先行研究が見出した知見を，著者に帰属させながら述べる．

◆According to Author (Year), there is no evidence that Ps are able to QQQ.

著者（発表年）によれば，PがQQQを行うことができるという証拠はない．

> According to Oden et al. (2001), there is no evidence that primates other than apes are able to solve analogies. (34)
> Odenら（2001）によれば，類人猿以外の霊長類が類推を解くことができるという証拠はない．

4.2 先行研究の知見

0145 先行研究が例証した知見を述べる.

◆ Author (Year) demonstrated that P required Q.

著者（発表年）は，PがQを要求することを例証した．

> For example, Thaler (1981) demonstrated that to delay a $15 lottery winning for 3 months people required an extra $15. (35)
> たとえば，Thaler（1981）は，15ドルの宝くじの賞金を3か月遅延するために人々はさらに15ドルを要求することを例証した．

0146 先行研究が報告した知見を意味とともに述べる.

◆ Author (Year) reports that XXX, suggesting that P develops over time.

著者（発表年）は，XXXということを報告し，Pは時間経過とともに発達することを示唆している．

> Gentner and Rattermann (1991) report that younger children (3 year-olds) showed poorer performance on this task in comparison with 4 year-olds, suggesting that the ability to reason about relations develops over time. (34)
> GentnerとRattermann（1991）は，さらに幼い子供（3歳）は4歳の子供と比べてこの課題での成績が悪いことを報告し，関係についての推論能力は時間経過とともに発達することを示唆している．

0147 先行研究がある課題を用いて見出した行動の確率についての知見を述べる.

◆ Using a[n] X, Author (Year) found that Ps were more likely to QQQ than were Rs.

Xを用いて，著者（発表年）は，PはRよりもQQQする確率が高いことを見出した．

> Using a conservation task, Church and Goldin-Meadow (1986) found that children who often produced gestures conveying different information from that conveyed in their speech were significantly more likely to profit from instruction in conservation than were children who produced few such gestures. (5)
> 保存課題を用いて，ChurchとGoldin-Meadow（1986）は，発話で伝えている情報とは異なる情報を伝えるジェスチャーをよく示す子供は，そのようなジェスチャーをほとんど示さない子供と比べて，保存課題の教示から学びとる確率が有意に高いことを見出した．

0148 古典的研究が見出した頻度についての知見を述べる.

◆ In a classic study [of X], the number of Ps was highest if QQQ (Author, Year).

[Xについての] 古典的な研究では，QQQの場合にPの数が最も多くなった（著者，発表年）．

> In an early classic study, when patients with panic attacks were asked to report which symptoms they experienced during their attacks, the number of symptoms was highest if assessed with a retrospective questionnaire (Margraf, Taylor, Ehlers, & Roth, 1987). (1)
> 初期の古典的な研究では，パニック発作の患者が発作中にどの症状を経験したかを聞かれた際に，回顧的な質問紙で評価された場合に症状数が最も多くなった（Margraf, Taylor, Ehlers, & Roth, 1987）．

4. 序文 (Introduction)

0149 尺度の得点についての知見を述べる．

◆ Author (Year) reported a score range of A to B (with a mean of C) on X administered to N individuals with Y.

著者（発表年）は，Y に罹患している N 名に実施した X において，A 点から B 点（平均が C 点）という得点の範囲を報告している．

> For instance, Streissguth, Barr, Kogan, and Bookstein (1996) reported a score range of 20 to 120 (with a mean of 79) on an IQ test administered to 178 individuals with FAS. (40)
> たとえば，Streissguth, Barr, Kogan, Bookstein（1996）は，FAS に罹患している 178 名に実施した IQ テストにおいて 20 点から 120 点（平均が 79 点）という得点の範囲を報告している．
>
> （訳者注：FAS; fetal alcohol syndrome, 胎児アルコール症候群）

0150 全国的研究による，ある参加者の割合についての知見を述べる．

◆ A nationwide study of X found that N% PPP (Author, Year).

X の全国的研究は，N% の X が PPP を行うことを見出した（著者，発表年）．

> A nationwide study of college students found that 71% overestimate the amount of alcohol used by peers (Perkins et al., 2005). (39)
> 大学生の全国的研究は，71% の大学生が，同輩のアルコール消費量を過大評価することを見出した（Perkins et al., 2005）．

0151 結果の分析により，一般的なパターンが見られたことを述べる．

◆ According to the results of their [meta-]analysis, the pattern of Ps remained generalizable (Author, Year).

彼らの[メタ]分析の結果によれば，P のパターンは一般化が可能なままであった（著者，発表年）．

> According to the results of their meta-analysis, more children than adults reported very severe levels of impairment, but the main patterns of GPD and PTS remained generalizable (Norris, Freidman, & Watson, 2002). (3)
> 彼らのメタ分析の結果によれば，大人より子供のほうが障害が大きいと報告したが，GPD と PTS のおもなパターンは相変わらず一般化が可能なままであった（Norris, Freidman, & Watson, 2002）．
>
> （訳者注：GPD; general psychological distress, 一般的心理的苦痛：PTS; posttraumatic stress, 心的外傷後ストレス）

0152 メタ分析による，ある結果の出現率についての知見を述べる．

◆ A meta-analysis of N X studies revealed Y in M% of the Z investigated (Author, Year).

N 個の X 研究のメタ分析は，研究された Z の中の M% において Y が見られることを明らかにした（著者，発表年）．

> A meta-analysis of 23 college drinking studies revealed misperceptions in 91% of the measures investigated (Borsari & Carey, 2008). (39)

4.2 先行研究の知見

大学生の飲酒に関する 23 の研究のメタ分析は，研究された測度の 91% において，誤った知覚が見られることを明らかにした（Borsari & Carey, 2008）．

0153 判別分析に基づく正しい分類の割合についての知見を述べる．
◆ Discriminant analysis indicated that P correctly classified N% of Q.
判別分析は P が Q の N% を正しく分類することを示した．

> Discriminant analysis indicated that multiple physiological measures contributed nonredundant information and correctly classified 95% of phobic and control participants. (1)
> 判別分析は，複数の生理学的測度が非冗長的な情報を提供し，恐怖症参加者と統制群参加者の 95% を正しく分類することを示した．

0154 先行研究の知見を強調して述べる．
◆ That XXX is an argument [first] made by Author[s] (Year) in his [/her /their] [seminal] paper on Y.
XXX ということは，著者（発表年）による Y についての [影響力のある] 論文において [最初に] なされた主張である．

> That different types of rules track the kind of structure the observer encounters is an argument first made by Shepard, Hovland, and Jenkins (1962) in their seminal paper on rule use and category structure. (24)
> 観察者の遭遇する構造の種類によって規則のさまざまな型が定まるということは，Shepard, Hovland, Jenkins（1962）による規則使用とカテゴリー構造についての影響力のある論文において最初になされた主張である．
>
> （訳者注：ここで，Xs track Ys. とは，X が，Y により定められる経路をたどる，すなわち，Y により X が定まる，ということを意味する）

4.2.2 逸話・事例・インタビューによる知見

0155 逸話に基づくアイデアを述べる．
◆ Anecdotal evidence suggests that P shapes Q.
P が Q を決めることを示唆する逸話的証拠がある．

> Strong anecdotal evidence suggests that an executive's ability to lead meetings shapes how team members perceive his or her effectiveness as a leader. (48)
> 幹部社員が会議をリードする能力が，チーム構成員が幹部社員のリーダーとしての有能さをどのように認識するかを決める，ということを示唆する強力な逸話的証拠がある．

0156 事例研究について述べる．
◆ An [/Another] interesting application was reported in a case study where P data were used to QQQ (Author, Year).
1 つの [/ もう 1 つの] 興味深い応用が，QQQ を行うために P のデータを用いた事例研究において報告されている（著者，発表年）．

Another interesting application was reported in a single case study where psychophysiological data collected with ambulatory assessment were used to correct biased perceptions of a patient's remaining symptoms after treatment (Hofmann, 1999). (1)
もう1つの興味深い応用が，治療後に残る患者の症状についての偏った知覚を修正するために，移動評価法により集めた心理生理学的データを用いた単一の事例研究において報告されている（Hofmann, 1999）．

0157 インタビュー研究の知見を述べる．
◆Interview-based studies indicate that Ps are noted by Qs (Author, Year).
インタビューに基づく研究は，QがPに言及することを示している（著者，発表年）．

Interview-based studies indicate that specific catastrophic cognitions are noted by panic patients (Breitholtz, Westling, & Ost, 1998). (1)
インタビューに基づく研究は，パニックの患者が特異的な破局的認知に言及することを示している（Breitholtz, Westling, & Ost, 1998）．

4.2.3 共通する知見

0158 いくつかの先行研究が，同じことを示していることを述べる．
◆Several studies have shown that Ps increase with Q.
いくつかの研究は，PはQが大きくなるにつれて増加することを示してきた．

Several studies have shown that misperceptions increase with social distance. (39)
いくつかの研究は，誤解は社会的距離が大きくなるにつれて増加することを示してきた．

0159 ある数以上の先行研究が同じことを明らかにしてきたことを述べる．
◆To date, more than N studies have revealed X.
これまでに，N以上の研究が，Xを明らかにしてきた．

To date, more than 25 studies have revealed misperceptions in peer drinking norms, with students consistently overestimating both the amount of drinking among their peers, and the extent to which they approve of heavy drinking. (39)
これまでに，25以上の研究が，同輩の飲酒規範における誤解を明らかにしてきており，学生は，同輩の飲酒量，および，同輩が深酒を是認する程度の両方を，一貫して過大評価することを示している．

0160 先行研究に共通した知見を述べる．
◆A common finding of these [/many /early] studies was that P decreased during Q.
これらの[/多くの/初期の]研究の共通した知見は，Q中にPが減少したということであった．

A common finding of early studies was that self-reported fear but not heart rate decreased during treatment. (1)
初期の研究の共通した知見は，治療中に自己報告による恐怖は減少したが，心拍数は減少しなかったということであった．

4.2 先行研究の知見

0161 複数の研究から同じ知見が得られたことを，意味とともに述べる．

◆ At least N pieces of research support X. Taken together, Author (Year) suggests that Ps were more likely than others to QQQ.

少なくとも，N 個の研究が X を支持している．それらを総合して，著者（発表年）は，P が QQQ する確率が他のものと比べてより高かったことを示唆している．

> At least four pieces of research support the impact of this ingredient on students' research attitudes and productivity. Taken together, Goodyear and Lichtenberg (1991), Mallinckrodt et al. (1990), and Royalty et al. (1986) suggest that training programs that were research productive and had an influence on students' research attitudes were more likely than others to promote the views inherent in the bubble hypothesis. (16)
> 少なくとも，4 つの研究が，学生の研究態度と生産性にこの要因が影響することを支持している．それらを総合して，Goodyear と Lichtenberg（1991），Mallinckrodt ら（1990），および Royalty ら（1986）は，研究面において生産的で学生の研究態度に影響を及ぼすような訓練プログラムは，それ以外のプログラムと比べて，バブル仮説に固有の見方を促進する確率がより高かったことを示唆している．
>
> （訳者注：バブル仮説；研究者は，あたかもガラスとシールの間の泡を潰すことに熱中するように，研究の欠点を取り除くことにとらわれることが多いが，実際には，自らの研究に欠点が残ることを受け入れる必要がある，という考え方のこと）

0162 いくつかの臨床研究に基づく，ある物質の役割についての知見を述べる．

◆ Clinical [/Preclinical] studies have indicated that P may play a key [/an important] role in Q. For example, XXX (Author, Year).

臨床 [/ 前臨床] 研究は，P が Q において重要な役割を果たしていることを示してきた．たとえば，XXX（著者，発表年）．

> Preclinical studies have indicated that serotonin may also play an important role in the behavioral effects of psychomotor stimulants. For example, (略). (30)
> 前臨床試験は，精神運動性興奮剤の行動への効果において，セロトニンもまた重要な役割を果たすことを示してきた．たとえば，（略）．

0163 いくつかの前臨床研究に基づく，ある実験的操作の効果についての知見を述べる．

◆ Preclinical [animal] research has shown that P can decrease [/increase] Q (Author, Year).

前臨床 [動物] 研究は，P が Q を減少 [/ 増加] させることを示している（著者，発表年）．

> Preclinical animal research has shown that presentation of novel stimuli or placement in a novel environment can decrease drug intake (Cain, Smith, & Bardo, 2004; Thompson & Ostlund, 1965). (49)
> 前臨床の動物研究は，新奇刺激の呈示や新奇な環境に置かれることが薬物摂取量を減少させることを示している（Cain, Smith, & Bardo, 2004; Thompson & Ostlund, 1965）．

4. 序文 (Introduction)

0164 一連の臨床研究から得られた知見を述べる．
◆ Compelling data have emerged from clinical research supporting X.
臨床研究から，Xを支持するきわめて説得力のあるデータが出現してきた．

> Compelling data have emerged from clinical research supporting indirect agonist-like pharmacotherapy for stimulant abuse and dependence. (30)
> 臨床研究から，興奮剤中毒と依存性に対する間接的作用薬のような薬物療法を支持するきわめて説得力のあるデータが出現してきた．

0165 経験的な証拠が数多くあることを述べる．
◆ There is now a substantial body of empirical evidence demonstrating X.
今やXを示す経験的な証拠が数多くある．

> There is now a substantial body of empirical evidence demonstrating time-inconsistent discounting. (35)
> 今や，時間軸上で一貫していない割引を示す経験的な証拠が数多くある．

0166 あることを示す先行研究が最近数多く累積していることを述べる．
◆ In [/Over] the last few years, an impressive number of studies demonstrating X have accumulated.
ここ2, 3年間に，Xを例証する非常に多くの研究が累積してきた．

> In the last few years, an impressive number of studies demonstrating reliability and validity of the IAT have accumulated. (13)
> ここ2, 3年間に，IATの信頼性と妥当性を例証する非常に多くの研究が累積してきた．

（訳者注：IAT; Implicit Association Test, 潜在的連合テスト）

0167 非常に多くの文献が示してきた知見を述べる．
◆ A large body of literature has shown that P can affect Q.
非常に多くの文献が，PがQに影響を及ぼすことがあることを示してきている．

> A large body of literature has shown that schools can affect children's academic performance. (23)
> 非常に多くの文献が，学校は子供の学業成績に影響を及ぼすことがあることを示してきている．

0168 特定の志向をもって行われてきた多くの研究が，ある知見をもたらしてきたことを述べる．
◆ A number of studies conducted within the X orientation (Author, Year) have shown that P can impair Q.
X志向で行われてきた多くの研究（著者，発表年）は，PがQを悪化させることがあることを示してきた．

4.2 先行研究の知見　　　53

> A number of studies conducted within the S–R orientation (Maltzman, Fox, & Morrisett, 1953; Spence, Farber, & McFann, 1956; Spence, Taylor, & Ketchel, 1956) have shown that a high drive can impair performance. (18)
> S–R 志向で行われてきた多くの研究（Maltzman, Fox, & Morrisett, 1953; Spence, Farber, & McFann, 1956; Spence, Taylor, & Ketchel, 1956）は，高い動因が成績を悪化させることがあることを示してきた．

（訳者注：S–R orientation; stimulus–response orientation, 刺激 – 反応志向）

0169　多くの研究者が同じ考えを主張していることを述べる．

◆ Many researchers have argued that Ps convey Q.

多くの研究者は，P が Q を伝達すると主張してきた．

> Many researchers have argued that the gestures speakers produce when they talk convey substantive information. (5)
> 多くの研究者は，話者が話すときに生成するジェスチャーが実質的な情報を伝達すると主張してきた．

0170　非常に多くの文献を要約する．

◆ A substantial body of X literature indicates that P becomes stronger with Q.

非常に多くの X 文献が，P は Q とともにより強くなることを示している．

> A substantial body of Western and cross-cultural literature indicates that competitive game-playing behavior and competitive attitudes become stronger with age, particularly among males and in urban/Westernized populations. (54)
> 非常に多くの欧米および異文化比較の文献が，競争的なゲーム遊びの行動と競争的態度が，特に男性，および，都会の母集団や西洋化された母集団において，年齢とともにより強くなることを示している．

4.2.4　研究グループによる知見

0171　研究グループによる先行研究が指摘した知見を述べる．

◆ As Author and colleagues (Author, Year) have pointed out, XXX.

著者らのグループ（著者，発表年）が指摘しているように，XXX である．

> As Schyns and colleagues (Schyns, Goldstone, & Thibaut, 1998; Schyns & Murphy, 1994) have pointed out, features are concepts in themselves. (24)
> Schyns らのグループ（Schyns, Goldstone, & Thibaut, 1998; Schyns & Murphy, 1994）が指摘しているように，特徴は，それ自体が概念である．

0172　研究グループによる研究の結論を述べる．

◆ Author and his [/her] colleagues (Year) concluded that the use of P is justified in Q.

著者らのグループ（発表年）は，Q における P の使用が正当化されると結論した．

4. 序文 (Introduction)

For example, in their analysis of the CGI-severity and CGI-improvement scales, Leon and his colleagues (1993) concluded that the use of the CGI-severity and CGI-improvement scales is justified in clinical trials. (26)
たとえば，Leon らのグループ（1993）は，CGI の重症度尺度と改善尺度の分析において，臨床治験におけるこれらの下位尺度の使用が正当化されると結論した．

（訳者注：CGI scale; Clinical Global Impression scale, 臨床全般印象尺度）

0173 研究グループによる研究が示した影響についての知見を述べる．

◆Author and colleagues (reviewed in [/by] Author, Year) have shown that P is influenced by Q.
著者らのグループ（著者，発表年で評論されている）は，P が Q により影響されることを示してきた．

> Chun and colleagues (reviewed in Chun, 2000) have shown that search for objects in scenes is influenced by the familiarity of distractor identity or of surround configuration. (24)
> Chun らのグループ（Chun, 2000 で評論されている）は，場面内における物体の探索が，妨害物の独自性や周囲の配置の熟知性により影響されることを示してきた．

0174 研究グループによる研究が示した反映についての知見を評論とともに述べる．

◆In a series of studies, Author and colleagues (for a review, see Author, Year) have shown that P reflects Q.
一連の研究において，著者らのグループ（評論については，著者，発表年を参照）は，P が Q を反映することを示してきた．

> In a series of studies, Rovee-Collier and colleagues (for a review, see Rovee-Collier, 1997) have shown that a failure of instrumental performance by young infants does not always reflect an absence of learning. (37)
> 一連の研究において，Rovee-Collier らのグループ（評論については Rovee-Collier, 1997 を参照）は，年少の乳児たちの道具的遂行行動の失敗が必ずしも学習の欠如を反映しないことを示してきた．

0175 1 人の研究者とそのグループによる一連の実験を報告する．

◆A series of experiments by Author and colleagues (e.g., Author, Year) reported XXX.
著者らのグループによる一連の実験（たとえば，著者，発表年）は，XXX ということを報告した．

> A series of experiments by Graham and colleagues (e.g., Davis et al., 1983; Graham, Kramer, & Haber, 1985) reported no effects of cuing on detection accuracy when two-interval forced choices were measured. (43)
> Graham らのグループによる一連の実験（たとえば，Davis et al., 1983; Graham, Kramer, & Haber, 1985）は，2 つの時間間隔の強制選択が測定された場合，手がかりが検出の正確さに影響しないことを報告した．

4.2.5 一貫した知見

0176 次第に一貫した知見が得られてきたことを述べる.

◆ Convergent results have been obtained from X studies, demonstrating that YYY.
X 研究の結果は収束してきており，YYY ということを例証しつつある.

> Convergent results have been obtained from event-related potential studies, demonstrating that the midfrontal FN400 old–new effect, which is typically correlated with familiarity-based recognition, is larger for associations that are rated as more unitized. (12)
> 事象関連電位研究の結果は収束してきており，通常は熟知性に基づく再認と相関する正中の FN400 の新奇・既知の効果が，よりユニット化されていると評定された連合に対してより大きくなることを例証しつつある.

0177 原因と結果について一貫した証拠があることを述べる.

◆ There is consistent evidence that Xs bring about Y.
X が Y を生じさせるという一貫した証拠がある.

> There is consistent evidence that feelings of belonging bring about action and reduce bystander behavior. (58)
> 所属意識が行為を生じさせ，傍観者行動を減少させる，という一貫した証拠がある.

0178 先行研究で一貫して得られた結果を述べる.

◆ A consistent observation in the study of X is Y.
X の研究において一貫して観察されてきたことは，Y である.

> A consistent observation in the study of aging and cognition is a decline in many perceptual and cognitive abilities across the adult life span. (47)
> 加齢と認知に関する研究において一貫して観察されてきたことは，多くの知覚的および認知的能力が成人の生涯を通して低下するということである.

0179 あることが強まるという一貫した証拠について述べる.

◆ The evidence consistently indicates that P strengthens during Q.
これまでの証拠は，Q の間に P が強まるを一貫して示している.

> The evidence consistently indicates that research attitudes do strengthen during training, if only modestly. (16)
> これまでの証拠は，訓練の間に，研究態度が，たとえ小幅であるとしても強まるのだということを一貫して示している.

0180 先行研究がある影響を一貫して強く支持することを述べる.

◆ Research has provided strong and consistent support for the impact of P on Q.
これまでの研究は，P が Q に影響することを一貫して強く支持してきた.

> Research has provided strong and consistent support for the impact of the advisor or mentor relationship on students' research attitudes. (16)

これまでの研究は，指導教員や指導者との関係が学生の研究態度に影響することを一貫して強く支持してきた．

4.2.6　一般的な知見

0181　一般的な知見を述べる．
◆ Research investigating X has reported Y [/that YYY].

X を分析した研究は，Y [/YYY ということ] を報告している．

> Research investigating the associations of RWA and SDO with Schwartz's social values, for example, has reported a recurrent pattern. (9)
> たとえば，シュワルツの社会的価値を用いて RWA と SDO の関連を分析した研究は，回帰的なパターンを報告している．
>
> （訳者注：RWA; right-wing authoritarianism, 右派権威主義：SDO; social dominance orientation, 社会的優位性志向）

0182　知見が十分に立証されていることを述べる．
◆ It is well established that XXX.

XXX ということは十分に立証されている．

> It is well established that many individuals with tinnitus complain of poor attention and concentration difficulties. (28)
> 耳鳴りのある多くの人々が，注意力が不足して注意集中が困難であると訴えることは，十分に立証されている．

0183　知見のパターンを述べる．
◆ This general pattern, indicating that XXX, has been reported in previous [/many /similar] studies.

この一般的なパターンは，XXX ということを示しており，先行 [/ 多くの / 類似の] 研究において報告が続いている．

> This general pattern, indicating that adolescents attain adult levels of competence to stand trial somewhere around age 15, has been reported in similar studies. (57)
> この一般的なパターンは，青年が裁判を受ける成人レベルの能力を 15 歳前後のどこかで獲得することを示しており，類似の研究において報告が続いている．

0184　評論から一般的な知見が明らかになることを述べる．
◆ In reviewing the literature on X, it becomes evident that YYY.

X についての文献を概観すれば，YYY であることが明らかになる．

> In reviewing the literature on using play therapy with special populations, it becomes evident that this modality is one that could prove beneficial in working with children diagnosed with FAS. (40)

4.2 先行研究の知見　　57

特定の母集団における遊戯療法の使用についての文献を概観すれば，この様式が，FAS と診断された子供の治療を手がける場合に有益であると実証される可能性があることが明らかになる．

（訳者注：FAS; fetal alcohol syndrome, 胎児アルコール症候群）

0185　決定的要因についての一般的な知見を述べる．
◆ Overall, this body of research indicates [clearly] that P is a crucial factor in Q.
全体的に，これら一連の研究は，P が Q における決定的な要因であることを [明確に] 示している．

> Overall, this body of research indicates clearly that resource loss is a crucial factor in individuals' trauma following disaster experiences.　　(3)
> 全体的に，これら一連の研究は，資源損失が災害経験の後に続く人々の心的外傷の決定的な要因であることを，明確に示している．

0186　原因と結果について一般的に同意が得られていることを述べる．
◆ There is general agreement that P results in [/leads to] Q.
P が Q を引き起こすことについては，一般的に同意されている．

> There is general agreement that acute psychological stress in humans leads to a cascade of hormonal changes.　　(1)
> ヒトにおける急性の心理的ストレスが一連のホルモン変化を引き起こすことについては，一般的に同意されている．

4.2.7　証拠・データ

0187　あることを示唆する証拠が多いことを述べる．
◆ The X literature has provided much evidence suggesting that YYY.
X の文献は，YYY ということを示唆する多くの証拠をもたらしてきた．

> The developmental literature has provided much evidence suggesting that prior knowledge plays a key role in forming effective problem-solving strategies.　　(34)
> 発達に関する文献は，事前の知識が効果的な問題解決ストラテジーの形成において重要な役割を果たすことを示唆する多くの証拠をもたらしてきた．

0188　証拠とその出典を述べる．
◆ Evidence that XXX comes from Y research [/studies].
XXX であることの証拠は，Y の研究から得られている．

> Evidence that habits can be performed without an available supporting explicit goal comes from naturalistic studies predicting the frequency with which people perform everyday behaviors such as watching TV, purchasing fast food, driving a car, and recycling.　　(62)
> 利用できる明示的な支持目標がなくても習慣を遂行できる証拠は，人々がテレビを見る，ファストフードを買う，自動車を運転する，リサイクルをするなどの日常的行動を行う頻度を予測する自然観察的な研究から得られている．

4. 序文（Introduction）

0189 研究が実質的な証拠を提供していることを述べる．
◆ Research on X provides substantial evidence of Y.
　X についての研究は，Y に関する実質的な証拠を提供している．
> Research on automatic goal pursuit provides substantial evidence of variability in responses promoted by the activation of nonconscious goals. (62)
> 自動的な目標追求についての研究は，無意識な目標の活性化により促進される反応の変動に関する実質的な証拠を提供する．

0190 重要な証拠の一部について述べる．
◆ Importantly, X has provided some of the most convincing evidence for Y.
　重要なことに，X は Y を支持する最も説得力のある証拠の一部をもたらしてきている．
> Importantly, this has provided some of the most convincing evidence for the validity of important models of psychopathology in panic disorder. (1)
> 重要なことに，このことは，パニック障害に関する精神病理学の重要なモデルの妥当性を支持する最も説得力のある証拠の一部をもたらしてきている．

0191 縦断的研究によるデータを述べる．
◆ Longitudinal studies have provided evidence [/data] demonstrating X.
　縦断的研究は，X を例証する証拠 [/ データ] を提供してきた．
> Longitudinal studies have provided data demonstrating the difficulties faced in school by children with FAS. (40)
> 縦断的研究は，FAS のある子供が学校で直面する困難さを例証するデータを提供してきた．

（訳者注：FAS; fetal alcohol syndrome, 胎児アルコール症候群）

0192 機序についての証拠を，あるアイデアとの一致とともに述べる．
◆ Consistent with this view, Author and his [/her] colleagues have provided evidence that Ps provide a mechanism for Q.
　この見方と一致して，著者らのグループは，P が Q の機序をもたらすという証拠を報告している．
> Consistent with this view, Mikulincer and his colleagues have provided evidence that priming thoughts of secure attachments and the maintenance of close relationships provide an alternative mechanism for quelling existential anxiety about death. (11)
> この見方と一致して，Mikulincer らのグループは，揺るぎない愛着についてのプライミング的な思考，および，親密な関係の維持が，死についての実存的不安を鎮める代替的な機序をもたらすという証拠を報告している．

0193 原因と結果についての説得力のある証拠をもたらしていることを述べる．
◆ Research on X provides convincing evidence that P results in [/leads to] Q.
　X についての研究は，P が Q につながるという説得力のある証拠をもたらしている．

4.2 先行研究の知見

> Research on the authority aspects of school climate provides convincing evidence that democratic exchange between students and school authority figures results in positive student outcomes. (58)
> 学校風土の権威的側面についての研究は，学生と権威者の間の民主的なやりとりは学生に有益な結果につながるという説得力のある証拠をもたらしている．

0194 決定要因についての説得力のある証拠を提供していることを述べる．

◆ This body of research [therefore] provides convincing evidence that P determines Q.
[それゆえ，]これら一連の研究は，PがQを決めるという説得力のある証拠を提供している．

> This body of research therefore provides convincing evidence that perceptual load determines the level of neural activity related to task-irrelevant stimuli. (43)
> それゆえ，これら一連の研究は，知覚的負荷が，課題とは無関連の刺激に関係する神経活動のレベルを決定するという説得力のある証拠を提供している．

0195 あることが起こるという証拠が十分に存在することを述べる．

◆ There is ample evidence that P occurs.
Pが起こるということを示す十分な証拠がある．

> However, there is ample evidence that adolescent violence toward parents also occurs (Paulson, Coombs, & Landsverk, 1990; Ulman & Straus, 2003), and that parent and adolescent violence within the dyad are related (Brezina, 1999; Browne & Hamilton, 1998; Ulman & Straus, 2003). (22)
> しかしながら，親に対する青年の暴力も起こること（Paulson, Coombs, & Landsverk, 1990; Ulman & Straus, 2003），そして，親子の組における親の暴力と青年の暴力の間には関連があること（Brezina, 1999; Browne & Hamilton, 1998; Ulman & Straus, 2003）を示す十分な証拠がある．

4.2.8 知見の具体的な内容

0196 可能性についての知見を述べる．

◆ Xs are likely to YYY.
Xは，YYYをする可能性が高い．

> That is, optimistic individuals facing a disaster are more likely to cope in a beneficial manner. (3)
> すなわち，災害に直面した楽観的な人々は，有益な仕方で対処行動を示す可能性がより高い．

0197 予測についての知見を述べる．

◆ X (e.g., A, B, C) predicted Y more strongly than did Z.
X（たとえば，A, B, C）は，Zよりもより強力にYを予測した．

For example, Chaney et al. (1997) found that increases in fathers' general distress (e.g., anxiety, depression, anger) over the course of one year predicted psychological functioning among children and adolescents with diabetes more strongly than did mothers' distress. (45)
たとえば，Chaney ら（1997）は，父親の一般的な苦痛（たとえば，不安，うつ，怒り）の1年間の増加のほうが，母親の悩みの増加よりも，糖尿病の子供や青年の心理的機能をより強力に予測することを見出した．

0198 発生状況についての知見を述べる．

◆A[n] X occurs when YYY.

　YYY のときに，X が起こる．

> A stressor occurs when an employee perceives an environmental demand as being exceeding, taxing, or threatening to his or her adaptive resources. (52)
> 環境の要求が過度である，負担が大きい，あるいは，適応資源にとって脅威となると被雇用者が知覚したときに，ストレス因子が発生する．

0199 背後にある機序についての知見を述べる．

◆The essential mechanism behind X involves Y.

　X の背後にある本質的な機序は，Y を含む．

> The essential mechanism behind direct cueing involves the cognitive neural changes that result from repeated coactivation of responses and contexts. (62)
> 直接的なキューイングの背後にある本質的な機序は，反応と文脈の反復的な同時活性化の結果として起きる認知的な神経変化を含む．

0200 相関についての知見を述べる．

◆X and Y have been found to be [weakly /moderately /strongly] correlated.

　X と Y は [弱く / 中程度に / 強く] 相関することが見出されてきた．

> Right-wing authoritarianism and social dominance orientation have been found to be weakly to moderately correlated. (9)
> 右派権威主義と社会的優位性志向は弱程度から中程度に相関することが見出されてきた．

0201 無相関についての知見を述べる．

◆There was no significant correlation between X and Y.

　X と Y の間に有意な相関はなかった．

> However, there was no significant correlation between the cortisol elevations during panic attacks and the severity of the attack. (1)
> しかしながら，パニック発作中のコルチゾールの上昇と発作の重症度の間に有意な相関はなかった．

0202 関連についての知見を述べる．

◆X has been associated with Y (see Author, Year, for review).

XはYと関連性をもち続けてきた（評論については，著者，発表年を参照）．

> Increased rates of car accidents have been associated with sections of road with greater numbers of roadside billboards (see B. Wallace, 2003, for review). (14)
> 自動車事故率の増加は，道路脇の広告板の数がより多い場所と関連性をもち続けてきた（評論については B. Wallace, 2003 を参照）．

> （訳者注：引用文献中に著者の異なる Wallace, 2003 が2つあり，それらを区別するために B. という名前のイニシャルが付されている）

0203 変数間の影響についての知見を，理論との一致とともに述べる．

◆ Consistent with X framework (Author, Year), Y appears to influence Z.

Xの枠組み（著者，発表年）と一致するように，YがZに影響しているように見える．

> Consistent with Kazak's social-ecological framework (Kazak, 1989), a child's illness itself appears to influence parents' stress responses. (45)
> Kazak の社会生態学的な枠組み（Kazak, 1989）と一致するように，子供の疾患自体が両親のストレス反応に影響しているように見える．

0204 ある母集団で実証されている現象についての知見を述べる．

◆ This phenomenon has been documented for participants [/children] from X (Author, Year) and Y (Author, Year) origins.

この現象は，X系（著者，発表年），および，Y系（著者，発表年）の参加者 [/子供] について，実証されてきている．

> This phenomenon has been documented for children of immigrants from both Asian (e.g., Zhou & Bankston, 1998) and Mexican (e.g., Matute-Bianchi, 1986; Valenzuela, 1999) origins. (23)
> この現象は，アジア系（たとえば，Zhou & Bankston, 1998），および，メキシコ系（たとえば，Matute-Bianchi, 1986; Valenzuela, 1999）の移民の子供について，実証されてきている．

0205 患者の行動傾向についての知見を述べる．

◆ When asked to XXX, individuals with Y tend to ZZZ.

XXX することを求められたとき，Yに罹患している人々は，ZZZ をする傾向がある．

> When asked to remember a specific event from their lives in response to a cue word (e.g., "happy"), individuals with depression show an overgeneral memory bias (OGM), that is, they tend to reply with descriptions that summarize several different events. (36)
> 手がかりとなる単語（たとえば，「うれしい」）に対して人生から特定の出来事を思い出すことを求められたとき，うつに罹患している人々は，概括化された記憶偏向（OGM）を示す．すなわち，彼らはいくつかの異なる出来事を要約する描写で答える傾向がある．

0206 参加者による報告についての知見を列挙する．

◆ Xs often report (a) A, (b) B, (c) C, and (d) D.

Xは，(a) A, (b) B, (c) C, (d) Dをしばしば報告する．

4. 序文 (Introduction)

> Runners often report (a) a feeling of euphoria after a strenuous bout of exercise (runner's high), (b) the need to increase the distance run to achieve feelings of well-being (tolerance), (c) difficulties in job performance and social interactions (addiction), and (d) symptoms of withdrawal, including depression, irritability, and anxiety, when prohibited from running (withdrawal). (33)
> ランナーは，(a) ひとしきり熱心に練習した後に多幸感を感じること（ランナーズ・ハイ），(b) 幸福感を得るために長距離走を増やしていく必要があること（耐性），(c) 仕事の遂行や社会的相互作用が難しくなること（嗜癖），(d) ランニングを禁止された場合に，うつ，易刺激性，不安を含む離脱症状を示すこと（離脱）を，しばしば報告する．

4.2.9 知見の強調

0207 たびたび報告される知見を述べる．
◆ It has been reported often that XXX.
　XXX ということがしばしば報告されてきている．

> For example, it has been reported often that many different agents, habits, or exogenous factors are capable of triggering attacks. (1)
> たとえば，多くの異なる作用物質，習慣，あるいは，外因的要因が発作の引き金となりうることがしばしば報告されてきている．

0208 知見の一部を強調する．
◆ Specifically, XXX (Author, Year).
　特に，XXX である（著者，発表年）．

> Specifically, individuals' feelings of safety, the strength of the disaster where they were located, or damage to their surrounding areas might not directly lead to loss of resources, but they remain indirectly associated with resource loss (Hobfoll, 2001). (3)
> 特に，人々が感じる安全性，移住した地域の災害強度，あるいは，周辺地域の被害は，資源損失に直接つながるものではないかもしれないが，それらは資源損失と間接的な関係を保ち続けている（Hobfoll, 2001）．

0209 視点を変えて強調する．
◆ In other words [/That is], XXX.
　言い換えれば，XXX．

> In other words, the task of expressing explicit knowledge can facilitate changes in that knowledge. (5)
> 言い換えれば，顕在的な知識を表現する課題は，その知識の変化を促進するかもしれない．

0210 異なる研究法を用いても，あることが重要であることを述べる．
◆ Congruent with X, Y also points to the importance of Z.
　X と同じように，Y も Z の重要性を示している．

Congruent with experimental manipulations in the laboratory, ambulatory assessment under natural conditions also points to the importance of expectancy in the onset of panic attacks. (1)

実験室における実験的操作と同じように，自然条件下での移動評価も，パニック発作開始時における期待の重要性を示している．

0211 知見のある側面が重要であることを述べる．

◆What is more important for our present concern is that P indicates that QQQ.

我々の今回の関心にとってより重要なことは，PがQQQを示すことである．

> What is more important for our present concern is that regardless of the initial perceptual error, the near congruence of the centroids for direct and indirect paths to the various targets for both vision and audition indicates that spatial updating was performed well for the two modalities. (42)
>
> 我々の今回の関心にとってより重要なのは，最初の知覚錯誤にかかわらず，直接的および間接的経路の重心が視覚および聴覚の多様な標的によく適合しているということから，これら2つのモダリティについて空間的更新がうまく実行されたことが示される，ということである．

4.2.10 最近の知見

0212 重要な要因についての最近の知見を引用する．

◆Recent research by Author (Year) identified X as a key factor.

著者（発表年）による最近の研究は，Xが重要な要因であることを証明した．

> Recent research by van Ginkel and van Knippenberg (2008) identified group members' understanding of the task as a key factor in this respect. (59)
>
> van Ginkelとvan Knippenberg（2008）による最近の研究は，グループ構成員の課題の理解がその点で重要な要因であることを証明した．

0213 最近の研究により，限界が例証されたことを述べる．

◆A recent study by Author (Year) illustrated the limitations of X.

著者（発表年）による最近の研究は，Xの限界を例証した．

> A recent study by Sanders Thompson and Alexander (2006) illustrated the limitations of relying on investigator-developed measures of the therapy process. (8)
>
> Sanders ThompsonとAlexander（2006）による最近の研究は，研究者が開発した治療過程測定に頼ることの限界を例証した．
>
> （訳者注：Sanders Thompsonは，1人の著者の名字である）

0214 あることを高めるという最近の研究の意味を述べる．

◆Recent research suggests that Ps heighten Q (Author, Year).

最近の研究は，PがQを高めることを示唆している（著者，発表年）．

64   4. 序文 (Introduction)

> Recent research suggests that experiences on the streets, in shelters, or in other homeless settings may heighten risk in this way among youth who are homeless, a process referred to as "risk amplification" (Whitbeck, Hoyt, & Yoder, 1999). (22)
> 最近の研究は，路上，シェルター，あるいは他のホームレス環境での経験が，ホームレスの若者の間でリスクをこのように高めるかもしれないことを示唆しており，これは「リスク増幅」(Whitbeck, Hoyt, & Yoder, 1999) と呼ばれる過程である．

0215　より最近の研究により，異なる概念化が提案されていることを述べる．

◆ More recently, however, many authors conceptualize X as Y.
しかし，最近では，多くの著者が X を Y として概念化している．

> More recently, however, many authors conceptualize these variables as ideological beliefs. (9)
> しかし，最近では，多くの著者がこれらの変数をイデオロギー的な信念として概念化している．

0216　より最近ではある研究が多いことを述べる．

◆ More recently, there have been numerous studies of X.
ごく最近では，X について多数の研究がある．

> More recently, there have been numerous studies of fathers across cultures. (3)
> ごく最近では，複数の文化にまたがる父親研究が数多くある．

0217　より新しい研究を引用する．

◆ Newer research is showing that XXX.
さらに最近の研究は，XXX ということを示している．

> Newer research is showing that paternal alcohol consumption may also transmit effects to the fetus through the sperm. (40)
> さらに最近の研究は，父親のアルコール消費もまた精子を通して胎児に効果を伝えるかもしれないことを示している．

4.2.11　追加的な知見

0218　類似した研究から得られた有意差についての追加的な知見を述べる．

◆ In a similar study, it was observed that Ps differed significantly between Q and R.
類似の研究において，P が Q と R で有意に異なることが観察された．

> In a similar study, it was observed that during a short commercial flight, a number of physiological measures, including heart rate, skin conductance level (SCL), and pauses in respiration, differed significantly between people with a phobia of flying and control participants. (1)
> 類似の研究において，民間機での短いフライト中に，心拍数，皮膚伝導水準 (SCL)，呼吸休止を含む多くの生理学的測度が，飛行恐怖患者と統制群参加者の間で有意に異なることが観察された．

4.2 先行研究の知見

0219 さらなる研究から得られたある傾向についての追加的な知見を紹介する.
◆ Further research indicates that P tends to QQQ.
さらなる研究は,PがQQQを行う傾向があることを示している.

> Further research indicates that alcohol consumption during the first two months of pregnancy tends to result in more adverse effects on the fetus than when alcohol consumption occurs later in pregnancy. (40)
> さらなる研究は,妊娠の最初の2か月間になされたアルコール消費が,それより後になされたアルコール消費に比べて,胎児により有害な影響をもたらす傾向があることを示している.

0220 同じ測度を用いた研究が見出した相関についての追加的な知見を述べる.
◆ Using the same measure as did Author (Year), these researchers found that Ps correlated significantly with Q.
著者(発表年)と同じ測度を用いて,これらの研究者はPがQと有意に相関することを見出した.

> Using the same measure as did Royalty et al. (see Gelso, Mallinckrodt, & Royalty, 1991), these researchers found that counseling psychologists' retrospective ratings of the faculty modeling ingredient correlated significantly with actual research productivity during their career. (16)
> Royaltyら(Gelso, Mallinckrodt, & Royalty, 1991を参照)と同じ測度を用いて,これらの研究者は,カウンセリング心理学者による教員のモデリング要因の回顧的評定が,キャリアにおける実際の研究生産性と有意に相関することを見出した.

0221 追跡研究により初期の知見が確かめられたことを述べる.
◆ Follow-up work on [/in] X confirmed these initial findings.
Xの追跡調査研究は,これらの初期の知見を確認した.

> Follow-up work in this sample with 14 years of additional mortality data confirmed these initial findings. (38)
> 14年に及ぶ死亡数についての追加的なデータを用いたこのサンプルの追跡調査研究は,これらの初期の知見を確認した.

0222 より参考になる追加的な研究において参加者に行われた課題を紹介する.
◆ In a more informative test of the idea that XXX, Author (Year) had participants YYY.
XXXという考えのより有益な検証において,著者(発表年)は,参加者にYYYさせた.

> In a more informative test of the idea that individuals abstract a rule during learning, DeLosh et al. (1997) had participants predict outputs from inputs sampled well outside of the training values. (44)
> 人々が学習中にルールを抽出するという考えのより有益な検証において,DeLoshら(1997)は,参加者に,訓練値から大きく外れて抽出されたインプットからアウトプットを予測させた.

4.2.12　矛盾した知見

0223　研究により，知見が一貫していないことを述べる．

◆ Findings are inconsistent for X.

X については，知見は一貫していない．

> However, findings are inconsistent for panic disorder patients outside the hospital or laboratory. (1)
> しかしながら，病院や実験室以外の場所におけるパニック障害患者については，知見は一貫していない．

0224　矛盾する結果が得られていることを述べる．

◆ Conflicting results were found between Xs [using the same Y].

[同一の Y を用いた] X の間で，矛盾する結果が得られた．

> Conflicting results were found between experiments using the same measure of distractor processing. (43)
> 妨害刺激の処理についての同一の測度を用いた実験間で，矛盾する結果が得られた．

0225　研究により結果が異なることを述べる．

◆ X varied considerably across studies.

X は，研究によりかなり異なっていた．

> Effect sizes and odds ratios in some cases varied considerably across studies. (27)
> いくつかの事例における効果量とオッズ比は，研究によってかなり異なっていた．

0226　先行研究における矛盾した知見について述べる．

◆ The literature shows inconsistent findings (Author, Year), with some studies reporting X (Author, Year) [,] whereas [/while] others report Y (Author, Year).

文献では，矛盾した知見が報告されており（著者，発表年），いくつかの研究は，X ということを報告している（著者，発表年）．一方，他の研究は，Y ということを報告している（著者，発表年）．

> The literature shows inconsistent findings (van Vreeswjik & de Wilde, 2004), with some studies reporting patients to be less specific in response to positive cues (McNally, Litz, Prassas, Shin, & Weathers, 1994; Williams & Scott, 1988), whereas others report OGM effects in response to negative cues, rather than positive and neutral cues (Jones et al., 1999; Mackinger, Pachinger, Leibetseder, & Fartacek, 2000). (36)
> 文献では，矛盾した知見が報告されており（van Vreeswjik & de Wilde, 2004），いくつかの研究は，患者が正の手がかりに対してあまり特異性を示さないことを報告している（McNally, Litz, Prassas, Shin, & Weathers, 1994; Williams & Scott, 1988）．一方，他の研究は，正や中立的な手がかりよりも，むしろ負の手がかりに対して，OGM 効果が見られることを報告している（Jones et al., 1999; Mackinger, Pachinger, Leibetseder, & Fartacek, 2000）．
>
> （訳者注：OGM; overgeneral memory bias，概括化された記憶偏向，過度に一般化された非特異的な記憶への偏りのこと）

4.2 先行研究の知見

0227 ある文献が他の文献とは対照的な結果を示していることを述べる．

◆ In contrast, the literature on X shows Y.

これとは対照的に，Xの文献は，Yということを示している．

> In contrast, the literature on age differences in psychosocial characteristics such as impulsivity, sensation seeking, future orientation, and susceptibility to peer pressure shows continued development. (57)
> これとは対照的に，衝動性，刺激欲求，未来志向，同輩からの圧力に対する脆さなどの心理社会学的特徴についての年齢差の文献は，継続的な発達が見られることを示している．

0228 一方の群ではある課題である知見が見られたが，もう一方の群では見られなかったことを述べる．

◆ They found X on Y tasks for A but not for B.

彼らは，A群ではY課題においてXを見出したが，B群では見出さなかった．

> They found reduced age-related differences on some dual tasks for older pilots but not for nonpilots. (47)
> 彼らは，いくつかの二重課題において，より高齢のパイロットでは年齢による差の減少を見出したが，パイロット以外の人間では年齢による差の減少を見出さなかった．

0229 先行研究が，対立する知見を示してきたことを述べる．

◆ Although research on X has consistently supported the proposition that AAA [/this proposition regarding A], research on Y also suggests that BBB.

Xについての研究は，AAAという提案[/Aに関するこの提案]を一貫して支持してきた．しかし，Yについての研究は，BBBということも示唆している．

> Although research on group decision making has consistently supported this proposition regarding the core role of group information elaboration, research on information sharing also suggests that groups with distributed information typically engage in less of this behavior. (59)
> 集団意思決定についての研究は，グループによる情報精緻化が果たすおもな役割に関するこの提案を一貫して支持してきた．しかし，情報共有についての研究は，情報が分散しているグループは概してそれほどこの行動に従事しないことも示唆している．

0230 モデルとの一致について対立する知見を述べる．

◆ On the one hand, X was not consistent with the prediction of A model. On the other hand, Y was better than predicted by B model.

一方で，Xは，Aモデルの予測と一致しなかった．もう一方で，Yは，Bモデルにより予測されるよりはよかった．

On the one hand, individuals' extrapolation performance for trained linear, exponential, and quadratic functions, though in the direction of the underlying function, was not consistent with the predictions of two standard rule models. On the other hand, extrapolation was better than predicted by the simple associative learning model. (44)
一方で，訓練された線形，指数，および，二次関数についての人々の推定の成績は，基礎となる関数の方向に沿ってはいたが，2つの標準的な規則モデルの予測とは一致しなかった．もう一方で，推定は，単純な連合学習モデルにより予測されるよりはよかった．

0231 関連性についての最近の知見が，過去の知見と矛盾することを述べる．
◆ In contrast with this pattern of results, a recent study by Author (Year) found that P was associated with Q.
このような結果パターンとは反対に，著者（発表年）による最近の研究は P が Q と関連することを見出した．

> However, in contrast with this pattern of results, a recent study by Staresina and Davachi (2006) found that activation in the hippocampus and the perirhinal cortex was associated with successful source encoding. (12)
> しかしながら，このような結果パターンとは反対に，Staresina と Davachi（2006）による最近の研究は，海馬と嗅周皮質の賦活が，成功裡に終わった情報源の符号化と関連することを見出した．

0232 ある能力についての最近の研究結果が，過去の結果と矛盾することを述べる．
◆ A more recent study by Author (Year), however, provided evidence that Ps are able to QQQ.
しかし，著者（発表年）によるより最近の研究は，P が QQQ することができるという証拠を提供した．

> A more recent study by Spinozzi, Lubrano, and Truppa (2004), however, provided evidence that monkeys are able to reason about abstract relations. (34)
> しかし，Spinozzi, Lubrano, Truppa（2004）によるより最近の研究は，サルが抽象的な関係について推論することができるという証拠を提供した．

4.3　先行研究の理論的・実践的な帰結

4.3.1　示唆・意味

0233 先行研究が全体として示唆することを述べる．
◆ Thus, the literature on X suggests that YYY.
それゆえ，X についての文献は，YYY ということを示唆している．

> Thus, the literature on peer intervention suggests that young people are willing to respond to the risky behaviors of others by taking socially responsible action. (58)

4.3 先行研究の理論的・実践的な帰結

それゆえ，同輩の介入についての文献は，若者が，社会的に責任のある行為を行うことにより，他者の危険な行動に対していとわずに反応することを示唆している．

0234 データの意味を述べる．

◆[Furthermore,] X data suggest that YYY.

[さらに，] X のデータは YYY ということを示唆している．

> Furthermore, longitudinal data suggest that women may be closing the gender gap. (39)
> さらに，縦断的なデータは，女性がジェンダー・ギャップを埋めつつあるかもしれないことを示唆している．

0235 これまでの研究による原因と結果についての意味を述べる．

◆Research suggests that P is a [/an /the] cause of Q (Author, Year).

これまでの研究は，P が Q の原因であることを示唆している（著者，発表年）．

> Research suggests that prenatal exposure to alcohol is not only the primary cause of mental retardation in the United States, but also the most readily preventable (Caley, Kramer, & Robinson, 2005; Harpur, 2001). (40)
> これまでの研究から，胎児期におけるアルコールへの曝露が，米国における精神遅滞のおもな原因であるのみならず，最も容易に予防可能でもあることを示唆している（Caley, Kramer, & Robinson, 2005; Harpur, 2001）．

0236 傾向があるという意味を述べる．

◆Prior research has suggested that Ps tend to QQQ.

先行研究は，P が QQQ を行う傾向があることを示唆してきた．

> Prior research has suggested that adaptive spiritual coping methods tend to decrease psychosocial distress over time, even after controlling for nonreligious coping methods when people face life stressors. (61)
> 先行研究は，人生のストレス要因に直面したときの非宗教的なコーピングの方法を制御した後でも，適応的であるスピリチュアルなコーピングの方法が心理社会的な苦痛を徐々に減少させる傾向があることを示唆してきた．

0237 条件により予測が異なるという意味を述べる．

◆Existing research has suggested that P may predict Qs differently across Rs.

既存の研究は，P による Q の予測が R により異なることを示唆してきた．

> Existing research has suggested that parent violence may predict behavioral health outcomes differently across gender and ethnic subgroups. (22)
> 既存の研究は，親の暴力による行動的な健康結果の予測が，性別と民族の下位集団により異なるかもしれないことを示唆してきた．

0238 複数の研究から，あることを反映するという意味を導くことを述べる．

◆Taken together, the above [/preceding] evidence suggests [/suggested] that Ps reflect Qs.

これらのことを総合すると，上記の [/ 前述の] 証拠は P が Q を反映することを示唆する [/ した].

> Taken together, the above evidence suggests that the spontaneous gestures that unsuccessful learners produce on a task can reflect the implicit steps that learners take on the road to mastering the task. (5)
> これらのことを総合すると，上記の証拠は，不成功に終わった学習者が課題において自発的に示すジェスチャーは，学習者がその課題をマスターする途上でたどる潜在的な段階を反映する可能性がある，ということを示唆している．

0239 先行研究がある理論の適切さを示唆することを述べる．

◆ Taken together, these studies suggested that P theory is salient for Q.

総合すると，これらの研究は，Q にとって P 理論が重要であることを示唆した．

> Taken together, these studies suggested that coping theory is salient for children's experiences of parental divorce. (61)
> 総合すると，これらの研究は，子供による両親の離婚の経験にとって，コーピング理論が重要であることを示唆した．

0240 知見がある概念間の依存関係を示唆することを，アイデアとの一致とともに述べる．

◆ These findings suggest that P depends on Q, in line with the R view.

これらの知見は，P が Q に依存することを示唆しており，R の考え方と一致する．

> These findings suggest that conscious perception depends on the allocation of attention, in line with the early selection view. (43)
> これらの知見は，意識知覚が注意配分に依存することを示唆しており，初期選択の考え方と一致する．

0241 先行研究がある理論にとって意味をもつことを述べる．

◆ This has important implications for theories of X that focus on Y.

このことは，Y に焦点を当てる X の理論にとって重要な意味をもっている．

> This has important implications for theories of panic disorder that focus on the biological underpinnings of the disorder. (1)
> このことは，障害の生物学的な土台に焦点を当てるパニック障害の理論にとって重要な意味をもっている．

0242 先行研究がモデルに基づいてあることを示唆したことを述べる．

◆ In their model framework for X, Authors (Year) have suggested that YYY.

著者（発表年）は，彼らの X のモデルの枠組みにおいて，YYY ということを示唆している．

> In their model framework for self-exclusion services, Blaszczynski, Ladouceur, and Nower (2007) have suggested that state governments should employ such an interventionist, called an educator. (46)

Blaszczynski, Ladouceur, Nower（2007）は，彼らの自己排除サービスのモデルの枠組みにおいて，州政府がエデュケータと呼ばれる前記のような介入員を雇用すべきであることを示唆している．

0243 先行研究の意味について，自分の意見を述べる．

◆ The literature on X seems to suggest that YYY.

X についての文献は，YYY ということを示唆しているように思われる．

> The literature on amygdala function seems to suggest that the amygdala is rather involved in anticipatory fear processing rather than in pain processing itself. (55)
> 扁桃体の機能についての文献は，扁桃体が，苦痛の処理自体よりも，むしろ予期的な恐怖の処理に関与していることを示唆しているように思われる．

0244 メタ分析の結果から，あることが効果的であることが示唆されたことを述べる．

◆ The results of meta-analyses of X suggest that Ps are effective Qs.

X のメタ分析の結果は，P が効果的な Q であることを示唆している．

> The results of meta-analyses of specific serotonin reuptake inhibitors suggest that these drugs are effective treatments for social anxiety disorder. (27)
> 特定のセロトニン再取り込み阻害薬のメタ分析の結果は，これらの薬物が社会不安障害の効果的な治療法であることを示唆している．

0245 メタ分析の結果と効果量から，あることが説明力をもたないことを述べる．

◆ Results of a meta-analysis have revealed that the overall effect size for each X is small, suggesting that Ps lack full explanatory power (Author, Year).

メタ分析の結果は，それぞれの X の全体的な効果量は小さいことを明らかにしており，P は十分な説明力をもたないことを示唆している（著者，発表年）．

> Results of a meta-analysis have revealed that the overall effect size for each theory is small, suggesting that these theories lack full explanatory power (Amato, 1993, 2001; Amato & Keith, 1991a). (61)
> メタ分析の結果は，各理論の全体的な効果量は小さいことを明らかにしており，これらの理論は十分な説明力をもたないことを示唆している（Amato, 1993, 2001; Amato & Keith, 1991a）．

4.3.2 予測の支持

0246 経験的な支持があることを述べる．

◆ There is empirical support for X (e.g., Author, Year).

X は，経験的に支持されている（たとえば，著者，発表年）．

> There is empirical support for this theoretical position (e.g., Jex, Beehr, & Roberts, 1992). (52)

この理論的立場は，経験的に支持されている（たとえば，Jex, Beehr, & Roberts, 1992）．

0247 いくつかの研究が支持することを述べる．
◆ Some research has supported X (e.g., Author, Year).
いくつかの研究は X を支持してきた（たとえば，著者，発表年）．

> Some research has supported Piaget's developmental analysis of immanent justice (e.g., Bibace & Walsh, 1981; Palmer & Lewis, 1976). (6)
> いくつかの研究は，ピアジェの内在的正義の発達分析を支持してきた（たとえば，Bibace & Walsh, 1981; Palmer & Lewis, 1976）．

0248 ある研究の評論がある予測を支持したことを述べる．
◆ A review of the X studies of Y provided support for these predictions (Author, Year).
Y についての X 研究の評論は，これらの予測を支持した（著者，発表年）．

> A review of the early and late selection studies of visual attention provided support for these predictions (Lavie & Tsal, 1994). (43)
> 視覚的注意についての初期選択および後期選択の研究の評論は，これらの予測を支持した（Lavie & Tsal, 1994）．

0249 先行研究が，ある分析を支持する結果を引用していることを述べる．
◆ Author (Year) cited [/found] support for this analysis in a study of X.
著者（発表年）は，この分析を支持する結果が，X に関する研究の中にあることを引用した [/ 見出した].

> He cited support for this analysis in a study of rumors that occurred following a major earthquake in India in 1934. (20)
> 彼は，この分析を支持する結果が，1934 年のインドの大地震後に起こった流言に関する研究の中にあることを引用した．

0250 大部分の研究がある関係についての命題を支持していることを述べる．
◆ Most X research on Y lends support to the thesis that Ps and Qs are related.
Y についての X 研究の大部分は，P と Q が関係するという命題を支持している．

> Most longitudinal research on burnout lends support to the thesis that chronic stressors at work and burnout are related in a bidirectional manner over time. (52)
> 燃え尽き症候群に関する縦断的研究の大部分は，仕事中の慢性的ストレス因子と燃え尽き症候群は長い時間をかけて双方向的に関係するという命題を支持している．

4.3.3 解釈・説明

0251 確信のもてる解釈を述べる．
◆ It is clear that XXX.
XXX ということは明らかである．

It is clear that self-esteem and optimism can provide insight into individual differences that
play a role in an individual's GPD and PTS following a disaster. (3)
自尊感情と楽天主義が災害後の人々の GPD と PTS に関与する個人差に洞察を与えることができる，ということは明らかである．

（訳者注：GPD; general psychological distress, 一般的心理的苦痛：PTS; posttraumatic stress, 心的外傷後ストレス）

0252 先行研究の結果の解釈を述べる．

◆ This can be interpreted as X.

このことは，X として解釈可能である．

> This can be interpreted as synchronous change. (1)
> このことは，同期変化として解釈可能である．

0253 他に考えられる説明を述べる．

◆ Another possible explanation is that XXX.

もう１つの可能な説明としては，XXX ということがある．

> Another possible explanation is that panic attacks are not uniform; the more severe experiences may overshadow less severe episodes in memory. (1)
> もう１つの可能な説明として，パニック発作は一様ではなく，より重度の経験が記憶内のそれほど重度ではないエピソードを覆い隠すということが考えられる．

0254 対照的な説明を紹介する．

◆ In contrast, it might be argued that XXX.

これとは対照的に，XXX という主張があるかもしれない．

> In contrast, it might be argued that the most potent way to enhance productivity is through the "input" factor. (16)
> これとは対照的に，生産性を高める有力な方法は「入力」要因の操作によるという主張があるかもしれない．

0255 異なる文脈における説明があることを述べる．

◆ Author (Year) discussed these points in the context of X, stating that YYY.

著者（発表年）は，これらの点を X の文脈で論じ，YYY と述べた．

> Gleason (1994) discussed these points in the context of developing gender roles, stating that whereas males are taught to strive for independence and influence over others, females are encouraged to be passive, accommodating, and respectful of others' feelings and opinions. (39)
> Gleason（1994）は，これらの点を性役割の発達の文脈で論じ，男性は主体性と他者への影響力を手に入れるために必死の努力をするように教えられるが，女性は受動的で，協調的で，他者の感情と意見を重んじるように奨励されると述べた．

0256 慎重な解釈が必要であることを述べる．

◆ Despite [the] well[-]documented X, this research must be interpreted with caution.

Xは十分に立証されているが，そのような研究は慎重に解釈する必要がある．

> Despite the well documented links between parental divorce and psychological maladjustment, this research must be interpreted with caution. (61)
> 親の離婚と心理的不適応の間の関連性は十分に立証されているが，そのような研究は慎重に解釈する必要がある．

0257 群間差についての最近の研究を解釈する．

◆ A recent study seems [/seemed] to indicate that Ps differ between Qs and Rs (Author, Year).

最近の研究は，PがQとRで異なることを示しているように思われる [/ 思われた]（著者，発表年）．

> A recent study seems to indicate that locomotor patterns do differ between panic patients and healthy control participants (Sakamoto et al., 2008). (1)
> 最近の研究は，運動パターンが，パニックの患者と健康な統制群の参加者で確かに異なっていることを示しているように思われる（Sakamoto et al., 2008）．

0258 説明の軸を述べる．

◆ Most efforts to explain X have centered around N theoretical perspectives: A, B, C, and D.

Xを説明するためのほとんどの努力は，N個の理論的な見方に集中している．すなわち，A, B, C, Dである．

> Most efforts to explain this variability have centered around five theoretical perspectives: the loss of the noncustodial parent, the adjustment of the custodial parent, interparental conflict, economic hardship, and the cumulative effect of stressful life changes. (61)
> この変動性を説明するためのほとんどの努力は，5つの理論的な見方に集中している．すなわち，保護観察権をもたない親の欠如，保護観察権をもつ親の適応，両親間の葛藤，経済的困難さ，ストレスの多い生活変化の累積的な影響である．

4.3.4 結　論

0259 先に述べた知見に基づいて結論することを述べる．

◆ Because of the strong empirical support just noted, one might conclude that XXX.

今述べたような強い経験的支持があることから，XXXと結論できるかもしれない．

> Because of the strong empirical support just noted, one might conclude that the "science as partly social experience" ingredient should be stated as a main effect. (16)
> 今述べたような強い経験的支持があることから，「ある程度社会的な経験としての科学」という因子が主効果と言うべきである，と結論できるかもしれない．

0260 知見から導かれる結論を述べる．

◆ Thus, it appears that XXX.

4.4 理論・モデル・仮説

　それゆえ，XXX と思われる．
　　Thus, it appears that the extent of heart rate changes during panic attacks is often relatively small. (1)
　　それゆえ，パニック発作中の心拍数変化の程度は多くの場合相対的に小さいと思われる．

0261　いまだに結論が得られていないことを述べる．
◆ Extensive research on X has not clarified definitively whether YYY.
　X についての広範な研究は，YYY かどうかについて，決定的な明確化までは至っていない．
　　Extensive research on the hypothalamic–pituitary–adrenal axis response to stress has not clarified definitively whether that axis is activated by phobic anxiety. (1)
　　ストレスに対する視床下部 – 脳下垂体 – 副腎軸の反応についての広範な研究は，恐怖症の不安によりこの軸が活性化されるかどうかについて，決定的な明確化までは至っていない．

0262　他の研究者が主張した結論を紹介する．
◆ The authors argued that these results provided evidence that XXX.
　著者らは，これらの結果が XXX の証拠を提供したと主張した．
　　The authors argued that these results provided evidence that capuchin monkeys can reason about abstract spatial relations. (34)
　　著者らは，これらの結果はオマキザルが抽象的な空間的関係について推論することができる証拠を提供した，と主張した．

0263　先行研究の結論を引用する．
◆ Author (Year) [has] concluded that "XXX" (p. N).
　著者（発表年）は，「XXX（p. N）」と結論した．
　　Wicklund and Brehm (1976) have concluded that "it is difficult to obtain evidence for selective avoidance of 'dissonance-arousing' information" (p. 189). (20)
　　Wicklund と Brehem (1976) は，「『不協和を引き起こす』情報の選択的回避を支持する証拠を得ることは難しい（p. 189）」と結論した．

4.4　理論・モデル・仮説

4.4.1　理　論

0264　理論のおもなアイデアを述べる．
◆ X theory proposes that YYY.
　X 理論は，YYY と提案している．
　　Terror management theory (TMT) proposes that humans need self-esteem to manage their existential anxiety about death. (11)

恐怖管理理論（TMT）は，死についての実存的不安を管理するために，人は自尊心を必要とすると提案している．

0265 理論から導かれるアイデアを述べる．

◆ According to X theory, YYY.

X 理論によれば，YYY.

> According to TMT, either people pursue self-esteem or they are overwhelmed with anxiety about death. (11)
> TMT によれば，人々は自尊心を追求するか，死の不安に飲み込まれてしまうかのどちらかである．
>
> （訳者注：TMT; terror management theory, 恐怖管理理論）

0266 理論の予測する比例的な減少を引用する．

◆ In X theory, P is reduced [/diluted] in proportion to Q.

X 理論では，P が Q に比例して弱くなる．

> In goal systems theory, the link between a goal and any one behavioral means is diluted in proportion to the number of other means to which the goal is linked. (62)
> 目標システム理論では，目標と何らかの行動手段の間の結びつきは，その目標が結びついている他の手段の数に比例して弱くなる．

0267 ある著者の理論が主張する内容を述べる．

◆ Author's X theory posits that YYY.

著者の X 理論によれば，YYY であるとされている．

> Lerner's just world theory posits that people need to believe they live in a world where people generally get what they deserve. (6)
> Lerner の公正世界理論によれば，人々は，自分でしたことの報いを自分自身で受けるような世界に住んでいる，と信じる必要があるとされている．

0268 理論が強調することを述べる．

◆ X theories of Y have emphasized the importance of Z.

Y について X 理論は，Z の重要性を強調してきた．

> Hyperventilation theories of anxiety (see Ley, 1985) and the suffocation false alarm hypothesis of panic (Klein, 1993) have emphasized the importance of respiratory measures for anxiety. (1)
> 不安について過換気理論（Ley, 1985 を参照）とパニックについての窒息誤警報仮説（Klein, 1993）は，不安についての呼吸測定の重要性を強調してきた．

0269 理論の仮定について述べる．

◆ X theory assumes that YYY.

X 理論では，YYY であると仮定している．

4.4 理論・モデル・仮説　　　　　　　　　　　　　　　　　77

Coping theory assumes that people are goal-directed individuals who actively seek to create and sustain significance in their lives. (61)
コーピング理論では，人間は，人生の意味を創造し維持することを積極的に求める目標志向的な人々である，と仮定されている．

0270 理論の目的を述べる．

◆ The overall aim of X theory is to YYY.
X 理論の全体的な目的は，YYY することである．

> The overall aim of the theory is to facilitate the creation of research training experiences that will result in more and better applied research in professional psychology. (16)
> この理論の全体的な目的は，専門職としての心理学においてより多くの，そして，よりよい応用研究をもたらす研究訓練経験の創出を促進することである．

0271 2 つの理論の焦点を比較する．

◆ Although X theory focuses on A, Y theory places a special [/specific] emphasis on B.
X 理論は，A に焦点を当てているけれども，Y 理論は B を特に強調している．

> Although many psychological theories of panic disorder focus on the role of bodily symptoms as triggers for panic attacks, cognitive theories place a specific emphasis on the spiraling function of bodily symptoms and cognitive evaluations into full-blown panic attacks. (1)
> パニック障害についての多くの心理学的な理論は，パニック発作の引き金としての身体症状の役割に焦点を当てているけれども，認知理論は，身体症状と認知的評価が螺旋状に悪化して全面的なパニック発作を引き起こす機能を特に強調している．

0272 理論における論点を，実際の研究動向をみきわめることにより明瞭化することを述べる．

◆ This point is illustrated by observing that XXX.
この論点は，XXX を観察することによって明瞭化にされる．

> This point may be illustrated by observing that contemporary dissonance theorists analyze the counterattitudinal role playing experiment. (20)
> この論点は，現代の不協和理論家が，態度に反する役割演技実験の分析を行っているのを観察することにより，明瞭化されるかもしれない．

0273 理論についての評判を述べる．

◆ The authors, along with many others, believe that X theory YYY.
著者らは，他の著者と同様に，X 理論は YYY であると信じている．

> The authors, along with many others, believe that dissonance theory has been an extremely stimulating force within and beyond social psychology. (20)
> 著者らは，他の著者と同様に，不協和理論は社会心理学の内外できわめて刺激的な推進力となってきたと信じている．

0274 理論に関する原因と結果についてのコメントを引用する.

◆ Author (Year) commented on Y by observing, "P is due to Q."

著者（発表年）はYについて論評し，「PはQのためである」と述べている．

> Wicklund and Brehm (1976) commented on the 20-year history of dissonance theory by observing, "To the extent that dissonance theory has evolved since 1957, the evolution has been primarily due to the discovery that responsibility is a prerequisite for effects that we call dissonance reduction" (p. 71). (20)
> Wicklund と Brehm（1976）は不協和理論の 20 年の歴史について論評し，「不協和理論が 1957 年から進化してきた範囲において，その進化をもたらしたのは，おもに，責任がいわゆる不協和低減効果の必要条件であるという発見であった（p. 71）」と述べている．

0275 理論の予測を述べる.

◆ In the present version of the theory, P is expected to QQQ.

この理論の現在のバージョンでは，PがQQQであることが予想される．

> In the present version of the theory, neither of these situations is expected to arouse dissonance because they have no apparent element of personal responsibility. (20)
> この理論の現在のバージョンでは，これらの場面は個人的責任の明白な要因を含まないので，どちらも不協和を喚起しないことが予想される．

0276 発達の土台の準備についての理論的な主張を述べる.

◆ X theorists have long argued that Ps set the stage for Q development.

Xの理論家は，PがQの発達の下地となると長い間主張してきた．

> Personality theorists have long argued that that early emerging personality characteristics may set the stage for later social, emotional, and personality development. (38)
> 性格の理論家は，初期に現れる性格的特徴が，後の社会的，情動的，性格的発達の下地となるかもしれないと長い間主張してきた．

0277 理論の現在の焦点を述べる.

◆ X theory seems now to be focused on Ps occurring in the service of Q.

Xの理論は，いまや，Qのために起こるPに焦点を当てているように思われる．

> The theory seems now to be focused on cognitive changes occurring in the service of ego defense. (20)
> この理論は，いまや，自我防衛のために起こる認知的な変化に焦点を当てているように思われる．

4.4.2 モデル

0278 ある学者があるモデルを開発したことを述べる.

◆ Author (Year) [recently] developed a conceptual model to facilitate research on X.

[最近,] 著者（発表年）は, X についての研究を促進する概念的なモデルを開発した．

Mahoney et al. (2008) recently developed a conceptual model to facilitate research on the role of spirituality in the context of a divorce. (61)

最近，Mahoney ら（2008）は，離婚という文脈におけるスピリチュアリティの役割についての研究を促進する概念的なモデルを開発した．

0279 知見に応じてモデルが開発されたことを述べる．

◆ In response to the X findings, Author (Year) developed the Y model.

著者（発表年）は，彼の X の知見に応じて，Y モデルを開発した．

> In response to their extrapolation findings, DeLosh et al. (1997) developed the EXAM model. (44)
> DeLosh ら（1997）は，彼らの外挿法の知見に応じて，EXAM のモデルを開発した．

（訳者注：EXAM; extrapolation–association model, 外挿連合モデル）

0280 複数過程モデルについて述べる．

◆ We present a N-process model of the task involving X. The first stage of the model is A. The second stage of the model is B.

我々は，X を含む課題の N 過程モデルを呈示する．モデルの最初の段階は A である．モデルの第二段階は B である．

> We present a two-process model of the task involving direct and indirect paths to a target. (略) The first stage of the model is stimulus encoding. (略) The second stage of the model is spatial updating. (42)
> 我々は，標的への直接的および間接的経路を含む課題の 2 過程モデルを呈示する．（略）モデルの最初の段階は，刺激符号化である．（略）モデルの第二段階は，空間的更新である．

0281 モデルの意味について述べる．

◆ The model also offers new insights into X, especially Y.

このモデルは，X，特に，Y に新しい洞察を与える．

> The model also offers new insights into established literatures, especially how to tailor behavior change interventions to maximize their impact on habits. (62)
> このモデルは，これまでに確立された文献，特に，行動修正的な介入を，習慣に及ぼす効果を最大化するように調整する方法に対してもまた，新しい洞察を与える．

0282 影響についてのモデルのアイデアについて述べる．

◆ The X model developed by Author and colleagues (Author, Year) indicates that Ps are influenced by Qs.

著者らのグループ（著者，発表年）により開発された X モデルは，P が Q により影響されることを示している．

> The integrative model developed by Garcia Coll and colleagues (Garcia Coll et al., 1996; Garcia Coll & Szalacha, 2004) indicates that children's behavioral, emotional, and cognitive development are greatly influenced by their daily experiences and surrounding environments, both of which are significantly shaped by class position, discrimination, and oppression. (23)

Garcia Coll らの研究グループ（Garcia Coll et al., 1996; Garcia Coll & Szalacha, 2004）により開発された統合モデルは，子供の行動的，情動的，認知的発達が日々の経験と周辺の環境により大きく影響され，さらに，それらの経験と環境は，学級内での地位，差別，抑圧によってその大部分が決まる，ということを示している．

4.4.3　等　式

0283　等式を述べる．

◆ Equation N represents X when YYY.

　等式 N は，YYY のときの X を表す．

> Equation 4 represents hyperbolic discounting when $0 < \beta < 1$. (35)
> 等式 4 は，$0 < \beta < 1$ のときの双曲線割引を表す．

0284　モデルの等式を述べる．

◆ Equation N denotes X over Y.

　等式 N は，Y の経過に伴う X を表す．

> Equation 2 denotes the internal discounting process over perceived time. (35)
> 等式 2 は，知覚時間の経過に伴う内的な割引過程を表す．

4.4.4　仮　説

0285　仮説の意味を述べる．

◆ The X hypothesis suggests that YYY.

　X 仮説は，YYY ということを示唆している．

> The affect-regulation hypothesis suggests that exposure to stressful events is a precursor of overgeneral memory. (36)
> 感情制御仮説は，ストレスのある出来事にさらされることが，概括化された記憶の前兆であることを示唆している．

0286　先行研究の仮説を述べる．

◆ In Author's (Year) statement, X was hypothesized to be Y.

　著者（発表年）の主張によれば，X は Y であると仮定されている．

> In Aronson's (1968) statement, dissonance was hypothesized to be a significant motivational force only when the self-concept or some other firmly held expectancy was involved. (20)
> Aronson（1968）の主張によれば，不協和は，自己概念や他の確固たる期待が含まれる場合にのみ，重要な動機づけ要因であると仮定されている．

0287　実験的操作がもたらす効果についての仮説を述べる．

◆ The X hypothesis states that P makes one prone to QQQ.

　X 仮説は，P が人を QQQ しやすくさせると述べている．

4.4 理論・モデル・仮説

> The anxiety-buffer hypothesis states that if a psychological structure (worldview faith or self-esteem) provides protection against anxiety, then strengthening that structure should make one less prone to exhibit anxiety or anxiety-related behavior in response to threats, and weakening that structure should make one more prone to exhibit anxiety or anxiety-related behavior in response to threats. (25)
> 不安バッファー仮説は，もしある心理学的な構造（世界観への信頼や自尊心）が不安に対する防衛となっているならば，その構造が増強されると，脅威に対して不安や不安関連行動をより示しにくくなり，その構造が弱化されると，脅威に対して不安や不安関連行動をより示しやすくなるはずである，と述べている．

0288 行為の困難さについての仮説の根拠を述べる．

◆There are reasons for believing [/to believe] that Ps might have difficulty [in] QQQ.
　P が QQQ することが難しいと考えるには理由がある．

> Moreover, there are reasons for believing that infants and young children might have difficulty in selecting an action on the basis of the current value of the outcome. (37)
> さらに，幼児と幼い子供は，結果の現在の価値に基づいて行為を選択することが難しいかもしれないと考えるには理由がある．

0289 先行研究の機序についての仮説を述べる．

◆Most notably, Author (Year) proposed that Ps are triggered by Qs.
　なかでも特に，著者（発表年）は，P が Q により引き起こされることを提案した．

> Most notably, William James (1890) proposed that habits are triggered spontaneously by sensory cues and preceding actions. (62)
> なかでも特に，William James（1890）は，習慣が感覚手がかりと先行する行為により自動的に引き起こされることを提案した．

0290 逸話的な証拠から示唆される原因についての仮説を述べる．

◆Anecdotal evidence suggests that P is attributable to Q.
　逸話的な証拠から，P は Q に帰せられることが示唆される．

> Anecdotal evidence suggests that the frequent coconsumption of ethanol and caffeine is attributable to the ability of caffeine to reverse ethanol-induced cognitive and motor deficits. (21)
> 逸話的な証拠から，エタノールとカフェインが高頻度に同時摂取されるのは，エタノールが誘発する認知的および運動的欠損を取り消す効果をカフェインがもっていることに帰せられることが示唆される．

4.4.5 仮　定

0291 モデルの仮定について述べる．

◆X models of Y postulate that ZZZ.
　Y についての X モデルは，ZZZ を仮定している．

Most cognitive models of panic disorder postulate that panic flares up in a positive feedback loop of bodily sensations and the cognitive response to these perceptions.　　(1)
パニック障害についての認知的モデルのほとんどは，身体感覚とそれらの知覚に対する認知的反応の正のフィードバック・ループの中で，パニックが突発することを仮定している．

0292　研究に共通する仮定を述べる．

◆A common assumption has been that XXX.
XXX ということが，共通の仮定とされてきた．

> A common assumption has been that when individuals learn predictive relationships between continuous variables, they abstract some sort of rule for mapping the values of one variable on to a value for another variable and then apply the rule to novel variables.　　(44)
> 連続変数間の予測的関係を学習する場合，人々は1つの変数の値をもう1つの変数に定位するためにある種のルールを抽出して，それからそのルールを新奇な変数の値に適用する，ということが，共通の仮定とされてきた．

0293　モデルの仮定について述べる．

◆Author's (Year) X model posits that Ps determine Q.
著者（発表年）の X モデルでは，P が Q を決定すると仮定されている．

> Lazarus and Folkman's (1984) stress-coping model posits that both the frequency of exposure and appraisal of the stressfulness of the event determine its impact on health outcomes.　(32)
> Lazarus と Folkman（1984）のストレスコーピングモデルでは，ストレスにさらされる頻度と，事象のストレスの程度の評価の両方が健康上の結果に及ぼす効果を決定すると仮定されている．

0294　研究アプローチの基本的な仮定を述べる．

◆A basic assumption of X is that P represents Q.
X の基本的な仮定は，P が Q を表すということである．

> A basic assumption of this research tradition is that nonverbal behavior represents a relatively spontaneous form of behavior.　　(13)
> この研究様式の基本的な仮定は，非言語的行動が，比較的自動的な行動形式を表すということである．

4.4.6　予　測

0295　モデルがあることを予測することを述べる．

◆This model [/theory] leads to the prediction that XXX.
このモデル [/ 理論] は，XXX ということを予測する．

> This model leads to the prediction that task-irrelevant stimuli will not be perceived.　　(43)
> このモデルは，課題に無関連な刺激が知覚されないことを予測する．

4.4 理論・モデル・仮説

0296 理論や研究に基づく予測について述べる.
◆ Overall, theory [and research] would predict that P is tied to Q.
全体的に，理論[と研究]は，PがQと結びついていることを予測するだろう．

> Overall, theory and research would predict that experiencing spiritual struggles about parental divorce would be tied to greater future psychological maladjustment. (61)
> 全体的に，理論と研究は，両親の離婚についてのスピリチュアルな苦闘の経験が，将来のより大きな心理的不適応と結びついていることを予測するだろう．

4.4.7 理論・モデル・仮説との一致・不一致

0297 研究の結果がモデルや理論と一致することを述べる.
◆ These results are consistent with models that postulate that P is critical for Q.
これらの結果は，PがQにとって重要であると仮定するモデルと一致する．

> These results are consistent with models that postulate that the hippocampus and parahippocampal cortex are critical for processing of episodic information that supports recollection-based discriminations. (12)
> これらの結果は，海馬と海馬傍回皮質が回想に基づく弁別を支えるエピソード情報の処理にとって重要であると仮定するモデルと一致する．

0298 モデルに対する支持がある研究に由来することを述べる.
◆ Support for the X model stems from research that indicates that P involves Q.
Xモデルに対する支持は，PがQを含むことを示す研究に由来する．

> Support for the associative network model stems from research that indicates that aversive stimulation does not necessarily have to involve direct provocation to prime hostility and aggression. (60)
> 連合ネットワークモデルに対する支持は，嫌悪刺激が，敵意と攻撃のきっかけとなる直接的な挑発を必ずしも含む必要はないことを示す研究に由来する．

0299 最近の実験的研究が仮説を支持することを述べる.
◆ More recent support for this hypothesis has been provided by experiments which have shown that increasing P by means of Q reduces R.
この仮説に対するさらに最近の支持は，QによるPの増加がRを減少させることを示した実験によりもたらされてきた．

> More recent support for this hypothesis has been provided by experiments which have shown that experimentally increasing self-esteem by means of bogus personality feedback or success on a supposed intelligence test reduces self-reported anxiety in response to a graphic death-related video. (25)
> この仮説に対するさらに最近の支持は，偽の性格のフィードバックや仮の知能検査での好成績により自尊心を実験的に高めると，死に関係する生々しいビデオに対する自己報告による不安を減少させることを示した実験によりもたらされてきた．

4.5 先行研究のトピック

4.5.1 先行研究における重要なトピックを述べる（テーマを述べる段落の最初の文章）

`0300`　テーマを直接的に述べる（明快な疑問文のよい例）．
◆ To what extent does XXX?
　どの程度まで XXX なのだろう．
> To what extent does conscious perception depend on attention? (43)
> 意識的知覚はどの程度まで注意に依存するのだろうか．

`0301`　心理学的な機序の問題を直接的に述べる（自問自答で議論を進めるよい例）．
◆ What are the possible mechanisms by which XXX?
　XXX の機序として考えられるものは何だろうか．
> What are the possible mechanisms by which overgeneral memory may put people at risk of chronic depression and PTSD after trauma? (36)
> 概括化された記憶が人々を心的外傷後の慢性うつ病と PTSD の危険にさらす機序として考えられるものは何だろうか．
>
> （訳者注：PTSD; posttraumatic stress disorder, 心的外傷後ストレス障害）

`0302`　重要な問題を述べる．
◆ X is one of the most significant Y issues in Z.
　X は，Z における最も重要な Y の問題の 1 つである．
> Homelessness is one of the most significant domestic policy and mental health issues in America. (41)
> ホームレスは，米国における国内政策上および精神保健上最も重要な問題の 1 つである．

`0303`　重要なトピックを述べる．
◆ X is critical to Y.
　X は，Y にとって不可欠である．
> The ability to attend to important information is critical to later recall of this information. (7)
> 重要な情報に注意を向ける能力は，その情報の後の想起にとって不可欠である．

`0304`　重要な治療法を述べる．
◆ The Nth treatment strategy is the use of Y.
　N 番目の治療の方略は，Y の使用である．
> The third pre-treatment strategy is the use of a developmental framework. (17)
> 第三の前治療の方略は，発達的枠組みの使用である．

`0305`　いまだに続いている重要な論争を述べる．
◆ An ongoing debate continues regarding X.

4.5 先行研究のトピック

Xについては，いまだに論争が進行中である．

> An ongoing debate continues regarding the risks of alcohol consumption during pregnancy, namely the amount of alcohol ingested and the period of pregnancy when consumption occurs. (40)
> 妊娠中のアルコール消費，すなわち，摂取されたアルコールの量と消費が起きた妊娠期間のリスクについては，いまだに論争が進行中である．

0306 何十年間にも及ぶ社会的な背景を述べる．

◆ Over [/In] the last N decades, Ps are witnessing Qs.

過去 N × 10 年間にわたり，P は Q に見舞われている．

> Over the last two decades, many Western countries are witnessing lower rates of fertility and higher life expectancy. (2)
> 過去 20 年間にわたり，西洋諸国の多くが，出生率の低下と平均寿命の増加に見舞われている．

0307 多くの分野で重要視されている原因と結果についての知見を述べる．

◆ X has been a central theme in many lines of research, with the main finding being that Ps lead to Qs.

X は多くの研究分野における主要なテーマであり，P が Q を引き起こすということがおもな知見として報告されてきている．

> The role of attention in memory performance has been a central theme in many lines of research, with the main finding being that distraction or divided attention lead to reductions in overall memory. (7)
> 記憶能力における注意の役割は多くの研究分野における中心テーマであり，そのおもな知見は，妨害や注意分割が全体的な記憶低下を引き起こすということである．

4.5.2 先行研究の中からテーマを絞る

0308 先行研究が主張したアイデアを述べる．

◆ It is [/has been] argued that XXX.

XXX ということが主張されている [/ されてきた]．

> It is argued that children initially respond to literal (physical) similarity between objects in terms of color, shape, and so forth. (34)
> 子供は最初に色，形などについての物体間の文字どおりの（物理的な）類似性に反応するということが主張されている．

0309 先行研究の中のある問題に注意を向けさせる．

◆ It is important to note [/worth noting] that XXX.

XXX ということは重要である [/ 注目に値する]．

It is worth noting that 7% of children (mostly those of Mexican origin) in the Early Childhood Longitudinal Survey—Kindergarten Cohort (ECLS-K) did not complete a direct reading assessment because of limited English proficiency in the fall of kindergarten.　　(23)
幼児期縦断的調査—幼稚園コホート群（ECLS-K）の 7% の子供（大部分はメキシコ系）が幼稚園の秋の時点で英語の習熟に限界があったために直読の評価を終えなかったことは注目に値する．

0310　先行研究が注意を払う必要があると主張した問題を述べる．

◆ Author (Year) reported that more attention must be paid to X in order to YYY.

著者（発表年）は，YYY を行うためには X にさらに注意を払う必要があると報告した．

> Streissguth et al. (1991) reported that more attention must be paid to the needs of these children in order to prevent future deleterious effects.　　(40)
> Streissguth ら（1991）は，将来の有害な効果を防ぐためには，これらの子供のニーズにさらに注意を払う必要があると報告した．

0311　先行研究がある研究法に問題があると主張したことを述べる．

◆ Recently, Author (Year) reviewed the extant literature on X and discussed limitations in Y.

最近，著者（発表年）は，X に関する現存の文献を概観し，Y の限界について論じた．

> Recently, Landrine and colleagues (2006) reviewed the extant literature on perceived discrimination and discussed limitations in the measurement of discrimination.　　(32)
> 最近，Landrine らのグループ（2006）は，被差別感に関する現存の文献を概観し，差別測定の限界について論じた．

0312　先行研究が重要な要因を示してきたことを述べる．

◆ X has been found to be a significant Y factor for Z.

X は Z の重要な Y 要因であることもまた示されてきている．

> Alcohol use has also been found to be a significant risk factor for sexual problems and other consequences.　　(39)
> アルコール使用は，性的問題およびその他の後禍における重要なリスク要因であることもまた示されてきている．

0313　先行研究が注目した比例的関係についての問題を述べる．

◆ Author (Year) noted that Ps with lower Q reported significantly higher Rs.

著者（発表年）は，Q がより低い P ほど，有意により高い R を報告したことに注目した．

> Vigil and Geary (2008) noted that adolescent survivors of Hurricane Katrina with lower self-esteem reported significantly higher levels of PTS.　　(3)
> Vigil と Geary（2008）は，自尊心がより低いハリケーン・カトリーナの青年生存者ほど，有意により高いレベルの PTS を報告したことに注目した．

（訳者注：PTS; posttraumatic stress, 心的外傷後ストレス）

0314 先行研究が提案した脳内機構の活性化についての問題を述べる.
◆ In prior work, X proposed that P activates Q.
先行研究で，XはPがQを活性化させることを提案した.

> In prior work, our research team proposed that stress exposure, even if impersonal in nature, activates brain mechanisms involved in approach motivation. (60)
> 先行研究で，我々の研究チームは，ストレスへの曝露が，たとえそれが本来個人にかかわらないものであっても，接近動機づけに含まれる脳内機序を活性化させることを提案した.

4.5.3　先行研究から導かれる問題

0315 先行研究からある問題が提起されることを述べる.
◆ This raises the issue of whether X [or Y] play[s] a role in the development of Z.
このことは，X [や Y] が Z の発症に関与しているのかどうかという問題を提起する.

> This raises the issue of whether stressful or traumatic life events play a role in the development of overgeneral memory retrieval. (36)
> このことは，ストレスのある，あるいは，心的外傷となるような人生の出来事が概括化された記憶想起の発症に関与しているのかどうかという問題を提起する.

0316 先行研究の応用可能性の問題について述べる.
◆ A valuable application of X research would [therefore] be to YYY.
[それゆえ，] X 研究の役立つ応用の1つは，YYY することであろう.

> A valuable application of attention research would therefore be to predict the type of stimuli that are likely to distract performance. (14)
> それゆえ，注意研究の役立つ応用の1つは，遂行を妨害する可能性の高い刺激のタイプを予測することであろう.

0317 先行研究から導かれる問題を疑問文で述べる（珍しいがよい表現）.
◆ This leads to the question, ["]XXX?["] [/This leads to the question: XXX? /This leads to the research question of why XXX.]
このことは，以下のような疑問につながる．すなわち，XXX なのだろうか．[/ このことは，XXX という疑問につながる．/ このことは，なぜ XXX なのだろうかという研究上の疑問につながる．]

> This leads to the question, What is the psychology underlying the inaction of fellow students who might have prevented harm by acting on their knowledge of a peer's dangerous intentions? (58)
> このことは，以下のような疑問につながる．すなわち，同輩の危険な意図を知った上で行動することで被害を防ぐことができたかもしれない同級生の無為の根底にある心理は何なのだろうか．

0318 先行研究から導かれる問題を提示する.

◆ The question is, then, XXX? [/The question, then, is XXX?]

そこで,問題は,XXX なのか,ということである.

> The question is, then, what factors might account for these diverging academic trajectories by racial-ethnic group? (23)
> そこで,問題は,人種民族グループにより大きく分かれてゆく学業成績の軌跡がどのような要因により説明されるか,ということである.

0319 先行研究の結果に基づいて,タイムリーな問題を述べる.

◆ Research on X is timely, given Y.

Yを考えれば,Xについての研究はタイムリーである.

> Research on the effects of stress on approach-related brain activity in the prefrontal cortices and its relationship to aggressive behavior is timely, given the demonstrated empirical association between approach motivation and aggressive responding. (60)
> 接近動機づけと攻撃反応の関連が経験的に例証されていることを考えれば,接近に関係する前頭前野皮質の脳活動にストレスが及ぼす効果,および,ストレスと攻撃行動との関連についての研究はタイムリーである.

0320 先行研究の知見から,今回の問題が重要であることを述べる.

◆ Given previous findings suggesting that XXX (Author, Year), Y may be important.

過去の知見が XXX ということを示唆している(著者,発表年)ことを考えれば,Yは重要であるかもしれない.

> Given previous findings suggesting that thought suppression will not work in the long term (Abramowitz et al., 2001), evaluating the effects of control strategies over time in consecutive trials may be important. (28)
> 過去の知見が思考抑制は長く続かないことを示唆している(Abramowitz et al., 2001)ことを考えれば,制御方略の効果を,連続する試行において時間経過に沿って評価することは重要であるかもしれない.

0321 基礎研究と応用研究の動向から,あるテーマが重要であることを述べる.

◆ An important challenge to research and practice in X, therefore, lies in Y.

それゆえ,Xの研究と実践にとって,Yが重要な課題となっている.

> An important challenge to research and practice in group decision making, therefore, lies in understanding the development of task representations in groups dealing with distributed information. (59)
> それゆえ,集団意思決定の研究と実践にとって,分散された情報を扱うグループにおける課題表象の発達を理解することが重要な課題となっている.

0322 過去の知見を要約し,研究すべき問題を指摘する.

◆ The evidence that we have reviewed so far suggests that (a) XXX, and (b) YYY. However, what remains unclear is whether ZZZ.

4.5 先行研究のトピック

これまでに概観した証拠は，(a) XXX，(b) YYY を示唆している．しかし，ZZZ かどうかについては，不明なままである．

> The evidence that we have reviewed so far suggests that (a) the perirhinal cortex supports familiarity-based recognition, and (b) unitization of item–item associations can increase the contribution of familiarity to associative recognition. However, what remains unclear is whether unitization of item and source information can increase the contribution of familiarity to source memory tests. (12)

これまでに概観した証拠は，(a) 嗅周皮質が熟知性を基盤とする再認を支えていること，および，(b) 項目－項目連合のユニット化が連合再認に対する熟知性の寄与を増加させうることを示唆している．しかし，項目情報と情報源の情報のユニット化が，情報源記憶テストに対する熟知性の寄与を増加させるかどうかについては，不明なままである．

4.5.4 数値データに基づく問題の重要性の指摘

0323 推定発生率を述べて重要性を強調する．

◆ X estimates have a range from L to M cases of X per N (Author, Year).

X の推定値は，N 人当たり X が L から M 症例の範囲である（著者，発表年）．

> FAS estimates have a worldwide range from 0.33 to 2.9 cases of FAS per 1,000 live births (Inaba & Cohen, 2004). (40)
> FAS の推定値は，世界中で，正常出産 1000 人当たり FAS が 0.33 から 2.9 症例の範囲である（Inaba & Cohen, 2004）．

（訳者注：FAS; fetal alcohol syndrome, 胎児アルコール症候群）

0324 罹患率を述べて重要性を強調する．

◆ A N prevalence study in X found that M% of Y had ZZZ.

X における N 年の罹患率研究は，Y の M% が ZZZ であったことがあることを見出した．

> A 1975 prevalence study in the United States found that 35% of adults 65 and over had gambled in their lifetime. (46)
> 米国における 1975 年の罹患率研究は，65 歳以上の成人の 35% が生涯に賭博を行ったことがあることを見出した．

0325 障害の推計罹患率を述べて重要性を強調する．

◆ It is estimated that nearly L% of X[,] and M% to N% of Y meet diagnostic criteria for this disorder.

X の L% 近く，および，Y の M% から N% がこの障害の診断基準を満たすと推計されている．

> It is estimated that nearly 2% of adults and 4% to 6% of adolescents meet diagnostic criteria for this disorder. (46)

成人の 2% 近く，および，青年の 4% から 6% がこの障害の診断基準を満たすと推計されている．

0326 推定摂取率を述べて重要性を強調する．
◆ Estimates suggest that N% of Xs take Y.
推計によると，N% の X が Y を摂取していることが示唆されている．

> Estimates suggest that more than 80% of Americans take at least one prescription drug, over-the-counter medication, or dietary supplement weekly. (29)
> 推計によると，80% 以上のアメリカ人が，少なくとも 1 種類の処方箋薬，市販薬，あるいは，栄養補助食品を毎週摂取していることが示唆されている．

0327 症候群の罹患率を述べて重要性を強調する．
◆ Recent studies suggest that between N% and M% of X experience Y.
最近の研究は，X の N% から M% が Y を経験していることを示唆している．

> Recent studies suggest that between 17% and 55% of older community-living women experience some type of urinary incontinence. (29)
> 最近の研究は，コミュニティに住む高齢女性の 17% から 55% がなんらかのタイプの尿失禁を経験していることを示唆している．

0328 あるカテゴリーの予想される割合を述べて重要性を強調する．
◆ Between N and M, Xs are expected to account for Y.
N 年から M 年の間に，X が Y を占めると予想されている．

> Between 1990 and 2010, children of immigrants are expected to account for more than half of the growth in the school-aged population. (23)
> 1990 年から 2010 年の間に，移民の子供が学童人口の増加分の半分以上を占めると予想されている．

4.5.5 障害の困難さに基づく重要性の強調

0329 患者が示す重要な困難さを述べて重要性を強調する．
◆ People with X often show difficulty in YYY.
X の患者はしばしば YYY することに困難を示す．

> People with major depression often show difficulty in retrieving specific autobiographical memories. (36)
> 大うつ病の患者は，しばしば特定の自伝的記憶を想起することに困難を示す．

0330 障害の特徴を述べて重要性を強調する．
◆ Numerous researchers have found X and Y as [/to be] common characteristics associated with Z.
多数の研究者が，X と Y が Z と関連する共通の特徴であることを見出してきた．

4.5　先行研究のトピック

Numerous researchers have found hyperactivity and attention problems to be common characteristics associated with FAS. (40)
多数の研究者が，多動性と注意の問題が FAS と関連する共通の特徴であることを見出してきた．

（訳者注：FAS; fetal alcohol syndrome, 胎児アルコール症候群）

0331 患者が示す共通の障害を述べて重要性を強調する．

◆ Among X samples, a large proportion of Y reported Z.
X のサンプルの中では，Y の人々のかなりの割合が Z を報告した．

Among depressed samples, a large proportion of individuals with overgeneral memory also reported a history of trauma and trauma-related intrusive and avoidance symptoms. (36)
うつ病のサンプルの中で，概括化された記憶を示す人々のかなりの割合が，心的外傷，および，心的外傷に関係する侵入・回避症状の病歴も報告した．

0332 共通して報告される症状を述べて重要性を強調する．

◆ Common themes [/symptoms] reported include X or Y.
共通して報告されるテーマ [/ 症状] は，X や Y を含む．

Common themes reported include feeling as though the older patient represents a parent's sexuality or the denial or exacerbation of existing fears of aging. (29)
共通して報告されるテーマは，高齢患者があたかも親の性的関心を象徴しているような感覚や，加齢に対する既存の恐怖の否認や悪化を含んでいる．

（訳者注：高齢患者の性的な問題を扱うカウンセラーが患者に対して無意識に抱く感情，すなわち，逆転移（counter transfer）の主題について述べた文章である）

4.5.6　自分の意見

0333 自分の意見を強調して述べる．

◆ It goes without saying that XXX.
XXX ということは言うまでもない．

It goes without saying that the faculty needs to be involved in research themselves. (16)
教員自身が研究に関与する必要があることは言うまでもない．

0334 他の意見に賛同できる点と賛同できない点があることを述べてから，自分の意見を述べる．

◆ One might argue that XXX. We agree that YYY. But, in our view, ZZZ.
XXX という主張もあるだろう．我々は，YYY ということには同意する．しかし，我々の見方によれば，ZZZ である．

One might argue that pursuing goals that are good for others and the self is simply another indirect means of obtaining self-esteem. We agree that the pursuit of goals that include others can result in increased self-esteem as an unintended consequence. But, in our view, the intention is crucial. (11)

他者と自己にとってよい目標を追求することは，自尊心を手に入れるためのもう1つの間接的な手段にすぎない，という主張もあるだろう．我々は，他者を含む目標の追求が，意図せぬ結果として自尊心の増大に帰結しうることには同意する．しかし，我々の見方によれば，意図が決定的な役割を果たす．

0335 他の意見と対比させながら，原因と結果についての意見を述べる．
◆ In our view, rather than XXX, P causes Q to RRR.
我々の見方では，XXX というよりもむしろ P は Q に RRR させてしまうことになる．

In our view, rather than helping people achieve their important goals, the pursuit of self-esteem causes people to lose sight of their most important goals. (11)
我々の見方では，自尊心の追求は，人々が大事な目的を達成するのを助けるよりもむしろ，最も大事な目的を見失わせてしまうことになる．

4.6 先行研究の問題点

4.6.1 先行研究が少ない

0336 ある年齢のグループの研究がないことを述べる．
◆ Studies of X among Y are lacking.
Y における X の研究は存在しない．

Although a few longitudinal studies of the impact of parent violence on adolescents exist (Smith, Ireland, & Thornberry, 2005), studies among adolescents who are homeless are lacking. (22)
親の暴力が青年に及ぼす影響についての少数の縦断的研究が存在する (Smith, Ireland, & Thornberry, 2005) が，ホームレスの青年における研究は存在しない．

0337 ある問題について研究がまったくないことを述べる．
◆ No research thus far has examined whether XXX.
XXX かどうかを調べた研究はこれまでに行われていない．

No research thus far has examined whether impersonal and interpersonal stressors elicit similar or distinct patterns of brain activity. (60)
個人に関しないストレス因子と，対人的なストレス因子が，類似した，あるいは，異なる脳活動のパターンを誘発するかどうかを調べた研究は，これまでに行われていない．

0338 あるトピックについて出版されている研究がないことを述べる．
◆ Despite the importance of X, there have been no published investigations of Y.
X の重要性にもかかわらず，Y の調査はこれまでに出版されていない．

Despite the importance of self-exclusion as a venue for intervention, there have been no published investigations of age-related characteristics of individuals who self-exclude from casinos. (46)

4.6 先行研究の問題点

介入の場として自己排除は重要であるにもかかわらず、カジノから自己排除を行う人々の、年齢に関連する特徴の調査はこれまでに出版されていない。

0339 不幸にも研究がないことを述べる．

◆ Unfortunately, there continues to be a dearth of X research [/research on X].
不幸にも，X の研究がない状態が続いている．

> Unfortunately, there continues to be a dearth of comparative research. (32)
> 不幸にも，比較研究がない状態が続いている．

0340 今日まで研究がないことを述べる．

◆ To date, no studies have investigated X.
今日まで，X を調べた研究はない．

> For example, to date, no studies have investigated the relationship between discrimination and state anxiety. (32)
> たとえば，今日まで，差別と状態不安の間の関係を調べた研究はない．

0341 診断のための検査がないことを述べる．

◆ No objective test currently exists for the diagnosis of X.
X の診断のための客観的な検査は，現時点では存在しない．

> No objective test currently exists for the diagnosis of FAS. (40)
> FAS の診断のための客観的な検査は，現時点では存在しない．

（訳者注：FAS; fetal alcohol syndrome, 胎児アルコール症候群）

0342 治療法についての研究がないことを述べる．

◆ Currently, no studies exploring the use of X therapy for Y exist.
現時点では，Y に対する X 療法の使用について調べた研究は存在しない．

> Currently, no studies exploring the use of play therapy for children with FAS exist. (40)
> 現時点では，FAS のある子供に対する遊戯療法の使用について調べた研究は存在しない．

（訳者注：FAS; fetal alcohol syndrome, 胎児アルコール症候群）

0343 あるトピックについての研究がほとんどないことを述べる．

◆ To date, few experimental analyses evaluating X are available.
現時点まで，X を評価する実験的分析はほとんどない．

> To date, few experimental analyses evaluating control on tinnitus reactions are available. (28)
> 現時点まで，耳鳴り反応の制御を評価する実験的分析はほとんどない．

0344 あることを明確化した先行研究がほとんどないことを述べる．

◆ Specifically, there is little research that delineates X.
特に，X を明確化した研究はほとんどない．

> Specifically, there is little research that delineates the type of discrimination that different ethnic groups face. (32)

特に，異なった民族グループが直面する差別のタイプを明確化した研究はほとんどない．

0345 あるトピックについて，ほとんど研究がなされていないことを述べる．
◆Published research on X appears to be limited to a handful of studies.
X についてこれまでに出版されている研究は，ほんの一握りに限定されるようである．

> Published research on coping theory and parental divorce appears to be limited to a handful of studies. (61)
> コーピング理論と両親の離婚についてこれまでに出版されている研究は，ほんの一握りに限定されるようである．

0346 機序についての先行研究が比較的少ないことを述べる．
◆Relatively few studies have examined how XXX.
どのようにして XXX となるかを調べた研究は比較的少ない．

> Relatively few studies have examined how experiences of homelessness may amplify risks because of parent–adolescent violence (Whitbeck & Hoyt, 1999). (22)
> ホームレスの経験が親子と青年の間の暴力のためにリスクをどのように増幅させる可能性があるのかを調べた研究は比較的少ない（Whitbeck & Hoyt, 1999）．

0347 あるトピックについて先行研究がわずかしかないことを述べる．
◆Only N study [/studies] so far [thus far] has [/have] investigated X while measuring Y.
Y を測定しながら X を調べた研究がこれまでに N 個だけ存在する．

> Only one study so far has investigated perceptual load while measuring participants' conscious perception of task-irrelevant stimuli. (43)
> 課題とは無関連である刺激の参加者による意識的な知覚を測定しながら知覚的負荷を調べた研究がこれまでに 1 つだけ存在する．

0348 わずかな研究しかないことを述べる（研究数がわかっているときにはよい表現）．
◆Only N published studies have explored X.
X を探求した研究はこれまでに N 編が出版されているのみである．

> Only three published studies have explored the characteristics of problem gamblers. (46)
> 問題賭博者の特徴を探求した研究は，これまでに 3 編が出版されているのみである．

0349 モデルを支持する研究が少ないことを述べる．
◆A handful of X studies were interpreted as supporting Y.
一握りの X 研究が，Y を支持すると解釈された．

> A handful of initial studies were interpreted as supporting these rule-learning models. (44)
> 一握りの初期研究が，これらのルール学習モデルを支持すると解釈された．

4.6 先行研究の問題点

0350 系統的な研究がないことを述べる（一般的な表現）．
◆ There has been little systematic research investigating X.
　X を調べた系統的研究はこれまでにほとんどなかった．

> There has been little systematic research investigating the nature and course of problem gambling among older adults. (46)
> 高齢者における問題賭博行動の性質と経過を調べた系統的研究はこれまでにほとんどなかった．

0351 限定された知識が単一のタイプの研究からもたらされているにすぎないことを述べる．
◆ What little is known about X comes from the literature on Y.
　X について知られているごくわずかの知識が，Y の文献によりもたらされているにすぎない．

> What little is known about bystander behavior in young people comes from the literature on bullying prevention. (58)
> 若者における傍観者行動について知られているごくわずかの知識が，いじめ防止についての文献によりもたらされているにすぎない．

0352 研究が比較的少ない状態が続いていることを述べる．
◆ There continues to be comparatively little research that examines X.
　X を調べる研究は比較的少ない状態が続いている．

> However, there continues to be comparatively little research that examines the impact of racial discrimination on other ethnic minority groups. (32)
> しかしながら，人種差別が他の民族的なマイノリティのグループに及ぼす影響を調べる研究は比較的少ない状態が続いている．

0353 あるトピックがほとんど研究されていないことを述べる．
◆ Little is known about X.
　X についてはほとんどわかっていない．

> Little is known about the gambling behavior of older adults. (46)
> 高齢者の賭博行動についてはほとんどわかっていない．

0354 ある知見は確立されているが，理由は知られていないことを述べる．
◆ While it has been established that XXX, less is known about why [/how] YYY.
　XXX ということは確立されているが，なぜ [/ どのように] YYY であるかについてはそれほどわかっていない．

> While it has been established that adults can make sense out of events through immanent justice reasoning, less is known about why they do so. (6)
> 大人が内在的正義推論を通して事象の意味を理解できるということは確立されている．だが，彼らがなぜそうするのかについては，それほどわかっていない．

0355 あるトピックは広く研究されているが，別のトピックはまだよくわかっていないことを述べる．

◆Extensive effort has been dedicated to documenting X. By contrast, relatively little is known about Y.

X を立証するために，これまでに広範囲にわたる努力が捧げられてきた．これとは対照的に，Y については比較的わかっていない．

> Extensive effort has been dedicated to documenting the effect and to providing various functional forms to model the data. By contrast, relatively little is known about the psychological mechanisms underlying hyperbolic discounting. (35)
> その効果を立証し，データのモデルとなるさまざまな関数形式を提供することに，これまでに広範囲にわたる努力が捧げられてきた．これとは対照的に，双曲線型の割引の基盤となる心理学的な機序については比較的わかっていない．

4.6.2　説明の矛盾・争点

0356 ある知見について複数の説明があることを述べる．

◆N possible explanations have emerged to date.

今日までに，N 個の説明の候補が出現している．

> Three possible explanations have emerged to date. (6)
> 今日までに，3 つの説明の候補が出現している．

0357 先行研究が，対立する説明を提案していることを述べる．

◆There are two primary explanations for X given in the literature. One explanation is that AAA. An opposing [/alternative] explanation argues that BBB.

X については，2 つの重要な説明が文献で提案されている．1 つの説明は，AAA というものである．それとは反対の [/ もう 1 つの] 説明は，BBB と主張する．

> There are two primary explanations for the relational shift given in the literature. One explanation is that children undergo a global shift in their cognitive abilities.（略）An opposing explanation argues that children are able to focus on relational similarities as a function of their knowledge base. (34)
> 関係シフトについては，2 つの重要な説明が文献で提案されている．1 つの説明は，子供が認知能力の全体的な変化を受けるというものである．（略）それとは反対の説明として，彼らの知識ベースに応じて関係的な類似性に焦点を当てることができるという主張がある．

0358 先行研究の理論的争点について述べる．

◆The central theoretical issue is what Ps are associated with Qs.

主要な理論的問題は，どのような P が Q と関連しているのかということである．

4.6 先行研究の問題点

> The central theoretical issue is what kinds of learning processes and representations are associated with the learning and transfer evidenced herein. (44)
> 主要な理論的問題は，どのような種類の学習過程と表象が，ここで示された学習と転移に関連しているのか，ということである．

4.6.3 先行研究の弱点

0359 先行研究の弱点を厳しく批判する．

◆ Significant weaknesses characterize the bulk of the small literature on X.

X についてのわずかな文献の大部分は，重大な弱点をもっている．

> Significant weaknesses characterize the bulk of the small literature on parental violence toward adolescents. (22)
> 青年に対する親の暴力についてのわずかな文献の大部分は，重大な弱点をもっている．

0360 先行研究の大部分がある要因に焦点を当ててきたにすぎないことを述べる．

◆ Most research on X has focused on Y.

X についての研究の大部分は，Y に焦点を当ててきた．

> Most research on parental stress related to caring for children with diabetes has focused on mothers and older children. (45)
> 糖尿病の子供の世話に関する親のストレスについての研究の大部分は，母親とより年長の子供に焦点を当ててきた．

0361 先行研究が用いてきた仮定に問題があることを述べる．

◆ The problem with the extant research is the assumption that XXX.

現存する研究の問題は，XXX という仮定を用いていることである．

> The problem with the extant research is the assumption that men have access and opportunity to express these social class/status expectations and roles. (41)
> 現存する研究の問題は，男性が，これらの社会的階層や地位の期待と役割に触れたり，それらを外に表現する機会がある，という仮定を用いていることである．

0362 先行研究がある点にのみ焦点を当てる傾向があったことを述べる．

◆ X research involving Y has tended to focus on Z.

Y を含む X 研究は，Z に焦点を当てる傾向があった．

> Psychotherapy research involving racial and ethnic minority clients has tended to focus on therapist characteristics, such as racial attitudes and multicultural counseling competence. (8)
> 人種および民族的な少数派のクライエントに関する精神療法研究は，人種に対する態度や多文化カウンセリング能力のような心理療法家の特徴に焦点を当てる傾向があった．

0363 先行研究の大部分が限られたサンプルを用いてきたことを述べる．

◆ In most previous investigations of X, researchers have examined participant samples drawn from Y.

Xについての先行研究の大部分においては，Yから抽出された参加者のサンプルが研究されてきた．

> In most previous investigations of political orientations, researchers have examined participant samples drawn from the general public or from university student populations. (9)
> 政治的志向についての先行研究の大部分においては，一般の人々や大学生の母集団から抽出された参加者のサンプルが研究されてきた．

0364 多くの研究があるが，あることができていないことを述べる．

◆ X has not been sufficiently studied [/investigated /addressed /extended].
X は十分に研究されて [/ 調査されて / 取り組まれて / 拡張されて] きていない．

> Although there are many studies that directly compare cardiovascular responding in healthy participants, this strategy has not been sufficiently extended to the study of anxiety disorders. (1)
> 健康な参加者の心臓血管反応を直接比較する研究は数多く存在するが，この方略が不安障害の研究まで十分に拡張されたことはなかった．

0365 ある問題が無視されてきたことを述べる．

◆ The question of why XXX has been mostly ignored by Ys.
どうして XXX であるのかという疑問を，Y はほとんど無視してきた．

> The question of why self-esteem is such a basic human need has been mostly ignored by contemporary self theorists. (25)
> どうして自尊心が人間のそのような基本的欲求であるのかという疑問を，現代の自己理論家はほとんど無視してきた．

4.6.4 展開の必要性

0366 研究が必要であることを述べる．

◆ There is a clear need to study X.
X を研究することが明らかに必要である．

> There is a clear need to study effects of control in clinical samples of individuals with tinnitus. (28)
> 耳鳴りのある人々の臨床サンプルにおいて制御の効果を研究することが明らかに必要である．

0367 あることを明らかにするために，研究が必要であることを述べる．

◆ Additional research is needed to clarify whether XXX.
XXX かどうかを明らかにするために，さらなる研究が必要とされる．

> Thus, additional research is needed to clarify whether parent–adolescent violence uniquely contributes to risk and therefore merits specialized intervention strategies. (22)

4.6 先行研究の問題点

そのため，親 – 青年間の暴力がリスクに対して一意的に寄与し，そして，それゆえに特化した介入の方略を受けるに値するかどうかを明らかにするために，さらなる研究が必要とされる．

0368 ある影響を評価するために，さらなる研究が必要であることを述べる．

◆More research is needed to evaluate the influence of X on Y.

X が Y に及ぼす効果を評価するためには，さらなる研究が必要である．

> More research is needed to evaluate the influence of age on an adolescent's GPD and PTS following a disaster. (3)
> 年齢が青年の災害後の GPD と PTS に及ぼす効果を評価するためには，さらなる研究が必要である．
>
> （訳者注：GPD; general psychological distress, 一般的心理的苦痛：PTS; posttraumatic stress, 心的外傷後ストレス）

0369 重要な報告が増えていることから，あるトピックの理解が必要であることを述べる．

◆Understanding of X is particularly important given the growing body of literature indicating Y.

Y を示す文献が増加していることを考えると，X を理解することは特に重要である．

> Finally, understanding of the relation between perceived discrimination and the well-being of Asian and Latino American college students is particularly important given the growing body of literature indicating greater psychological distress and depression in these two groups than in their European American counterparts. (32)
> 最後に，ヨーロッパ系アメリカ人学生と比べて，アジア系アメリカ人およびラテンアメリカ系アメリカ人の大学生グループでは心理的苦痛とうつがより大きいことを示す文献が増加していることを考えると，後者の 2 つのグループにおける被差別感と健康の間の関係を理解することは特に重要である．

0370 いくつかの論点から，研究の必要性が強調されることを述べる．

◆These points underscore the need to explore X, especially Y.

これらの論点は，X，特に Y を研究する必要性を強調する．

> These points underscore the need to explore gender issues in alcohol use, especially the motivational factors driving women's drinking. (39)
> これらの論点は，アルコール使用における性別の問題，特に女性を飲酒に駆り立てる動機づけ要因を研究する必要性を強調する．

0371 あるサンプルに焦点を当てる必要性を強調する．

◆There are compelling reasons to study X with respect to Y.

Y に関して X を研究することには説得力のある理由がある．

> There are compelling reasons to study Asian Americans and Latinos with respect to racial discrimination and to study the groups together. (32)

人種差別に関してアジア系アメリカ人とラテンアメリカ系アメリカ人を研究すること、および、それら2つのグループを一緒に研究することには説得力のある理由がある.

0372 変数間の関係についてさらなる研究が必要であることを述べる.

◆The relationship between X, Y, and Z appears complex and warrants further exploration.

X, Y, Z の間の関係は複雑のようであり、さらなる研究が当然必要である.

> The relationship between gender, GPD, and PTS appears complex and warrants further exploration. (3)
> 性、GPD、PTS の間の関係は複雑のようであり、さらなる研究が当然必要である.
>
> (訳者注：GPD; general psychological distress, 一般的心理的苦痛：PTS; posttraumatic stress, 心的外傷後ストレス)

0373 研究が必要な複数の論点を列挙する.

◆Several issues require [/required] further study. First, XXX. Second, YYY. Third, ZZZ.

いくつかの問題については、さらなる研究が必要である [/であった]. 第一に、XXX. 第二に、YYY. 第三に、ZZZ.

> Several issues required further study. First, (略). Second, (略). Third, (略). (3)
> いくつかの問題については、さらなる研究が必要であった. 第一に、(略). 第二に、(略). 第三に、(略).

0374 ある研究を追跡調査することが必要であることを述べる.

◆It is [/was] essential to follow up on research by Author (Year), which suggested that XXX.

著者（発表年）により行われた XXX を示唆する研究をさらに追跡調査することが不可欠である [/であった].

> It was essential to follow up on research by Galea et al. (2007) and Kessler et al. (2008), which suggested that being a member of a displaced group was a strong predictor of psychological trauma after Hurricane Katrina. (3)
> Galea ら（2007）、および、Kesseller ら（2008）の研究は、ハリケーン・カトリーナ後に退去させられたグループの構成員であることが心的外傷の強力な予測因子であることを示唆しており、これらの研究をさらに追跡調査することが不可欠であった.

0375 あるアイデアの例証が必要であることを述べる.

◆It remains to be demonstrated [/seen] whether XXX.

XXX かどうかについては、これからの例証を待たなければならない.

> It remains to be demonstrated whether the simple coactivation in direct cuing (e.g., representations of popcorn + movie theater) provides a sufficient impetus to initiate an overt habit response. (62)

4.7 本研究のテーマ・関心・目的　　　101

直接的な手がかりにおける単純な同時活性化（たとえば，ポップコーンの表象＋映画館）が顕在的な習慣反応を起こすための本質的な刺激となるかどうかについては，これからの例証を待たなければならない．

0376 問題の系統的な研究が必要であることを述べる．

◆ Systematic research on when [/where /which /why /how] XXX is needed.

いつ [/ どこで / どれが / なぜ / どのように（どれくらい）] XXX なのかについての系統的な研究が必要とされる．

> Nevertheless, systematic research on how well patients tolerate such procedures or how this may alter their behavior is needed. (1)
> それにもかかわらず，患者がそのような手続きにどれくらい耐えられるか，あるいは，そのことが患者の行動をどのように変えるのかについて系統的な研究が必要とされる．

4.7　本研究のテーマ・関心・目的

4.7.1　テーマ・関心

0377 研究全体を導くテーマについて述べる．

◆ The thesis guiding [/that guided] the present study is [/was] that XXX.

本研究のテーマは，XXX ということである [/ であった]．

> The thesis guiding the present study is that students' perceptions of a democratic, cohesive school climate will positively relate to their willingness to act on knowledge of a peer's intention to do something dangerous by seeking the assistance of an adult or directly intervening. (58)
> 本研究のテーマは，民主的で団結的な学校風土を学生が感じることが，同輩が危険なことを行おうとする意図を知ったときに大人の援助を求めたり直接的に介入することにより行動する意思と正の関係にある，ということである．

0378 全体的なテーマについて述べる．

◆ The present study concerns the expression of X in the transition to Y.

本研究は，Y への過渡期における X の表出に関係する．

> The present study concerns the expression of cooperativeness, competitiveness, individualism and interpersonalism in the transition to Japanese adolescence. (54)
> 本研究は，青年への過渡期における日本人の協調性，競争性，個人主義，間人主義の表出に関係する．

0379 関心のあるテーマを述べる．

◆ We were interested in the effects of X on Y.

我々は，X が Y に及ぼす効果に関心があった．

> We were interested in the effects of the experimental manipulation on reported intrusiveness of tinnitus and on cognitive functioning. (28)
> 我々は，実験的な操作が，各個人の感じる耳鳴りの侵入性と認知的機能に及ぼす効果に関心があった．

0380 特に関心のあるテーマを述べる．

◆ Of primary interest is [/was] whether XXX.
特に関心があるのは，XXX かどうかということである [/ であった]．

> Of primary interest is whether memory quantity and efficiency are both impaired in AD relative to healthy younger and older adults. (7)
> 特に関心があるのは，AD においては，健康な若者や高齢者と比べて，記憶の量と効率の両方が損なわれているのかどうかということである．

（訳者注：AD; Alzheimer's disease, アルツハイマー病）

0381 主な関心と副次的な関心を述べる．

◆ Our principal interest in this research is in X. However, a subsidiary issue here is whether YYY.
本研究における我々のおもな関心は，X にある．しかし，ここでの副次的な問題は，YYY かどうかということである．

> Our principal interest in this research is in the results obtained with 10 sighted, blindfolded observers. However, a subsidiary issue here is whether spatial updating of targets specified by 3-D and SL is exhibited by blind observers. (42)
> 本研究における我々のおもな関心は，目隠しをされた視力のある 10 名の観察者の結果についてである．しかし，ここでの副次的な問題は，3-D と SL で明記される標的の空間的更新が盲目の観察者によって示されるかどうかということである．

（訳者注：SL; spatial language, 空間的言語）

4.7.2 単独の目的

0382 目的を述べる．

◆ The goal of this article was [/is] to XXX.
本論文の目的は，XXX することであった [/ である]．

> The goal of this article was to provide psychologists with current information regarding sexuality and aging. (29)
> 本論文の目的は，性的関心と年齢についての現時点の情報を心理学者に提供することであった．

0383 研究の全体的な目的を述べる．

◆ The X study was designed to YYY.
X 研究は，YYY を行うために計画された．

4.7　本研究のテーマ・関心・目的

The MacArthur Juvenile Capacity Study was designed to examine age differences in a variety of cognitive and psychosocial capacities that are relevant to debates. (57)
マッカーサー青年能力研究は，ディベートに関連するさまざまな認知的および心理社会的能力における年齢差を調べるために計画された．

0384　新たに着手する，という目的を述べる．

◆ We set out to XXX.

我々は，XXX に着手した．

> In the present study, we set out to examine the effects of perceptual load on conscious perception in a modified inattentional blindness paradigm in which an expected "critical" stimulus was presented in multiple trials. (43)
> 今回の研究において，我々は，予期された「重要な」刺激が複数の試行で呈示される，修正された不注意盲目パラダイムにおいて，知覚的負荷が意識的知覚に及ぼす効果の研究に着手した．

0385　調べる，という目的を述べる．

◆ The present study examines [/examined] X.

本研究は，X を調べる [/ 調べた]．

> The present study examines the contributions of both parent and adolescent violence in prospective prediction of later behavioral health problems. (22)
> 本研究は，後年の行動的な健康問題の前向き予測における親と青年の暴力の両方の寄与を調べる．

0386　程度を決定する，という目的を述べる．

◆ The purpose of this study was to determine the degree to which XXX.

本研究の目的は，XXX である程度を決定することであった．

> The purpose of this study was to determine the degree to which the capacity to understand and use analogies is present in a New World monkey species. (34)
> 本研究の目的は，類推を理解し，使用する能力が新世界ザル種に存在する程度を判定することであった．

0387　真偽を決める，という目的を述べる．

◆ The current study aimed to determine whether XXX.

今回の研究は，XXX かどうかを決定することを目的とした．

> The current study aimed to determine whether capuchin monkeys were capable of solving a complex analogical task that more closely mirrored those that have been solved by young children and chimpanzees. (34)
> 本研究は，オマキザルが，幼児とチンパンジーが解くことのできる問題をより密接に反映した複雑な類推的課題を解くことができるかどうかを明らかにすることを目的とした．

4. 序文 (Introduction)

0388 効果を調べる，という目的を述べる．
◆ In the present study, we examined the effects of P on Q[, R, and S].
本研究において，我々はPがQ [, R, S] に及ぼす効果を調べた．

> In the present study, we set out to examine the effects of perceptual load on conscious perception. (43)
> 本研究において，我々は，知覚的負荷が意識的知覚に及ぼす効果の分析に着手した．

0389 変数間の関係の有無を調べる，という目的を述べる．
◆ We studied whether P is related to Q[, R, and S].
我々は，PがQ [, R, S] と関係があるかどうかを調べた．

> We studied whether memory specificity is related to major depression, acute stress disorder, and specific assault-related phobia at 2 weeks postassault. (36)
> 我々は，暴力後2週間の時点で，記憶特異性が，大うつ，急性ストレス障害，暴力に関連する特定の恐怖症と関係があるかどうかを調べた．

0390 測度の信頼性を調べる，という目的を述べる．
◆ This study examines the internal consistency and stability of the X Test [/Scale].
本研究は，X検査 [/ 尺度] の内的整合性と安定性を調べる．

> This study examines the internal consistency and stability of the IAT-Anxiety. (13)
> この研究は，IAT-不安の内的整合性と安定性を調べる．

（訳者注：IAT; Implicit Association Test, 潜在的連合テスト）

0391 比較する，という目的を述べる．
◆ The present study was developed to directly compare X with Y.
本研究はXをYと直接比較するために開発された．

> The present study was developed to directly compare brain activity induced by impersonal stress with that induced by interpersonal stress. (60)
> 本研究は，個人に関しないストレスにより引き起こされる脳活動を，対人関係のストレスにより引き起こされる脳活動と直接比較するために，開発された．

0392 異なる研究を統合する，という目的を述べる．
◆ The present study sought to integrate X with Y.
本研究は，XをYと統合することを目的とした．

> The present study sought to integrate research on the stress–aggression relationship with recent work emphasizing motivational systems and brain processes that promote anger and aggression. (60)
> 本研究は，ストレスと攻撃の関係についての研究を，怒りと攻撃を増進する動機づけ系および脳過程を強調する最近の研究と統合することを目的とした．

0393 概念化の枠組みを提案する，という目的を述べる．
◆ We propose a[n] X framework for conceptualizing Y.

4.7 本研究のテーマ・関心・目的　　105

我々は，Yを概念化するためのXの枠組みを提案する．
> We propose an emic and etic framework for conceptualizing and understanding discrimination across groups. (32)
> 我々はグループを通して差別を概念化し理解するためのエミック（文化内）およびエティック（文化外）な枠組みを提案する．
>
> （訳者注：エミック；emic, 文化現象を住民がどのように意識しているかを分析する立場のこと：エティック；etic, 文化現象を観察者の視点から客観的に分析する立場のこと）

0394　アイデアの検証により文献に寄与する，という目的を述べる．

◆ The present study aimed to make an important contribution to the X literature by testing Y.

本研究は，Yを検証することによりXの文献に重要な寄与を行うことを目的とした [/する]．

> The present study aimed to make an important contribution to the team reflexivity literature by testing a central tenet in team reflexivity theory, i.e., that team reflexivity is conducive to the development of shared task representations that are conducive to group performance. (59)
> 本研究は，チーム内省理論の中心的な教義，すなわち，チームの内省はグループの成績に資する共有された課題表象の発達につながるということを検証することによって，チーム内省の文献に重要な寄与を行うことを目的とした．

0395　未解決の問題に取り組むことにより先行研究を拡張する，という目的を述べる．

◆ The present study extends previous research on X in [/by] addressing N unresolved questions.

本研究は，未解決であるN個の疑問に取り組むことにより，Xに関する先行研究を拡張する．

> The present study extends previous research on empathy in addressing two distinct, currently unresolved questions. (55)
> 本研究は，現在未解決である2つの異なる疑問に取り組むことにより，共感に関する先行研究を拡張する．

0396　新しい話題に焦点を当てることにより先行研究を拡張する，という目的を述べる．

◆ This work extends that of Author (Year) by focus[s]ing on X.

この研究は，Xに焦点を当てることにより，著者（発表年）の研究を拡張する．

> This work extends that of Duriez et al. (2005) by focussing explicitly on the extent of the correspondence between the two dimensions of these three domains. (9)
> 本研究は，これら3つの領域における2つの次元の間の対応の範囲に明示的に焦点を当てることにより，Duriezら（2005）の研究を拡張する．

4. 序文 (Introduction)

0397 モデルを検証する，という目的について述べる．
◆ We tested a model in which XXX.
我々は XXX というモデルを検証した．

> Finally, we tested a model (Model C) in which the two political orientation factors described earlier were hypothesised to be moderately intercorrelated. (9)
> 最後に，我々は先に述べた 2 つの政治的志向という要因が中程度に相関すると仮定するモデル（モデル C）を検証した．

0398 モデルを比較する，という目的を述べる．
◆ This study compared [/was designed to compare] the N competing models.
この研究は N 個の競合するモデルを比較した [/ 比較するために計画された]．

> Accordingly, this study was designed to compare the two competing models on the basis of their ability to predict. (44)
> したがって，本研究は，2 つの競合するモデルをそれらの予測力に基づいて比較するために計画された．

0399 現象をモデルで説明する，という目的を述べる．
◆ The present study represents an attempt to conceptualize the X phenomenon in terms of a[n] Y model.
本研究は，X の現象を Y モデルにより概念化する試みについて述べる．

> The present study represents an attempt to conceptualize the functional fixedness phenomenon (e.g., Adamson, 1952; Duncker, 1945) in terms of an S–R model. (18)
> 本研究は，機能的固定の現象（たとえば，Adamson, 1952; Duncker, 1945）を S–R モデルにより概念化する試みについて述べる．

0400 著者のモデルを他のモデルと対比させる，という目的を述べる．
◆ We contrast these explanations with a X model [/account].
我々はこれらの説明を X のモデル [/ 説明] と対比させる．

> We contrast these explanations with our perceived-time-based account, which centers on the perception of time rather than devaluation of outcomes. (35)
> 我々は，これらの説明を，知覚時間を基盤とする我々の説明と対比させる．我々の説明は，結果の価値低下よりもむしろ時間知覚に重点をおいている．

0401 薬物により誘発される現象の調節を調べる，という目的を述べる．
◆ The current study [/research] examined whether P modulates Q-induced changes in R.
本研究は，Q により誘発される R の変化を P が調節するかどうかを調べた．

> The current research examined whether caffeine interacts to modulate ethanol-induced changes in anxiety, locomotion, and learning in the plus-maze discriminative avoidance task (PMDAT). (21)

4.7 本研究のテーマ・関心・目的   *107*

本研究は，十字型迷路弁別回避課題（PMDAT）において，エタノールにより誘発される不安，運動，学習の変化を，カフェインが調節するように相互作用するかどうかを調べた．

0402　薬物による治療効果を分析する，という目的を述べる．

◆In the present paper, we have studied the efficacy of a treatment of X with Y.

本論文において，我々はYによるXの治療の効果を調べた．

> In the present paper, we have studied the efficacy of a treatment of CHI with intravenous pyruvate, and evaluated the contribution of Pyr blood Glu scavenging activity to its neuroprotective properties. (64)
> 本論文において，我々はピルビン酸の静脈内投与によるCHIの治療の効果を調べて，ピルビン酸の血液中のグルタミン酸塩排除活動の神経保護的な特性への寄与を評価した．

（訳者注：CHI; closed head injury, 閉鎖性頭部外傷）

4.7.3　複数の目的

0403　2つの目的を列挙する．

◆We first XXX. We then YYY.

我々は，最初に，XXXを行う．次に，我々はYYYを行う．

> We first review current explanations of hyperbolic discounting, contrasting various behavioral theories with our perceived-time-based model. We then present an experiment designed to empirically test this model. (35)
> 我々は，最初に，さまざまな行動理論を知覚時間を基盤とする我々のモデルと対比させながら，双曲線型割引についての現在の説明を概観する．次に，我々は，このモデルを経験的に検証するために設計された実験を示す．

0404　複数の目的を，複数の文章により列挙する．

◆The purpose of the current [/this] study was N-fold. First, XXX. Second, YYY. [Third, ZZZ.]

本研究の目的はN個であった．第一に，XXX．第二に，YYY．[第三に，ZZZ.]

> Therefore, the purpose of the current study was twofold. First, in Experiment 1, we characterized the relation between conditioned novelty and cocaine reward by assessing competition across a range of cocaine doses. Second, in Experiment 2, we determined whether novelty's ability to compete with cocaine persisted or if the initial drug preference returned after a period of abstinence. (49)
> それゆえ，本研究の目的は2つであった．第一に，実験1において，コカインのある範囲の投与量にまたがって競合を評価することにより条件性新奇性とコカイン報酬の関係の特性を描き出した．第二に，実験2において，新奇性がコカインと競合する能力は持続するのか，あるいは，ある期間の禁断後に薬物に対する初期の選好が回復するのかを明らかにした．

4. 序文 (Introduction)

0405 複数の目的を，文章中で列挙する．

◆ The goals of this study were to (a) XXX, and (b) YYY.

今回の研究の目的は，(a) XXX すること，および，(b) YYY することであった．

> The goals of this study were to (a) examine the impact of perceived racial discrimination on various mental health outcomes for Asian Americans and Latinos, and (b) expand the range of our understanding of racial discrimination and its mental health associations. (32)
> 本研究の目的は，(a) アジア系アメリカ人とラテンアメリカ系アメリカ人について，被差別感が精神保健に関するさまざまな結果に及ぼす効果を調べ，(b) 人種差別，および，人種差別と精神保健の関連についての我々の理解を広げることであった．

0406 複数の目的を，コロンと不定詞を用いて列挙する．

◆ The project described herein accomplished two goals: (a) to XXX, and (b) to YYY.

ここで報告されるプロジェクトは，2つの目的を達成した．すなわち，(a) XXX すること，および，(b) YYY することであった．

> The class project described herein accomplished two goals: (a) to enhance a Tests and Measurements class, and (b) to devise a college-wide course ratings form. (53)
> ここで報告される授業プロジェクトは，2つの目的を達成した．すなわち，(a)「検査と測定」の授業の質を高めること，および，(b) 大学規模の科目評定尺度質問用紙を考案することであった．

0407 取り組む問題を，コロンと疑問文を用いて列挙する．

◆ This study aimed to XXX. N general questions were addressed: (a) AAA? (b) BBB? [and] (c) CCC?

本研究は，XXX することを目的とした．N個の一般的な問題に取り組んだ．すなわち，(a) AAA か，(b) BBB か，(c) CCC か，である．

> This study aimed to describe such commonalities and to provide information on how executive coaching can help executives improve meeting leadership. Three general questions were addressed: (a) Can more effective meeting behaviors be identified? (b) Can the identified behaviors be changed through executive coaching? (c) Will such behavioral changes lead to positive outcomes from the meetings for the participants and for their organizations? (48)
> 本研究は，このような共通性を記述し，幹部社員コーチングが幹部社員の会議における指導力の改善をどのように手助けできるのかについての情報を提供することを目的とした．3つの一般的な問題に取り組んだ．(a) より効果的な会議行動を同定することはできるのだろうか，(b) 同定された行動は，幹部社員コーチングにより変容することができるのだろうか，(c) そのような行動の変化は参加者と組織にとって有益な会議結果につながるのだろうか．

0408 焦点を当てる問題を，コロンと疑問文を用いて列挙する．

◆ This study [/It] focused on the following questions: (a) XXX? (b) YYY? and (c) ZZZ?

本研究 [/それ] は，以下の問題に焦点を当てた．(a) XXX か．(b) YYY か．(c) ZZZ か．

4.7 本研究のテーマ・関心・目的　　　109

It focused on the following questions: (a) How do adolescents' reports on their closest grandparent's involvement vary in different family structures? (b) What are the associations between grandparent involvement and adolescents' emotional and behavioral adjustment? and (c) Do the associations between grandparent involvement and adolescents' adjustment vary across different family structures? (2)

それは，以下の問題に焦点を当てた．(a) 最も近しい祖父母の関与についての青年の報告は，家族構造の違いによりどのように異なるか．(b) 祖父母との関与と青年の情動的および行動的適応の間の関連は，どのようなものであるか．(c) 祖父母の関与と青年の適応の間の関係は，家族構造の違いにより異なるか．

4.7.4　目的と研究内容

0409　理解を深めるという目的を，研究内容とともに述べる．

◆ To better understand X, this study examined Y.

　X をよりよく理解するために，本研究は Y を調査した．

> To better understand this community, this study qualitatively examined the experiences of homelessness among men at a rural homeless shelter. (41)
> このコミュニティをよりよく理解するために，本研究は，地方のホームレスシェルターにおいて男性のホームレスの経験を質的に調査した．

0410　影響を調べるという目的を，変数の関係を調べるという研究内容とともに述べる．

◆ To understand how X affects [/influences] Y, this study [/we] examined the relationship between A, B, [and] C and D.

　X が Y にどのように影響するかを理解するために，A, B, C と D の間の関係を調べた．

> To understand how school climate influences young people's willingness to intervene in the dangerous plan of a peer, we examined the relationship between adolescents' perceptions of the adult authority at school as democratic and open, school solidarity, and personal feelings of belonging and how they respond to a hypothetical vignette in which a peer is planning to do something dangerous at school. (58)
> 同輩の危険な計画に若者が介入しようとする意思に学校風土が及ぼす効果を理解するために，学校にいる大人の権威者が民主的で開放的であるという青年の認識，学校の団結，および，個人の所属意識と，同輩が学校で危険なことを企てる架空の短文に対してどのように反応するか，ということとの間にどのような関係があるかを調べた．

0411　あることを評価するという目的を，薬物が誘発する症状を調べるという研究内容とともに述べる．

◆ To evaluate the X properties of Y, we injected rats with A and observed them for symptoms of B.

　Y の X 的な特徴を評価するために，我々はラットに A を注射し，B の症状につい

て彼らを観察した．

> To evaluate the addictive properties of running, we injected active and inactive male and female rats with the opioid antagonist naloxone and observed them for symptoms of precipitated withdrawal. (33)
> ランニングの中毒的な特徴を評価するために，我々は活動的および非活動的な雄と雌のラットに，オピオイド拮抗体であるナロキソンを注射し，誘発離脱症状について観察した．

0412 目的とする論理的帰結を，研究内容とともに述べる．

◆ By studying X, we may gain a better understanding of Y.
X を調べることにより，我々は Y をよりよく理解できるかもしれない．

> By studying the ability of nonhuman primates to use analogies to solve problems, we may gain a better understanding of our own reasoning ability. (34)
> 人間以外の霊長類が問題解決のために類推を使用する能力を調べることにより，我々は，自分自身の推論能力について，より深い理解を得ることができるかもしれない．

4.7.5 目的と理由

0413 経験的データがないという理由に基づいて，研究の目的を述べる．

◆ Currently, little empirical data is [/are] available about X. Our primary goal in this study was to YYY.
現在，X についての経験的データはほとんどない．この研究における我々の第一の目的は，YYY することである．

> Currently, little empirical data are available about the positive or negative roles that specific spiritual beliefs or practices may play in youth's psychological adjustment when their parents divorce. Our primary goal in this study was to fill this gap. (61)
> 現在，両親が離婚するときに，特定のスピリチュアルな信念や習慣が，若者の心理的適応において果たす正および負の役割についての経験的データはほとんどない．この研究における我々の第一の目的は，このギャップを埋めることである．

0414 重要な問題が取り組まれていないという理由に基づいて，あることを確立するという目的を述べる．

◆ The existing X tasks do not address the important issue of what [/when /how] YYY. The purpose of the present study was therefore to establish Z.
既存の X 課題は，何が [/ いつ / どのように] YYY かという重要な問題に取り組んでいない．それゆえ，本研究の目的は，Z を確立することであった．

4.7 本研究のテーマ・関心・目的　　　　111

The existing distractor tasks do not address the important issue of what determines distraction by stimuli that are entirely irrelevant to the task at hand as they bear no response or feature relevance to the task stimuli, and appear in an irrelevant location. The purpose of the present study was therefore to establish a new distractor paradigm in which, as often is the case in daily life, the distractor stimuli may attract attention despite being entirely irrelevant to the task. (14)

既存の妨害課題は，課題刺激とは反応的あるいは特徴的な関連がなく，しかも無関係な場所に呈示されることから，当面の課題とは完全に無関係である刺激による妨害を決定するものは何かという重要な問題に取り組んでいない．それゆえ，本研究の目的は，日常生活においてしばしばそうであるように，妨害刺激が課題とは完全に無関係であるにもかかわらず注意を引くかもしれないような，新しい妨害パラダイムを確立することであった．

4.7.6 一連実験の目的

0415 一連の実験の目的を，複数の文章に分けて述べる．

◆ The purpose of the present series of experiments was therefore to determine whether XXX. Experiment 1 demonstrated that YYY. Experiments 2 and 3 then investigated whether ZZZ.

したがって，今回の一連の実験の目的は，XXX かどうかを明らかにすることであった．実験 1 は YYY を例証した．次に，実験 2 と 3 は，ZZZ かどうかを調べた．

> The purpose of the present series of experiments was therefore to determine whether instrumental actions performed by young children are sensitive to devaluation of the outcome. Experiment 1 demonstrated that children are sensitive to the instrumental contingency between the target response (touching an icon on a touch sensitive screen) and the outcome (the presentation of a short video clip). Experiments 2 and 3 then investigated whether devaluing the outcome by specific satiety had an effect on the subsequent instrumental behavior of children ranging between 18 and 48 months of age. (37)
>
> したがって，今回の一連の実験の目的は，幼い子供の行う道具的な行為が結果の価値低下に敏感であるかどうかを明らかにすることであった．実験 1 は，子供が標的反応（タッチパネルの画面上のアイコンに触れること）とその結果（短いビデオクリップの呈示）の間の道具的な随伴性に敏感であることを例証した．次に，実験 2 と 3 は，結果の価値を特異的な飽和により低下させることが，18〜48 月齢の子供のその後の道具的行動に影響を及ぼすかどうかを調べた．

0416 一連の研究の複数の目的を，文章内で列挙する．

◆ N studies were conducted to (a) XXX, (b) YYY, and (c) ZZZ.

（a）XXX を行う，（b）YYY を行う，（c）ZZZ を行うために，N 個の研究が行われた．

112　　　　　　　　　　　　　4.　序文（Introduction）

Four studies (including one pilot study) were conducted to (a) assess immanent justice reasoning using a measure that unambiguously assesses participants' causal inferences, (b) examine the role of deservingness in immanent justice reasoning, and (c) provide support for the notion that immanent justice reasoning can serve to protect the belief in a just world when the belief is threatened. (6)
(a) 参加者の因果的推論を明確に評価する測度を用いて内在的正義推論を評価するため，(b) 内在的正義推論における賞罰の当然性の役割を調べるため，(c) 内在的正義推論は公正世界の信念が脅かされたときにそれを守るのに役立つという主張に支持を与えるために，4つの研究（1個の予備的研究を含む）が行われた．

0417 一連の実験の目的を，1文で述べる．
◆We conducted N experiments aimed at addressing [the questions of] whether XXX and whether YYY.
我々は，XXX かどうか，および，YYY かどうか，[という問題]に取り組むことを目的とする N 個の実験を行った．

> We conducted three experiments aimed at addressing the questions of whether it is possible to unitize item information and source information and whether this unitization leads to increased familiarity-based memory. (12)
> 我々は，項目情報と情報源情報をユニット化することができるかどうか，および，そのようなユニット化が熟知性を基盤とする記憶の増加につながるかどうか，という問題に取り組むことを目的とする3つの実験を行った．

0418 いくつかの可能な説明を検討するという一連の実験の目的を述べる．
◆We examined X by addressing alternative accounts in terms of A (Experiments L), B (Experiment M), and C (Experiment N).
A（実験L），B（実験M），および，C（実験N）による代わりの説明に取り組むことにより，X を分析した．

> In addition, with the following experiments we also examined the specificity of the effect of perceptual load by addressing alternative accounts in terms of memory (Experiments 2 and 3), response prioritization or goal neglect (Experiment 4), and strategy (Experiment 5). (43)
> 加えて，引き続く実験で，記憶（実験2と3），反応優先順位または目標無視（実験4），および，方略（実験5）による代わりの説明に取り組むことにより，知覚的負荷効果の特異性も分析した．

4.7.7　評論のテーマ・目的

0419 ある文献を概観するという目的を述べる．
◆We review a [/the] literature on X. [/We review N relevant literatures: A, B, and C.]
我々は，X の文献を概観する．[/ 我々は，N 個の関連文献，すなわち，A, B, C を評論する．]

4.7 本研究のテーマ・関心・目的   113

We briefly review here three relevant literatures: research on the neural systems underpinning repeated responding, computational models of the cognitive processes that underlie routine action, and animal learning studies. (62)
我々は，ここで，3つの関連文献を簡潔に概観する．すなわち，反復反応を支える神経系の研究，決まりきった行為の基礎となる認知的過程についての計算論的モデル，および，動物学習の研究である．

0420 評論があるテーマに焦点を当てることを述べる．
◆ The focus of this [critical] review is on X.
この [批判的な] 評論は，X に焦点を当てる．

> The focus of this critical review is on two particular anxiety disorders: panic disorder and specific phobia. (1)
> この批判的な評論は，2つの特定の不安障害，すなわち，パニック障害と特定恐怖症に焦点を当てる．

0421 評論が，あるテーマではなく，別のテーマに焦点を当てることを述べる．
◆ This article focuses more on X and less on Y.
本論文は，おもに X に焦点を当て，Y にはあまり焦点を当てない．

> Ultimately, the article focuses more on psychophysiological assessment and less on subjective reports of mood states or cognitions. (1)
> 最後に，本論文は，おもに心理生理学的な評価に焦点を当て，気分や認知についての主観的な報告にはあまり焦点を当てない．

0422 評論が，あるテーマが重要である理由を強調することを述べる．
◆ This review highlighted two main reasons why XXX. First, YYY. Second, ZZZ.
本評論は，なぜ XXX であるかについて，2つのおもな理由を強調した．第一に，YYY．第二に，ZZZ．

> This review highlighted two main reasons why ambulatory assessment is particularly important in research on anxiety disorders. First, (略). Second, (略). (1)
> 本評論は，なぜ移動評価が不安障害の研究において特に重要であるかについて，2つのおもな理由を強調した．第一に，(略)．第二に，(略)．

0423 評論がいくつかの例を示すことを述べる．
◆ This review provide[d] several examples of XXX.
本評論は，XXX のいくつかの例を示す [/ 示した]．

> Although this review provided several examples of how monitoring change during (exposure) therapy can provide useful data, the existing literature is mostly limited to "guided" therapy sessions. (1)
> 本評論は（曝露）療法中の変化をモニターすることが有用なデータを提供することができるいくつかの例を示したが，既存の研究はその大部分が「付き添いつきの」療法のセッションに限定されている．

4.8 内容の予告

4.8.1 仮説・予測

0424 仮説を述べる.

◆We hypothesized that XXX.

我々は，XXX という仮説を立てた.

> We hypothesized that female college students would overestimate the amount of alcohol that male students want them to drink. (39)
> 我々は，女子大生は男子学生が彼女たちに飲んでほしいと思うアルコールの量を過大評価するという仮説を立てた.

0425 仮説を主張する.

◆We contend that XXX. [/In our view, XXX.]

我々は，XXX と主張する.

> We contend that a probable dynamic underlying this association is the sense of identification with the common good. (58)
> 我々は，この関係の根底にある原動力として有望なものは公益と一体であるという意識であると主張する.

0426 仮説を，改行・字下げした文章で述べる.

◆I hypothesized the following: [/I explored the following hypothesis:]

   Hypothesis 1: XXX.

私は以下の仮説を立てた.

   仮説 1：XXX.

> Thus, I hypothesized the following:
>   *Hypothesis 1*: Executive coaching will significantly increase the percentage of process behaviors and significantly decrease the percentage of content behaviors observed among meeting leaders. (48)
> それゆえ，私は以下の仮説を立てた.
>   仮説 1：幹部社員コーチングは，会議のリーダーにおいて観察される進行にかかわる行動の割合を有意に増大させ，内容にかかわる行動の割合を有意に減少させる.

0427 前提と仮説を述べる.

◆We assume that XXX, and [/but] we postulate that YYY.

我々は XXX を前提としている. そして [/ しかし]，YYY と仮定する.

> We assume that the "true" internal discounting process is exponential, but we postulate that the values of delayed outcomes are internally discounted based not on calendar time t but rather on subjective estimates of the objective time T. (35)

我々は,「真の」内的な割引過程は指数関数的であることを前提としているが,遅延される結果の価値は,暦時間である t ではなく,客観的時間の主観的な推定値である T に基づいて内的に割り引かれると仮定する.

0428 　調整変数についての仮説を述べる.

◆We [/I /This study] considered A, B, and C as potential moderators of the relationship between X and Y.

我々[/私/本研究]は,A, B, CがXとYとの関係の潜在的な調整変数であると考えた.

> We considered history of childhood abuse, history of major depression, sex, and ethnicity as potential moderators of the relationship between memory specificity and posttrauma psychopathology. (36)
> 我々は,児童期における虐待の病歴,大うつ病の病歴,性別,民族性が記憶特異性と心的外傷後の精神病理との関係の潜在的な調整変数であると考えた.

0429 　過去の知見に基づいて,仮説を立てたことを述べる.

◆Based on these findings and a pathway analysis approach, we hypothesized that XXX.

これらの知見およびパスウェイ解析のアプローチに基づいて,XXX という仮説を立てた.

> Based on these findings and a pathway analysis approach, we hypothesized that KIBRA activity would be altered via the RhoA/ROCK/Rac pathway through the putative modulation of PKC-ζ (Van Kolen & Slegers, 2006). (31)
> これらの知見およびパスウェイ解析のアプローチに基づいて,KIBRA の活動性が PKC-ζ の推定上の調節を通して,RhoA/ROCK/Rac 経路経由で,変化させられるという仮説を立てた (Van Kolen & Slegers, 2006).

(訳者注:KIBRA は記憶に関連する遺伝子の名称:PKC-ζ は記憶に関連する酵素の名称:ROCK はシナプス形成に関連する酵素の名称:RhoA と Rac はタンパク質の名称)

0430 　先行研究に基づいて,媒介変数についての仮説を立てたことを述べる.

◆Because X has been found to YYY (Author, Year), we hypothesized that P would mediate Q.

X は YYY することが見出されてきている (著者,発表年) ことから,我々は,P が Q を媒介するという仮説を立てた.

> Because age and AD have both been found to reduce the efficiency of the working memory system (Logie et al., 2004), we hypothesized that that age and AD related changes in working memory capacity would mediate, to some degree, any changes seen in selective encoding. (7)
> 加齢と AD はどちらも作業記憶システムの効率を減少させることが見出されてきている (Logie et al., 2004) ことから,我々は,加齢と AD に関連する作業記憶容量の変化が,選択的符号化において見られるすべての変化をある程度媒介している,という仮説を立てた.

(訳者注:AD; Alzheimer's disease, アルツハイマー病)

4. 序文 (Introduction)

0431 過去の知見を統合して，仮説を立てたことを述べる．
◆ Taken together, these findings prompted the authors to conclude that XXX.
これらの知見を総合した結果，XXX と結論するに至った．

> Taken together, these findings prompted the authors to conclude that the students in these schools may have felt that they had "nowhere to turn" with their concerns, creating a climate of silence and inaction. (58)
> これらの知見を総合した結果，これらの学校の生徒は心配事をもっていくところがどこにもないと感じ沈黙と無為という学校風土をつくった，と結論するに至った．

0432 仮説を検証したことを述べる．
◆ We tested the hypothesis that P would reduce [/increase] the effects that Q has on R.
我々は，Q が R に及ぼす効果を P が減少させる [/ 増加させる] という仮説を検証した．

> We tested the hypothesis that higher levels of self-esteem would reduce the effects that mortality salience has on worldview defense. (25)
> 我々は，自尊心のレベルが高くなるほど，死の顕現性が世界観の防衛に及ぼす効果が減少する，という仮説を検証した．

0433 実験により仮説を検証したことを述べる．
◆ We tested these hypotheses in an experiment in which we manipulated whether XXX.
我々は，XXX かどうかを操作した実験においてこれらの仮説を検証した．

> We tested these hypotheses in an experiment in which we manipulated whether groups engaged in reflection. (59)
> 我々は，グループが内省を行うかどうかを操作した実験においてこれらの仮説を検証した．

0434 仮説に基づく予測を述べる．
◆ The X hypothesis of Y predicts that ZZZ.
Y の X 仮説は，ZZZ を予測する．

> The approach-motivation hypothesis of stress-induced aggression (Hypothesis 1) predicts that either type of stressor will foster left lateralized frontal brain activity indicative of approach motivation. (60)
> ストレス誘発性攻撃行動についての接近動機づけ仮説（仮説 1）は，どちらのタイプのストレス因子も，接近動機づけの指標である左半球に側性化した前頭脳活動を増進することを予測する．

0435 先行研究に基づく予測を述べる．
◆ Based on X research, the Y sampled here could be expected to ZZZ.
X 研究を踏まえれば，ここで抽出された Y は ZZZ を行うことが期待されるかもしれない．

Based on such research, the 5th graders sampled here could be expected to express cooperativeness and interpersonalism and a strong task involvement rather than competitiveness or individualism. (54)

そのような研究を踏まえれば，ここで抽出された 5 年生は，競争性や個人主義よりもむしろ，協調性と間人主義と課題への強い関与を表現することが期待されるかもしれない．

4.8.2　具体的な内容

0436　課題の内容を述べる．

◆ The task was to XXX.

課題は，XXX を行うことであった．

> The task was to remove each of the balls from its box. (5)
> 課題は，その箱から各ボールを取り出すことであった．

0437　参加者と課題の内容を述べる（**our study** より **the study** がよい）．

◆ The [/Our] study employed X and Y, who [collectively] performed Z.

今回の研究では X と Y を雇用して，Z を [集団で] 行ってもらった．

> Our study employed older and younger professional air traffic controllers and age-matched noncontrollers, who collectively performed a battery of cognitive tasks and simulated ATC tasks that varied in difficulty. (47)
> 今回の研究では，高齢および若年のプロの航空管制官と，年齢がマッチさせられた管制官ではない参加者を雇用して，難易度の異なる認知課題と模擬的な ATC 課題のバッテリーを集団で行ってもらった．
>
> （訳者注：ATC; air-traffic control, 航空管制）

0438　調査票を配布し回収したことを述べる．

◆ X and Y completed self-administered surveys distributed and collected by Z.

X と Y が，Z により配布・回収される自問自答型の調査票に記入した．

> Teachers and administrators completed self-administered surveys distributed and collected by field supervisors. (23)
> 先生と管理者が，現地指導員により配布・回収される自問自答型の調査票に記入した．

0439　実験的操作の前後で尺度に回答してもらったことを述べる．

◆ Participants indicated their X at Y and after Z on an L-item scale (e.g., "A," "B," "C") ranging from M (not at all) to N (very).

参加者は，Y および Z 後に，X を，M（まったく違う）から N（とても）までの範囲をもつ，L 項目（たとえば，「A」，「B」，「C」）の尺度上で示した．

> Participants indicated their state anxiety at baseline and after the stress induction on an eight-item scale (e.g., "worry," "nervous," "tense") ranging from 0 (not at all) to 5 (very). (13)

4. 序文 (Introduction)

参加者は，ベースラインおよびストレス導入後の時点で，状態不安を，0（まったく違う）から 5（とても）までの範囲をもつ 8 項目（たとえば，「心配して」，「神経質で」，「緊張して」）の尺度上で示した.

0440 異なる条件を設定したことを述べる.

◆ In the X condition AAA, and in the Y condition BBB.

X 条件では，AAA であり，Y 条件では，BBB であった.

> In the high perceptual load condition the non-target letters were H, K, M, W, and Z, and in the low perceptual load condition they were all Os. (43)
> 高知覚的負荷条件では，非標的刺激の文字は H, K, M, W, Z であり，低知覚的負荷条件では，それらはすべて O であった.

0441 課題や測度の選定理由を述べる.

◆ The tasks [/measures] were selected to XXX.

課題 [/ 測度] は，XXX のために選ばれた.

> The tasks in the cognitive task battery were selected to provide measures of both ATC domain-relevant abilities and less relevant measures of different aspects of cognition (see Wickens, Mavor, & McGee, 1997). (47)
> 認知課題バッテリーの課題は，ATC 領域関連の能力の測度と，ATC とはあまり関連のないさまざまな認知的側面の測度を提供するために選ばれた（Wickens, Mavor, & McGee, 1997 を参照）.

（訳者注：ATC; air-traffic control, 航空管制）

0442 課題や実験の特徴を列挙する.

◆ An important aspect of this task [/experiment] is that XXX. Another novel feature of the paradigm is that YYY. A third feature of the task [/experiment] concerns Z.

今回の課題 [/ 実験] の 1 つの重要な側面は，XXX である．このパラダイムのもう 1 つの新しい特徴は，YYY である．この課題 [/ 実験] の 3 つ目の特徴は，Z に関係する.

> An important aspect of this experiment is that we adopted training functions that have not been examined in previous research. (略) Another novel feature of the paradigm is that one side of the function was sparsely trained to parallel EXAM's assumption that a few (e.g., two) values are retrieved to prepare a transfer (generalization) response. (略) A third feature of the experiment concerns the sequencing of the training stimuli. (44)
> 今回の実験の 1 つの重要な側面は，先行研究では分析されたことのない訓練関数を採用したことである．(略) このパラダイムのもう 1 つの新しい特徴は，転移（般化）反応を準備するために少数の（たとえば 2 個の）値が想起されるという EXAM のモデルの仮説に対応して，関数の片側がまばらに訓練されることである．(略) この実験の 3 つ目の特徴は，訓練刺激の順序に関係する.

（訳者注：EXAM; extrapolation–association model, 外挿連合モデル）

4.8.3 研究計画の根拠

0443 計画の理論的根拠を，複数の文章により列挙する．

◆ The rationale behind X is N-fold. First, AAA. The second rationale for Y is BBB.

Xの理論的根拠は，N個ある．第一に，AAA．Yの第二の理論的根拠は，BBB．

> The rationale behind familiarizing students with varied methods and facilitating students' use of them is twofold. First, doing so will give students the greatest degrees of freedom in fitting the method to their research questions. (略) The second rationale for teaching and facilitating the use of varied methodologies may be even more important, although it is generally not acknowledged in our field. (略) (16)
> 学生たちにさまざまな方法に慣れさせ，それらの使用を促進させることの背後にある理論的根拠は，2つである．第一に，そうすることにより，研究問題に方法を合わせる場合に最も大きな自由度を学生に与えることになるということである．(略) 多様な方法論の使用を教授し促進する第二の理論的根拠は，我々の分野では概して知られていないが，さらに重要であるかもしれない．(略)

0444 アプローチの理論的根拠を，文章内で列挙する．

◆ The underlying rationale of this approach was that (a) AAA, (b) BBB, and (c) CCC.

このアプローチの基礎となる理論的根拠は，(a) AAA, (b) BBB, (c) CCC, であった．

> The underlying rationale of this approach was that (a) certain individuals are inaccurate in their responses to trait anxiety questionnaires, (b) these individuals could be detected by high scores on social desirability scales, and (c) thus, the use of social desirability scores in addition to anxiety scores would enhance the prediction of anxiety-related behaviors. (13)
> このアプローチの基礎となる理論的根拠は，(a) ある人々は特性不安質問紙に対する反応が正確ではない，(b) これらの人々は社会的望ましさ尺度における高得点により検出されうるであろう，(c) そのため，不安尺度に加えて社会的望ましさ尺度を使用することにより不安関連行動の予測が向上するだろう，というものであった．

0445 計画の前提となる仮定を，コロンを用いて列挙する．

◆ N assumptions undergird the propositions I will offer: (a) AAA, and (b) BBB.

私の提案する計画は，以下のN個の仮定を根拠としている．すなわち，(a) AAA, および，(b) BBB である．

> Two assumptions undergird the propositions I will offer: (a) the production of more and better science (research and theory) is a desirable goal in professional psychology, and (b) the most effective setting in which to influence scientific production is the graduate training situation. (16)
> 私の提案する計画は，以下の2つの仮定を根拠としている．すなわち，(a) 専門職としての心理学においては，より多くの，そしてよりよい科学（研究と理論）の生産が望ましい目標である，および，(b) 科学的な生産に影響する最も効果的な環境は大学院での訓練場面である．

4.8.4 先行研究をヒントにした

0446 今回の研究が先行研究を模していることを述べる.
◆ This study was modeled from [/after] a task that has previously been used to test X.
本研究は，X をテストするために過去に用いられてきた課題をもとにつくられた.

> This study was modeled from a task that has previously been used to test the analogical reasoning abilities of children. (34)
> 本研究は，子供の類推的推論の能力をテストするために過去に用いられてきた課題をもとにつくられた.

0447 今回の研究が先行研究における最近の動向を参考にしていることを述べる.
◆ The present study draws on recent trends in X research that emphasize Y.
本研究は，Y を強調する X 研究における最近の動向を資源として利用している.

> The present study draws on recent trends in process and outcome research that emphasize the role of client perceptions and contributions to positive outcomes (Tallman & Bohart, 1999). (8)
> 本研究は，クライエントの認識の役割および有益な結果への寄与を強調するプロセス研究とアウトカム研究の最近の動向を資源として利用している（Tallman & Bohart, 1999）.

0448 今回の研究が，先行研究の評論に基づいて，あることを行ったことを述べる.
◆ According to several review papers (Author, Year; Author, Year), we XXX.
いくつかの評論（著者，発表年；著者，発表年）に従って，我々は XXX を行った.

> According to several review papers (Furuya et al., 2006; Stores, 2007), we developed diagnostic criteria consisting of a central and core features to classify the ghost tales as far as possible into the four types described below (see Table 1). (15)
> いくつかの評論（Furuya et al., 2006; Stores, 2007）に従って，我々は，幽霊物語を以下に述べる 4 つのタイプ（表 1 を参照）にできる限り分類するための中心的・核心的な特徴から成る診断基準を開発した.

0449 今回の研究がある理論の示唆に基づいていることを述べる.
◆ The present study is [/was] guided by X theory (Author, Year), which suggests that YYY.
本研究は X 理論（著者，発表年）に基づいており，この理論は，YYY ということを示唆している.

> The present study is guided by social ecological theory (Bronfenbrenner, 1979), which suggests that to understand children's development, we should take into account not only the children and their immediate circles' characteristics, but also experiences with other family members outside of the immediate family's residence. (2)

本研究は社会生態学的理論（Bronfenbrenner, 1979）に基づいており，この理論は，子供の発達を理解するためには，子供と子供の身近な環境の特徴を考慮するのみならず，身近な家族の居住地の外に住んでいる他の家族構成員との経験もまた考慮するべきであることを示唆している．

0450 今回の研究が先行研究に基づいてあることを調べたことを述べる．

◆On the basis of previous research (Author, Year), the present study [/we] explored whether XXX.

先行研究（著者，発表年）に基づいて，XXX かどうかを調べた．

> On the basis of previous research (Landrine et al., 2006), we explored whether Asian Americans and Latinos would experience similar amounts of recent discrimination and similar appraisals of the stressfulness of these events. (32)
> 先行研究（Landrine et al., 2006）に基づいて，アジア系アメリカ人とラテンアメリカ系アメリカ人が，同じような量の最近の差別を経験し，それらの出来事について同じ程度のストレス度の評価を経験するかどうかを調べた．

0451 今回の研究が先行研究と同一の論理を用いたことを述べる．

◆We applied the same logic to investigate whether XXX.

我々は，XXX かどうかを研究するために同じ論理を用いた．

> We applied the same logic to investigate whether young children represent their own instrumental actions in terms of specific action–outcome relationships. (37)
> 我々は，幼い子供が，自らの道具的行為を特定の行為 – 結果関係により表象するかどうかを研究するために，同じ論理を応用した．

4.9 一連の実験をつなぐ

4.9.1 前の実験をまとめる

0452 前の実験のおもな知見を述べる．

◆The major finding of Experiment N was that XXX.

実験 N のおもな知見は，XXX ということであった．

> The major finding of Experiment 1 was that increasing self-esteem decreased the worldview defense that occurs in response to reminders of mortality. (25)
> 実験 1 のおもな知見は，自尊心を高めると，死を連想させるものに反応して起こる世界観の防衛を減少させるということであった．

0453 前の実験の知見とその意味を述べる．

◆The key finding of Experiment N was X, which suggests that YYY.

実験 N の重要な知見は，X であり，このことは，YYY を示唆している．

122　　　　　　　　　　4. 序文（Introduction）

The key finding of Experiment 2 was the significant devaluation effect observed in the two older age groups, which suggests that the children of approximately 32 months and above were capable of goal-directed action. (37)
実験2の重要な知見は，2つの年長群で観察された有意な価値低下効果であり，このことは，約32か月齢以上の子供が目標指向性行為を行うことができることを示唆している．

0454　　前の実験により決まったことを述べる．
◆ The previous experiment determined whether XXX [/the extent that XXX].
　先の実験は，XXX かどうか [/XXX である程度] を判定した．

> The previous experiment determined the extent that novelty conditioned reward competed with cocaine conditioned stimuli. (49)
> 先の実験は，新奇性に条件づけられた報酬が，コカインに条件づけられた刺激と競合する程度を判定した．

0455　　前の実験が仮説を支持したことを述べる．
◆ The results from [/of] Experiment N supported the X hypothesis.
　実験 N の結果は X 仮説を支持した．

> The results from Experiment 1 supported the unitization hypothesis. (12)
> 実験1の結果はユニット化仮説を支持した．

0456　　前の実験の結果が別の実験の結果と一致したことを述べる．
◆ The results of Experiment N are [generally] consistent with the results of Experiment M.
　実験 N の結果は，実験 M の結果と [大体において] 一致した．

> The results of Experiment 2 are generally consistent with the results of Experiment 1. (25)
> 実験2の結果は，実験1の結果と大体において一致した．

4.9.2　次の実験につなげる

0457　　前の実験の結果から次の問題が浮かび上がることを述べる．
◆ The present findings raise an obvious question: XXX?
　今回の知見から，明白な問題が浮かび上がる．すなわち，XXX なのだろうか？

> The present findings raise an obvious question: Does encouraging children to gesture, which (as Study 1 demonstrates) elicits new and correct strategies expressed uniquely in gesture, increase the likelihood that children will profit from instruction in mathematical equivalence? (5)
> 今回の知見から，明白な問題が浮かび上がる．すなわち，子供たちに，（研究1が例証するように）ジェスチャーに一意的に表現されている新しい正解方略を誘発するジェスチャーをすることを勧めることによって，子供たちが数学的な等価についての教示から恩恵を被る確率が大きくなるのだろうか？

4.9 一連の実験をつなぐ

0458 次の実験手続きの違いを述べる.
◆Experiment N was identical to Experiment M, except that XXX.
実験 N は，XXX である点を除けば，実験 1 と同一であった．

> Experiment 2 was identical to Experiment 1, except that the unitized and nonunitized encoding tasks were modified to control for overall differences in performance. (12)
> 実験 2 は，成績の全体的な差を制御するために，ユニット化された，および，ユニット化されない符号化課題を修正した点を除いては，実験 1 と同一であった．

0459 次の実験のデザインと選定理由を，前の実験と対比させながら述べる.
◆Experiment N used the design to assess X. Experiment M used a variant of this design to extend Y [/contrast Ys].
実験 N は，X を評価するためにこのデザインを用いた．実験 M は，Y を拡張する [/ 対比させる] ために，このデザインを変形したものを用いた．

> Experiment 1 used the design that was outlined earlier to assess the prediction that contextual modulation of similarity can be observed in rats. Experiment 2 used a variant of this design to both extend the generality of the results of interest, and to contrast two theoretical interpretations for them. (10)
> 実験 1 は，ラットにおいて類似性の文脈的調節が観察されうるという予測を評価するために，先に概説したデザインを用いた．実験 2 は，これまでに得られた興味深い結果の一般性を拡張し，かつ，それらの結果についての 2 つの理論的解釈を対比させるために，このデザインを変形したものを用いた．

0460 次の実験で新しい参加者を募集したことを述べる.
◆N new participants were recruited from X.
N 名の新しい参加者が，X から募集された．

> Sixteen new participants were recruited from UCL. (43)
> 16 名の新しい参加者が，UCL から募集された．

（**訳者注**：UCL; University College London, ユニバーシティ・カレッジ・ロンドン）

5 方法（Method）

5.1　参加者・被験体
5.2　装　置
5.3　材料・刺激・薬品・課題
5.4　教　示
5.5　場　所
5.6　データ
5.7　心理検査
5.8　研究デザイン
5.9　具体的な手続き
5.10　試行・ブロック・セッション
5.11　予備的研究
5.12　観察者による符号化・点数化
5.13　操作チェック
5.14　インタビュー
5.15　ウェブ調査
5.16　倫理的ガイドラインの遵守
5.17　動物学習
5.18　薬物・神経科学
5.19　データの欠損
5.20　統　計
5.21　メタ分析
5.22　統計ソフトウェア

5.1　参加者・被験体

5.1.1　学生の参加者

0461　心理学入門コースの大学生が，研究参加の単位得点と引き換えに参加したことを述べる．

◆L introductory psychology students (M women and N men) at X University

participated in this study in exchange for research participation credit.
X 大学の L 名の心理学入門科目の学生（女性 M 名，男性 N 名）が，研究参加の単位得点と引き換えにこの研究に参加した．

> Forty-one introductory psychology students (33 women and 8 men) at Johannes Gutenberg-University Mainz participated in this study in exchange for research participation credit. (13)
> ヨハネス・グーテンベルク大学マインツの 41 名の心理学入門科目の学生（女性 33 名，男性 8 名）が，研究参加の単位得点と引き換えにこの研究に参加した．

0462 大学生が，心理学コースの単位と引き換えに参加したことを述べる．

◆ N students at X University in Y, Z participated in exchange for course credit in a first-year psychology course.
Z の Y にある X 大学の N 名の大学生が，第 1 学年の心理学科目の単位得点と引き換えに参加した．

> Eighty-three students at McMaster University in Hamilton, Ontario, Canada, participated in exchange for course credit in a first-year psychology course. (24)
> カナダ，オンタリオ州ハミルトンのマクマスター大学の 83 名の大学生が，第 1 学年の心理学科目の単位得点と引き換えに参加した．

0463 学部学生が，心理学コースの割り増し単位得点を得るために参加したことを述べる．

◆ L (M female, N male) University of X undergraduate students taking psychology courses participated for bonus course credits.
心理学科目を受講している X 大学の L 名の学部学生（女性 M 名，男性 N 名）が，割増の単位得点を得るために参加した．

> Thirty-eight (35 female, 3 male) University of Calgary undergraduate students taking psychology courses participated for bonus course credits. (6)
> 心理学の科目を受講しているカルガリー大学の 38 名の学部学生（女性 35 名，男性 3 名）が，割り増しの単位得点を得るために参加した．

0464 大学生の参加者の学年について述べる．

◆ Class standing was A% freshman, B% sophomore, C% junior, and D% senior.
学年は，A% が 1 年生，B% が 2 年生，C% が 3 年生，D% が 4 年生であった．

> Class standing was 19.0% freshman, 24.8% sophomore, 27.1% junior, and 29.1% senior. (39)
> 学年は，19% が 1 年生，24.8% が 2 年生，27.1% が 3 年生，29.1% が 4 年生であった．

0465 生徒の参加者のサンプルのサイズ，および，学校の種類と場所を述べる．

◆ Participants were N boys [/girls] from a[n] X school in Y.
参加者は Y にある X 校の N 名の男子生徒 [/ 女子生徒] であった．

Participants were 84 boys from a school complex affiliated with a national (public) university in central Tokyo. (54)
参加者は，東京中心部の国立（公立）大学の付属一貫校の 84 名の男子生徒であった．

0466 生徒の参加者の性別，学校がある場所，個別検査について述べる．
◆Participants were L children (M girls, N boys)[,] who were tested individually at their schools in the X area.
参加者は L 名の子供（M 名が少女，N 名が少年）で，X 地域の学校において個別にテストされた．

Participants were 106 children (55 girls, 51 boys), who were tested individually at their schools in the Chicago area. (5)
参加者は 106 名の子供（55 名が少女，51 名が少年）で，シカゴ地域の学校において個別にテストされた．

5.1.2 社会人の参加者

0467 社会人の参加者，および，群の人数を述べる．
◆N X and M non[-]X served as participants, with P Y and Q Z per group.
N 名の X と M 名の X ではない人が参加者であった．各群の中で，P 名が Y，Q 名が Z であった．

Thirty-six licensed ATC controllers and 36 noncontrollers served as participants, with 18 older and 18 younger adults per group. (47)
36 名の免許のある航空管制官と 36 名の管制官ではない人が参加者であった．各群の中で，18 名が高齢者，18 名が若年者であった．

（訳者注：ATC; air-traffic control, 航空管制）

0468 社会人の参加者の年齢，家族状況，勤続年数を述べる．
◆On average, respondents were N years old, A% of them were married, and of the latter category B% were married with children. Respondents were predominantly women (C%); their mean seniority (length of service in X) was M years.
平均すると，回答者は N 歳で，A% が既婚者であり，その中の B% が子供のいる既婚者であった．回答者は女性が多数（C%）を占めていた．平均的な勤続年数（X に従事している長さ）は M 年間であった．

On average, respondents were 36.2 years old, 85% of them were married, and of the latter category 86% were married with children. Respondents were predominantly women (82%); their mean seniority (length of service in teaching) was 11 years. (52)
平均すると，回答者は 36.2 歳で，85% が既婚者であり，その中の 86% が子供のいる既婚者であった．回答者は女性が多数（82%）を占めていた．平均的な勤続年数（教職に従事している長さ）は 11 年間であった．

5.1.3 参加者の年齢・性別・男女の割合

0469 参加者の年齢を述べる．
◆ Their ages ranged from A to B (*M* = C, *SD* = D).
彼らの年齢は A 歳から B 歳（平均 C 歳，標準偏差 D）であった．

> Their ages ranged from 18 to 25 (*M* = 18.9, *SD* = 1.17). (61)
> 彼らの年齢は，18 歳から 25 歳（平均 18.9 歳，標準偏差 1.17）であった．

0470 サンプルに占める男女の割合を述べる．
◆ N percent of the X students were female [/male].
X 学生の N% は女性 [/ 男性] であった．

> Fifty-three percent of the high school students were female. (58)
> その高校生の 53% は女性であった．

0471 男女の割合がほぼ同じであったことを述べる．
◆ There was [a] relatively equal distribution between women (A%, *n* = B) and men (C%, *n* = D).
男性（A%, *n* = B）と女性（C%, *n* = D）の配分は相対的に等しかった．

> There was relatively equal distribution between women (49.8%, *n* = 797) and men (50.2%, *n* = 804). (46)
> 男性（49.8%, *n* = 797）と女性（50.2%, *n* = 804）の配分は相対的に等しかった．

0472 サンプルの男女の割合と年齢を述べる．
◆ The sample consisted of [approximately] equal percentages of males (A%) and females (B%) ages C to D years (*M* = E, *SD* = F).
サンプルは男性（A%）と女性（B%）の割合が [ほぼ] 等しく，年齢は C 歳から D 歳（平均 E 歳，標準偏差 F）であった．

> The sample consisted of approximately equal percentages of males (51.3%) and females (48.7%) ages 11 to 16 years (*M* =13.38, *SD* = 1.39). (2)
> サンプルは男性（51.3%）と女性（48.7%）の割合がほぼ等しく，年齢は 11 歳から 16 歳（平均 13.38 歳，標準偏差 1.39）であった．

0473 参加者の年齢と男女の割合の偏りについて述べる．
◆ These participants ranged in age from A to B years (*M* = C, *SD* = D), and the majority was female [/male] (E%).
これらの参加者は，年齢が A 歳から B 歳（平均 C 歳, 標準偏差 D）で，女性 [/ 男性] のほうが多かった（E%）．

> These participants ranged in age from 18 to 25 years (*M* = 19.87, *SD* = 1.35), and the majority was female (62.0%). (39)

これらの参加者は，年齢が 18 歳から 25 歳（平均 19.87 歳，標準偏差 1.35）で，女性のほうが多かった（62.0%）．

5.1.4 参加者の教育歴・収入・過去経験

0474 参加者が報告した教育歴について述べる．

◆X reported N mean years of formal education, and Y reported M years of formal education.

X は平均 N 年の公的な教育歴があると報告し，Y は平均 M 年の公的な教育歴があると報告した．

> Healthy older adults reported 15.2 mean years of formal education, and individuals with AD reported 14.7 years of formal education. (7)
> 健康な高齢者は平均 15.2 年の公的な教育歴があると報告し，AD のある人々は平均 14.7 年の公的な教育歴があると報告した．
>
> （訳者注：AD; Alzheimer's disease, アルツハイマー病）

0475 参加者の給与や年収について述べる．

◆Estimated annual salaries (*n* = N) ranged from $A to $B, with a median annual salary of $C.

推定年俸 (*n* = N) は，A ドルから B ドルの範囲であり，年俸の中央値は C ドルであった．

> Estimated annual salaries (*n* = 18) ranged from $100,000 to $30,000,000, with a median annual salary of $272,500. Bonuses were not included in these estimates. (48)
> 推定年俸（*n* = 18）は，100000 ドルから 30000000 ドルの範囲であり，年俸の中央値は 272500 ドルであった．これらの推定年俸にボーナスは含まれていなかった．

0476 参加者の学歴，年収，家族状況，就労状況を述べる．

◆The majority of the Xs were Y graduates (A%, *M* years of education = B, *SD* = C) and Xs reported an annual family income of over $D (E%). Nearly all Xs were married (F%) and worked outside of the home full-time (G%).

X の大多数は，Y 卒であり（A%，平均教育歴 B 年，標準偏差 C），家族の年収が D ドルを超えている（E%），と報告した．ほぼすべての X は結婚しており（F%），家の外でフルタイムで働いていた（G%）．

> The majority of the fathers were high school graduates (84%, *M* years of education = 16.3, *SD* = 2.4) and fathers reported an annual family income of over $75,000 (78%). Nearly all fathers were married (98%) and worked outside of the home full-time (98%). (45)
> 父親の大多数は，高卒であり（84%，平均教育歴 16.3 年，標準偏差 2.4），家族の年収が 75000 ドルを超えている（78%），と報告した．ほぼすべての父親は結婚しており（98%），家の外でフルタイムで働いていた（98%）．

0477　生徒の参加者のサンプルサイズ，学校がある場所，世帯収入について述べる．
◆Participants were N students at X schools located in Y. The median household income was $A for B and $C for D (Author, Year).

参加者は，YにあるX校に通うN名の生徒であった．Bの世帯収入の中央値はAドル，DではCドルであった（著者，発表年）．

> Participants were 636 students at two public high schools located in separate towns in Louisiana's Tangipahoa Parish (county). The median household income was $24,067 for the first town and $22,244 for the second town (U.S. Census Bureau, 2000).　　　　(3)
> 参加者は，ルイジアナのタンギパホア地方行政区（地域）の異なる町にある2つの公立高校に通う636名の生徒であった．1番目の町の世帯収入の中央値は24067ドル，2番目の町は22244ドルであった（U.S. Census Bureau, 2000）．

（訳者注：地方行政区は他州の郡に相当）

0478　参加者の過去経験の可能性を述べる．
◆Xs were likely to have YYY.

XはYYYを行っていた可能性が高かった．

> Compared to younger adults, older adults were more likely to have gambled longer.　　　　(46)
> 若年者と比べて，高齢者は，すでにより長い間賭博を行っていた可能性がより高かった．

5.1.5　参加者の人種

0479　参加者の民族的・人種的な背景を述べる．
◆With regard to the ethnic or racial origin of the participants, A% were X, B% were Y, and C% were Z.

参加者の民族的あるいは人種的な出自は，A%がX，B%がY，C%がZであった．

> With regard to the ethnic or racial origin of the participating candidates, 93.2% were White, 1.1% were Arab/West Asian, 1.1% were Aboriginal Canadians, 0.5% were Black, 0.5% were South Asian, 0.5% were Chinese, 0.5% were Korean, 0.5% were members of another visible minority, and 2.1% did not indicate their ethnicity.　　　　(9)
> 参加候補者の民族的あるいは人種的な出自は，93.2%が白人，1.1%がアラブ人/西アジア人，1.1%がアボリジニ系カナダ人，0.5%が黒人，0.5%が南アジア人，0.5%が中国人，0.5%が韓国人，0.5%が容貌から判断できる別の少数派のメンバーであり，2.1%は民族性を示さなかった．

0480　大学生の参加者の人種，性別，データ収集の場所を述べる．
◆Data were collected from A (n = L) and B (n = M) college students at a university located in the C region of D. The student sample consisted of X men (A = P; B = Q) and Y women (A = R, B = S).

DのC地域に位置している大学のA（n = L）とB（n = M）の大学生から，データが集められた．この学生サンプルは，X名の男性（AがP名，BがQ名）とY名

130 5．方法（Method）

の女性（A が R 名，B が S 名）から成っていた．
> Data were collected from 186 Asian American (*n* = 107) and Latino American (*n* = 79) college students at a university located in the Rocky Mountain region of the United States. The student sample consisted of 67 men (Asian American = 36; Latino = 31) and 119 women (Asian American = 71; Latina = 48). (32)
> 米国のロッキー山脈地域に位置している大学の 186 名のアジア系アメリカ人（*n* = 107）とラテンアメリカ系アメリカ人（*n* = 79）の大学生から，データが集められた．この学生サンプルは，67 名の男性（アジア系アメリカ人が 36 名，ラテンアメリカ系アメリカ人が 31 名）と 119 名の女性（アジア系アメリカ人が 71 名，ラテンアメリカ系アメリカ人が 48 名）から成っていた．

0481 サンプルにおける移民の割合について述べる．

◆ About N% of the sample was composed of [children of] immigrants [from X].
サンプルの約 N% は，[X からの] 移民 [の子供] から成り立っていた．
> About 12% of the sample was composed of children of immigrants. (23)
> サンプルの約 12% は，移民の子供から成り立っていた．

0482 参加者が人種を名乗ったことを述べる．

◆ N participants identified themselves as X.
N 名の参加者は，自分が X であると名乗った．
> Eleven participants identified themselves as White. (41)
> 11 名の参加者は，自分が白人であると名乗った．

5.1.6 参加者の人口統計学的情報の収集

0483 民族的背景についての回答の分類を述べる．

◆ X responses were categorized as A, B, and C.
X の回答は，A, B, C という範疇に分類された．
> Ethnicity responses were categorized as Caucasian, African American, Latino/Latina, Asian, and Other-Not Listed. (3)
> 民族的背景についての回答は，白人，アフリカ系アメリカ人，ラテンアメリカ系アメリカ人，アジア人，リストにないその他，という範疇に分類された．

0484 参加者の背景や人口統計学的な情報を得るために質問紙を用いたことを述べる．

◆ A background questionnaire was used to obtain demographic and X information, including Y and Z.
背景についての質問紙が，Y と Z を含む人口統計学的および X 的情報を得るために用いられた．

A background questionnaire was used to obtain demographic and medical information, including child age and ethnicity, family income, parent employment and education history, date of diagnosis, and current medical regimen. (45)
背景についての質問紙が，子供の年齢と民族性，家族の収入，両親の職業と教育歴，診断日時，現在の医学療法を含む人口統計学的および医学的情報を得るために用いられた．

0485 参加者の人口統計学的な情報を収集したことを述べる．

◆Participants provided information about their X, Y, and Z.
参加者は，X, Y, Z についての情報を提供した．

> Participants provided information about their age, gender, ethnicity, and highest level of education within their household. (57)
> 参加者は，彼らの年齢，性別，民族性，世帯の中で最も高い教育水準についての情報を提供した．

0486 参加者の人口統計学的な変数が記録されたことを述べる．

◆Participants' X, Y, and Z were recorded.
参加者の X, Y, Z が記録された．

> Participants' age, gender, and ethnicity were recorded. (3)
> 参加者の年齢，性別，民族的背景が記録された．

0487 参加者の人口統計学的，および，臨床的な性質を表に示したことを述べる．

◆Table N presents the demographic and clinical characteristics of the participants [/the study sample].
表 N に，参加者 [/ 研究サンプル] の人口統計学的および臨床的特徴を表す．

> Table 1 presents the demographic and clinical characteristics of the study sample. (36)
> 表 1 に，研究サンプルの人口統計学的および臨床的特徴を表す．

5.1.7 募集方法

0488 募集の場所を表す．

◆They were recruited from X.
彼らは，X で募集された．

> They were recruited from an audiology department at a university hospital. (28)
> 彼らは，大学病院の耳鼻咽喉科で募集された．

0489 募集の時期と場所を述べる．

◆Xs were recruited between A and B from Y in Z.
X が，Z にある Y から，A と B の間に募集された．

132   5. 方法（Method）

Adolescents in the homeless sample were recruited between October 1997 and August 2000 from shelters in the five-county metropolitan areas, including all existing shelters in the area at the time of the outset of the study. (22)
研究開始時にその地域に存在したすべてのシェルターを含む，5 つの地方の首都圏のシェルターから，1997 年 10 月と 2000 年 8 月の間に，ホームレスのサンプル内の青年が募集された．

0490 募集の場所と回数を述べる．

◆Xs were recruited N times [/in N waves] from Y.
X は，Y から N 回にわたって募集された．

> Participants were recruited in two waves from a Midwestern university. (61)
> 参加者は，ミッドウェスタン大学から 2 回にわたって募集された．

0491 ボランティアの参加者を，参加者プールとチラシにより募集したことを述べる．

◆The sample consisted of N volunteers (M women) recruited from a university psychology department participant pool and via flyers posted on campus and in the community.
サンプルは，大学の心理学科の参加者プール，および，学内とコミュニティ内に掲示した広告により募集された N 名のボランティア（女性が M 名）であった．

> The sample consisted of 135 volunteers (61 women) recruited from a university psychology department participant pool and via flyers posted on campus and in the community. (60)
> サンプルは，大学の心理学科の参加者プール，および，キャンパスとコミュニティ内に掲示した広告から募集された 135 名のボランティア（女性が 61 名）であった．

0492 参加者を，広告により募集したことを述べる．

◆Participants were recruited across X via Y advertisements posted [/placed] on [/in] Z.
参加者は，Z に掲載された Y の広告により，X の全域で募集された．

> Participants were recruited across New York City via multilingual advertisements posted on electronic and community bulletin boards and local newspapers. (8)
> 参加者は，電子的なおよびコミュニティの掲示板と地方新聞に多言語で掲載された広告により，ニューヨーク市の全域で募集された．

0493 子供の参加者を，親への連絡により募集したことを述べる．

◆Parents of identified Xs were contacted by Y and a follow-up Z by a trained research assistant who introduced the study, answered questions, and determined eligibility.
同定された X の両親とは，Y，および，訓練を受けた研究補助者によるフォローアップの Z により連絡を行った．その研究補助者は，研究内容を紹介し，質問に答え，さらに，参加資格を有しているかどうかを決めた．

5.1 参加者・被験体　　　　　　　　　133

Parents of identified children were contacted by mail and a follow-up telephone call by a trained research assistant who introduced the study, answered questions, and determined eligibility. (45)
同定された子供の両親とは，郵便，および，訓練を受けた研究補助者によるフォローアップの電話により連絡を行った．その研究補助者は，研究内容を紹介し，質問に答え，さらに，参加資格を有しているかどうかを決定した．

0494 子供の参加者を，親に手紙を送ることにより募集したことを述べる．

◆Letters were sent home to the parents of X from two public high [/elementary /middle] schools.
2つの公立高校 [/ 小学校 / 中学校] の X の親の自宅宛に手紙が送られた．

> Letters were sent home to the parents or guardians of randomly selected nondisplaced students and selected displaced students from two public high schools. (3)
> 2つの公立高校から無作為に選ばれた，非退去学生，および，退去学生の親あるいは保護者の自宅宛に手紙が送られた．

0495 子供の参加者を，人を介して募集したことを述べる．

◆The children were introduced to the apparatus and the investigator by X.
子供は，X によって，装置と研究者に引きあわされた．

> They were introduced to the apparatus and the investigator by a member of the nursery staff well known to the child. (37)
> 子供は，その子供がよく知っている保育所スタッフによって，装置と研究者に引きあわされた．

0496 ウェブ調査の参加者を電子メールにより募集したことを述べる．

◆A total of N e-mail messages were sent out, inviting candidates to participate in an online survey, "XXX."
「XXX」というオンライン調査への参加を勧誘する N 通の電子メールが参加候補者に送られた．

> A total of 938 e-mail messages were sent out shortly after the election inviting candidates to participate in an online survey, "Political Attitudes in Canada." (9)
> 選挙のすぐ後に，「カナダにおける政治的態度」というオンライン調査への参加を勧誘する 938 通の電子メールが参加候補者に送られた．

0497 ウェブ調査の参加者を電子メールにより募集したことを，報酬・インフォームドコンセントとともに述べる．

◆Students responded to X-approved advertisements sent through Y, and inviting them to participate in an Internet-based research study on Z. Informed consent was obtained. Students were administered the survey via the Internet and were paid $N [/M yen].

学生は，Z についてのインターネット上での研究に参加するように勧誘する X によって承認された Y による広告に対して，返信を行った．インフォームドコンセントが得られた．学生は，インターネットを通して調査に回答し，N ドル [/M 円] が支払われた．

> Students responded to IRB-approved advertisements sent through e-mail, and inviting them to participate in an Internet-based research study on student health. Informed consent was obtained. Students were administered the survey via the Internet and were paid $10.　　(32)
> 学生は，学生の健康についてのインターネット上での研究に参加するように勧誘するIRB によって承認された電子メールの広告に対して，返信を行った．インフォームドコンセントが得られた．学生は，インターネットを通して調査に回答し，10 ドルが支払われた．

（訳者注：IRB; Institutional Review Board, 施設内倫理委員会）

0498 募集のための電子メールが配信できなかったこと，および，ウェブ調査を完了した参加者の数を表す．

◆ N of the e-mail messages were returned as undeliverable. Thus, of the M individuals who were invited to participate, A% of them (n = B) completed the online survey.
N 通の電子メールは配信不能であった．そのため，参加を勧誘された M 名の中で，A% (n = B) がオンラインの調査を完了した．

> However, 67 of the e-mail messages were returned as undeliverable. Thus, of the 871 individuals who were invited to participate, 22% of them (n = 190) completed the online survey.　　(9)
> しかし，67 通の電子メールは配信不能であった．そのため，参加を勧誘された 871 名の中の 22% (n =190) がオンライン調査を完了した．

5.1.8　参加者への報酬

0499 参加者が，調査への参加に対して報酬をもらったことを述べる．

◆ Participants received $N [/M yen] compensation for completing the survey.
参加者は調査への回答に対して N ドル [/M 円] の報酬を受け取った．

> Participants received $20 compensation for completing the survey.　　(39)
> 参加者は調査への回答に対して 20 ドルの報酬を受け取った．

0500 参加者が，自発的な参加に対して報酬をもらったことを述べる．

◆ Each participant was paid N dollars [/M yen] for his/her voluntary participation.
各参加者には，自発的な参加に対して N ドル [/M 円] が支払われた．

> Each participant was paid 20 dollars for her/his voluntary participation.　　(41)
> 各参加者には，自発的な参加に対して 20 ドルが支払われた．

5.1　参加者・被験体

0501　参加者が，実験終了時に報酬をもらったことを述べる．

◆ Participants received X at the end of the experiment.

参加者は，実験終了時にXを受け取った．

> Participants received a movie ticket or three lottery tickets at the end of the experiment. (28)
> 参加者は，実験終了時に，映画のチケットか3枚の宝くじ券を受け取った．

0502　参加者が，あることを終了した時点で報酬をもらったことを述べる．

◆ Participants received $N [/M yen] at the conclusion of the X.

研究参加者は，Xの終了時点で，Nドル[/M円]を受け取った．

> Research participants received $20 at the conclusion of the baseline and 1.5 year follow-up interviews. (22)
> 研究参加者は，ベースラインと1年半の事後インタビューが終了した時点で，20ドルを受け取った．

0503　参加者に報酬が支払われ，追跡研究への参加を打診されたことを述べる．

◆ At the end of the interview [/experiment], participants were paid $N [/M yen] for their participation and asked whether they would be willing to be contacted X later for Y.

インタビュー[/実験]の終了時に，参加への報酬として参加者にNドル[/M円]が支払われ，さらに，YのためにX後にコンタクトをとってもかまわないかどうかを尋ねられた．

> At the end of the interview, participants were paid $30 for their participation and asked whether they would be willing to be contacted a week later for a brief follow-up conversation. (8)
> インタビューの終了時に，参加への報酬として参加者に30ドルが支払われ，さらに，短い追跡的な会話を行うために1週間後にコンタクトをとってもかまわないかどうかを尋ねられた．

5.1.9　参加者の参加資格・スクリーニングと除外・参加拒否

0504　参加者の資格要件を列挙する．

◆ Eligibility requirements for participation in the study were: (a) A, (b) B, (c) C, and (d) D.

本研究への参加資格要件は以下のとおりであった．（a）A，（b）B，（c）C，（d）D．

> Eligibility requirements for participation in the study were: (a) child age between 2.0 and 6.0 years at the time of questionnaire completion, (b) at least 6-month duration of child's diagnosis of Type 1 diabetes, (c) absence of other chronic illness or developmental diagnosis, and (d) parent fluency in English. (45)

本研究への参加資格要件は以下のとおりであった．(a) 質問紙への回答の時点で子供の年齢が2から6歳であること，(b) 少なくとも6か月間子供が1型糖尿病であると診断されていること，(c) 他の慢性疾患や発達上の診断がないこと，(d) 親が英語を流暢に話すこと．

0505 参加者の資格要件を述べる．

◆ To be eligible for the study, participants had to be able to XXX.

本研究への参加資格として，参加者は，XXXすることができる必要があった．

> To be eligible for the study, participants had to understand and speak English fluently enough to be able to answer interview questions and fill out questionnaires. (36)
> 本研究への参加資格として，参加者は，インタビューの質問に答え質問紙に回答するのに十分なほど流暢に英語を理解し話せる必要があった．

0506 一部の参加者が，インフォームドコンセントが得られないために除外されたことを述べる．

◆ N% of potential participants were excluded from the survey [/study] because of refusal to consent by X.

参加者になる可能性のある人たちの中のN%は，Xによる同意が得られなかったために除外された．

> Only 3% of potential participants were excluded from the study because of refusal to consent by parents or other legal caregivers, and none of the youth who were approached refused assent. (22)
> 参加者になる可能性のある人たちの中の3%だけが，親あるいは法律上の介護者による同意が得られなかったために除外された．打診された若者は1人も同意を拒否しなかった．

0507 参加者の学習達成の基準を述べる．

◆ Only participants who XXX were treated as having learned sufficiently for analysis.

XXXであった参加者だけが，分析に値する学習を達成したとみなされた．

> Only participants who achieved over 70% accuracy on both assessment rounds were treated as having learned the material sufficiently for analysis. (24)
> 2回の評価の両方で70%以上の正確さを示した参加者だけが，分析に値する材料の学習を達成したとみなされた．

0508 あることを保証するために，参加者のスクリーニングが行われたことを述べる．

◆ Participants were prescreened to ensure that they XXX.

参加者がXXXであることを保証するための事前のスクリーニングが行われた．

> All participants were first prescreened to ensure that they were in good health, after which they were assigned to their respective age and experience groups. (47)

5.1 参加者・被験体

まず，参加者が健康であることを保証するための事前のスクリーニングが全参加者に対して行われ，その後，各年齢および経験群に割り当てられた．

0509 参加者のスクリーニングがある基準に基づいて行われたことを述べる．
◆ Participants were screened out if they XXX.
参加者は，XXX である場合に，研究から除外された．

> Participants were screened out if they did not live in the shelter, had any severe mental health problems, or did not have a job. (41)
> 参加者は，シェルターで生活していない場合，重度の精神保健上の問題がある場合，あるいは，仕事がない場合に，研究から除外された．

0510 参加者を除外した追加的な基準を述べる．
◆ An additional N Xs who YYY, or ZZZ, were omitted from the study.
これ以外に，YYY であったり，ZZZ であった N 名の X は，研究から除外された．

> An additional 25 adolescents who did not answer this question, or reported that they lived with someone else, were omitted from the study. (2)
> これ以外に，この質問に回答しなかったり，他の誰かと住んでいると答えた 25 名の青年は，研究から除外された．

0511 参加基準を満たさなかったため，あるいは，欠損値のために，参加者を除外したことを述べる．
◆ N participants were dropped from the study because they did not meet the inclusion criterion, and another M participants were dropped because of missing data.
N 名の参加者は，参加基準を満たさなかったために，本研究から除外された．さらに M 名の参加者が，データに欠損値があったために除外された．

> Forty-eight participants were dropped from the study because they did not meet the inclusion criterion that their parents' divorce occurred at or after age 13, and another 19 participants were dropped because of missing data. (61)
> 48 名の参加者は，両親の離婚が 13 歳以上で起こったという参加基準を満たさなかったために，本研究から除外された．さらに 19 名の参加者が，データに欠損値があったために除外された．

0512 参加者が他の参加者と交代させられたことを述べる．
◆ L children did not complete the session because XXX (M) or because of Y (N) and were therefore replaced.
L 名の子供は，XXX であったため（M 名），あるいは，Y のため（N 名）にセッションを終えることができず，それゆえ交代させられた．

> Four children did not complete the session because they became distracted (2) or because of interference by other children (2) and were therefore replaced. (37)

4名の子供は，気が散ってしまったため（2名），あるいは，他の子供に邪魔されたため（2名）に，セッションを終えることができず，それゆえ交代させられた．

0513 参加者を交代させるための追加募集について述べる．

◆N new participants were recruited from X.

N 名の新しい参加者が X から募集された．

> Sixteen new participants were recruited from University College London. (43)
> 16 名の新しい参加者がユニバーシティ・カレッジ・ロンドンから募集された．

0514 より大きなサンプルから選ばれた参加者の一部が除外されたことを述べる．

◆Xs were drawn from a larger group of Y, from which N participants were excluded because of Z.

X は Y というより大きなグループから抽出され，その中の N 名の参加者は Z のために除外された．

> These youth were drawn from a larger group of 398 adolescents, from which 23 were excluded because of their self-identification as belonging to ethnic groups (e.g., Latino Whites) that were poorly represented in the overall sample. (22)
> これらの若者は，398 名のより大きな青年グループから抽出された．その中の 23 名は，全体的なサンプルを代表しない民族グループ（ラテンアメリカ系白人など）に所属していると本人が報告したために除外された．

0515 拒否した参加者の割合，および，有効な調査を完了した参加者の数を述べる．

◆Less than N% of participants refused [to participate]. In total, M students completed valid surveys.

[参加を] 拒否した参加者は N% 以下であった．全体で，M 名の学生が有効な調査を完了した．

> Less than 5% of participants in any of the districts refused or gave unusable survey data. In total, 1,933 students completed valid surveys. (58)
> どの地域でも，拒否した，あるいは，使用不能な調査データを示した参加者は 5% 以下であった．全体で，1933 名の学生が有効な調査を完了した．

0516 参加者の拒否率について述べる．

◆The refusal rate of those participants who returned parental consent forms varied by district [/school], ranging from N% to M%.

親の同意書の用紙を返送してきた参加者の拒否率は地域 [/ 学校] によって異なり，N% から M% の範囲であった．

> The refusal rate of those participants who returned parental consent forms varied by district, ranging from 5% to 10%. (58)
> 親の同意書の用紙を返送してきた参加者の拒否率は地域によって異なり，5% から 10% の範囲であった．

5.1 参加者・被験体

0517 親の同意の要求により回答率が低下したことを述べる．
◆ Requiring active parental consent lowered the [/our] overall response rate to N%.
親の積極的な同意を要求したことにより，全体的な回答率は N% まで減少した．

> Requiring active parental consent lowered our overall response rate to 54%. (58)
> 親の積極的な同意を要求したことにより，全体的な回答率は 54% まで減少した．

5.1.10 より大きいサンプルとの関係

0518 サンプルが，より大きなサンプルから抽出されたことを述べる．
◆ This sample was drawn from a larger sample of N individuals who XXX.
このサンプルは，XXX を行った N 名のより大きなサンプルから抽出された．

> This sample is drawn from a larger sample of 2,668 individuals who applied for self-exclusion. (46)
> このサンプルは，自己排除に応募した 2668 名の人々のより大きなサンプルから抽出された．

0519 データが，あるデータセットの下位サンプルから得られたことを述べる．
◆ Data were [/are] from a sub[-]sample of X.
データは，X の下位サンプルから得られた [/ 得られる]．

> Data are from a subsample of the Providence cohort of the National Collaborative Perinatal Project (NCPP). (38)
> データは，国家共同周産期プロジェクト（NCPP）のプロビデンス市のコホートの下位サンプルから得られる．
>
> （訳者注：コホートとは，同齢の集団のことである）

0520 無作為サンプルが，より大きな抽出枠の中から抽出されたことを述べる．
◆ A random probability sample of X was drawn from the sampling frame of Y.
Y の抽出枠の中から，X の無作為確率サンプルが選ばれた．

> A random probability sample of 30 high schools was drawn from the sampling frame of 240 Hebrew-language, nonvocational, and nonboarding high schools located north of Be'er-Sheva in Israel. (52)
> イスラエルのベエルシェバの北に位置し，職業高校や寄宿学校ではなく，ヘブライ語を言語とする 240 の高校の抽出枠の中から，30 の高校の無作為確率サンプルが選ばれた．

0521 1 次サンプル単位について述べる．
◆ The primary sampling units (PSU) were X made up of Ys.
1 次サンプル単位（PSU）は，Y から成る X であった．

> The primary sampling units (PSU) were geographic areas made up of counties or groups of counties. (23)
> 1 次サンプル単位（PSU）は，地方，あるいは，地方のグループから成る地理的な地域であった．

140   5. 方法（Method）

> **0522** 研究で，大規模な縦断的データセットを用いたことを述べる．

◆ This study used a large longitudinal dataset, the X.

本研究は，大きな縦断的データセットであるX群を使用した．

> This study used a large, contemporary longitudinal dataset, the Early Childhood Longitudinal Survey—Kindergarten Cohort.　　　　　　　　　　　　　　　　　　　　　　　　(23)
> 本研究は，現代の大規模な縦断的データセットである，幼児期縦断的調査—幼稚園コホートを使用した．

（訳者注：コホートとは，同齢の集団のことである．）

> **0523** サンプルが母集団を代表するものであったことを述べる．

◆ Overall, the demographics of the X samples at the N Y schools were representative of their respective X populations.

全体的に，NつのY学校のXサンプルの人口統計は，それぞれのXの母集団を代表するものであった．

> Overall, the demographics of the student samples at the two high schools were representative of their respective student populations.　　　　　　　　　　　　　　　　(3)
> 全体的に，2つの高校の学生サンプルの人口統計は，それぞれの学生の母集団を代表するものであった．

> **0524** サンプルのグループサイズが母集団を反映するものであったことを述べる．

◆ The sizes of these X groupings [/groups] reflected the overall student populations in the school district.

これらのXのグループのサイズは，その学区の全体的な学生の母集団を反映するものであった．

> The sizes of these ethnic groupings reflected the overall student populations in the school districts.　　　　　　　　　　　　　　　　　　　　　　　　　　　　　　　　　(58)
> これらの民族的なグループのサイズは，その学区の全体的な学生の母集団を反映するものであった．

> **0525** サンプルが母集団を代表するものであったかどうかを調べたことを述べる．

◆ To test whether the sample was representative of Xs, we compared their demographic characteristics to [/with] those of a random sample drawn from all N Xs during a period of Y.

サンプルがXを代表するものであるかどうかを調べるために，彼らの人口統計学的な特徴を，Yの期間中の全N名のXからの無作為サンプルの特徴と比較した．

> To test whether the sample was representative of assault survivors presenting to this emergency department, we compared their demographic characteristics with those of a random sample drawn from all 2,785 assault survivors treated in the department during a period of 1 year.　　　　　　　　　　　　　　　　　　　　　　　　　　　　　　　　(36)

5.1 参加者・被験体　　　*141*

サンプルが救急部門に来る暴力被害者を代表するものであるかどうかを調べるために，彼らの人口統計学的な特徴を，1 年間に救急部門で治療された 2785 名の被害者からの無作為サンプルの特徴と比較した．

5.1.11　参加者のグループ分け

0526　参加者をパーセンタイルによりグループ分けしたことを述べる．

◆We categorized participants who scored about the Lth percentile (greater than A) of the distribution on the X Scale as high in Y, and those who scored between the Mth (B) and Nth percentiles (C) of the distribution as moderate in Y.

我々は，X 尺度の分布の L パーセンタイル以上（A 点以上）の参加者を高い Y，M パーセンタイル（B 点）から N パーセンタイル（C 点）の間の参加者を中程度の Y と分類した．

> We categorized participants who scored above the 75th percentile (greater than 36) of the distribution on the Rosenberg Self-Esteem Scale (Rosenberg, 1965) as high in self-esteem (M = 38.4) and those who scored between the 25th (28) and 50th percentiles (32) of the distribution as moderate in self-esteem (M = 30.4). (25)
>
> 我々は，Rosenberg の自尊心尺度（Rosenberg, 1965）の分布の 75 パーセンタイル以上（36 点以上）の参加者を高い自尊心（M=38.4），25 パーセンタイル（28 点）から 50 パーセンタイル（32 点）の間の参加者を中程度の自尊心（M=30.4）と分類した．

0527　測度を用いて参加者を分類するための得点（識別点）を述べる．

◆Cut-off scores for the X/Y range were N for A and M for B.

X 域と Y 域の識別得点は，A については N 点，B については M 点であった．

> Cut-off scores for the borderline/abnormal range were 16 for total difficulties, and 6 for emotional symptoms. (2)
>
> 境界域と異常域の識別得点は，全体的な困難さについては 16 点，情動性症状については 6 点であった．

0528　参加者の移民的地位を質問への回答により決定したことを述べる．

◆X status was determined by Y's response to the questions of (a) AAA and (b) BBB.

X の地位は（a）AAA，および，（b）BBB，という質問に対する Y の回答により決定された．

> Immigrant status was determined by the parent's response to the questions of (a) whether he or she was born in the United States (which was asked in the spring that the child was in first grade) and (b) whether the child was born in the United States (which was asked in the spring that the child was in kindergarten). (23)
>
> 移民であるか否かは，(a) 米国で生まれたか（その子供が 1 年生のときの春に聞いた），および，(b) 子供は米国内で生まれたか（その子供が幼稚園のときの春に聞いた），という質問に対する親の回答により決定された．

5.1.12　参加者の匿名性と機密性

0529　臨床研究における匿名性について述べる．

◆For confidentiality purposes, all X names referenced below are pseudonyms.
　機密保持のため，以下で言及するすべてのXの名は偽名である．

> For confidentiality purposes, all participant names referenced below are pseudonyms.　　(8)
> 機密保持のため，以下で言及するすべての参加者の名は偽名である．

0530　参加者に機密が保持されることを告げたことを述べる．

◆Participants were informed that their Xs were confidential and would not be connected to their names or e-mail addresses.
　参加者には，彼らのXについては機密が保持され，名前や電子メールアドレスとは結びつけられないことが告げられた．

> Participants were informed that their responses were confidential and would not be connected to their names or e-mail addresses.　　(39)
> 参加者には，彼らの反応については機密が保持され，名前や電子メールアドレスとは結びつけられないことが告げられた．

0531　参加者を取り扱う倫理的ガイドライン（匿名性，機密性）が守られたことを述べる．

◆Xs were guaranteed anonymity and confidentiality of Ys.
　Xには，Yの匿名性と機密性が保証された．

> Respondents were guaranteed anonymity and confidentiality of individual responses.　　(52)
> 回答者には，個人の反応の匿名性と機密性が保証された．

5.1.13　事例研究の参加者

0532　治療を受けている参加者について述べる．

◆X was a N-year-old Y being treated for A at B.
　Xは，BにおいてAの治療を受けているN歳のYであった．

> Roy was a 70-year-old man being treated for major depression in individual psychotherapy at his local hospital's outpatient mental health center.　　(29)
> Royは，地元の病院の外来精神衛生センターで大うつ病の治療のために個人的な精神療法を受けている70歳の男性であった．

0533　精神療法を求めている参加者について述べる．

◆X was a N-year-old Y who sought psychotherapy for Z.
　Xは，Zのために精神療法を求めているN歳のYであった．

> Martha was a 67-year-old married woman who sought psychotherapy for anxiety and depression.　　(29)

5.1 参加者・被験体　　　143

Martha は，不安とうつのために精神療法を求めている 67 歳の既婚女性であった．

5.1.14　被験体（動物）

0534　被験体の入手先，年齢，実験開始時の体重，飼育場所，明暗サイクルを述べる．

◆N Xs, M weeks [/months] of age and weighing between A and B g at the beginning of the experiment, were housed in Y on a C:D light–dark cycle.

実験開始時の年齢が M 週 [/ か月] 齢で体重が A g から B g である，N 匹の X が，Y の中で，C：D の明暗サイクルで飼育された．

> Forty-four female Long-Evans rats (Charles River Laboratories, Raleigh NC), 8 weeks of age and weighing between 150 and 175 g at the beginning of the experiment, were housed in a temperature-controlled room (21℃ ± 2℃) maintained on a 12:12 reverse light–dark cycle (lights on at 20:00). (33)
>
> 実験開始時の年齢が 8 週齢で体重が 150 g から 175 g である，44 匹の雌のロングエバンス系ラット（チャールズ・リバー・ラボラトリーズ社，ノースカロライナ州ローリー市）が，温度が管理された部屋（21℃ ± 2℃）の中で，12 時間：12 時間の昼夜が逆転した明暗サイクル（20:00 に点灯）で飼育された．

0535　被験体の年齢と入手先を述べる．

◆N-month-old Xs were obtained from Y, City, Country.

N か月齢の X が，国の市にある Y から導入された．

> Two-month-old male Wistar rats were obtained from the Central Animal Research Facility of the National Institute of Mental Health and Neuro Sciences (NIMHANS), Bangalore, India. (50)
>
> 2 か月齢の雄のウィスター系ラットが，インドのバンガロール市にある国立精神保健神経科学研究所（NIMHANS）の中央動物研究施設から導入された．

0536　実験的にナイーブな被験体の体重，飼育条件，明暗サイクルを述べる．

◆Experimentally naïve Xs (N = A) were B to C g at the time of delivery. They were individually housed in a temperature and humidity controlled colony on a D-hr light–dark cycle in E.

実験的にナイーブな X（N = A）は，配達時の体重が B g から C g であった．それらの X は，温度と湿度が制御された飼育地域内において，D 時間の明暗サイクルの下で，E の中で，個別に飼育された．

> Experimentally naïve male Sprague-Dawley rats (N = 143) were 250 to 300 g at the time of delivery. They were individually housed in a temperature and humidity controlled colony on a 12-hr light–dark cycle in plastic cages 48.3 × 24.1 × 21.0 cm (l × w × h) with stainless steel lids. (49)

実験的にナイーブな雄のスプラーグドーリーラット（N = 143）は，配達時の体重が250 g から 300 g であった．それらのラットは，温度と湿度が制御された飼育地域内において，12 時間の明暗サイクルの下で，ステンレススチール製の蓋のついた長さ 48.3 × 幅 24.1 × 高さ 21.0 cm のプラスチック製ケージの中で，個別に飼育された．

0537 実験的にナイーブな被験体の入手先と体重の維持について述べる．

◆ N experimentally naïve Xs (*Latin name*) obtained from Y were maintained at A% of their free feeding weights (mean = B g; range = C – D g).

Y から入手された N 匹の実験的にナイーブな X（ラテン名）が，自由摂食時の A% の体重（平均 = B g; レンジ = C – D g）に維持された．

> Sixteen experimentally naïve male Lister hooded rats (*Rattus norvegicus*) obtained from OLAC (Bicester, United Kingdom) were maintained at 80% of their free feeding weights (mean = 397 g; range = 360–423 g) by giving them a restricted quantity of food. (10)
> OLAC 社（ビスター市，英国）から入手された 16 匹の実験的にナイーブな雄のリスター系の頭巾ネズミ（*Rattus norvegicus*）が，食物量を制限することにより，自由摂食時の 80% の体重（平均 = 397 g; レンジ = 360 〜 423 g）に維持された．

0538 霊長類研究の場所，および，用いた母集団を述べる．

◆ All studies were conducted at X, in adult male and female Y (*Latin name*) and adult male Z (*Latin name*).

すべての研究は，X において，成体の雌と雄の Y（ラテン名），および，成体の雄の Z（ラテン名）を使って行われた．

> All studies were conducted at the Yerkes National Primate Research Center, Emory University, in adult male and female rhesus monkeys (*Macaca mulatta*) and adult male squirrel monkeys (*Saimiri sciureus*). (30)
> すべての研究は，エモリー大学のヤーキーズ国立霊長類研究センターにおいて，成体の雌と雄のアカゲザル（*Macaca mulatta*），および，成体の雄のリスザル（*Saimiri sciureus*）を使って行われた．

0539 被験体への食物と水の与え方を述べる．

◆ X was presented in Y food cups [with lids]. Water was available in Z bottles [fitted with drip-proof stainless steel stoppers].

X は，[蓋つきの] Y 製の食物カップ内に呈示された．水は [防滴型のステンレススチール製の栓が取りつけられた] Z 製の瓶から摂取可能であった．

> Chow was presented in stainless steel food cups with lids. The food cups were clipped to the cage floors to prevent spillage. Water was available in glass bottles fitted with drip-proof stainless steel stoppers. (33)
> 飼料は，蓋つきのステンレススチール製の食物カップ内に呈示された．その食物カップは，こぼれないようにケージの床に固定されていた．水は，防滴型のステンレススチール製の栓が取りつけられたガラス瓶から摂取可能であった．

5.1 参加者・被験体

0540 被験体の個別飼育，および，食物と水について述べる．
◆ Each subject was housed individually and fed A (X, City, Prefecture [/State]), B, and C. Water was continuously available.
各被験体は個別に飼育され，A（X 社製，県 [/ 州]，市），B, C を与えられた．水は常に摂取可能であった．

> Each subject was housed individually and fed Purina monkey chow (Ralston Purina, St. Louis, MO), fruits, and vegetables. Water was continuously available. (30)
> 各被験体は個別に飼育され，ピュリナ・サル飼料（ラルストン・ピュリナ社，ミズーリ州セントルイス市），果物，野菜を与えられた．水は常に摂取可能であった．

0541 被験体のグループ飼育，および，食物と水への自由摂取について述べる．
◆ Xs were housed in groups of N per cage and had *ad libitum* access to food and water.
X は，1 個のケージにつき N 匹のグループで飼育され，食物と水を随時摂取することができた．

> Mice were housed in groups of 4 mice per cage and had *ad libitum* access to food and water. (21)
> マウスは，1 個のケージにつき 4 匹のグループで飼育され，食物と水を随時摂取することができた．

0542 被験体の飼育ケージ，室温，および，明暗サイクルについて述べる．
◆ The Xs were housed in polypropylene cages (dimensions A × B × C cm) at room temperature (D ± E°C) and were maintained on 12-hr light–dark cycles.
X は，室温（D ± E°C）下で，ポリプロピレン製のケージ（寸法は A × B × C cm）内で飼育され，12 時間の明暗サイクルで維持された．

> The rats were housed in polypropylene cages (dimensions 22.5 × 35.5 × 15 cm) at room temperature (26 ± 2°C) and were maintained on 12-hr light–dark cycles. (50)
> ラットは，室温（26 ± 2°C）下で，ポリプロピレン製のケージ（寸法は 22.5 × 35.5 × 15 cm）内で飼育され，12 時間の明暗サイクルで維持された．

0543 被験体の選定理由を述べる．
◆ The Xs in the current study were chosen because they YYY.
本研究の X は，彼らが YYY であったことから選ばれた．

> The capuchin subjects in the current study were chosen because they have had many years of experience solving experimental problems, particularly spatial relational problems such as navigating two-dimensional mazes and using a variety of tools. (34)
> 本研究のオマキザルの被験体は，実験課題，特に，2 次元迷路の通り抜けと多様な道具の使用のような空間的関係の課題を解くことを何年間も経験していたことから選ばれた．

5. 方法 (Method)

0544 被験体の年齢，研究参加の経験を述べる．

◆ These Xs ranged in age from N to M years old. All subjects had several years of experience with Y.

これらの X の年齢は N 歳から M 歳であった．すべての被験体は，Y を数年間経験していた．

> These monkeys ranged in age from 10 to 20 years old. All subjects had several years of experience with instrumental spatial problem-solving tasks. (34)
>
> これらのサルの年齢は 10 歳から 20 歳であった．すべての被験体は道具的な空間的問題解決課題を数年間経験していた．

0545 動物の飼料，および，APA の要求する動物の倫理的取り扱いについて述べる（標準的表現）．

◆ The Xs received a diet of Y. The care and experimental treatment of the Xs followed local and federal regulations concerning humane care and treatment.

X は，Y の食事を与えられた．X の世話と実験的な取り扱いは，人道的な世話と取り扱いに関する地方条例および連邦規則に従って行われた．

> The monkeys received a diet of Purina monkey chow and fruit. The care and experimental treatment of the monkeys followed local and federal regulations concerning humane care and treatment. (34)
>
> サルは，ピュリナ社製サル飼料の規定食と果物を与えられた．サルの世話と実験的な取り扱いは，人道的な世話と取り扱いに関する地方条例および連邦規則に従って行われた．

5.2 装　　　置

5.2.1 実験装置

0546 視覚刺激を呈示するための装置と性能を述べる．

◆ The Xs were presented in a Y, described in detail by Author (Year). This instrument permits Z ranging from A s to B min.

X が，著者（発表年）に詳細に記述されている，Y により呈示された．この装置は，A 秒から B 分間の範囲の Z を実行することが可能であった．

> The 12 word pairs were presented in a modified Dodge tachistoscope, described in detail by Karlin (1955). This instrument permits exposure durations ranging from .001 s to 2 min. (18)
>
> 12 個の単語の組が，Karlin（1955）の中で詳細に記述されている，改造されたドッジ社のタキストスコープにより呈示された．この装置では，0.001 秒から 2 分間の範囲の露出時間を実行することが可能であった．

5.2 装置

0547 聴覚刺激を呈示するためのスピーカーについて述べる.

◆ N external computer speakers connected to the X were situated behind the touch screen.

X に接続された N 台のコンピュータ用外部スピーカーが，タッチスクリーンの後ろに置かれていた.

> Two external computer speakers (HK 195) connected to the laptop were situated behind the touch screen. (37)
> ラップトップ・コンピュータに接続された 2 台のコンピュータ用外部スピーカー (HK 195) が，タッチスクリーンの後ろに置かれていた.

0548 材料や刺激の呈示方法を述べる.

◆ The X were presented to the subjects on [/via] a[n] Y.

X は，Y の上に載せて [/ を経由して] 被験体に呈示された.

> The stimuli were presented to the subjects on a metal cart that was pushed up to the Plexiglas panel of the test cage. (34)
> 刺激は，テストケージのプレクシグラス板上に押しつけられる金属製の荷車の上に載せて被験体に呈示された.

0549 迷路の材料について述べる.

◆ The X consisted of a A base and B floors and walls with a C top [/no top].

X は，A 製の土台と，C 製の天井がある [/ 天井のない] B 製の床と壁からできていた.

> The modified elevated plus-maze consisted of a wood base and gray Plexiglas floors and walls with no top. (21)
> 改造された高架式十字迷路は，木製の土台と，天井のない灰色のプレクシグラス製の床と壁からできていた.

0550 放射状迷路について述べる.

◆ The N-arm X maze is a Y maze (Manufacturer, City, Prefecture [/State] [, Country]) consisting of N equally spaced arms radiating from a central platform. Each arm is A cm long, B cm high, and C cm wide.

N 本のアームの X 迷路とは，中央プラットフォームから等間隔で放射状に広がる N 本のアームから成る Y 迷路 (製造会社，[国，] 県 [/ 州], 市) である. 各アームの大きさは，長さ A cm, 高さ B cm, 幅 C cm である.

> The eight-arm radial maze is a computer-monitored plexiform maze (Columbus Instruments, Columbus, OH, USA) consisting of eight equally spaced arms radiating from an octagonal central platform. Each arm is 42 cm long, 11.4 cm high, and 11.4 cm wide. (50)
> 8 本のアームの放射状迷路とは，八角形の中央プラットフォームから等間隔で放射状に広がる 8 本のアームから成る，コンピュータでモニターされた叢状迷路 (コロンバス・インスツルメンツ社, 米国オハイオ州コロンバス市) である. 各アームの大きさは，長さ 42 cm, 高さ 11.4 cm, 幅 11.4 cm である.

5. 方法（Method）

0551 動物実験で用いられたケージの大きさと材料を述べる．
◆ Subjects were tested in a cage (A cm × B cm × C cm) composed of X.
被験体は，Xでつくられたケージ（A cm × B cm × C cm）の中でテストされた．
> Subjects were tested in a cage (64 cm × 47 cm × 78 cm) composed of metal mesh and two Plexiglas side panels. (34)
> 被験体は，金属製の網と2つのプレクシグラス製の側面パネルから成るケージ（64 cm × 47 cm × 78 cm）の中でテストされた．

0552 動物実験で用いられた固定装置について述べる．
◆ The animals were fixed on a[n] X instrument.
動物は，X装置に固定された．
> The animals were fixed on a stereotaxic instrument. (50)
> 動物は，定位固定装置に固定された．

0553 脳イメージングで用いられた装置について述べる．
◆ Functional magnetic resonance imaging [/Brain imaging] was performed at the X on a Y scanner.
機能的磁気共鳴画像法 [/ 脳イメージング] は，Xにおいて，Yを用いて行われた．
> All brain imaging was performed at the Emory University PET Center on a Siemens 951 scanner. (30)
> すべての脳イメージングは，エモリー大学PETセンターにおいて，シーメンス社951スキャナーにより行われた．

5.2.2 コンピュータ

0554 コンピュータを用いて，実験を行ったことを述べる．
◆ The experiment was run on a[n] X computer connected to a stand-alone flat panel Y LCD monitor with an effective display area of A × B cm and a screen resolution of C × D.
実験は，有効表示域がA × B cmで画面解像度がC × Dの，Yの独立型フラットパネルLCDモニターに接続された，Xのコンピュータで行われた．
> The experiment was run on a Sony Vaio laptop computer (F808K and GRX315MP) connected to a stand-alone flat panel Taxan CV600 LCD monitor with an effective display area of 21.5 × 16 cm and a screen resolution of 640 × 480. (37)
> 実験は，有効表示域が21.5 × 16 cmで，画面解像度が640 × 480のタクサン社製の独立型フラットパネルCV600 LCDモニターに接続された，ソニー製のVaioラップトップコンピュータ（F808KとGRX315MP）で行われた．

0555 心理学実験ソフトウェアを用いて，実験をプログラムしたことを述べる．
◆ The experiment was programmed and run with the use of X.

5.3　材料・刺激・薬品・課題　　　　　149

実験は，X を用いてプログラムされ，実行された．
> The experiment was programmed and run with the use of E-Prime.　　　　(14)
> 実験は，E-Prime を用いてプログラムされ，実行された．

0556　研究者が開発した専用ソフトウェアを用いて，課題を実施したことを述べる．
◆ The X was administered on a personal computer with the program Y (Author, Year).
X は，Y というプログラム（著者，発表年）を用いてパソコン上で実施された．
> The IATs were administered on personal computers with the program FIAT for Windows 2.3 (Farnham, 1998).　　　　(13)
> IAT は，Windows 2.3 用の FIAT というプログラム（Farnham, 1998）を用いて，パソコン上で実施された．

（訳者注：IAT; Implicit Association Test, 潜在的連合テスト）

0557　プログラミング言語を用いて，刺激呈示と反応記録用のソフトウェアを開発したことを述べる．
◆ The software used for controlling stimulus presentation and recording of responses was written and compiled using X.
刺激呈示と反応記録を制御するために用いられたソフトウェアは，X を使って書かれ，コンパイルされた．
> The software used for controlling stimulus presentation and recording of responses was written and compiled using Microsoft Visual Basic Professional 6.0.　　　　(37)
> 刺激呈示と反応記録を制御するために用いられたソフトウェアは，マイクロソフト社の Visual Basic Professional 6.0 を使って書かれ，コンパイルされた．

5.3　材料・刺激・薬品・課題

5.3.1　材　料

0558　課題で用いた材料と呈示方法について述べる．
◆ The following materials were presented on a[n] X in standard positions in front of the participants: A, B, C, and D.
以下の材料が，参加者の前にある X 上の標準的な位置に呈示された．すなわち，A, B, C, D であった．
> The following materials were presented on a table in standard positions in front of the participants: a round thumbtack box, approximately 50 thumbtacks, a rectangular pocket-size matchbox, approximately 35 safety matches, and one wax candle.　　　　(18)
> 以下の材料が，参加者の前にあるテーブル上の標準的な位置に呈示された．すなわち，丸い画鋲の箱，約 50 個の画鋲，長方形のポケットサイズのマッチ箱，約 35 本の安全マッチ，1 本のろうそくであった．

5. 方法（Method）

0559 報酬として用いたビデオクリップについて述べる。

◆During pretraining, N A-s clips were used, whereas M B-s clips constituted the outcomes during acquisition and reversal.

前訓練中は，N 個の A 秒間のクリップが用いられた．一方，獲得と逆転中は，M 個の B 秒間のクリップが結果として用いられた．

> During pretraining, four 10-s clips were used, whereas four different 24-s clips constituted the outcomes during acquisition and reversal. (37)
> 前訓練中は，4 個の 10 秒間のクリップが用いられた．一方，獲得と逆転中は，4 個の 24 秒間のクリップが結果として用いられた．

0560 実験で用いたシナリオの内容を述べる。

◆In the X scenario, YYY.

X のシナリオでは，YYY．

> In the orchard scenario, two boys steal apples in an orchard. (6)
> 果樹園のシナリオでは，2 人の少年が果樹園のリンゴを盗む．

0561 記憶実験で用いた材料を連続して呈示したことを述べる。

◆Participants were presented with N lists in succession.

参加者には，N 個のリストが連続して呈示された．

> Participants were presented with eight different lists in succession. (7)
> 参加者には，8 個の異なるリストが連続して呈示された．

0562 課題で用いたテスト項目を述べる。

◆Test items consisted of X.

テスト項目は X であった．

> Test items consisted of equivalents of the training overlap exemplars and were made by skewing the features of training items 20° clockwise and 20° counterclockwise, producing two skewed versions of each feature. (24)
> テスト項目は訓練時の重複する見本と同じものであり，訓練項目の各特徴を時計回りに 20 度，および，反時計回りに 20 度曲げることで，各特徴を曲げた 2 つのバージョンがつくられた．

0563 材料のリストについて，提示順の異なるバージョンを作成して参加者に割り当てたことを述べる。

◆N versions of the order of the M lists were created, and participants were assigned to one of the [/these] N versions.

M 個のリストの順序について N つの異なるバージョンが作成され，参加者はそれら N つのバージョンの中の 1 つに割り当てられた．

> Finally, three different versions of the order of the eight lists were created, and participants were assigned to one of the three versions. (7)

5.3 材料・刺激・薬品・課題　　　　　　　　　　　　　　　　　　　　　　　　　　*151*

最終的に，8個のリストの順序について3つの異なるバージョンが作成され，参加者は
それら3つのバージョンの中の1つに割り当てられた．

5.3.2 刺　激
0564　実験刺激の内容，数，大きさを述べる．
◆The experimental stimuli consisted of X.
　実験刺激は，Xであった．
> The experimental stimuli consisted of two sets of eight plastic stacking cups (children's toys), spray-painted black. The cups in these sets ranged in diameter from 5.08 cm to 8.89 cm.　(34)
> 実験刺激は，スプレーで黒く塗装された8個のプラスチック製積み重ねカップ（子供用のおもちゃ）の2組であった．これらの組の中のカップは，直径が5.08 cmから8.89 cmであった．

0565　先行研究を参考にして刺激を作成したことを述べる．
◆The stimulus display for X trials consisted of Y (as in Author, Year).
　Xの試行の刺激表示は，Yで構成されていた（著者，発表年の実験と同様である）．
> The stimulus display for training trials consisted of three side-by-side vertical bars (as in DeLosh et al., 1997).　(44)
> 訓練試行の刺激表示は，3つの平行な垂直の棒で構成されていた（DeLosh et al.,1997の実験と同様である）．

0566　視覚刺激のスクリーンでの呈示方法と大きさを述べる．
◆Stimuli consisted of X displayed by a[n] Y and measuring approximately N cm × M cm on the screen.
　刺激は，Yに表示される，スクリーン上で約 N cm × M cmの大きさのXであった．
> Stimuli consisted of line drawings of imaginary animals displayed by an overhead projector and measuring approximately 20 cm × 35 cm on the screen.　(24)
> 刺激は，OHPのスクリーンに表示される，スクリーン上で約20 cm × 35 cmの大きさの架空の動物の線画であった．

0567　視覚刺激の呈示時間を述べる．
◆Each item was presented for N ms followed by a M-ms fixation.
　各項目はN msの間呈示され，その後，M msの注視時間が設定された．
> Each item was presented for 4,500 ms followed by a 500-ms fixation.　(12)
> 各項目は4500 msの間呈示され，その後，500 msの注視時間が設定された．

0568　視覚刺激の呈示方法（コンピュータ画面）と観察距離を述べる．
◆All stimuli were presented on a N-in. computer screen at a viewing distance of M cm.

152　　　　　　　　　　　5.　方法（Method）

すべての刺激は，観察距離が M cm である N インチのコンピュータ画面上に呈示された．

> All stimuli were presented on a 15-in. computer screen at a viewing distance of 60 cm.　　(14)
> すべての刺激は，観察距離が 60 cm である 15 インチのコンピュータ画面上に呈示された．

0569　言語刺激の呈示方法（コンピュータ画面）とフォントを述べる．

◆ The Xs were presented on the center of a computer screen in P Y N-point font, on a Q background.
コンピュータ画面の中央に，X が，Q 色の背景上に，P 色の N ポイントの Y のフォントで呈示された．

> The words were presented on the center of a computer screen in white Times New Roman 48-point font, on a black background.　　(7)
> コンピュータ画面の中央に，単語が，黒い背景上に白色の Times New Roman の 48 ポイントのフォントで呈示された．

0570　刺激項目を無作為な順序で呈示したことを述べる．

◆ The experimenter presented the N test items individually in a randomly generated order.
実験者は，無作為に生成された順序に従って，N 個のテスト項目を個別に呈示した．

> The experimenter presented the 24 test items individually in a randomly generated order held constant across all participants.　　(24)
> 実験者は，全参加者で同一の，無作為に生成された順序に従って，24 のテスト項目を個別に呈示した．

5.3.3　薬　品

0571　薬品の購入先を述べる．

◆ A, B, C, and D were purchased from X.
A, B, C, D が，X から購入された．

> L-Glutamate, pyruvate, porcine heart glutamate-pyruvate transaminase, NAD, glycine, and hydrazine hydrate were purchased from Sigma.　　(64)
> L–グルタミン酸塩，ピルビン酸，ブタ心臓グルタミン酸塩ピルビン酸トランスアミナーゼ，NAD，グリシン，ヒドラジン水和物が，シグマ社から購入された．

>（訳者注：NAD; nicotinamide adenine dinucleotide, ニコチンアミドアデニンジヌクレオチド）

0572　薬品の購入先，製剤法，投与法を述べる．

◆ X was purchased from Y (City, Prefecture [/State] [, Country]), dissolved in Z (N% NaCl) and injected intraperitoneally [/intravenously] at a volume of M ml/kg.
X は Y 社（市，県 [/ 州][, 国]）から購入され，Z（N% の NaCl）に溶かされて，M ml/kg の量で腹腔内 [/ 静脈内] に注射された．

Cocaine hydrochloride was purchased from Sigma Chemicals (St. Louis, MO), dissolved in saline (0.9% NaCl) and injected intraperitoneally at a volume of 1 ml/kg. (49)
塩酸コカインはシグマ・ケミカルズ社（ミズーリ州セントルイス市）から購入され，生理食塩水（0.9%のNaCl）に溶かされて，1 ml/kgの量で腹腔内に注射された．

5.3.4 課　題

0573　課題の内容を述べる．

◆ The participants' task was to XXX.

参加者の課題は，XXX することであった．

> The participants' task was to retrieve and briefly describe a specific personal memory, in response to each cue word. (36)
> 参加者の課題は，各手がかり語に対して，特定の個人的記憶を想起し簡潔に記述することであった．

0574　課題の要求を述べる．

◆ The X task required participants to YYY.

X課題では，参加者はYYYすることを要求された．

> The reading span task required participants to read sentences on a computer screen. (7)
> 読み取り範囲課題では，参加者はコンピュータ画面上の文章を読むことを要求された．

0575　問題の組を解くという課題の要求を述べる．

◆ We asked X to solve N sets of M Y problems.

Xに，M個のY問題のN組を解くことを求めた．

> We asked children to solve two sets of six mathematical equivalence problems. (5)
> 子供に，6個の数学的な等価性問題の2組を解くことを求めた．

0576　ある能力を測定するために用いられた課題を述べる．

◆ X, which refers to Y, was measured using the Z (Author, Year).

XとはYのことであり，Zを用いて測定された（著者，発表年）．

> Visual spatial processing, which refers to an individual's ability to process objects and events in space, was measured using the mental rotation task (Cooper & Shepard, 1973). (47)
> 視覚的空間的処理とは空間内にある対象と事象を処理する個人の能力のことであり，メンタルローテーション課題を用いて測定された（Cooper & Shepard, 1973）．

0577　材料の呈示と課題の内容を詳しく述べる．

◆ Each child [/participant] was first shown X and was asked to YYY. The experimenter then ZZZ.

各子供[/参加者]は，最初にXを見せられ，YYYをするように求められた．次に実験者がZZZを行った．

> Each child was first shown two rows containing the same number of checkers and was asked to verify that the rows had the same number. The experimenter then spread out the checkers in one row, leaving the second row unchanged, and asked the child whether the transformed row had the same or a different number of checkers as the untransformed row. (5)
> 各子供は，最初に同じ数のチェッカーが入っている2列を見せられ，2つの列には同じ数が入っていることを確かめるように求められた。次に実験者が1つの列のチェッカーを広げて置き，2つ目の列はそのままにして，子供たちに，形が変わった列には，形が変わっていない列と同じ数のチェッカーがあるのか，違う数のチェッカーがあるのか，を聞いた。

0578 一連の課題を行ったことを述べる．

◆ Participants completed a series of X and Y tasks.

参加者は，一連のX課題とY課題を行った．

> Participants completed a series of cognitive and ATC tasks. (47)
> 参加者は，一連の認知課題とATC課題を行った．
>
> （訳者注：ATC; air-traffic control, 航空管制）

0579 課題獲得後にテストを行ったことを，実施期間とともに述べる．

◆ X test was carried out N days following acquisition of the task.

課題の獲得後に，XテストがN日間行われた．

> Retention test was carried out 10 days following acquisition of the task. (50)
> 課題の獲得後に，保持テストが10日間行われた．

0580 課題が先行研究をヒントに作成されたことを述べる．

◆ The task used in this study was a[n] X task inspired by [/based on] the Y task (Author, Year).

本研究で用いられた課題は，Y課題（著者，発表年）からヒントを得た [/ に基づいた] X課題であった．

> The task used in this study was a cooperative decision-making task inspired by the Towers Market task (Weingart, Bennet, & Brett, 1993). (59)
> 本研究で用いられた課題は，タワーマーケット課題（Weingart, Bennet, & Brett, 1993）からヒントを得た協調的な意思決定課題であった．

5.4 教　　示

5.4.1 教示の内容

0581 各条件における教示を，改行・字下げした文章で述べる．

◆ In the X condition, participants received the following instruction:
　YYY.

5.4 教　　示

X条件では，参加者は以下の教示を受けた：
YYY.

> In the faking condition, participants received the following instruction:
> Imagine that you were applying for a job in a large international consulting company. To get this job, you should try to make a very good impression. (13)
> だまし条件では，参加者は以下の教示を受けた．
> あなたは国際的なコンサルティング会社での仕事に応募していると想像してください．あなたは，この仕事を手に入れるために，よい印象を与えるようにしなければなりません．

0582 教示を簡潔に述べる．

◆Participants were told that XXX. [/The researcher told the participants that XXX].
参加者には，XXX であると告げられた．[/ 研究者が参加者に XXX であると告げた．]

> Participants were told that the event could be important or trivial. (36)
> 参加者には，その出来事は重要である，または，ささいであると告げられた．

0583 研究内容についての教示を述べる．

◆Participants were told that they were participating in a study examining X.
参加者は，X を調べる研究に参加していると告げられた．

> Participants were told that they were participating in a study examining the perception of emotional cues in events portrayed through different forms of media. (6)
> 参加者は，形式の異なるメディアを通して描写された事象における情動的手がかりの知覚を調べる研究に参加していると告げられた．

0584 課題についての教示を述べる．

◆Participants were instructed that they would be X-ing.
参加者は，X をしてもらうことになるでしょう，と教示された．

> Participants were instructed that they would be making a series of category judgments. (13)
> 参加者は，カテゴリー判断を連続して行ってもらうことになるでしょう，と教示された．

0585 実験開始時に与えられた課題についての教示を述べる．

◆Participants were told at the start of training [/the experiment] that their task was to XXX.
参加者は，訓練 [/ 実験] の開始時に，彼らの課題は XXX することであると伝えられた．

> Participants were told at the start of training that their task was to learn a set of four species of imaginary animals. (24)
> 参加者は，訓練開始時に，彼らの課題は 4 つの架空の動物種の組を学習することであると伝えられた．

5.4.2 教示の操作

0586 群により異なる教示を与えたことを述べる.
◆ Children in the X group (*n* = N) were asked [/told] to AAA; children in the Y group (*n* = M) were asked [/told] to BBB.
X群（*n* = N）の子供は AAA を求められた．Y群（*n* = M）の子供は，BBB を求められた．

> Children in the told-to-gesture group (*n* = 33) were asked to use their hands when they explained how they solved the problems; children in the told-not-to-gesture group (*n* = 35) were asked to keep their hands still when explaining their solutions. (5)
> ジェスチャー指示群（*n* = 33）の子供は，問題の解き方を説明するときに，手を用いることを求められた．ジェスチャー非指示群（*n* = 35）の子供は，解き方を説明するときに，手を動かさないことを求められた．

0587 条件により異なる教示を与えたことを述べる.
◆ In the X condition, participants were told to AAA, and in the Y condition[,] participants were told to BBB.
X条件では，参加者は，AAA を行うように告げられた．Y条件では，参加者は BBB を行うように告げられた．

> In the unitized source condition, participants were told to form a mental image of the item in the same color as the background color on the screen and to make a key press indicating whether or not the item was plausible in the background color. In the nonunitized source condition, participants were told to make an animacy judgment if the item was presented on a red background and to make a size judgment if the item was presented on a yellow background. (12)
> ユニット化される情報源条件では，参加者は，画面の背景色と同じ色の項目の心的イメージを形成し，背景色の項目がもっともらしいかどうかを示すキー押しを行うように告げられた．ユニット化されない条件では，参加者は項目が赤い背景上に呈示されたときには生物かどうかの判断を，黄色い背景上に呈示されたときには大きさの判断をするように告げられた．

0588 2つの群に与える教示をある方向に沿って操作したことを述べる.
◆ The instructions were manipulated between subjects such that the participants in the X condition were given instructions that AAA, whereas participants in the Y condition were given B instructions.
被験者間で教示が操作され，X条件の参加者には，AAA という教示が与えられ，Y条件の参加者には B の教示が与えられた．

The instructions were manipulated between subjects such that participants in the unitized source condition were given instructions that encouraged them to unitize the item and source information, whereas participants in the nonunitized source condition were given typical source task instructions. (12)
被験者間で教示が操作され，ユニット化される情報源条件の参加者には，項目と情報源の情報を結合することを奨励する教示が与えられ，ユニット化されない情報源条件の参加者には，典型的な情報源課題の教示が与えられた．

0589　2群に異なる教示が与えられたことを述べる（部分的な違いのみを述べて紙面を節約する）．

◆X subjects were told: "AAA." In place of the above instructions given to the X subjects, the Y subjects were told: "BBB."
Xの被験者は，「AAA」と告げられた．Yの被験者は，Xの被験者に与えられた上記の教示の代わりに，「BBB」と告げられた．

Low-drive Ss were told: "We are doing pilot work on various problems in order to decide which will be the best ones to use in an experiment we plan to do later. We would like to obtain norms on the time needed to solve." In place of the above instructions given to low-drive Ss, high-drive Ss were told: "Depending on how quickly you solve the problem you can win $5.00 or $20.00. The top 25% of the Ss in your group will win $5.00 each; the best will receive $20.00. Time to solve will be the criterion used." (18)
低動因の被験者は，「私たちは，後に実施が計画されている実験において用いるにはどの問題が最善であるかを決めるために，さまざまな問題についての予備的研究を行っています．私たちは，問題解決にかかる時間についての基準を得たいと思っています．」と告げられた．高動因の被験者は，低動因の被験者に与えられた上記の教示の代わりに，「あなたがどれくらい早く問題を解いたかにより5ドルか20ドルを勝ち得ることができます．あなたのグループの中の上位25％は各自5ドル，最も成績がよい人は20ドルを勝ち得るのです．解決時間が基準として用いられます．」と告げられた．

（訳者注：Ss; subjects, 被験者）

5.4.3　教示の呈示法

0590　教示をコンピュータ画面上に呈示したことを述べる．

◆Task instructions were presented on a [/the] screen in white on black (N point X).
課題教示は，黒地に白色の文字（NポイントのX）で画面上に呈示された．

Task instructions were presented on the screen in white on black (12 point Arial). (56)
課題教示は，黒地に白色の文字（12ポイントのArial）で画面上に呈示された．

0591　教示を書面により与えたことを述べる．

◆In the X condition, Y received a written instruction that ZZZ.
X条件で，Yは，ZZZである書面による教示を受け取った．

In the team reflection condition, group members received a written instruction that discussed the relevance of reflecting on the task. (59)
チーム内省条件で，グループ構成員は課題の内省の適切さについて論じた書面による教示を受けた．

0592 テーブルについて座らされた参加者に教示を与えたことを述べる．
◆ The participants were seated at the table and given instructions on X.
参加者はテーブルについて座らされ，Xについての教示が与えられた．

> The participants were seated at the table and given instructions on the requirements of the problem. (18)
> 参加者は，テーブルについて座らされ，問題の要件についての教示が与えられた．

0593 実験者による実地説明により説明したことを述べる．
◆ The experimenter demonstrated and explained X to the participant [/child] on the Y trials.
Y試行において，参加者 [/ 子供] に対して，実験者がXを実際に示し説明した．

> To train children to perform the required instrumental actions, the experimenter demonstrated and explained the movement sequence to the child on the first two practice trials. (37)
> 子供に要求される道具的行為を行うように訓練するために，最初の2回の練習試行において，実験者が一連の運動を子供に実際に示して説明した．

5.5 場　　所

0594 実験が行われた場所を述べる．
◆ The experiment took place in X on [/at] Y.
実験は，YにあるXで行われた．

> The experiment took place in a flat grassy field without obstructions on the UCSB campus. (42)
> 実験は，UCSBのキャンパスの障害物のない平らな芝生の上で行われた．
>
> （訳者注：UCSB; University of California, Santa Barbara, カリフォルニア大学サンタバーバラ校）

0595 実験が行われた場所と状況を述べる．
◆ The participants [/children] were tested while seated at a table within easy reach of the X in a Y room in their Z.
参加者 [/ 子供] は，Zの中のYの部屋で，Xに容易に手が届くようにしてテーブルについて座った状態で，テストされた．

In this and all of the following experiments, the children were tested while seated at a table within easy reach of the touch-sensitive monitor in a familiar room in their regular day nursery. (37)
この実験，および，以下の全実験において，子供は，行きつけの保育所の中にある慣れた部屋で，タッチパネルつきのモニターに容易に手が届くようにしてテーブルについて座った状態で，テストされた．

0596 データ収集が 2 つの場所で行われたことを述べる．
◆ Data collection took place either at X or at Y.
データ収集は，X か Y で行われた．

Data collection took place either at one of the participating university's offices or at a convenient location in the community. (57)
データ収集は，参加している大学の研究室か，コミュニティの利便な場所で行われた．

0597 データ収集が複数の場所で行われたことを述べる．
◆ There were N data collection sites in the study: A; B; C; and D.
この研究では，N か所のデータ収集場所があった．すなわち，A, B, C, そして，D であった．

There were five data collection sites in the study: Los Angeles; Irvine, CA; Denver; Philadelphia; and Washington, DC. (57)
この研究では，5 か所のデータ収集場所があった．すなわち，ロサンゼルス市，アーバイン市（カリフォルニア州），フィラデルフィア市，デンバー市，そしてワシントン D.C. であった．

5.6　デ　ー　タ

5.6.1　反　応

0598 反応を，ある能力の指標として測定したことを述べる．
◆ X was measured as the ability to YYY.
X は，YYY を行う能力として測定された．

Source recollection was measured as the ability to remember the color associated with each item. (12)
情報源の想起は，各項目と結びついた色を思い出す能力として測定された．

0599 反応を，ある方法により測定・記録したことを述べる．
◆ X was measured and recorded by [/in] Y.
X が Y により測定・記録された．

Locomotor activity was measured and recorded continuously in an accelerometer equipped in the watch-type computer. (1)

歩行活動が，腕時計型コンピュータ内に取りつけられた加速度計により，連続的に測定・記録された．

0600 反応を，ある期間中に記録したことを述べる．
◆ Recordings of X were obtained during Y.
Y 中に X の記録がとられた．

> Recordings were obtained during everyday activities of 26 patients with panic disorder, 40 patients with generalized anxiety disorder, and 24 control participants. (1)
> パニック障害のある 26 名の患者，全般性不安障害のある 40 名の患者，および，統制群の 24 名の参加者において，日常の活動中に記録がとられた．

（訳者注：「記録」とは，心拍などの記録のことである）

0601 適切な反応に対してフィードバックを与えたことを述べる．
◆ When a response was selected with a [/the] click [/press] of a mouse [/button /key], a feedback stimulus was presented for N s showing the proper response.
マウス [/ ボタン / キー] のクリック [/ 押し下げ] により反応が選択された場合，適切な反応であることを示すフィードバック刺激が N 秒間呈示された．

> When a response was selected with a click of the left mouse button, a feedback stimulus was presented for 1.5 s showing the proper response. (44)
> マウスの左ボタンのクリックにより反応が選択された場合，適切な反応であることを示すフィードバック刺激が 1.5 秒間呈示された．

0602 ある期間の反応をベースラインとして用いたことを述べる．
◆ Data collected in X served as an individual baseline from which Ys were calculated.
X の期間に集められたデータが，Y を計算するための各個人のベースラインとして用いられた．

> For each subject, data collected in the same time period on a comparison nondriving day served as an individual baseline from which cortisol response scores were calculated. (1)
> 各被験者について，比較のための運転しない日の同じ時間帯に集められたデータが，コルチゾール反応得点を計算するための個人のベースラインとして用いられた．

5.6.2 観察・報告

0603 観察をビデオに記録したことを述べる．
◆ A video camera was used to record X to allow playback for scoring purposes.
後で再生し点数化できるように，ビデオカメラを用いて X が録画された．

> A video camera was used to record testing sessions to allow playback for scoring purposes. (34)
> 後で再生し点数化できるように，ビデオカメラを用いてテストセッションが録画された．

0604 言語的な報告と心理検査を併用したことを述べる．

◆In this study, we measured X in N ways. First, we tapped Y. Second, we measured Z.

本研究において，我々は，XをN通りの方法で測定した．まず，Yを採取した．さらに，Zを測定した．

> In this study, we measured middle and high school students' sense of community at school in two ways. First, we tapped their reports of the general climate and relationships among students at school. Second, we measured students' personal assessment of how they and their friends fit into the culture of their schools. (58)
> 本研究において，我々は，中学生と高校生の学校におけるコミュニティ感覚を2つの方法で測定した．まず，全般的な学校風土についての学生の報告と学校における学生関係についての学生の報告を採取した．さらに，学生本人や学生の友達が学校の文化に合っているかどうかについての学生の個人的な評価を測定した．

0605 日記によりあるデータを記録させたことを述べる．

◆The diaries required X to write down Y.

日記は，YについてYを書きとめることをXに要求した．

> The diaries required patients to write down panic attacks and instances of self-exposure using paper diaries. (1)
> 紙面による日記を用いて，患者にパニック発作と自己曝露の例を日記に書きとめることを要求した．

5.7 心 理 検 査

5.7.1 内容・目的

0606 心理検査の実施と目的を述べる．

◆X tests were administered to assess Y.

X検査が，Yを評価するために行われた．

> A number of neuropsychological tests were administered to assess basic cognitive abilities. (47)
> 多くの神経心理学的検査が，基本的な認知能力を評価するために行われた．

0607 あることを質問紙で評価したことを述べる．

◆X was assessed using the Y (Abbreviation for Y; Author, Year).

Xは，Y（Yの略語；著者，発表年）により評価された．

> Quantity of alcohol consumption was assessed using the Daily Drinking Questionnaire (DDQ; Collins, Parks, & Marlatt, 1985). (39)
> アルコール消費量は，日常的飲酒質問紙（DDQ; Collins, Parks, & Marlatt, 1985）により評価された．

0608 あることを尺度で評価したことを述べる.

◆ Author's (Year) scale of X was used to assess Y.

著者（発表年）のX尺度が，Yを評価するために用いられた.

> Elder and Conger's (2000) scale of grandparent–grandchild relationships was used to assess the emotional closeness of the adolescents with their grandparents. (2)
> Elder と Conger（2000）の祖父母 – 孫関係尺度が，青年と祖父母の情動的な親密さを評価するために用いられた.

0609 2つの質問紙に回答させたことを，目的とともに述べる.

◆ All participants filled out the X ([Abbreviation for X;] Author, Year), a questionnaire used to assess A, and Y ([Abbreviation for Y;] Author, Year), which is used to assess B.

すべての参加者は，Aを評価するための質問票の1つであるX（[Xの略語;] 著者，発表年），および，Bを評価するためのY（[Yの略語;] 著者，発表年）に回答した.

> All participants filled out the Interpersonal Reactivity Index (IRI; Davis, 1980), a questionnaire used to assess empathy, and the State–Trait Anxiety Inventory (STAI; Spielberger, Gorsuch, Lushene, Vagg, & Jacobs, 1983), which is used to assess anxiety level. (55)
> すべての参加者は，共感を評価するために用いられる質問紙の1つである対人反応性指標（IRI; Davis, 1980），および，不安レベルを評価するための状態 – 特性不安検査（STAI; Spielberger, Gorsuch, Lushene, Vagg, & Jacobs, 1983）に回答した.

0610 知能検査の使用を目的とともに述べる.

◆ The X was used to produce an estimate of Y based on Z.

Xが，Zに基づいてYを推定するために用いられた.

> The Wechsler Abbreviated Scale of Intelligence (WASI) Full-Scale IQ Two-Subtest (FSIQ-2) was used to produce an estimate of general intellectual ability based on two (Vocabulary and Matrix Reasoning) of the four subtests. (57)
> ウェクスラー短縮版知能検査（WASI）の全検査IQの2つの下位検査（FSIQ-2）が，4つの下位検査中の2つの下位検査（単語と行列推理）に基づいて一般的知能を推定するために用いられた.

0611 異性についての質問紙に回答させたことを述べる（能動態なのでよい表現）.

◆ Female [/Male] participants responded to N sets of questions assessing X of opposite sex (male [/female]) Y.

女性[/男性]の参加者は，異性（男性[/女性]）のYについてのXを評価するためのN組の質問セットに答えた.

> Female participants responded to two sets of questions assessing perceptions of opposite sex (male) drinking preferences. (39)

5.7 心理検査

女性の参加者は，異性（男性）の飲酒に関する選好についての認識を評価するための2組の質問セットに答えた．

0612 質問紙に回答させたことを目的とともに述べる．

◆Participants completed a questionnaire that included items designed to XXX.

参加者はXXXを行うために考案された項目を含む質問紙に回答した．

> Participants subsequently completed a questionnaire that included items designed to facilitate the believability of the cover story. (6)
> 引き続いて，参加者は，作り話の信憑性を高めるために考案された項目を含む質問紙に回答した．

0613 質問紙（目録）の内容を述べる．

◆The X Inventory is a well-validated[,] N-item[,] self-report measure of Y (Author, Year).

X目録は，妥当性が十分に確認されている，YについてのN項目から成る自己報告型の測度である（著者，発表年）．

> The Brief Symptom Inventory (BSI) is a well-validated 53-item self-report measure of psychological distress (Derogatis & Melisaratos, 1983). (32)
> 簡易的症状目録（BSI）は，妥当性が十分に確認されている，心理的苦痛についての53項目から成る自己報告型の測度である（Derogatis & Melisaratos, 1983）．

0614 尺度の出典・由来を表す．

◆The X (Abbreviation for X) was adapted by Author (Year) from the Y originally developed by Author (Year).

X（Xの略語）は，もともと著者（発表年）によって開発されたYを，著者（発表年）が改訂したものである．

> The Resource Loss Scale for Children (RLSC) was adapted by Jones and Ollendick (1994) from the Resources Questionnaire originally developed by Freedy et al. (1992). (3)
> 子供用資源損失尺度（RLSC）は，もともとFreedyら（1992）によって開発された資源質問紙を，JonesとOllendick（1994）が改訂したものである．

0615 質問紙の最初の内容が，人口統計学的な質問であることを述べる．

◆The first section of the questionnaire asked X to provide demographic information, including A, B, and C.

質問紙の最初の部分は，XにA, B, Cを含む人口統計学的な情報を提供することを求めるものであった．

> The first section of the questionnaire asked adolescents to provide demographic information, including age, gender, free school meals (FSM) eligibility (in the UK FSMs are given to students of families receiving benefits because of low income), and ethnicity. (2)

質問紙の最初の部分は，青年に，年齢，性別，無料給食（FSM）受給資格（英国では，低収入により給付を受けている家庭の学生に対して，無料給食が与えられている），民族，を含む人口統計学的な情報を記入することを求めるものであった．

0616 質問紙（目録）の特徴について述べる．

◆ The N-item version of the Author (Year) X Inventory was used to measure Y. This is a widely used measure with high internal consistency ($\alpha = A$).

著者（発表年）のX目録のN項目版が，Yを測るために用いられた．これは，内的整合性が高く（$\alpha = A$），広く用いられている測度である．

> The ten-item version of the Rosenberg (1965) Self-Esteem Inventory was used to measure students' self-esteem. This is a widely used measure with high internal consistency ($\alpha = .85$). (3)
> Rosenberg（1965）の自尊心目録の10項目版が，学生の自尊心を測るために用いられた．これは，内的整合性が高く（$\alpha = .85$），広く用いられている測度である．

0617 質問紙が求める評価の内容を述べる．

◆ The X asks Ys to rate the A and B of C commonly reported by Zs.

Xは，Zが共通して報告するCのAとBを評価することをYに求めるものである．

> The PIP asks parents to rate the frequency and perceived difficulty of 42 events commonly reported by parents of children with a chronic illness. (45)
> PIPは，慢性疾患のある子供の親が共通して報告する42の出来事の頻度と困難感を評定することを両親に求めるものである．

（訳者注：PIP; Pediatric Inventory for Parents, 親のための小児科質問紙）

0618 尺度が DSM に基づいていることを述べる．

◆ The N-item scale follows DSM-IV criteria for X.

このN項目の尺度は，XについてのDSM-IVの診断基準に従っている．

> This 10-item scale follows DSM-IV criteria for specific phobias. (36)
> この10項目の尺度は，特定恐怖症についてのDSM-IVの診断基準に従っている．

（訳者注：DMS-IV; Diagnostic and Statistical Manual of Mental Disorders, 4th edition, 米国精神医学会による『精神疾患の診断統計マニュアル 第4版』）

0619 質問紙の出典と内容を述べる．

◆ The N-item X (Abbreviation for X) was developed by Author (Year) to assess Y. The X contains M factors: A, B, and C.

N項目のX尺度（Xの略語）は，Yを評価するために著者（発表年）によって開発された．Xは，A, B, CというM個の要因を含んでいる．

> The twelve-item General Health Questionnaire-12 (GHQ-12) was developed by Goldberg, Gater, Sartorius, and Ustun (1997) to assess an individual's GPD. The GHQ-12 contains three factors: Anxiety and Depression, Social Dysfunction, and Loss of Confidence. (3)

12 項目の一般健康質問票 -12（GHQ-12）は，個人の GPD を評価するために Goldberg, Gater, Sartorius, Ustun（1997）によって開発された．GHQ-12 は，「不安と抑うつ」，「社会的機能障害」，「自信喪失」という 3 つの要因を含んでいる．

（訳者注：GPD; general psychological distress, 一般的心理的苦痛）

0620　ある検査の下位検査を用いたことを述べる．

◆ The X subtest was adopted for the present study.

本研究では，X という下位検査が採用された．

> The Digit-Symbol subtest included in the Wechsler Adult Intelligence Scale-Revised test battery was adopted for the present study.　　　　　　　　　　　　　　　　(28)
> 本研究では，改訂版ウェクスラー成人知能検査に含まれる数字記号下位検査が採用された．

0621　検査が他の検査と類似していることを述べる．

◆ The X test was similar to that in the Y.

X 検査は，Y に含まれるものと類似していた．

> The digit-span memory test was similar to that in the Wechsler scales.　　　　(57)
> 数唱記憶検査は，ウェクスラー尺度に含まれるものと類似していた．

0622　ある調査の短縮版を用いたことを述べる．

◆ The short [version of] X (Abbreviation for X; Author1, Year, based on the original Y of Author2, Year) was used to assess Z.

Z を評価するために，短縮版の X（X の略語；著者 1，発表年，著者 2，発表年によるオリジナルの Y に基づくもの）が用いられた．

> The Short Schwartz Value Survey (SSVS; Lindeman & Verkasalo, 2005, based on the original Schwartz Value Survey of Schwartz, 1992, 1996) was used to assess participants' values.　(9)
> 参加者の価値観を評価するために，短縮版のシュワルツ価値観調査（SSVS; Lindeman & Verkasalo, 2005, Schwartz, 1992, 1996 によるオリジナルの価値観調査に基づくもの）が用いられた．

0623　有名な測度の修正版を用いたことを述べる．

◆ X was assessed using a modified version of a widely used measure developed by Author (Year).

X は，著者（発表年）により開発され，広く用いられている測度の修正版を使って評価された．

> Risk perception was assessed using a modified version of a widely used measure developed by Benthin, Slovic, and Severson (1993).　　　　　　　　　　　　　　　　　　　(57)
> リスク認知は，Benthin, Slovic, Severson（1993）により開発され，広く用いられている測度の修正版を使って評価された．

5. 方法（Method）

0624 ある測度の修正版を用いたことを述べる．
◆ The current study used a modified version of the X that was adapted to measure Y.
本研究は，Y を測るように修正された X の改訂版を用いた．

> The current study used a modified version that was adapted to measure parents' beliefs about their ability to manage their child's diabetes. (45)
> 本研究は，子供の糖尿病を管理する能力についての親の信念を測るように改訂された版を用いた．

0625 ある尺度の修正版を用いたことを述べる．
◆ A modified N-item version of the X was used to assess Y.
X を修正した N 項目の版が，Y を評価するために用いられた．

> A modified 5-item version of the Scale for Suicidal Ideation (SSI) was used to assess current conscious suicidal intent. (32)
> 自殺念慮尺度（SSI）を修正した 5 項目の版が，その時点での意識的な自殺意思を評価するために用いられた．

5.7.2 リッカート法

0626 リッカート法を用いて頻度を測定したことを述べる．
◆ Respondents were asked to report, on a N-point scale, how often they had experienced (a) A, (b) B, (c) C, (d) D, and (e) E.
回答者は，(a) A，(b) B，(c) C，(d) D，(e) E をどれくらいの頻度で経験するかを，N 点の尺度上で答えるように求められた．

> Respondents were asked to report, on a 7-point scale, how often they had experienced (a) headaches, (b) inability to concentrate, (c) colds, (d) sore throats, and (e) dizziness. (52)
> 回答者は，どれくらいの頻度で（a）頭痛，(b) 集中不能，(c) 風邪，(d) のどの痛み，(e) 目眩を経験するかを，7 点の尺度上で答えるように求められた．

0627 リッカート法を用いて同意の程度を測定したことを述べる．
◆ Participants had to rate on a scale ranging from 1 (completely disagree) to N (completely agree) the extent to which they agreed with X.
参加者には，X に同意する程度を，1（完全に不同意）から N（完全に同意）までの尺度で評定することが求められた．

> Participants had to rate on a scale ranging from 1 (completely disagree) to 7 (completely agree) the extent to which they agreed with the statements. (59)
> 参加者には，記述に同意する程度を，1（完全に不同意）から 7（完全に同意）までの尺度で評定することが求められた．

0628 リッカート法を用いて同意の強さを測定したことを述べる．
◆ Participants responded to each of these items by indicating on a[n] N-point scale

5.7 心理検査　　　*167*

their level of agreement (1 = strongly disagree, to N = strongly agree).
参加者は，これらの各項目に対してどの程度同意するかを，N 点の尺度上（「1 = 強く同意しない」から「N = 強く同意する」まで）で答えた．

> Participants responded to each of these items by indicating on a 5-point scale their level of agreement (1 = strongly disagree, to 5 = strongly agree). (58)
> 参加者は，これらの各項目に対してどの程度同意するかを，5 点の尺度上（「1= 強く同意しない」から「5= 強く同意する」まで）で答えた．

0629　リッカート法を用いて確信度を測定したことを述べる．

◆ Participants [/They] were asked to give X/Y responses on a confidence scale from 1 to N, with 1 representing A and N representing B.

参加者 [/ 彼ら] は，1 が「A」反応を，N が「B」反応を表す，1 から N までの確信度尺度上で，X/Y についての反応を行うように要求された．

> They were asked to give old/new responses on a confidence scale from 1 to 6, with 6 representing the most confident old responses and 1 representing the most confident new responses. (12)
> 彼らは，6 が「古いと最も確信する」反応を，1 が「新しいと最も確信する」反応を表す 1 から 6 までの確信度尺度上で，「古い / 新しい」についての反応を行うように要求された．

0630　リッカート法によりあることの高低を評価したことを述べる．

◆ Participants were asked to rate, on a scale from N (low) to M (high), (a) X [/XXX], (b) Y [/YYY], and (c) Z [/ZZZ].

参加者は，N（低い）から M（高い）までの尺度上で，(a) X [/XXX], (b) Y [/YYY], (c) Z [/ZZZ]，について評定するように求められた．

> Participants were asked to rate, on a scale from 0 (low) to 10 (high), (a) the severity of damage to their neighborhood, (b) how afraid they were during the storm, and (c) how safe they felt during the storm. (3)
> 参加者は，0 点（低い）から 10 点（高い）までの尺度上で，(a) 近隣の損害のひどさ，(b) 嵐の間にどれぐらい怖いと感じたか，(c) 嵐の間どれくらい安全だと感じたか，について評定するように求められた．

0631　リッカート法における選択肢の範囲を述べる．

◆ The X uses a[n] N-point Likert-type scale for Y ranging from A to B, and not at all C to extremely C for Z.

X は，Y について「A」から「B」まで，Z について「まったく C でない」から「かなり C である」までの N 段階のリッカート型の尺度を用いる．

> The GED uses a 6-point Likert-type scale for exposure to discrimination ranging from never to almost all of the time, and not at all stressful to extremely stressful for stress associated with each type of discrimination. (32)

GED は，差別への曝露について「まったくない」から「ほぼいつもある」まで，各差別タイプと関連するストレスについて「まったくストレスを感じない」から「きわめてストレスを感じる」までの 6 段階のリッカート型の尺度を用いている．

（訳者注：GED; General Ethnic Discrimination scale, 全般的民族差別尺度）

5.7.3 標準化・下位尺度・複合尺度

0632 測度が標準化されたことを述べる．

◆All measures were standardized with a mean of N and [a] standard deviation of M.
すべての測度は，平均が N で標準偏差が M となるように標準化された．

> All measures were standardized with a mean of 0 and standard deviation of 1. (38)
> すべての測度は，平均が 0 で標準偏差が 1 となるように標準化された．

0633 因子分析を用いて尺度を構成したことを表す．

◆Participants' scores on scales assessing X and Y were constructed on the basis of the factor analysis results.
因子分析の結果に基づいて，X と Y を評価する尺度における参加者の得点が構成された．

> Participants' scores on scales assessing attitudes toward social policies (i.e., social conservatism attitudes) and economic policies (i.e., economic competition attitudes) were constructed on the basis of the factor analysis results. (9)
> 因子分析の結果に基づいて，社会政策（すなわち，社会的保守主義態度）と経済政策（すなわち，経済的競争態度）に対する態度を評価する尺度における参加者の得点が構成された．

0634 ある質問紙の下位尺度に回答させたことを述べる．

◆Participants completed the N-item X subscale from the Y Questionnaire (Abbreviation for Y; Author, Year).
参加者は，Y 質問紙（Y の略語；著者，発表年）の中の N 項目からなる X の下位尺度に回答した．

> Participants also completed a trait version of the 17-item Anxious Arousal subscale of the Mood and Anxiety Symptom Questionnaire (MASQ; Watson et al., 1995) and the 12-item Rumination subscale from the Rumination-Reflection Questionnaire (RRQ; Trapnell & Campbell, 1999). (60)
> 参加者は，気分不安症状質問紙（MASQ; Watson et al., 1995）の中の 17 項目からなる不安覚醒下位尺度の特性版，および，自己反芻・自己内省質問紙（RRQ; Trapnell & Campbell, 1999）の中の 12 項目からなる反芻の下位尺度に回答した．

0635 尺度中の一部の項目のみを使用した理由を述べる．

◆N of the M original items were chosen because they evidenced high X and because they represented a range of Y.

もとのM項目中のN項目が，Xが高いこと，かつ，それらが幅広いYを示すことから，選ばれた．

> Five of the 19 original items were chosen because they evidenced high item-total correlations and because they represented a range of suicidal types of ideation. (32)
> もとの19項目中から5項目が選ばれた．その理由は，それらの項目の全体的な相関が高いため，かつ，それらは幅広い自殺観念のタイプを示すためであった．

0636 リッカート尺度への回答に基づいて，下位尺度を計算したことを述べる．

◆Participants responded to items using a N-point Likert scale anchored at 1 (X) and N (Y), and each subscale was summed for analyses.

参加者は，1（X）からN（Y）までのN点のリッカート尺度を使って項目に回答し，分析のために各下位尺度の得点が合計された．

> Participants responded to items using a 5-point Likert scale anchored at 1 (strongly disagree) and 5 (strongly agree), and each subscale was summed for analyses. (61)
> 参加者は，1（強く同意しない）から5（強く同意する）までの5点のリッカート尺度を使って項目に回答し，分析のために各下位尺度の得点が合計された．

0637 下位尺度をまとめて要約変数を作成したことを述べる．

◆These subscales were combined into one overall X score. They were first standardized and then summed such that YYY.

これらの下位尺度が1つの全体的なX得点にまとめられた．まず，それらの下位尺度は標準化され，次に，YYYになるように合計された．

> These subscales were combined into one overall discrimination score. They were first standardized and then summed such that both subscales carried equal weighting in the discrimination total score. (32)
> これらの下位尺度が1つの全体的な差別得点にまとめられた．まず，それらの下位尺度は標準化され，次に，両方の下位尺度が等しい重みで差別総得点に寄与するように合計された．

0638 項目をまとめて指標を作成したことを述べる．

◆A[n] X index was formed by combining 3 items: (a) A, (b) B, and (c) C.

X指数が，(a) A, (b) B, (c) C, という3つの項目をまとめることにより形成された．

> An intrinsic job dissatisfaction index was formed by combining three items: dissatisfaction with (a) the autonomy level, (b) opportunities for professional growth, and (c) opportunities for the implementation of valued educational goals. (52)
> 仕事本来の不満足指標が，(a) 自主性のレベルについての不満，(b) 職業的に成長する機会についての不満，および，(c) 価値ある教育目標を達成する機会についての不満という3つの項目をまとめることにより形成された．

170   5. 方法（Method）

0639 複数の項目を合わせて複合測度をつくったことを述べる．

◆ The X measure (α = N) was created to assess Y.

X 測度（α = N）が，Y を評価するためにつくられた．

> The Democratic Authority Structure measure (α = .69) was created to assess adolescents' perceptions of the school authority structure as democratic and open.　　　　　(58)
> 民主的権威構造測度（α = .69）が，学校の権威構造が民主的で開放的であるかどうかについての青年の認識を評価するためにつくられた．

0640 複合的な測度をつくるためにまとめられた複数の項目について述べる．

◆ The N items in the X measure (α = M) asked Y whether (a) AAA; (b) BBB; (c) CCC; (d) DDD; and (e) EEE.

X 測度における N 個の項目（α = M）は，Y に（a）AAA,（b）BBB,（c）CCC,（d）DDD,（e）EEE かどうかを問うものであった．

> The five items in the School Solidarity measure (α= .85) asked students whether in their school (a) students have a lot of school spirit; (b) students feel like they are an important part of the school; (c) everyone tries to keep the school looking good; (d) most students take pride in the school; and (e) most students seem to care about each other, even people they do not know well.　　　　　(58)
> 学校の団結測度の 5 つの項目（α=.85）は，学生に学校では（a）学生が愛校心を多くもっているか，（b）学生が自分は学校の重要な一部であると感じているか，（c）みんなが学校をよく見せようとしているか，（d）大部分の学生が学校を誇りに思っているか，（d）大部分の学生が，たとえ知らない相手であっても互いを気にかけているか，を問うものであった．

0641 質問紙への反応を複数のカテゴリーに分類したことを述べる．

◆ Responses were grouped into three categories: (a) A; (b) B; and (c) C.

反応は，（a）A,（b）B,（c）C という 3 つのカテゴリーに分類された．

> Responses were grouped into three categories: (a) demographic characteristics—age at application, household income, race, employment (full-time vs. other) and educational status (college graduate vs. non-college graduate), marital status (married vs. unmarried); (b) gambling behavior—years spent gambling, age of gambling onset, strategic versus nonstrategic and mixed forms of gambling (e.g., pai gow poker, craps vs. slot machines, lottery tickets); and (c) reasons for self-exclusion.　　　　　(46)
> 反応は，（a）人口統計学的特徴：応募時の年齢，世帯の収入，人種，雇用（フルタイム対その他），学歴（大卒対非大卒），および，婚姻の状態（既婚対独身），（b）賭博行動：賭博に費やされた年数，賭博開始年齢，方略的対非方略的および混合型形式賭博（たとえば，パイ・ゴウ・ポーカー，クラップス対スロットマシーン，宝くじ券），（c）自己排除に応募した理由，という 3 つのカテゴリーに分類された．

5.7.4 逆転項目

0642 逆転項目を用いた測度について述べる.
◆ The X (α = M) measure consisted of N items[,] which were reverse coded.
X 測度（α = M）は N 個の項目から成り立っており，それらは逆転項目であった．
> The Personal Belonging (α= .56) measure consisted of two items, which were reverse coded. (58)
> 個人的所属測度（α=.56）は，2 つの項目から成り立っており，それらは逆転項目であった．

0643 逆転項目で矛盾した反応が見られたので，一部のデータを除外したことを述べる.
◆ Data from X were not included because of inconsistent responses across two or more of the reverse-scored measures.
X のデータは，2 つ以上の逆転項目測度で矛盾した反応を示したので除外された．
> Data from 17 participants were not included in the analyses because of inconsistent responses (e.g., choosing all 1s or 5s) across two or more of the reverse-scored measures. (3)
> 17 名の参加者のデータは，2 つ以上の逆転項目の測度で矛盾した反応（たとえばすべて 1 か 5 を選ぶなど）を示したために分析から除外された．

0644 得点を逆転させた採点により，ある複合測度を形成したことを述べる.
◆ A composite measure of X was formed by reverse-scoring the measures of A and B, so that higher scores indicated greater Y.
X の複合的な測度が，高得点が高い Y を示すように，A と B の得点を逆転させた採点法により形成された．
> A composite measure of psychosocial maturity was formed by reverse-scoring the measures of impulsivity and sensation seeking so that higher scores indicated greater maturity. (57)
> 心理社会的な成熟度の複合的な測度が，高得点が高い成熟度を示すように，衝動性測度と刺激欲求測度の得点を逆転させた採点法により形成された．

0645 いくつかの項目を組み合わせて，ある尺度を計算したことを述べる.
◆ To calculate a scale for X, we combined the A and B items with the C, D, and E items.
X の尺度を計算するために，我々は，A と B の項目を，C, D, E の項目と組み合わせた．
> To calculate a scale for conservation (vs. openness to change), we combined the self-direction and stimulation items with the (reversed) conformity, tradition, and security items. (9)
> 保護主義（対，変化に対する寛大さ）の尺度を計算するために，我々は，自己志向と刺激の項目を，（逆転された）同調，伝統，安全の項目と組み合わせた．

5.7.5 試行後質問紙

0646 試行後質問紙を与えたことを述べる.

◆ After each of the N trials, participants were given the same post-trial questionnaire.
N 試行のそれぞれの後で，参加者に，同一の試行後質問紙が与えられた.

> After each of the four trials, participants were given the same post-trial questionnaire. (54)
> 4回の各試行の後で，参加者に，同一の試行後質問紙が与えられた.

0647 各試行後に，経過観察のための質問紙に回答させたことを述べる.

◆ After each trial during X, participants completed a follow-up questionnaire and rated their Y.
X 中の各試行の後で，参加者は経過観察の質問紙に回答し，Y を評定した.

> After each trial during the experimental phase, participants completed the follow-up questionnaire and rated their tinnitus interference. (28)
> 実験段階中の各試行の後で，参加者は経過観察の質問紙に回答し，自分の耳鳴りの干渉性を評定した.

5.7.6 質問項目の具体的な内容

0648 質問項目の実際の言葉遣いについて述べる.

◆ The item assessing X read, [/read as follows:] "YYY?"
X を評価する項目は,「YYY ですか?」という内容であった.

> The item assessing immanent justice reasoning read, "To what extent do you feel Roger Wilson's winning of the lottery was the result of the kind of person he is?" which was anchored from 1 (not at all) to 7 (a great deal). (6)
> 内在的正義推論を評価する項目は,「ロジャー・ウィルソンが宝くじに当たったのは，どの程度，彼の人柄の結果であると感じますか?」という内容であり, 1 (まったくそうではない) から 7 (かなりの程度) までの間で評価された.

0649 質問項目の具体例を述べる.

◆ Questions aimed to determine X were testing for Y, such as "AAA?" and "BBB?"
X を判定するための質問は,「AAA」，および,「BBB」というような, Y について調べるものであった.

> Questions aimed to determine the level of agreement among the group were testing for consensus, such as "Can we move ahead to the next item now?" and "Are we ready to adopt those two points?" (48)
> グループの中の合意のレベルを判定するための質問は,「さて次の項目に進んでもいいですか?」，および,「これら2つの点を採用する準備は整っているでしょうか?」というような, 同意について確認するものであった.

5.7 心理検査

0650 回答のための選択肢の内容を述べる．

◆Response options for all questions were as follows: 0 (*A woman who never Xs any Y*), 1 (*A woman who Xs 1 or 2 Zs*), 2 (*A woman who Xs 3 or 4 Zs*), and 3 (*A woman who Xs 5 or more Zs*).

すべての質問に対する反応の選択肢は，以下のとおりであった．0（Y をまったく X しない女性），1（1 か 2 の Z を X する女性），2（3 か 4 の Z を X する女性），3（5 以上の Z を X する女性）．

> Response options for all three questions were as follows: 0 (*A woman who never drinks any alcohol*), 1 (*A woman who drinks 1 or 2 drinks when she drinks*), 2 (*A woman who drinks 3 or 4 drinks when she drinks*), and 3 (*A woman who drinks 5 or more drinks when she drinks*). (39)
> 3 つの質問のすべてに対する反応の選択肢は以下のとおりであった．0（アルコールをまったく飲まない女性），1（飲酒時に 1, 2 杯飲む女性），2（飲酒時に 3, 4 杯飲む女性），3（飲酒時に 5 杯以上飲む女性）．

0651 質問項目のリストを表に示したことを述べる．

◆The list of [standard] questions asked of each participant is presented in Table N.

各参加者に尋ねられた [標準的な] 質問のリストを，表 N に示す．

> The list of standard questions asked of each participant is presented in Table 2. (8)
> 各参加者に尋ねられた標準的な質問のリストを，表 2 に示す．

0652 測度と項目のサンプルを表に示したことを述べる．

◆Table N lists the [/these] measures and provides sample items for [/from] each.

表 N にこれらの測度と，各測度の見本項目を示す．

> Table 2 lists these measures and provides sample items from each. (57)
> 表 2 にこれらの測度と，各測度の見本項目を示す．

0653 質問項目の正確な表現が，著者から入手できることを述べる．

◆The exact wording of the X is available from the authors upon request.

X の正確な言い回しは，著者に要求すれば入手可能である．

> The exact wording of the items used is available from the authors upon request. (52)
> 用いられた項目の正確な言い回しは，著者に要求すれば入手可能である．

5.7.7 テストバッテリー

0654 テストバッテリーの内容を述べる．

◆The [test] battery included measures of A, B, and C.

テストバッテリーは，A, B, C という測度を含んでいた．

> The battery included measures of tinnitus distress and disability, anxiety and depression symptoms, and problems with sleep. (28)

テストバッテリーは，耳鳴りの苦痛と障害，不安とうつ症状，および，不眠の測度を含んでいた．

0655 テストバッテリーの構成と内容を述べる．

◆ The [test] battery included several X tests, including A, B, and C.
テストバッテリーは，数個の X 検査から成っており，A, B, C を含んでいた．

> The test battery included several widely used tests of basic cognitive skills, including a test of resistance to interference in working memory, a digit-span memory test, and a test of verbal fluency.　(57)
> テストバッテリーは，数個の広く用いられている基本的な認知的技能の検査から成っており，作業記憶における干渉への抵抗力の検査，数唱記憶検査，言語流暢性検査を含んでいた．

5.7.8　期間・回数・方法

0656 測定の期間と時点を述べる．

◆ The data were collected at N points in time [/N time points][,] over a[n] X-year [/month] period.
X 年間 [/X か月間] の期間中の N 回の時点において，データが収集された．

> The data were collected at two time points over a 5-year period.　(2)
> 5 年間の期間中の 2 つの時点において，データが収集された．

0657 検査の回数を述べる．

◆ The X was administered [once /twice /N times].
X が [1 回 /2 回 /N 回] 実施された．

> As part of a larger project, the IAT–Anxiety was administered twice.　(13)
> 大きなプロジェクトの一部として，IAT- 不安が 2 回実施された．
>
> （訳者注：IAT; Implicit Association Test, 潜在的連合テスト）

0658 参加者に実験室に来てもらい，測度に回答させたことを述べる．

◆ On arrival at the laboratory, participants were greeted by N experimenters and completed the X and Y measures.
実験室に到着すると，参加者は N 名の実験者に出迎えられ，X 測度と Y 測度に回答した．

> On arrival at the laboratory, participants were greeted by two experimenters and completed the IAT–Anxiety and the explicit trait measures.　(13)
> 実験室に到着すると，参加者は 2 名の実験者に出迎えられ，IAT- 不安と顕在的な特性の測度に回答した．
>
> （訳者注：IAT; Implicit Association Test, 潜在的連合テスト）

5.7 心理検査

0659 調査票を授業で配布したことを述べる.

◆Surveys were distributed to Lth–Mth grade students via their N-min X classes in the Y of Z.
調査票は，Z年のYの季節に，N分間のXの授業において，L年生からM年生の生徒に配布された．

> Surveys were distributed to 7th–12th grade students via their 45-min social studies classes in the spring of 2004. (58)
> 調査票は，2004年春に，45分間の社会研究の授業において，7年生から12年生の生徒に配布された．

0660 質問紙を郵送により返送してもらったことを述べる.

◆Xs were asked to complete the Y questionnaires on their own time, and to mail them back to the researcher's university address using a pre-paid, pre-addressed envelope.
Xは自由時間にY質問紙に回答し，あらかじめ宛名書きされた先払いの（料金別納の）封筒を使って，回答した質問紙を研究者の大学の住所に送り返すように求められた．

> Teachers were asked to complete the T2 questionnaires on their own time, and to mail them back to the researcher's university address using a pre-paid, pre-addressed envelope. (52)
> 教師は自由時間にT2質問紙にすべて回答し，あらかじめ宛名書きされた先払いの（料金別納の）封筒を使って，回答した質問紙を研究者の大学の住所に送り返すように求められた．

5.7.9 妥当性と信頼性

0661 測度が頑健であることを述べる.

◆X have robust psychometric properties.
Xは頑健な計量心理学的特性をもっている．

> These measures have robust psychometric properties. (28)
> これらの測度は，頑健な計量心理学的特性をもっている．

0662 妥当性と信頼性が確立されていることを述べる.

◆Previous studies (Author, Year) established the reliability and validity of the X.
先行研究（著者，発表年）が，Xの信頼性と妥当性を立証した．

> Previous studies (D. Shwalb & B. Shwalb, 1985; Zander, 1971) established the reliability and validity of the two orientation scales. (54)
> 先行研究（D. Shwalb & B. Shwalb, 1985; Zander, 1971）が，2つの志向尺度の信頼性と妥当性を立証した．

5. 方法 (Method)

0663 検査が優れた内的整合性，妥当性，信頼性をもつことを述べる．

◆Previous research [has] indicated that the X demonstrates high internal consistency (α = A – B), N-month test-retest reliability (*r* = C – D) and validity (Author, Year).

Xが高い内的整合性 (α = A – B)，Nか月離れた再テスト信頼性 (*r* = C – D)，および，妥当性を示すことが，これまでの研究により明らかにされている（著者，発表年）．

> Previous research has indicated that the GED demonstrates high internal consistency (α = .94–.95), 1-month test-retest reliability (*r* = .95–.96) and validity (Klonoff & Landrine, 1999, 2000; Landrine & Klonoff, 1996, 2000; Landrine et al., 2006). (32)
> GEDが高い内的整合性 (α = .94–.95)，1か月離れた再テスト信頼性 (*r* = .95–.96)，および，妥当性を示すことが，これまでの研究により明らかにされている（Klonoff & Landrine, 1999, 2000; Landrine & Klonoff, 1996, 2000; Landrine et al., 2006）．

（訳者注：GED; General Ethnic Discrimination Scale, 全般的民族差別尺度）

0664 尺度の信頼性と妥当性が，開発段階で証明されていることを述べる．

◆The X evidenced good internal consistency (α = N), test-retest reliability (*r* = M), and validity (content, criterion, and convergent) in its development [/validation /instrumentation] study (Author, Year).

Xは，その開発 [/ 妥当性 / 計装] 研究において，優れた内的整合性 (α = N)，再テスト信頼性 (*r* = M) および，妥当性 (内容妥当性，基準関連妥当性，収束的妥当性) を示した（著者，発表年）．

> The HDI evidenced good internal consistency (α = .93), test-retest reliability (*r* = .95), and validity (content, criterion, and convergent) in its development study (Dozois, 2003; Reynolds & Kobak, 1995). (32)
> HDIは，その開発研究において，優れた内的整合性 (α = .93)，再テスト信頼性 (*r* = .95) および，妥当性 (内容妥当性，基準関連妥当性，収束的妥当性) を示した（Dozois, 2003; Reynolds & Kobak, 1995）．

（訳者注：HDI; Hamilton Depression Inventory, ハミルトンうつ尺度）

0665 内的整合性の程度について述べる．

◆The scale showed excellent [/adequate /moderate /low] internal consistency (α = N).

この尺度は，優れた [/ 十分な / 中程度の / 低い] 内的整合性を示した (α = N)．

> The scale showed excellent internal consistency (α = .94). (36)
> この尺度は，優れた内的整合性を示した (α = .94)．

0666 先行研究における内的整合性の程度を述べる．

◆Internal consistency in previous research was reported to be high [/low /moderate], α = N.

先行研究における内的整合性は高く [/ 低く / 中程度で]，α = N であった．

> Internal consistency in previous research was reported to be high, α = .94. (3)
> 先行研究における内的整合性は高く，α = .94 であった．

5.7 心理検査

0667 内的整合性の信頼性（α 係数）を表す．

◆The internal consistency reliability [/reliabilities] (coefficient alphas) of the X and Y scales was [/were] N for X and M for Y.

X と Y の尺度の内的整合性の信頼性（α 係数）は，X で N，Y で M であった．

> The internal consistency reliabilities (coefficient alphas) of the two scales were .87 for RWA and .81 for SDO. (9)
> これら 2 つの尺度の内的整合性の信頼性（α 係数）は，RWA で .87, SDO で .81 であった．
> （訳者注：RWA; right-wing authoritarianism, 右派権威主義：SDO; social dominance orientation, 社会的優位志向）

0668 あるサンプルにおける内的整合性の程度について述べる．

◆In the X sample, Y displayed excellent [/adequate /moderate /low] internal consistency (α = N).

X のサンプルでは，Y が優れた [/ 十分な / 中程度の / 低い] 内的整合性を示した（α = N）．

> In the current sample, the ECBI problem scale displayed excellent internal consistency (α = .90). (45)
> 今回のサンプルでは，ECBI の問題尺度が優れた内的整合性を示した（α = .90）．
> （訳者注：ECBI; Eyberg Child Behavior Inventory, アイバーグ子供行動目録）

0669 内的整合性の信頼性係数（クロンバックの α）を表に示したことを述べる．

◆Internal consistency reliabilities (Cronbach's alpha) for all X variables are presented in Table N.

すべての X 変数に関する内的整合性の信頼性係数（クロンバックの α）を表 N に示す．

> Internal consistency reliabilities (Cronbach's alpha) for all stressor variables are presented in Table 1. (52)
> すべてのストレス因子の変数に関する内的整合性の信頼性係数（クロンバックの α）を表 1 に示す．

0670 複合的指標と信頼性係数（α 係数）の値を述べる．

◆Scores on these N items were combined to form an index of X (Index Name: α = M).

これらの N 個の項目の得点をまとめた値が，X の指標とされた（指標の名前；α = M）．

> Scores on these four items were combined to form an index of global religiousness and spirituality (global R–S; α =.78). (61)
> これらの 4 つの項目の得点をまとめた値が，全体的な宗教性とスピリチュアリティの指標とされた（global R–S; α =.78）．

0671 質問紙が優れた妥当性をもつことを述べる．

◆The X has been used in previous studies of Y and has demonstrated good validity

178　　　　　　　　　　　5．方法（Method）

(Author, Year).
Xは，Yについての先行研究で用いられてきており，優れた妥当性をもつことが例証されてきている（著者，発表年）．

> The DDQ has been used in previous studies of college student drinking and has demonstrated good validity (Larimer et al., 2001; Marlatt et al., 1998). (39)
> DDQは，大学生の飲酒についての先行研究で用いられてきており，優れた妥当性をもつことが例証されてきている（Larimer et al., 2001; Marlatt et al., 1998）．

（訳者注：DDQ; Daily Drinking Questionnaire, 日常的飲酒質問紙）

0672　測度が内的，収束，弁別，および，増分妥当性をもつことを述べる．

◆The measure has [previously] demonstrated adequate internal, convergent, discriminant, and incremental validity (Author, Year).
この測度は，十分な内的，収束的，弁別，および，増分妥当性をもつことが [以前に] 例証されている（著者，発表年）．

> The measure has demonstrated adequate internal, convergent, discriminant, and incremental validity (Snyder et al., 1991). (45)
> この測度は，十分な内的，収束的，弁別，および，増分妥当性をもつことが例証されている（Snyder et al., 1991）．

0673　再テスト信頼性係数を述べる．

◆Reliability studies of X have found test-retest coefficients ranging from A for Y[,] to B for Z.
Xの信頼性についての研究は，再テスト信頼性係数がYについてのAから，ZについてのBの範囲であることを見出してきた．

> Reliability studies of CTS2 have found test-retest coefficients ranging from the mid .7s for Psychological Aggression to the high .8s and low .9s for Physical Assault and Injury Scales. (22)
> CTS2の信頼性についての研究は，再テスト信頼性係数が心理的攻撃尺度の.7の中間から，身体的虐待と傷害尺度の.8の上のほうから.9の低いほうくらいまでの範囲であることを見出してきた．

（訳者注：CTS2; Revised Conflict Tactics Scales, 改訂版葛藤戦略尺度）

5.8　研究デザイン

5.8.1　独立変数と従属変数

0674　呈示を変えることにより，独立変数を操作したことを述べる．

◆X was manipulated by offering different Y and the A was controlled by B.
Xは，異なるYを呈示することにより操作され，AはBにより制御された．

Drive was manipulated by offering different incentives and the response hierarchies were controlled by the manner in which the problem was arranged. (18)
動因は異なる誘因を提供することにより操作され，反応ヒエラルキーは問題の配置の仕方により制御された．

0675　課題変数を変化させることにより，独立変数を操作したことを述べる．

◆X was manipulated by varying Y.
　Xは，Yを変化させることにより操作された．

> Task difficulty was manipulated by varying the entry rate of aircraft into the sector, resulting in low and high airspace load. (47)
> 課題の難易度は，航空機の領域内への進入率を変化させて航空領域の負荷に高低をもたらすことにより操作された．

0676　従属変数として，ある測定値を用いたことを述べる．

◆The total [/Total] number of X per minute into Y was used as an index of Z.
　1分間当たりのYへのXの総数が，Zの指標として用いられた．

> Total number of entries per minute into all arms was used as an index of locomotion. (21)
> すべてのアームに1分間当たりに入った回数の総数が，運動の指標として用いられた．

0677　従属変数として，ある測度を用いたことを述べる．

◆X and Y served as dependent measures.
　XとYが従属測度とされた．

> Self-reported tinnitus interference and the Digit-Symbol subtest served as dependent measures. (28)
> 自己報告による耳鳴りの干渉性と数字記号の下位検査が従属測度とされた．

0678　セッション中の従属変数として，ある測定値を用いたことを述べる．

◆The main dependent measure during X sessions was Y.
　Xセッション中のおもな従属測度はYであった．

> The main dependent measure during habituation and all ensuing test sessions was time spent (in seconds) in each compartment. (49)
> 馴化および続くすべてのテストセッション中のおもな従属測度は，各コンパートメント内において費やされた時間（秒単位）であった．

0679　従属変数（結果変数）が選ばれた理由を述べる．

◆X was selected as an outcome [/a dependent variable] because YYY [/because of Y].
　Xが，YYYということから [/Yのために] 結果 [/従属] 変数として選ばれた．

> Alcohol use problems were selected as an outcome because of their higher base rate in the population relative to other types of substances. (22)
> アルコール使用の問題は，他のタイプの物質と比較して母集団内の基本的な出現率が高いことから，結果変数として選ばれた．

5.8.2 条件の設定

0681 各条件の設定について述べる.

◆ In the first condition, XXX. In the second condition, YYY.

第一条件では, XXX. 第二条件では, YYY.

> In the first condition, participants read that prior to the accident Donald was involved in an extramarital affair with a female travel agent he met at a company party. In the second condition, Donald did not have an extramarital affair but had dealt with the agent to purchase a similar vacation for his family. (6)
> 第一条件では, 参加者は, 事故の前にドナルドは会社のパーティで会った旅行会社の女性販売員と不倫関係にあったという内容を読まされた. 第二条件では, ドナルドは不倫をしていたのではなく, 家族のために同じようなバカンスを購入しようとして, その販売員と取引をしていたという内容を読まされた.

0682 ある条件の下で, 参加者が経験させられたことを述べる.

◆ Participants in the X condition were exposed to Y.

次に, X 条件の参加者は Y にさらされた.

> Participants in the impersonal and interpersonal stress conditions were then exposed to the same stressor. (60)
> 次に, 個人に関しないストレス条件, および, 対人関係的ストレス条件の参加者は, 同じストレス因子にさらされた.

0683 異なる条件の下で, ある効果を分析したことを述べる.

◆ The effects of X were investigated under two conditions: Y and Z.

X の効果が, Y と Z という 2 つの条件の下で分析された.

> The effects of drive were investigated under two conditions: dominant response correct (Dm+), and incorrect (Dm−). (18)
> 動因の効果が, 優勢正反応 (Dm+) と優勢誤反応 (Dm−) という, 2 つの条件の下で分析された.

0684 薬物投与の有無という条件の下で, テストが行われたことを述べる.

◆ Rats [/Subjects] were tested in a drug free and X state.

ラット [/ 被験体] は, 薬物のない状態と X 投与状態でテストされた.

0680 従属変数（結果変数）を用いた目的を述べる.

◆ A total of N variables were used to evaluate X.

合計で N 個の変数が X を評価するために用いられた.

> A total of nine variables were used to evaluate the advantages and disadvantages of the schools. (23)
> 合計で 9 個の変数が, 学校の長所と短所を評価するために用いられた.

Rats were tested in a drug free and cocaine state. (49)
ラットは，薬物のない状態とコカイン投与状態でテストされた．

5.8.3 デザイン

0685 実験ブロックと統制ブロックからなるブロックデザインについて述べる．
◆ The experimental blocks were followed by a control block of trials in which the participants were asked to XXX.
実験ブロックの後には，統制ブロックの試行が行われ，そこでは参加者にXXXすることが求められた．

> The experimental blocks were followed by a control block of trials in which the participants were asked to not perform the letter search task and to just detect the CS. (43)
> 実験ブロックの後には，統制ブロックの試行が行われ，そこでは，文字探索課題を行わずCSを検出することだけが参加者に求められた．

（訳者注：CS; conditioned stimulus, 条件刺激）

0686 第一ブロックと第二ブロックからなるブロックデザインについて述べる．
◆ In Block 1, participants XXX. In Block 2, they YYY.
第一ブロックでは，参加者はXXXを行った．第二ブロックでは，参加者はYYYを行った．

> In Block 1, participants practiced the target concept discrimination by categorizing stimuli into self and other categories. In Block 2, they did the same for the attribute discrimination by sorting items into anxiety and calmness categories. (13)
> 第一ブロックでは，参加者は，刺激を自己と他者のカテゴリーに分類することにより，標的概念弁別を練習した．第二ブロックでは，参加者は，項目を不安と冷静のカテゴリーに分類することにより，属性弁別について同じ練習を行った．

0687 連続ブロックからなるブロックデザインについて述べる．
◆ The X comprises a sequence of N blocks.
Xは，N個の連続するブロックから成り立っている．

> The IAT–Anxiety comprises a sequence of five blocks (see Figure 1 for an overview). (13)
> IAT-不安は5つの連続するブロックから成り立っている（概要については図1を参照）．

（訳者注：IAT; Implicit Association Test, 潜在的連合テスト）

0688 2要因デザインについて述べる．
◆ The experiment had a 2 (X: A/B) × 2 (Y: C/D) design.
実験は，2（X：AかBか）×2（Y：CかDか）のデザインで行われた．

> The experiment had a 2 (team reflection: yes/no) × 2 (task representations: not all appropriate/all appropriate) design. (59)

実験は，2（チーム内省：あり / なし）× 2（課題表象：すべてが適切とは限らない / すべてが適切である）のデザインで行われた．

5.8.4 条件への割り当て

0689 参加者を，実験条件と統制条件に無作為に配置したことを述べる．
◆ Participants were randomly assigned to a[n] X condition or a control condition.
参加者は，X 条件と統制条件に無作為に割り当てられた．
> Participants were randomly assigned to a faking condition or a control condition. (13)
> 参加者は，だまし条件と統制条件に無作為に割り当てられた．

0690 ある人数の大学生を，2 つの実験条件に無作為に配置したことを述べる．
◆ L students from the University of X participated in the experiment. M participants were randomly assigned to the A condition, and N participants were randomly assigned to the B condition.
X 大学の L 名の学生が，実験に参加した．M 名の参加者が，A 条件に無作為に割り当てられ，N 名の参加者が B 条件に無作為に割り当てられた．
> Sixty-nine students from the University of California, Davis, participated in the experiment for partial course credit. Thirty-four participants were randomly assigned to the unitized source condition, and 35 participants were randomly assigned to the nonunitized source condition. (12)
> カリフォルニア大学デービス校の 69 名の学生が，単位の部分的な得点のために実験に参加した．34 名の参加者が，ユニット化される情報源条件に無作為に割り当てられ，35 名の参加者がユニット化されない情報源条件に無作為に割り当てられた．

0691 障害をもつ参加者を 2 つのグループに無作為に配置したことを述べる．
◆ N participations with A were randomly assigned to B or [to] C.
N 名の A をもつ参加者が，B と C のどちらかに無作為に割り当てられた．
> Thirty-seven participants with panic disorder were randomly assigned to biofeedback or to a delayed-treatment control group. (1)
> 37 名のパニック障害をもつ参加者が，バイオフィードバック群と遅延治療統制群に無作為に割り当てられた．

0692 決められた人数の参加者を，2 つの実験条件へ配置したことを述べる．
◆ N participants [/children] aged between A and B years [/months] were assigned to the X condition (C boys, D girls) and the Y condition (E boys, F girls).
A から B 歳 [/ 月齢] の N 名の参加者 [/ 子供] が，X 条件（C 名の少年，D 名の少女）と Y 条件（E 名の少年，F 名の少女）に配置された．
> Seventy-two children aged between 17.7 and 46.7 months were assigned to the extinction condition (18 girls, 18 boys) and the reacquisition condition (17 girls, 19 boys). (37)

5.8 研究デザイン

17.7 〜 46.7 か月齢の 72 名の子供が，消去条件（18 名の少女，18 名の少年）と再獲得条件（17 名の少女，19 名の少年）に配置された．

0693 参加者を，決められた人数のグループに配置したことを述べる．
◆ Participants [/They] were assigned to N M-person groups.
参加者 [/ 彼ら] は N 個の M 人グループに割り当てられた．

> They were assigned to 84 three-person groups. (59)
> 彼らは 84 の 3 人グループに割り当てられた．

0694 参加者を，2 × 2 要因のデザインに無作為に配置したことを述べる．
◆ Participants were randomly assigned to conditions of the 2 (X: A vs. B) × 2 (Y: C vs. D) factorial design.
参加者は，2（X：A vs. B）× 2（Y：C vs. D）要因のデザインの各条件に無作為に配置された．

> Participants were randomly assigned to conditions of the 2 (personality feedback: neutral vs. positive) × 2 (mortality salience treatment: mortality salience vs. control) factorial design. (25)
> 参加者は，2（性格フィードバック：中性 対 正）× 2（死の顕現性の扱い方：死の顕現性群 対 統制群）要因のデザインの各条件に無作為に配置された．

0695 参加者を，3 人組に無作為に配置したことを述べる．
◆ Xs were randomly assigned to Y triads [/trios /threesomes].
X は，Y の 3 人組に無作為に割り当てられた．

> Boys were randomly assigned to same-grade, same-homeroom triads, and were videotaped constructing card houses with playing cards during two experimental sessions. (54)
> 男子生徒は，同じ学年の，同じホームルームの 3 人組に無作為に割り当てられ，2 回の実験セッション中にトランプを使ってカードハウスを組み立てる様子をビデオに録画された．

0696 一部のグループのみが分析されたことを表す．
◆ Only data from the X and Y were analyzed.
X および Y のデータのみが分析された．

> Only data from the drug-only and placebo arms were analyzed. (27)
> 薬物のみの治験グループ，および，偽薬が与えられた治験グループのデータだけが分析された．

5.8.5 参加者のマッチング

0697 まれな参加者を除外することで，参加者群を同等にそろえたことを述べる．
◆ To make the groups as comparable as possible, we eliminated the few X who YYY.

これらの群をできるだけ同等にするために，我々は YYY であった数少ない X を研究から除外した．

> To make the groups as comparable as possible, we eliminated the few children who solved any problems correctly from the study. (5)
> これらの群をできるだけ同等にするために，我々はどんな問題も正確に解いた数少ない子供を研究から除外した．

0698 統制群が，いくつかの次元で実験群とマッチさせられたことを述べる．

◆Control group participants [/Controls] were matched on A, B, C, and D.

統制群は，A, B, C, D について，マッチさせられた．

> Controls were matched on sex, race, birth date, Full Scale IQ, maternal age, and maternal education. (38)
> 統制群は，性別，人種，誕生日，全検査 IQ，母親の年齢，母親の教育について，マッチさせられた．

（訳者注：マッチさせられた；これらの次元で実験群と一致するように構成された）

0699 ある得点が同一になるという制限をつけて，2 つの群に割り当てたことを述べる．

◆Subjects [/Rats] were assigned to X or Y groups with a restriction that the groups did not differ on the Z score.

被験体 [/ ラット] は，Z の得点が 2 群で異ならないという制限をつけて，X 群か Y 群のどちらかに割り当てられた．

> Rats were assigned to control or novelty groups with a restriction that the groups did not differ on the initial place conditioning score. (49)
> ラットは，場所条件づけの最初の得点が 2 群で異ならないという制限をつけて，統制群か新奇群のどちらかに割り当てられた．

0700 マッチドペア法の使用について述べる．

◆A [stratified,] matched pairs design was used to XXX.

XXX するために，[階層化された] マッチドペア法が用いられた．

> A stratified, matched pairs design was used to isolate the factors that predicted racial/ethnic minorities' satisfaction with cross-racial therapy. (8)
> 人種間の精神療法に対する人種的・民族的マイノリティの満足度を予測する因子を分離するために，階層化されたマッチドペア法が用いられた．

5.9 具体的な手続き

5.9.1 先行研究の踏襲

0701 方法が先行研究から採用されたことを述べる.
◆ The method was adopted from Author (Year).
　その方法は，著者（発表年）から採用された．
> The method was adopted from Rao, Hattiangady, and Shetty (2006). (50)
> その方法は，Rao, Hattiangady, Shetty（2006）から採用された．

0702 先行研究の手続きに基づいていることを述べる.
◆ Following previous research on X, YYY.
　Xの先行研究に従って，YYYが行われた．
> Following previous research on group decision making, part of the decision-relevant information was given to all group members. (59)
> 集団意思決定の先行研究に従って，意思決定関連情報の一部はすべてのグループ構成員に与えられた．

0703 今回のアプローチが先行研究からヒントを得たことを述べる.
◆ The X approach to the study was informed by Y research.
　本研究のXアプローチは，Y研究にヒントを得た．
> The qualitative approach to the study was informed by phenomenology and consensual qualitative research. (8)
> 本研究の質的なアプローチは，現象学，および，合議制質的研究法からヒントを得た．

0704 手続きの詳細が先行研究で説明されていることを述べる.
◆ These procedures were previously described in [/by] Author (Year).
　これらの手続きは，著者（発表年）の論文で，すでに説明されている．
> These procedures were previously described in Reichel and Bevins (2008). (49)
> これらの手続きは，ReichelとBevins（2008）の論文で，すでに説明されている．

0705 先行研究に基づいて，参加者に求めたことを述べる.
◆ Drawing from [/on] the X and Y literature[s], we asked students [/participants] to indicate Z.
　XとYの文献に基づいて，学生 [/ 参加者] にZを示すことを求めた．
> Drawing from the developmental and bystander literatures, we asked students to indicate the likelihood that they would ignore it because they did not believe it would really happen. (58)
> 発達的および傍観者の文献に基づいて，学生に対して，そのことが実際に起こるとは思えないので無視する確率を示すことを求めた．

5.9.2 一連の研究の手続き

0706 一連の実験段階で，用いた手続きはほぼ同一であるが，一部が異なっていたことを述べる．

◆ The procedures used in these phases were identical to those described for Experiment N, except that XXX.

これらの段階で用いられた手続きは，XXX であったことを除き，実験 N で使用された手続きと同じであった．

> The procedures used in these phases were identical to those described for Experiment 1, except that rats were assigned to one of three retention conditions (1, 14, or 28 days) and the dose of cocaine was 10 mg/kg. (49)
>
> これらの段階で用いられた手続きは，ラットが3つの保持条件（1, 14, 28 日）の1つに割り当てられたこと，および，コカインの投与量が 10 mg/kg であったことを除き，実験 1 で用いられた手続きと同じであった．

0707 一連の実験で，先行実験と類似した方法を用いたことを述べる．

◆ The apparatus, stimuli, and procedure were the same as in Experiment N[,] except that [the] participants were instructed to XXX.

装置，刺激，手続きは実験 N と同一であったが，参加者が XXX を行うように教示された点だけが異なっていた．

> The apparatus, stimuli, and procedure were the same as Experiment 1 except that the participants were instructed to make their response to the letter search task 2 s after stimulus presentation. (43)
>
> 装置，刺激，手続きは実験 1 と同一であったが，文字探索課題に対する反応を，刺激呈示の 2 秒後の時点で行うように参加者に教示した点だけが異なっていた．

0708 一連の実験で，用いられた手続きの細かな違いを述べる．

◆ The stimuli and procedure were identical to that of Experiment N, with the following exception[s]. In both experiments XXX. In Experiment A[,] YYY, whereas in experiment B[,] ZZZ.

刺激と手続きは，以下の点を除いて，実験 N と同一であった．まず，両方の実験において，XXX とされた．また，実験 A では YYY であったが，実験 B では ZZZ であった．

> The stimuli and procedure were identical to that of Experiment 1, with the following exception. For both experiments the target, nontarget, and distractor-letter stimuli were displayed for only 100 ms. A 2-s time window was allowed for responses, after which a beep was heard. In Experiment 2(a) the irrelevant distractor was displayed until response, whereas in Experiment 2(b) the irrelevant distractor was displayed only for 100 ms. (14)

刺激と手続きは，以下の点を除いて，実験1と同一であった．まず，両方の実験において，標的刺激，非標的刺激，および，妨害文字刺激は100 msのみ呈示された．反応のために2秒間の時間枠が設定され，それが終わるとビープ音が呈示された．また，実験2(a)では無関連妨害刺激は反応が行われるまで呈示されていたが，実験2(b)では無関連妨害刺激は100 msのみ呈示された．

<u>0709</u> 一連の調査で，先行調査と類似した測度を用いたことを述べる．

◆The X used in this study was identical to that used in Study N. In addition, participants completed the Y.

この研究で用いられたXは，研究Nで用いられたものと同一であった．加えて，参加者はYに回答した．

> The IAT-Anxiety used in this study was identical to that used in Study 1. In addition, participants completed the German version of the Trait form of the STAI. (13)
> この研究で用いられたIAT-不安は，研究1で用いられたものと同一であった．加えて，参加者はSTAIの特性不安のドイツ語版に回答した．

(**訳者注**：IAT; Implicit Association Test, 潜在的連合テスト：STAI; State-Trait Anxiety Inventory, 状態−特性不安検査)

5.9.3　研究の実施者

<u>0710</u> 研究の実施者について述べる．

◆Xs were conducted by Y and Z.

Xは，YとZにより行われた．

> Interviews were conducted by paid full-time interviewers and advanced undergraduate and graduate student volunteers. (22)
> インタビューは，有給の専任のインタビュアー，および，高学年の学部学生と大学院の学生のボランティアにより行われた．

5.9.4　キー押し

<u>0711</u> キーを使った手続きについて述べる．

◆Participants were instructed to press the X key when AAA[,] and the Y key when BBB.

参加者は，AAAのときはXのキーを，BBBのときはYのキーを押すように教示された．

> Participants were instructed to press the A key when the CS was absent and the S key when it was present. (43)
> 参加者は，CSがないときはAのキーを，CSがあるときはSのキーを押すように教示された．

(**訳者注**：CS; conditioned stimulus, 条件刺激)

5.9.5 評価テスト

0712 紙と鉛筆による評価テストを事後的に述べる.

◆After the X, children [/participants] were given a [paper-and-pencil] post[-]test containing Y.

X 後,子供 [/ 参加者] に,Y を含む [紙と鉛筆による] 事後テストが与えられた.

> After the lesson, children were given a paper-and-pencil posttest containing the same types of problems as those given at baseline, to assess the effects of the lesson. (5)
> 授業後に,子供には,授業の効果を評価するために,ベースラインで与えられたものと同じタイプの問題を含む紙と鉛筆による事後テストが与えられた.

0713 実験的操作の後で評価テストを行ったことを述べる.

◆We experimentally manipulated X and added a post[-]test to assess Y.

我々は X を実験的に操作し,Y を評価するために事後テストを行った.

> To address this question, we experimentally manipulated children's gestures as in Study 1 and added a lesson and posttest to assess learning. (5)
> この問題に取り組むために,我々は,研究 1 のように子供のジェスチャーを実験的に操作し,さらに,学習を評価するために授業と事後テストを行った.

0714 評価テストの内容を述べる.

◆The assessment included questions on A, B, C, and D.

評価テストは,A, B, C, D についての質問を含んでいた.

> The remainder of the assessment included questions on measurement, geometry and spatial sense, data analysis, statistics and probability, and patterns, algebra, and functions. (23)
> 評価テストの残りは,測定,幾何学と空間感覚,データ解析,統計と確率,図形と代数と関数についての質問を含んでいた.

0715 最初のテストの結果に応じてその後のテスト内容を選ぶ段階的な評価テストについて述べる.

◆The tests were conducted in a N-stage process. Xs were first given Y as a routing section. Z varied in [/with] regard to difficulty level, and Xs were administered Z on the basis of their performance on Y.

テストは N 段階の手順で実施された.まず,X に,行き先を選定するためのセクションとして,Y が与えられた.Z は難しさのレベルがさまざまに異なっており,Y の成績に応じて,X には Z が実施された.

> The tests were conducted in a two-stage process. Children were first given a common set of questions as a routing section with 12–20 items covering a broad range of difficulty. The second set of questions varied in regard to difficulty level, and children were administered these sections on the basis of their performance on the first set of questions. (23)

検査は，2段階の手順で実施された．まず，子供に，幅広い範囲の難易度を含む 12 〜 20 の項目のある行き先選定のセクションとして，共通の質問セットが与えられた．第二の質問セットは，困難さのレベルがさまざまに異なっており，最初の質問セットの成績に応じて，これらのセクションが子供に与えられた．

5.9.6 小論を書かせる
0716 小論を書かせる手続きについて述べる．
◆ Participants completed an essay in which they described X.
参加者は，X について述べる小論を書いた．

All participants completed an essay in which they described themselves and their strengths and weaknesses. (60)
すべての参加者は，自分自身と自分の長所と短所について述べる小論を書いた．

5.9.7 内容分析
0717 内容分析（テキスト分析）について述べる．
◆ We analyzed L narratives [/stories /tales] from A and M narratives [/stories /tales] from B. The classifications of these narratives [/stories /tales] are shown in Table N.
我々は，A の中の L 個の説話 [/ 物語 / お話] と，B の中の M 個の説話 [/ 物語 / お話] を分析した．これらの説話 [/ 物語 / お話] の分類を表 N に示す．

We analyzed 41 tales from the "Tohno Folktales" (Supplement 1) and 142 tales from the "Ghosts Tales of Japan" (Supplement 1). The classifications of these tales are shown in Table 2. (15)
我々は，『遠野物語』（付録 1）の中の 41 の物語と『日本の幽霊物語』（付録 1）の中の 142 の物語を分析した．これらの物語の分類を表 2 に示す．

5.9.8 得 点
0718 点数の与え方について述べる．
◆ A score of N was given when XXX. A score of M was given when YYY.
XXX のときには N 点が与えられた．YYY のときには，M 点が与えられた．

A score of 1 was given when all information was completely ignored by all three group members. A score of 2 was given when one of the members mentioned a crucial item of information. (59)
すべての情報が 3 人のグループの全構成員に無視されたときには 1 点が与えられた．構成員の 1 人が決定的な情報項目について述べたときには，2 点が与えられた．

5.9.9 基準の達成

0719 基準の達成まで手続きを繰り返したことを述べる．

◆This procedure was repeated until XXX.
この手続きは，XXX するまで繰り返された．

> This procedure was repeated until the child had explained all six problems. (5)
> この手続きは，子供が6個の問題のすべてを説明しおわるまで，繰り返された．

0720 基準の達成までテストを続けたことを述べる．

◆Each subject continued testing until he [/she] reached a criterion of L correct trials out of M consecutive trials in N consecutive testing sessions.
各被験体は，N回の連続するテストセッションにおいてM回の連続する試行中でL試行が正答であるという基準を満たすまで，テストを続けた．

> Each subject continued testing until he reached a criterion of 9 correct trials out of 11 consecutive trials in two consecutive testing sessions. (34)
> 各被験体は，2回の連続するテストセッションにおいて11回の連続する試行中で9試行が正答であるという基準を満たすまで，テストを続けた．

5.9.10 ディブリーフィング（研究後の内容説明）

0721 研究内容についてのディブリーフィングについて述べる．

◆Xs were then debriefed.
その後，Xは，研究内容の説明を受けた．

> Participants were then fully debriefed and thanked for their time. (6)
> その後，参加者は，すべての研究内容について説明され，さらに，実験に時間を割いてくれたことを感謝された．

0722 「ディセプション（だまし）」を含む実験におけるディブリーフィングを詳細に述べる．

◆All participants were fully debriefed. They were given an explanation of the true intentions and hypotheses of the experiment, provided justification for using deception in X studies, and [were] encouraged to YYY.
すべての参加者に，研究内容が完全に説明された．参加者は，実験の真の意図と仮説について説明され，X研究においてだましを用いることの正当性が説明され，そして，YYYをするように奨励された．

> All participants were fully debriefed. They were given an explanation of the true intentions and hypotheses of the experiment, provided justification for using deception in aggression studies, and encouraged to voice any concerns to the experimenter. (60)

すべての参加者に，研究内容が完全に説明された．参加者は，実験の真の意図と仮説について説明され，攻撃研究においてだましを用いることの正当性が説明され，さらに，実験についての懸念があれば表明するように奨励された．

5.10 試行・ブロック・セッション

5.10.1 試　行

`0723` 各参加者の試行数を述べる．

◆Training continued for N trials for every participant.

訓練は，各参加者について N 試行まで続けられた．

> Training continued for 200 trials for every participant. (44)
> 訓練は，各参加者について 200 試行まで続けられた．

`0724` 総試行数について述べる．

◆The subject completed a total of N X trials.

被験体は，計 N 回の X 試行を完了した．

> The subject completed a total of 60 transfer trials (30 trials involving sets of two stimuli and 30 involving sets of three stimuli). (34)
> 被験体は，計 60 回の転移試行（2 つの刺激の組を含む 30 試行と 3 つの刺激の組を含む 30 試行）を完了した．

`0725` 例題試行，練習試行，実験ブロックから成る系列について述べる．

◆Participants performed L example trials and M practice trials, followed by N experimental blocks.

参加者は，L 回の例題試行と M 回の練習試行を行い，その後で，N 回の実験ブロックを行った．

> Participants performed 12 slow example trials and 24 practice trials, followed by eight experimental blocks. (14)
> 参加者は，12 回のゆっくりとした例題試行と 24 回の練習試行を行い，その後で，8 回の実験ブロックを行った．

`0726` 練習試行，実験ブロック，本試行について述べる．

◆Following a brief practice which consisted of N trials, the experimental block began, during which M trials were administered.

N 試行の短い練習の後，実験ブロックが開始され，M 試行が行われた．

> Following a brief practice which consisted of 16 trials, the experimental block began, during which 96 trials were administered. (47)
> 16 試行の短い練習の後，実験ブロックが開始され，96 試行が行われた．

192 5. 方法（Method）

0727 実演試行と練習試行について述べる．
◆After observing X complete N demonstration trials, the child [/participant] completed M practice trials that were identical to the demonstration trials.
X が N 回の実演試行を行うのを観察した後で，子供 [/ 参加者] は，実演試行と同一の M 回の練習試行を行った．

> After observing the experimenter complete two demonstration trials, one with the left icon and the other with the right icon, the child completed two practice trials that were identical to the demonstration trials. (37)
> 実験者が 2 回の実演試行を 1 回は左のアイコンを，もう 1 回は右のアイコンを使って行うのを観察した後で，子供は，実演試行と同一の 2 回の練習試行を行った．

0728 実験前に例題試行を見せたことを述べる．
◆Before starting the experiment, participants were shown N example trials with X, followed by M example trials with Y.
実験開始前に，参加者は，X のある例題試行を N 回，その後，Y のある例題試行を M 回見せられた．

> Before starting the experiment, the participants were shown nine example trials with no CS, followed by six example trials with the CS. (43)
> 実験開始前に，参加者は，CS が呈示されない例題試行を 9 回，その後に CS が呈示される例題試行を 6 回見せられた．

> （訳者注：CS; conditioned stimulus, 条件刺激）

5.10.2 ブロック

0729 訓練ブロックの内容と材料の呈示順序を述べる．
◆There were L training blocks, for each training block all M Xs were each presented once (N trials total), and there was random and ordered presentation of the Xs.
L 個の訓練ブロックが設けられ，それぞれの訓練ブロックについて M 個の X がそれぞれ 1 回呈示され（合計で N 試行），X については無作為な呈示と規則的な呈示が設定された．

> There were 10 training blocks, for each training block all 20 input values were each presented once (200 trials total), and there was random and ordered presentation of the input values. (44)
> 10 個の訓練ブロックが設けられ，各訓練ブロック中に，20 個の入力値がそれぞれ 1 回呈示された（計 200 試行）．さらに，入力値については，無作為な呈示と規則的な呈示が設定された．

0730 ブロックがある回数の試行から成り立っていたことを述べる．
◆The X block was composed of N trials of Y.

5.10 試行・ブロック・セッション　　193

X ブロックは，Y の N 試行から成り立っていた．
　The transfer block was composed of 31 trials of input values not presented during training. (44)
　転移ブロックは，訓練中に呈示されなかった入力値が呈示される 31 試行から成り立っていた．

5.10.3 実験段階

`0731`　2 つの実験段階を設定したことを，内容とともに述べる．

◆The N testing days were blocked into 2 phases: the initial phase consisting of testing Days A to B, which was considered X, and the later [/latter] phase consisting of Days C to D, which was considered Y.
N 日間のテスト日は，2 段階に分けられていた．最初の段階は，第 A 日から第 B 日までのテスト日であり，X であるとみなされた．後の段階は第 C 日から第 D 日であり，Y であるとみなされた．

　The 11 testing days were blocked into two phases: the initial phase consisting of testing Days 2 to 7, which was considered an acquisition measure as used in the learning index measure described below, and the latter phase consisting of Days 8 to 12, which was considered a more steady-state measure of memory. (31)
　11 日間のテスト日は，2 つの段階に分けられていた．最初の段階は，第 2 日から第 7 日までのテスト日であり，以下に説明する学習指標で使用される獲得の測度であるとみなされた．後の段階は第 8 日から第 12 日であり，より定常的な記憶測度であるとみなされた．

5.10.4 セッション

`0732`　各セッションの長さと 1 日当たりの最大試行数を述べる．

◆Each testing session lasted approximately N min and consisted of no more than M trials per X.
各テストセッションは約 N 分間であり，X につき最大で M 試行から成っていた．

　Each testing session lasted approximately 30 min and consisted of no more than 22 trials per day. (34)
　各テストセッションは約 30 分間であり，1 日当たり最大で 22 試行から成っていた．

`0733`　セッションと試行について述べる．

◆Each testing session consisted of N trials involving X and M trials involving Y, [presented] in random order.
各テストセッションは，無作為な順序で呈示される，X を用いた N 回の試行と，Y を用いた M 回の試行から成り立っていた．

Each testing session consisted of four trials involving yellow cubes (transfer trials) and seven trials involving black cups (familiar trials), in random order. (34)
各テストセッションは，無作為な順序で呈示される，黄色の立方体を用いた4回の試行（転移試行）と，黒いカップを用いた7回の試行（熟知試行）から成り立っていた．

0734 セッションの間隔について述べる．

◆ N to M weeks [/days /months] intervened between successive sessions.
連続するセッションは，N〜M週間[/日間/月間]の間隔をあけて行われた．

> Three to 4 weeks intervened between successive testing sessions. (18)
> 連続するテストセッションは，3〜4週間の間隔をあけて行われた．

0735 セッションについて述べる．

◆ Participants came for N sessions scheduled, on average, M days apart (M = A days, SD = B, minimum = C, maximum = D).
参加者は，平均でM日間（平均A日，標準偏差B，最小C，最大D）おきに設定されたN回のセッションのために来訪した．

> Participants came for two sessions scheduled, on average, 10 days apart (M = 10.4 days, SD = 4.33, minimum = 2, maximum = 14). (55)
> 参加者は，平均で10日間（平均10.4日，標準偏差4.33，最小2，最大14）おきに設定された2回のセッションのために来訪した．

0736 実験状況とセッションを述べる．

◆ Participants were tested in groups of A to B at computer stations that blocked the view of participants from one another. L sessions were completed within a M hr N min sitting.
参加者は，互いに視覚的に遮られたコンピュータステーションにおいて，A人からB人のグループでテストされた．L回のセッションは，M時間N分間の着席の間に終了した．

> Participants were tested in groups of 8 to 15 at computer stations that blocked the view of participants from one another. Both sessions were completed within a single 1 hr 15 min sitting. (44)
> 参加者は，互いに視覚的に遮られたコンピュータステーションにおいて，8人から15人のグループでテストされた．両方のセッションは，1時間15分の長さの1回の着席の間に終了した．

5.10.5 順序の無作為化

0737 実施順序を無作為化したこと，および，課題にかかった時間を述べる．

◆ The order in which the Xs were administered was randomized across Ys, and the task took approximately N min to complete.

5.10 試行・ブロック・セッション

Xの実施順序はYを通して無作為化された．課題の完了にはおよそN分間を要した．

> The order in which the trials were administered was randomized across participants, and the task took approximately 45 min to complete. (47)
> 試行の実施順序は参加者を通して無作為化された．課題の完了にはおよそ 45 分間を要した．

0738 試行順序を無作為化したこととその目的，および，従属変数について述べる．

◆The trial order was randomized to avoid [possible] order effects, and X served as the dependent variable.
試行順序は，[起こるかもしれない]順序効果の出現を避けるために無作為化され，Xが従属変数とされた．

> The trial order was randomized to avoid possible order effects, and response time served as the dependent variable. (47)
> 試行順序は，起こるかもしれない順序効果の出現を避けるために無作為化され，反応時間が従属変数とされた．

0739 条件の順序が，セッション内およびセッション間で無作為化されたことを表す．

◆X performed under the following N M-minute conditions, randomized for order within and between sessions.
Xは，セッション内およびセッション間で順序が無作為化された，以下のN個のM分間条件の下で課題を行った．

> Specifically, boys performed under the following four 8-minute conditions, randomized for order within and between sessions. (54)
> 特に，男子生徒は，セッション内およびセッション間で順序が無作為化された，以下の4つの8分間条件の下で課題を行った．

5.10.6 カウンターバランス（相殺）

0740 いくつかの条件をカウンターバランスして作成した刺激を用いたことを述べる．

◆A counterbalanced set of L different Xs, employed across M blocks of N trials, consisted of Y.
カウンターバランスされたL個の異なるXの組が，N試行から成るM個のブロックを通して用いられた．それらN個の組は，Yから成り立っていた．

> A counterbalanced set of 144 different stimulus displays, employed across two blocks of 72 trials, consisted of each load condition (2), each of the target letters (2) in each of the letter circle positions (6), either with or without the CS in each position (6). (43)

カウンターバランスされた144個の異なる刺激表示の組が，72試行から成る2つのブロックを通して用いられた．それら144個の刺激表示の組は，各負荷条件（2通り），各円形文字位置（6通り）の各標的文字（2通り），各位置でのCSの有無（6通り）から成り立っていた．

（訳者注：CS; conditioned stimulus, 条件刺激）

0741 ブロックの順序をカウンターバランスしたことを述べる．

◆The order of the N blocks was counterbalanced across [the] Xs.

N個のブロックの呈示順序は，Xを通してカウンターバランスされた．

> The order of the eight blocks was counterbalanced across participants. (56)
> 8個のブロックの呈示順序は，参加者を通してカウンターバランスされた．

0742 セッションの順序をカウンターバランスしたことを述べる．

◆Half of the rats received sessions with presentations of stimulus A on Day 1 and stimulus B on Day 2, and the remainder received the reverse arrangement.

ラットの半数は，第1日目に刺激Aが呈示されるセッションを，そして，第2日目に刺激Bが呈示されるセッションを経験した．残りの半数は，その反対の配置のセッションを経験した．

> Half of the rats received sessions with presentations of stimulus X on Day 1 and stimulus Y on Day 2, and the remainder received the reverse arrangement. (10)
> ラットの半数は，第1日目に「刺激X」が呈示されるセッションと第2日目に「刺激Y」が呈示されるセッションを経験した．残りの半数は，その逆の配置のセッションを経験した．

（訳者注：この論文では，一連のクリック音（a train of clicks）を刺激X，2000Hzの連続音（a 2000 Hz constant tone）を刺激Yと名づけている）

0743 検査の複数のバージョンを，順序をカウンターバランスして実施したことを述べる．

◆N different versions of the test were constructed, which were administered in a counterbalanced order.

この検査の異なるN個のバージョンがつくられ，それらがカウンターバランスされた順序で実施された．

> Four different versions of the test were constructed (i.e., the order of the numbers), which were administrated in a counterbalanced order. (28)
> この検査の異なる4つのバージョン（すなわち数字の呈示順序をかえたもの）がつくられ，それらがカウンターバランスされた順序で実施された．

0744 テストの反復において，順序の無作為化とカウンターバランスを行ったこと，および，テストの間隔を述べる．

◆The order of X testing was randomized and counterbalanced across treatment

conditions, and at least N separated [the] repeated tests [/determinations].
Xテストの順序は無作為化され，治療条件を通してカウンターバランスされた．さらに，[その]反復するテスト[/測定]の間は，少なくともNの間隔が設けられた．

> The order of drug testing was randomized and counterbalanced across treatment conditions, and at least one week separated the repeated determinations. (30)
> 薬物テストの順序は無作為化され，治療条件を通してカウンターバランスされた．さらに，反復する測定の間は，少なくとも1週間の間隔が設けられた．

5.10.7 手続きや実験に要した時間

0745 検査にかかった時間を述べる．
◆ The test took approximately N hr [/min] to administer.
検査を実施するのに，およそN時間[/分間]を要した．

> The test battery took approximately 6 hr to administer. (47)
> テストバッテリーを実施するのに，およそ6時間を要した．

0746 実験手続きの全体的な長さを述べる．
◆ In all, the experiment took approximately N hr.
実験は，全体でおよそN時間かかった．

> In all, the experiment took approximately 2.5 hr. (60)
> 実験は，全体でおよそ2.5時間かかった．

0747 手続きの長さを述べる．
◆ The X lasted between N and M hr [/min /s].
XはN時間[/分間/秒間]からM時間[/分間/秒間]続いた．

> The semistructured face-to-face interview lasted between 1 hr and 3 hr. (8)
> 半構造化された対面式のインタビューは1時間から3時間続いた．

0748 研究全体の長さ，および，週当たりのテスト日数を述べる．
◆ Testing occurred over a span of approximately L days [/months], during which [time] subjects were tested between M and N days per week.
テストは約L日[/Lか月]の期間にわたって行われ，その期間中，被験体は1週間にM日からN日テストされた．

> Testing occurred over a span of approximately 9 months, during which time subjects were tested between 4 and 7 days per week. (34)
> テストは約9か月の期間にわたって行われ，その期間中，被験体は1週間に4日から7日テストされた．

5.11 予備的研究

0749 予備的研究で記述式の質問紙を用いたことを述べる.

◆In a pilot study, N Xs completed Y questionnaires in which they were requested to describe Z.

予備的研究では, N 名の X が, Z について記述してもらう Y 形式の質問紙に答えた.

> In a pilot study, 53 junior high school teachers completed open-ended questionnaires in which they were requested to describe stressful situations experienced at work. (52)
> 予備的研究では, 53 名の中学校の教師が, 仕事で経験するストレスの強い場面について記述してもらう自由回答形式の質問紙に答えた.

0750 予備的研究の結果を簡潔に述べる.

◆A pilot study with X indicated that YYY.

X を用いた予備的研究は, YYY ということを示した.

> A pilot study with several observers indicated that they had difficulty performing the walking tasks in the SL condition when they were asked to imagine the mere location. (42)
> 数名の観察者を用いた予備的研究は, 観察者が単なる位置だけを想像するように求められた場合には SL 条件で歩行課題を行うことは困難であることを示した.
>
> (訳者注：SL; spatial language, 空間的言語)

0751 予備的な研究を行い, 本研究に還元させたことを述べる.

◆A pilot interview [/study] was conducted with X, resulting in feedback for Y.

X に対して予備的なインタビュー [/ 研究] が行われ, その結果が Y にフィードバックされた.

> Lastly, a pilot interview was conducted with a participant at the shelter house, resulting in feedback for a fifth and final version of the interview protocol. (41)
> 最後に, シェルターハウスで 1 名の参加者に対して予備的なインタビューが行われ, その結果が第 5 版となる最終のインタビュー手順へのフィードバックをもたらした.

5.12 観察者による符号化・点数化

5.12.1 符号化・点数化の方法

0752 データがあるシステムに従って符号化されたことを述べる.

◆All of the participants' [/children's] speech [and gestures] was [/were] transcribed and coded according to a previously developed system (Author, Year).

参加者 [/ 子供] の発言 [とジェスチャー] のすべては, 以前に開発されたシステム (著者, 発表年) に従って文字に書き起こされ, 符号化された.

5.12 観察者による符号化・点数化

All of the children's speech and gestures were transcribed and coded according to a previously developed system (Perry et al., 1988). (5)
子供の発言とジェスチャーのすべては，以前に開発されたシステム（Perry et al., 1988）に従って文字に書き起こされ，符号化された．

0753 符号化に用いられるカテゴリーの内容を述べる．

◆Participants' Xs were coded using a N-category scheme: (a) A; (b) B; (c) C; and (d) D.
参加者のXは，N個のカテゴリーの図式によって，符号化された．それらのカテゴリーは，(a) A，(b) B，(c) C，(d) Dであった．

> Participants' rationales for their ratings of immanent justice were coded using a four-category scheme with each rationale assigned as many codes as applied: (a) chance, coincidence, fluke, random; (b) fate, predestined but no mention of justice, punishment, or reward; (c) justice, punishment, reward, karma, justice maxims (e.g., "what goes around comes around"); and (d) other. (6)
> 参加者の内在的正義の評定の理論的根拠は，4個のカテゴリーの図式によって，符号化された．各根拠には，適用できる限り多くの符号が割り当てられた．それらのカテゴリーは，(a) 偶然, 同時発生, まぐれ, ランダム，(b) 運命, 運命づけられていたが正義, 罰, 報酬には触れないもの，(c) 正義, 罰, 報酬, 宿命, 正義の格言（たとえば，「因果応報だ」），および (d) その他，であった．

0754 あることを知らされない2人の符号化担当者が，独立して符号化を行ったことを述べる．

◆The coding was conducted independently by X and a second coder who were blind to the Y.
符号化は，Yを知らされていないXともう1人の符号化担当者が，それぞれ独立に行った．

> The coding was conducted independently by the first author and a second coder who were blind to the immanent justice ratings associated with each rationale and condition. (6)
> 符号化は，各理論的根拠および各条件と関連する内在的正義の評定を知らされていない，第一著者，および，もう1人の符号化担当者が，それぞれ独立に行った．

0755 目的を知らされない観察者が点数をつけたことを述べる．

◆X was determined by a blind[ed] observer.
Xが，目的を知らされていない観察者によって判定された．

> The NSS was determined by a blinded observer. (64)
> NSSが，目的を知らされていない観察者によって判定された．

（訳者注：NSS; neurological severity score, 神経学的重症度得点）

0756 あることを知らされないもう1人の独立した評定者が，あることを点数化したことを述べる．

◆A second independent rater who was blind to participants' X scored a random sample of N Ys.

参加者のXを知らされていないもう1人の独立した評定者が，N個のYの無作為抽出サンプルを点数化した．

> A second independent rater who was blind to participants' diagnostic status scored a random sample of 50 oral AMT responses. (36)
> 参加者の診断の状態を知らされていないもう1人の独立した評定者が，50個の口頭によるAMT反応の無作為抽出サンプルを点数化した．

（訳者注：AMT; Autobiographical Memory Test, 自伝的記憶テスト）

5.12.2 信頼性のチェック

0757 観察者間の信頼性チェックを行ったことを述べる．

◆ Observers naïve to X conducted inter[-]observer reliability checks on Y.

Xについて先入的な知識のない観察者が，Yについて観察者間の信頼性チェックを行った．

> Observers naïve to the experimental conditions conducted interobserver reliability checks on both measures. (49)
> 実験条件について先入的な知識のない観察者が，両方の測度について観察者間の信頼性チェックを行った．

0758 符号化の信頼性を査定する手続きを述べる．

◆ Reliability was assessed by having a second experimenter independently code a random subset of the X.

信頼性は，Xの無作為な部分集合を，第二の実験者に独立して符号化してもらうことにより査定された．

> Reliability was assessed by having a second experimenter independently code a random subset of the explanations. (5)
> 信頼性は，説明の無作為な部分集合を，第二の実験者に独立して符号化してもらうことにより評価された．

5.12.3 評定者間の一致度

0759 評定者間の一致度（カッパ係数）について述べる．

◆ Good inter[-]rater agreement was obtained for X (κ = N) and for Y (κ = M).

X（κ = N）およびY（κ = M）について，評定者間に高い一致度が得られた．

> Good interrater agreement was obtained for the categorization of specific versus nonspecific responses (κ = .87) and for the categorization of assault-relatedness (κ = .78). (36)
> 特異的反応と非特異的反応の分類（κ = .87）および暴行関連性の分類（κ = .78）について，評定者間に高い一致度が得られた．

0760 評定法と評定者間の一致度（カッパ係数）について述べる．

◆Two raters (unaware of the experimental conditions) watched the X and rated Y (κ = N).

実験条件を知らない2人の評定者が，Xを見てYを評定した（κ = N）．

> Two raters (unaware of the experimental conditions) watched the recordings and rated elaboration (κ = 0.82). (59)
> 実験条件を知らない2人の評定者が，記録を見て，精緻化を評定した（κ = 0.82）．

0761 予測について知らされない状態で符号化したこと，および，評定者間の一致度（相関係数）を述べる．

◆The Nth coder was blind with respect to the predictions for each rat. The inter[-]rater correlations (r) exceeded A, ps < B.

N番目の符号化担当者は，各ラットの予測について知らされていなかった．評定者間の相関係数（r）はAを超えた（すべての場合でp < B）．

> The second coder (R.C.H.) was blind with respect to the individual predictions for each rat. The interrater correlations (r) exceeded 0.95 in both Experiments 1 and 2. ps < .001. (10)
> 2番目の符号化担当者（R.C.H.）は，各ラットの個々の予測については知らされていなかった．評定者間の相関係数（r）は，実験1と2の両方で0.95を超えた（すべての場合でp < .001）．

0762 評定者間の一致度（百分率）を述べる．

◆Inter[-]rater agreement was A% for X and B% for Y, with the final coding resolved by the two coders.

2人の符号化担当者が最終的な符号を決定した結果，評定者間の一致度は，Xについては A% であり，Yについては B% であった．

> Interrater agreement was 86.25% for the accident and 91.25% for the lottery, with the final coding resolved by the two coders. (6)
> 2人の符号化担当者が最終的な符号を決定した結果，評定者間の一致度は，事故条件については 86.25% であり，宝くじ条件については 91.25% であった．

5.13 操作チェック

0763 操作チェックのために，参加者による評定を用いたことを述べる．

◆Participants' ratings of X served as a manipulation check.

参加者によるXの評定が，操作チェックとして役立った．

> Participants' ratings of David's character on a 7-point scale ranging from 1 (very bad) to 7 (very good) served as a manipulation check. (6)

0764 操作チェックのために，参加者に評定を求めたことを述べる．
◆For a [/the] manipulation check, participants were asked to rate X.
操作チェックのために，X を評定することが，参加者に求められた．

> For the manipulation check, participants were asked to rate the extent to which Kerry was suffering from her HIV status, using a scale ranging from 1 (minimally) to 7 (a great deal). (6)
> 操作チェックのために, ケリーが HIV という状態にどの程度苦しめられていたかを, 1 (最小限に)から 7 (かなりの程度)までの尺度を使って評定することが, 参加者に求められた．

0765 操作チェックとして，参加者に要約を求めたことを述べる．
◆As a manipulation check for the X, participants were asked to summarize Y.
X の操作チェックとして，参加者に Y を要約することが求められた．

> As manipulation check for the task representations, participants were asked to summarize their perceptions of the task before they engaged in the group task. (59)
> 課題表象の操作チェックとして，グループ課題に従事する前に，参加者に課題の認識を要約することが求められた．

5.14 インタビュー

0766 インタビューの目的を述べる．
◆The purpose of the interview was to gain an understanding of (a) X, (b) Y, and (c) Z.
インタビューの目的は，(a) X，(b) Y，(c) Z について，理解することであった．

> The purpose of the interview was to gain a qualitative understanding of (a) the participant's life experiences and perceptions of homelessness, (b) the participant's perceptions of his own masculinity, and (c) the social class concerns of this population. (41)
> インタビューの目的は，(a) 参加者の人生経験とホームレスに対する認識，(b) 自分の男性性についての参加者の認識，(c) この母集団の社会的階層への関心について，質的に理解することであった．

0767 インタビューの場所を述べる．
◆All interviews were conducted in X.
すべてのインタビューは，X で行われた．

> All interviews were conducted in lab offices on campus. (8)
> すべてのインタビューは，キャンパスの研究室で行われた．

0768 インタビュアーの特徴を参加者の特徴とマッチさせたことを述べる．
◆Interviewers were matched with participants on X, Y, and Z.

インタビューを行う人は，参加者と，X, Y, Z が一致するようにマッチされた．
> Interviewers were matched with participants on race/ethnicity, gender, and language preference. (8)
> インタビューを行う人は，参加者と，人種や民族性，性別，言語選択が一致するようにマッチされた．

0769 インタビューが録音され文字に書き起こされたことを述べる．
◆ Each interview was [digitally] audiotaped and transcribed.
各インタビューは，[デジタルで] 録音され，文字に書き起こされた．
> Each interview was digitally audiotaped and transcribed. (8)
> 各インタビューは，デジタル録音され，文字に書き起こされた．

0770 インタビューで用いるプロトコル（会話の手順）の構成について述べる．
◆ The finalized protocol consisted of N sections: a X portion, a Y portion and a Z portion.
最終的に決められたプロトコルは，N 個の部分から成り立っていた．すなわち，X の部分，Y の部分，Z の部分であった．
> The finalized protocol consisted of two sections: a demographics portion and an open-ended portion. (41)
> 最終的に決められたプロトコルは，2 つの部分から成り立っていた．すなわち，人口統計学的な部分，および，自由回答形式の部分であった．

5.15 ウェブ調査

0771 ウェブ調査で，サンプルのタイプとサイズ，研究のタイプ，場所，タイミングなどを 1 つの文章で述べる（密度が高くてよい表現）．
◆ A random sample of N students stratified across class year and equally portioned from two universities (a[n] A university and a[n] B university on [/located in] C) was invited to complete a web-based survey during the D semester.
学年ごとに分けられ，2 つの大学（C にある A 大学と B 大学）から等しく無作為に抽出された N 名の学生が，D 学期の間に，ウェブ上の調査に答えるように勧誘された．
> A random sample of 7,000 students stratified across class year and equally portioned from two universities (a private mid-size university and a large public university on the West Coast) was invited to complete a web-based survey during the fall semester of 2007. (39)
> 学年ごとに分けられ，2 つの大学（西海岸にある中規模の私立大学と大規模の公立大学）から等しく無作為に抽出された 7000 名の学生が，2007 年の秋学期の間に，ウェブ上の調査に答えるように勧誘された．

0772 ウェブ調査で，参加者に同意を求める手続きを述べる．
◆ Those who agreed to XXX were required to check off a box indicating their consent. XXX することに同意する人には，同意を示すボックス内に印を入れることが要求された．

> Those who agreed to participate were required to check off a box indicating their consent. (9)
> 参加に同意する人には，同意を示すボックス内に印を入れることが要求された．

0773 ウェブ調査で，ディブリーフィング（研究後の内容説明）を行う手続きを述べる．
◆ Once participants completed the online survey, they were directed to a page with a debriefing form explaining X.
参加者がオンライン調査を完了すると，X を説明するディブリーフィングの書式のページに導かれた．

> Once participants completed the online survey, they were directed to a page with a debriefing form explaining the specific purpose of the research. (9)
> 参加者がオンライン調査を完了すると，この研究の詳しい目的を説明するディブリーフィングの書式のページに導かれた．

5.16 倫理的ガイドラインの遵守

0774 インフォームドコンセント，および，研究が研究倫理委員会により承認されたことを述べる．
◆ All Xs gave [/provided] [written] informed consent and the study was approved by the Y research ethics committee.
すべての X は [書面による] インフォームドコンセントを与え，研究は Y の研究倫理委員会により承認された．

> All participants gave informed consent and the study was approved by the local research ethics committee. (55)
> すべての参加者はインフォームドコンセントを与え，研究は地域の研究倫理委員会により承認された．

0775 手続きの詳細が倫理委員会による審査を受けたことを述べる．
◆ A, B, and C were reviewed by the Ethical Committee [/Institutional Review Board] of X University.
A, B, C は，X 大学の倫理委員会による審査を受けた．

> Questionnaires, procedures, and informed consent forms and instructions were reviewed by the Ethical Committee of the University of Oxford. (4)

質問紙，手続き，および，インフォームドコンセントの書式と教示は，オックスフォード大学倫理委員会による審査を受けた．

（訳者注：米国では，Institutional Review Board のほうが一般的である）

0776 動物実験の手続きが指針を遵守し，倫理委員会により承認されたことを述べる．

◆The experimental protocols followed the "Guide for the Care and Use of Laboratory Animals" (Author, Year) and were approved by X university Institutional Animal Care and Use Committee.

実験手続きは，「実験動物の世話と使用に関する指針」（著者，発表年）を遵守しており，X 大学の動物実験委員会により承認された．

> The experimental protocols followed the "Guide for the Care and Use of Laboratory Animals" (National Research Council, 1996) and were approved by the University of Nebraska-Lincoln Institutional Animal Care and Use Committee. (49)
> 実験手続きは，「実験動物の世話と使用に関する指針」（National Research Council, 1966）を遵守しており，ネブラスカ大学リンカーン校の動物実験委員会により承認された．

0777 動物実験の手続きが倫理委員会により承認され，基準を遵守していたことを述べる．

◆All procedures were approved by the X committee and adhered to Y.

すべての手続きは，X 委員会により承認され，Y を遵守していた．

> All procedures were approved by the local IACUC committee and adhered to NIH standards. (31)
> すべての手続きは，地域の IACUC により承認され，NIH の基準を厳守していた．

（訳者注：IACUC; the Institutional Animal Care and Use Committee, 動物実験委員会：NIH; National Institute of Health, 国立衛生研究所）

5.17 動 物 学 習

5.17.1 訓練手続き

0778 条件づけの手続きを紹介する．

◆One way to compare the impact of X on Y is with a variation of the Z procedure.

Y に対する X の影響を比較する 1 つの方法では，Z 手続きを改変したものを用いている．

> One way to compare the impact of conditioned associations on choice behavior is with a variation of the traditional place conditioning procedure. (49)
> 選択行動に対する条件性連合の影響を比較する 1 つの方法では，伝統的な場所条件づけ手続きを改変したものを用いている．

5. 方法 (Method)

0779 特定の訓練日における手続きを述べる.
◆ During the Nth day of training, XXX.
訓練 N 日目の間は，XXX であった.

> During the second day of training, the plastic flaps were lowered to their normal positions, and rats had to move the flaps to gain access to the food pellets. (10)
> 訓練 2 日目の間は，プラスチックの垂れ蓋が通常の位置に下げられ，ラットは食物ペレットを得るためにはその垂れ蓋を動かさなければならなかった．

0780 条件づけの第一段階の手続きを述べる.
◆ During the first stage of X conditioning, YYY.
X 条件づけの第一段階の間，YYY した.

> During the first stage of appetitive conditioning, rats were placed in four visually distinct experimental chambers. (10)
> 食餌条件づけの第一段階の間，ラットは，視覚的に異なる 4 つの実験箱に入れられた．

0781 刺激の呈示，および，要求された反応について述べる.
◆ X was presented with N stimuli[,] and was required to YYY.
X には，N 個の刺激が呈示され，YYY を行うことが要求された.

> Sarah was presented with three stimuli in this form and was required to choose one item from a pair of objects. (34)
> サラには，この形式で 3 つの刺激が呈示され，1 対の対象物から 1 つの項目を選ぶことが要求された．
>
> (訳者注：サラは被験体の名前である)

0782 電気ショックの呈示について述べる.
◆ Shocks were delivered at the rate of N per [/every] minute [/min].
電気ショックは，1 分間に N 回の出現率で与えられた.

> Shocks were delivered at the rate of one every min. (10)
> 電気ショックは，1 分間に 1 回の出現率で与えられた．

0783 マウスの迷路実験の報告において，迷路の探索，データの記録，迷路の清掃について述べる.
◆ For the testing session N hours later, each mouse was returned to the center of the apparatus and, for a period of M min, was again free to explore the maze. Time in each X and X entries were recorded. No Ys were turned on during the testing. The maze was cleaned with Z before each training and testing session.
N 時間後のテストセッションでは，各マウスは装置の中央に戻され，M 分の間，迷路を再び自由に探索することができた．各 X に滞在した時間と入った回数が記録された．テスト中，Y は呈示されなかった．迷路は，各訓練およびテストセッション前に Z で清掃された．

For the testing session 24 hours later, each mouse was returned to the center of the apparatus and, for a period of 3 min, was again free to explore the maze. Time in each arm and arm entries were again recorded. No cues were turned on during the testing. The maze was cleaned with 70% ethanol before each training and testing session. (21)
24時間後のテストセッションでは，各マウスは装置の中央に戻され，3分の間，迷路を再び自由に探索することができた．各アームに滞在した時間と入った回数が再び記録された．テスト中，手がかり刺激は呈示されなかった．迷路は，各訓練およびテストセッション前に 70% エタノール溶液で清掃された．

0784 強化スケジュールの下で反応したことを述べる．

◆Subjects responded for X under a Y schedule of reinforcement, as described previously (Author, Year).
被験体は，X を得るために，先行研究において記述されている Y 強化スケジュール（著者，発表年）の下で反応を行った．

> Subjects responded for intravenous infusions of cocaine under a second-order schedule of reinforcement, as described previously (Howell et al., 2007). (30)
> 被験体は，コカインの静脈内注入を得るために，先行研究に記述されている 2 次強化スケジュール（Howell et al., 2007）の下で反応を行った．

0785 強化スケジュール値の操作について述べる．

◆Initially, the fixed ratio (FR) was N (FR N) and gradually increased to FR M.
最初，定比率（FR）は N（FR N）とされ，段階的に FR M まで増加された．

> Initially, the fixed ratio (FR) was one (FR 1) and gradually increased to FR 20. (30)
> 最初，定比率（FR）は 1（FR 1）とされ，段階的に FR 20 まで増加された．

0786 あるスケジュールで維持された被験体に起きたことを述べる．

◆Xs maintained on Y schedule ZZZ.
Y のスケジュールで維持された X は，ZZZ した．

> Within 7 to 10 days, rats maintained on this schedule died of starvation. (33)
> このスケジュールで維持されたラットは，7 日から 10 日以内に餓死した．

5.17.2 試行とセッション

0787 予備的訓練，および，訓練試行について述べる．

◆After completing preliminary training, subjects were exposed to basic X trials.
予備的訓練の後，被験体は基本的な X 試行にさらされた．

> After completing preliminary training, subjects were exposed to basic MTS trials. (34)
> 予備的訓練の後，被験体は基本的な MTS 試行にさらされた．

（訳者注：MTS; matching-to-sample, 見本合わせ）

5. 方法 (Method)

0788 獲得試行，および，逆転試行の系列について述べる。
◆After the N acquisition trials had been completed, the X contingency was reversed for a further M trials.
N 回の獲得試行が完了した後，X の随伴性がその後の M 試行で逆転された。

> After the eight acquisition trials had been completed, the response-outcome contingency was reversed for a further eight trials. (37)
> 8 回の獲得試行が完了した後，反応結果の随伴性がその後の 8 試行で逆転された。

0789 1 日当たりの試行数，および，訓練の長さを述べる。
◆Animals performed for N trials each day for M days.
動物は，1 日 N 試行を M 日間行った。

> Animals performed for four trials each day for 12 days. (31)
> 動物は，1 日 4 試行を 12 日間行った。

0790 訓練セッション，および，セッションの間隔について述べる。
◆On each day, [the] rats received N sessions of training that were separated by a[n] M-hr interval.
各訓練日に，ラットは M 時間の時間間隔で隔てられた N 回の訓練セッションを経験した。

> On each day, rats received two sessions of training that were separated by a 2-hr interval. (10)
> 各訓練日に，ラットは 2 時間の時間間隔で隔てられた 2 回の訓練セッションを経験した。

0791 複数の刺激の 1 つを用いたセッションについて述べる。
◆Xs received N session[s] of training with each of the M Y stimuli (A, B, C, and D).
X は，M 個の各 Y 刺激（A, B, C, D）を用いた N セッションの訓練を受けた。

> On each day of training, rats received one session of training with each of the four visual stimuli (A, B, C, and D). (10)
> 各訓練日に，ラットは，A, B, C, D という 4 つの各視覚刺激を用いた 1 セッションの訓練を受けた。
>
> （訳者注：ここで, A, B, C, D は，実験箱内でラットに呈示される視覚刺激に与えられた呼称である）

0792 実験セッションの長さと場所を述べる。
◆Daily sessions lasted for approximately N hr and were conducted within a X.
1 日のセッションはおよそ N 時間であり，X の中で行われた。

> Daily sessions lasted for approximately 4 hr and were conducted within a ventilated, sound-attenuating chamber. (30)
> 1 日のセッションはおよそ 4 時間であり，換気された防音室内で行われた。

5.18 薬物・神経科学

0793 薬物実験における薬物の注入について述べる.
◆A volume of N ml/infusion was delivered over M s [/min].
1回の注射当たり N ml の量が，M 秒 [/分] 間かけて注入された．

> A volume of 2.0 ml/infusion was delivered over 7 s. (30)
> 1回の注射当たり 2.0 ml の量が，7秒間かけて注入された．

0794 異なる動物群が異なる量の薬物を投与されたことを述べる.
◆There were three experimental groups: L animals received X, M animals received Y at a dose of A mg, and N animals received Z at a dose of B.
3つの実験群が設けられた．すなわち，L 匹の動物が X を与えられ，M 匹の動物が Y を A mg の投与量で与えられ，そして，N 匹の動物が Z を B mg の投与量で与えられた．

> There were three experimental groups: nine animals received saline vehicle ("aged vehicle"), nine animals received hydroxyfasudil (Sigma-Aldrich, St. Louis, MO) at a dose of 0.1875 mg ("aged low dose"), and nine animals received hydroxyfasudil at a dose of 0.3750 mg ("aged high dose"). (31)
> 3つの実験群が設けられた．すなわち，9匹の動物が生理食塩水の賦形剤を与えられ（老齢賦形剤群），9匹の動物が塩酸ファスジル（シグマアルドリッチ社，ミズーリ州セントルイス市）を 0.1875 mg の投与量で（老齢低投与量群），そして，9匹の動物が塩酸ファスジルを 0.3750 mg の投与量で（老齢高投与量群）与えられた．

0795 被験体に麻酔をかけた方法を述べる.
◆Male [/Female] rats weighing A–B g were anesthetized with a mixture of X (initial inspired concentration C%) in D% oxygen (E L/min).
体重が A 〜 B g の雄 [/ 雌] のラットが，濃度 D% の酸素（E L/min）中の X 混合物（最初の吸入濃度は C%）により麻酔された．

> Spontaneously breathing male Sprague Dawley rats weighing 200–300 g were anesthetized with a mixture of isoflurane (initial inspired concentration 2%) in 100% oxygen (1 L/min). (64)
> 体重が 200 〜 300 g の自発的に呼吸している雄のスプラーグドーリーラットが，濃度 100% の酸素（1 L/min）中のイソフルラン混合物（最初の吸入濃度は 2%）により麻酔された．

0796 薬物実験における投与量について述べる.
◆In regards to X doses, rats [/monkeys] received A mg/kg (B injections of C mg/kg) to D mg/kg (E injections of F mg/kg) over G days.
X の投与量に関しては，ラット [/ サル] は，A mg/kg（C mg/kg を B 回注射）から

D mg/kg（F mg/kg を E 回注射）を，G 日間にわたって受けた.
> In regards to our cocaine doses, rats received 30 mg/kg (4 injections of 7.5 mg/kg) to 120 mg/kg (4 injections of 30 mg/kg) over 8 days. (49)
> コカイン投与量に関しては，ラットは，30 mg/kg（7.5 mg/kg を 4 回注射）から 120 mg/kg（30 mg/kg を 4 回注射）を，8 日間にわたって受けた.

0797 薬物の相互作用を分析したことを述べる.

◆ To determine whether X interacts with Y to modulate A, B, or C, we coadministered doses of both drugs that have been shown to alter behavior in the Z.

X が，A, B, C を調節するように Y と相互作用するかどうかを明らかにするために，Z において行動を変化させることが示されている投与量の 2 つの薬物を，同時投与した.

> Finally, to determine whether caffeine interacts with ethanol to modulate anxiety, locomotion, or learning, we coadministered doses of both drugs that have been shown to alter behavior in the PMDAT. (21)
> 最後に，カフェインが，不安，運動，学習を調節するようにエタノールと相互作用するかどうかを明らかにするために，PMDAT において行動を変化させることが示されている投与量の 2 つの薬物を，同時投与した.

（訳者注：PMDAT; plus-maze discriminative avoidance task, 十字型迷路弁別回避課題）

0798 ラットの脳に細胞を移植した後で，群に分けて迷路を用いた行動研究を行ったことを述べる.

◆ Behavioral studies were carried out following N months of transplantation using a[n] M-arm radial maze and X maze tasks in separate groups of rats.

移植の N か月後に，ラットが異なる群に分けられ，M 個のアームの放射状迷路課題と X の迷路課題を用いた行動研究が行われた.

> Behavioral studies were carried out following 2 months of transplantation using an eight-arm radial maze and Morris water maze tasks in separate groups of rats. (50)
> 移植の 2 か月後に，ラットが異なる群に分けられ，8 つのアームのある放射状迷路課題とモリス水中迷路課題を用いた行動研究が行われた.

5.19 データの欠損

0799 データの欠損を表す.

◆ Of the N participants who provided data, M were missing data indicating [/for] their X [or Y].

データを提供した N 名の参加者の中で，M 名は X [や Y] を示すデータが欠損していた.

5.20 統　　計

Of the 1,933 participants who provided data, 193 were missing data indicating their school and grade. (58)
データを提供した 1933 名の参加者の中で，193 名は学校と学年を示すデータが欠損していた.

0800　欠損データの範囲を表す.

◆For the X items, the percentage of cases classified as missing ranged from A% to B% across the sample.
X の項目については，欠損値に分類された事例の割合はサンプルを通して A% から B% の範囲であった.

For the construct items, the percentage of cases classified as missing ranged from 1% to 5% across the sample. (58)
構成項目については，欠損値に分類された事例の割合はサンプルを通して 1% から 5% の範囲であった.

5.20　統　　計

5.20.1　記述統計

0801　記述統計が行われたことを述べる.

◆Descriptive statistics were examined for X.
X について記述統計が分析された.

First, descriptive statistics were examined for all variables of interest in this study. (45)
最初に，本研究で興味の対象とされているすべての変数について記述統計が分析された.

5.20.2　t 検定

0802　群間差についての仮説と t 検定によるテストについて述べる.

◆The *a priori* hypothesis was that X would differ for treatment groups versus controls. Accordingly, this comparison was made with a *t*-test.
演繹的な仮説は，X が治療群と統制群により異なるだろうということであった. したがって，この比較が t 検定を用いて行われた.

The *a priori* hypothesis was that the Glu concentrations in blood samples would differ for treatment groups versus controls. Accordingly, this comparison was made with a *t*-test. (64)
演繹的な仮説は，血液サンプル中の Glu の濃度が治療群と統制群により異なるだろうということであった. したがって，この比較が t 検定を用いて行われた.

（訳者注：Glu, glutamic acid, グルタミン酸）

0803　標準化 t 検定の使用について述べる.

◆Standardized t tests (M = A, SD = B) were used to examine X.

5. 方法（Method）

標準化 t 検定（M = A, SD = B）が，X を分析するために用いられた．

> Standardized *t* tests (*M* = 50, *SD* = 10) were used to examine reading and math outcomes via a transformed measure of the IRT scale score. (23)
> IRT の尺度得点の変換測度により読書と算数の成績結果を分析するために，標準化 *t* 検定（*M* = 50, *SD* = 10）が用いられた．

（訳者注：IRT; item response theory, 項目反応理論）

0804 有意水準，t 検定のタイプについて述べる．

◆All tests of statistical significance reported in this study used a $p < N$ level of significance, and all *t* tests used a X test.

本研究における統計的な有意性の検定はすべて $p < N$ の有意水準を使用し，すべての *t* 検定は X 検定を使用した．

> All tests of statistical significance reported in this study used a $p < .05$ level of significance, and all *t* tests used a two-tailed test. (52)
> 本研究における統計的な有意性の検定はすべて $p < .05$ の有意水準を使用し，すべての *t* 検定は両側検定を使用した．

0805 有意水準について述べる．

◆Alpha was set at N for all analyses.

すべての分析で，有意水準は N に設定された．

> Alpha was set at .05 for all analyses. (34)
> すべての分析で，有意水準は .05 に設定された．

5.20.3 相関と回帰

0806 ピアソンの相関係数と分散分析の使用について述べる．

◆Bivariate associations among the variables were estimated using Pearson product-moment correlations and N-way ANOVAs.

2 変数間の結びつきが，ピアソンの積率相関係数と N 要因の分散分析により推定された．

> Next, bivariate associations among the variables were estimated using Pearson product-moment correlations and one-way ANOVAs. (45)
> 次に，2 変数間の結びつきがピアソンの積率相関係数と 1 要因の分散分析により推定された．

0807 相関分析を行ったことを述べる．

◆Correlations were calculated across participants between [the] X and Y.

X と Y の間の相関が，参加者を通して計算された．

> Correlations were calculated across participants between the physiological variable of heart rate and self-reported heart pounding. (1)

心拍数という生理学的変数と自己報告による心臓の鼓動の間の相関が，参加者を通して計算された．

0808　線形重回帰を行ったことを述べる．
◆A linear multiple regression was conducted to examine the associations of X with A and B.
AおよびBと，Xの間の結びつきを分析するために，線形重回帰が行われた．

> Finally, a linear multiple regression was conducted to examine the associations of fathers' pediatric parenting stress with mother-reported child behavior problems and fathers' psychological resources. (45)
> 最後に，母親が報告する子供の行動問題，および，父親の心理的資源と，父親の小児科での育児ストレスの間の結びつきを分析するために，線形重回帰が行われた．

0809　ロジスティック回帰分析を行ったことを述べる．
◆Logistic regression analyses were conducted to investigate the predictor variables that distinguish X from Y, controlling for Z.
Zを制御しながらXとYを区別する予測変数を調べるために，ロジスティック回帰分析が行われた．

> Logistic regression analyses were conducted to investigate the predictor variables that distinguish older adult self-excluders from those who were middle-aged or younger, controlling for demographic variables. (46)
> 人口統計学的な変数を制御しながら，高齢の自己排除者と，中年や若年の自己排除者を区別する予測変数を調査するために，ロジスティック回帰分析が行われた．

5.20.4　分散分析

0810　群間差を分散分析により分析したことを述べる．
◆Differences between groups were analyzed by N-way analysis of variance (ANOVA).
群間差が，N要因の分散分析（ANOVA）により分析された．

> Differences between groups were analyzed by one-way or two-way analysis of variance (ANOVA). (21)
> 群間差が，1要因あるいは2要因の分散分析（ANOVA）により分析された．

0811　混合デザインの分散分析を行ったことを述べる（過去形のほうがよい）．
◆This was [/is] confirmed by a[n] N × M mixed-design analysis of variance (ANOVA) on X, with Y condition (A, B) as a between-subjects factor and Z (C, D) as a within-subjects factor.
このことは，Y（AかBか）を被験者間要因とし，Z（CかDか）を被験者内要因とする，XについてのN×Mの混合型デザインの分散分析（ANOVA）により確認された [/ される]．

This is confirmed by a 2 × 2 mixed-design analysis of variance (ANOVA) on training accuracy, with test-item condition (familiar overlap, novel overlap) as a between-subjects factor and assessment round (end of training, after test) as a within-subjects factor.　(24)
このことは，テスト項目条件（熟知性が重複するか，新奇性が重複するか）を被験者間要因とし，評価の期間（訓練の終わりか，テスト後か）を被験者内要因とする，訓練の正確さについての2×2の混合型デザインの分散分析（ANOVA）により確認される．

0812　繰り返しのある分散分析の使用について述べる．

◆N-way repeated measures analysis of variance [/ANOVA] with X as a within subjects factor and Y as a between subjects factor were used to ZZZ.

ZZZを行うために，Xを被験体内要因とし，Yを被験体間要因とするN要因の繰り返しのある分散分析が用いられた．

> Two-way repeated measures ANOVA with days as within subjects factor and treatment as between subjects factor were used to assess behavioral performance on radial arm maze and water maze tasks.　(50)
> 放射状迷路と水迷路における行動成績を評価するために，日数を被験体内要因とし，治療を被験体間要因とする2要因の繰り返しのある分散分析が用いられた．

0813　テューキーの事後比較検定が用いられたことを述べる．

◆X was controlled for by Tukey's honestly significant difference (HSD) post hoc comparisons.

Xは，テューキーの事後比較（HSD）検定により制御された．

> Type I error rate was controlled for by Tukey's honestly significant difference (HSD) post hoc comparisons.　(49)
> 第一種の過誤は，テューキーの事後比較（HSD）検定により制御された．

0814　分散分析，t検定，カイ二乗検定の使用について述べる．

◆Tests of differences in X, Y, and Z were investigated using analysis of variance (ANOVA) or t-tests for continuous variables, and chi-square for categorical variables.

X, Y, Zの差の検定は，連続変数については分散分析（ANOVA）かt検定，カテゴリー変数についてはカイ二乗検定を用いて分析された．

> Tests of differences in demographic, clinical, and trial demand characteristics were investigated using analysis of variance (ANOVA) or t-tests for continuous variables, and chi-square for categorical variables.　(28)
> 人口統計学的，臨床的，試行による要求特性の差の検定は，連続変数については分散分析（ANOVA）かt検定，カテゴリー変数についてはカイ二乗検定を用いて分析された．

5.21 メタ分析

5.21.1 文献検索とデータの抽出

0815 メタ分析における電子検索の方法を述べる.

◆Using the search terms A and B combined sequentially with C, D, and E in the X electronic search engine, we searched for peer-reviewed papers reporting F.

電子検索エンジンであるXにおいて,AとBに,C, D, Eという用語を逐次的に組み合わせた検索語を用いて,Fを報告している査読論文を検索した.

> Using the search terms social phobia and social anxiety disorder combined sequentially with the generic names of the selective reuptake inhibitors citalopram, escitalopram, and sertraline in the PsycINFO electronic search engine, we searched for peer-reviewed papers reporting the results of randomized, placebo-controlled trials of selective serotonin reuptake inhibitors in social anxiety disorder. (26)
> 電子検索エンジンの PsycINFO において,社会恐怖と社会不安障害に,選択的再取り込み阻害薬の一般的名称である citalopram, escitalopram, sertraline という用語を逐次的に組み合わせた検索語を用いて,無作為化され,偽薬コントロールが行われている,社会不安障害における選択的セロトニン再取り込み阻害薬の治験の結果を報告している査読論文が検索された.

0816 メタ分析における文献検索の方法を述べる.

◆X and Y electronic databases were searched through N for A, B, and C trials of D involving E and F.

EとFを含むDの,A, B, Cである治験について,XとYの電子データベースがN年を通して検索された.

> PubMed and PsycINFO electronic databases were searched through 2004 for double-blind, placebo-controlled, randomized clinical trials of social anxiety disorder (social phobia) in adults involving the selective serotonin reuptake inhibitors citalopram and escitalopram. (27)
> 選択的セロトニン再取り込み阻害薬のシタロプラムとエスシタロプラムを含む大人の社会不安障害(社会恐怖)の,二重盲検法を用いており,偽薬コントロールが行われ,無作為化されている臨床治験について,PubMed と PsycINFO の電子データベースが 2004 年を通して検索された.

0817 メタ分析において特定のデータを抽出したことを述べる.

◆A, B, C, and D were extracted and recorded[,] and then verified independently by a second investigator.

A, B, C, D が抽出・記録され,第二の研究者により正当性が独立して確かめられた.

> Study design, subject number, drug and dose, trial length, rating instruments, and baseline and end point data including standard deviation and standard error were extracted and recorded and then verified independently by a second investigator. (27)

研究デザイン，被験者数，薬物と投与量，治験の長さ，評定道具，標準偏差と標準誤差を含むベースラインと終了時のデータが抽出・記録され，第二の研究者により正当性が独立して確かめられた．

0818 メタ分析の対象から除外する際の基準を表す．

◆Articles that reported A, B, or C were excluded from further analysis.

A, B, C についての研究は，以後の分析から除外された．

> Articles that reported the results of case studies, case series, or open-label trials were excluded from further analysis. (27)
> 症例研究，症例集積研究，非盲検の治験の結果は，以後の分析から除外された．

0819 メタ分析で用いられる公式について述べる．

◆The basic formula used for X is Y.

X のために用いられた公式は，Y である．

> The basic formula used for the standardized difference between means for the quantitative rating scales is (略). (26)
> 定量的評定尺度の平均間の標準化された差のために用いられた公式は，（略）である．

5.21.2 統計量の計算

0820 メタ分析における Q 統計量の計算を表す．

◆The Q statistic, a measure of homogeneity between studies (Author, Year), was computed for effect sizes for both binary (Θ log-odds ratios) and quantitative (d statistics) data.

研究間の等質性の測度である Q 統計量（著者，発表年）が，2 値データ（Θ オッズ比の対数）と量的データ（d 統計量）の両方の効果量について計算された．

> The Q statistic, a measure of homogeneity between studies (Whitehead, 2002), was computed for effect sizes for both binary (Θ log-odds ratios) and quantitative (d statistics) data. (27)
> 研究間の等質性の測度である Q 統計量（Whitehead, 2002）が，2 値データ（Θ オッズ比の対数）と量的データ（d 統計量）の両方の効果量について計算された．

0821 メタ分析における効果量の計算方法を表す．

◆Effect scores for X were calculated by computing the Hedges g.

X の効果量の得点が，ヘッジズの不偏推定値 g を計算することにより算出された．

> Effect scores for the remaining scales were calculated by first computing the Hedges g. (27)
> 残った尺度の効果量の得点が，最初にヘッジズの不偏推定値 g を計算することにより算出された．

0822 メタ分析における効果量の平均を表す．

◆To obtain overall mean effect sizes for each of the scales and to compare effect sizes between Xs, a mean *d* score was calculated according to the method outlined by Author (Year).

各尺度ごとの平均効果量を算出し，効果量をXの間で比較するために，著者（発表年）により概説されている方法に従って，*d*得点の平均が計算された．

> To obtain overall mean effect sizes for each of the scales and to compare effect sizes between drugs, a mean *d* score was calculated according to the method outlined by Whitehead (2002). (27)
> 各尺度ごとの平均効果量を算出し，効果量を薬物間で比較するために，Whitehead（2002）により概説されている方法に従って，*d*得点の平均が計算された．

0823 メタ分析における効果量の計算について述べる．

◆Effect sizes based upon *d* scores were computed for A, B, and C.

*d*得点に基づく効果量がA, B, Cについて計算された．

> Effect sizes based upon *d* scores were computed for the Liebowitz Social Anxiety Scale, Brief Social Phobia Scale, and Hamilton Depression Scale. (27)
> *d*得点に基づく効果量がリーボウィッツ社会不安尺度，簡易版社会恐怖尺度，ハミルトンうつ尺度について計算された．

0824 メタ分析の統計的手法について述べる．

◆The *g* score was then adjusted to obtain a *d* score.

その後，*g*得点を調整することにより，*d*得点が得られた．

> The *g* score was then adjusted to obtain a *d* score, which is an unbiased estimator of effect size (Θ). (27)
> その後，*g*得点を調整することにより，*d*得点が得られた．ここで，*d*得点とは効果量（Θ）の不偏推定量である．

5.22 統計ソフトウェア

0825 分析を行った統計ソフトウェアを述べる．

◆Analyses were conducted [/carried out] using X for Y, Version N.

分析は，Y用XのバージョンNを用いて行われた．

> Analyses were conducted using SPSS for Windows, Version 16. (46)
> 分析は，Windows用SPSSのバージョン16を用いて行われた．

0826 データ分析に用いた統計ソフトウェアを述べる．

◆Data were analyzed with X N for Y.

データはY用XのバージョンNを用いて分析された．

| Data were analyzed with SPSS 15.0 for Windows. (33)
| データは Windows 用の SPSS 15.0 を用いて分析された.

0827　複数の統計ソフトウェアのどれかを用いたことを述べる.

◆All analyses were conducted using X Version N or Y Version M.
すべての分析は X のバージョン N か Y のバージョン M を用いて行われた.

| All analyses were conducted using SPSS Version 16.01 or Mplus Version 5.2. (28)
| すべての分析は SPSS のバージョン 16.01 か MPlus のバージョン 5.2 を用いて行われた.

6
結果 (Results)

6.1 参加者
6.2 データの分析と結果の傾向
6.3 統計的解析
6.4 表への言及
6.5 図への言及
6.6 付録への言及

6.1 参 加 者

6.1.1 参加者の動向

0828 各群に最終的に割り当てられた参加者数を述べる．

◆Of the L participants, M were in the X group[,] while N were in the Y group.

L名の参加者の中で，M名はX群であり，N名はY群であった．

> Of the 13 participants, 8 were in the unsatisfied group, while 5 were in the satisfied group. (8)
> 13名の参加者の中で，8名は不満足群であり，5名は満足群であった．

0829 ある変数に従って2群を区別したことを述べる．

◆A[n] X factor that distinguished Y from Z participants was A.

Yの参加者をZの参加者と区別するX要因は，Aであった．

> A second client factor that distinguished satisfied from unsatisfied participants was a personal history of oppression or alienation from members of one's own group. (8)
> 満足群の参加者を不満足群の参加者と区別するクライエント側の第二の要因は，自分のグループの構成員から抑圧されたり疎外されたという個人的な履歴であった．

0830 参加者の中にある感情を示した人がいたことを，人数とともに述べる．

◆Out of the N participants, M expressed X feelings about Y.

N名の参加者の中で，M名はYについてXの感情を表現した．

> Out of the 15 participants, 12 expressed negative feelings about being homeless. (41)
> 15名の参加者の中で，12名はホームレスであることについて否定的な感情を表現した．

220 6．結果（Results）

0831 参加者が共通して訴えた主訴の内容を，人数とともに述べる．
◆The most common presenting complaints [/chief complaints /presenting symptoms /presenting problems] (not mutually exclusive) were "X" (L), "Y" (M), and "Z" (N).
最も共通していた主訴（相互に排他的ではない）は，「X」（L 名），「Y」（M 名），「Z」（N 名）であった．

> The most common presenting problems (not mutually exclusive) were "loneliness/isolating myself from other people" (9), "mood swings or depression" (9), "career/work-related stress" (9), "family conflicts" (8), and "feeling anxious for either known or unknown reasons" (5). (8)
> 最も共通していた主訴（相互に排他的ではない）は，「孤独，あるいは，自分が他の人々から隔離されている」（9 名），「気分が変わりやすいあるいはうつ」（9 名），「キャリア，あるいは，仕事に関連するストレス」（9 名），「家族の葛藤」（8 名），「わかっている，あるいは，わかっていない原因により不安を感じること」（5 名）であった．

6.1.2 参加者の割合

0832 ある反応を示した参加者の割合を述べる．
◆The percentage of X who YYY was as follows: A (L%), B (M%), and C (N%).
YYY であった X の割合は，A で L%，B で M%，C で N% であった．

> The percentage of females who overestimated males' actual preference mean score for each item was as follows: drinks per occasion (70.8%), maximum drinks (73.5%), friends (69.7%), sexual partners (65.5%), and dating partners (43.1%). (39)
> 各項目について男性の実際の選好の平均得点を過大評価した女性の割合は，機会当たりの飲酒量で 70.8%，最大飲酒量で 73.5%，友人で 69.7%，性的パートナーで 65.5%，デートのパートナーで 43.1% であった．

0833 ある反応を示した参加者のおおよその割合を述べる．
◆Overall, [approximately] half [/a majority /a third] of the participants (N out of M) XXX.
全体として，参加者の [約] 半分 [/ 大多数 /3 分の 1]（M 名中の N 名）が，XXX であった．

> Overall, half of the participants (8 out of 16) described their therapists as attentive, caring, and sensitive. (8)
> 全体として，参加者の半分（16 名中 8 名）が，彼らを担当しているセラピストは傾聴的で，思いやりがあり，感受性が高いと述べた．

0834 参加者が印をつけた項目の数，および，ある項目に印をつけた参加者の割合を述べる．
◆Xs endorsed [/agreed with /checked off] an average of N Ys, with A% endorsing [/agreeing with /checking off] B.
X は平均して N 個の Y に印をつけ [/ 同意し / チェックマークをつけ]，A% は B に印をつけた [/ 同意した / チェックマークをつけた]．

Younger adults endorsed an average of four activities, with 59.4% (*n* = 291) endorsing blackjack, along with slots (65.9%, *n* = 323), video poker (33.9%, *n* = 163), and lottery tickets (46.7%, *n* = 229). (46)
若い成人は平均して4つの遊びに印をつけ，59.4%（*n* = 291）はブラックジャックに印をつけ，その他に，スロット（65.9%, *n* = 323），ビデオ・ポーカー（33.9%, *n* = 163），および，宝くじ券（46.7%, *n* = 229）に印をつけた．

0835 参加者がもっていた疾患を，割合とともに述べる．
◆A% of the participants had X, B% had Y, and C% had Z.
参加者のA%はXを，B%はYを，そして，C%はZをもっていた．

At 6 months, 16.3% of the participants had major depression, 24.2% had PTSD, and 20.0% had an assault-related specific phobia. (36)
6か月の時点で，参加者の16.3%は大うつを，24.2%はPTSDを，そして，20.0%は暴行関連の特定恐怖症をもっていた．

（訳者注：PTSD; posttraumatic stress disorder, 心的外傷後ストレス障害）

0836 あることを報告したのは参加者の一部であったことを述べる．
◆Only N% of the sample reported X (*n* = A).
Xを報告したのはサンプルのN%（*n* = A）にすぎなかった．

Only 10.7% of the sample reported any illness (*n* = 61). (38)
なんらかの疾患を報告したのはサンプルの10.7%（*n* = 61）にすぎなかった．

6.2 データの分析と結果の傾向

6.2.1 分析の方針

0837 ある操作がある指標に及ぼす効果を分析したことを述べる．
◆We examined whether the X manipulations affected Y responding.
我々はX操作がY反応に影響を及ぼすかどうかを調べた．

We examined whether the stress manipulations affected subsequent aggressive responding. (60)
我々は，ストレス操作が続いて起こる攻撃反応に影響を及ぼすかどうかを調べた．

0838 ある指標を探索的に分析したことを述べる．
◆We conducted [/planned to conduct] exploratory analyses of X.
我々はXを探索的に分析した [/ 分析することを計画していた]．

As mentioned in the Introduction, we also planned to conduct exploratory analyses of the mean levels of the political parties on each of the six scales. (9)
序文で述べたように，我々は，6つの各尺度における政党の平均値についての探索的な分析を行うことも計画していた．

0839　先に述べた方法で分析したことを述べる.
◆Xs were analyzed as previously described.
　Xは，先に説明した方法で分析された.
> The data were analyzed as previously described. (49)
> データは，先に説明した方法で分析された.

6.2.2　計算方法
0840　時間当たりの反応数を計算したことを述べる.
◆The number of responses per minute [/second /hour] was calculated for the time during which YYY.
　YYYであった時間について，1分間 [/1秒間 /1時間] 当たりの反応数が計算された.
> The number of responses per minute was calculated for the time during which the children had opportunity to respond to the butterfly icons. (37)
> 子供が蝶のアイコンに反応する機会があった時間について，1分間当たりの反応数が計算された.

0841　ある得点を平均することにより，全体的な得点を計算したことを述べる.
◆An overall X score was computed by averaging Y across Zs.
　全体的なX得点は，Zを通じてYを平均することにより計算された.
> An overall accuracy score was computed by averaging the number of correct responses across all test trials. (57)
> 全体的な正確性得点は，全テスト試行の正反応数を平均することにより計算された.

0842　総反応の平均点を算出したことを，その意味とともに述べる.
◆The total responses for each X were averaged; higher mean scores indicated Y [/YYY].
　各Xに対する総反応が平均された. その平均点が高いほど，Yを [/YYYということを] 意味していた.
> The total responses for each living grandparent were averaged; higher mean scores indicated a closer grandchild–grandparent relationship. (2)
> 生存している各祖父母に対する総反応が平均された. その平均点が高いほど，祖父母と孫の関係がより親密であることを示していた.

6.2.3　外れ値
0843　外れ値を分析から除外したことを述べる.
◆Xs longer than [/greater than /greater than or equal to /less than /less than or equal to] N were considered outliers and were excluded from the analyses.

Nより長い [/ を超える / 以上の / 未満の / 以下の] X は外れ値とされ，分析から除外された．

> Response times longer than 2 s were considered outliers and were excluded from the analyses. (14)
> 2秒間より長い反応時間は外れ値とされ，分析から除外された．

6.2.4 データの分割

0844 データを項目グループに分割したことを述べる．

◆ The data were broken down into X items (A), Y items (B), and Z items (C).
データは，X項目（A），Y項目（B），Z項目（C）に分割された．

> The recall data were broken down into primacy items (recall of words in serial position 1–4), middle items (serial position 5–8), and recency items (serial position 9–12). (7)
> 想起データは，初頭項目（系列位置が1～4番目の単語の想起），中央項目（系列位置が5～8），親近項目（系列位置が9～12）に分割された．

0845 現象学的研究において，ある概念を下位概念に分割したことを述べる．

◆ X was conceptualized as composed of N subcategories: (a) AAA, (b) BBB, and (c) CCC.
Xとは，N個の下位カテゴリーからなると概念化された．すなわち，(a) AAA，(b) BBB，(c) CCC，という下位カテゴリーである．

> Active style was conceptualized as composed of three subcategories, all of which were more common in satisfied participants: (a) offering concrete advice, suggestions, and skill development, (b) asking thought-provoking questions and challenging the client's thinking, and (c) providing psychoeducation. (8)
> 能動的な様式は，満足している参加者の回答により共通して見られるものであり，3つの下位カテゴリーからなると概念化された．すなわち，(a) 具体的なアドバイス，示唆，および，技能の開発を提案する，(b) 思考を促進する質問を行いクライエントの考えに異議を唱える，(c) 心理教育を行う，という下位カテゴリーであった．

（訳者注：能動的な様式（active style）とは，セラピストの能動的な治療方法のことである）

6.2.5 平均と標準偏差

0846 平均と標準偏差を述べる．

◆ The mean level of X was A (*SD* = B), and the mean level of Y was C (*SD* = D).
Xの平均レベルはA（*SD* = B）であり，Yの平均レベルはC（*SD* = D）であった．

> The mean level of religiousness was 2.01 (*SD* = 1.03), and the mean level of spirituality was 2.21 (*SD* = 1.12). (61)
> 宗教性の平均レベルは2.01（*SD* = 1.03）であり，スピリチュアリティの平均レベルは2.21（*SD* = 1.12）であった．

224　　　　　　　　　　　　6.　結果（Results）

0847　全群を通じた平均と標準偏差を述べる．
◆ Across the groups, children X-ed a mean number of N Ys (*SD* = M).

全群を通じて，子供は平均 N 個の Y（*SD* = M）を X した．

> Across the groups, children added a mean number of 0.30 strategies (*SD* = 0.60) to their repertoires during the manipulation. (5)
> 全群を通じて，子供は，操作中に平均 0.3 個の方略（*SD* = 0.60）をレパートリーに追加した．

0848　試行を通じた平均と標準偏差について述べる．
◆ On average, participants X-ed *M* = A (*SD* = B) Y across the N trials (C%).

平均すると，参加者は N 試行を通して *M* = A（*SD* = B）個の Y を X した（C%）．

> On average, participants retrieved *M* = 7.63 (*SD* = 2.51) specific memories across the 12 trials (64%). (36)
> 平均すると，参加者は 12 試行を通して *M* = 7.63（*SD* = 2.51）個の特定の記憶を想起した（64%）．

6.2.6　結果の傾向

0849　正選択試行や誤反応試行の割合を述べる．
◆ Overall, X made correct choices [/errors] on L out of M (N%) Y trials.

全体で，X は，M 回の Y 試行の中の L 回（N%）で正選択 [/ 誤反応] を示した．

> Overall, Mickey made errors on 28 out of 105 (27%) familiar trials with black cups and on 23 out of 60 (38%) transfer trials involving the novel yellow cubes. (34)
> 全体で，ミッキーは黒色カップを用いた 105 回の熟知試行の中の 28 回（27%），および，新奇な黄色立方体を含む 60 回の転移試行の中の 23 回（38%）で誤反応を示した．
>
> （訳者注：ミッキーとは，被験体の名前である）

0850　差の程度と意味を述べる．
◆ The magnitude of the difference between Xs [/the X differential] was Y, indicating that ZZZ.

X の差の強度は Y であった．このことは，ZZZ ということを示している．

> The magnitude of the score differential was smaller, indicating that at least some of the differences may have been attributable to school-level factors. (23)
> 得点差の強度はより小さかった．このことは，それらの差の少なくともある部分は学校のレベルという要因に帰せられうるものであったかもしれないことを示している．
>
> （訳者注：score differential は少し大げさな表現であり， the difference between scores のほうがよい）

0851　被験者の回答例を列挙する．
◆ Examples included XXX, YYY, or ZZZ.

例としては，XXX, YYY, ZZZ などがあった．

Examples included coming to sessions late or canceling sessions altogether, answering the phone or doing paperwork during the session, or violating confidentiality. (8)
回答例としては，セッションに遅れたり完全にキャンセルする，セッション中に電話に出たり書類事務をしたりする，あるいは，秘密を守らない，などがあった．

0852　2つの変数間に密接な対応関係があったことを述べる．

◆There was a close correspondence between X and Y.

　XとYの間には，密接な対応関係があった．

> Hence, there was a close correspondence between the time course of drug uptake in the brain and drug-induced increases in extracellular dopamine. (30)
> それゆえ，脳内における薬物取り込みの時間経過と，薬物により誘発される細胞外ドーパミンの増加の間には，密接な対応関係があった．

0853　参加者が一方の反応をより多く行うことにより，ある効果を示したことを述べる．

◆The children [/participants] showed a[n] X effect by performing Y more than Z.

　子供 [/ 参加者] は，ZよりもYをより多く行うことにより，X効果を示した．

> As Figure 3 and Table 3 illustrate, the children showed a devaluation effect in the extinction test by performing the response trained with the valued outcome relatively more than those trained with the devalued outcome. (37)
> 図3と表3に示したように，子供は，消去テストにおいて，価値が低下した結果で訓練された反応よりも価値ある結果で訓練された反応を相対的により多く行うことにより，価値低下効果を示した．

0854　ある操作を省略したことにより反応が消去したことを述べる．

◆In the X condition, omission of the Y produced extinction of Z.

　X条件において，Yが省略されるとZが消去した．

> In the extinction condition, omission of the video outcome on test produced rapid extinction of responding, and some children failed to respond at all in the second minute of the extinction test. (37)
> 消去条件では，テストにおいてビデオという反応結果の呈示が省略されると反応は急速に消去し，なかには消去テストの2分目においてまったく反応しなくなった子供もいた．

0855　ある操作によりある時間が増加したことを述べる．

◆X resulted in more time spent in Y.

　Xの結果，Yにおける滞在時間が増加した．

> For control rats (n = 12), conditioning with 7.5 mg/kg cocaine (Figure 2A, upper left graph) resulted in more time spent in the cocaine-paired compartment on all 3 test days. (49)
> 統制群のラット（n = 12）では，7.5 mg/kgのコカインを用いた条件づけの結果（図2A，上段左の図），3日間のテスト日のすべてにおいて，コカインと対にされたコンパートメントで費やされた時間が増加した．

6. 結果 (Results)

0856　薬物の投与が実験段階により異なる効果をもたらしたことを述べる.
◆ X administered at training had no effect on Y at training but altered Z assessed at testing.
訓練時に投与された X は，訓練時の Y には影響を及ぼさなかったが，テスト時に評価された Z を変化させた.

> Caffeine administered at training had no effect on learning-related behavior at training but altered learning assessed at testing. (21)
> 訓練時に投与されたカフェインは，訓練時の学習に関係する行動には影響を及ぼさなかったが，テスト時に評価された学習を変化させた.

0857　毒素の注入により脳の損傷に成功したことを述べる.
◆ X was lesioned completely (see Figures N and M) following Y infusion.
X が，Y 注入後に完全に損傷された（図 N と M を参照）.

> Ventral subiculum was lesioned completely (see Figures 1B and 1C, and 2A and 2B) following ibotenic acid infusion. (50)
> 腹側鉤状回が，イボテン酸注入後に完全に損傷された（図 1B, 1C, 2A, 2B を参照）.

6.2.7　操作チェック

0858　操作チェックを行ったことを，目的とともに述べる.
◆ To assess the effectiveness of the X manipulation, we performed a Y analysis on the item that assessed how ZZZ.
X の操作の有効性を評価するために，どれくらい ZZZ かを評価する項目について，Y 分析を行った.

> To assess the effectiveness of the self-esteem manipulation, we performed a 2 (personality feedback) × 2 (mortality salience) analysis of variance (ANOVA) on the item that assessed how good the personality assessment made participants feel about themselves. (25)
> 自尊心の操作の有効性を評価するために，その性格評価により参加者が自分にどれくらい自信がもてるようになったかを評価する項目について，2（性格のフィードバック）× 2（死の顕現性）の分散分析（ANOVA）を行った.

0859　操作チェックの結果，操作の有効性が確認されたことを述べる.
◆ The results confirm[ed] that the X manipulation was effective.
これらの結果は，X の操作が有効であったことを確認する [/ した].

> These results confirm that the perceptual load manipulation was effective. (43)
> これらの結果は，知覚的負荷の操作が有効であったことを確認する.

6.3 統計的解析

6.3.1 カイ二乗検定

0860 カイ二乗検定と分散分析を用いて差を分析したことを述べる。

◆Using chi-square tests, we examined whether there were significant differences between the X participants and the Y participants.
カイ二乗検定を用いて，XとYの参加者間に有意差があるかどうかを分析した．

> Using chi-square and ANOVA tests, we first examined whether there were significant differences between the 125 participants excluded and 569 participants included in the current analyses. (38)
> カイ二乗検定と分散分析を用いて，まず，現行の分析から除外された125名の参加者と現行の分析に含まれた569名の参加者の間に有意差があるかどうかを分析した．

0861 カイ二乗分析により有意差が見出されたことを述べる．

◆Chi-square analyses on X revealed Y differences for N items: 'A,' Statistics, 'B,' Statistics, and 'C,' Statistics.
Xについてのカイ二乗分析は，N個の項目について，Yによる差を見出した．それらは，「A」[統計量]，「B」[統計量]，「C」[統計量]の項目であった．

> Chi-square analyses on each of the 24 items revealed age differences for only three items: 'participating in homeroom activities,' $\chi^2(1, N = 84) = 8.77, p < .001$; 'preparing for entrance examinations,' $\chi^2(1, N = 84) = 19.01, p < .001$; and 'helping a peer weaker in sports,' $\chi^2(1, N = 84) = 19.01, p < .001$. (54)
> 24個の各項目についてのカイ二乗分析は，3つの項目についてのみ，年齢差を見出した．それは，「ホームルーム活動への参加」，$\chi^2(1, N = 84) = 8.77, p < .001$，「入試への準備」，$\chi^2(1, N = 84) = 19.01, p < .001$，「スポーツで弱い仲間を助ける」，$\chi^2(1, N = 84) = 19.01, p < .001$，の項目であった．

0862 最尤カイ二乗分析により，2つの指標の間に有意差が見出されたことを述べる．

◆A maximum likelihood chi-square analysis on the distribution of X and Y across Z groups found a significant difference between the A's B and that of C, Statistics.
Z群を通じたXとYの分布に関する最尤カイ二乗分析は，AのBとCのBとの間に有意差を見出した[統計量]．

> A maximum likelihood chi-square analysis on the distribution of persistence and revision responses across strategy groups found a significant difference between the feature-listing rule producers' response pattern and that of their yoked partners, $G^2(1) = 4.25, p < .05$. (24)
> 全方略群を通じた忍耐力と修正反応の分布に関する最尤カイ二乗分析は，特徴リスト規則の生成者の反応パターンと，連動統制群の相手の反応パターンとの間に，有意差を見出した[$G^2(1) = 4.25, p < .05$]．

> **0863**　カイ二乗検定により，有意な条件差が見られたことを，統計量とともに述べる．

◆[The frequency of] X was significantly lower in the Y condition than in the Z condition, Statistics.

X [の頻度] は，Z 条件よりも，Y 条件において，有意に低かった [統計量]．

> The frequency of chance accounts was significantly lower in the prolonged suffering condition than in the ended suffering condition, $\chi^2(1, N = 80) = 5.48, p < .02$. (6)
> 偶然による説明の頻度は，終了した苦痛条件よりも，長引く苦痛条件において，有意に低かった [$\chi^2(1, N = 80) = 5.48, p < .02$]．

6.3.2　t 検定

> **0864**　t 検定により，2 つの指標の間に有意差が見られたことを述べる．

◆Independent samples t-tests revealed that X's Y were significantly higher than Z's Y, for A and B, ps < N.

独立サンプルについての t 検定は，A と B について，X の Y が Z の Y よりも有意に高いことを示した（すべての場合において $p < $ N）．

> Independent samples t-tests revealed that females' perceived reflective normative preferences were significantly higher than males' actual normative preferences, for drinks per occasion and maximum drinks in the past week, ps < .001. (39)
> 独立サンプルについての t 検定は，機会当たりの飲酒量と過去 1 週間の最大飲酒量について，男性が女性に対してもつと感じられる規範的選好が男性の実際の規範的選好よりも有意に高いことを示した（すべての場合において $p < .001$）．

> **0865**　対応のある t 検定により，平均値に有意差が見られなかったことを述べる．

◆A paired t-test found no significant difference[s] in the mean X between A and B, Statistics.

対応のある t 検定の結果，A と B の間で，X の平均に有意差はなかった [統計量]．

> A paired t-test found no significant differences in the mean number of overlap responses made between each yoked group and that of their rule-producing partners, $t(9) = 1.03, SE = 2.0, p > .30$. (24)
> 対応のある t 検定の結果，各連動統制群と規則を生成する相手群の間で，重複反応数の平均に有意差はなかった [$t(9) = 1.03, SE = 2.0, p > .30$]．

> **0866**　有意な条件差があったことを，t 検定の統計量とともに述べる．

◆X were significantly higher in the Y than in the Z condition, Statistics.

X は，Z 条件よりも Y 条件において有意に高かった [統計量]．

> They were significantly higher in the self than in the other condition, placebo: $t(19) = 4.20, p < .01$; OT: $t(19) = 3.32, p < .01$. (55)
> それらのデータは，他者条件よりも自己条件において有意に高く，偽薬群では，$t(19) = 4.20, p < .01$，OT 群では，$t(19) = 3.32, p < .01$ であった．

(訳者注：OT; oxytocin, オキシトシン)

0867 一連の t 検定の結果を述べる．

◆A series of *t*-tests indicated that XXX.

　一連の *t* 検定は，XXX ということを示した．

> A series of *t*-tests indicated that eighth graders felt most strongly that they had 'worked alone.' (54)
> 一連の *t* 検定は，8 年生が最も強く「1 人で作業している」と感じたことを示した．

6.3.3 その他の検定

0868 ノンパラメトリック法を用いたことを有意水準とともに述べる．

◆Nonparametric procedures and a standard alpha level of N were used for all statistical tests.

　ノンパラメトリック法と N という標準的な有意水準がすべての統計的検定で使用された．

> Nonparametric procedures and a standard alpha level of .05 were used for all statistical tests. (48)
> ノンパラメトリック法と .05 という標準的な有意水準がすべての統計的検定で使用された．

0869 二項検定により，得られた結果がチャンスレベルより高いことを述べる．

◆X was significantly above a chance level [/chance], according to binomial tests.

　二項検定によれば，X はチャンスレベルより有意に高かった．

> This performance was significantly above chance according to binomial tests. (34)
> 二項検定によれば，この成績はチャンスレベルより有意に高かった．

6.3.4 有意差の有無

0870 2 群間に有意差があったことを述べる．

◆X reported significantly higher levels of Y than [did] Z.

　X は，Z より，有意に高いレベルの Y を報告した．

> Displaced adolescents reported significantly higher levels of PTS than nondisplaced adolescents. (3)
> 退去させられた青年は，退去させられなかった青年より，有意に高いレベルの PTS を報告した．

(訳者注：PTS; posttraumatic stress, 心的外傷後ストレス)

0871 連動群の間に有意差がなかったことを述べる．

◆There was no reliable [/significant] difference between A and B in X.

　A 群と B 群で，X に信頼できる [/ 有意な] 差はなかった．

There was no reliable difference between the yoked groups in the accuracy of filling in the category-by-feature table at the end of training. (24)
訓練終了時に，2つの連動する群で，特徴によるカテゴリー表を埋める正確さに信頼できる差はなかった．

0872 群間に有意差がなかったことを述べる．
◆ There were no statistically significant group differences on any of the X measures (all ps > N).
どの X 測度についても，統計的に有意な群間差はなかった（すべての場合において p > N）．

There were no statistically significant group differences on any of the self-report measures (all ps > .07). (28)
どの自己申告測度についても，統計的に有意な群間差はなかった（すべての場合において p > .07）．

0873 いくつかの条件で，有意な効果が見られたことを述べる．
◆ Analyses of X confirmed that the N Y conditions elicited significant Z.
X の分析の結果は，N 個の Y 条件が有意な Z を誘発したことを確認した．

Analyses of lateral frontal sites confirmed that the two stress conditions elicited significant shifts in frontal brain activity. (60)
外側前頭部位の分析の結果は，2つのストレス条件が前頭脳活動において有意な変化を誘発したことを確認した．

0874 2つの条件で平均値に有意差がなかったことを表す．
◆ There were no significant differences in the mean levels of X [and Y] between A and B.
A と B で，X [と Y] の平均レベルに有意差はなかった．

There were no differences in the mean levels of the stressors and strains between T1 and T2. (52)
T1 と T2 で，ストレス因子と過労の平均レベルに差はなかった．
（訳者注：ここで，T1 と T2 は，調査の実施時期を表す略称である）

0875 変数の間に有意な関連はなかったことを述べる．
◆ No significant associations emerged between X and Y.
X と Y の間には有意な関連が出現しなかった．

No significant associations emerged between fathers' pediatric parenting stress and demographic characteristics (age, education, employment, income). (45)
父親の小児科での育児ストレスと人口統計学的な特徴（年齢，教育，雇用，収入）の間には，有意な関連が出現しなかった．

6.3 統計的解析

0876 予測されたとおり差が消失したことを述べる.

◆As predicted, there was no longer a difference between X and Y, Statistics.

予想どおり,もはやXとYで差はなかった[統計量].

> As predicted, with the 2-s delay of the search response there was no longer a difference in search RTs between the high (M = 337 ms) and the low (M = 335 ms) perceptual load conditions, $F < 1$. (43)
> 予想どおり,探索反応に2秒の遅延があると,高知覚的負荷条件(M = 337 ms)と低知覚的負荷条件(M = 335 ms)の間に,探索RTの差はもはやなかった($F < 1$).

(訳者注:RT; reaction time,反応時間)

0877 すべての効果が有意ではなかったことを述べる.

◆No effects were significant (all $ps > N$).

どの効果も有意ではなかった(すべての場合で $p > N$).

> No effects were significant (all $ps > .34$). (25)
> どの効果も有意ではなかった(すべての場合で $p > .34$).

0878 ある変数の効果が有意でないので,その変数に沿ってデータを畳んだことを述べる.

◆The analysis revealed no significant effects of the X variable, and therefore we collapsed the Y across this variable.

分析の結果,X変数の効果は有意ではなかったため,X変数値の異なるYを畳んで1つにまとめた.

> The analysis revealed no significant effects of the response variable, and therefore we collapsed the discrimination ratios across this variable. (37)
> 分析の結果,反応変数の効果は有意ではなかったため,反応変数値の異なる弁別比を畳んで1つにまとめた.

6.3.5 有意差傾向 ($p < .10$)

0879 有意差傾向とその理由を,統計量とともに述べる.

◆The A group had a marginally higher X compared to the B group, Statistics. This marginal finding may be due to Y.

A群は,B群と比べてXがより高いという有意差傾向があった[統計量].この有意差傾向の知見は,Yのためかもしれない.

> The aged low dose group had only a marginally higher learning index for working memory incorrect errors compared to the aged vehicle group, $t(16) = 1.79$; $p < .09$. This marginal finding may be due to a slight under-powering in the aged low dose animals. (31)
> 高齢の低投与量群は,高齢の賦形剤投与群と比べて,作業記憶の不正解の誤反応について,学習指標がより高いという有意差傾向のみがあった[$t(16) = 1.79$; $p < .09$].この有意差傾向の知見は,高齢の低投与量群のほうがわずかに体力が低かったためかもしれない.

0880 有意差傾向とその意味を，統計量とともに述べる．

◆A marginal [/marginally significant] main effect for X was found, Statistics, which indicated that YYY.

Xについて有意差に近い主効果が見出された [統計量]．このことは，YYY ということを示していた．

> An unexpected, marginally significant main effect for mortality salience (MS) also was found, $F(1,45) = 3.55$, $p < .07$, which indicated that MS participants felt worse about themselves ($M = 6.46$) than did control participants ($M = 7.16$). (25)
> 期待とは異なり，死の顕現性（MS）についても，有意差に近い主効果が見出された [$F(1,45) = 3.55, p < .07$]．このことは，MS の参加者（$M = 6.46$）が統制群の参加者（$M = 7.16$）と比べて，自分がより嫌になったことを示していた．

0881 主効果や交互作用に有意差傾向が見られたことを述べる．

◆A marginally significant main effect [/interaction /interaction term] was evident [/found] for X ($p = N$).

X ($p = N$) についての主効果 [/ 交互作用 / 交互作用項] に有意差傾向が明らかであった [/ 見られた]．

> A marginally significant interaction term was evident for behavioral inhibition ($p = .09$) and attention ($p = .09$). (38)
> 行動制止（$p = .09$）と注意（$p = .09$）について有意に近い交互作用項が明らかであった．

0882 2つの条件下で相関が見られたが，一方の相関は有意差傾向にとどまったことを述べる．

◆A positive relationship was observed between X and Y at A (Statistics) and B (Statistics), although the latter correlation was only a marginal [/a nonsignificant] trend.

X と Y の間には，A（統計量）と B（統計量）において，正の相関が見られた．ただし，後者の相関は有意差傾向にとどまった．

> A positive relationship was observed between BAS reward and frontal asymmetry at baseline ($\beta = .24$, $p = .02$) and post-condition assignment ($\beta = .20$, $p = .06$), although the latter correlation was a nonsignificant trend. (60)
> BAS の報酬と前頭の非対称性の間には，ベースライン（$\beta = .24, p = .02$）と条件後配置（$\beta = .20, p = .06$）において，正の相関が観察された．ただし，後者の相関は有意差傾向にとどまった．

（訳者注：BAS; behavioral approach system, 行動活性化システム）

6.3.6 分散分析の実施

0883 2要因の繰り返しのある分散分析を用いた分析を用いたことを述べる.

◆Two-way repeated measures analysis of variance, for the effects of X and Y, was conducted on the Z.

Zについて，XとYの効果を調べるための繰り返しのある2要因の分散分析が行われた.

> Two-way repeated measures analysis of variance, for the effects of age level and competitive/non-competitive trials, was conducted on the proportions of time during which cards were being stacked in each of three structures. (54)
> 3つの各構造物にカードが積まれていた時間の割合について，年齢水準と競争的/非競争的試行の効果を調べるための繰り返しのある2要因の分散分析が行われた.

0884 混合型の分散分析を用いたことを述べる.

◆Data from the X were analyzed with mixed-mode analyses of variance.

Xから得られたデータは，混合型の分散分析により分析された.

> Data from the cognitive test battery were analyzed with mixed-mode analyses of variance. (47)
> 認知テストバッテリーのデータは，混合型の分散分析により分析された.

0885 混合型の分散分析を用いたことを，各変数の意味とともに述べる.

◆The Xs were analyzed by a mixed analysis of variance (ANOVA), with the between-participants [/children] Y variable differentiating Z. The within-participant [/child] variables of A and B distinguished C during D and E and C on the different Fs, respectively.

Xが，Zを区別するY変数を参加者[/子供]間変数として，混合型の分散分析（ANOVA）により分析された．AとBという参加者[/子供]内変数が，DとE中のC，および，異なるFにおけるCをそれぞれ区別した.

> The ratios were analyzed by a mixed analysis of variance (ANOVA), with the between-children response variable differentiating performance when right or left responses were correct during acquisition. The within-child variables of phase and trial distinguished performance during acquisition and reversal and on the different trials of each phase, respectively. (37)
> その比は，獲得中に右か左の反応が正しかったときの成績を区別する反応変数を子供間変数として，混合型の分散分析（ANOVA）により分析された．段階と試行という子供内変数が，獲得と逆転における成績，および，各段階の異なる試行における成績を，それぞれ区別した.
>
> （訳者注：between-childrenはbetween-participantsに，within-childはwithin-participantに書き換えたほうがよい）

o886 3要因の混合型の分散分析を実施したことを述べる.

◆We performed a L (X) × M (Y) between-participants [/subjects] × N (Z) within-participants [/subjects] ANOVA on A.

我々は,Aについて,L(X:参加者 [/ 被験者] 間)× M(Y:参加者 [/ 被験者] 間)× N(Z:参加者 [/ 被験者] 内)の分散分析を行った.

> We performed a 2 (personality feedback) × 2 (MS) between-subjects × 2 (time of completing accessibility measures) within-subjects ANOVA on the accessibility of television-related words. (25)
> 我々は,テレビに関連する単語への接触性について,2(性格フィードバック:被験者間)× 2(MS:被験者間)× 2(接触性測度に記入した時期:被験者内)の分散分析を行った.

(訳者注:MS は,死の顕現性(mortality salience)の実験的操作を示す)

o887 3要因の混合型の分散分析を,目的とともに述べる.

◆To test whether XXX, we performed a[n] L × M × N ANOVA with A as a between-participants [/subjects] factor and B and C as within-participant [/subject] factors.

XXX かどうかを分析するために,Aを参加者 [/ 被験者] 間要因,BとCを参加者 [/ 被験者] 内要因として,L × M × N の分散分析を行った.

> To test whether the two types differed with respect to their behavioral unpleasantness ratings, we performed a 2 × 2 × 2 analysis of variance (ANOVA) with prosociality (prosocial/selfish) as a between-subjects factor and drug (OT/placebo) and target (self/other) as within-subject factors. (55)
> それら 2 つのタイプが行動の不快性の評定について異なるかどうかを分析するために,向社会性(向社会的 / 利己的)を被験者間要因,薬物(OT/ 偽薬)とターゲット(自己 / 他者)を被験者内要因として,2 × 2 × 2 の分散分析(ANOVA)を行った.

(訳者注:OT; oxytocin, オキシトシン)

o888 3要因の混合型の分散分析を用いて得点を分析したことを述べる.

◆These scores were analyzed by [/with] a L × M × N mixed ANOVA, with X as the within-participants [/subjects] factor and Y (A, B) and Z (C, D) as the between-participants [/subjects] factors.

これらの得点は,Xを参加者 [/ 被験者] 内要因とし,Y(A, B)とZ(C, D)を参加者 [/ 被験者] 間要因とする,L × M × N の混合型分散分析により分析された.

> These error scores were analyzed with a 4 × 2 × 2 mixed ANOVA, with transfer region as the within-participants factor and presentation type (ordered, random) and function shape (convex, concave) as the between-participants factors. (44)
> これらの誤反応得点は,転移領域を参加者内要因とし,呈示型(規則的,無作為)と関数の形(凸状,凹状)を参加者間要因とする,4 × 2 × 2 の混合型分散分析により分析された.

6.3 統計的解析

0889　分散分析において交互作用を分析したことを，目的とともに述べる．
◆We examined how X interacted with Y, to determine whether A would alter B.
AがBを変化させるかどうかを明らかにするために，XがYとどのように交互作用するかを調べた．

> We examined how the 40 mg/kg dose of caffeine interacted with the 1.4 g/kg dose of ethanol, to determine whether coadministration of an anxiogenic dose of caffeine and an anxiolytic dose of ethanol would alter learning. (21)
> 不安を惹起する投与量のカフェインと不安を低減する投与量のエタノールの同時投与が学習を変化させるかどうかを明らかにするために，40 mg/kg のカフェインの投与が 1.4 g/kg のエタノールの投与とどのように交互作用するかを調べた．

6.3.7　多変量分散分析の実施

0890　多変量分散分析を行ったことを，目的とともに述べる．
◆A multivariate analysis of variance (MANOVA) was conducted to assess the effects of X on A, B, C, and D.
XがA, B, C, Dに及ぼす効果を評価するために，多変量分散分析（MANOVA）が行われた．

> A multivariate analysis of variance (MANOVA) was conducted to assess the effects of displacement on resource loss, age, gender, and relocation distance. (3)
> 退去が，資源損失，年齢，性別，移住距離に及ぼす効果を評価するために，多変量分散分析（MANOVA）が行われた．

6.3.8　分散分析の主効果と交互作用

0891　反応数に群間差があり，1要因の分散分析から群の主効果が有意であったことを述べる．
◆The X Y-ed more Z than the other groups, and a one-way ANOVA showed the main effect of group [/group effect] on A, Statistics.
Xは他の群よりも多くのZをYした．1要因の分散分析の結果，群の要因がAに及ぼす主効果は有意であることが示された [統計量]．

> The younger adults recalled more words than the other groups, and a one-way ANOVA showed a main effect of group on recall performance, $F(3, 194) = 73.99$, $MSE = .952$, $\eta^p_2 = .53$, $p < .0001$. (7)
> 若年成人は他の群よりも多くの単語を想起した．1要因の分散分析の結果，群の要因が想起成績に及ぼす主効果は有意であることが示された [$F(3, 194) = 73.99$, $MSE = .952$, $\eta^p_2 = .53$, $p < .0001$]．

236　　　　　　　　　　6．結果（Results）

0892　　**1 要因の分散分析から，成績に有意な群間差が見られたことを述べる．**
◆One-way ANOVA revealed significant group differences in the X performance as assessed by Y, Statistics.
1 要因の分散分析は，Y により評価される X の成績 [統計量] において，有意な群間差があることを示した．
> One-way ANOVA revealed significant group differences in the task performance as assessed by percent of correct choices, $F(3, 31) = 104.20$, $p < .001$, and working memory errors, $F(3, 31) = 216$, $p < .001$. (50)
> 1 要因の分散分析は，正選択率により評価される課題成績 $[F(3, 31) = 104.20, p < .001]$，および，作業記憶の誤反応により評価される課題成績 $[F(3, 31) = 216, p < .001]$ において，有意な群間差があることを示した．

0893　　**1 要因の分散分析の結果，得点が条件の関数として有意に変化したことを述べる．**
◆X scores varied significantly as a function of Y, Statistics.
X 得点は，Y の関数として有意に変化した [統計量]．
> Total withdrawal scores after injection of 1.0 mg/kg sc naloxone varied significantly as a function of activity and feeding condition, $F(4, 39) = 15.53$, $p < .001$. (33)
> 1.0 mg/kg のナロキソンを皮下注射した後の総離脱症状得点は，活動性と給餌条件の関数として有意に変化した $[F(4, 39) = 15.53, p < .001]$．

> （訳者注：sc は subcutaneous injection（皮下注射）の略語．他に，im（intramuscular injection，筋肉内注射），iv（intravenous injection，静脈内注射）などがある）

0894　　**平均得点を列挙し，1 要因の分散分析からそれらの値に差が見られなかったことを述べる．**
◆Averaged X scores for the Y were L for A, M for B, and N for C. These differences were not significant according to ANOVA.
Y についての X 得点の平均は，A で L，B で M，C で N であった．これらの差は分散分析では有意ではなかった．
> Averaged d scores for the individual four drugs in Table 3 were 0.52 for paroxetine (five trials), 0.58 for fluvoxamine (three trials), 0.34 for sertraline (two trials), and 0.03 for fluoxetine (one trial). These differences were not significant according to ANOVA. (27)
> 表 3 に示されている 4 つの個々の薬物についての平均 d 得点は，パロキセチンで 0.52（5 つの治験），フルボキサミンで 0.58（3 つの治験），セルトラリンで 0.34（2 つの治験），フルオキセチンで 0.03（1 つの治験）であった．これらの差は分散分析によれば有意ではなかった．

0895　　**2 要因の分散分析の結果，主効果は有意であったが交互作用は有意ではなかったことを述べる．**
◆The ANOVA with the factors of X and Y conditions revealed main effects for X,

Statistics, and for Y, Statistics, but no interaction of X and Y, Statistics.
X条件とY条件を要因とする分散分析の結果，X [統計量] とY [統計量] の主効果が有意であることが示された．しかし，XとYの間の交互作用は有意ではなかった [統計量].

> The ANOVA with the factors of load and irrelevant-distractor conditions revealed main effects for load, $F(1,15) = 107.73$, $MSE = 12,927.06$, $p < .001$, $\eta^p_2 = .88$, and for the irrelevant distractor condition, $F(1,15) = 11.05$, $MSE = 3,336.68$, $p = .005$, $\eta^p_2 = .42$, but no interaction of load and irrelevant-distractor condition, $F < 1$. (14)
> 負荷と無関係妨害刺激条件を要因とする分散分析の結果，負荷 [$F(1,15) = 107.73$, $MSE = 12927.06$, $p < .001$, $\eta^p_2 = .88$] と無関係妨害刺激条件 [$F(1,15) = 11.05$, $MSE = 3336.68$, $p = .005$, $\eta^p_2 = .42$] の主効果が有意であることが示された．しかし，負荷と無関連妨害刺激条件の間の交互作用は有意ではなかった（$F < 1$）．

0896 2要因の分散分析の結果，主効果が有意であったことを述べる．

◆ Comparing Xs with N × M analyses of variance yielded significant differences for the Y versus Z manipulation, Statistics.
N × Mの分散分析によりXを比べると，YとZの操作についての有意差が見られた [統計量].

> Comparing the mean number of representations with 2 × 2 analyses of variance yielded significant differences only for the not-all appropriate versus all-appropriate representations manipulation, $F(1, 81) = 58.26$, $p < .01$, $\eta^2 = .54$. (59)
> 2 × 2の分散分析により平均表象数を比べると，必ずしもすべてが適切ではない操作と，すべてが適切である表象操作についてのみ有意差が見られた [$F(1, 81) = 58.26$, $p < .01$, $\eta^2 = .54$].

0897 分散分析の結果，主効果が有意ではなかったことを述べる．

◆ No X was obtained for measures of Y, Statistics, or Z, Statistics.
Y [統計量] やZ [統計量] について，Xは見られなかった．

> Also consistent with our hypotheses, based on an analysis of the ATC task, no experience-based sparing was obtained for measures of processing speed, $F(1, 68) = 0.01$, $\eta^2 = .00$, $p < .96$, or inductive reasoning, $F(1, 68) = 0.03$, $\eta^2 = .00$, $p < .87$. (47)
> 我々の仮説が予測するとおり，ATC課題の分析に基づくと，処理速度 [$F(1, 68) = 0.01$, $\eta^2 = .00$, $p < .96$] や演繹的推論 [$F(1, 68) = 0.03$, $\eta^2 = .00$, $p < .87$] について，経験に基づく節約は見られなかった．

（訳者注：ATC; air-traffic control, 航空管制）

0898 2要因の分散分析から，群間差が有意ではなかったことを述べる．

◆ A N (X) × M (Y) ANOVA found no significant group differences on Z (Statistics).
N（X）× M（Y）の分散分析は，Zについて，有意な群間差を見出さなかった（統計量）.

A 2 (group) × 4 (time) ANOVA found no significant group differences on loudness levels of background sounds across trials ($F = .01; p = .93$). (28)
2（群）× 4（時間）の分散分析は，試行を通じた背景音の大きさのレベルについて，有意な群間差を見出さなかった（$F = .01; p = .93$）．

0899　分散分析の結果，交互作用が有意であったことを述べる．
◆A significant interaction was observed between X and Y, with a smaller Y-related difference in Z between the A and B than between the C and D.
XとYの間に有意な交互作用が観察され，CとDの間よりも，AとBの間のほうが，YによるZの差は小さかった．

> On these two abilities, a significant interaction was observed between experience and age, with a smaller age-related difference in cognition between the young and older controllers than between the young and old noncontrollers. (47)
> これらの2つの能力について，経験と年齢の間に有意な交互作用が観察され，若年と高齢の非管制官群の間よりも，若年と高齢の管制官群の間のほうが，年齢による認知の差は小さかった．

0900　分散分析の結果，ある主効果は有意ではなかったが，別の主効果と交互作用が有意であったことを述べる．
◆A N-way ANOVA revealed no significant effect of X, a significant effect of Y, Statistics, as well as a significant interaction, Statistics.
N要因の分散分析によりXの有意な効果は見られなかったが，Yの有意な効果 [統計量]，および，有意な交互作用 [統計量] が見出された．

> At training, two-way ANOVA revealed no significant effect of drug treatment, a significant effect of arm, $F(1, 17) = 90.12, p < .001$, as well as a significant interaction, $F(2, 16) = 6.89, p < .01$. (21)
> 訓練では，2要因分散分析により薬物治療の有意な効果は見られなかったが，走路の有意な効果 [$F(1, 17) = 90.12, p < .001$]，および，有意な交互作用 [$F(2, 16) = 6.89, p < .01$] が見出された．

0901　分散分析の結果，主効果は有意ではなかったが，交互作用は有意であったことを示す．
◆There were no main effects of X or Y (Fs < A), but there was a significant interaction between these factors, Statistics.
XあるいはYの主効果は見られなかった（すべての場合で $F < A$）．しかし，これらの要因間の交互作用は有意であった [統計量]．

> There were no main effects of visual or auditory stimulus (Fs < 1), but there was a significant interaction between these factors, $F(1, 15) = 41.90, p < .001$. (10)
> 視覚あるいは聴覚刺激の主効果は見られなかった（すべての場合で $F < 1$）．しかし，これらの要因間の交互作用は有意であった [$F(1, 15) = 41.90, p < .001$]．

6.3 統計的解析

0902 仮説のとおり，分散分析により有意な交互作用が示されたことを述べる．
◆ Consistent with Hypothesis N, an analysis of variance of X showed an interaction between Y and Z.
仮説 N のとおり，X の分散分析は，Y と Z の間に交互作用があることを示した．

> Consistent with Hypothesis 1, an analysis of variance of shared task representations showed an interaction between reflection and all-appropriate versus not-all-appropriate representations. (59)
> 仮説1のとおり，共有課題表象についての分散分析は，内省と，「すべて適切な表象」および「すべてが適切とは限らない表象」の間に交互作用があることを示した．

0903 分散分析の結果，一部の交互作用のみが有意であったことを述べる．
◆ There was a significant interaction between X and Y, Statistics; no other interactions between factors were significant.
X と Y の間には有意な交互作用があった [統計量]．要因間の他の交互作用は有意ではなかった．

> There was a significant interaction between discrimination type and reinforcement, $F(1, 15) = 13.84, p < .003$; no other interactions between factors were significant. (10)
> 弁別のタイプと強化の間には有意な交互作用があった [$F(1, 15) = 13.84, p < .003$]．要因間の他の交互作用は有意ではなかった．

0904 分散分析の結果，交互作用はどれも有意ではなかったことを述べる．
◆ No interaction terms [/None of the interaction terms] were significant.
交互作用についての項は，どれも有意ではなかった．

> None of the interaction terms were significant. (55)
> 交互作用についての項は，どれも有意ではなかった．

6.3.9 多変量分散分析の主効果と交互作用

0905 ある目的で多変量分散分析を実施し，有意な主効果と交互作用が見出されたことを述べる．
◆ A multivariate analysis of variance (MANOVA) was conducted on A to determine whether X-based Y-related B would be observed. Significant main effects were obtained for X, Statistics, and Y, Statistics, as well as for an X × Y interaction, Statistics.
X 要因を基盤とし，Y 要因の変化に伴う B が見られるかどうかを明らかにするために，A について，多変量分散分析（MANOVA）が行われた．X 要因（統計量），Y 要因（統計量）の有意な主効果，および，X × Y の有意な交互作用（統計量）が見出された．

A multivariate analysis of variance (MANOVA) was conducted on measures from each of the four ATC tasks to determine whether experienced-based age-related sparing would be observed. Significant main effects were obtained for age, $F(1, 65) = 28.6$, $\eta^2 = 64$, $p < .01$, and experience, $F(1, 6) = 22.4$, $\eta^2 = .58$, $p < .01$, as well as for an Age × Experience interaction, $F(1, 68) = 7.6$, $\eta^2 = .32$, $p < .01$. (47)

経験を基盤とする，年齢による節約が観察されるかどうかを明らかにするために，4つの各ATC課題から得られた測度について，多変量分散分析（MANOVA）が行われた．有意な主効果が，年齢要因では $F(1, 65) = 28.6$, $\eta^2 = 64$, $p < .01$ で，経験要因では $F(1, 6) = 22.4$, $\eta^2 = .58$, $p < .01$ で見出され，さらに，年齢 × 経験の有意な交互作用が $F(1, 68) = 7.6$, $\eta^2 = .32$, $p < .01$ で見出された．

（訳者注：ATC; air-traffic control, 航空管制）

0906 ある変数について多変量分散分析を実施したが，有意な効果が見られなかったことを述べる．

◆A multivariate analysis of variance (MANOVA) performed on X revealed no significant effects (all ps > N).

Xについて多変量分散分析（MANOVA）が行われた結果，有意な効果は見出されなかった（すべての場合で p > N）．

> A multivariate analysis of variance (MANOVA) performed on the 11 subscales of the PANAS-X revealed no significant effects (all ps > .10). (25)
> PANAS-Xの11個の下位尺度について多変量分散分析（MANOVA）が行われた結果，有意な効果は見出されなかった（すべての場合で p > .10）．

（訳者注：PANAS-X; Positive and Negative Affect Scales—Expanded Form, ポジティブ感情・ネガティブ感情尺度—拡張版）

6.3.10 分散分析の下位検定

0907 事後分析の結果，有意な条件差が示されたことを述べる．

◆Post hoc analysis showed that X were significantly higher than Y, ps < A.

事後分析の結果，XはYよりも有意に高いことが示された（すべての場合で p < A）．

> Post hoc analysis showed that withdrawal scores of active food-restricted rats were significantly higher than the scores of rats in the three inactive conditions, ps < .001. (33)
> 事後分析の結果，食物を制限された活動的なラットの離脱症得点が，3つの非活動的条件のラットの離脱症得点よりも有意に高いことが示された（すべての場合で p < .001）．

0908 事後検定の結果，差がまったく見られなかったことを述べる．

◆Post hoc comparisons did not reveal any X differences.

事後比較の結果，Xの差はまったく見られなかった．

> However, post hoc comparisons did not reveal any group differences. (49)
> しかし，事後比較の結果，群間差はまったく見られなかった．

6.3 統計的解析

0909 テューキーの事後比較検定の結果，群間差が有意であったことを述べる．

◆ Post hoc Tukey's test showed that the X group had significantly lower Y compared with the Z group (Statistics).

テューキーの事後比較検定により，X 群は，Z 群と比べて Y が有意により低くなることを示した（統計量）．

> Post hoc Tukey's test showed that the VSL had significantly lower percent correct choices compared with the NC group (t = 18.73, p < .001). (50)
>
> テューキーの事後比較検定により，VSL 群の正選択率は NC 群と比べて有意に低いことを示した（t = 18.73, p < .001）．

(訳者注：VSL; ventral subicular lesioned, 腹側鉤状回損傷の：NC; normal control, 正常対照の)

0910 テューキーの事後比較検定の結果，差が有意でなかったことを述べる．

◆ Post hoc (Tukey) tests showed that X and Y did not differ from one another (p < N) in terms of Z.

テューキーの事後比較検定の結果，Z について，X と Y は互いに異ならないことが示された（p < N）．

> Post hoc (Tukey) tests showed that younger and older adults did not differ from one another (p < .81) in terms of the mean SI. (7)
>
> テューキーの事後比較検定の結果，平均 SI について，若年者と高齢者は互いに異ならないことが示された（p < .81）．

(訳者注：SI; selectivity index, 選択性指標)

0911 ボンフェローニの一対比較法による検定の結果，群間差が有意であったことを述べる．

◆ Pairwise comparisons using a Bonferroni correction indicated significant differences in X between N groups.

ボンフェローニの修正を用いた一対比較は，N 群の間で X に有意差があることを示した．

> Pairwise comparisons using a Bonferroni correction indicated significant differences in general cognitive capacity between each of the first four age groups. (57)
>
> ボンフェローニの修正を用いた一対比較は，最初の 4 つの各年齢群の間で，一般的認知能力に有意差があることを示した．

0912 シェフェ法による検定の結果，群間差が有意であったことを述べる．

◆ Post hoc Scheffé comparisons noted [/indicated] significant differences between [/among] N groups, Statistics.

事後比較のシェフェ法により，N 群のすべての間に有意差が見られた [統計量]．

> Similarly, post hoc Scheffé comparisons noted significant differences among all three groups, $F(2, 1598)$ = 316.76, p < .0001. (46)

同様に，事後比較のシェフェ法により，3つの群のすべての間に有意差が見られた [$F(2, 1598) = 316.76, p < .0001$]．

0913 単純主効果の分析により，有意な効果が確認されたことを述べる．
◆Analysis of simple main effects confirmed that XXX.
単純主効果の分析により，XXX ということが確認された．

> Analysis of simple main effects confirmed that AX elicited greater freezing than CX, $F(1, 15) = 11.13, p < .006$, and CY elicited greater freezing than AY, $F(1, 15) = 11.05, p < .006$. (10)
> 単純主効果の分析により，刺激 AX は刺激 CX と比べてより大きなフリージングを誘発し [$F(1, 15) = 11.13, p < .006$]，刺激 CY は刺激 AY と比べてより大きなフリージングを誘発した [$F(1, 15) = 11.05, p < .006$] ことが確認された．
>
> (訳者注：AX, CX, AY, CY は実験刺激の名称である)

6.3.11 因子分析（探索的因子分析）

0914 因子分析の基本的な手続きを述べ，さらに，因子負荷量の表に言及する．
◆We conducted a common factor analysis on the L X items, extracting M factors and applying an oblique rotation (i.e., Promax, with *kappa* set to P). The loadings of the items on these Q Promax-rotated factors are shown in Table N.
我々は，L 個の X の項目について共通因子分析を行い，M 個の因子を抽出し，斜交回転（すなわち，カッパを P に設定したプロマックス）を行った．これら Q 個のプロマックス回転因子に関する項目の負荷量を表 N に示す．

> We conducted a common factor analysis on the 22 political attitude issue items, extracting two factors and applying an oblique rotation (i.e., Promax, with *kappa* set to 4). The loadings of the items on these two Promax-rotated factors are shown in Table 3. (9)
> 我々は，22 の政治的態度問題の項目について共通因子分析を行い，2 つの因子を抽出し，斜交回転（すなわち，カッパを 4 に設定したプロマックス）を行った．これら 2 つのプロマックス回転因子に関する項目の負荷量を表 3 に示す．

0915 因子分析から導き出された因子を羅列し，それらの要因が先行研究で報告されていたことを述べる．
◆Factor analysis of X produced N dimensions: A, B, and C, all of which had been noted in previous research.
X の因子分析は，N 個の次元をもたらした．すなわち，A, B, C であった．これらの次元はすべて先行研究で報告されていたものであった．

> Factor analysis of these ratings produced three dimensions: dynamic communication, organization, and concern for individuals, all of which had been noted in previous research. (53)

これらの評定の因子分析は，3つの次元をもたらした．すなわち，動的コミュニケーション，組織化，個人への関心であった．これらの次元はすべて先行研究で報告されていたものであった．

0916 因子分析において，回転された因子の意味について述べる．

◆The first rotated factor was defined by X.

最初に回転された因子は，Xにより定義された．

> The first rotated factor was defined by support for policies such as criminal charges for marijuana possession, repealing same-sex marriage, closer alignment with U.S. foreign policy, and opposition to political policies such as easier access to abortion and publicly funded day care. (9)
> 最初に回転された因子は，マリファナ所持の起訴，同姓結婚の廃止，米国の外交政策とのより密接な提携などの政策に対する支持，妊娠中絶利用の容易化，公的費用による介護などの政策に対する反対により定義された．

0917 因子分析において，各因子による分散の説明率を述べる．

◆These factors accounted for A%, B%, and C% of variance in scores, respectively, collectively explaining D% of the total variance.

これらの各因子は，それぞれ得点の分散のA%, B%, C%を説明し，合わせて全分散のD%を説明した．

> These factors accounted for 37.1%, 10.8%, and 8.2% of the variance in scores, respectively, collectively explaining 56.7% of the total variance. (22)
> これらの各因子は，それぞれ得点の分散の37.1%, 10.8%, 8.2%を説明し，合わせて全分散の56.7%を説明した．

0918 因子分析において，ある因子が含まれなかったことを述べる．

◆X was not included as a factor in the analyses reported.

報告される分析に，Xは要因として含まれなかった．

> Gender was not included as a factor in the analyses reported. (60)
> 報告される分析に，性別は要因として含まれなかった．

0919 因子分析において，標準化された負荷量の範囲を述べる．

◆The standardized item loadings range [/ranged] from A to B.

項目の標準化された負荷量は，AからBの範囲である[/であった]．

> The standardized item loadings range from .56 to .93 (see Table 1). (58)
> 項目の標準化された負荷量は，.56から.93の範囲である（表1を参照）．

0920 因子分析において，交互作用の意味を述べる．

◆An interaction involving X and Y (Statistics) showed that effects of A on the B were limited to the C group.

XとYに交互作用があったことから（統計量），AのBに対する効果はCの群に限

定されることが示された.
> As shown in Figure 1, an interaction involving housing and parent violence (B = –.37, t = –2.28; p < .05) showed that the longitudinal effects of parental violence on the GSI were limited to the housed group. (22)
> 図1に示されているように,住居と親の暴力の間に交互作用があったことから(B = –.37, t = –2.28; p < .05),親の暴力の GSI に対する縦断的な効果は,住居がある群に限定されることが示された.

(訳者注:GSI; General Severity Index, 全般的重症度指標)

6.3.12　因子分析(確証的因子分析)

0921　あるソフトウェアを用いた確証的因子分析の実施を,目的とともに述べる.
◆To test the N models outlined in the Introduction, we conducted confirmatory factor analyses (CFA) using X software (Version M).
序文で概説された N 個のモデルを検証するために,我々は,X ソフトウェア(バージョン M)を使って,確証的因子分析を行った.
> To test the three models outlined in the Introduction, we conducted confirmatory factor analyses (CFA) using AMOS software (Version 7.0). (9)
> 序文で概説された3つのモデルを検証するために,我々は,AMOS ソフトウェア(バージョン 7.0)を使って,確証的因子分析を行った.

0922　確証的因子分析において,モデルへの適合度を述べる.
◆A confirmatory factor analysis indicated that the X model fit the data well (Statistics).
確証的因子分析の結果,X モデルはデータとよく一致することが示された(統計量).
> A confirmatory factor analysis indicated that the composite model fit the data well (comparative fit index = .95, root mean square error of approximation = .075). (57)
> 確証的因子分析の結果,複合モデルはデータとよく一致することが示された(比較適合度指標 CFI = .95, 近似誤差平均平方根 RMSEA = .075).

0923　確証的因子分析において,標準化得点と適合度指標を述べる.
◆For each of the N models, standardized scores of the observed variables were used. The fit of each model was assessed using the chi-square statistic, the comparative fit index (CFI), and the root mean square error of approximation (RMSEA).
N 個の各モデルについて,観察された変数の標準化得点が用いられた.各モデルへの適合が,カイ二乗統計,比較適合度指数(CFI),近似誤差平均平方根(RMSEA)を用いて評価された.
> For each of the three models, standardized scores of the observed variables were used. The fit of each model was assessed using the chi-square statistic, the comparative fit index (CFI), and the root mean square error of approximation (RMSEA). (9)

3つの各モデルについて，観察された変数の標準化得点が用いられた．各モデルへの適合が，カイ二乗統計，比較適合度指標（CFI），近似誤差平均平方根（RMSEA）を用いて評価された．

0924 確証的因子分析において，モデルの適合度を述べる．
◆ This X model provided a good [/poor] fit to the data.
このXモデルは，データへの当てはまりがよかった [/ 悪かった].
> This model provided a rather poor fit to the data (see Table 4). (9)
> このモデルは，データへの当てはまりがかなり悪かった（表4を参照）．

0925 確証的因子分析において，2つのモデルの適合度指標を比較する．
◆ Model X provided a better fit to the data compared to Model Y [/than did Model Y].
モデルXは，モデルYよりもデータへの当てはまりがよかった．
> Model B provided a better fit to the data than did Model A. (9)
> モデルBは，モデルAよりもデータへの当てはまりがよかった．

0926 確証的因子分析において，潜在因子間の相関を述べる．
◆ In this model, the correlation between the latent factors was N.
このモデルでは，潜在因子間の相関がNであった．
> In this model, the correlation between the latent factors was .46. (9)
> このモデルでは，潜在因子間の相関が.46であった．

6.3.13 構造方程式モデリング（共分散構造分析）

0927 構造方程式モデリングで，関係がある要因により媒介されていることを述べる．
◆ The relationships linking X[,] to Y[,] are [/were] partially mediated by Z.
XをYと結びつける関係は，Zにより部分的に媒介されている [/ いた].
> The relationships linking both perceptions of teachers as democratic and feelings of personal belonging, to ignoring, are partially mediated by students' beliefs that confiding in a teacher may result in more trouble. (58)
> 教師が民主的であるという認識，および，個人の所属意識の両方を，無視と結びつける関係は，教師に打ち明けるとより大きなトラブルがもたらされるかもしれない，という学生の信念によって部分的に媒介されている．

0928 構造方程式モデリングにおける直接効果，間接効果，総合効果について述べる．
◆ There was a significant negative indirect effect and non-significant direct and total effect of the X factors on Y.
X要因は，Yに対して，有意な負の間接効果，および，有意でない直接効果と総合効果を及ぼした．

There was a significant negative indirect effect and non-significant direct and total effect of each of the three school climate factors on the likelihood of telling a friend but not an adult a peer's plan to do something dangerous. (58)
学校風土の3つの各要因は，同輩が危険なことを計画していることを大人ではなく友人に言う確率に対して，有意な負の間接効果，および，有意でない直接効果と総合効果を及ぼした．

0929 構造方程式モデリングにおいて，変数と因子の間に一貫した関係があることを述べる.
◆There was a consistent relationship between X and Y.
XとYの間には一貫した関係が見られた．

There was also a consistent relationship between being female and three of the response strategies. (58)
女性であることと，3つの反応方略の間にも，一貫した関係が見られた．

0930 構造方程式モデリングにおける共変量について述べる.
◆X was used as a covariate. [/X served as a covariate.]
Xが共変量として用いられた．

Thus, gender was used as a covariate. (58)
それゆえ，性別が共変量として用いられた．

0931 構造方程式モデリングにおいて，潜在的構成概念を構成する項目について述べる.
◆These N items make up the latent X construct (α= A).
これらのN個の項目が，Xという潜在的構成概念を構成した（α = A）．

These four items make up the latent Ignore construct (α = .91). (58)
これらの4つの項目が無視という潜在的構成概念を構成した（α=.91）．

0932 構造方程式モデリングを行う複数のステップについて述べる.
◆The analysis consisted of 3 steps. First, a confirmatory factor analysis was performed to show that the measurement model provided [an] adequate fit for the data. Second, a structural equation model was estimated in which XXX. Third, a structural equation model was estimated that YYY.
分析は3段階から成り立っていた．第一に，測定モデルがデータに適切に一致することを示すために，確証的因子分析が行われた．第二に，XXXである構造方程式モデルが推定された．第三に，YYYである構造方程式モデルが推定された．

6.3 統計的解析

The analysis consisted of three steps. First, a confirmatory factor analysis was performed to show that our measurement model provided an adequate fit. Second, a structural equation model was estimated in which the response strategies were regressed on students' perceptions of their schools' authority structure, perceptions of school solidarity, personal sense of belonging at school, being in high school versus being in middle school, and the covariates. Third, a structural equation model was estimated that included students' beliefs about getting into trouble as a mediator of the relationship between students' perceptions of school climate and the response strategies. (58)

分析は3段階から成り立っていた．第一に，測定モデルが適切に一致することを示すために，確証的因子分析が行われた．第二に，反応方略が，学校の権威構造に対する生徒の認識，学校団結の認識，個人の所属意識，高校か中学か，および，共変量に回帰される構造方程式モデルが推定された．第三に，学生の学校風土の認識と反応方略の間の媒介要因として，トラブルに巻き込まれることについての学生の信念を含む構造方程式モデルが推定された．

0933 構造方程式モデリングの因果モデルについて述べる．

◆A[n] Nth structural equation model was estimated with X as a mediator. In this model, Ys were regressed on the Z.

N番目の構造方程式モデルは，Xを媒介変数として推定された．このモデルでは，YがZに回帰された．

> A second structural equation model was estimated with students' beliefs that they would get into trouble if they confided in a teacher included as a mediator. In this model, the four response strategies were regressed on the school climate factors and students' beliefs about getting into trouble. (58)
> 2番目の構造方程式モデルは，先生に打ち明けるとトラブルに巻き込まれるという学生の信念を媒介変数として推定された．このモデルでは，4つの反応方略が，学校風土という要因，および，トラブルに巻き込まれることについての学生の信念に回帰された．

0934 構造方程式モデリングを，適合度指標の全体的パターンに基づいて評価したことを述べる．

◆We assessed model fit by evaluating the overall pattern of [the] fit indices, including X, Y, and Z.

我々は，X, Y, Zを含む適合度指標の全体的パターンを評価することにより，モデル適合度を評価した．

> We assessed model fit by evaluating the overall pattern of the fit indices, including chi-square, comparative fit index (CFI), and root-mean-square error of approximation (RMSEA). (58)
> 我々は，カイ二乗値，比較適合度指標（CFI），近似誤差平均平方根（RMSEA）を含む適合度指標の全体的パターンを評価することにより，モデル適合度を評価した．

0935 構造方程式モデリングにおいて，適合度指標の値を述べる．

◆The fit indices of this model were χ^2(A, N = B) = C, p = D; TLI = E; CFI = F.

このモデルの適合度指標は χ^2(A, N = B) = C, p = D; TLI = E; CFI = F であった.
> The fit indices of this model were χ^2(5, N = 35) = 8.76, p = .12; TLI = .87; CFI = .89. (28)
> このモデルの適合度指標は χ^2(5, N = 35) = 8.76, p = .12; TLI = .87; CFI = .89 であった.

(訳者注：TLI; Tucker–Lewis index, タッカー・ルイス指標：CFI; comparative fit index, 比較適合度指標)

6.3.14 主成分分析

0936 主成分分析の実施を，因子，固有値，分散の説明率とともに述べる.

◆We subjected the N items to a principal[-]components factor analysis with X rotation. Examination of the scree plot revealed M factors, with eigenvalues of A and B, accounting for C% and D% of the variance.

我々は，これら N 個の項目について，X 回転の主成分分析を行った．スクリープロットを調べた結果，M 個の因子が明らかになり，それぞれの固有値は A と B で，分散の C% と D% を説明した．

> We subjected the five items to a principal-components factor analysis with Varimax rotation. Examination of the scree plot revealed two factors, with eigenvalues of 1.38 and 1.28, accounting for 27.7% and 25.5% of the variance. (25)
> 我々は，これら 5 つの項目について，バリマックス回転の主成分分析を行った．スクリープロットを調べた結果，2 つの要因が明らかになり，それぞれの固有値は 1.38 と 1.28 で，分散の 27.7% と 25.5% を説明した．

0937 主成分の抽出により同定された因子と固有値について述べる.

◆Principal components extraction identified N factors with eigenvalues greater than A.

主成分抽出により，固有値が A 以上である N 個の因子を同定した.

> Principal components extraction identified four factors with eigenvalues greater than 1.0. (22)
> 主成分抽出により，固有値が 1.0 以上である 4 つの因子を同定した．

6.3.15 相関と偏相関

0938 2 つの変数の間に有意な相関があったことを述べる.

◆X and Y were significantly correlated (r = A, p = B).

X と Y は，有意に相関した（r = A, p = B）.

> Immanent justice reasoning and deservingness were again significantly correlated (r = .33, p = .002). (6)
> 内在的正義推論と賞罰の当然性は，再び有意に相関した（r = .33, p = .002）.

0939 測度の得点と行動の間に有意な相関があったことを述べる.

◆Scores on the X were significantly correlated with Y behavior.

X の得点は，Y の行動と有意に相関した.

Scores on the sensation-seeking questionnaire were significantly correlated with sensation-seeking behavior. (57)
刺激欲求質問紙の得点は，刺激欲求行動と有意に相関した．

0940 正または負の有意な相関が見られたことを述べる．

◆A correlational analysis using X revealed a significant positive [/negative] relationship between Y and Z ($r = A$, $p < B$).

Xを用いた相関分析は，YとZの間に有意な正の[/負の]相関があることを示した（$r = A$, $p < B$）．

> A correlational analysis using all active rats revealed a significant positive relationship between total withdrawal scores and the number of wheel turns on the day preceding testing ($r = .453$, $p < .05$). (33)
> すべての活動的なラットを用いた相関分析は，総離脱症得点とテスト前日の輪まわし回数の間に，有意な正の相関があることを示した（$r = .453$, $p < .05$）．

0941 測度の得点がある指標と有意に相関したことを述べる．

◆Scores on the X measure were significantly and positively [/negatively] related to Y.

X測度の得点は，Yと，正の[/負の]有意な相関関係を示した．

> In our sample, scores on the impulsivity self-report measure were significantly and negatively related to the amount of time participants waited before making their first move on a Tower of London task. (57)
> 我々のサンプルにおいて，自己報告による衝動性測度の得点は，ロンドン塔課題において参加者が最初に駒を動かすまでの待ち時間との間に，有意な負の相関関係を示した．

0942 変数の間に強い相関関係があったことを述べる．

◆There was a strong relationship between X and Y.

XとYの間には強い関係があった．

> There was a strong relationship between therapist self-disclosure of personal history and treatment satisfaction. (8)
> セラピストの個人的な履歴の自己開示と治療の満足の間には，強い関係があった．

0943 相関の程度を述べる．

◆The N Xs were modestly [/moderately /strongly] intercorrelated (rs range from A to B; average $r = C$).

N個のXは，互いに弱い[/中程度の/強い]相関関係にあった（rはAからBの範囲で，rの平均はCであった）．

> The five indicators were modestly, but significantly, intercorrelated (rs range from .14 to .38; average $r = .26$). (57)
> 5つの指標は，互いに，弱い程度の有意な相関関係を示した（rは.14から.38の範囲で，rの平均は.26であった）．

0944 有意な相関を，意味とともに述べる．

◆ A significant correlation (Statistics) was obtained, strongly suggesting that XXX.

有意な相関（統計量）が得られたことから，XXX ということが強く示唆された．

> A significant correlation ($r^2 = 0.19$; $p = 0.023$) was obtained, strongly suggesting that the Pyr-induced decrease of blood Glu levels contributes to the NSS improvement after CHI. (64)
> 有意な相関（$r^2 = 0.19$; $p = 0.023$）が得られたことから，Pyr により誘発される血液中の Glu レベルの減少が CHI 後の NSS の改善に寄与していることが強く示唆された．
>
> （訳者注：Pyr; pyruvate, ピルビン酸：Glu; glutamic acid, グルタミン酸：NSS; neurological severity score, 神経学的重症度得点：CHI; closed head injury, 閉鎖性頭部外傷）

0945 有意な相関を，比較級を用いて述べる．

◆ Results indicated that X-er Ps were significantly associated with Y-er Qs (R^2 = A).

結果は，より X である P が，より Y である Q と有意に関連していることを示した（R^2 = A）．

> Results indicated that fewer years in school were significantly associated with higher psychological distress ($R^2 = .04$). (32)
> 結果は，学校にいる年数がより少ないことが，より強い心理的苦痛と有意に関連していることを示した（$R^2 = .04$）．

0946 有意な相関がなかったことを述べる．

◆ Correlational analyses revealed no significant relationship between X and Y.

相関分析の結果，X と Y の間に有意な相関は見出されなかった．

> Correlational analyses revealed no significant relationship between the number of wheel turns on the day preceding testing and total withdrawal scores. (33)
> 相関分析の結果，テスト前日の輪まわし回数と離脱症状得点の間に有意な相関は見出されなかった．

0947 偏相関を計算したが，有意ではなかったことを述べる．

◆ Partial correlations were computed to assess the relationship between X, Y, and Z after controlling for A, B, and C. The partial correlations were not significant.

A, B, C を制御した後の X, Y, Z の間の関係を評価するために，偏相関が計算された．偏相関は有意ではなかった．

> Partial correlations were computed to assess the relationship between displacement, GPD, and PTS after controlling for age, relocation time, and relocation distance. The partial correlations were not significant. (3)
> 年齢，移住時間，移住距離を制御した後の，退去と GPD と PTS の間の関係を評価するために，偏相関が計算された．それらの偏相関は有意ではなかった．
>
> （訳者注：GPD; general psychological distress, 一般的心理的苦痛：PTS; posttraumatic stress, 心的外傷後ストレス）

6.3.16 単回帰分析

0948 単回帰分析の結果と説明率について述べる。

◆A linear function fit the X data with an intercept of A and a slope of B, and accounted for C% of the variance.

Xのデータに対して，傾きがBでy切片がAの線形関数が当てはめられた．その関数は分散のC%を説明した．

> A linear function fit the SL data with an intercept of –6.3° and a slope of 1.03, and accounted for 99.3% of the variance. (42)
> SLのデータに傾きが1.03でy切片が–6.3°の線形関数が当てはめられた．その関数は分散の99.3%を説明した．

（訳者注：SL; spatial language, 空間的言語）

6.3.17 重回帰分析

0949 多変量回帰モデルにより説明される分散の割合を述べる．

◆The [full] model accounted for A% of the variance in X.

モデル[全体]でXの分散のA%を説明した．

> The full model accounted for 61% of the variance in fathers' pediatric parenting stress (see Table 3). (45)
> モデル全体で父親の小児科での育児ストレスの分散の61%を説明した（表3を参照）．

0950 許容度（トレランス統計量）のレベルについて述べる．

◆Tolerance was within acceptable limits for X variables in Y models.

許容度は，YのモデルにおけるXの変数について，受容できる限界内であった．

> Tolerance was within acceptable limits for all variables in all models. (22)
> 許容度は，すべてのモデルにおけるすべての変数について，受容できる限界内であった．

6.3.18 階層的重回帰分析

0951 階層的重回帰分析の実施を，目的とともに述べる．

◆Hierarchical regression analyses were conducted to examine the relationship between X and Y.

XとYの間の関係を調べるために，階層的重回帰分析が行われた．

> Hierarchical regression analyses were conducted to examine the relationship between independent variables and mental health outcomes. (32)
> 独立変数と精神保健についての結果変数の間の関係を調べるために，階層的重回帰分析が行われた．

6. 結果 (Results)

0952 階層的重回帰分析を用いて検定を行ったことを述べる.

◆ Hierarchical regression analyses were used to test X.

X を検定するために，階層的重回帰分析が用いられた.

> Hierarchical regression analyses were used to test these hypotheses (Baron & Kenny, 1986; Yzerbyt, Muller, & Judd, 2004). (59)
> これらの仮説 (Baron & Kenny, 1986; Yzerbyt, Muller, & Judd, 2004) を検証するために，階層的重回帰分析が用いられた.

0953 一連の階層的重回帰分析モデルの推定を，目的とともに述べる.

◆ A series of hierarchical multivariate regression models were estimated to predict each of N dependent variables: A, B, C,..., and Z.

A, B, C,..., Z という N 個の従属変数のそれぞれを予測するために，一連の階層的多変量重回帰モデルが推定された.

> A series of hierarchical multivariate regression models were estimated to predict each of the six dependent variables: emotional symptoms, conduct problems, hyperactivity, peer problems, prosocial behavior, and total difficulties. (2)
> 情動的症状，素行障害，過活動，同輩との問題，向社会的行動，全体的な困難さ，という 6 つの各従属変数を予測するために，一連の階層的多変量重回帰モデルが推定された.

0954 階層的多変量重回帰モデルの各ステップの操作について述べる.

◆ In the first step, A, B, and C were included. The second step added D. In the third step[,] E was added, and the fourth [/final] step included F.

第一段階では, A, B, C が含まれた. 第二段階では, D が追加された. 第三段階では, E が含まれ，第四 [/ 最終] 段階では F が含まれた.

> In the first step, the sociodemographic characteristics of the adolescents (age, gender, exclusion from school, receipt of free school meals, and ethnicity) were included. The second step added family structure. In the third step, grandparent involvement was added, and the fourth step included the terms that interact with grandparent involvement and family structure. (2)
> 第一段階では，青年の社会人口統計学的な特性（年齢，性別，学校からの阻害，無料給食の受領，民族性）が含まれた. 第二段階では，家族構造が追加された. 第三段階では，祖父母の関与が含まれ，第四段階では，祖母の関与および家族構造と交互作用する項が含まれた.

0955 階層的重回帰分析における各ステップで，ある変数が入力されたことを述べる.

◆ X was entered in the first step. In the second step, either Y or Z were entered.

第一段階で，X が入力された. 第二段階で Y または Z が入力された.

> Time in days from baseline was entered in the first step. In the second step, either the GSI score at baseline or the number of alcohol problems were entered. (22)

第一段階で，日数で表されたベースラインからの時間が入力された．第二段階で，ベースラインにおける GSI 得点，または，アルコール問題の数が入力された．
(訳者注：GSI; General Severity Index, 一般的重症度指標)

0956 階層的重回帰分析における各ステップで，調整変数や交互作用を投入したことを述べる．

◆ To test for moderation, we entered X in the first step of a hierarchical multiple regression analysis, followed by the moderator variable under investigation, followed by the interaction of X and the moderator.

調整について検定するために，我々は，X を階層的重回帰分析の第一ステップに入れ，次に調べようとする変数を調整変数として入れ，さらに，X と調整変数の交互作用を入れた．

> To test for moderation, we entered memory specificity in the first step of a hierarchical multiple regression analysis, followed by the moderator variable under investigation, followed by the interaction of memory specificity and the moderator. (36)
> 調整について検定するために，我々は，記憶特異性を階層的重回帰分析の第一ステップに入れ，次に調べようとする変数を調整変数として入れ，さらに，記憶特異性と調整変数の交互作用を入れた．

0957 階層的重回帰モデルの第一ステップで，ある変数が共変量とされたことを述べる．

◆ In Step 1, X, Y, and Z served as the covariates.

第一ステップでは，X, Y, Z が共変量とされた．

> In Step 1 of both models, race/ethnicity, Greek status, class standing, and perceived same sex norms served as the covariates. (39)
> 両モデルの第一ステップでは，人種/民族性，ギリシア人であるか否か，学年，同性がもっていると認識される規範が共変量とされた．

0958 階層的重回帰モデルの予測変数を述べる．

◆ The hierarchical regression model used the predictors of (a) X, (b) Y, and (c) Z.

階層的重回帰モデルは，(a) X, (b) Y, (c) Z という予測変数を使用した．

> The first hierarchical regression model used the predictors of (a) age, (b) resource loss, and (c) relocation time. (3)
> 最初の階層的重回帰モデルは，(a) 年齢，(b) 資源損失，(c) 移住時間という予測変数を使用した．

0959 階層的重回帰分析の結果を簡潔に述べる．

◆ In the regression models, the X step explained a statistically significant proportion of the variance in Y.

この回帰モデルにおいては，X のステップが Y における分散の統計的に有意な部

分を説明した.

In both regression models, the perceived reflective normative preferences step explained a statistically significant proportion of the variance in drinking. (39)

両方の回帰モデルにおいては，相手が自分に対してもつと感じられる規範的選好のステップが，飲酒における分散の統計的に有意な部分を説明した．

0960 階層的重回帰モデルがあることを有意に予測したことを述べる．

◆ The model was significantly predictive of X, with R^2 = A, $F(B, C)$ = D, SE = E, p < F.

このモデルは X を有意に予測し，R^2 = A, $F(B, C)$ = D, SE = E, p < F であった．

The model was significantly predictive of GPD, with R^2 = .296, $F(8, 549)$ = 28.92, SE = 4.17, p < .001. (3)

このモデルは GPD を有意に予測し，R^2 = .296, $F(8, 549)$ = 28.92, SE = 4.17, p < .001 であった．

（訳者注：GPD; general psychological distress, 一般的心理的苦痛）

0961 階層的重回帰分析の N 番目のモデルの予測を述べる．

◆ In the first [/second /third] model, X was predicted by Y.

1 [/2 /3] 番目のモデルにおいて，X は Y により予測された．

In the second model, alcohol use was predicted by membership in a Greek sorority. (39)

2 番目のモデルにおいて，アルコール使用はギリシア女子学生社交クラブのメンバーであることにより予測された．

0962 階層的重回帰モデルにおいて，モデルに寄与する変数を羅列する．

◆ X and Y both contributed significantly to the model in Step N.

X と Y の両方が，第 N ステップにおいて有意にモデルに寄与した．

Relocation time and resource loss both contributed significantly to the model in Step 1. (3)

移住時間と資源損失の両方が，第一ステップにおいて有意にモデルに寄与した．

0963 階層的重回帰分析において，変数間の関連と効果量について述べる．

◆ X was significantly associated with Y, which constituted a small [/medium /large] effect (φ^2 = A).

X は Y と有意に結びついており，その効果量は小さかった [/ 中程度であった / 大きかった] (φ^2 = A).

Financial stress was significantly associated with state anxiety, which constituted a small effect (φ^2 = .04). (32)

経済的なストレスは状態不安と有意に結びついており，その効果量は小さかった（φ^2 = .04）．

0964 階層的重回帰分析における調整変数について述べる．

◆ X moderated the effect of Y on Z, as indicated by a significant interaction.

有意な交互作用によって示されているように，X が，Y が Z に及ぼす効果を調整し

ていた．
> History of major depression prior to the assault moderated the effect of memory specificity on depression severity, as indicated by a significant interaction. (36)
> 有意な交互作用によって示されているように，暴行前の大うつの病歴が，記憶特異性がうつの重症度に及ぼす効果を調整していた．

6.3.19 階層的ロジスティック回帰分析

0965 階層的ロジスティック回帰分析の実施を，その目的とともに述べる．

◆Hierarchical logistic regression analyses were used to determine the relationship between X and Y.

階層的ロジスティック回帰分析が，XとYの関係を判定するために用いられた．

> Hierarchical logistic regression analyses were used to determine the relationship between variables and clinical depression. (32)
> 階層的ロジスティック回帰分析が，変数と臨床的うつの関係を判定するために用いられた．

6.3.20 媒介分析

0966 回帰分析による媒介分析について述べる．

◆We used mediation analyses to test [/Mediation analysis tested] whether X and Y mediated the effects of A on B and C, using the N-step regression analyses approach suggested by Author (Year).

我々は，著者（発表年）によって示唆されているNステップの回帰分析のアプローチを用いて，XとYが，AがBとCに及ぼす影響を媒介するかどうかを検定するために，媒介分析を用いた．

> We used mediation analyses to test whether rumination and permanent change mediated the effects of memory specificity on PTSD and depression, using the three-step regression analyses approach suggested by Baron and Kenny (1986). (36)
> 我々は，BaronとKenny（1986）によって示唆されている3ステップの回帰分析のアプローチを用いて，反芻と恒久的な変化が，記憶特異性がPTSDとうつに及ぼす影響を媒介するかどうかを検定するために，媒介分析を用いた．

（訳者注：PTSD; posttraumatic stress disorder, 心的外傷後ストレス障害）

0967 階層線形モデルにおける媒介分析の結果について述べる．

◆X was shown to mediate the relation between Y and Z.

Xは，YとZの間を媒介していることが示された．

> Finally, as predicted in Hypothesis 5, group information elaboration was shown to mediate the relation between shared task representations emphasizing information elaboration and decision quality. (59)

最後に，仮説5が予測するように，グループによる情報精緻化は，情報精緻化を重視する共有された課題表象と，意思決定の質の間を媒介していることが示された．

6.3.21　変数の制御

0968　重回帰分析において，すべての分析がある変数を制御したことを述べる．
◆All analyses control [/controlled] for X, Y, and Z.
すべての分析は，X, Y, Z を制御する [/ した]．

> All analyses controlled for race/ethnicity, childhood SES, learning disability status, and child health status. (38)
> すべての分析は，人種 / 民族性，子供の SES, 学習障害の状態，子供の健康状態を制御した．

（訳者注：SES; socioeconomic status, 社会経済的地位）

0969　重回帰分析において，ある要因を制御することにより得られた結果を述べる．
◆Controlling for these factors, it was found that X had more A and B, than [did] Y.
これらの要因が制御された結果，Y よりも，X のほうが，より多くの A や B をもつことが見出された．

> Controlling for these factors, it was found that respondents raised in stepfamilies and lone-parent families had more conduct problems and more total difficulties than those from two-parent biological families. (2)
> これらの要因が制御された結果，2 人の両親がいる生物学的な家族で育った回答者よりも，義理の家族や親が独身である家族で育った回答者のほうが，より多くの素行の問題や全体的な困難さをもつことが見出された．

0970　重回帰分析において，ある変数を制御することにより得られた結果を述べる．
◆Controlling for X, A and their interactions with B predicted change in both C and D scores over the N to M time period.
X を制御したところ，A, および，A と B の交互作用が，C と D の得点の変化を N から M の期間にわたって予測した．

> Controlling for family environment variables, violence factors and their interactions with background variables predicted change in both the GSI and alcohol problem scores over the baseline to 1.5 year time period. (22)
> 家族環境の変数を制御したところ，暴力要因，および，暴力要因と背景変数の交互作用が，GSI とアルコール問題の両方の変化をベースラインから 1.5 年の期間にわたって予測した．

（訳者注：GSI; General Severity Index, 全般的重症度指標）

0971　重回帰分析において，交絡因子を制御したことを述べる．
◆Multivariable models controlled for potential confounds including X, Y, and Z.
多変量モデルにより，X, Y, Z を含む潜在的な交絡因子が制御された．

6.3 統計的解析

Multivariable models controlled for potential confounds including gender, race (white, black), learning disability status, SES at birth, and child health status. (38)
多変量モデルにより，性別，人種（白人，黒人），学習障害の状態，誕生時の SES，子供の健康状態を含む潜在的な交絡因子が制御された．

（訳者注：SES; socioeconomic status, 社会経済的地位）

6.3.22 成長曲線モデル

0972 成長曲線モデルを用いたことを述べる．

◆N-level growth curve modeling was used to estimate the associations between X and Y.
N 段階の成長曲線モデルが，X と Y の関連を推定するために用いられた．

> Three-level growth curve modeling was used to estimate the associations between immigrant status and children's academic trajectories. (23)
> 3 段階の成長曲線モデルが，移民であるか否かと子供の学業成績の軌跡の関連を推定するために用いられた．

0973 成長曲線モデルにおいて，当てはめられた予測曲線を，傾きと y 切片とともに示す．

◆The average X had a fitted trajectory with an intercept of A and a slope of B.
平均的な X は，切片が A で傾きが B の軌跡を示した．

> The average child of immigrants from East Asia had a fitted trajectory with an intercept of 60.20 and a slope of 0.95. (23)
> 西アジアからの移民の平均的な子供は，切片が 60.20 で傾きが 0.95 の軌跡を示した．

0974 成長曲線モデルにおいて，適合度の評価について述べる．

◆The fit of X model was evaluated with N goodness-of-fit indices.
X のモデルの適合度が，N 個の適合度指標により評価された．

> The fit of each model presented in Table 2 was evaluated with three goodness-of-fit indices. (23)
> 表 2 に示されている各モデルの適合度が，3 つの適合度指標により評価された．

6.3.23 メタ分析と効果量

0975 メタ分析において，同定した治験の数を述べる．

◆We identified N randomized [, double-blind, placebo-controlled] trials of [/experiments on] X.
我々は，無作為化された [，二重盲検法で，偽薬コントロールされている] X についての N 個の治験 [/ 実験] を同定した．

We initially identified 20 double-blind, placebo-controlled trials of selective serotonin reuptake inhibitors in social anxiety disorder. (26)
我々は，二重盲検法で，偽薬コントロールされている，社会不安障害におけるセロトニン再取り込み阻害薬の 20 個の治療を最初に同定した．

0976 メタ分析において，包含される基準を満たした先行研究の数を述べる．
◆ Only N studies met inclusion criteria.
N 個の研究のみが，包含されるための基準を満たした．

> Overall, only 16 studies met inclusion criteria. (26)
> 全体的に，16 の研究のみが包含されるための基準を満たした．

0977 メタ分析において，得られた平均値を述べる．
◆ A meta-analytic study of N Xs from Y studies of Z (Author, Year) found an average A of B.
Z についての Y 研究から集められた N 個の X のメタ分析研究（著者，発表年）は，A の平均が B であることを見出した．

> A meta-analytic study of 1,861 correlations from largely cross-sectional studies of stressor–strain relationships (Crampton & Wagner, 1994) found an average correlation of .07. (52)
> ストレス因子と過労の関係についての広範な横断的研究から集められた 1861 個の相関のメタ分析研究（Crampton & Wagner, 1994）は，相関係数の平均が .07 であることを見出した．

0978 メタ分析において，効果量の値を述べる．
◆ Effects sizes as measured with X for Y and Z factors were A and B, respectively.
X によって測定された Y と Z の要因の効果量は，それぞれ A と B であった．

> Effects sizes as measured with Cohen's f^2 for the slope and intercept factors were .36 and .01, respectively. (28)
> コーエンの f^2 によって測定された傾きと切片の要因の効果量は，それぞれ .36 と .01 であった．

0979 メタ分析において，コーエンの d の範囲を述べる．
◆ Cohen's d ranged from A to B.
コーエンの d は A から B であった．

> Cohen's d ranged from .31 to .67. (39)
> コーエンの d は .31 から .67 であった．

0980 メタ分析において，効果量の大きさについて述べる．
◆ The differences were small to moderate [/moderate to large] in effect size (d = A).
差は，効果量では小から中 [/ 中から大] であった（d = A）．

> Both differences were small to moderate in effect size (d = .43). (32)
> 両方の差は，効果量では，小から中であった（d = .43）．

0981 メタ分析において,Q統計量が有意であったことを,その意味とともに述べる.
◆Significant Q statistics were found for A, B, and C, indicating XXX.
有意なQ統計量が,A, B, Cについて見出された.このことは,XXXということを示している.

> Significant Q statistics were found for the Liebowitz Social Anxiety Scale, Hamilton Anxiety Scale and Fear of Negative Evaluation Scale, indicating significant heterogeneity across trials in the results from these scales. (27)
> 有意なQ統計量が,リーボウィッツ社会不安尺度,ハミルトン不安尺度,否定的評価恐怖尺度について見出された.このことは,これらの尺度から得られた結果には,治験を通して有意な異質性があったことを示している.

0982 メタ分析において,Q統計量が有意でなかったことを述べる.
◆The Q statistics for the X and Y studies were not significant.
XとY研究についてのQ統計量は有意ではなかった.

> The Q statistics for the sertraline and fluvoxamine studies were not significant. (27)
> セルトラリンとフルボキサミン研究についてのQ統計量は有意ではなかった.

6.4　表への言及

6.4.1　人口統計学的なデータの表

0983 人口統計学的なデータを表に示したことを述べる.
◆Table N summarizes demographic and other key characteristics of the M participants [/subjects].
表Nに,M名の参加者[/被験者]の人口統計学的およびその他の重要な特徴の要約を示す.

> Table 1 summarizes demographic and other key characteristics of the 569 subjects. (38)
> 表1に,569名の被験者の人口統計学的およびその他の重要な特徴の要約を示す.

6.4.2　記述統計の表

0984 記述統計を表に示したことを述べる.
◆Descriptive statistics for X are presented [/summarized] in Table N.
Xの記述統計を表Nに示す[/要約する].

> Descriptive statistics for all measures used in this study are summarized in Table 1. (61)
> 本研究で用いられたすべての測度の記述統計を表1に要約する.

6.4.3　平均と標準偏差（標準誤差）の表

0985　平均と標準偏差を，表に示したことを述べる．
◆ Table N shows the means and standard deviations of [/for] X, Y, and Z.
　表 N に，X, Y, Z の平均と標準偏差を示す．

> Table 2 shows the means and standard deviations of the scales measuring attitudes toward political issues, the ideological belief scales, and the value dimension scales.　　(9)
> 表 2 に，政治的問題に対する態度を測定する尺度，イデオロギー的な信念尺度，価値次元尺度の平均と標準偏差を示す．

0986　平均，標準偏差，有意差検定を，表に示したことを述べる．
◆ The means, standard deviations, and significance tests for X effects, for Y, are given in Table N.
　Y について，平均，標準偏差，X の効果の有意差検定が，表 N に示されている．

> The means, standard deviations, and significance tests for age effects, for the post-treatment questionnaire responses, are given in Table 2.　　(54)
> 治療後質問紙への反応について，平均，標準偏差，年齢の効果の有意差検定が表 2 に示されている．

0987　平均を，異なる条件ごとに表に示したことを述べる．
◆ Table N presents the mean results in the different X conditions.
　表 N に，異なる X 条件における平均の結果を示す．

> Table 1 presents the mean results in the different experimental conditions.　　(14)
> 表 1 に，異なる実験条件における平均の結果を示す．

0988　平均と標準偏差を，条件と時間ごとに表に示したことを述べる．
◆ Means and standard deviations for X and Y are displayed by A and B in Table N.
　X と Y の平均と標準偏差が，A と B ごとに表 N に示されている．

> Means and standard deviations for self-reported fear and hostility are displayed by stress condition and time in Table 1.　　(60)
> 自己報告による恐怖と敵意の平均と標準偏差が，ストレス条件と計測の時期ごとに表 1 に示されている．

0989　平均値と標準偏差を，2 つの表に示したことを述べる．
◆ The mean and standard deviation values of X and Y are presented in Tables N and M, respectively.
　X と Y の平均と標準偏差の値が，表 N と表 M にそれぞれ示されている．

> The mean and standard deviation values of stressor and strain measures are presented in Tables 1 and 2, respectively.　　(52)
> ストレス因子と過労の測定の平均と標準偏差の値が，表 1 と表 2 にそれぞれ示されている．

6.4 表への言及

0990 平均と標準誤差を，複数の表に示したことを述べる．

◆ Means and standard errors for X are presented in Tables N through M.

X の平均と標準誤差が，表 N から M に示されている．

> Means and standard errors for different cognitive battery task conditions are presented in Tables 1 through 4. (47)
> それぞれの認知的テストバッテリー課題条件における平均と標準誤差が，表 1 から表 4 に示されている．

6.4.4 相関係数の表

0991 相関係数を表に示したことを，目的とともに述べる．

◆ A complete list of bivariate correlations is displayed in Table N to address X.

X に取り組むために，2 変数間の相関の完全なリストを表 N に示す．

> A complete list of bivariate correlations is displayed in Table 2 to address the relationships between the various predictors, displacement, GPD, and PTS. (3)
> さまざまな予測指数，退去，GPD，PTS の間の関係に取り組むために，2 変数の相関の完全なリストを表 2 に示す．

> （訳者注：GPD; general psychological distress, 一般的心理的苦痛；PTS; posttraumatic stress, 心的外傷後ストレス）

0992 複数の指標間の相関係数を表に示したことを述べる．

◆ Correlations among the N Xs, as well as the Y and Z, are contained [/included] in Table M.

N 個の X，および，Y と Z の間の相関を，表 M に示す．

> Correlations among the five norms items, as well as same-sex norms and drinking variables for females, are contained in Table 2. (39)
> 5 つの規範項目，および，女性における同性の規範と飲酒変数の間の相関を，表 2 に示す．

0993 静的相関，および，交差遅延相関を表に示したことを表す．

◆ The static and cross-lagged correlations among the X are presented in Table N.

X 間の静的相関および交差遅延相関が，表 N に示されている．

> The static and cross-lagged correlations among the stressors and the strains are presented in Table 3. (52)
> ストレス因子と過労の間の静的相関および交差遅延相関が表 3 に示されている．

0994 N 次相関を表に示したことを述べる．

◆ The zero [/first /second /third]-order correlations among Xs are displayed in Table N.

X 間の 0 [/1 /2 /3] 次相関が，表 N に示されている．

> The zero-order correlations among the scales are also displayed in Table 2. (9)
> 尺度間の 0 次相関も，表 2 に示されている．

6.4.5　結果の要約の表

0995　おもな分析の結果を，表に示したことを述べる．
◆ Results of the main analyses are displayed in Table N.
おもな分析の結果は表 N に示されている．
> Results of the main analyses are displayed in Table 5. (13)
> おもな分析の結果は表 5 に示されている．

0996　結果の要約を，表に示したことを述べる．
◆ See Table N for a summary of X. [/ Table N presents a summary of X.]
X のまとめについては表 N を参照されたい．[/X のまとめを表 N に示す．]
> See Table 1 for a summary of mean scores. (45)
> 平均得点のまとめについては表 1 を参照されたい．

0997　複数の得点を，表に示したことを述べる．
◆ Table N presents the X scores for Y and Z.
表 N に，Y と Z についての X 得点を示す．
> Table 1 presents the memory scores for item recognition and source recognition. (12)
> 表 1 に，項目再認と情報源再認についての記憶得点を示す．

0998　実験段階の結果を，ブロックごとに，表に示したことを述べる．
◆ The results from the L stage of X training are presented in M-day blocks in Table N.
X 訓練の第 L 段階の結果が，M 日のブロックごとに，表 N に示されている．
> The results from the first stage of appetitive training are presented in 8-day blocks in Table 2. (10)
> 食餌訓練の第一段階の結果が，8 日間のブロックごとに，表 2 に示されている．

0999　シミュレーションの結果を，表に示したことを述べる．
◆ Table N presents the results of M simulations that illustrate the influence of X on the trajectories of Y.
表 N は，X が Y の軌跡に及ぼす効果を例証する M 個のシミュレーションの結果を示している．
> Table 4 presents the results of two simulations that illustrate the influence of school-level factors on the trajectories of the children of immigrants. (23)
> 表 4 は，学校のレベルという要因が移民の子供の軌跡に及ぼす効果を例証する 2 つのシミュレーションの結果を示している．

6.4.6　因子・パス係数・効果分解の表

1000　因子分析において，因子負荷量を表に示したことを述べる．
◆ Table N reports the standardized factor loadings for X.

表Nに，Xの標準化された因子負荷量を示す．
> Table 1 reports the descriptive statistics for the variables used in the analysis and the unstandardized and standardized factor loadings for each item in a latent construct. (58)
> 表1に，分析に用いられた変数の記述統計と，潜在的構成概念における各項目の標準化されていない，および，標準化された因子負荷量を示す．

1001 因子分析において，回転された因子パターンを表に示したことを述べる．

◆ The rotated factor pattern is displayed in Table N.
回転された因子パターンを表Nに示す．
> The rotated factor pattern is displayed in Table 2. (22)
> 回転された因子パターンを表2に示す．

1002 確証的因子分析において，あるモデルの標準化されたパス係数を，表に示したことを述べる．

◆ Table N displays the standardized path coefficients for the model regressing X on the Y factors and covariates.
表Nに，XをY要因と共変量に回帰させるモデルについての標準化されたパス係数を示す．
> Table 4 displays the standardized path coefficients for the model regressing adolescent response strategies on the school climate factors and covariates. (58)
> 表4に，青年の反応方略を学校風土要因と共変量に回帰させるモデルについての，標準化されたパス係数を示す．

1003 確証的因子分析の結果を，表に要約したことを述べる．

◆ Results of the confirmatory factor analyses [/CFAs] for each model are summarized in Table N.
各モデルについての確証的因子分析 [/CFA] の結果が，表Nに要約されている．
> Results of the CFAs for each model are summarized in Table 4. (9)
> 各モデルについてのCFAの結果が，表4に要約されている．

1004 確証的因子分析において，因子間の相関を表に示したことを述べる．

◆ Table N reports the correlations of the factors in the measurement [/structural /mediation] model.
表Nに，測定 [/ 構造 / 媒介] モデルにおける因子間の相関を示す．
> Table 3 reports the correlations of the factors in the measurement model. (58)
> 表3に，測定モデルにおける因子間の相関を示す．

1005 構造方程式モデリングにおいて，直接効果と間接効果への分解を表に示したことを述べる．

◆ A decomposition of the effect of X on Y is presented in Table N.

XがYに及ぼす効果の分解を表Nに示す．
> A decomposition of the effect of the school climate factors on each of the four ways of responding to a peer's dangerous plan is presented in Table 6. (58)
> 学校風土という要因が，同輩の危険な計画に対する4つの各反応法に及ぼす効果の分解を，表6に示す．

1006 成長曲線モデルにおいて，複数のモデルの結果を表に示したことを述べる．
◆ Tables N and M present the X and Y results for Models A–B.
表NとMに，モデルA～BについてXとYの結果を示す．
> Tables 2 and 3 present the reading and math results for Models 1–3. (23)
> 表2と3に，モデル1～3について読書と数学の結果を示す．

6.4.7　メタ分析の表

1007 先行研究のオッズ比の対数を，表に示したことを述べる．
◆ In Table N, the log-odds ratios are reported for the X scale for the studies reporting data from this scale.
表Nに，X尺度について，この尺度のデータを報告している研究のオッズ比の対数を示す．
> In Table 2, the log-odds ratios are reported for the Clinical Global Impression of Improvement Scale for the studies reporting data from this scale. (27)
> 表2に，臨床全般印象改善尺度について，この尺度のデータを報告している研究のオッズ比の対数を示す．

1008 先行研究の効果量を，表に示したことを述べる．
◆ Table N shows effect sizes for the X scale for the studies that reported data from this scale.
表Nに，X尺度について，この尺度のデータを報告している研究の効果量を示す．
> Table 3 shows effect sizes for the Liebowitz Social Anxiety Scale for the studies that reported data from this scale. (27)
> 表3に，リーボウィッツ社会不安尺度について，この尺度のデータを報告している研究の効果量を示す．

6.4.8　表から示される結果

1009 表から，特徴的な差が示されたことを述べる．
◆ As depicted in Table N, there were X differences in Y.
表Nに示されているように，YにXの差が見られた．
> As depicted in Table 1, there were positive linear differences in the age of gambling onset. (46)
> 表1に示されているように，賭博開始年齢には正の線形の差が見られた．

6.4 表への言及

1010 表から，試行による差が見られることを述べる．

◆Inspection of Table N suggests that there was greater X on Y trials than on Z trials.

表 N を詳しく見れば，Z 試行よりも Y 試行において X が多いことが示唆される．

> Inspection of Table 2 suggests that from the first block there was greater responding on the reinforced than on the nonreinforced trials. (10)
> 表 2 を詳しく見れば，最初のブロックから，非強化試行よりも強化試行のほうが反応が多いことが示唆される．

1011 表から，複数の興味深いパターンが明らかになったことを述べる．

◆The results displayed in Table N reveal [/revealed] two [/three /some] interesting patterns.

表 N に示した結果から，2 つの [/3 つの / いくつかの] 興味深いパターンが明らかである [/ 明らかにされた]．

> The results displayed in Table 5 reveal some interesting patterns. (9)
> 表 5 に示した結果から，いくつかの興味深いパターンが明らかである．

1012 表から，有意な相関が示されたことを述べる．

◆As shown in Table N, [the] results indicate[d] significant positive [/negative] correlations between X and Y.

表 N に示されるように，結果は，X と Y の間に有意な正の [/ 負の] 相関があることを示している [/ いた]．

> As shown in Table 2, results indicate overall significant positive correlations between discrimination and psychological distress, anxiety, and clinical depression. (32)
> 表 2 に示されるように，結果は，差別と心理的苦痛，不安，臨床的うつの間に全体的に有意な正の相関があることを示している．

1013 表から，全変数において有意な相関が示されたことを述べる．

◆As shown in Table N, A, B, and C were all significantly correlated with D.

表 N に示されているように，A, B, C は，どれも D と有意に相関した．

> As shown in Table 2, sacred loss and desecration, spiritual struggles, and adaptive spiritual coping were all significantly correlated with global R–S. (61)
> 表 2 に示されているように，神聖さの喪失と神聖冒涜，スピリチュアルな苦闘，適応的であるスピリチュアルなコーピングは，どれも全体的 R–S と有意に相関した．

（訳者注：R–S; religiousness and spirituality, 宗教性とスピリチュアリティ）

6.5 図への言及

6.5.1 グラフの内容

1014 折れ線グラフに示したことを，横軸と縦軸とともに述べる．

◆ Figure N displays X based on Y.

図 N に Y に基づく X を示す．

> Figure 1 displays the probability of recalling a word based on the point value of each word. (7)
> 図 1 に，各単語の得点値に基づく単語想起の確率を示す．

1015 散布図の具体的な内容について述べる．

◆ We constructed plots of X for each Y point[,] for the N blocks of each Z group.

我々は，各 Z 群の N ブロックについて，各 Y 時点での X の図を描いた．

> We constructed plots of performance for each training point (averaged over participants' individual training performances) for the first 4 blocks of each learning group. (44)
> 我々は，各学習群の最初の 4 ブロックについて，各訓練時点での成績（参加者個人の訓練成績の平均）の図を描いた．

1016 テスト結果を，グラフに示したことを述べる．

◆ Figure N shows the test results from X.

図 N は，X のテスト結果を示している．

> Figure 2 shows the test results from Experiment 2. (10)
> 図 2 は，実験 2 のテスト結果を示している．

1017 ある群の結果を，グラフに示したことを述べる．

◆ Figure N shows the data for X.

図 N に，X のデータを示す．

> Figure 2C shows the data for rats conditioned with 30 mg/kg cocaine. (49)
> 図 2C に，30 mg/kg のコカインで条件づけが行われたラットのデータを示す．

1018 学習結果を，グラフに詳細に示したことを述べる．

◆ Figure N provides the details of X learning in the Y maze.

図 N に，Y 迷路における X 学習の詳細を示す．

> Figure 10 provides the details of task learning in the eight arm radial maze. (50)
> 図 10 に，8 本のアームの放射状迷路における課題学習の詳細を示す．

6.5.2 図から示される結果

1019 棒グラフから，差が示されたことを述べる．

◆ Inspection of this figure reveals that X Y-ed more [/greater] Z.

この図を詳しく見れば，X はより多くの Z を Y したことが明らかである．

Inspection of this figure reveals that B elicited greater freezing than D. (10)
この図を詳しく見れば，D よりも B のほうが，より多くのフリージングを誘発したことは明らかである．

（訳者注：ここで，D と B は，実験で用いられた刺激の名称である）

1020 棒グラフから，有意な効果が示されたことを述べる．

◆ Figure N illustrates that X significantly Y-ed in comparison to Z.
図 N は，X が Z と比べて有意に Y したことを示している．

Figure 1b illustrates that Pyr significantly decreased blood Glu levels in comparison to saline measured at the outcome of the 30-min-long intravenous treatments. (64)
図 1b は，30 分間の静脈内治療の結果として評価された場合，Pyr が，生理食塩水と比べて，血液中の Glu レベルを有意に減少させたことを示している．

（訳者注：Pyr; pyruvate, ピルビン酸：Glu; glutamic acid, グルタミン酸）

6.6 付録への言及

1021 すべての材料を，付録に掲載したことを述べる．

◆ All Xs are displayed in Appendix N.
すべての X を，付録 N に掲載する．

All items are displayed in the Appendix. (61)
すべての項目を，付録に掲載する．

1022 すべての結果を，付録に要約したことを述べる．

◆ A summary of all Xs is given in Appendix N.
すべての X を，付録 N に要約して示す．

A summary of all non-rule response frequencies is given in Appendix C. (24)
すべての非規則的な回答の頻度を，付録 C に要約して示す．

7 考察 (Discussion)

7.1　目的・仮説・内容の再確認
7.2　知見の再確認
7.3　仮説や予測との一致・不一致
7.4　先行研究との一致・不一致
7.5　知見の意味
7.6　知見の説明・原因・理由
7.7　知見の重要性・貢献
7.8　限界・短所・長所
7.9　今後の展開の可能性
7.10　要約と結論

7.1　目的・仮説・内容の再確認

7.1.1　目的の再確認

1023　研究のおもな目的を再確認する.

◆ The main purpose of this study is [/was] to examine whether XXX.

本研究のおもな目的は，XXX かどうかを調べることである [/ であった].

> The main purpose of this study was to examine whether the association between grandparent involvement and adolescents' adjustment varied across different family structures. (2)
> 本研究のおもな目的は，祖父母の関与と青年の適応の間の関連が家族構造の差異によって異なるかどうかを調べることであった.

1024　仮説を検証するという目的を再確認する.

◆ The present study was conducted to test the hypothesis that XXX.

本研究は，XXX という仮説を検証するために行われた.

> The present study was conducted to test the initial hypothesis that childhood personality attributes are associated with adult health. (38)
> 本研究は，幼年時代の性格属性が成人時の健康と関連するという初期の仮説を検証するために行われた.

1025　ある効果を評価するという実験デザインの目的を再確認する.

◆ The present study was designed to evaluate the effects of X on Y.

7.1 目的・仮説・内容の再確認

本研究は，X が Y に及ぼす効果を評価するために計画された．
> The present study was designed to evaluate the effects of control and no control of background sounds on measures of tinnitus interference in a sample of participants with chronic tinnitus. (28)
> 本研究は，慢性の耳鳴りをもつ参加者サンプルにおいて，背景音の制御と非制御が耳鳴りの干渉性の測度に及ぼす効果を評価するために計画された．

1026 研究が取り組んだ問題を再確認する．

◆ An important [subsidiary] issue addressed by this study is [/was] whether XXX.
本研究が取り組んだ重要な [副次的] 問題は，XXX かどうかということである [/ であった].

> An important subsidiary issue addressed by this study is whether individuals with essentially no visual experience are able to perform spatial updating. (42)
> 本研究が取り組んだ最も重要な副次的問題は，本質的に視覚経験のない人々が空間的更新を実行することができるかどうかということである．

1027 目的を，研究の焦点とともに再確認する．

◆ The [Nth] goal of this study is [/was] to investigate whether XXX. To this end, we first focused on Y.
本研究の [N 番目の] 目的は，XXX かどうかを調べることである [/ であった]．このために，まず，Y に焦点を当てた．

> The second goal of this study was to investigate whether there is a predictive link between prosocial behavior and empathic brain responses. To this end, we first focused only on the placebo condition and compared brain responses. (55)
> 本研究の第二の目的は，向社会的行動と脳の共感的反応の間に予測的な関連性があるかどうかを調べることであった．このために，まず，偽薬条件だけに焦点を当てて脳反応を比較した．

1028 一連の実験が，ある効果を評価するという目的で行われたことを再確認する．

◆ The present series of studies evaluated the effects of X on Y in Z.
今回の一連の研究は，Z において，X が Y に及ぼす効果を評価した．

> The present series of studies also evaluated the effects of combined DAT and SERT inhibitor on cocaine self-administration in rhesus monkeys. (30)
> 今回の一連の研究は，アカゲザルにおいて，DAT と SERT の複合抑制薬がコカインの自己投与に及ぼす効果もまた評価した．

> （訳者注：DAT; dopamine transporter, ドーパミン・トランスポーター：SERT; serotonin transporter, セロトニン・トランスポーター）

1029 さまざまな仮説や仮定を検証するという複数の目的を再確認する．

◆ The aim of this study was N-fold. First, we wanted to test the hypothesis that XXX. The second goal of the study was to test another assumption, that YYY.

本研究の目的は，N 個あった．1 つには，XXX という仮説を検証しようとした．第二の目的は，YYY というもう 1 つの仮定を検証することであった．

> The aim of this study was twofold. First, using a classical empathy paradigm, we wanted to test the hypothesis that administration of OT enhances empathy. (略) The second goal of the study was to test another implicit, but never tested, assumption about the empathic brain, namely that individual differences in prosocial behavior predict empathic brain responses. (55)
> 本研究の目的は，2 つであった．第一に，古典的な共感パラダイムを用いて，OT の投与が共感を強めるという仮説を検証しようとした．（略）第二の目的は，暗黙の，しかし，いまだに検証されていないもう 1 つの共感脳の仮定，すなわち，向社会的行動の個人差が脳の共感的反応を予測するという仮定を検証することであった．

（訳者注：OT; oxytocin, オキシトシン）

7.1.2 仮説の再確認

1030 おもな仮説を再確認する．

◆ The primary hypothesis for Study N was that XXX.
研究 N のおもな仮説は，XXX ということであった．

> The primary hypothesis for Study 3 was that participants whose justice concerns were aroused from viewing the HIV victim video would evidence more immanent justice reasoning for the subsequent unrelated stories than would those who learned that the young woman's suffering had ended. (6)
> 研究 3 のおもな仮説は，HIV の患者のビデオを見ることで正義への関心が喚起された参加者は，その若い女性患者の苦しみが終わったことを知った参加者と比べて，その後の無関係な物語に対して内在的正義推論をより多く示すであろう，ということであった．

1031 作業仮説を再確認する．

◆ Our current working hypothesis is that XXX.
我々の現在の作業仮説は，XXX というものである．

> Our current working hypothesis is that PKC-ζ activity modulation alters learning and memory through KIBRA. (31)
> 我々の現在の作業仮説は，PKC-ζの活動性調節が KIBRA を通して学習と記憶を変容させるというものである．

（訳者注：PKC-ζ; protein kinase C-zeta, プロテイン・キナーゼ C ツェータ：KIBRA は記憶に関連する遺伝子の名称）

1032 先行研究の仮定を再確認する．

◆ According to Author (Year), the basic assumption underlying X is that YYY.
著者（発行年）によれば，X の基礎となる仮定は，YYY ということである．

> According to Neighbors, Larimer, and Lewis (2004), the basic assumption underlying normative feedback interventions is that students care about how they compare with their peers. (39)
> Neigbors, Larimer, Lewis（2004）によれば，規範をフィードバックする介入の基礎となる仮定は，学生が自分は同輩と比べてどうであるかを気にするということである.

7.1.3 重要な手続きの再確認

1033 教示による操作を再確認する.

◆X was manipulated by instructing groups to YYY.
YYY するようにグループに教示することにより，X が操作された.

> In the present study, team reflection was manipulated by instructing groups to reflect before the group task only. (59)
> 本研究では，グループに課題前だけ内省するように教示することにより，チームの内省が操作された.

1034 ある可能性を排除するための実験デザインを再確認する.

◆To rule out this possibility, it was necessary to assess the effect[s] of X on Y in a design in which ZZZ.
この可能性を排除するために，ZZZ のデザインにおいて，X が Y に及ぼす効果を評価することが必要であった.

> To rule out this possibility, it was necessary to assess the effect of perceptual load on CS detection in a design in which the RT for the letter search task was equal in the low and high perceptual load conditions. (43)
> この可能性を排除するためには，低知覚的負荷条件と高知覚的負荷条件で文字探索課題の RT が等しくなるようなデザインにおいて，知覚的負荷が CS の検出に及ぼす効果を評価することが必要であった.

（訳者注：RT; reaction time, 反応時間：CS; conditioned stimulus, 条件刺激）

1035 ある変数を一定に保ちながら調べたことを再確認する.

◆The present research examined [the] X while holding constant A of B.
今回の研究は，B の A を一定に保ちながら，X を調べた.

> The present research examined the importance of intensity or salience of the cocaine US while holding constant the intensity of the novel object US. (49)
> 今回の研究は，新奇な物体という US の強度を一定に保ちながら，コカインという US の強度と顕著性の重要性を調べた.

（訳者注：US; unconditioned stimulus, 無条件刺激）

1036 先行研究のアイデアに基づいて行われたことを再確認する.

◆Drawing on assertions by Author (Year), the present research examined XXX.
著者（発表年）の主張に基づいて，本研究は，XXX を調べた.

272　　　　　　　　　　　　　　7．考察（Discussion）

Drawing on assertions by Duckitt and colleagues (Duckitt, 2001; Duckitt et al., 2002) and Duriez et al. (2005), the present research examined the relation among social and economic political orientation dimensions in a sample of politically sophisticated participants.　　(9)
Duckitt らのグループ（Duckitt, 2001; Duckitt et al., 2002）および Duriez ら（2005）の主張に基づいて，本研究は，政治的に洗練された参加者サンプルにおいて，社会的および経済的な論点についての複数の政治的志向の次元の間の関係を調べた．

1037　一部の参加者を除外したことを再確認する．

◆ We reanalyzed the X data from the present study after dropping Y.
　我々は，Y を除いた後に，本研究から得られた X のデータを再分析した．

> We reanalyzed the cognitive capacity data from the present study after dropping the 10-year-olds.　　(57)
> 我々は，10 歳の参加者を除いた後に，本研究から得られた認知的能力のデータを再分析した．

1038　変数の効果を制御したことを再確認する．

◆ We controlled for the effects of X and Y variables before investigating the effects of Z.
　我々は，Z の効果を研究する前に，X と Y の変数の効果を制御した．

> That is, we controlled for the effects of ethnicity- and socioeconomic status-related variables before investigating the effects of discrimination.　　(32)
> すなわち，我々は，差別の効果を研究する前に，民族性，および，社会経済的地位に関連する変数の効果を制御した．

7.2　知見の再確認

7.2.1　おもな知見

1039　研究の知見を述べる．

◆ The present study shows [/showed] that XXX.
　本研究は，XXX ということを示している [/ 示した]．

> The present study shows that ERPs add to RTs in the evaluation of decision making, and allow evaluating ongoing brain processes, while decision making under affective influences takes place.　　(56)
> 本研究は，意思決定の評価において ERP が RT の一助となり，感情的な影響下にある意思決定が起こっている間に進行する脳過程を評価することを可能にする，ということを示している．

（訳者注：ERP; event related potential, 事象関連電位：RT; reaction times, 反応時間）

1040　研究のおもな知見を述べる．

◆ The main findings of the study show [/showed /were] that XXX.
　本研究のおもな知見は，XXX ということを示している [/ 示した / であった]．

7.2 知見の再確認

The main findings of the study showed that greater grandparent involvement was associated with fewer emotional problems and with more prosocial behavior. (2)
本研究のおもな知見は，祖父母の関与が大きいほど情動的な問題が少なくなり，かつ，向社会的行動が多くなるという関連があることを示した．

1041 一連の実験のおもな知見について述べる．

◆ The main finding from this series of experiments is [/was] that XXX.
今回の一連の実験のおもな知見は，XXX ということである [/ であった]．

> The main finding from this series of experiments is that children over 3 years of age are capable of goal-directed action as assessed by the outcome devaluation paradigm. (37)
> 今回の一連の実験のおもな知見は，価値低下パラダイムで評価されたように，3 歳以上の子供は目標志向的行為ができるということである．

1042 全体的な知見を要約する．

◆ These findings generally show [/showed] that XXX.
これらの知見は，総じて，XXX ということを示している [/ 示した]．

> Thus, these findings generally show that men who are homeless, especially those in a shelter setting, are well aware of the barriers in their recovery. (41)
> それゆえ，これらの知見は，ホームレスの男性，特に，シェルターという環境にいる男性は，立ち直りを妨げる障壁を十分承知している，ということを総じて示している．

7.2.2 重要な知見

1043 最も重要な知見を端的に述べる．

◆ The most important finding of this study is [/was] X.
本研究の最も重要な知見は，X である [/ であった]．

> The most important finding of this study is the occurrence of spatial updating in the SL condition. (42)
> 本研究の最も重要な知見は，SL 条件において空間的更新が起こることである．

（訳者注：SL; spatial language, 空間的言語）

1044 最も重要な結果について説明する．

◆ The most significant finding of this study is [/was] that XXX.
本研究の最も重要な知見は，XXX ということである [/ であった]．

> The most significant finding of this study was that one subject, Mickey, used a relational matching rule to match items from two physically dissimilar sets of stimuli (the final test phase). (34)
> 本研究の最も重要な知見は，1 匹の被験体（ミッキー）が物理的に類似していない 2 つの刺激セット（最終テスト段階）の項目を合わせるために，関係見本合わせ規則を使用したことである．

1045 知見に留意することが重要であることを述べる.

◆It is important to note that XXX.
XXX に留意することは重要である.

> It is important to note that the children in our study were not actively gesturing during the math lesson—all of their gesturing was done before the lesson began. (5)
> 我々の研究対象の子供は数学の授業中に積極的にジェスチャーを行っていたのではなく，彼らのジェスチャーのすべては授業が始まる前に行われていたことに留意することは重要である.

1046 興味深い知見に焦点を当てる.

◆One of the interesting findings in this study was that XXX.
本研究における興味深い知見の 1 つは，XXX ということであった.

> One of the interesting findings in this study was that many of the men did not believe that their masculinity changed. (41)
> 本研究における興味深い知見の 1 つは，男性の多くは自分の男性性が変化したと思っていなかったことである.

1047 もう 1 つの重要な知見を述べる.

◆Another key finding was that XXX.
もう 1 つの重要な知見は，XXX ということであった.

> Another key finding was that EXAM's ability to more accurately predict human transfer behavior held across training situations that varied with regard to the presence of tick marks. (44)
> もう 1 つの重要な知見は，目盛りの存在に関して異なるさまざまな訓練場面を通して，ヒトの転移行動をより正確に予測する EXAM の能力が保たれたことであった.
>
> （訳者注：EXAM; extrapolation-association model, 外挿連合モデル）

1048 もう 1 つの注目すべき知見に焦点を当てる.

◆Another noteworthy finding is [/was] that XXX.
もう 1 つの注目すべき知見は，XXX ということである [/ であった].

> Another noteworthy finding is that an exploratory factor analysis revealed two distinct factors related to recall of high and low value items. (7)
> もう 1 つの注目すべき知見は，探索的因子分析により，高値と低値の項目の想起に関係する 2 つの異なる要因が明らかにされたことである.

1049 議論が必要なもう 1 つの重要な知見に焦点を当てる.

◆Another point that warrants discussion is [/was] the observation that XXX.
議論が必要なもう 1 つのポイントは，XXX という観察結果である [/ であった].

> Another point that warrants discussion is the observation that younger noncontrollers performed as well as younger and older controllers on the ATC task battery. (47)

7.2　知見の再確認

議論が必要なもう 1 つのポイントは，ATC 課題バッテリーにおいて，若年の非管制官が若年の管制官や高齢の管制官と同じくらい上手に課題を遂行したという観察結果である．

（訳者注：ATC; air-traffic control, 航空管制）

7.2.3　結果のまとめ（「6. 結果」に収録されている表現も参照）

1050　結果をまとめる．

◆XXX, indicating that YYY.

XXX であった．このことは，YYY ということを示していた．

> There was a significant negative correlation between recall of low-value and high-value items in healthy older adults and individuals with AD, indicating that when participants recalled more of the higher value items they also recalled fewer lower value items. (7)
> 健康な高齢者と AD の人々において，低値項目と高値項目の想起の間に，有意な負の相関があった．このことは，参加者が高値項目をより多く想起する場合には，低値項目をより少なく想起することを示していた．

（訳者注：AD; Alzheimer's disease, アルツハイマー病）

1051　ある視点から結果をまとめる．

◆From the point of view of X, YYY.

X という点では，YYY であった．

> From the point of view of number of source studies contributing to a meta-analysis, the most robust results from this study are for the Liebowitz Social Anxiety Scale. (26)
> メタ分析に寄与した研究の数という点では，この研究から得られた最も頑健な結果はリーボウィッツ社会不安尺度に関するものであった．

1052　ある条件の下で得られた結果と意味をまとめる．

◆In the X condition, YYY, suggesting that ZZZ.

X 条件では，YYY であった．このことは，ZZZ ということを示唆していた．

> In the positive-personality-feedback condition, responses to the self-esteem manipulation check correlated negatively with pro-U.S. bias, suggesting that increased self-esteem reduced pro-U.S. bias. (25)
> 正の性格フィードバック条件では，自尊心操作チェックに対する反応が，親米的な偏向と負の相関関係にあった．このことは，自尊心を増加させると親米的な偏向が減少することを示唆していた．

1053　異なる条件の比較により得られた結果をまとめる．

◆The following trends were notable comparing A and B: (1) XXX; (2) YYY; and (3) ZZZ.

A と B を比較すると，以下の傾向が顕著であった．(1) XXX．(2) YYY．(3) ZZZ．

The following trends were notable comparing male Japanese 5th and 8th graders: (1) individualistic orientations and behavior were more notable in older boys; (2) group-centered orientations and behavior gave some ground to individualism, but were still an integral aspect of behavior in young adolescents; (3) competitiveness was treated differently from individualistic striving and was evaluated negatively at both ages; and (4) cooperation was highly evident and valued at both ages. (54)

日本人の5学年と8学年を比較すると，以下の傾向が注目に値した．(1) 個人主義的な志向と行動は，年長の少年においてより顕著であった．(2) グループ中心的な志向と行動は，個人主義にとって代わられるが，それでもなお若い青年の行動のある不可欠な側面となっていた．(3) 競争性は個人主義的努力とは違うものとしてとらえられており，どちらの年齢でも否定的に見られていた．(4) 協力は両方の年齢において非常に顕著であり，高く評価されていた．

7.3 仮説や予測との一致・不一致

7.3.1 仮説や予測との一致

1054 仮説が支持されたことを述べる．

◆ Support was found for the hypothesis that XXX.

XXX という仮説が支持された．

> Support was found for the hypothesis that participants experiencing just world threat would view an unrelated negative event more in immanent justice terms than would participants not experiencing just world threat. (6)
> 公正世界の脅威を経験した参加者は，それを経験していない参加者と比べて，関連のない否定的な事象を内在的正義の用語でとらえることが多いだろうという仮説が支持された．

1055 仮説がどのように支持されたかを述べる．

◆ In support of these hypotheses [/this hypothesis], XXX.

これらの [/ この] 仮説を支持する結果として，XXX であった．

> In support of these hypotheses, individuals receiving the instructions to control the background sounds exhibited a significantly steeper increase of tinnitus interference than those receiving the no control instructions. (28)
> これらの仮説を支持する結果として，背景音を制御するようにという教示を受けた人々は，制御の教示を受けなかった人々と比べて，有意により急激な耳鳴り干渉性の増加を示した．

1056 知見が仮説を予備的に支持することを述べる．

◆ These findings provide preliminary evidence [/support] for the hypothesis that XXX.

これらの知見は XXX という仮説に対して予備的な証拠 [/ 支持] を与える．

These findings provide preliminary evidence for the hypothesis that the level of perceptual load in a task dictates whether any additional stimuli unrelated to the search task can be consciously detected. (43)
これらの知見は，課題における知覚的負荷のレベルが，探索課題に無関連の追加的な刺激が意識上で検出されるかどうかを規定する，という仮説に対して予備的な証拠を与える．

1057 知見が先行研究の著者による仮説を支持することを述べる．

◆ This finding supports the hypothesis of Author (Year) that XXX.
この知見は，XXX という著者（発表年）の仮説を支持する．

> This finding supports the hypothesis of Duckitt and his colleagues (Duckitt, 2001; Duckitt et al., 2002) and Duriez et al. (2005) that the two dimensions of political orientation should be moderately correlated when assessed in samples of politically sophisticated persons. (9)
> この知見は，政治的志向の 2 つの次元が，政治的に洗練された人のサンプルにおいて評価された場合には中程度に相関する，という Duckitt らのグループ（Duckitt, 2001; Duckitt et al., 2002），および Duriez ら（2005）の仮説を支持する．

1058 仮説から予測されたとおりの結果を述べる．

◆ As predicted in [/by] the X hypothesis, YYY.
X の仮説から予測されたように，YYY であった．

> As predicted in the third hypothesis, higher levels of adaptive spiritual coping at the time of the divorce were correlated with higher levels of perceived posttraumatic growth resulting from the divorce ($r = .32$, $p \leq .001$) and spiritual growth after controlling for global religiousness (partial $r = .41$, $p \leq .01$). (61)
> 3 番目の仮説から予測されたように，離婚時に適応的であるスピリチュアルなコーピングのレベルが高いことは，離婚によってもたらされる心的外傷後の成長感（$r = .32$, $p \leq .001$），および，全体的な宗教性を制御した後のスピリチュアルな成長感（偏相関係数 $r = .41$, $p \leq .01$）のレベルが高いことと相関した．

1059 結果が，ある予測を証明したことを述べる．

◆ The results provided evidence consistent with the X predictions.
結果は，X の予測と一致する証拠をもたらした．

> The results provided evidence consistent with the experimental predictions. (18)
> 結果は，実験的な予測と一致する証拠をもたらした．

1060 結果が，事前の予想を確認したことを述べる．

◆ These results confirmed the [/our] expectation [/prediction] that XXX.
これらの結果は，XXX という [我々の] 予想を確認するものであった．

> These results confirmed our expectation that learning about the prolonged suffering of the young woman living with HIV would lead to an increased activation of justice concepts. (6)

これらの結果は，HIV とともに生きる若い女性が長い間苦しんでいることについて学習することで正義の概念がより活性化されるだろう，という我々の予想を確認するものであった．

1061 理論の予測が確認されたことを，予測の内容とともに述べる．
◆ The major prediction of the theory, that XXX, was confirmed.
XXX という，その理論のおもな予測は確認された．

> The major prediction of the theory, that there is an interaction between drive level and nature of the dominant response, was confirmed. (18)
> 動因レベルと優勢反応の性質の間には交互作用があるという，その理論のおもな予測は確認された．

1062 予想に一致した傾向が見られたことを述べる．
◆ As expected [/Not surprisingly], Xs were more [/less] likely to YYY.
予想されたように，X は YYY する傾向がより強かった [/ 弱かった]．

> As expected, youth were more likely to say that they would ignore their peer's dangerous plan or talk about it among friends (but not with an adult), to the extent that they believed that going to an adult would result in more trouble. (58)
> 予想されたように，大人のところに相談に行くともっとトラブルがもたらされると信じている限り，若者は，同輩の危険な計画を無視するか，友人間でそれについて話し合う（しかし，大人とは話さない）つもりであると答える傾向がより強かった．

7.3.2　仮説や予測との不一致

1063 知見が仮説に反していたことを，仮説の根拠とともに述べる．
◆ These findings were contrary to the hypotheses [/predictions][,] which were based on X.
これらの知見は，仮説 [/ 予測] に反していた．その仮説 [/ 予測] は，X に基づいていた．

> These findings were contrary to our predictions, which were based on longitudinal research highlighting the ameliorative impact that adaptive spiritual coping strategies typically have over time. (61)
> これらの知見は，我々の予測に反していた．その予測は，適応的でスピリチュアルなコーピングが長い年月をかけて示す改善的な効果を強調した縦断的研究に基づくものであった．

1064 予想外の知見を述べる．
◆ An unexpected finding was X.
予想外の知見は，X であった．

> An unexpected finding was the equivalent level of self-esteem reported by displaced and nondisplaced participants. (3)

予想外の知見は，退去させられた参加者と退去させられなかった参加者が同じ程度の自尊心を報告したことであった．

1065 驚くべき結果を述べる．

◆ We were surprised to find that XXX.

XXX ということを発見して驚いた．

> We were surprised to find that therapist cultural competence was not associated with treatment satisfaction whereas cultural incompetence—that is, behavior suggesting lack of cultural awareness, knowledge, or therapeutic skill—was associated with treatment dissatisfaction only. (8)
> セラピストの文化的な能力は治療に対する満足と関連がなく，文化的な無能力（すなわち，文化的な気づき，知識，あるいは治療的技能の欠如を示唆する行動）が治療の不満足のみと関連があったことを発見して驚いた．

1066 結果がある仮説を部分的にしか支持しないことを，理由とともに述べる．

◆ The results of the [/our] analyses only partially supported this hypothesis, as XXX.

XXX ということから，この [/ 我々の] 分析結果はこの仮説を部分的に支持したにすぎない．

> The results of our analyses, however, only partially supported this hypothesis, as the two student community measures operate somewhat differently in the model. (58)
> しかし，学生コミュニティについての 2 つの測度がモデルの中でやや異なる作用をするため，我々の分析結果はこの仮説を部分的に支持したにすぎない．

7.4 先行研究との一致・不一致

7.4.1 論点の再確認（「4.2 先行研究の知見」に収録されている表現も参照）

1067 序文で述べた論点を再確認する．

◆ As noted in the introduction to this article, XXX.

本論文の序文において言及したように，XXX である．

> As noted in the introduction to this article, naturalistic paradigms reveal substantial covariation between contexts and responses that can form the basis for outsourcing behavioral control. (62)
> 本論文の序文において言及したように，自然観察法のパラダイムは，行動制御を外部委託するための基盤となる文脈と反応の間の実質的な共変動を明らかにしている．

1068 以前に述べた論点を再確認する．

◆ As discussed earlier, XXX.

以前に論じたように，XXX である．

> As discussed earlier, reflection is likely to increase the likelihood of teams developing appropriate representations. (59)
> 以前に論じたように，内省はチームが適切な表象を発達させる確率を高める可能性が高い．

1069 先に述べた論点を要約して再確認する．

◆ To summarize X, YYY.

X を要約すれば，YYY である．

> To summarize motivated cueing, models of the neurotransmitter processes that underlie instrumental learning provide a mechanism by which the context cues reliably associated with response outcomes can come to motivate habit performance. (62)
> 動機づけキューイングを要約すれば，道具的学習の基盤となる神経伝達物質過程のモデルが，反応の結果と確実に結びついている文脈的手がかりが習慣の遂行を動機づけるに至ることができる機序をもたらすということである．

7.4.2 先行研究との一致

1070 結果が，先行研究を支持することを述べる．

◆ The present data offer further corroboration of the findings of Author (Year).

今回のデータは，著者（発表年）の知見にさらなる確証を与える．

> The present data offer further corroboration of the findings of Mills et al. (2007) and Galea et al. (2008). (3)
> 今回のデータは，Mills ら（2007）と Galea ら（2008）の知見にさらなる確証を与える．

1071 結果が，最近増加しつつある一連の研究と一致することを述べる．

◆ The current results join a growing body of research indicating that XXX (Author, Year).

今回の結果は，XXX を示す現在増加中の研究（著者，発表年）と一致する．

> The current results join a growing body of research indicating that the contribution of familiarity to memory for arbitrary associations is increased if the information is encoded as an integrated unit (Giovanello et al., 2006). (12)
> 情報が統合された単位として符号化される場合に，任意の連合についての記憶に対する熟知性の寄与が増加することを示す研究が増えており（Giovanello et al., 2006），今回の結果はそれらの研究と一致する．

1072 結果が，別のサンプルを用いた研究の知見と一致することを述べる．

◆ This corroborates [/supports] Author and [his /her] colleagues' (Author, Year) findings from a sample of X.

このことは，X のサンプルにおける著者らのグループ（著者，発表年）の知見に確証を与える [/ を支持する] ものである．

7.4 先行研究との一致・不一致

This corroborates Streisand and colleagues' (Streisand et al., 2008) previous findings from a sample of parents of older children with diabetes, that mothers and fathers' pediatric parenting stress were associated with greater anxiety. (45)
このことは，母親と父親の小児科での育児ストレスがより大きな不安と関連しているという，より年長の糖尿病の子供の親のサンプルから得られた，Streisand らのグループによる以前の知見（Streisand et al., 2008）に確証を与えるものである.

1073 過去の知見と類似している結果を述べる.

◆ As found in other studies, XXX.
他の研究においても見出されているように，XXX である.

> As found in other studies, Latinos did report feeling like they have been accused of doing something wrong more than Asian Americans. (32)
> 他の研究においても見出されているように，ラテンアメリカ系アメリカ人は，アジア系アメリカ人よりも，何か悪いことをしたと責められてきたような感情をより多く報告したのである.

1074 結果が最近の研究と一致していることを，研究例とともに述べる.

◆ The present results are in line with recent X studies: [/.] Author (Year) published a study that YYY.
今回の結果は，最近の X 研究と一致している．すなわち，著者（発表年）は，YYY という研究を出版した．

> The present results are in line with recent neuroeconomic fMRI studies: Knutson, Rick, Wimmer, Prelec, and Loewenstein (2007) published a neuroeconomic study that was thematically related, but（略）. (56)
> 今回の結果は，最近の神経経済学的な fMRI 研究と一致している．すなわち，Knutson, Rick, Wimmer, Prelec, Loewenstein（2007）は，本研究に関係するテーマの神経経済学研究を出版した．しかし，（略）．

1075 結果が先行研究と一致することを，先行研究の内容とともに述べる.

◆ This is consistent with the findings of Author (Year) which suggested that XXX.
これは，XXX を示唆した著者（発表年）の知見と一致する.

> This is consistent with the findings of Barrett et al. (2008) which suggested that older adolescents would fare worse than their younger counterparts. (3)
> このことは，年少の青年よりも，年長の青年のほうが，うまくやっていけないことを示唆した Barrett ら（2008）の知見と一致する.

1076 今回の知見が先行研究と一致することを，先行研究の内容とともに述べる.

◆ The findings of the current study correspond with those of Author (Year), who demonstrated that XXX.
本研究の知見は著者（発表年）と一致する．彼らは，XXX ということを例証した．

The findings of the current study correspond with those of Spinozzi et al. (2004), who demonstrated that capuchins could match images on the basis of abstract spatial relations (above and below). (34)
本研究の知見は Spinozzi ら（2004）と一致する．彼らは，オマキザルが抽象的な空間的関係（上と下）に基づいてイメージの見本合わせができることを例証した．

1077 結果が先行研究の主張と一致していることを，主張の内容とともに述べる．

◆The current study lends empirical support to Author and [his /her] colleagues' assertion that XXX.
本研究は，XXX という著者らのグループの主張に経験的支持を与える．

> The current study lends empirical support to Young and colleagues' assertion that women's drinking is based on their perceptions of men's expectations. (39)
> 本研究は，女性の飲酒が男性の期待についての女性の認識に基づいている，という Young らのグループの主張に経験的支持を与える．

1078 結果が先行研究の主張を支持することを，主張の内容とともに述べる．

◆This finding provides further empirical support for the assertion that XXX.
この知見は，XXX という主張に対してさらなる経験的支持を与える．

> This finding provides further empirical support for the assertion that political ideology is comprised of two components. (9)
> この知見は，政治的イデオロギーが2つの構成要素から成るという主張に対してさらなる経験的支持を与える．

1079 結果が評論研究の結論を支持することを，結論の内容とともに述べる．

◆The results are in line with a recent review which concluded that XXX (Author, Year).
これらの結果は，XXX と結論した最近の評論（著者，発表年）と一致する．

> The results are in line with a recent review which concluded that trauma exposure *per se* is unlikely to be the primary mechanism leading to overgenerality (Moore & Zoellner, 2007). (36)
> これらの結果は，心的外傷への曝露自体が概括化につながる基本的な機序である可能性は低いと結論した最近の評論（Moore & Zoellner, 2007）と一致する．

1080 他の研究者のアイデアと一致している知見を述べる．

◆Consistent with ideas expressed by other scholars (Author, Year), our findings suggest that XXX.
他の研究者が述べている考え（著者，発表年）と一致して，我々の知見は XXX ということを示唆している．

7.4 先行研究との一致・不一致

Consistent with ideas expressed by other scholars (Fischer, Jome, & Atkinson, 1998), our findings suggest that there are critical ingredients of care that appear to be equally important for racially or culturally mismatched dyads and matched dyads. (8)
他の研究者が述べている考え (Fischer, Jome, & Atkinson, 1998) と一致して，我々の知見は，人種的あるいは文化的に一致していない組，および，一致している組にとって同程度に重要と思われるケアの要因があることを示唆している．

1081 今回の知見が先行研究の理論と一致していることを，理論の内容とともに述べる．

◆ Findings from this study are consistent with theory [and research] suggesting that XXX.
この研究から得られた知見は，XXX を示唆する理論 [と研究] と一致する．

> Findings from this study are consistent with theory and empirical work suggesting that temperament and personality show meaningful continuities across time. (38)
> この研究から得られた知見は，気質と性格が時を超えて意味のある連続性を示すことを示唆する理論および経験的研究と一致する．

1082 今回の知見が先行研究の理論を支持することを，理論の内容とともに述べる．

◆ This finding is in line with the X theories which suggest that YYY.
この知見は，YYY ということを示唆する X 理論と一致する．

> This finding is in line with the social ecological paradigm and family systems theories which suggest that supportive relationships with family members outside the immediate family are linked to better adjustment for children and adolescents. (2)
> この知見は，身近な家族以外の家族構成員との支援的な関係が，子供や青年にとってよりよい適応と結びついている，ということを示唆する社会生態学的なパラダイム，および，家族システム理論と一致する．

1083 結果が，ある予測変数についての先行する知見と一致したことを述べる．

◆ These results were consistent with the findings of Author (Year), that X was a strong predictor of Y.
これらの結果は，X が Y を強く予測するという著者（発表年）の知見と一致した．

> These results were consistent with the findings of Galea et al. (2007) and Kessler et al. (2008), that being a member of a displaced group was a strong predictor of psychological trauma after Hurricane Katrina. (3)
> これらの結果は，退去させられたグループの構成員であることがハリケーン・カトリーナ後の心的外傷の強力な予測変数であるという Galea ら (2007) および Kessler ら (2008) の知見と一致した．

7.4.3　先行研究の再現

1084　結果が，先行研究の知見を再現したことを述べる．

◆ The present research replicated Xs that have been observed in previous work.

本研究は，先行研究で観察されてきた X を再現した．

> The present research also replicated relations among the three domains that have been observed in previous work. (9)
> 本研究は，先行研究で観察されてきた 3 つの領域間の関係もまた再現した．

1085　一連の実験において，先の実験で見られた効果を再現したことを述べる．

◆ Experiment N replicated the X effect on Y found in Experiment M.

実験 N は，実験 M で見出された X が Y に及ぼす効果を再現した．

> Experiment 3, therefore, replicated the perceptual load effect on CS detection found in Experiments 1 and 2. (43)
> それゆえ，実験 3 は，実験 1 と 2 で見出された知覚的負荷が CS の検出に及ぼす効果を再現した．
>
> （訳者注：CS; conditioned stimulus, 条件刺激）

7.4.4　先行研究の拡張

1086　得られた知見が先行研究を支持し拡張することを，先行研究の内容とともに述べる．

◆ The present results [/findings] support and extend Author's (Year) important work demonstrating that XXX.

今回の結果 [/ 知見] は，XXX ということを例証した著者（発表年）の重要な研究を支持し拡張する．

> The present findings support and extend Raman and Winer's (2002, 2004) important work demonstrating that adults under certain circumstances will engage in immanent justice reasoning. (6)
> 今回の知見は，ある環境の下で大人は内在的正義推論を行うことを例証した Raman と Winer（2002, 2004）の重要な研究を支持し拡張する．

1087　今回の知見が文献を拡張することを，文献の内容とともに述べる．

◆ The [/Our] findings extend the X literature, demonstrating Y.

この [/ 我々の] 知見は，Y を例証してきた，X の文献を拡張する．

> Our findings also extend the interruption-management literature, demonstrating interference from interruptions that clearly require no response. (14)
> 我々の知見は，反応を明らかに要求しない割り込みによる干渉を例証してきた，割り込み管理の文献もまた拡張する．

1088　今回の知見がある機序についての研究を基礎とし，その研究を拡張すること

7.4 先行研究との一致・不一致

を述べる.
◆ This finding [/This] builds on research that examines how XXX, and extends this work to Y.
この知見 [/ このこと] は,どのようにして XXX が起こるのかを調べた研究を基礎とし,そのような研究を Y にまで拡大する.

> This builds on research that examines how attentional control and working memory are affected by AD, and extends this work to control over encoding operations in light of prioritizing items in memory. (7)
> このことは,AD により注意制御と作業記憶がどのように影響されるのかを調べた研究を基礎とし,そのような研究を,記憶における項目の優先順位づけを考慮した符号化操作の制御にまで拡大する.

(訳者注:AD; Alzheimer's disease, アルツハイマー病)

1089 先行研究と比較することにより,知見を拡張する.
◆ In comparison to previous studies with [/of] X, the results of this study suggest that YYY.
X についての先行研究と比べると,本研究の結果は YYY ということを示唆している.

> In comparison to previous studies with mothers (e.g., Streisand et al., 2008), the results of this study suggest that child disease characteristics may have weaker associations with fathers' than mothers' pediatric parenting stress. (45)
> 過去の母親研究(たとえば,Streisand et al., 2008)と比べると,本研究の結果は,子供の病気の性質と父親の小児科での育児ストレスの関連が,子供の病気の性質と母親の小児科での育児ストレスとの関連よりも弱いかもしれないことを示唆する.

7.4.5 先行研究との不一致

1090 先行研究の知見と一致しないことを,知見の内容とともに述べる.
◆ These findings contrast [/contrasted] with those of Author (Year), who found that XXX.
これらの知見は,XXX を見出した著者(発表年)の知見とは対照的である [/ であった].

> These findings contrast with those of Lewis and Neighbors (2004), who found that gender nonspecific and opposite-sex norms did not account for drinking. (39)
> これらの知見は,異性のもっている性別に非特異的な規範が飲酒を説明しないことを見出した Lewis と Neighbors(2004)の知見とは対照的である.

(訳者注:ここでは,過去形の contrasted のほうがよい)

1091 ある現象が再現されず,先行研究の知見と矛盾することを述べる.
◆ In the current study, X failed to YYY. This finding contradicts [/contradicted] work by

Author (Year) who found that ZZZ.
本研究では，X が YYY することができなかった．この知見は，ZZZ ということを見出した著者（発表年）の研究と矛盾する [/ した]．

> In the current study, caffeine failed to reverse ethanol-induced learning deficits. On the surface, this finding contradicts work by Silva and Frussa-Filho (2000), who found that caffeine reversed memory deficits in mice when coadministered with a memory-impairing dose of the benzodiazepine chlordiazepoxide. (21)
> 本研究では，カフェインが，エタノールにより誘発される学習欠損を覆すことができなかった．この知見は，Silva と Frussa-Filho（2000）の研究と表面上矛盾する．彼らは，マウスにおいて，記憶欠損を発生させる量のベンゾジアゼピン系のクロルジアゼポキシドと同時投与した場合に，カフェインが記憶欠損を覆すことを見出したのである．

（訳者注：ここでは，過去形の contradicted のほうがよい）

1092 意外な結果が得られたことを述べる．

◆ It was [somewhat] surprising that XXX.
XXX ということは，[やや] 意外であった．

> It was somewhat surprising that there was a performance advantage in the nonspeeded condition for the unitized condition. (12)
> ユニット化条件については，非高速化条件において成績の改善が見られたことが，やや意外であった．

1093 無視できない例外があったことを述べる．

◆ The exception to these findings that cannot be ignored is [/was] X.
これらの知見に対する無視できない例外は，X である [/ であった]．

> The exception to these findings that cannot be ignored is the diversity among children of Asian origin. (23)
> これらの知見に対する無視できない例外は，アジア系の子供に見られる多様性である．

7.5 知見の意味

7.5.1 示唆

1094 データから示唆されることを述べる（現在形がよい）．

◆ The data suggest [/indicate] that XXX.
これらのデータは，XXX ということを示唆している [/ 示している]．

> These data suggest that in the face of age-related decline across many basic cognitive abilities, seasoned older professionals may use alternative strategies (Backman & Dixon, 1992) that employ domain-relevant knowledge to efficiently manage complex sociotechnical systems. (47)

7.5 知見の意味

これらのデータは，経験豊かな高齢の専門家が，多くの基本的な認知能力にまたがる加齢性の能力低下に直面した場合，複雑な社会技術システムを効果的に管理するために，領域関連知識を用いた代替的な方略（Backman & Dixon, 1992）を用いるかもしれないことを示唆している．

1095　分析から示唆されることを述べる．

◆ Our analysis of X suggests that YYY.

X についての我々の分析は，YYY ということを示唆する．

> Our analysis of therapist factors suggests that minority clients working with racially or culturally dissimilar therapists may have different expectations and standards for evaluating therapeutic expertise, credibility, and competence. (8)
> セラピストの要因についての我々の分析は，人種的・文化的に異なるセラピストの治療を受けているマイノリティのクライエントは，治療についての専門的技術，信頼性，能力の評価に対して異なる期待と基準をもっているかもしれないことを示唆する．

1096　今回の研究を他の研究と合わせて示唆されることを述べる．

◆ These findings, in conjunction with results of studies demonstrating that XXX, suggest that YYY.

これらの知見は，XXX を示した研究結果とともに，YYY ということを示唆する．

> These findings, in conjunction with results of studies demonstrating that intake of drugs of abuse and running activates the endogenous opioid and dopamine reward systems, suggest that it might be possible to substitute drug-taking behavior with naturally rewarding behavior. (33)
> これらの知見は，中毒薬物の摂取とランニングが内因的なオピオイドおよびドーパミン報酬系を活性化することを示した研究結果とともに，薬物摂取行動を，生来報酬性をもつ行動と置き換えることが可能であるかもしれないことを示唆する．

1097　可能性についての示唆を述べる．

◆ These results suggest the possibility that XXX.

これらの結果は，XXX という可能性を示唆している．

> These results also suggest the possibility that criteria may be useful to classify the hallucinations experienced by people with neurological disorders in order to clarify the mechanism. (15)
> これらの結果は，神経障害をもつ人々が経験する幻覚をその機序の解明を目的として分類するために，基準が有用である可能性も示唆している．

1098　総合的な見方から，ある可能性が示唆されることを述べる．

◆ Taken together, these Xs suggest that Ps are likely to QQQ.

総合すると，これらの X は P が QQQ する可能性が高いことを示唆している．

Taken together, these results suggest that as youth attempt to integrate a parental divorce into their spiritual orienting system, those who also become embroiled in spiritual struggles are particularly likely to face ongoing psychological difficulties. (61)
総合すると，これらの知見は，若者は両親の離婚を彼らのスピリチュアルな定位システムに統合しようと試みるので，スピリチュアルな苦闘にも巻き込まれることになる若者は進行している心理的困難さと特に直面しやすい，ということを示唆している．

1099 証拠から，部分的影響が示唆されることを述べる．
◆X evidence suggests that P is partially influenced by Q.
Xの証拠は，PがQに部分的に影響されることを示唆している．

> Other evidence suggests that the perceived reliability of feature representation is partially influenced by the relative predictiveness of categorical identity. (24)
> 他の証拠は，特徴表象の主観的な信頼性がカテゴリー独自性の相対的予測性に部分的に影響されることを示唆している．

1100 全体として，弱化が示唆されることを述べる．
◆Collectively [/Overall], the Xs suggest that P attenuates Q.
全体として，Xは，PがQを弱めることを示唆する．

> Collectively, the results suggest that increasing brain serotonin activity can attenuate the reinforcing and brain activating effects of cocaine. (30)
> 全体として，これらの結果は，脳内セロトニンの活動性を高めることにより，コカインの強化効果および脳内活性化効果を弱めることができることを示唆する．

1101 分析から，あることの危機が示唆されることを述べる．
◆The X analyses suggest that Ps threaten Q.
X分析は，PがQを危うくすることを示唆する．

> The mediational analyses further suggest that when a youth interprets a parental divorce as a sacred loss or desecration, such perceptions threaten his or her spiritual orienting system. (61)
> 媒介分析は，若者が両親の離婚を神聖さの喪失や神聖冒涜と解釈する場合には，そのような認識が彼らのスピリチュアルな定位システムを危うくする，ということをさらに示唆する．

1102 報告された結果から，統計的な区別の困難さが示唆されることを述べる．
◆The results reported herein suggest that Ps are statistically indistinguishable from Qs.
ここで報告された結果は，PがQと統計的に区別することができないことを示唆している．

> The results reported herein suggest that the standardized mean difference between proportions from the CGI-I scale are statistically indistinguishable from effect sizes for the Liebowitz Social Anxiety Scale. (26)

ここで報告された結果は，CGI-I 尺度から得られた比率間の標準化された平均差はリーボウィッツ社会不安尺度の効果量と区別がつかないことを示唆している．

(訳者注：CGI-I scale; Clinical Global Impression-Improvement scale, 臨床全般印象改善尺度)

7.5.2　理論的・実践的な帰結

1103　結果の意味を述べる．

◆ The results of our study [/studies] imply that XXX.

我々の研究結果は，XXX ということを意味している．

> The results of our studies imply that decision making in categorization is at least partially dependent on how features are encoded and on what level of feature representation seems most reliable in a given context. (24)
> 我々の研究結果は，カテゴリー化における意思決定が，特徴がどのようにコード化されるか，および，所定の文脈においてどのレベルの特徴表象が最も信頼できるように見えるかに少なくとも部分的に依存していることを意味している．

1104　結果が例証することを述べる．

◆ The results of the analyses illustrate that XXX.

我々の分析結果は，XXX ということを例証する．

> The results of our analyses illustrate that sociocontextual factors such as school climate and relationships with others at school have a potential role in preventing dangerous behavior at school. (58)
> 我々の分析結果は，学校風土と学校における他者との関係のような社会文脈的要因が，学校での危険な行動の防止において潜在的な役割を果たす可能性があることを例証する．

1105　研究が実証したことを述べる．

◆ This study demonstrated that XXX.

本研究は，XXX ということを実証した．

> This study demonstrated that Japanese children and adolescents differ in the relative value they place on cooperation, individualism and interpersonalism. (54)
> 本研究は，日本人の子供と青年では，協力，個人主義，間人主義に対してもつ相対的な価値が異なることを実証した．

1106　結果が主張することを述べる．

◆ The results reported herein argue that XXX.

ここで報告された結果は，XXX ということを主張する．

> The results reported herein argue that the CGI-I is indeed an effective method of assessing clinical change in a subject. (26)
> ここで報告された結果は，CGI-I が被験者の臨床的変化を評価するためのまさに効果的な方法であることを主張する．

(訳者注:CGI-I; Clinical Global Impression-Improvement scale, 臨床全般印象改善尺度)

1107 研究があることの重要性を示すことを述べる.

◆ This work has underlined the importance of X.

本研究は,Xの重要性を強調した.

> This work has underlined the importance of deservingness in defining reactions to the fate of others. (6)
> 本研究は,他者の運命に対する態度の明確化における賞罰の当然性の重要性を強調した.

1108 結果を総合することにより確認されることを述べる.

◆ Taken together, our results confirm X [/that XXX].

総合すると,我々の結果はX [/XXX ということ] を確認する.

> Taken together, our results confirm two major ways in which anticipatory time perception determines temporal discounting. (35)
> 総合すると,我々の結果は,予期的な時間知覚が時間割引を決定する2つのおもな道筋を確認する.

1109 研究がある事柄に対する洞察をもたらすことを述べる.

◆ The current X provides some insight into Y.

今回のXは,Yに対する洞察をもたらす.

> The current study provides some insight into the progression of preferences for gambling activities. (46)
> 今回の研究は,賭博活動に対する選好の進行に対する洞察をもたらす.

1110 知見が現在進行中の研究に対して意味をもつことを述べる.

◆ These Xs have implications for continued [/continuing /ongoing] research on Y.

これらのXは,Yに関する現在進行中の研究に対して意味をもつ.

> These findings have implications for continued research on contextual and brain factors that promote dysregulated behaviors. (60)
> これらの知見は,調整不全行動を増進する文脈と脳の要因に関する現在進行中の研究に対して意味をもつ.

1111 結果が,あるトピックについて,これまでに最も説得力のある証拠を与えることを述べる.

◆ The results provide the most compelling evidence so far [/thus far /to date] in support of the claim that XXX.

これらの結果は,XXXという主張に対して,これまでに最も説得力のある証拠を与える.

> The results provide the most compelling evidence so far in support of the claim that the level of perceptual load in a task determines the extent to which any additional task-irrelevant stimuli are consciously perceived. (43)

これらの結果は，課題の知覚的負荷のレベルが，課題とは無関連の追加刺激が意識上で知覚される程度を決定する，という主張に対して，これまでに最も説得力のある証拠を与える．

1112 結果が命題や理論を強固なものにすることを述べる．

◆ The [previous] results strengthen the proposal [/proposition] that XXX.

[先行] 研究の結果は，XXX という提案を強固なものにする．

> The previous results strengthen the proposal that running and drugs of abuse activate similar neural pathways. (33)
> 先行研究の結果は，ランニングと中毒薬物が類似した神経回路を活性化するという提案を強固なものにする．

1113 予備的なものであるが，結果が，あることを意味することを述べる．

◆ While [very] preliminary, these results imply that XXX.

[きわめて] 予備的ではあるが，これらの結果は，XXX ということを意味している．

> While very preliminary, these results imply that various psychological variables that have been shown to be associated with differences in discount rates, such as age, income, or intelligence, may be due to the individuals' perception of time delays rather than differences in impulsive reactions. (35)
> きわめて予備的ではあるが，これらの結果は，年齢，収入，知性などの，割引率の差と関連することが示されてきているさまざまな心理学的な変数が，衝動的な反応の差よりも，むしろ時間遅延についてのその人々の知覚に帰されるかもしれないことを意味している．

1114 結果を総合することにより，2 つの間の関連性が例証されることを述べる．

◆ Taken together, these Xs demonstrate the association between P and Q.

総合すると，これらの X は，P と Q の間には関連があることを例証している．

> Taken together, these findings demonstrate the association between perceiving the school climate as democratic and cohesive and students' motivation to speak up and take action. (58)
> 総合すると，これらの知見は，民主的および団結した学校風土を認識することと，意見を言い行動を起こす学生の動機づけの間には，関連があることを例証している．

1115 結果を要約すると，ある効果が予想とは異なることを述べる．

◆ In summary, Xs are more [/less] than [would be] expected on the basis of Y.

要するに，X は，Y から予想されるものよりも多い [/ 少ない]．

> In summary, observable heart rate changes during panic attacks are indeed less than would be expected on the basis of patient self-reports. (1)
> 要するに，パニック発作中に観察可能な心拍数の変化は，患者の自己報告から予想されるものよりも実際には少ない．

1116 研究が，ある効果を例証したことを述べる．

◆ Our Xs have demonstrated the effect of P on Q.

我々のXは，PがQへ及ぼす効果を例証した．
> Our experiments have demonstrated the effect of perceptual load on conscious perception. (43)
> 我々の実験は，知覚的負荷が意識的知覚へ及ぼす効果を例証した．

1117 研究が，研究領域の潜在的な有望性を強調することを述べる．

◆ These Xs underscore the potential of the promises of P studies.

これらのXは，P研究の潜在的な有望性を強調する．

> These findings underscore the potential of the promises of genome-wide association studies. (31)
> これらの知見は，ゲノムワイド関連研究の潜在的な有望性を強調する．

1118 研究が，ある見方の重要性を支持することを述べる．

◆ These Xs affirm the importance of a[n] P perspective.

これらのXは，Pという見方の重要性を支持する．

> These findings affirm the importance of adopting an idiographic perspective. (8)
> これらの知見は，個性記述的な見方を採用することの重要性を支持する．

1119 データが，構成についての主張を支持する傾向があることを述べる．

◆ The Xs tend to support the contention that the Ps comprise Q.

Xは，PがQを構成するという主張を支持する傾向にある．

> The data tend to support the contention that the five highest value items comprise one factor. (7)
> データは，最も値の高い5つの項目が1つの要因を構成するという主張を支持する傾向がある．

1120 結果が，ある課題を遂行する能力についての証拠を提供することを述べる．

◆ X provides [compelling] evidence that P can solve Q[s].

Xは，PがQを解くことができるという[説得的な]証拠を提供する．

> Mickey's performance provides compelling evidence that a member of a New World monkey species can solve a problem involving analogical reasoning. (34)
> ミッキーの成績は，新世界ザル種の一員が類推的推論を含む課題を解くことができるという説得的な証拠を提供する．

（訳者注：ミッキーとは，被験体の名前である）

1121 結果が，ある過程への関与を意味することを述べる．

◆ The X presented here implicate P in the processes of both Q and R.

ここで示したXは，QとRの両方の過程にPが関与していることを意味している．

> The data presented here implicate ROCK activity in the processes of both learning and the ability to handle a high working memory load. (31)

ここで示したデータは，学習，および，高い作業記憶負荷を扱う能力の両方の過程にROCK 活性が関与していることを意味している．

(訳者注：ROCK; Rho-associated coiled-coil-containing protein kinase, セリン・スレオニンタンパク質リン酸化酵素)

7.6 知見の説明・原因・理由

7.6.1 説　明

1122　結果に可能な説明を与える．

◆A possible explanation for X might be Y.

X の可能な説明の1つとしては，Y が挙げられるかもしれない．

> A possible explanation for the absence of the risk amplification pattern might be the nature of the sample. (22)
> 危険増幅パターンが見られなかったことについて考えられる1つの説明としては，サンプルの性質が挙げられるかもしれない．

1123　知見の可能な説明について詳しく述べる．

◆One possible explanation for X is that YYY.

X の可能な説明の1つは，YYY ということである．

> One possible explanation for this finding is that the feelings of solidarity students report having with their peers lead them to feel bonded against the administration. (58)
> この知見の可能な説明の1つは，学生が同輩と共有していると報告する団結感のために，学生は，管理者側に対抗して結束していると感じるようになるということである．

1124　1 つの説明を提案する．

◆It is possible that XXX.

XXX という可能性がある．

> It is possible that gamblers who take the step to approach casino personnel for self-exclusion may be more motivated to seek services than other problem gamblers. (46)
> 自己排除のためにカジノの職員にアプローチする手続きをとる賭博者は，他の問題賭博者よりも，助けを求めるようにより強く動機づけられているかもしれない，という可能性がある．

1125　知見が，あることにより部分的に説明されることを述べる．

◆This result may be explained in part [/partly] by X.

この結果は，X により部分的に説明されるかもしれない．

> This result may, in part, be explained by the discrete levels of community tapped by these measures. (58)
> この結果は，これらの測度により取り出されたコミュニティのレベルが離散的であることにより，部分的に説明されるかもしれない．

1126　結果が，ある影響を反映していることを述べる．

◆ These results may reflect the influences of X on Y.

これらの結果は，X が Y に及ぼす影響を反映しているのかもしれない．

> These results may reflect the influences of classroom experiences on orientations toward the self, peers, and tasks. (54)
> これらの結果は，学級での経験が自己，同輩，課題に対する態度に及ぼす影響を反映しているのかもしれない．

1127　結果が，ある観点から理解できることを述べる．

◆ From a developmental [/social psychological /clinical /theoretical] perspective, it is understandable why XXX: YYY.

発達心理学的 [/ 社会心理学的 / 臨床的 / 理論的] な観点からは，どうして XXX なのか，ということは理解できる．すなわち，YYY なのである．

> From a developmental perspective, it is understandable why this strategy is the preferred response for adolescents: not only does it sidestep the possibility of involving adults, which may invite trouble, but also it reflects their growing sense of autonomy. (58)
> 発達心理学的な観点からは，どうしてこの方略が青年に好まれる反応であるのかは理解できる．すなわち，そのような反応は，大人を巻き込み，トラブルを招くかもしれない可能性を回避するのみならず，自律性の意識が成長しつつあることを反映しているのである．

1128　結果の説明が複数あることを述べる．

◆ There are N notable theoretical accounts that could explain X. According to the Y account, AAA. Alternatively, the Z account suggests that BBB.

X を説明できる N 個の注目すべき理論的説明がある．Y による説明によれば，AAA であるとされる．代わりの考え方として，Z による説明によれば，BBB ということが示唆される．

> There are two notable theoretical accounts that could explain the lack of effect of either novelty or cocaine after a long retention interval: stimulus generalization or the context-change account of forgetting. According to the stimulus generalization account, recall of detailed stimulus properties within a learning situation is transient because specific attributes of stimuli are forgotten. Alternatively, the context-change account suggests that perception of contextual cues present at the time of conditioning changes with the passage of time. (49)
> 長い保持間隔の後では新奇性とコカインのどちらも効果がないことを説明できる2つの注目すべき理論的説明がある．すなわち，忘却の刺激般化，あるいは，文脈変化による説明である．刺激般化による説明によれば，刺激の特定の属性が忘却されるために，学習場面内の詳細な刺激特性の想起は一過性のものであるとされる．代わりの考え方として，文脈変化による説明によれば，条件づけのときに存在した文脈手がかりの知覚が時間経過とともに変化することが示唆される．

7.6 知見の説明・原因・理由

1129 複数の理由を挙げて，自らの解釈を主張する（明快でよいパターン）．

◆We would argue that XXX for N [primary] reasons. First, YYY. Second, ZZZ.

我々は，以下のN個の[おもな]理由からXXXと主張したい．その第一の理由は，YYYである．第二の理由として，ZZZということがある．

> We would also argue that the analogical task solved by Mickey in the current study was more challenging than the spatial task performed by the monkeys in Spinozzi et al.'s study for two primary reasons. First, the subjects in the current study were required to direct their attention to the location of hidden food that was unattainable and use this information to search under the object of analogous size in their own set. (略) A second difference between Spinozzi et al.'s task and the current study was the number of stimuli the subjects had to choose from. (34)
> また，我々は，本研究においてミッキーが解いた類推的課題は，以下の2つのおもな理由から，Spinozziらの研究でサルが取り組んだ空間的課題よりも難しいと主張したい．その第一の理由は，今回の研究の被験体は，手の届かない隠された食物の位置に注意を向け，その情報を自分の組の中で類似している大きさの対象の下を探索するのに使用することを要求されたことである．（略）本研究とSpinozziらの課題との第二の差異は，被験体が選択しなければならない刺激の数であった．

（訳者注：ミッキーとは，被験体の名前である）

1130 ある説明を述べ，その説明が正しくないと論駁する．

◆One could argue that XXX. However, it has been established that YYY.

XXXという主張があるかもしれない．しかし，YYYであることが立証されてきている．

> One could argue that Pyr and GPT exert some of their neuroprotective effects in the brain compartment rather than the blood compartment since CHI causes an opening of the blood-brain barrier. However, it has been established that the latter opening after CHI is transient. (64)
> CHIは脳血液関門の開通を引き起こすので，PyrとGPTは，血液区画よりもむしろ脳区画において神経保護的な効果を発揮する，という主張があるかもしれない．しかし，CHI後の後者の開通は一過性であることが立証されてきている．

（訳者注：CHI; closed head injury, 閉鎖性頭部外傷：Pyr; pyruvate, ピルビン酸：GPT; glutamate-pyruvate transaminase, グルタミン酸ピルビン酸トランスアミナーゼ）

1131 代わりの説明が考えられることを述べる．

◆An alternative explanation for X is that YYY.

Xの代わりの説明としては，YYYということが挙げられる．

> An alternative explanation for the results of Experiment 3 is that unitization may increase the speed of the recollection process. (12)
> 実験3の結果の代わりの説明としては，ユニット化が回想過程の速度を増加させるかもしれない，ということが挙げられる．

1132 代わりの説明が除外されたことを述べる.

◆X ruled out alternative explanations of the Y effects in terms of Z.

X は，Z により Y 効果が起こるという代わりの説明を除外した．

> Experiment 4 ruled out alternative explanations of the perceptual-load effects in terms of a difference in the search strategy employed. (14)
> 実験 4 は，採用される探索方略の差異により知覚的負荷効果が起こる，という代わりの説明を除外した．

1133 結果が，仮説とは関係のない変数によるものではないことを述べる.

◆These findings were not due to a[n] X account or to differences in Y.

これらの知見は，X による説明に帰されず，また，Y の差異によるものではない．

> More important, these findings were not due to a stimulus generalization account or to differences in activity impacting compartment choice. (49)
> さらに重要なことは，これらの知見は刺激般化による説明に帰されず，また，コンパートメントの選択に影響する活動性の差異によるものでもない，ということである．

1134 結果が真の群間差を反映しているのか，それとも偶然なのかを確定することができないことを述べる.

◆It cannot be determined whether X reflects genuine group [/sex] differences, or if it merely occurred by chance.

X が，真の群間差 [/ 性差] を反映しているのか，それとも，単なる偶然によるものなのかについては，確定することができない．

> However, it cannot be determined whether this observation reflects genuine sex differences, the greater level of running in females than in males, or if it merely occurred by chance. (33)
> しかしながら，この観察結果が，雄よりも雌のほうが走行レベルが高いという真の性差を反映しているのか，それとも，単なる偶然によるものなのかについては，確定することができない．

7.6.2 原因・理由

1135 知見の理由を述べる.

◆A possible contributor to this finding might have been X.

この知見の一因としては，X が挙げられるかもしれない．

> A possible contributor to this finding might have been attenuation in the homeless group. (22)
> この知見の一因としては，ホームレスグループの弱化ということがあったのかもしれない．

1136 知見の他の理由を述べる.

◆A more plausible reason for the [/our] finding could be that XXX.

7.6 知見の説明・原因・理由

この [/ 我々の] 知見のよりもっともらしい理由としては，XXX ということが考えられる．

A more plausible reason for our finding could be that, given that the experience of interacting with the ATC simulation platform is analogous to playing an interactive video game, younger inexperienced adults are much better suited for such tasks compared with their older counterparts. (47)

我々の知見のよりもっともらしい理由としては，ATC のシミュレーションプラットホームとの対話的なやりとりの経験が対話型ビデオゲームで遊ぶことと類似しているとすれば，若年の非経験者が高齢の非経験者と比べてそのような課題にははるかに向いているため，ということが考えられるだろう．

（訳者注：ATC; air-traffic control, 航空管制）

1137 天井効果が原因であることを述べる．

◆X may be attributed to the fact that performance of the Y may have been too easy, producing a ceiling effect.

X は，Y を行うことがあまりにやさしかったために，天井効果を生み出していたかもしれない，ということに帰せられるかもしれない．

The failure to obtain a significant effect in Cond. Dm+ may be attributed, in part, to the fact that the performance of the correct response may have been too easy, producing a ceiling effect. (18)

Dm+ 条件で有意な効果が見られなかったことは，正反応の遂行があまりにやさしかったために，天井効果を生み出していたかもしれない，ということに部分的に帰せられるかもしれない．

1138 先行研究の知見が得られなかった理由を 2 つ述べる．

◆This was not the case in the present study for two reasons. First, XXX. A second explanation concerns Y.

このことは，本研究では見出されなかった．それには 2 つの理由が考えられる．第一に，XXX である．第二の説明は Y に関係するものである．

This was not the case in the present study for two reasons. First, on self-report measures and in most Western game-playing tasks thought to tap competitive motivation, behavior which maximizes the individual's rewards (individualistic acts) is defined as competitive. (略) A second explanation concerns cultural values. (54)

このことは，本研究では見出されなかった．それには，2 つの理由が考えられる．第一に，競争的動機づけをとらえているとされる自己報告型の測度，および，たいていの欧米のゲーム遊び型課題では，個人の報酬を最大化する行動（個人主義的な行為）が競争的と定義されていることである．（略）第二の理由は，文化的な価値観に関係するものである．

（訳者注：文頭の「このこと」とは，「欧米の男子は青年期により競争的になる」という先行研究の知見をさす）

1139 原因がよくわからないが，推論は可能であること，また，それでも不明な点

があることを述べる.

◆It is not clear why XXX. It is possible that YYY. It remains unclear, however, why ZZZ.

なぜ XXX であるかについてはわからない．YYY という可能性はある．しかし，ZZZ である理由については明らかではない．

> It is not clear why this particular task appealed to him more than others presented in our lab, although it is possible that Mickey showed greater motivation for this task because it involved actively searching for food. It remains unclear, however, why Mickey performed better on this task in comparison with the three other monkeys tested. (34)
> なぜこの特定の課題が実験室で呈示された他の課題よりもミッキーの興味をより強く引いたのかについてはわからない．ただ，この課題が食物の能動的な探索を含むために，ミッキーがより強い動機づけを示した，という可能性はある．しかし，テストされた他の3個体のサルと比べて，ミッキーが成績がよかった理由については明らかではない．

（訳者注：ミッキーとは，被験体の名前である）

1140 因果関係を示すことはできないが，あることを示している可能性があることを述べる.

◆Although the current study cannot determine causal implications [/causality], these findings may indicate that XXX.

本研究は因果関係を明らかにすることはできないが，これらの知見は XXX ということを示しているのかもしれない．

> Although the current study cannot determine causal implications, these findings may indicate that grandchildren in lone-parent and step-families are the chief beneficiaries of grandparent contact and that this contact is an important protective resource in their lives. (2)
> 本研究は因果関係を明らかにすることはできないが，これらの知見は，ひとり親の家庭や再婚家庭で暮らす孫は祖父母の接触が大きな利益をもたらす対象であること，および，この接触が彼らの人生における保護的な資源であることを示しているのかもしれない．

7.6.3 推　論

1141 個人的推論を述べる.

◆It appears that XXX.

XXX であると思われる．

> It appears that electronic diaries will be increasingly popular tools in routine clinical assessment. (1)
> 電子的な日記が日常の臨床評価における道具としてますます普及すると思われる．

1142 最初に推論を述べ，議論を始める.

◆We speculate that XXX. [The] Y data suggest that ZZZ.

我々は，XXX であると推論する．Y のデータは ZZZ を示唆している．

7.6 知見の説明・原因・理由

We speculate that attention to action is another factor that promotes activation of goals despite continued repetition. Neuroimaging data suggest that automatic responses that receive attention during execution are likely to engage systems involved in goal pursuit. (62)
我々は，行為に対する注意が，連続反復にもかかわらず目標活性化を促進するもう1つの要因であると推測する．神経イメージング的なデータは，実行中に注意を受ける自動的な反応は目標追求に含まれるシステムを働かせやすいことを示唆している．

1143 複数の知見から推測されることを述べる．

◆In light of these findings, it is reasonable to assume that XXX.
これらの知見から，XXX と推測することは理にかなっている．

> In light of these findings, it is reasonable to assume that some adolescents view teachers as a viable outlet to whom they could go, without getting into trouble, if they need adult guidance regarding concerns about another's dangerous intentions. (58)
> これらの知見から，同輩の危険な意図に関する心配事について大人の指導が必要な場合に，教師を，トラブルに巻き込まれることなく相談に行ける実行可能なはけ口であると思い込む青年もいる，と考えることは理にかなっている．

1144 今回の知見を過去の知見と照らし合わせて，ある推論を述べる．

◆On the basis of the present study, as well as previous research, it seems reasonable to XXX.
本研究，および，先行研究を基盤とすれば，XXX することは理にかなっているように思われる．

> On the basis of the present study, as well as previous research, it seems reasonable to distinguish between two very different decision-making contexts. (57)
> 本研究，および，先行研究を基盤とすれば，2つのまったく異なる意思決定の文脈を区別することは理にかなっているように思われる．

1145 手続きの特徴を述べ，それから推測される解釈を述べる．

◆In the current experiment[s], XXX. Thus, Y presumably ZZZ.
今回の実験では，XXX であった．それゆえ，Y は ZZZ なのであろう．

> In the current experiments, rats experienced the rewarding aspects of systemic cocaine by alternating daily placements into the chamber. Thus, an association is presumably formed between the physiological effects of cocaine (US) and the features of the environment (the CS). (49)
> 今回の実験では，ラットは実験箱への配置を毎日交代されることにより全身投与コカインの報酬的な側面を経験した．それゆえ，おそらく，コカインの生理的な効果（US）と環境の特徴（そのCS）の間に連合が形成されるのであろう．
>
> （訳者注：US; unconditioned stimulus, 無条件刺激：CS; conditioned stimulus, 条件刺激）

1146 推論を次々に提案する．

◆We must also consider the impact that Xs have. At the same time, YYY. It is also

possible that ZZZ.
我々は，X の影響についても考慮しなければならならない．同時に，YYY である．また，ZZZ ということも考えられる．

> We must also consider the impact that school policies (e.g., zero tolerance) have in creating an atmosphere in which students feel they can (or cannot) confide in a teacher or principal. In this post-Columbine era, public education has seen an increase in zero tolerance policies. At the same time, policy discussions such as the one led by Verdugo and Glenn (2002) suggest that zero tolerance policies are only partially effective, and in some cases may exacerbate the problem behavior. It is also possible that these policies create an environment that actually discourages students from revealing their concerns to teachers because of the increased "costs" of revelation. (58)
> 我々は，学校の方針（たとえば，ゼロ・トレランス方式）が，教師や校長に打ち明けられる（あるいは打ち明けられない）と感じる雰囲気をつくる際にもつ影響についても考慮しなければならならない．コロンバイン高校事件後の時代に，公立学校では，ゼロ・トレランス方式が増加している．同時に，Verdugo と Glenn（2002）を旗頭としてなされているような方針についての議論は，ゼロ・トレランス方式が部分的にしか有効ではなく，事例によっては問題行動を悪化させることを示唆している．これらの方針は，問題発覚の「コスト」を増加させることから，心配事を先生に教えようという学生の勇気を実際にくじく環境をつくっている，ということも考えられる．

（訳者注：ゼロ・トレランス方式とは不寛容の厳罰主義のことである）

7.7　知見の重要性・貢献

7.7.1　重要性

1147　ある知見が特に重要であることを，先行研究から示される理由とともに述べる．

◆ This is especially important, as [/because /in that] XXX.
XXX なので，このことは特に重要である．

> This is especially important, as research shows that the emotional benefits of grandparent contact may persist into adulthood. (2)
> 祖父母との接触の情動的な利点が成人まで続くことを示す研究があるので，このことは特に重要である．

1148　問題が特に重要であることを，臨床的な理由とともに述べる．

◆ This issue is particularly important because X treatment approaches rely on Y.
X の治療アプローチは Y に頼ることから，この問題は特に重要である．

> This issue is particularly important because many novel treatment approaches rely less on direct therapeutic guidance but use new technologies for remote care. (1)

多くの新しい治療アプローチは直接的な治療指導にあまり頼らず，遠隔医療のための新しい技術を用いることから，この問題は特に重要である．

1149 研究により明らかにされた要因が，実際の社会問題と関連することを述べる．

◆These factors are particularly relevant to the risk of X.
これらの要因は，X のリスクと特に関連している．

> These factors are particularly relevant to the risk of suicide in older adult gamblers. (46)
> これらの要因は，高齢の賭博者における自殺のリスクと特に関連している．

1150 結果が多くの実用場面で重要であることを，例とともに述べる．

◆Results from this study have a number of practical implications. For example, XXX.
本研究の結果は，数多くの実用的な意味をもっている．たとえば，XXX．

> Results from this study have a number of practical implications. For example, conducting workshops and support groups that acknowledge the experience of discrimination across many settings with some specific tailoring by group might aid in promoting the value of diversity and cultural acceptance. (32)
> 本研究の結果は，数多くの実用的な意味をもっている．たとえば，各グループに特異的な調整をしながら多くの場面にまたがって見られる差別の経験を知らせるワークショップやサポートグループを実践することは，多様性と文化受容の価値を高めるのに役立つかもしれない．

1151 今回の研究が，日常生活の場面において実用的意味をもつことを述べる．

◆The present research has promising practical implications for X in daily life.
今回の研究は，日常生活における X にとって，有望な実用的意味をもつ．

> The present research has promising practical implications for determining the situations in which people are particularly susceptible to distraction in daily life. (14)
> 今回の研究は，日常生活で人々が特に妨害されやすい状況の判定にとって，有望な実用的意味をもつ．

7.7.2 貢　献

1152 研究の独自の貢献を直接述べる．

◆The unique contribution of this study is that XXX.
本研究の独自の貢献は，XXX である．

> The unique contribution of this study is that we manipulated a vehicle through which implicit knowledge is often expressed (gesture) and observed the effect of that manipulation on learning. (5)
> 本研究の独自の貢献は，暗黙的知識が表現されることが多い媒体（ジェスチャー）を操作して，その操作が学習に及ぼす効果を観察したことである．

302   7. 考察（Discussion）

1153　今回の結果が文献に数多くの点で貢献することを述べる．
◆The results from [/of] this study contribute to the X literature in a number of ways.
本研究の結果は，X についての文献に多くの点で貢献する．
> The results from this study contribute to the discrimination–health literature in a number of ways. (32)
> 本研究の結果は，差別と健康の関連性の文献に多くの点で貢献する．

1154　研究が貢献した点を系統的に示す．
◆The present study contributes to the literature in N ways. First, XXX. Second, YYY. Third, ZZZ.
本研究は，N の点でこの分野の文献に貢献する．まず第一に，XXX．そして第二に，YYY．さらに第三に，ZZZ．
> The present study contributes to the literature in several ways. First, it contributes to theory on the use of distributed information in decision-making groups.（略）Second, the present study contributes to what we know about team reflection by demonstrating how shared task representations can explain some of the effects of team reflection.（略）Third, the present study contributes to research on the development of shared (task) cognition. (59)
> 本研究は，いくつかの点でこの分野の文献に貢献する．まず第一に，意思決定グループにおける分配情報の使用についての理論に貢献する．（略）そして第二に，本研究は，共有される課題表象がチーム内省の効果のある部分をどのように説明するかを例証することにより，チーム内省についての我々の知識に貢献する．（略）さらに第三に，本研究は共有される（課題）認知の発達についての研究に貢献する．

1155　あることを例証することにより，トピックの文献を発展させることを主張する．
◆The present study advances the X literature by demonstrating Y.
本研究は，Y を例証することにより，X の文献を発展させる．
> The present study advances the executive coaching literature by demonstrating the perceived efficacy of this increasingly popular form of development. (48)
> 本研究は，普及しつつあるこの開発形式の効力感を例証することにより，幹部社員コーチングの文献を発展させる．

1156　あるトピックをこれまでとは異なる方法で調べたという貢献を述べる．
◆We examined X under conditions that have received very little attention in the literature.
我々は，これまでの文献ではほとんど注目されてこなかった条件の下で，X を調べた．
> We examined function learning and extrapolation under exposure conditions that have received very little attention in the literature. (44)

7.7 知見の重要性・貢献 303

我々は，これまでの文献ではほとんど注目されてこなかった曝露条件の下で，関数学習と外挿を調べた．

1157 2つのアプローチを1つにするという貢献を述べる．

◆The results from [/of] the experiment[s] presented here illustrate the utility of bridging the X and Y literatures on Z.

ここで報告した実験の結果は，ZについてのXとYの文献の間に橋渡しをすることの有用性を例証している．

> The results from the experiments presented here illustrate the utility of bridging the behavioral and neuroimaging literatures on source recognition. (12)
> ここで報告した実験の結果は，情報源再認についての行動研究と神経イメージング研究の文献の間に橋渡しをすることの有用性を例証している．

1158 2つの研究トピックの間の空白部分を埋めたことを述べる．

◆The analyses addressed gaps in the research on X and Y.

この分析は，X研究とY研究の間の空白部分に取り組んだ．

> The analyses addressed gaps in the research on family violence among adolescents who are homeless and family violence among adolescents more generally. (22)
> この分析は，ホームレスの青年の家庭内暴力研究と，青年の家庭内暴力研究の間の空白部分に，より広く取り組んだ．

1159 あるトピックを調べた最初の研究であることを述べる．

◆This study was [/is] the first to examine X.

本研究は，Xを調べた最初の研究であった [/である]．

> This study is the first to examine age differences in the demographic characteristics and gambling preferences of casino self-excluders. (46)
> 本研究は，カジノの自己排除者の人口統計学的特徴と賭博選好における年齢差を調べた最初の研究である．

1160 あることを調べた研究がこれまでにないことを述べる．

◆These findings are important because no research to date has explored X.

Xを調べた研究はこれまでに存在しないので，これらの知見は重要である．

> These findings are important because no research to date has explored the ways in which youths' spiritual beliefs about or responses to their parents' divorce relate to their psychological or spiritual adjustment. (61)
> 両親の離婚についての若者のスピリチュアルな信念や反応が彼らの心理的あるいはスピリチュアルな適応にどのように関係するかを調べた研究はこれまでに存在しないので，これらの知見は重要である．

1161 トピックをある方向に沿って調べた最初の研究であることを，成果とともに

述べる.

◆Although further experiments are necessary to confirm X, the present results can be considered an initial step in that direction, providing Y.

X を確認するためにはさらなる実験が必要であるが，今回の結果はその方向に向けての最初のステップであると考えられ，Y をもたらした.

> Although further experiments are necessary to confirm the mechanisms underlying hydroxyfasudil-induced functional improvements on learning and memory, the present results can be considered an initial step in that direction, providing support for hypothesis that ROCK inhibition initiates a cascade of events that can influence cognition. (31)
> 塩酸ファスジルに誘発される学習と記憶の機能的改善の基盤となる機序を確認するためにはさらなる実験が必要であるが，今回の結果はこの方向に沿った最初のステップであると考えられ，ROCK の抑制が認知に影響しうる連続的な事象を開始させるという仮説に対する支持をもたらした.

（訳者注：ROCK; Rho-associated coiled-coil-containing protein kinase, セリン・スレオニンタンパク質リン酸化酵素）

7.8　限界・短所・長所

7.8.1　限界・短所

1162　サンプルサイズと人口統計学的特徴に問題があったことを述べる.

◆This sample of N participants is [/was] small and limited with regard to X as well as Y and Z.

N 名の参加者という今回のサンプルは数が少なく，かつ，X，および，Y と Z の点で限定されたものである [/ であった].

> First, this sample of 43 fathers is small and limited with regard to ethnicity as well as marital and socioeconomic status. (45)
> 第一に，43 名の父親という今回のサンプルは数が少なく，かつ，民族性，および，婚姻の状態，社会経済的地位の点で限定されたものである.

1163　研究デザインに不備があったことを認める.

◆We also acknowledge [/It is also acknowledged] that XXX.

我々は，XXX ということも認めなければならない.

> We also acknowledge that the use of a longitudinal design would have afforded us the opportunity to control for selective attrition effects. (47)
> 我々は，縦断的なデザインを用いていたならば，選択的な摩滅効果を制御する機会があったであろう，ということも認めなければならない.

1164　手続き上，2 つの要因に混同があったことを述べる.

◆It is important to note that P and Q were confounded with one another.

P と Q が互いに混同されていることに注意することは重要である.

It is important to note that age and experience were confounded with one another in the controller group. (47)

管制官の群では年齢と経験が互いに混同されていることに注意することは重要である.

1165 手続き上,結果には偏りがあるかもしれないことを述べる.

◆The present results may be biased because XXX.

XXX なので,今回の結果には偏りがあるかもしれない.

The present results may be biased because some children did not complete a reading assessment at some data points. (23)

データ収集のいくつかの時点で読書の評価を終えていなかった子供がいたことから,今回の結果には偏りがあるかもしれない.

1166 1つの限界を述べる.

◆One limitation of the study was its reliance on X.

本研究の限界の1つは,X に依存したことであった.

One limitation of the study was its reliance on single informant (i.e., adolescent self-report) measurement of parent–adolescent violence. (22)

本研究の限界の1つは,親 – 青年の暴力について単一の情報提供者(すなわち,青年の自己報告)による測度に依存したことであった.

1167 複数の限界に注意する必要があることを述べる.

◆Several [/Some] limitations to [/of] this X study [/research] should be noted.

今回の X 研究には,いくつかの限界があることに注意しなければならない.

Several limitations to this initial validation study of the IAT–Anxiety should also be noted. (13)

IAT– 不安の妥当性に関する今回の初めての研究には,いくつかの限界があることに注意しなければならない.

(訳者注:IAT; Implicit Association Test, 潜在的連合テスト)

1168 考慮すべき複数の限界を述べる.

◆Several limitations require consideration concerning X.

X に関しては,いくつかの限界について考慮する必要がある.

Several limitations require consideration concerning this study. (27)

本研究に関しては,いくつかの限界について考慮する必要がある.

1169 複数の明白な限界を具体的に述べる.

◆The current study has obvious limitations, such as X, Y, and Z.

今回の研究には,X, Y, Z のように,明らかな限界がある.

The current study has obvious limitations, such as the use of categorical variables and the absence of valid screening instruments. (46)

今回の研究には，カテゴリー変数を使用したことや，妥当なスクリーニング法が欠如していたことなど，明らかな限界がある．

1170 留意すべき複数の短所を述べる．

◆ When interpreting the results of X, readers should bear N caveats in mind.

X の結果を解釈する際には，N つの重要な警告を心に留めておくべきである．

> When interpreting the results of the present study, readers should bear several caveats in mind. (58)
> 今回の研究結果を解釈する際には，いくつかの重要な警告を心に留めておくべきである．

1171 複数の問題点を詳しく列挙する．

◆ Our findings should be considered with the following reservations and caveats in mind. First, XXX. Second, YYY. Third, ZZZ.

我々の知見は，以下の制限と警告を心に留めながら考察されるべきである．第一に，XXX．第二に，YYY．第三に，ZZZ．

> Our findings should be considered with the following reservations and caveats in mind. First, a major criticism of longitudinal research is that the initial measurement does not reflect a no-cause baseline or a "steady state" and that the time lag chosen is not optimal. (略) Second, the influence flows we identified may be spurious because they were induced by variables that remain exogenous to our model. (略) Third, our two-wave design is but an inferior alternative to a true time-series design with many data collection points, which allows for testing the rate of change and nonlinear change patterns. (52)
> 我々の知見は，以下の制限と警告を心に留めながら考察されるべきである．第一に，縦断的研究に対するおもな批判として，最初の測定が原因を含まないベースライン，あるいは，定常状態を反映しておらず，選ばれた時間差は最適ではないというものがある．(略) 第二に，我々が同定した影響の流れは，我々のモデルにとってはいまだに外因的であるような変数により引き起こされたために，擬似的なものであるかもしれない．(略) 第三に，我々の 2 回データを収集するデザインは，多くのデータ収集時点を含む真の時系列デザインと比べると，見劣りする選択肢にすぎないことである．そのような真の時系列デザインを用いれば，変化率や非線形的変化パターンを検証することが可能になる．

1172 いくつかの長所はあるが，いくつかの限界もあることを述べる（**several** よりも **some** のほうが限界が少なく感じる）．

◆ Although the study has [/had] several strengths, including X, Y, and Z, it also has [/had] several [/some] limitations.

この研究は X, Y, Z などのいくつかの長所をもつ [/ もっていた] が，いくつかの [/ ある程度の] 限界もある [/ あった]．

> Although the study has several strengths, including a large sample size, recruitment soon after a trauma, and a prospective longitudinal design, it also has several limitations. (36)
> この研究はサンプルサイズが大きいこと，心的外傷直後に募集を行ったこと，前向きの縦断的デザインであることなどの長所をもつが，いくつかの限界もある．

1173 知見は既存の文献に寄与するが，研究には多くの短所があることを述べる．

◆ Although the findings from this study add to the existing literature on X and Y, a number of limitations deserve mention. First, AAA. In addition, BBB. Third, CCC.

本研究から得られた知見はXとYに関する既存の文献に寄与するけれども，多くの限界があることは言及に値する．第一に，AAAである．加えて，BBBである．第三に，CCCである．

> Although the findings from this study add to the existing literature on discrimination and mental health outcomes, a number of limitations deserve mention. First, data were collected on college students who are a select and resilient group, able to overcome barriers, and perhaps have particular coping strategies. (略) In addition, there are dozens of distinct Asian and Latino ethnic groups with different backgrounds, status, and experiences. (略) Third, like most discrimination studies, data were cross-sectional and directionality of effects cannot be certain. (32)
>
> 本研究から得られた知見は差別と精神保健の結果変数に関する既存の文献に寄与するけれども，数多くの限界があることは言及に値する．第一に，優秀で回復力のあるグループに属しており，障壁を乗り越える能力があり，おそらくは特定のコーピング方略をもっている大学生から，データが得られていることである．（略）加えて，それぞれ異なる背景，地位，経験をもつ何ダースもの異なるアジア系およびラテンアメリカ系民族グループがいるということである．（略）第三に，大部分の差別研究がそうであるように，データは横断的なものであり，効果の方向性は判然としない．

1174 探索的な研究のために，結論と意味に複数の限界があることを述べる．

◆ Because X was an exploratory study, [its] conclusions and implications should be considered in light of its [/some] limitations.

Xは探索的な研究であり，[その] 結論と意味については，その [/いくつかの] 限界を考慮しながら考察されるべきである．

> Because this was an exploratory study, conclusions and implications should be considered in light of some potential limitations. (41)
>
> 今回は探索的な研究であり，結論と意味については，いくつかの潜在的な限界を考慮しながら考察されるべきである．

7.8.2　長　所

1175 研究の長所を述べる．

◆ The present study has [/had] a number of strengths, including A [, B, and C].

本研究は，A [, B, C] を含む，数多くの長所をもっている [/いた]．

> The present study has a number of strengths, including the integration of a unique set of stress inductions and multiple methodologies (electrophysiological, overt behavior, self-report mood) into a unified experimental paradigm. (60)

本研究は，ストレス誘導の独自の組と複数の方法論（電気生理学的，観察可能な行動，自己報告による気分）を単一の実験パラダイムに統合したことを含む，数多くの長所をもっている．

1176 多少の問題があっても，長所があることを述べる．

◆ Nevertheless, we do believe that the present results provide X.

にもかかわらず，我々は今回の結果が X を提供すると信じている．

> Nevertheless, we do believe that the present results provide accurate information regarding the benefits of experience. (47)
> にもかかわらず，我々は今回の結果が経験の恩恵に関する正確な情報を提供すると信じている．

1177 短所はあるが，ある考えを支持するという長所もあることを述べる．

◆ Despite these limitations, the [/our] study provides support for the notion that XXX.

これらの限界があるにもかかわらず，この [/ 我々の] 研究は XXX という考えを支持する．

> Despite these limitations, our study provides support for the notion that actual control of background sounds can have a negative effect on tinnitus interference. (28)
> これらの限界があるにもかかわらず，我々の研究は，背景音を実際に制御することが耳鳴りの干渉性に対して負の効果をもつ可能性があるという考えを支持する．

1178 短所はあるが，先行研究の理論と一致するという長所もあることを述べる．

◆ In spite of these limitations, the [/our] findings are consistent with extant theories in the literature concerning X.

これらの限界はあるが，この [/ 我々の] 知見は X についての文献に現存する理論と一致する．

> In spite of these limitations, our findings are consistent with extant theories in the literature concerning the consequences of parental absence for the development of adolescents. (2)
> これらの限界はあるが，我々の知見は，親の不在が青年の発達にもたらす結果についての文献に現存する理論と一致する．

1179 研究に限界はあるが，研究文献を進展させるという長所もあることを述べる．

◆ Despite these limitations, the present results advance the research literature on X.

これらの限界があるにもかかわらず，本研究の結果は X についての研究文献を進展させる．

> Despite these limitations, the present results advance the research literature on motivational states and aggression. (60)
> これらの限界があるにもかかわらず，本研究の結果は動機づけ状態と攻撃についての研究文献を進展させる．

7.9 今後の展開の可能性

7.9.1 追試の必要性

1180 知見の再現性を確かめるために，さらなる研究が必要があることを述べる．
◆Further research is needed to replicate the current findings on X.
  X に関する今回の知見を再現するために，さらなる研究が必要である．

> Previous research has provided few explanations as to why these patterns should be present, and further research is needed to replicate the current findings on relocation. (3)
> これまでの研究はなぜこれらのパターンが存在するに至ったのかについてほとんど説明を与えておらず，移住に関する今回の知見を再現するために，さらなる研究が必要である．

1181 より実質的な結論を得るために，追試が必要であることを述べる．
◆More evidence is warranted before reaching [/we reach] definitive [/substantive] conclusions about X.
  X について決定的な [/ 実質的な] 結論を得るためには，さらなる証拠が必要である．

> More empirical evidence seems warranted before we reach more substantive conclusions about the effects of reflection on team performance. (59)
> 内省がチームの成績に及ぼす効果についてより実質的な結論を得るためには，さらなる経験的な証拠が必要であろう．

(訳者注：ここでは substantive よりも，definitive や definite を用いるほうがより一般的でよい)

1182 追試を正当化し，その内容を示唆する．
◆Clearly, replication of this [/our] study is necessary, and future studies should XXX.
  明らかにこの [/ 我々の] 研究の再現が必要であり，今後の研究は XXX を行う必要がある．

> Clearly, replication of our study is necessary, and future studies should directly compare the performance of monkeys presented with problems in this manner to the performance of monkeys that are required to solve the problem with no other prior problem-solving experience. (34)
> 明らかに我々の研究の再現が必要であり，今後の研究は，問題をこのような仕方で呈示されたサルの成績を，事前の問題解決経験が他にない状態でその問題を解くことを要求されたサルの成績と，直接比較するべきである．

1183 結果は特定の母集団に限定されるものであり，他の母集団でも再現されるべきであることを述べる．
◆The results are limited to X, and they need to be replicated with Y populations.
  これらの結果は X に限定されるものであり，Y の母集団で再現される必要がある．

> The results are therefore limited to survivors of physical assaults, and they need to be replicated with other trauma populations. (36)

したがって，これらの結果は身体的暴行の生存者に限定されるものであり，他の心的外傷の母集団で再現される必要がある．

7.9.2 今後取り組むべき問題

1184 今後取り組むべき1つの問題を述べる．

◆ One [/Another] question worthy of future research is XXX.

今後の研究に値する1つの [/もう1つの] 問題は，XXX ということである．

> Another question worthy of future research is how self-esteem derived from different aspects of the worldview relates to MS-produced worldview defense. (25)
> 今後の研究に値するもう1つの問題は，世界観の異なった側面に由来する自尊心が，MSにより生ずる世界観の防衛にどのように関係するのかということである．
>
> （訳者注：MS; mortality salience, 死の顕現性）

1185 今後研究されるべき重要な問題を述べる．

◆ What remains a particularly interesting and largely unanswered question is X.

特に興味深く，かつ，ほとんど答えが得られていない問題として，X がある．

> What remains a particularly interesting and largely unanswered question is that of the function that each domain serves in relation to the other. (9)
> 特に興味深く，かつ，ほとんど答えが得られていない問題として，各領域が他の領域との関係において果たしている機能の問題がある．

1186 今回の研究から促される研究上の問題について述べる．

◆ A general question prompted by the present research is why XXX.

本研究から引き出される一般的な疑問は，なぜXXX なのか，ということである．

> A general question prompted by the present research is why the behavioral effects of the conditioned rewarding effects of novelty or cocaine do not survive indefinitely. (49)
> 本研究から引き出される一般的な疑問は，新奇性やコカインの条件性報酬効果がもつ行動上の効果がどうしていつまでも続かないのか，ということである．

1187 ある問題に取り組むことが有益であることを示唆する．

◆ Future research might focus usefully on X.

今後の研究は，X に集中していくことが有益かもしれない．

> Future research might focus usefully on the development of adequate behavioral measures that are able to differentiate between different forms of prosociality and their underlying motivation so that, for example, fairness-based cooperative behavior can be distinguished from empathy-based helping behavior. (55)
> 今後の研究は，形式の異なる向社会性とその基盤となる動機づけの区別を可能にすることで，たとえば，公平に基づく協調的行動を，共感に基づく援助行動と区別できるような，適切な行動測度の開発に集中していくことが有益かもしれない．

7.9 今後の展開の可能性

1188 今後の研究の焦点を述べる．

◆An important focus for future X research is [/would be] to YYY.

今後のX研究にとっての重要な焦点は，YYYすることである[/であろう]．

> An important focus for future ambulatory assessment research is to document how patients transfer behavioral changes to their everyday lives. (1)
> 今後の移動評価研究の重要な焦点は，患者が行動変容をどのようにして日常生活に転移させるのかを実証することである．

1189 今後取り組むべき複数の議論があることを述べる．

◆There are several pressing research questions that may be answered with future X studies.

今後のX研究が答えていかなければならない差し迫った研究問題がいくつかある．

> There are several pressing research questions that may be answered with future ambulatory assessment studies. (1)
> 今後の移動評価研究が答えていかなければならない差し迫った研究問題がいくつかある．

1190 将来の研究が取り組むべきいくつかの問題を述べる．

◆There are several important unanswered [/open] research questions concerning X.

Xについては，いくつかの重要な未解決の研究問題がある．

> There are several important open research questions concerning the IAT. (13)
> IATについては，いくつかの重要な未解決の研究問題がある．
>
> （訳者注：IAT; Implicit Association Test, 潜在的連合テスト）

1191 今後は，頑健性の検証に取り組む必要があることを示唆する．

◆Future research [/researchers] should examine the extent to which the Xs are robust across different Ys.

今後の研究[/研究者]は，Xが異なるYを通して頑健である範囲を分析する必要がある．

> Future researchers should examine the extent to which these results are robust across different participant samples and across different measures of the constructs. (9)
> 今後の研究者は，これらの結果が，異なる参加者サンプル，および，この構成概念についての異なる測度を通して，頑健である範囲を分析する必要がある．

1192 将来の研究がより広い問題に取り組むことを推奨する．

◆We recommend that future research broaden the scope of X and investigate Y.

今後の研究がXの範囲をさらに広げて，Yを調べることを推奨する．

> We recommend that future research broaden the scope of the current examination and investigate the contribution of the involvement of more than one grandparent. (2)

今後の研究では，今回の調査の範囲をさらに広げ，1人以上の祖父母の関与がもたらす寄与を調べることを推奨する．

1193 今後は，より綿密な研究が必要であることを述べる．

◆Further in-depth research is needed to identify X.
Xを同定するために，綿密な研究をさらに行う必要がある．

> Further in-depth research is needed to identify characteristics of older adult problem gamblers in casinos. (46)
> カジノの高齢の問題賭博者の特徴を同定するために，綿密な研究をさらに行う必要がある．

1194 今後は，ある要因を考慮すべきであることを示唆する．

◆Future research should consider X.
今後の研究は，Xを考慮に入れなければならない．

> Future research should consider a broader array of factors impacted by child health. (45)
> 今後の研究は，子供の健康により影響を受ける，さらに幅広い要因を考慮に入れなければならない．

1195 現在の結果が，将来の研究で検証すべき仮説を示唆することを述べる．

◆The present results suggest a hypothesis that can be tested in future X studies.
今回の結果は，今後のX研究でテスト可能な仮説を示唆する．

> The present results suggest a clear hypothesis that can be tested in future imaging studies. (12)
> 今回の結果は，今後のイメージング研究でテストすることのできる明確な仮説を示唆する．

1196 今後は，よりよい測定法の開発が必要であることを述べる．

◆Future research should work toward[s] establishing a standardized assessment with psychometric evaluation regarding X.
今後の研究は，Xに関する精神測定学的な評価を用いた標準化判定法の確立に向けて努力すべきである．

> Future research should work towards establishing a standardized assessment with psychometric evaluation regarding construct validity. (39)
> 今後の研究は，構成概念妥当性に関する精神測定学的な評価を用いた標準化判定法の確立に向けて努力すべきである．

1197 今後はある変数の制御が必要であることを，推論される理由とともに述べる．

◆While [very] speculative, this may indicate that XXX. Future research controlling [for] Y should further investigate this question.
[かなり]推論的ではあるが，このことは，XXXということを示しているかもしれない．Yを制御した今後の研究により，この問題がさらに分析されるべきである．

7.9 今後の展開の可能性

While very speculative, this may indicate that perceived duration is more contracted in anticipation than in experience. Future research controlling the length of the duration should further investigate this question. (35)
かなり推論的ではあるが，このことは，知覚される時間間隔が，経験よりも期待において より縮小されることを示しているかもしれない．時間の長さを制御した今後の研究により，この問題がさらに分析されるべきである．

1198 今後は別の被験体を用いる必要があることを，理由とともに述べる．

◆ To more directly determine the effects of X on Y, future studies will need to use Zs.
X が Y に及ぼす効果をより直接的に判定するために，今後の研究は，Z を用いる必要があるだろう．

To more directly determine the effects of reduced body weight on symptoms of precipitated withdrawal, future studies will need to use a group of inactive rats whose body weight is paired to that of active food-restricted rats. (33)
体重減少が誘発性の離脱症状に及ぼす効果をより直接的に判定するために，今後の研究は，食物を制限された活動的なラット群と体重をそろえられた非活動的なラット群を用いる必要があるだろう．

1199 今後は，薬品の効果について治験が行われるべきであることを述べる．

◆ The wide therapeutic action of X and large number of clinical indications warrants the conduct of clinical trials.
X の広範な治療的作用，および，非常に多くの臨床的適応を考えると，臨床治験の実施は当然のことである．

The wide therapeutic action of Pyr, its apparent lack of toxicity and large number of clinical indications warrants now the conduct of clinical trials. (64)
Pyr の広範な治療的作用，毒性の明白な欠如，および，非常に多くの臨床的適応を考えると，臨床治験の実施は今や当然のことである．

（訳者注：Pyr; pyruvate, ピルビン酸）

7.9.3 よりよい方法論の示唆

1200 より厳密な方法を示唆する．

◆ This methodology [probably] provides a [more] stringent test of the hypothesis that XXX.
この方法論により，[おそらく] XXX という仮説の [より] 厳密な検証が可能になるだろう．

This methodology probably provides a more stringent test of the hypothesis that control over uncontrollable internal events (i.e., tinnitus) has a negative long-term effect regardless of the intent or knowledge of the participant. (28)

7. 考察 (Discussion)

おそらく，この方法論により，制御不能である内的な事象（すなわち，耳鳴り）の制御は参加者の意図や知識にかかわらず長期にわたり負の効果をもつという仮説のより厳密な検証が可能になるだろう．

1201 よりよい研究デザインとして，ある方向を示唆する．

◆ The optimal study design might be [envisioned] to XXX.

最適な研究デザインは，XXX することである [と予想される] かもしれない．

> The optimal study design might be envisioned to directly pharmaceutically target KIBRA. (31)
> 最適な研究デザインは，KIBRA を直接，製薬ターゲットにすることであると予想されるかもしれない．
>
> （訳者注：KIBRA は記憶に関連する遺伝子の名称）

1202 より有用な方法として，影響を比較する研究を示唆する．

◆ It would be useful to examine the extent to which X affects Y in comparison with Z[,] by AAA.

AAA することにより，Z と比べて X が Y に影響する程度を調べることは有用であろう．

> It would be useful to examine the extent to which experience specific to this task affects performance in comparison with general problem-solving experience gained outside of this task by presenting experimentally naïve monkeys with this same set of problems. (34)
> 同じ問題の組を実験的にナイーブなサルに呈示することで，この課題とは別のところで獲得された一般的な問題解決経験と比べて，この課題に特有の経験が成績に与える影響の程度を調べることは有用であろう．

1203 自然な場面で再現することにより，研究がより進展することを述べる．

◆ It would be valuable to replicate the [/these] results in a field setting using X.

X を使ったフィールド環境で，この [/ これらの] 結果を再現することに価値はあるだろう．

> It would of course be valuable to replicate the results in a field setting using preexisting teams in organizations to establish that the same relationships may obtain in organizational settings. (59)
> もちろん，組織環境で同じ関係が見られることを立証するために，組織内にある既存のチームを使ったフィールド環境において，今回の結果を再現することには，もちろん価値があるだろう．

1204 洗練化された分析と縦断的なデザインを用いることにより，洞察がより深まることを述べる．

◆ Further testing of this model with longitudinal data and more sophisticated analyses (i.e. [/e.g.], X) would offer better causal insights into Y.

このモデルを縦断的データとより洗練化された分析（すなわち [/ たとえば]，X)

を用いてさらに検証することにより，Y について，因果的な洞察を深めることができるだろう．

> Further testing of this model with longitudinal data and more sophisticated analyses (i.e., structural equation modeling) would offer better causal insights into the various spiritual appraisal and coping pathways linked with distress. (61)
> このモデルを縦断的データとより洗練化された分析（すなわち，構造方程式モデリング）を用いてさらに検証することにより，苦痛と関連するさまざまなスピリチュアルな評価とコーピングの経路について，因果的な洞察を深めることができるだろう．

1205 将来の研究が，重要なトピックの理解をより深めることを述べる．

◆ Such research would expand further our understanding of X.

そのような研究は，X についての我々の理解をさらに広げるであろう．

> Such research would expand further our understanding of the structure of political orientation. (9)
> そのような研究は，政治的志向の構造についての我々の理解をさらに広げるであろう．

1206 あまり研究されていないトピックの研究が，ある人々に恩恵をもたらすことを述べる．

◆ X will [only] benefit from closer examination of this critically important but typically understudied topic.

きわめて重要だが概して研究が不十分であったこのトピックをより詳しく調べることによって [のみ]，X は恩恵を被るだろう．

> Our patients will only benefit from closer examination of this critically important but typically understudied topic. (29)
> きわめて重要だが概して研究が不十分であったこのトピックをより詳しく調べることによってのみ，我々の患者は恩恵を被るだろう．

1207 ある枠組みに沿った研究がよりよい理解につながることを述べる．

◆ Investigating [/Investigation of] X within this framework will lead to a more comprehensive picture of Y.

この枠組みの中で X を調べることにより，Y をより包括的に描き出すことができるようになるであろう．

> Investigating older adult gambling within these frameworks will lead to a more comprehensive picture of the development of gambling problems. (46)
> これらの枠組みの中で高齢者の賭博を調べることにより，賭博問題の発症をより包括的に描き出すことができるようになるであろう．

7.10　要約と結論

7.10.1　全体の要約

1208　論文全体を要約する.

◆ In closing [/In summary], this study [/review] has demonstrated that XXX.
最後に [/ 要約すれば]，本研究 [/ 評論] は XXX ということを実証した.

> In closing, this review has demonstrated that ambulatory assessment is particularly valuable to research on anxiety disorders. (1)
> 最後に，本評論は移動評価が不安障害の研究にとって特に役に立つことを実証した.

1209　論文の要点を述べる.

◆ This article highlighted X [/how XXX /why XXX].
本論文は，X [/ どれくらい XXX であるか / なぜ XXX であるか] を強調した.

> This article highlighted potential advantages of ambulatory assessment over data collection using cross-sectional questionnaires or interviews. (1)
> 本論文は，横断的質問紙やインタビューを用いたデータ収集と比べて移動評価が潜在的に優れていることを強調した.

1210　評論論文を要約する.

◆ In this review [/article], I have discussed how XXX [/why XXX].
本評論 [/ 論文] で，どのように XXX であるか [/ なぜ XXX であるか] を議論してきた.

> In this article, I have discussed how graduate students' research attitudes (interest in doing research and belief in the value of research in their subsequent careers) and eventual research productivity may be enhanced by the presence of certain ingredients in the research training environment. (16)
> 本論文で，大学院生の研究態度（研究を行うことへの興味と，後のキャリアにおける研究の価値についての信念）と最終的な研究生産性が，研究訓練環境におけるある要因の存在によってどのように強められるかについて議論してきた.

7.10.2　知見についての結論

1211　全体的な結論を述べる.

◆ In conclusion, XXX.
結論として，XXX.

> In conclusion, in contemporary consulting engagements, clients are increasingly asking for performance data to support the return on their coaching dollars. (48)
> 結論として，現代のコンサルティング契約においては，顧客がコーチング費用により得られる利得を証拠立てる性能データをますます求めるようになっている.

7.10 要約と結論

1212 知見から導かれる結論を述べる．

◆Based on these findings, it appears that XXX.

これらの知見に基づくと，XXX であると思われる．

> Based on these findings, it appears that use of the CGI-I scale is an appropriate method of determining clinical change in trials of social anxiety disorder. (26)
> これらの知見に基づくと，CGI-I 尺度の使用は社会不安障害の治験において臨床的変化を判定する適切な方法であると思われる．

（訳者注：CGI-I scale; Clinical Global Impression-Improvement scale, 臨床全般印象改善尺度）

1213 知見から導かれる一連の結論を羅列する．

◆In sum, we may draw a number of conclusions from these results. First, XXX. Second, YYY. Third, ZZZ.

要約すると，我々はこれらの結果から多くの結論を引き出すことができるだろう．第一に，XXX．第二に，YYY．さらに第三に，ZZZ．

> In sum, we may draw a number of conclusions from these results. First, from a theoretical standpoint, experience appears to moderate the effects of age-related decline on only a subset of the most relevant of cognitive abilities that underlie complex task performance. Second, the magnitude of experience benefits appears to be largely a result of the knowledge older workers use to mitigate the impact of age-related cognitive decrements as task complexity increases. Third, our results suggest that mandatory retirement policies introduced several decades ago to ensure safety across myriad complex professions should perhaps be reexamined. (47)
> 要約すると，我々はこれらの結果から多くの結論を引き出すことができるだろう．まず第一に，理論的な点として，経験は，年齢による低下が，複雑な課題遂行の基盤となる認知的能力の中で最も関連があるものの部分集合だけに及ぼす効果を調整しているようである．そして第二に，経験による恩恵の大きさは，高齢の作業者が課題の複雑さが増すにつれて，年齢による認知機能低下の影響を補うために用いる知識によっておもに定まるようである．さらに第三に，我々の結果は，無数の複雑な職業にまたがり安全性を確保するために数十年前に導入された定年制の方針は，おそらく見直されなければならないということを示唆している．

（訳者注：第一の結論における「年齢による低下」とは，認知機能の低下のことである）

1214 あることが類似していることを例証したという結論を述べる．

◆In conclusion, the results of the present experiment demonstrate that P shares similarities with Q.

結論として，今回の実験の結果は，P が Q と類似している部分があることを例証する．

> In conclusion, the results of the present experiment demonstrate that excessive running shares similarities with drug-taking behavior. (33)
> 結論として，今回の実験の結果は，過剰なランニングが薬物摂取行動と類似している部分があることを例証する．

1215 あることを無視できない，という結論を述べる．

◆ It can be concluded that it should not be neglected that Ps are Qs.
Ｐ は Ｑ であることを無視すべきでない，と結論することができる．

> It can be concluded that it should not be neglected that human beings are social beings when modeling human decision making. (56)
> 人間の意思決定をモデル化する場合，人間は社会的な存在であることを無視すべきでない，と結論することができる．

1216 効果の拮抗を例証したという結論を述べる．

◆ To conclude, this experiment demonstrated that the P effects of Q competed with R.
結論として，今回の実験により，Ｑ の Ｐ 効果は Ｒ と拮抗することが例証された．

> To conclude, this experiment demonstrated that the conditioned rewarding effects of novelty competed with those of cocaine following a 14-day retention interval in the drug free state. (49)
> 結論として，今回の実験により，新奇性の条件性報酬の効果は，薬物がない状態で 14 日間の保持間隔を経た後のコカインの条件性報酬の効果と拮抗することが例証された．

7.10.3 仮説・理論についての結論

1217 研究が仮説を経験的に支持すると結論する．

◆ In conclusion, these studies [/this study] provide[s] empirical support for the idea [/hypothesis] that XXX.
結論として，これらの研究 [/ 本研究] は，XXX という考え [/ 仮説] を経験的に支持する．

> In conclusion, these studies provide empirical support for the idea that drug treatment programs may use novelty to enhance intervention programs by providing new learning histories that are incompatible with drug use. (49)
> 結論として，これらの研究は，薬物治療プログラムが，薬物使用と相容れない新しい学習履歴の提供により介入プログラムの質を高めるために，新奇性を使用してもよい，という考えを経験的に支持する．

1218 理論がある研究分野に拡張されたと結論する．

◆ In conclusion it should be noted that P theory has been successfully extended to Q.
結論として，Ｐ 理論が Ｑ にうまく拡張されたことに留意すべきである．

> In conclusion it should be noted, first, that neobehavioristic drive theory has been successfully extended to two different areas. (18)
> 結論として，まず第一に，新行動主義的な動因理論が 2 つの異なる分野にうまく拡張されたことに留意すべきである．

7.10.4　今回の研究の意義についての結論

1219　新しいアイデアを提案すると結論する．

◆In conclusion, we propose the possibility that XXX.

結論として，我々は XXX という可能性を提案する．

> In conclusion, we propose the possibility that two thirds of the ghost tales may be classified into one of four types of hallucinations experienced by normal people.　(15)
> 結論として，我々は幽霊物語の3分の2は健常者の経験する幻覚の4つのタイプの1つに分類されるかもしれないという可能性を提案する．

1220　理解への第一歩であると結論する．

◆This study represents an important first step in understanding [/toward an understanding of] X.

本研究は，X を理解する重要な第一歩である．

> This study represents an important first step in understanding the experiences of fathers of young children with Type 1 diabetes.　(45)
> 本研究は，1型糖尿病の幼い子供をもつ父親の経験を理解する重要な第一歩である．

1221　証拠を提供すると結論する．

◆This study provides evidence that XXX.

本研究は，XXX ということの証拠を提供する．

> This study provides evidence that Asian American and Latino American college students experience discrimination across a variety of social and professional settings.　(32)
> 本研究は，アジア系アメリカ人とラテンアメリカ系アメリカ人の大学生がさまざまな社会的および職業的な環境にまたがり差別を経験していることの証拠を提供する．

1222　関係の明確化に役立つと結論する．

◆The present findings help clarify the links between X and Y.

今回の知見は X と Y の間の関連を明らかにすることに役立つ．

> The present findings help clarify the links between affective states and particular motivational tendencies.　(60)
> 今回の知見は，感情状態と特定の動機づけ傾向の間の関連を明らかにすることに役立つ．

1223　あることを支持する初めての研究であると結論する．

◆In sum, the present study provides the first [detailed] X support for Y.

要約すると，本研究は，Y に対して，X による初めての [詳細な] 支持をもたらす．

> In sum, the present study provides the first detailed ERP support for cognitive tuning effects on decision making, more specifically on decision making in the context of purchasing.　(56)
> 要約すると，本研究は，認知的調整効果が，意思決定（より具体的には，購買の文脈における意思決定）に及ぼす効果に対して，ERP による初めての詳細な支持をもたらす．

（訳者注：ERP; event-related potential, 事象関連電位）

7. 考察 (Discussion)

1224 あることを行った最初の研究であると結論する.
◆ In conclusion, the current study is [/was] the first to XXX.
結論として,本研究は,XXX を行った最初の研究である [/ であった].

> In conclusion, the current study is the first to quantify the difference between the amount heterosexual women believe men want them to drink, and the drinking behaviors that heterosexual men actually prefer. (39)
> 結論として,本研究は,異性愛の女性が信じる男性が望む飲酒量と,異性愛の男性が実際に望む飲酒行動の差異を定量化した最初の研究である.

1225 応用的な意義の可能性があると結論する.
◆ Our conclusions about X are relevant to [/might improve /contribute to] Y.
X に関する我々の結論は,Y に関係する [/ 改善するかもしれない / 寄与する].

> Our conclusions about spatial updating are relevant to the design of navigation systems for the visually impaired. (42)
> 空間的更新に関する我々の結論は,視覚障害をもつ人々のためのナビゲーションシステムのデザインに関係する.

1226 独自の洞察を与えると結論する.
◆ Overall, the present study offers a unique insight into X.
全体として,今回の研究は,X に対して独自の洞察を与えるものである.

> Overall, the present study offers a unique insight into the psychology of adolescents who were exposed to Hurricane Katrina. (3)
> 全体として,今回の研究は,ハリケーン・カトリーナにさらされた青年の心理に対して独自の洞察を与える.

1227 理解を前進させると結論する.
◆ This study takes a step toward better understanding of X.
本研究は,X の理解を一歩前進させる.

> This study takes a step toward better understanding the complexities and impact of perceived discrimination in Asian American and Latino college students. (32)
> 本研究は,アジア系アメリカ人とラテンアメリカ系アメリカ人の大学生における被差別感の複雑さとその影響の理解を一歩前進させる.

8
表 の 説 明

8.1 題　名
8.2 一般注
8.3 特定注と確率注

8.1　題名（題名はイタリック体で書くことに注意）

1228　人口統計学的特徴の表（同時にサンプル数も示す）．
◆ Table N
Demographic Characteristics of X (N = M)
表 N. X の人口統計学的特徴（N = M）．
> Table 1
> *Demographic Characteristics of the Sample* (*N* = 935)　　　　　　　　　　　　(57)
> 表 1. サンプルの人口統計学的特徴（*N* = 935）．

1229　条件の関数としての，ある行動を示したサンプルの数の表．
◆ Table N
Number of X Displaying Y as a Function of Z Conditions
表 N. Z 条件の関数としての，Y を示した X の数．
> Table 1
> *Number of Female Rats Displaying Individual Withdrawal Symptoms as a Function of Exercise and Feeding Conditions*　　　　　　　　　　　　(33)
> 表 1. 運動と給餌条件の関数としての，個々の離脱症状を示した雌のラットの数．

1230　条件の関数としての，平均，標準誤差，誤反応の割合の表．
◆ Table N
Mean X (SE in Parentheses) and Percentage Error Rates as a Function of Y
表 N. Y の関数としての，X の平均（括弧内は標準誤差）と誤反応率の割合．
> Table 2
> *Experiment 2: Mean RTs (SE in Parentheses) and Percentage Error Rates as a Function of Distractor Condition and Load*　　　　　　　　　　　　(14)
> 表 2. 実験 2 の結果：妨害刺激条件と負荷の関数としての，平均 RT（括弧内は標準誤差），および，誤反応率の割合．

(訳者注：RT; reaction time, 反応時間)

1231 相関係数の表．

◆ Table N
Correlations Between A and B, C, and D
表 N. A と，B, C, D の間の相関係数．

Table 5
Correlations Between Working Memory Capacity and Recall of Low-Value Items (Recall 1–7), High-Values Items (Recall 8–12), and Selectivity Index (7)
表 5. 作業記憶容量と，低値項目（想起 1 〜 7）の想起，高値項目（想起 8 〜 12）の想起，選択性指標の間の相関係数．

8.2 一 般 注

8.2.1 データについての一般注

1232 サンプルサイズ，欠損値を述べる．

◆ *Note.* N = X. M [additional] participants had missing data [that prevented classification].
注：N = X である．M 名の [追加的な] 参加者は [分類できない] 欠損値を示した．

Note. N = 1,990. Twelve participants had missing data that prevented classification. (51)
注：N = 1990 である．12 名の参加者は分類できない欠損値を示した．

1233 構造方程式モデルの標準化パス係数の表の注で，適合度の値を述べる．

◆ *Note.* Model fit: χ^2(X) = A; comparative fit index [/CFI] = B; root-mean-square error of approximation [/RMSEA] = C.
注：モデル適合度：χ^2(X) = A，比較適合度指標 [/CFI] = B，近似誤差平均平方根 [/RMSEA] = C．

Note. Model fit: χ^2(179) = 720.220; comparative fit index = .967; root-mean-square error of approximation = .040. (58)
注：モデル適合度：χ^2(179) = 720.220，比較適合度指標 = .967，近似誤差平均平方根 = .040．

1234 得点を算出するための計算式を述べる．

◆ *Note.* X, Y, and Z scores were computed using the following formula: A + B + C.
注：X, Y, Z 得点は，以下の公式を用いて計算された．A + B + C

Note. Bullying, victim, and witness chronicity scores were computed using the formula: number of types of bullying/victimization/witness + frequency of bullying/victimization/witness + number of locations for bullying/victimization/witness. (51)

注：いじめ，被害者，目撃者の慢性度得点は，以下の公式を用いて計算された．（いじめのタイプの数 / 被害 / 目撃）+（いじめの頻度 / 被害 / 目撃）+（いじめの場所の数 / 被害 / 目撃）．

8.2.2 記号，略語についての一般注

1235 記号の用法を定義する．

◆ *Note.* X, Y[,] and Z are A, B, and C.

注：X, Y, Z は，それぞれ A, B, C である．

Note. $n_1, \hat{\mu}_1$ and $\hat{\sigma}_1$ are the sample size, sample mean, and sample standard deviation. (4)

注：$n_1, \hat{\mu}_1, \hat{\sigma}_1$ は，それぞれ，サンプルサイズ，サンプル平均，サンプルの標準偏差である．

1236 略字の意味を定義する．

◆ *Note.* A = X, B = Y, C = Z.

注：A は X，B は Y，C は Z を表す．

Note. I = incongruent distractor, C = congruent distractor, ID = irrelevant distractor, ND = no distractor. (14)

注：I は不適合的妨害刺激（incongruent distractor），C は適合妨害刺激（congruent distractor），ID は無関連妨害刺激（irrelevant distractor），ND は妨害刺激なし（no distractor）を表す．

1237 カテゴリー変数の記号を定義する．

◆ *Note.* For X: 0 = *A*, 1 = *B*. For Y: 0 = *C*, 1 = *D*. For class standing: 1 = *freshman*, 2 = *sophomore*, 3 = *junior*, 4 = *senior*.

注：X については，0 が A，1 が B．Y については，0 が C，1 が D．学年については，1 が 1 年生，2 が 2 年生，3 が 3 年生，4 が 4 年生．

Note. For race/ethnicity: 0 = *all other racial groups*, 1 = *White/Caucasian*. For Greek status: 0 = *non-Greek*, 1 = *Greek*. For class standing: 1 = *freshman*, 2 = *sophomore*, 3 = *junior*, 4 = *senior*. (39)

注：人種 / 民族性については，0 がその他のすべての人種グループ，1 が白人 / コーカサス人．ギリシア人であるか否かについては，0 が非ギリシア人，1 がギリシア人．学年については，1 が 1 年生，2 が 2 年生，3 が 3 年生，4 が 4 年生．

1238 リッカート尺度の範囲とカテゴリー，二件法のカテゴリーを述べる．

◆ *Note.* All items range from N = *A* to M = *B*, except [for] the X question, which was dichotomous (0 = *C* and 1 = *D*).

注：すべての項目は「N = A」から「M = B」までの範囲であったが，例外は X の質問であり，これは二件法（「0 = C」と「1 = D」）であった．

Note. All items range from 1 = *never* to 5 = *very often*, except for the roommate question, which was dichotomous (0 = *no* and 1 = *yes*). (19)

注：すべての項目は「1 = 決してない」から「5 = かなりしばしば」までの範囲であったが，例外はルームメイトについての質問であり，これは二件法（「0 = いいえ」と「1 = はい」）であった．

1239 測度の範囲とカテゴリー，リッカート尺度の範囲とカテゴリー，サンプル数について述べる．

◆ *Note.* X ranges from P (*Below A*) to Q (*Above [/Over] B*). Y ranges from R (*Extremely C*) to S (*Extremely D*). Z sample consists of E.

注：Xは，P（A以下）からQ（B以上）の範囲である．Yは，R（きわめてC）からS（きわめてD）までの範囲である．Zサンプルは，E名から成る．

> *Note.* Childhood household income ranges from 1 (*Below $10,000*) to 8 (*Over $500,000*). Political Orientation ranges from 1 (*Extremely Liberal*) to 5 (*Extremely Conservative*). Volunteer sample consists of 1,963 people. (19)
> 注：子供の頃の世帯収入は1（10000ドル以下）から8（500000ドル以上）の範囲である．政治的志向は，1（きわめてリベラル）から5（きわめて保守的）までの範囲である．志願者サンプルは，1963名から成る．

8.2.3　データの見方についての一般注

1240 括弧内の数値について述べる．

◆ *Note.* Xs are presented in parentheses.

注：Xが括弧内に示されている．

> *Note.* Standard deviations are presented in parentheses. (6)
> 注：標準偏差が括弧内に示されている．

1241 適合度の見方を示す．

◆ *Note.* A more positive [/negative] value indicates a better fit.

注：値がプラス [/ マイナス] であるほどよりよく適合していることを示す．

> *Note.* A more positive value indicates a better fit. (44)
> 注：値がプラスであるほどよりよく適合していることを示す．
> （訳者注：ここで，値とは対数尤度値のことである）

8.3　特定注と確率注

8.3.1　一部のデータについての特定注

1242 ある行は，尺度が逆転されていることを述べる．

◆ *Note.* [a] [The] X scale was [/is] reversed.

注：[a] Xの尺度は，逆転されていた [/ いる]．

> *Note.* ᵃ Attitudes Favoring Equal Opportunity scale is reversed. (19)
> 注：ᵃ 機会均等選好態度の尺度は，逆転されている．

1243 ある行は合算値であることを述べる．

◆ *Note.* ᵃ Combined X.

注：ᵃ 合わせた X を示す．

> *Note.* ᵃ Combined household income. (19)
> 注：ᵃ 合わせた世帯収入を示す．

8.3.2 一般注・特定注・確率注を含む注

1244 一般注で，サンプルサイズの値，略語の定義を述べる．確率注で，有意水準を述べる（一般注の終わりは改行すること，および，確率注は最後に書くことに注意）．

◆ *Note.* N = X. A = P; B = Q; C = R.
$*p < .05. **p < .01. ***p < .001$ (two-tailed).
注：N = X. A は P，B は Q，C は R である．
$*$ は $p < .05$，$**$ は $p < .01$，$***$ は $p < .001$（両側検定）を表す．

> *Note.* N = 62. IAT = Implicit Association Test-Anxiety; STAI = Trait form of the State–Trait Anxiety Inventory.
> $*p < .05. **p < .01. ***p < .001$ (two-tailed). (13)
> 注：N = 62. IAT は潜在連合検査（Implicit Association Test-Anxiety）を，STAI は状態‐特性不安検査（Trait form of the State–Trait Anxiety Inventory）を表す．
> $*$ は $p < .05$，$**$ は $p < .01$ を表し，$***$ は $p < .001$ を表す（両側検定）．

1245 一般注で，サンプルサイズの範囲，相関の計算方法，単位を述べる．特定注で，記号の意味を述べる．確率注で，有意差傾向を含む p 値を述べる（一般注，特定注，確率注はこの順番で書くこと，および，**3 種類の注ごとに改行することに注意**）．

◆ *Note.* Ns range from A to B. Correlations are based on X. For Y, the unit is Z.
ᵃ C = 1, D = 2.
$† p < .10. *p < .05. **p < .01. ***p < .001$.
注：N の値は A から B の範囲である．相関は X に基づいている．Y については，単位は Z である．
ᵃ C が 1，D が 2 である．
$†$ は $p < .10$，$*$ は $p < .05$，$**$ は $p < .01$，$***$ は $p < .001$ を表す．

Note. Ns range from 11,055 to 12,189. Correlations are based on pairwise deletion. For total wealth, the unit is 100,000 dollars.
[a] Male = 1, female = 2.
† $p < .10$. * $p < .05$. ** $p < .01$. (63)
注：N の値は 11055 から 12189 の範囲である．相関はペアワイズ法に基づいている．総資産については，単位は 100000 ドルである．
[a] 男性が 1 で，女性が 2 である．
† は $p < .10$, * は $p < .05$, ** は $p < .01$ を表す．

9 図 の 説 明

9.1 題　名
9.2 上下，または，左右のパネルの説明
9.3 縦軸と横軸・凡例・略語・再掲の説明

9.1　題　名

9.1.1　イラスト，写真の題名

1246　実験装置のイラスト．
◆A schematic of the X is shown in Figure N.
X の概略図を図 N に示す．
> A schematic of the water radial-arm maze is shown in Supplementary Figure 1A. (31)
> 放射状水迷路の概略図を付録図 1A に示す．

1247　ある実験の刺激配置のイラスト．
◆*Figure N.* Stimulus layout of [an experiment on] X.
図 N. X [についての実験] の刺激配置．
> *Figure 1.* Stimulus layout and results of an experiment on spatial updating of visual and auditory targets. (42)
> 図 1. 視覚的および聴覚的標的の空間的更新についての実験の刺激配置と結果．

1248　課題の刺激配置のイラスト（一定の縮尺で描かれていない）．
◆*Figure N.* Depiction of stimulus arrangement for X tasks. Note that objects pictured are not drawn to scale.
図 N. X 課題の刺激配置の描写図（物体は一定の縮尺で描かれていないことに注意）．
> *Figure 1.* Depiction of stimulus arrangement for five matching tasks. Note that objects pictured are not drawn to scale. (34)
> 図 1. 5 つの見本合わせ課題の刺激配置の描写図（物体は一定の縮尺で描かれていないことに注意）．

328   9. 図 の 説 明

1249   2次元空間内における刺激配置のイラスト．
◆ *Figure N.* The spatial layout of X as a function of distance and azimuth from the origin.

図 N. 原点からの距離と方位角の関数としての X の空間的配置．

> *Figure 5.* The spatial layout of the targets as a function of distance and azimuth from the origin. (42)
> 図 5. 原点からの距離と方位角の関数としての標的の空間的配置．

1250   ある実験条件における刺激表示例のイラスト．
◆ *Figure N.* Example of the stimulus display used in the X condition.

図 N. X 条件で用いられた刺激表示の例．

> *Figure 1.* Example of the stimulus display used in the high perceptual load condition. (43)
> 図 1. 高知覚的負荷条件で用いられた刺激表示の例．

1251   ある刺激を含む刺激表示例のイラスト（一定の縮尺で描かれていない）．
◆ *Figure N.* An example stimulus display (not to scale) with X in the Y condition.

図 N. Y 条件における，X のある刺激表示の例（一定の縮尺で描かれていない）．

> *Figure 1.* An example stimulus display (not to scale) with an irrelevant distractor in the low load condition. (14)
> 図 1. 低負荷条件における，無関係妨害刺激のある刺激呈示の例（一定の縮尺で描かれていない）．

1252   仮説のイラスト．
◆ *Figure N.* Schematic of X hypotheses regarding YYY.

図 N. YYY に関する X 仮説の概略図．

> *Figure 2.* Schematic of two hypotheses regarding how familiar-looking features influence categorization decisions. (24)
> 図 2. 熟知しているように見える特徴がカテゴリーの決定にどのように影響を与えるかに関する 2 つの仮説の概略図．

1253   各実験段階の条件設定のイラスト．
◆ *Figure N.* X throughout the experimental phases are represented by [/in] the [/this] schematic representation.

図 N. 実験段階を通しての X を，略図で表す．

> *Figure 1.* Compartment placements throughout the experimental phases are represented in this schematic representation. (49)
> 図 1. 実験段階を通してのコンパートメントの配置を，略図で表す．

1254   異なる群から得られた典型的なデータ例のイラスト．
◆ *Figure N.* Representative examples of X during the Y performance from different

groups: A, B, and C participants [/rats].

図 N. 異なる群（A 群，B 群，C 群の参加者 [/ ラット]）から得られた，Y 遂行中の X の代表的な例．

> *Figure 11.* Representative examples of swim path during the water maze performance from different groups: the normal control (NC), ventral subicular lesioned (VSL), VSL vehicle control (VC), and VSL rats transplanted with H3-GFP cell lines (VSL + H3-GFP). (50)
> 図 11. 異なる群から得られた，水迷路遂行中の水泳経路の代表的な例．異なる群とは，正常対照群（NC），腹側鉤状回損傷群（VSL），VSL 溶媒対照群（VC），腹側鉤状回損傷 H3-GFP 細胞株移植群（VSL + H3-GFP）である．

1255 モデルのルールのイラスト．

◆ *Figure N.* Illustration of the X rule used by the Y model.

図 N. Y モデルで用いられた X ルールの図解．

> *Figure 1.* Illustration of the extrapolation rule used by the extrapolation-association model. (44)
> 図 1. 外挿連合モデルで用いられた外挿ルールの図解．

1256 複数のパネルに示された脳切片の写真．

◆ *Figure N.* Photographs [/Photomicrographs] of the coronal [/sagittal /axial /oblique] P brain sections at the level of Q in X (A), Y (B), and Z (C) Ps.

図 N. X 群（A），Y 群（B），Z 群（C）の P における，P の脳の Q の平面における冠状面 [/ 矢上面 / 体軸断面 / 斜断面] の写真 [/ 顕微鏡写真]．

> *Figure 1.* Photomicrographs of the cresyl violet-stained coronal rat brain sections at the level of ventral subiculum in normal control (NC) (A), ventral subicular lesioned (VSL) (B), and VSL lesioned rats transplanted with green fluorescent protein (GFP)-labeled hippocampal cell line (H3-GFP) (VSL + H3-GFP) (C) rats. (50)
> 図 1. 正常統制（NC）群（A），腹側鉤状回損傷（VSL）群（B），VSL を損傷され緑色蛍光タンパク質（GFP）でラベルされた海馬細胞株（H3-GFP）を移植された（VSL + H3-GFP）群（C）のラットにおける，クレシルバイオレットにより染色された脳の腹側鉤状回の平面における冠状面の顕微鏡写真．

（訳者注：体軸断面を表すために，axial の代わりに transverse が用いられることもある：矢状面は「しじょうめん」と読む）

9.1.2 グラフの題名

1257 実験群と統制群の平均値を比較する棒グラフ．

◆ *Figure N.* Mean X for participants [/rats /monkeys] trained [/conditioned] with Y in the control and Z groups.

図 N. Y で訓練された [/ 条件づけられた] 統制群と Z 群の参加者 [/ ラット / サル] の平均 X．

Figure 3. Mean activity counts (± SEM) for rats conditioned with 7.5, 20, or 30 mg/kg cocaine in the control and novelty groups for Experiment 1. (49)
図3. 7.5, 20, 30 mg/kg のコカインで条件づけられた実験1の統制群と新奇群のラットの平均活動得点（±標準誤差）.

1258 参加者の平均反応をある変数の関数としてブロックごとにプロットしたグラフ.

◆ *Figure N.* Mean participant responses during X blocks when trained on the Y condition.
図N. Y条件で訓練された場合のXブロック中の参加者の平均反応.

Figure 4. Mean participant responses during the first four training blocks when trained on the concave ordered condition. (44)
図4. 凹状の順序条件で訓練された場合の最初の4つの訓練ブロック中の参加者の平均反応.

1259 異なる参加者群の平均データを比較する棒グラフ.

◆ *Figure N.* Mean percentages of X, in Y with and without A, B, and C, respectively.
図N. A, B, Cのそれぞれのある Y, および, それらのない YにおけるXの平均割合.

Figure 1. Mean percentages of specific autobiographical memories in assault survivors with and without acute stress disorder (ASD), depression, and assault-related phobia, respectively. (36)
図1. 急性ストレス障害（ASD），うつ，暴行関連恐怖のある暴力被害者，および，それらのない暴力被害者における，特異的な自伝的記憶の平均割合.

1260 異なる条件ごとに分けて計算された平均データの変化を示す折れ線グラフ.

◆ *Figure N.* Mean X rates calculated separately for Y and Z.
図N. YおよびZについてそれぞれ分けて計算された平均のX率.

Figure 2. Mean annual compound discount rates calculated separately for objective and subjective time. (35)
図2. 客観的および主観的時間についてそれぞれ分けて計算された年間の複合割引率の平均.

1261 ある条件において複数の推定値を比較する棒グラフ.

◆ *Figure N.* X estimates from Y in the Z conditions.
図N. Z条件におけるYから得られたXの推定値.

Figure 2. Parameter estimates from the individual source receiver operating characteristics in the unitized source and nonunitized source conditions for Experiment 1. (12)
図2. 実験1のユニット化されたおよびユニット化されない情報源条件における個々の情報源の受信者動作特性のパラメータ推定値.

9.2　上下，または，左右のパネルの説明　　　*331*

1262　独立変数の操作が従属変数に一貫した効果をもたらすことを示す箱ひげ図．
◆ *Figure N*. X treatment is associated with Y.
　図 N. X 治療は，Y と関連がある．

> *Figure 1.* Hydroxyfasudil treatment is associated with a dose-related increase in learning proficiency in aged rats. (31)
> 図 1. 塩酸ファスジル治療は，高齢ラットにおける投与量に応じた学習上達度の増加と関連がある．

1263　強化スケジュールで維持されている従属変数の折れ線グラフ．
◆ *Figure N*. X maintained by Y.
　図 N. Y で維持されている X.

> *Figure 3.* Self-administration of RTI-177 maintained by a second-order schedule of intravenous drug delivery in individual rhesus monkeys. (30)
> 図 3. 個々のアカゲザルにおける，腹腔内薬物投与の 2 次スケジュールで維持されている RTI-177 の自己投与量．
>
> （訳者注：RTI-177 はモノアミン酸化酵素阻害薬の一種）

1264　個人の参加者の反応データの図．
◆ *Figure N*. An individual participant's responses during X.
　図 N. X 中のある個人の参加者の反応．

> *Figure 8.* An individual participant's responses during the last two training blocks and the transfer block when trained in the convex ordered condition. (44)
> 図 8. 凸状順序条件で訓練された場合の最後の 2 つの訓練ブロックおよび転移ブロック中の，ある個人の参加者の反応．

1265　確証的因子分析のパス図．
◆ *Figure N*. Confirmatory factor analysis of the revised Model X, with standardized coefficients.
　図 N. 改訂されたモデル X の確証的因子分析と標準化係数．

> *Figure 1.* Confirmatory factor analysis of the revised Model C, with standardized coefficients. (9)
> 図 1. 改訂されたモデル C の確証的因子分析と標準化係数．

9.2　上下，または，左右のパネルの説明

1266　上下のパネルに示された刺激を説明する．
◆ *Figure N*. Upper panel: X for Experiment Y. Lower panel: Z used in Experiment Y.
　図 N. 上のパネル：実験 Y の X. 下のパネル：実験 Y で用いられた Z.

Figure 3. Upper panel: Training stimuli for Hannah and Brooks (2006) and Experiment IA. Shown above training prototypes (upper row) are the defining features for each category. Lower panel: Two test items used in Experiment IA. (24)

図3. 上のパネル：Hannah と Brooks（2006）および実験 IA の訓練刺激．訓練の原型の図（上の列）の上に，各カテゴリーを決定する特徴を示す．下のパネル：実験 IA で用いられた2つのテスト項目．

1267 上下のパネルに示されたデータを説明する．

◆ *Figure N.* Mean X by the different Y groups during Z in the A condition (top panel) and B condition (bottom panel) for the responses trained with C.

図 N. C により訓練された反応について，A 条件（上のパネル）と B 条件（下のパネル）における，Z 中の，異なる Y 群による平均 X．

Figure 2. Mean percentage responding by the different age groups during the test in the extinction condition (top panel) and reacquisition condition (bottom panel) for the responses trained with the valued and devalued outcomes. (37)

図 2. 価値のある結果と価値の低下した結果により訓練された反応について，消去条件（上のパネル）と再獲得条件（下のパネル）における，テスト中の異なる年齢群による平均反応率．

1268 左右のパネルに示された個人のデータを説明する．

◆ *Figure N.* Left panel: An individual participant's X that YYY. Right panel: An individual participant's X that ZZZ.

図 N. 左のパネル：YYY するある個人の X．右のパネル：ZZZ するある個人の X．

Figure 10. Left panel: An individual participant's transfer responses that the POLE model predicted well. Right panel: An individual participant's transfer responses that the EXAM model predicted well. (44)

図 10. 左のパネル：POLE モデルがよく予測するある個人の参加者の転移反応．右のパネル：EXAM モデルがよく予測するある個人の参加者の転移反応．

（訳者注：EXAM; extrapolation-association model, 外挿連合モデル：POLE; population of linear experts model, 線形エキスパート群モデル）

9.3　縦軸と横軸・凡例・略語・再掲の説明

1269 横軸と縦軸，実線と点線を説明する．

◆ *Figure N.* (略) Abscissae: A. Ordinates: B. Solid [/Full] lines indicate [/represent] C. Dashed [/Broken] lines indicate [/represent] D.

図 N.（略）横軸は，A を表す．縦軸は，B を表す．実線は，C を表す．点線は D を表す．

9.3　縦軸と横軸・凡例・略語・再掲の説明　　　*333*

Figure 3.（略）Abscissae: unit dose, log scale. Ordinates: response rate in responses/s. Solid lines indicate mean rates of responding maintained by the training dose of cocaine. Dashed lines indicate the upper limit of responding during saline extinction. (30)
図 3.（略）横軸は，投与量の単位を対数目盛りで表す．縦軸は，反応率を反応数 / 秒で表す．実線は，コカインの訓練投与量により維持された平均反応率を表す．点線は生理食塩水による消去中の反応の上限を表す．

1270　横軸のカテゴリーを説明する．

◆ *Figure N.*（略）X indicates the A for B, and Y indicates the C for D.
　図 N.（略）X は，B の A を，Y は，D の C を示す．

> *Figure 2.*（略）Recollection (yellow) indicates the recollection estimate for items studied on a yellow background, and recollection (red) indicates the recollection estimate for items studied on a red background. (12)
> 図 2.（略）Recollection（yellow）は，黄色い背景上で調べられた項目の想起推定値を，Recollection（red）は赤色の背景上で調べられた項目の想起推定値を示す．

1271　符号を説明する．

◆ *Figure N.*（略）Black [/White] dots [/circles /squares] indicate X.
　図 N.（略）黒い [/ 白い] 点 [/ 円 / 四角] は X を表す．

> *Figure 8.*（略）A solid line indicates the trained function, and black dots indicate participant responses. (44)
> 図 8.（略）実線は訓練された関数を，黒い点は参加者の反応を表す．

1272　棒グラフのシェーディング（濃淡），**ns**，*p* 値の記号を説明する．

◆ *Figure N.*（略）Black bars = X; gray bars = Y; ns = non-significant. **p < .01.
　図 N.（略）黒いバーは X を，灰色のバーは Y を示す．ns は，有意でないことを表す．** は *p* < .01 を示す．

> *Figure 1.*（略）Black bars = positive cues; gray bars = negative cues; ns = non-significant. **p < .01. (36)
> 図 1.（略）黒いバーは正の手がかりを，灰色のバーは負の手がかりを示す．ns は有意でないことを表す．** は *p* < .01 を示す．

1273　グラフの凡例の略語，エラーバー（誤差範囲）を説明する．

◆ *Figure N.*（略）A is a[n] B, and C is a[n] D. Error bars indicate E.
　図 N.（略）A は B を，C は D を表す．エラーバーは E を表す．

> *Figure 2.*（略）*R* is a perceived-time-based discount rate, and *r* is a calendar-time-based discount rate. Error bars indicate *SEM*. (35)
> 図 2.（略）*R* は知覚時間に基づく割引率を，*r* は暦時間に基づく割引率を表す．エラーバーは標準誤差を表す．

1274 エラーバー（誤差範囲）つきグラフをまとめて説明する．

◆ *Figure N.*（略）Shown are the *X* ± *Y*.
図 N.（略）*X* ± *Y* が示されている．

> *Figure 1.*（略）Shown are the *M* ± *SE*. (31)
> 図 1.（略）平均±標準誤差が示されている．

1275 先行研究からの再掲であることを述べる．

◆ *Figure N.*（略）Reprinted from "Title," by Authors, Year, Citation. Copyright Year by X.
図 N.（略）以下の論文より再掲．タイトル，著者，発表年，引用情報．著作権は X（年号）に帰属する．

> *Figure 1.*（略）Reprinted from "The Conceptual Basis of Function Learning and Extrapolation: Comparison of Rule and Associative Based Models," by M. A. McDaniel and J. R. Busemeyer, 2005, *Psychonomic Bulletin & Review*, *12*, Figure 1, p. 28. Copyright 2005 by Psychonomic Society Publications. (44)
> 図 1.（略）以下の論文より再掲．"The Conceptual Basis of Function Learning and Extrapolation: Comparison of Rule and Associative Based Models," by M. A. McDaniel and J. R. Busemeyer, 2005, *Psychonomic Bulletin & Review*, *12*, Figure 1, p. 28. 著作権は Psychonomic Society Publications（2005）に帰属する．

引用文献

第2章以降で引用した文献のリストを示す．文献の番号は，本文中の例文に付されている番号に対応している．第1章で述べたように，本書で引用した例文の中には，正確さやわかりやすさのために，原文を一部省略または改変したものがある．

(1) Alpers, G. W. (2009). Ambulatory assessment in panic disorder and specific phobia. *Psychological Assessment*, **21(4)**, 476-485. doi: 10.1037/a0017489

(2) Attar-Schwartz, S., Tan, J., Buchanan, A., Flouri, E., & Griggs, J. (2009). Grandparenting and adolescent adjustment in two-parent biological, lone-parent, and step-families. *Journal of Family Psychology*, **23(1)**, 67-75. doi: 10.1037/a0014383

(3) Blaze, J. T., & Shwalb, D. W. (2009). Resource loss and relocation: A follow-up study of adolescents two years after Hurricane Katrina. *Psychological Trauma: Theory, Research, Practice, and Policy*, **1(4)**, 312-322. doi: 10.1037/a0017834

(4) Bonett, D. G. (2009). Meta-analytic interval estimation for standardized and unstandardized mean differences. *Psychological Methods*, **14(3)**, 225-238. doi: 10.1037/a0016619

(5) Broaders, S. C., Cook, S. W., Mitchell, Z., & Goldin-Meadow, S. (2007). Making children gesture brings out implicit knowledge and leads to learning. *Journal of Experimental Psychology: General*, **136(4)**, 539-550. doi: 10.1037/0096-3445.136.4.539

(6) Callan, M. J., Ellard, J. H., & Nicol, J. E. (2006). The belief in a just world and immanent justice reasoning in adults. *Personality and Social Psychology Bulletin*, **32(12)**, 1646-1658. doi: 10.1177/0146167206292236

(7) Castel, A. D., Balota, D. A., & McCabe, D. P. (2009). Memory efficiency and the strategic control of attention at encoding: Impairments of value-directed remembering in Alzheimer's disease. *Neuropsychology*, **23(3)**, 297-306. doi:10.1037/a0014888

(8) Chang, D. F., & Berk, A. (2009). Making cross-racial therapy work: A phenomenological study of clients' experiences of cross-racial therapy. *Journal of Counseling Psychology*, **56(4)**, 521-536. doi: 10.1037/a0016905521

(9) Choma, B. L., Ashton, M. C., & Hafer, C. L. (2010). Conceptualizing political orientation in Canadian political candidates: A tale of two (correlated) dimensions. *Canadian Journal of Behavioural Science*, **42(1)**, 24-33. doi: 10.10371/a0015650

(10) Close, J., Hahn, U., & Honey, R. C. (2009). Contextual modulation of stimulus generalization in rats. *Journal of Experimental Psychology: Animal Behavior Processes*, **35(4)**, 509-515. doi: 10.1037/a0015489

(11) Crocker, J., & Nuer, N. (2004). Do people need self-esteem? Comment on Pyszczynski et al. (2004). *Psychological Bulletin*, **130(3)**, 469-472. doi: 10.1037/0033-2909.130.3.469

(12) Diana, R. A., Yonelinas, A. P., & Ranganath, C. (2008). The effects of unitization on familiarity-based source memory: Testing a behavioral prediction derived from neuroimaging data. *Journal of Experimental Psychology: Learning, Memory, and Cognition*, **34(4)**, 730-740. doi: 10.1037/0278-7393.34.4.730

(13) Egloff, B., & Schmukle, S. C. (2002). Predictive validity of an Implicit Association Test for assessing anxiety. *Journal of Personality and Social Psychology*, **83(6)**, 1441–1455. doi: 10.1037//0022-3514.83.6.1441
(14) Forster, S., & Lavie, N. (2008). Failures to ignore entirely irrelevant distractors: The role of load. *Journal of Experimental Psychology: Applied*, **14(1)**, 73–83. doi: 10.1037/1076-898X.14.1.73
(15) Furuya, H., Ikezoe, K., Shigeto, H., Ohyagi, Y., Arahata, H., Araki, E., & Fujii, N. (2009). Sleep- and non-sleep-related hallucinations—Relationship to ghost tales and their classifications. *Dreaming*, **19(4)**, 232–238. doi: 10.1037/a0017611
(16) Gelso, C. J. (2006). On the making of a scientist-practitioner: A theory of research training in professional psychology. *Training and Education in Professional Psychology*, **S(1)**, 3–16. doi: 10.1037/1931-3918.S.1.3
(17) Glickman, N. S. (2009). Adapting best practices in CBT for deaf and hearing persons with language and learning challenges. *Journal of Psychotherapy Integration*, **19(4)**, 354–384. doi: 10.1037/a0017969
(18) Glucksberg, S. (1962). The influence of strength of drive on functional fixedness and perceptual recognition. *Journal of Experimental Psychology*, **63(1)**, 36–41.
(19) Gottfredson, N. C., Panter, A. T., Daye, C. E., Allen, W. A., Wightman, L. F., & Deo, M. E. (2008). Does diversity at undergraduate institutions influence student outcomes? *Journal of Diversity in Higher Education*, **1(2)**, 80–94. doi: 10.1037/1938-8926.1.2.80
(20) Greenwald, A. G., & Ronis, D. L. (1978). Twenty years of cognitive dissonance: Case study of the evolution of a theory. *Psychological Review*, **85(1)**, 53–57.
(21) Gulick, D., & Gould, T. J. (2009). Effects of ethanol and caffeine on behavior in C57BL/6 mice in the plus-maze discriminative avoidance task. *Behavioral Neuroscience*, **123(6)**, 1271–1278. doi: 10.1037/a0017610
(22) Haber, M. G., & Toro, P. A. (2009). Parent-adolescent violence and later behavioral health problems among homeless and housed youth. *American Journal of Orthopsychiatry*, **79(3)**, 305–318. doi: 10.1037/a0017212
(23) Han, W. J. (2008). The academic trajectories of children of immigrants and their school environments. *Developmental Psychology*, **44(6)**, 1572–1590. doi: 10.1037/a0013886
(24) Hannah, S. D., & Brooks, L. R. (2009). Featuring familiarity: How a familiar feature instantiation influences categorization. *Canadian Journal of Experimental Psychology*, **63(4)**, 263–275. doi: 10.1037/a0017919
(25) Harmon-Jones, E., Simon, L., Greenberg, J., Pyszczynski, T., Solomon, S., & McGregor, H. (1997). Terror management theory and self-esteem: Evidence that increased self-esteem reduces mortality salience effects. *Journal of Personality and Social Psychology*, **72(1)**, 24–36.
(26) Hedges, D. W., Brown, B. L., & Shwalb, D. A. (2009). A direct comparison of effect sizes from the clinical global impression-improvement scale to effect sizes from other rating scales in controlled trials of adult social anxiety disorder. *Human Psychopharmacology*, **24(1)**, 35–40. doi: 10.1002/hup.989
(27) Hedges, D. W., Brown, B. L., Shwalb, D. A., Godfrey, K., & Larcher, A. M. (2007). The efficacy of selective serotonin reuptake inhibitors in adult social anxiety disorder: A meta-analysis of double-blind, placebo-controlled trials. *Journal of Psychopharmacology*, **21(1)**, 102–111. doi: 10.1177/0269881106065102
(28) Hesser, H., Pereswetoff-Morath, C. E., & Andersson, G. (2009). Consequences of controlling background sounds: The effect of experiential avoidance on tinnitus interference. *Rehabilitation*

Psychology, **54(4)**, 381-389. doi: 10.1037/a0017565
(29) Hillman, J. (2008). Sexual issues and aging within the context of work with older adult patients. *Professional Psychology: Research and Practice*, **39(3)**, 290-297. doi: 10.1037/0735-7028.39.3.290
(30) Howell, L. L. (2008). Nonhuman primate neuroimaging and cocaine medication development. *Experimental and Clinical Psychopharmacology*, **16(6)**, 446-457. doi: 10.1037/a0014196
(31) Huentelman, M. J., Stephan, D. A., Talboom, J., Corneveaux, J. J., Reiman, D. M., Gerber, J. D., ... Bimonte-Nelson, H. A. (2009). Peripheral delivery of a ROCK inhibitor improves learning and working memory. *Behavioral Neuroscience*, **123(1)**, 218-223. doi: 10.1037/a0014260
(32) Hwang, W., & Goto, S. (2009). The impact of perceived racial discrimination on the mental health of Asian American and Latino college students. *Asian American Journal of Psychology*, **S(1)**, 15-28. doi: 10.1037/1948-1985.S.1.15
(33) Kanarek, R. B., D'Anci, K. E., Jurdak, N., & Mathes, W. F. (2009). Running and addiction: Precipitated withdrawal in a rat model of activity-based anorexia. *Behavioral Neuroscience*, **123(4)**, 905-912. doi: 10.1037/a0015896
(34) Kennedy, E. H., & Fragaszy, D. M. (2008). Analogical reasoning in a capuchin monkey (*Cebus apella*). *Journal of Comparative Psychology*, **122(2)**, 167-175. doi: 10.1037/0735-7036.122.2.167
(35) Kim, K., & Zauberman, G. (2009). Perception of anticipatory time in temporal discounting. *Journal of Neuroscience, Psychology and Economics*, **2(2)**, 91-101. doi: 10.1037/a0017686
(36) Kleim, B., & Ehlers, A. J. (2008). Reduced autobiographical memory specificity predicts depression and posttraumatic stress disorder after recent trauma. *Journal of Consulting and Clinical Psychology*, **76(2)**, 231-242. doi: 10.1037/0022-006X.76.2.231
(37) Klossek, U. M. H., Russell, J., & Dickinson, A. (2008). The control of instrumental action following outcome devaluation in young children aged between 1 and 4 years. *Journal of Experimental Psychology: General*, **137(1)**, 39-51. doi: 10.1037/0096-3445.137.1.39
(38) Kubzansky, L. D., Martin, L. T., & Buka, S. L. (2009). Early manifestations of personality and adult health: A life course perspective. *Health Psychology*, **28(3)**, 364-372. doi: 10.1037/a0014428
(39) LaBrie, J. W., Cail, J., Hummer, J. F., Lac, A., & Neighbors, C. (2009). What men want: The role of reflective opposite-sex normative preferences in alcohol use among college women. *Psychology of Addictive Behaviors*, **23(1)**, 157-162. doi: 10.1037/a0013993
(40) Liles, E. E., & Packman, J. (2009). Play therapy for children with fetal alcohol syndrome. *International Journal of Play Therapy*, **18(4)**, 192-206. doi: 10.1037/a0015664
(41) Liu, W. M., Stinson, R., Hernandez, J., Shepard, S., & Haag, S. (2009). A qualitative examination of masculinity, homelessness, and social class among men in a transitional shelter. *Psychology of Men & Masculinity*, **10(2)**, 131-148. doi: 10.1037/a0014999
(42) Loomis, J. M., Lippa, Y., Golledge, R. G., & Klatzky, R. L. (2002). Spatial updating of locations specified by 3-D sound and spatial language. *Journal of Experimental Psychology: Learning, Memory, and Cognition*, **28(2)**, 335-345. doi: 10.1037//0278-7393.28.2.335
(43) Macdonald, J. S. P., & Lavie, N. (2008). Load induced blindness. *Journal of Experimental Psychology: Human Perception and Performance*, **34(5)**, 1078-1091. doi: 10.1037/0096-1523.34.5.1078
(44) McDaniel, M. A., Dimperio, E., Griego, J. A., & Busemeyer, J. R. (2009). Predicting transfer performance: A comparison of competing function learning models. *Journal of Experimental Psychology: Learning, Memory, and Cognition*, **35(1)**, 173-195. doi: 10.1037/a0013982
(45) Mitchell, S. J., Hilliard, M. E., Mednick, L., Henderson, C., Cogen, F. R., & Streisand, R. (2009).

Stress among fathers of young children with type 1 diabetes. *Families, Systems, & Health*, **27(4)**, 314–324. doi: 10.1037/a0018191

(46) Nower, L., & Blaszczynski, A. (2008). Characteristics of problem gamblers 56 years of age or older: A statewide study of casino self-excluders. *Psychology and Aging*, **23(3)**, 577–584. doi: 10.1037/a0013233

(47) Nunes, A., & Kramer, A. F. (2009). Experience-based mitigation of age-related performance declines: Evidence from air traffic control. *Journal of Experimental Psychology: Applied*, **15(1)**, 12–24. doi: 10.1037/a0014947

(48) Perkins, R. D. (2009). How executive coaching can change leader behavior and improve meeting effectiveness: An exploratory study. *Consulting Psychology Journal: Practice and Research*, **61(4)**, 298–318. doi: 10.1037/a0017842

(49) Reichel, C. M., & Rick, A. (2010). Competition between novelty and cocaine conditioned reward is sensitive to drug dose and retention interval. *Behavioral Neuroscience*, **124(1)**, 141–151. doi: 10.1037/a0018226

(50) Rekha, J., Chakravarthy, S., Veena, L. R., Kalai, V. P., Choudhury, R., Halahalli, H. N., ... Kutty, B. M. (2009). Transplantation of hippocampal cell lines restore spatial learning in rats with ventral subicular lesions. *Behavioral Neuroscience*, **123(6)**, 1197–1217. doi: 10.1037/a0017655

(51) Rivers, I., Poteat, V. P., Noret, N., & Ashurst, N. (2009). Observing bullying at school: The mental health implications of witness status. *School Psychology Quarterly*, **24(4)**, 211–223. doi: 10.1037/a0018164

(52) Shirom, A., Oliver, A., & Stein, E. (2009). Teachers' stressors and strains: A longitudinal study of their relationships. *International Journal of Stress Management*, **16(4)**, 312–332. doi: 10.1037/a0016842

(53) Shwalb, B. J., & Shwalb, D. W. (1992). Development of a course ratings form by a tests and measurements class. *Teaching of Psychology*, **19(4)**, 232–234.

(54) Shwalb, D., Shwalb, B., & Murata, K. (1989). Cooperation, competition, individualism and interpersonalism in Japanese fifth and eighth grade boys. *International Journal of Psychology*, **24(5)**, 617–630.

(55) Singer, T., Snozzi, R., Bird, G., Petrovic, P., Silani, G., Heinrichs, M., & Dolan, R. J. (2008). Effects of oxytocin and prosocial behavior on brain responses to direct and vicariously experienced pain. *Emotion*, **8(6)**, 781–791. doi: 10.1037/a0014195

(56) Steffen, A. C., Rockstroh, B., & Jansma, R. (2009). Brain evoked potentials reflect how emotional faces influence our decision making. *Journal of Neuroscience, Psychology, and Economics*, **2(1)**, 32–40. doi: 10.1037/a0015464

(57) Steinberg, L., Cauffman, E., Woolard, J., Graham, S., & Banich, M. (2009). Are adolescents less mature than adults?: Minors' access to abortion, the juvenile death penalty, and the alleged APA "flip-flop." *American Psychologist*, **64(7)**, 583–594. doi: 10.1037/a0014763

(58) Syvertsen, A. K., Flanagan, C. A., & Stout, M. D. (2009). Code of silence: Students' perceptions of school climate and willingness to intervene in a peer's dangerous plan. *Journal of Educational Psychology*, **101(1)**, 219–232. doi: 10.1037/a0013246

(59) van Ginkel, W., Tindale, R. S., & van Knippenberg, D. (2009). Team reflexivity, development of shared task representations, and the use of distributed information in group decision making. *Group Dynamics: Theory, Research, and Practice*, **13(4)**, 265–280. doi: 10.1037/a0016045

(60) Verona, E., Sadeh, N., & Curtin, J. J. (2009). Stress-induced asymmetric frontal brain activity and

aggression risk. *Journal of Abnormal Psychology*, **118(1)**, 131–145. doi: 10.1037/a0014376
(61) Warner, H. L., Mahoney, A., & Krumrei, E. J. (2009). When parents break sacred vows: The role of spiritual appraisals, coping, and struggles in young adults' adjustment to parental divorce. *Psychology of Religion and Spirituality*, **1(4)**, 233–248. doi: 10.10371/a0016787
(62) Wood, W., & Neal, D. T. (2007). A new look at habits and the habit-goal interface. *Psychological Review*, **114(4)**, 843–863. doi: 10.1037/0033-295X.114.4.843
(63) Zhan, Y., Wang, M., Liu, S., & Shultz, K. S. (2009). Bridge employment and retirees' health: A longitudinal investigation. *Journal of Occupational Health Psychology*, **14(4)**, 374–389. doi: 10.1037/a0015285
(64) Zlotnik, A., Gurevich, B., Cherniavsky, E., Tkachov, S., Matuzani-Ruban, A., Leon, A., ... Teichberg, V. I. (2007). The contribution of the blood glutamate scavenging activity of pyruvate to its neuroprotective properties in a rat model of closed head injury. *Neurochemical Research*, **33(6)**, 1044–1050. doi: 10.1007/s11064-007-9548-x

索引

語の後の数字は例文番号を示す．🔲 は類義語，
🔲 は対義語，［主語］は対応する主語の例を示す．

◆ A

a priori 802
abbreviation 107, 113, 128, 134, 607, 609, 614, 619, 622, 634
ability 598, 🔲 power
able (be — to) 144, 232, 505
above 238, 589, 869, 1239
abscissa 1269
acceptable 950
access 48, 541, 🔲 approach
accompany (be —ed by) 111
accomplish 406
according to 102, 144, 151, 265, 448, 752, 822, 869, 894, 1032, 1128, 🔲 as stated by
accordingly 802, 🔲 therefore
account (n) 400, 418, 1128, 1133, 🔲 explanation
account (v) (— for) 328, 936, 948, 949, 🔲 explain, form a part of
　［主語］
　　因子 917
accumulate 166, 🔲 build up
acknowledge 12, 15, 1163, 🔲 thank, admit
acquisition 559, 579, 788
action 1199
activate 314
　［主語］
　　証拠 88
active 517
ad libitum 541
adapt 624
　［主語］
　　検査 614
add 954
　　— to 1173
　［主語］
　　我々（著者） 713
additional 367, 510, 1232

address (n) 30, 31, 530, 660, 🔲 location
address (v) 71, 78, 364, 395, 417, 418, 991, 1026, 🔲 approach
　［主語］
　　課題 414
　　研究 80
　　研究者 84
　　分析 1158
　　問題 407
　　連絡先 30, 31
adequate 665, 668, 672, 932, 🔲 equal
adhere 777
adjust 824, 🔲 adapt, correct, set
administer 149, 556, 715, 737, 743, 745, 856, 🔲 conduct, give
　［主語］
　　学生 497
　　検査 606, 657
　　試行 726
adopt 🔲 follow
　［主語］
　　下位検査 620
　　方法 701
adult 538
advance 🔲 progress, 🔲 retard
　［主語］
　　結果 1179
　　研究 1155
advertisement 492, 497
affect 167, 410, 1202, 🔲 influence
　［主語］
　　操作 837
affiliate (be —d with) 6
affiliation 30, 31, 🔲 association, tie
affirm 1118, 🔲 confirm
again 783
age 469, 472, 473, 534, 544, 692
agree 628, 🔲 consent, 🔲 disagree

342　　　　　　　　　　　　索　　引

［主語］
　参加者　627
　我々（著者）　334
agreement　186, 628, 759, 762, ▆ assent, consent
aim (n)　270, 1029
aim (v)（— to）　387, 394, 407, 649, ▆ attempt, intend
allow　603, ▆ permit
alpha　667, 669, 805, 868
also　118, 210, 229, 281, 1146, 1163, 1172
alter　797, 856, 889
alternative　357, 418, 1131, 1132
alternatively　1128
among　912
ample　195
analysis　16, 54, 151, 153, 249, 343, 429, 507, 633, 636, 805, 809–812, 814, 818, 825, 827, 838, 843, 858, 861, 862, 873, 878, 883–885, 890, 896, 902, 905–907, 913–915, 918, 921, 922, 932, 936, 940, 946, 951, 952, 956, 965, 966, 968, 995, 1003, 1066, 1095, 1101, 1104, 1158, 1204, 1265
analyze　696, 839, 885, ▆ analyse, examine, study
［主語］
　群間差　810
　データ　39, 826, 884
　得点　888
　我々（著者）　717
anchor　636
anecdotal　155, 290
anesthetize　795
animal　163, 552, 776, 789, 794
annual　26, 27, 475, 476, ▆ biennial
anonymity　531
another　79, 119, 156, 253, 442, 511, 736, 910, 1029, 1047–1049, 1164, 1184
ANOVA　806, 810–812, 814, 885–888, 891, 892, 894, 895, 898, 900
answer　493, 1189, ▆ resolve, respond
apart　735
apparatus　495, 707, 783
appear　57, 203, ▆ seem
［主語］
　it　260, 1141, 1212
　関係　372
　研究　345
appendix　1021, 1022
application　156, 316

apply　79, 914, ▆ utilize
［主語］
　我々（著者）　100, 451
appreciation　16, ▆ gratitude
approach　120–122, 429, 444, 703, 966, 1148
approve
［主語］
　研究　774
　実験手続き　776
　手続き　777
approximately　39, 472, 566, 732, 737, 745, 746, 748, 792, 833
approximation　923, 1233
area　79, 466, 554, ▆ region
argue　▆ debate
［主語］
　it　254, 308
　one　334, 1130
　結果　1106
　研究者　169
　説明　357
　著者　262
　理論家　276
　我々（著者）　1129
argument　66, 154, ▆ disagreement
arm　550
arrangement　742, 1248, ▆ formation, layout, order
array　141
arrival　658
article　20–22, 25, 30, 31, 99, 382, 421, 818, 1067, 1209, 1210
ask　205, 503, 617, 651, 660, ▆ demand, inquire, interview
［主語］
　回答者　626
　項目　640
　子供　577, 586
　参加者　629, 630, 685, 764, 765
　質問紙　615
　著者　130
　我々（著者）　575, 705
aspect　442
assertion　1036, 1077, 1078
assess　128, 134, 459, 606–609, 611, 619, 622, 623, 625, 633, 639, 648, 713, 856, 858, 890, 892, 947, 1034

［主語］
　各モデルへの適合　923
　信頼性　758
　著者　130
　我々（著者）　45, 934
assessment　714, 1196
assign (be —ed to)　563, 689–695, 699,
　　■ commission, set
assistance　11–17
assistant　493, ■ subordinate
associate (be —d with)　32, 202, 231, 330, 358, 945,
　　963, 1262, ■ connect, link, relate
association　114, 140, 142, 806, 808, 875, 972, 1114
assume　1143, ■ presume, suppose, think
［主語］
　理論　269
　我々（著者）　427
assumption　38, 292, 294, 361, 445, 1029, 1032
attempt　128, 399, ■ effort, try
attention　310, 1156
attenuate　1100
attitude　41
attributable　290
attribute　1137
audiotape　769
author　15, 18, 116, 215, 262, 273, 431, 653
available　539, 540
［主語］
　経験的データ　413
　実験的分析　343
　正確な言い回し　653
average　468, 735, 834, 841, 848, 894, 943, 973, 977
［主語］
　総反応　842
avoid　738
axial　1256
azimuth　1249

◆ B

back　660
background　484, 569
bar　1272, 1273, ■ line
base　429, 435, 549, 580, 610, 622, 823, 1014, 1212,
　　■ found
　be —d on　25, 1063, 1245
baseline　602

basic　294, 787, 819, 1032
basis　450, 633, 715, 1115, 1144, ■ foundation
battery　654, 655
bear　79, ■ carry
［主語］
　readers　1170
because　679, 1147
become　170, ■ get, go, turn
［主語］
　it　184
begin　726, ■ start, 対 end
beginning　534, ■ first, origin, root, start, 対 end,
　　middle
behavior　797, 939, ■ conduct
behavioral　798
believe　288
［主語］
　我々（著者）　273, 1176
beneficial　89
benefit　1206
best　54
between-participant(s)　885–888
between-subject(s)　811, 812
bias　1165
biennial　26
binary　820
binomial　869
bivariate　806, 991
blind　754–756
［主語］
　符号化担当者　761
block　685–687, 725, 726, 729, 730, 736, 740, 741,
　　998, 1015, 1258
［主語］
　テスト日　731
board　775, ■ management
body　87, 89, 92, 93, 140, 165, 167, 170, 185, 194,
　　369, 1071
Bonferroni's correction　911
bonus　463
bottle　539
bottom　1267, 対 top
box　772
boy　44, 465, 466, 692
brain　553, 1256
break　844, ■ separate, split, 対 make

索　引

bridge　1157
brief　726
bring (— about)　177, 题 convey
broken　1269
build (— on)　1088
bulk　359, 题 volume
button　601

◆ C

cage　541, 542, 551
calculate　602, 645, 1260, 题 compute
　［主語］
　　相関　807
　　得点　821, 822
　　反応数　840
call　107
camera　603
campus　491
candidate　496
care　545, 776, 题 keeping
carry (be —ed out)　题 conduct, convey, express
　［主語］
　　研究　798
　　テスト　579
　　分析　825
case　156, 323, 800, 1138, 题 example, fact
categorical　814
categorize
　be —d as　483
　［主語］
　　我々（著者）　526
category　468, 641
causal　1140, 1204
causality　1140
cause　235, 335, 题 origin, reason
caution　256, 题 care, caveat
caveat　1170, 1171
ceiling　1137
center　47, 569, 783, 题 middle
　— around　258
central　307, 358, 550
CFI　923
challenge　321
chance　869, 1134
change　401, 970
characteristic　330, 487, 525, 983, 1228

characterize
　be —d by　110–112
　［主語］
　　重大な弱点　359
check　17, 757, 763–765, 772, 题 examine, test
chi-square　814, 860–862, 923
chief　831
child　39, 204, 466, 468, 481, 495, 512, 577, 586, 593, 595, 692, 712, 727, 752, 847, 853, 885, 题 parent
choice　849, 题 option, selection
choose　题 pick, select
　［主語］
　　項目　635
　　被験体　543
circle　1271
citation　1275, 题 reference
cite　249
City（市の名称）　1–7, 26, 27, 535, 540, 550, 572
claim　1111, 题 assertion
clarify　367, 1222
　［主語］
　　研究　261
class　42, 464, 659, 771, 1237, 题 course, grade, group, lesson, year
classic　148
classification　717, 1232
classify　153, 800, 题 arrange, organize
clean　783
clear　366, 题 unclear
　it be — that　251
　it be — why　1139
clearly　185, 1182, 题 obviously
click　601
clinical　162, 164, 487, 1127, 1199
clip　559
close　852, 1206, 1208, 题 open
cm　542, 550, 551, 554, 566, 568
coadminister　797
code　642, 753, 758
　［主語］
　　説明　752
coder　754, 761, 762
coding　754, 762
coefficient　667, 673, 1002, 1265
Cohen's *d*　979

cohort 124
coin 101
　［主語］
　　用語 113
collapse 878, ▣ crumple
colleague 171-175, 192, 282, 1072, 1077
collect 124, 438, 602
　［主語］
　　データ 480, 656
collection 14-16, 596, 597
collectively 437, 917, 1100
college 480
colony 536
combine 638, 815
　［主語］
　　下位尺度 637
　　得点 670
　　我々（著者） 645
combined 1243
come ▣ arrive, emerge, originate, ▣ go
　— from 188, 351
　［主語］
　　参加者 735
comment 13, 18, 20-22
　［主語］
　　著者 274
committee 774-777
common 136, 160, 292, 330, 332, 831, 914,
　　▣ individual
commonly 617
community 491
comparable 697
comparative 923, 1233
comparatively 352
compare 391, 778, 822, 879, 896, 909, 925, 1053
　［主語］
　　研究 398
　　我々（著者） 525
comparison 802, 813, 908, 911, 912, 1020, 1089,
　　1202, ▣ contrast, distinction
compelling 164, 371, 1111, 1120
compensation 499
compete 28, 398, ▣ fight, race
　［主語］
　　効果 1216
　　参加者 498

compile 557
complaint 831
complete 43, 131, 438, 498, 499, 660, 709, 737, 749,
　　771, 787, 991, ▣ finish, perfect
　［主語］
　　子供 512
　　参加者 41, 44, 515, 578, 612, 634, 647, 658, 716,
　　　773
　　試行 788
　　実験者 727
　　セッション 736
　　被験体 724
completely 627, 857
complex 372, ▣ simple
comply 29
component 936, 937, ▣ factor
compose (be —d of) 481, 551, 730, 845, ▣ comprise
composite 644
comprehensive 1207
comprise 687, 1119
compute 821
　be —d as 132
　［主語］
　　効果量 823
　　統計量 820
　　得点 841, 1234
　　偏相関 947
computer 547, 554, 556, 568, 569, 736
concentration 795, ▣ distribution
conceptual 278
conceptualize 393, 399, 845
　be —d as 108
　［主語］
　　著者 215
concern (n) 211
concern (v) ▣ be relevant to, regard
　［主語］
　　研究 378
　　説明 1138
　　特徴 442
concerning 21, 30, 31, 545, 1168, 1178, 1190
conclude 431, 1079, 1216, ▣ decide, judge
　it be —d that 1215
　［主語］
　　one 259
　　著者 172, 263

346　　　　　　　　　索　　引

我々（著者）　60
conclusion　502, 1174, 1181, 1211, 1213, 1214, 1217–1219, 1224, 1225, 🔃 deduction, findings
condition　440, 581, 587, 588, 591, 681–683, 689, 690, 692, 694, 739, 744, 760, 811, 854, 863, 866, 873, 895, 987, 1052, 1156, 1229, 1250, 1251, 1258, 1261, 1267, 🔃 requirement, state
conditioned　1257
conditioning　780
conduct　13, 17, 168, 710, 1199, 🔃 behave, do, perform
　［主語］
　インタビュー　751, 767
　階層的重回帰分析　951
　観察者　757
　研究　416, 538, 1024
　研究者　84
　セッション　792
　線形重回帰　808
　多変量分散分析　890, 905
　追跡調査研究　221
　テスト　715
　符号化　754
　分散分析　883
　分析　825, 827
　ロジスティック回帰分析　809
　我々（著者）　417, 838, 914, 921
conference　26
confidence　629
confidential　530
confidentiality　529, 531
confirm　221, 811, 1161, 🔃 affirm, corroborate, support, validate
　［主語］
　結果　63, 859, 1060, 1108
　実験　62
　分析　873, 913
　予測　1061
confirmatory　54, 921, 922, 932, 1003, 1265
conflict　28, 224
confound (n)　971, 🔃 confounding variable
confound (v)　1164, 🔃 confuse
congruent　210
conjunction　1096
connect　530, 554, 🔃 join, link, tie

［主語］
　スピーカー　547
consecutive　720
consent　497, 506, 516, 517, 772, 774
consider　731, 843, 🔃 regard, think
　［主語］
　意味　1174
　結果　1161
　結論　1174
　研究　1194
　知見　1171
　我々（著者）　428, 1146
considerably　225
consideration　1168
consist (— of)　124, 472, 480, 491, 549, 550, 562, 564–566, 642, 726, 731–733, 740, 770, 932, 1239, 🔃 comprise
consistency　390, 616, 663–669, 🔃 constancy, uniformity
consistent　57, 141, 177, 178, 180, 192, 203, 902, 929, 1059, 1080, 🔃 inconsistent
　be — with　230, 297, 456, 1075, 1081, 1083, 1178
consistently　179, 229
constant　1035
constitute　559, 963, 🔃 comprise, form
construct　97, 931, 🔃 compose, build, make
　［主語］
　テスト　743
　得点　633
　我々（著者）　1015
consultation　13, 🔃 interview
contact　503
　［主語］
　両親　493
contain　619, 712, 🔃 hold, include
　［主語］
　相関　992
contend　425, 🔃 assert
content　664
contention　1119
context　255
contingency　788
continue　1110
　— to　339, 352

［主語］
　訓練　723
　被験体　720
　論争　305
continuous　814
continuously　540
contradict　1091
contrary　66
［主語］
　知見　1063
contrast　227, 231, 254, 355, 459
［主語］
　知見　1090
　我々（著者）　400
contribute　23, 962, ▨ play a part
　— to　40
［主語］
　結果　1153
　結論　1225
　研究　1154
contribution　394, 1152, ▨ addition
contributor　1135
control　536, 557, 674, 685, 689, 698, 802, 809, 813, 947, 969, 970, 975, 1197, 1257, ▨ govern, manage, standard of comparison
［主語］
　多変量モデル　971
　分析　968
　我々（著者）　1038
convergent　135, 176, 664, 672
convey　169
convincing　190, 193, 194
copyright　1275
coronal　1256
correct　720, 849, ▨ right
correction　911
correctly　153, ▨ accurately, rightly
correlate
　— with　220
　be —d　200, 938
　be —d with　939, 1013
correlation　141, 201, 761, 806, 807, 882, 926, 944, 947, 991–994, 1004, 1012, 1231, 1245
correlational　940, 946
correspond　1076
correspondence　30, 31, 852

corroborate　1072, ▨ support
corroboration　1070
counterbalance　740, 743
［主語］
　順序　744
　呈示順序　741
Country（国の名称）　1–7, 26, 535, 550, 572, ▨ state
course　462, 463, ▨ class, curriculum
covariate　930, 957, 1002
create　▨ make
［主語］
　測度　639
　バージョン　563
credit　461–463
criterion　325, 511, 618, 664, 720, 976, ▨ standard
critical　297, 420
　be — to　303
critically　1206
criticism　19
Cronbach's alpha　669
cross　46, ▨ blend
cross-lagged　993
crucial　185, ▨ important
cup　539
current　29, 40, 387, 401, 404, 543, 624, 1031, 1071, 1076, 1077, 1091, 1109, 1140, 1145, 1169, 1180, 1224
currently　6, 7, 341, 342, 413
curve　972
cut-off　527
cycle　534, 536, 542

◆ D

daily　792, 1151
dashed　1269
data　14–16, 25, 26, 39, 156, 164, 191, 234, 413, 480, 511, 519, 596, 597, 602, 643, 656, 696, 799, 820, 826, 844, 884, 922, 924, 925, 932, 948, 1007, 1008, 1017, 1037, 1070, 1094, 1142, 1204, 1232, ▨ information, statistics
database　816
dataset　522
dearth　339
debate　94, 305
debrief　721, 722, 773

〔主語〕
　参加者　722
decade　93, 94, 306
deception　722
declare　28
decomposition　1005
decrease　53, 160, 163, 🔁 increase
dedicate　355
define　🔁 delineate, describe
　be —d as　101–103, 105
　〔主語〕
　　因子　916
definitive　1181
definitively　261
degree　386, 🔁 grade, level, point, stage
delineate　344, 🔁 define, describe
deliver　🔁 give, present
　〔主語〕
　　注射量　793
　　電気ショック　782
delivery　536
demographic　484, 487, 523, 525, 615, 983, 1228
demonstrate　165, 166, 176, 191, 375, 663, 671, 1076, 1086, 1087, 1096, 1114, 1116, 1155
　〔主語〕
　　確証的因子分析　54
　　研究　37, 142, 1105, 1208
　　実験　415, 1214, 1216
　　実験者　593
　　測度　672
　　著者　145
demonstration　727
denote　100, 🔁 designate
　〔主語〕
　　等式　284
department　1, 3–5, 491, 🔁 division, section
depend (— on)　240
dependent　677–679, 738, 953, 🔁 independent
depict　1009
depiction　1248
describe　109, 406, 546, 706, 716, 749, 784, 839, 🔁 delineate, depict, draw
　〔主語〕
　　手続き　704
descriptive　801, 984
deserve　1173

design　46, 459, 612, 688, 694, 700, 1034, 1201, 🔁 outline, plan
　〔主語〕
　　研究　383, 398, 1025
detail　546, 1018, 1223, 🔁 specifics
determination　744
determine　194, 293, 386, 387, 415, 493, 649, 755, 797, 889, 905, 965, 1198, 🔁 ascertain, identify
　〔主語〕
　　it　1134
　　研究　1140
　　参加者　528
　　実験　454
develop　76, 127, 146, 614, 623, 752, 🔁 grow
　〔主語〕
　　研究　391
　　研究者　78
　　参加者　42
　　尺度　619
　　著者　278, 279
　　モデル　282
development　276, 315, 664
developmental　1127
deviation　632, 985, 986, 988, 989, 🔁 departure, discrepancy
diagnosis　341
diagnostic　325
diary　605
dichotomous　1238
diet　545
differ　802, 🔁 equal
　— between　218, 257
　— from　910
　〔主語〕
　　2群　699
difference　810, 813, 814, 850, 860–862, 865, 871, 872, 874, 876, 892, 894, 896, 898, 899, 908, 911, 912, 980, 1009, 1133, 1134
different　126, 674, 740, 743, 885, 987, 1191, 1254, 1267, 🔁 same
differential　850
differentiate　885, 🔁 integrate
differently　237
difficulty　288, 329, 715
digitally　769
dilute　266

dimension 542, 915
direct 50, 928, 🟦 lead, straight, 🟦 indirect
　［主語］
　参加者 773
direction 1161, 🟦 instruction, way
directly 391, 1198, 🟦 right
disagree 627, 628, 🟦 differ, 🟦 agree
discriminant 135, 153, 672
discuss 1068, 1210
　［主語］
　意味 73
　知見 74
　著者 255, 311
discussed 311
discussion 1049, 🟦 debate
disorder 112, 325, 🟦 order
display 554, 565, 566, 668, 1011, 1021, 1229, 1250, 1251, 🟦 presentation, show
　［主語］
　因子パターン 1001
　結果 995
　図 1014
　相関 994
　表 1002
　標準偏差 988
　平均 988
　リスト 991
dissolve 572, 🟦 melt
distance 568, 1249, 🟦 length, space
distinguish 809, 829, 🟦 differentiate, separate
　［主語］
　変数 885
distribute 438, 🟦 allocate, deliver
　［主語］
　調査票 659
distribution 471, 526, 862, 🟦 concentration
district 516, 524
diverse 141
do 48, 197, 220, 300, 511, 512, 699, 870, 908, 910, 925, 969, 🟦 come, make, perform
doctoral 24
document 256, 355
　［主語］
　現象 204
dollar 500
dose 794, 796, 797

dose-dependently 53
dose-independently 53
dot 1271
double-blind 975
down 605, 844
draft 20, 21
draw 🟦 extract, sketch
　be —n from 363, 514, 518, 520, 525
　［主語］
　研究 447
　物体 1248
　我々（著者） 1213
drip-proof 539
drop 1037
　［主語］
　参加者 511
drug 684, 797
due (be — to) 14, 274, 879, 1133

◆ E

e.g. 116, 123, 175, 197, 246, 247, 439, 1204
early 22, 81, 82, 160, 1068, 🟦 late, middle
easy 595, 1137
education 474, 476, 🟦 instruction, training
effect 36, 45, 55, 89, 137, 245, 379, 388, 432, 683, 738, 820–823, 853, 856, 877, 878, 880, 881, 883, 890, 891, 895, 900, 901, 905, 906, 913, 920, 928, 963, 964, 966, 978, 980, 986, 1005, 1008, 1025, 1028, 1034, 1038, 1085, 1116, 1132, 1137, 1198, 1216
effective 57, 244, 554
　［主語］
　操作 859
effectiveness 858
efficacy 402
effort 77, 258, 355
eigenvalue 936, 937
electronic 815, 816
elementary 494
elicit 873
eligibility 493, 504
eligible 505
eliminate 697
email 30, 31
emerge

［主語］
　　関連　875
　　説明　356
　　データ　164
emphasis　72, 271
emphasize　447
　［主語］
　　理論　268
empirical　71, 165, 246, 259, 413, 1077, 1078, 1217, 🔄 theoretical
empirically　63, 78
employ
　［主語］
　　組　740
　　研究　437
encourage　722
end　501, 503, 1027, 🔄 last, purpose, remainder, 🔄 beginning, middle
endorse　834
engine　815
ensure　508
enter　47, 124, 955, 🔄 come in
　［主語］
　　我々（著者）　956
entry　783
envelope　660
envision　1201
equal　471, 472, 843
equally　23, 550, 771
equation　283, 284, 932, 933
error　849, 923, 990, 1230, 1233, 1273
especially　97, 281, 370, 1147
essay　716
essential　199
　［主語］
　　it　374
establish　414, 1196, 🔄 certify, confirm, constitute
　［主語］
　　it　182, 354, 1130
　　研究　662
　　知見　69
estimate　323, 325, 326, 475, 610, 972, 1261, 🔄 assess, evaluate
　［主語］
　　it　325
　　階層的多変量重回帰モデル　953

　　構造方程式モデル　932, 933
　　2変数間の結びつき　806
ethic　774
ethical　775
ethnic　479
evaluate　121, 343, 368, 411, 680, 934, 1025
　［主語］
　　研究　1028
　　適合度　974
evaluation　1196, 🔄 rating
every　723, 782
evidence　66, 87, 88, 123, 140, 144, 155, 165, 177, 179, 187–195, 232, 238, 262, 290, 322, 664, 1056, 1059, 1099, 1111, 1120, 1181, 1221
　［主語］
　　項目　635
evident　184
　［主語］
　　主効果　881
exact　653
examination　936, 1206, 🔄 test, testing
examine　39, 43, 61, 352, 583, 803, 808, 951, 1023, 1088, 1159, 1202, 🔄 analyze, inspect, study
　［主語］
　　researchers　363
　　記述統計　801
　　研究　35, 83, 337, 346, 385, 390, 401, 409, 410, 1035, 1036, 1191
　　研究領域　79
　　心理学者　76
　　我々（著者）　388, 418, 837, 860, 889, 1156
example　81, 115, 162, 423, 725, 728, 851, 1150, 1250, 1251, 1254, 🔄 case, instance
exceed　761, 🔄 top
excellent　665, 668
exception　708, 1093
exchange　461, 462
exclude　843, 🔄 omit, 🔄 include
　［主語］
　　研究　818
　　参加者　506, 514
exclusive　831
exist　237, 414, 1173
　［主語］
　　研究　342
　　検査　341

索　引　　*351*

expand　1205
expect　58, 275, 328, 435, 1062, 1115
expectation　1060
experience　327, 544, 🔄 have, receive, see
　[主語]
　　回答者　626
experiment　13, 61, 62, 116, 175, 299, 415, 417, 418,
　　433, 442, 452–456, 458, 459, 501, 503, 534, 554,
　　555, 585, 594, 688, 690, 706–708, 722, 728, 746,
　　975, 1041, 1085, 1145, 1157, 1161, 1214, 1216,
　　1247, 1266
experimental　46, 343, 545, 564, 685, 725, 726, 760,
　　776, 794, 1253
experimentally　536, 537, 713
experimenter　570, 577, 593, 658, 758
explain　258, 773, 917, 959, 1128
　[主語]
　　結果　1125
　　構造　54
　　実験者　593
explanation　253, 356, 357, 400, 722, 1122, 1123,
　　1131, 1132, 1138, 🔄 account
explanatory　245
exploration　372
exploratory　838, 1174
explore　40, 114, 342, 370, 783, 1160
　[主語]
　　研究　75, 348, 450
　　私（著者）　426
expose　🔄 display
　[主語]
　　参加者　682
　　被験体　787
express　1080, 🔄 show, state
　[主語]
　　参加者　830
　　我々（著者）　16
expression　378, 🔄 manifestation
extant　311, 361, 1178
extend　57, 364, 459, 🔄 enhance, expand
　[主語]
　　結果　1086
　　研究　395, 396
　　知見　1087, 1088
　　理論　1218
extensive　261, 355

extent　300, 454, 627, 1191, 1202
external　547, 🔄 internal
extinction　854
extract　49, 817, 914
extraction　937
extremely　631, 1239

◆ F

facilitate　278
fact　1137
factor　54, 76, 87, 92, 185, 212, 312, 619, 633, 811,
　　812, 829, 887, 888, 895, 901, 903, 914–918,
　　921, 922, 926, 928, 932, 936, 937, 969, 978,
　　1000–1004, 1149, 1265
factorial　694
faculty　42
fail (— to)　1091, 🔄 not succeed
family　476, 🔄 home, house, household
far　322, 337, 347, 373, 1111, 1193, 1197, 1205
feature　442, 🔄 characteristic, property
federal　545
feed　537, 🔄 serve
　[主語]
　　被験体　540
feedback　601, 751
feeling　830
female　463, 470, 472, 473, 538, 611, 795, 🔄 male
few　35, 166, 343, 346, 697, 🔄 many
field　90, 1203
figure　857, 1014, 1016–1020, 1246–1275
fill (— out)　609, 🔄 fulfill
final　762, 954
finalize　770
financial　28
find　33, 86, 140, 143, 147, 150, 200, 220, 224, 228,
　　231, 249, 312, 324, 330, 430, 673, 862, 865, 880,
　　881, 898, 969, 977, 981, 1054, 1065, 1073, 1085,
　　1090, 1091, 🔄 discover, notice, realize
　[主語]
　　it　969
　　彼ら　228
　　Q 統計量　981
　　結果　224
　　研究　33, 140, 150, 231, 324, 673, 977
　　研究者　220, 330
　　最尤カイ二乗分析　862

支持　1054
主効果　880
著者　143, 147
t 検定　865
文献　86
分散分析　898
finding　64, 69, 74, 160, 221, 223, 226, 240, 279, 307, 320, 429, 431, 452, 453, 457, 879, 1040–1044, 1046–1048, 1056, 1057, 1063, 1064, 1070, 1072, 1075, 1076, 1078, 1080–1083, 1086–1088, 1090, 1091, 1093, 1096, 1133, 1135, 1136, 1140, 1143, 1160, 1171, 1173, 1178, 1180, 1212, 1222
first　128, 154, 280, 373, 403, 404, 422, 443, 577, 604, 615, 637, 681, 715, 780, 916, 932, 954–956, 961, 994, 1027, 1029, 1129, 1138, 1154, 1171, 1173, 1213, 1220, 1223, 対 last, second
〔主語〕
　研究　1159, 1224
first-year　462
fit　539, 922–925, 932, 934, 935, 974, 1233, 1241, 類 adjust, match
〔主語〕
　線形関数　948
fitted　973
fix　785, 類 determine, place
〔主語〕
　動物　552
fixation　567
flat　554
floor　549, 類 base, level, story
flyer　491
focus　420, 1188, 類 concentrate, direct, spotlight
— on　77, 91, 241, 271, 277, 360, 362, 396, 408, 421, 1027, 1187
〔主語〕
　研究　408
　努力　77
　文献　91
follow　374, 567, 579, 648, 650, 702, 725, 726, 728, 798, 832, 857
〔主語〕
　尺度　618
　手続き　776
　被験体　545
　ブロック　685
　我々（著者）　956

follow-up　221, 493, 647
following　408, 426, 558, 581, 708, 739, 1053, 1171, 1234
font　569, 類 character
food　539, 541
for　799, 985
form　516, 670, 773, 類 constitute, make
— part of　24
〔主語〕
　指数　638
　測度　644
formal　474
formula　819, 1234, 類 procedure, rule
frame　520
framework　203, 242, 393, 1207
free　537, 684, 783
frequency　863
freshman　464, 1237
front　558, 対 back
full　245, 949, 1269
full-time　476
fully　722, 類 completely, entirely, perfectly, totally
function　893, 948, 1229, 1230, 1249
functional　553
fund　10
　be —ed by　9
further　219, 372, 788, 818, 1070, 1078, 1161, 1180, 1204
furthermore　234
future　1182, 1184, 1187–1189, 1191, 1192, 1194–1198, 対 present

◆ G
g（単位）　53, 534, 536, 537, 795
gain　766, 類 collect, gather, obtain, 対 reduce
〔主語〕
　我々（著者）　412
gap　1158
gather　119, 類 collect, gain, obtain
general　183, 186, 407, 1186, 対 local, specific
generalizable　151
generally　456, 1042, 対 specifically
generate　570
genuine　1134
gesture　752
girl　44, 465, 466, 692, 類 miss

give　319, 320, 357, 369, 589, 629, 715, 722, 774,
　　 類 apply, dedicate, pay, present, yield, 対 take
　［主語］
　　検定　986
　　参加者　588, 592, 646, 712
　　点　718
　　標準偏差　986
　　平均　986
　　要約　1022
go (it — without saying)　333, 類 come
goal　382, 405, 406, 413, 1027, 1029, 類 end
good　230, 409, 412, 664, 671, 759, 924, 925, 1204, 1227, 1241
goodness-of-fit　974
grade　44, 659, 類 level, score
gradually　785
graduate　476
grant　8–10
grateful (be — to)　13, 20
gratefully　12
great　526, 644, 843, 937, 1010, 1019
greet　658
group　467, 514, 524, 541, 586, 693, 697–699, 736, 794, 798, 802, 810, 828, 847, 862, 872, 879, 891, 892, 898, 909, 911, 912, 920, 1015, 1033, 1134, 1254, 1257, 1267, 類 cluster, set
　［主語］
　　反応　641
grouping　524
grow　87–92, 369, 1071, 類 develop, produce, raise
growth　972, 類 development
guarantee　531, 類 ensure, warrant
guide　377, 779, 類 direct, lead, teach
　［主語］
　　研究　449

◆ H

half　742, 833
hand
　on the one —　34, 230
　on the other —　34, 230
handful　345, 349
have　10, 33, 35, 75–80, 83, 84, 92–94, 103, 105, 107, 113, 114, 122, 123, 129, 137–142, 158, 159, 162–164, 166–169, 171, 173, 174, 176, 180, 181, 183, 187, 190–192, 200, 202, 204, 207, 216, 229, 236, 237, 242, 245, 247, 258, 261, 263, 268, 276, 292, 299, 307, 308, 312, 322, 324, 330, 337, 338, 340, 346–348, 350, 354–356, 360, 362–365, 402, 430, 432, 446, 478, 505, 507, 541, 544, 626, 627, 661, 663, 671–673, 758, 788, 797, 915, 969, 973, 1084, 1107, 1116, 1130, 1135, 1137, 1146, 1151, 1156, 1160, 1208, 1210, 1218, 類 bear, experience, hold, make, ought, 対 lack
　— a range　323
　— access to　48
　— data　1232
　— difficulty in　288
　— effect on　89, 856
　— implications　241, 1110
　— interests　28
　— limitations　1169, 1172
　— strengths　1172, 1175
　— ties to　97
　［主語］
　　群　879, 909
　　結果　1150
　　参加者　835
　　実験　688
　　著者　222
Hedges g　821
heighten　214
help　14
　［主語］
　　知見　1222
helpful　13, 18, 21
herein　406, 1102, 1106
hierarchical　951–953, 956, 958, 965
high　148, 313, 494, 526, 550, 616, 630, 635, 644, 663, 666, 842, 864, 866, 870, 879, 907, 対 low
highlight
　［主語］
　　評論　422
　　論文　1209
historical　97
hold　1035, 類 bear, carry, contain, give, have, make, support
home　476, 494, 類 family, house
homogeneity　820
honestly　813
hour　783, 840
house　534, 536, 540–542

household 477
how 354, 376, 414, 1209
however 215, 232, 322, 381, 1130, 1139, 類 but, nevertheless, though
hr（単位） 746, 747, 790, 792
humane 545
humane care 545
humidity 536
hypothesis 64, 285, 287, 299, 426, 432–434, 455, 722, 802, 902, 1024, 1029–1031, 1054–1058, 1063, 1066, 1195, 1200, 1217, 1252, 類 assumption, proposition, theory
hypothesize
 　be ―d to 286
 　［主語］
 　　私（著者） 426
 　　我々（著者） 424, 429, 430

◆ I
i.e. 1204
idea 82, 222, 1080, 1217
identical (be ― to) 458, 706, 708, 709, 727
identify 49, 493, 1193, 類 diagnose, pinpoint, recognize
 　［主語］
 　　研究 92, 212
 　　参加者 482
 　　主成分抽出 937
 　　我々（著者） 975
ignore 1093, 対 know
 　［主語］
 　　疑問 365
illustrate 999
 　［主語］
 　　結果 1104, 1157
 　　研究 213
 　　図 1020
 　　論点 272
illustration 1255
image 553
immigrant 481
impact 180, 778, 1146
impair 168
implicate 1121
implication 70, 73, 74, 241, 1110, 1140, 1150, 1151, 1174

imply 1103, 1113, 類 indicate, mean, suggest
importance 68, 210, 268, 338, 1107, 1118
important 87, 138, 162, 211, 241, 320, 321, 394, 414, 442, 1026, 1043, 1086, 1188, 1190, 1206, 1220
 　［主語］
 　　it 309, 1045, 1164
 　　知見 1147, 1160
 　　問題 1148
 　　理解 369
importantly 59, 190, 類 significantly
impressive 166
improve 1225
improvement 57, 類 advance
in addition 709, 1173
in order to 310
in other words 209
in-depth 1193
include 141, 484, 612, 615, 918, 934, 954, 971, 992, 1172, 1175, 対 exclude
 　［主語］
 　　意味 70
 　　データ 643
 　　テーマ 332
 　　テストバッテリー 654, 655
 　　評価テスト 714
 　　文献 85
 　　例 851
inclusion 511, 976
income 476, 477
inconsistent 226, 643, 対 consistent
 　［主語］
 　　知見 223
increase 53, 158, 163, 299, 432, 類 advance, grow, 対 decrease
 　［主語］
 　　比率 785
incremental 672
independent 756, 864, 類 free, 対 dependent
independently 754, 758, 817
index 638, 670, 676, 923, 934, 935, 974, 1233
indicate 52, 89, 101, 183, 211, 257, 282, 298, 369, 628, 644, 705, 772, 799, 842, 850, 880, 945, 964, 981, 1050, 1071, 1094, 1270, 類 point, show, suggest

［主語］
　this　1197
　一対比較　911
　エラーバー　1273
　確証的因子分析　922
　結果　1012
　研究　157, 162, 185, 219, 663, 750
　参加者　439
　実験　61
　シェフェ法　912
　証拠　179
　線　1269
　知見　1140
　t 検定　867
　点　1271
　値　1241
　判別分析　153
　文献　170
　平均点　842
indication　1199
indirect　928, 🆚 direct
indistinguishable　1102
individual　149, 205, 498, 518, 602, 1264, 1268, 🆚 common
individually　466, 536, 540, 570, 🆚 separately
influence (n)　37, 368, 999, 1126
influence (v)　76, 203, 410, 🆚 affect, control, guide
　be —d by　173, 282, 1099
inform
　［主語］
　　アプローチ　703
　　参加者　530
information　119, 484, 485, 615
informative　222
informed consent　497, 774
infusion　857, 🆚 fill
initial　221, 731, 795, 1161
initially　785
inject　572
　［主語］
　　我々（著者）　411
injection　796
insight　281, 1109, 1204, 1226
insightful　22
inspection　1010, 1019, 🆚 examination, review
inspire　580, 795

instigate　120
institutional　775, 776
instruct　1033
　［主語］
　　参加者　584, 707, 711
instruction　46, 581, 588–592, 🆚 direction, order
instrument　546, 552, 🆚 apparatus, tool
instrumentation　664
integrate　392, 🆚 differentiate
intention　722
inter-　757, 759, 761, 762
interact　797, 889
interaction　881, 895, 899–905, 920, 956, 964, 970
intercept　948, 973
intercorrelate (be —d)　943
interest　28, 90, 380, 381, 🆚 benefit, concern
interested　379
interesting　156, 1011, 1046, 1185
internal　390, 616, 663–669, 672, 🆚 external
internet　497
internet-based　497
interpret　1170, 🆚 render, understand
　be —ed as　349
　［主語］
　　研究　256
　　知見　252
interval　790
intervene　734
interview　157, 503, 751, 766, 767, 769
interviewer　768
intraperitoneally　572
intravenously　572
intrigue　94
introduce　493, 🆚 initiate, present
　［主語］
　　子供　495
　　手段　134
introduction　921, 1067, 🆚 entry
introductory　461
invaluable　11
inventory　613, 616
investigate　152, 181, 350, 364, 451, 809, 1027, 1038, 1192, 1207
　［主語］
　　研究　36, 93, 137, 340, 347, 1197
　　検定　814

356　　　　　　　　　索　引

効果　683
実験　415
著者　81
investigation　338, 363, 956, 1207
investigator　495, 817
invite　496–498
　[主語]
　学生　771
involve　280, 298, 362, 733, 816, 920, 🔃 include
　[主語]
　機序　199
issue　78, 79, 302, 315, 358, 373, 381, 414, 1026, 1148, 🔃 problem, question
item　562, 567, 570, 612, 628, 635, 636, 638, 640, 642, 645, 648, 652, 670, 800, 844, 858, 861, 914, 919, 931, 936, 1238, 🔃 object, point

◆ J

join　1071
junior　464, 1237
just　259
justification　722
justify　172, 🔃 support, warrant

◆ K

key　162, 212, 453, 601, 711, 983, 1047
kg（単位）　53, 572, 796
know　351, 🔃 perceive, realize, recognize, 🔃 ignore
　[主語]
　less　354
　little　353, 355

◆ L

laboratory　114, 658, 776
lack　245
　[主語]
　研究　336
large　84, 93, 140, 167, 331, 514, 518, 522, 963, 980, 1199, 🔃 little, small
largely　1185, 🔃 mostly
last　166, 306, 747, 🔃 first
　[主語]
　セッション　792
　テストセッション　732
late　731, 🔃 belated, 🔃 early, middle
latent　926, 931

later　130, 503, 783
Latin　537, 538
latter　468, 731, 882
law　29
layout　1247, 1249
lead (— to)　94, 186, 193, 295, 307, 317, 1207, 🔃 command, conduct, direct, guide
learn　507, 1018, 🔃 discover, master, memorize, understand
least　161, 744, 🔃 most
lend　🔃 add, bring, contribute
　— support to　250, 1077
　[主語]
　研究　250, 1077
length　468
lesion　857
less　354, 421, 515, 1062, 1115, 🔃 more
letter　494
level　45, 628, 715, 804, 846, 868–870, 874, 1256
lid　539
lie (— in)　321, 🔃 stand
life　1151
light　1143, 1174
light–dark　534, 536, 542
like (v)　11, 22
like (prep)　128
likelihood　862
likely (be — to)　147, 161, 196, 478, 1062, 1098
Likert(-type) scale　631, 636
limit　345, 950, 🔃 confine, restrict
　[主語]
　結果　1183
　効果　920
　サンプル　1162
limitation　213, 311, 1166–1169, 1172–1174, 1177–1179, 🔃 reservation, restraint, restriction
line　307, 1269, 🔃 direction
　be in — with　240, 1074, 1079, 1082
linear　808, 948
link　927, 1222, 🔃 tie
list　561, 563, 651, 991, 🔃 inventory
　[主語]
　表　652
literature　40, 85, 86, 89, 91, 93, 167, 170, 184, 187, 226, 227, 233, 243, 311, 351, 357, 359, 369, 394, 419, 705, 1087, 1153–1157, 1173, 1178, 1179

little 344, 350–353, 355, 413, 1156, 対 much
loading 914, 919, 1000
local 545, 対 general
locate 477, 480, 771, 類 place, put
log 820, 1007
logic 451
logistic 809, 965, 類 logistical
logistical 14
long 276, 550, 843, 876, 対 short
long-standing 94
longitudinal 191, 522, 1204
low 313, 630, 665, 666, 668, 863, 909, 1266, 対 high
lower 517, 対 raise

◆ M

magnetic 553
magnitude 850
mail 660, 類 post, send
main 307, 422, 678, 880, 881, 891, 895, 901, 905, 913, 995, 1023, 1040, 1041
maintain 786, 1263
［主語］
　被験体 537, 542
major 42, 452, 1061, 類 main, main subject
majority 473, 476, 833, 類 bulk
make 154, 287, 394, 521, 697, 類 create, do, work, 対 break
　— choices 849
　— up 931
　— responses 126
［主語］
　比較 802
male 463, 470, 472, 473, 538, 611, 795, 対 female
man 461, 471, 480
manipulate 433, 674, 675, 1033, 類 control, operate
［主語］
　教示 588
　我々（著者） 713
manipulation 763–765, 837, 858, 859, 896, 類 control, operation
MANOVA 890, 905, 906
manufacturer 550
manuscript 12
many 83, 85, 123, 160, 169, 183, 215, 273, 307, 対 few
marginal
879, 880, 882
marginally 879–881
marry 468, 476, 類 unite
match 700, 類 agree, correspond, fit, 対 mismatch
［主語］
　インタビューを行う人 768
　統制群 698
material 558
maximum 735, 862
maze 550, 783, 798, 1018
mean 119, 149, 299, 468, 474, 537, 632, 822, 842, 846, 847, 865, 874, 923, 985–990, 1230, 1257–1260, 1267
measure 41, 45, 65, 69, 128, 129, 132, 133, 136, 220, 347, 441, 566, 576, 598, 599, 613, 616, 623, 624, 632, 639, 640, 642–644, 652, 654, 658, 672, 677, 678, 812, 820, 872, 883, 897, 941, 978, 類 assess, evaluate, quantify
［主語］
　我々（著者） 604
measurement 134, 932, 1004, 類 assessment, evaluation, quantification
mechanism 114, 192, 199, 301
median 475, 477
mediate 51, 430, 966, 967
［主語］
　関係 927
mediation 966, 1004
mediator 933
medium 963
meet 325, 511, 類 bear, cross, encounter, satisfy
［主語］
　研究 976
meeting 27
member 42
mention 1173, 類 reference
merely 1134, 類 just, only
message 496, 498, 類 letter
meta-analysis 151, 152, 245
meta-analytic 977
method 123, 701, 822
methodology 1200
middle 494, 対 beginning, end
might 1225
min（単位） 47, 659, 676, 732, 736, 737, 745, 747,

索　引

782, 783, 793, 795, 840
mind　1170, 1171, 🔁 brain, head
minimum　735, ↔ maximum
minute　676, 739, 782, 840
miss　511, 799, 800, 1232, 🔁 lack, ↔ successive
mixed　885, 888
mixed-design　811
mixed-mode　884
mixture　795
ml（単位）　572
model　65, 118, 230, 242, 278–282, 291, 293, 295, 297, 298, 397–400, 921–926, 932–935, 949, 950, 953, 958–962, 971, 974, 1002–1004, 1006, 1204, 1233, 1255, 1265, 🔁 example, framework, modeling, paradigm, pattern, simulaion
　［主語］
　　研究　446
modeling　972
moderate　526, 665, 666, 668, 964, 980, 🔁 average, mild, modest
moderately　200, 943
moderation　956
moderator　428, 956
modestly　943
modified　623–625
modulate　401, 797
monitor　554
monkey　796
month　534, 656, 692, 734, 748, 798
more　57, 93, 147, 159, 161, 197, 211, 215, 216, 222, 232, 299, 310, 368, 421, 643, 650, 732, 853, 855, 891, 969, 1019, 1062, 1115, 1136, 1181, 1198, 1200, 1204, 1207, 1241, ↔ less
most　139, 190, 250, 258, 289, 302, 360, 363, 831, 1043, 1044, 1111, ↔ least
mostly　365
mouse　601, 783
ms（単位）　567
much　187, ↔ little
multiple　808, 956
multivariable　971
multivariate　890, 905, 906, 953
mutually　831

◆ N

naïve　536, 537, 757

name　30, 31, 529, 530, 537, 538, 670, 🔁 title
narrative　717, 🔁 story, tale
nationwide　150
nearly　325, 476
necessary
　［主語］
　　it　1034
　　再現　1182
　　実験　1161
need　366, 370, 🔁 require, want
　［主語］
　　結果　1183
　　研究　367, 368, 376, 1180, 1193, 1198
negative　928, 940, 1012, 1241, ↔ positive
negatively　941
neglect (it should not be —ed that)　1215, 🔁 drop, ignore, miss, omit
never　650
nevertheless　1176
new　69, 134, 281, 460, 513, ↔ old
newer　217
non　467
non(-)significant　882, 928, 1272
none　904
nonparametric　868
notable　1128
　［主語］
　　傾向　1053
notably　289
note (n)　1232–1245
note (v)　157, 259, 309, 915, 1045, 1067, 1164, 1218, 1248, 🔁 indicate, mention, observe
　［主語］
　　限界　1167
　　シェフェ法　912
　　著者　104, 313
noteworthy　1048
notion　1177
novel　442
now　7, 31, 165, 277
number　9, 84, 92, 148, 166, 168, 676, 840, 847, 1150, 1153, 1173, 1175, 1199, 1213, 1229, 🔁 figure, quantity
numerous　142, 216, 330

索　引

◆ O

object　1248
objective　341
oblique　914, 1256
observation　178, 1049
observe　218, 272, 274, 727, 905, 928, 1084,
　　　☒ conform, mention, note, watch, ☒ overlook
　［主語］
　　交互作用　899
　　相関　882
　　我々（著者）　411
observer　755, 757
obtain　484, 497, 537, 822, 824, 897
　［主語］
　　一致度　759
　　記録　600
　　結果　176
　　主効果　905
　　証拠　123
　　相関　944
　　被験体　535
obvious　457, 1169
occur　195, 198, 277, 1134, ☒ exist, happen
　［主語］
　　テスト　748
odds ratio　820, 1007
off　772, 834
offer　445, 674, ☒ provide, suggest, tender
　［主語］
　　研究　1226
　　検証　1204
　　データ　1070
　　モデル　281
often　96, 122, 206, 207, 329, 626
old　468, 544, ☒ new
omission　854
omit (be —ted from)　510
on the one hand　34, 230
on the other hand　34, 230
once　657, 729, 773
one-way　891, 892
ongoing　305, 1110
online　496, 498, 773
only　347, 348, 507, 696, 836, 882, 976, 1206
open　1190, ☒ uncovered, unresolved

operationalize (be —d as)　96
oppose　357, ☒ fight, object, resist
opposite　611, ☒ different, reverse
optimal　1201
option　650, ☒ alternative, choice
order　563, 570, 729, 733, 737–739, 741, 743, 744,
　　　☒ sequence, sort out, ☒ disorder
ordinate　1269
organization　2, 5, ☒ association, company
orientation　168
origin　204, 479, 1249, ☒ birth, root, source
original　622, 635
originally　614
other　34, 230, 891, 903, 983, 1073, 1080, ☒ same
others　161, 226, 273
our　437, 517, 1060, 1066, 1087, 1136, 1177, 1178,
　　　1182
out　171, 384, 496, 509, 579, 609, 798, 825, 1034,
　　　1132
outcome　136, 559, 679
outlier　843
outline　822, 921
over　166, 1239
overall　185, 245, 270, 296, 517, 523, 524, 637, 822,
　　　833, 841, 849, 934, 1100, 1226
own　660
oxygen　795

◆ P

page　773
pair　700
paired　865
pairwise　911
panel　554, 1266–1268, ☒ board
paper　154, 402, 448, 815
paper-and-pencil　712
paradigm　114, 115, 117, 118, 442
parent　493, 494, ☒ child
parental　516, 517
parenthesis　1230, 1240
part　24, 25, 1125, ☒ component, piece, portion,
　　　section
partial　947
partially　8, 927, 1066, 1099, ☒ incompletely, partly
participant　41, 48, 115, 117, 126, 204, 222, 363,
　　　439, 460, 465–467, 473, 477, 479, 482, 485–487,

491, 492, 499–503, 505–509, 511, 513–516, 526, 530, 558, 561, 563, 573, 574, 577, 578, 581–585, 587, 588, 592, 593, 595, 609, 611, 612, 627–630, 633, 634, 636, 646, 647, 651, 658, 682, 685, 686, 689, 690, 692–694, 698, 705, 707, 709, 711, 712, 716, 722, 723, 725, 727, 728, 735, 736, 752, 753, 756, 763–765, 768, 773, 799, 807, 828–830, 833, 835, 848, 853, 860, 983, 1162, 1232, 1254, 1257, 1258, 1264, 1268
participate　498, 515
　— in　496, 497, 690
　〔主語〕
　　参加者　583
　　大学生　461–463
participation　461, 500, 503, 504, 691
particularly　369, 1148, 1149, 1185, 類 especially
partly　1125
path　1002, 類 course
pathway　429
patient　130
pattern　141, 151, 183, 231, 934, 1001, 1011
pay　497, 660
　〔主語〕
　　参加者　500, 503
　　注意　310
Pearson product-moment correlation　806
peer-reviewed　815
people　329
percent　470
percentage　472, 800, 832, 1230, 1259, 類 percent
percentile　526
perform　116, 125, 437, 739, 853, 906, 932, 類 complete, do, execute
　〔主語〕
　　機能的磁気共鳴画像法　553
　　参加者　115, 725
　　動物　789
　　我々（著者）　858, 886, 887
performance　715, 892, 1137, 1254
period　525, 656, 783, 970, 類 interval, term, time, phase
permit　546, 類 allow
personal　556
perspective　258, 1118, 1127
phase　706, 731, 1253, 類 period, stage, step
phenomenon　107, 204, 399

photograph　1256, 類 picture
photomicrograph　1256
picture　1207, 1248, 類 depict, depiction, image, show
piece　161
pilot　749–751
place　47, 72, 271, 492, 589, 類 area, classify, lay, position, put, space
　〔主語〕
　　理論　271
placebo　975
　placebo-controlled　975
plan　838
platform　550, 類 program, stage
plausible　1136
play (— a role)　162, 315, 類 perform
playback　603
plot　936, 1015
point (n)　255, 272, 590, 1015, 1049, 1051, 類 aim, dot, item, moment, place, subject
point (v)　370, 656, 類 direct, indicate
　— out　171
　— to　210
　〔主語〕
　　結果　68
polypropylene　542
pool　491
poor　924
population　523, 524, 1183
portion (n)　26, 770
portion (v)　771
posit
　〔主語〕
　　モデル　293
　　理論　267
position　558, 類 attitude, perspective, place, post, view
positive　882, 940, 1012, 1241, 対 negative
positively　941
possibility　1034, 1097, 1219
possible　253, 301, 356, 697, 738, 1122, 1123, 1135
　it be — that　1124, 1139, 1146
post hoc　813, 907–910, 912
post (v)　491, 492
post-　646, 712, 713, 類 after, later
postulate　297, 427, 類 hypothesize, posit, suppose
　〔主語〕
　　モデル　291

potential 428, 506, 971, 1117, 関 possible
power 245
practical 1150, 1151
practice 70, 321, 725–727, 関 application, exercise, rehearsal
pre- 559, 660
preceding 238
preclinical 162, 163
predict 197, 230, 237, 876, 953, 961, 970, 1058, 関 foretell, portend
　[主語]
　　仮説 434
　　理論 296
prediction 230, 248, 295, 761, 1059–1061, 1063
predictive 960
predictor 56, 809, 958, 1083
predominantly 468
Prefecture (県の名称) 540, 550, 572
preliminary 27, 787, 1056, 1113
preparation 12, 対 ignorance
prescreen 508
present (adj) 36, 37, 211, 275, 377, 378, 385, 388, 391, 392, 394, 395, 399, 402, 414, 415, 447, 449, 450, 457, 620, 1024, 1025, 1028, 1035–1037, 1039, 1070, 1074, 1084, 1086, 1138, 1144, 1151, 1154, 1155, 1161, 1165, 1175, 1176, 1179, 1186, 1195, 1214, 1222, 1223, 1226, 関 current, existing, nearby, 対 future
present (v) 25, 539, 546, 548, 569, 729, 733, 781, 996, 1121, 1157, 1240, 関 bestow, display, introduce
　be —ed with 117, 561
　[主語]
　　教示 590
　　結果 998
　　研究 26
　　項目 567
　　材料 558
　　刺激 568
　　実験者 570
　　信頼性係数 669
　　相関 993
　　著者 82
　　統計 984
　　表 487, 987, 997, 999, 1006
　　フィードバック刺激 601

分解 1005
平均と標準誤差 990
平均と標準偏差 989
リスト 651
我々（著者） 280
presentation 557, 729, 742, 関 demonstration, introduction
presenting complaint/symptom/problem 831
press 601, 711, 1189
presumably 1145
pretraining 559
prevalence 324
prevent 1232
previous 21, 33, 57, 66, 183, 320, 363, 395, 450, 454, 662, 663, 666, 671, 702, 915, 1084, 1089, 1112, 1144
previously 446, 672, 704, 752, 784, 839
primarily 111
primary 357, 380, 413, 521, 1030, 1129
principal 381, 936, 937
prior 236, 314
probability 520, 関 chance, likelihood
probably 1200, 関 likely
problem 361, 575, 831
procedure 704, 706–708, 719, 777, 778, 868, 関 method, process
process 715, 1121, 関 course, procedure
produce 610, 1137, 関 create, make
　[主語]
　　因子分析 915
　　省略 854
product-moment 806
program (n) 556
program (v) 555
project 11, 406
Promax 914
promise 1117
　[主語]
　　研究 1151
promising 1151
prompt 1186, 関 cause, inspire, instigate
　[主語]
　　知見 431
prone 287
proper 601
property 411, 661, 関 attribute, dimension

proportion 266, 331, 959, 圜 dimension, ratio
proposal 1112, 圜 offer, suggestion
propose 314, 圜 offer, suggest
　［主語］
　　著者 289
　　理論 264
　　我々（著者） 393, 1219
proposition 229, 445, 1112
protocol 770, 776
prototypical 116
provide 133, 190, 615, 722, 774, 799, 924, 925, 932, 1109, 1120, 1161, 1176
　be —d by 10
　［主語］
　　結果 262, 1059, 1111
　　研究 180, 189, 191, 193, 194, 232, 1177, 1217, 1221, 1223
　　参加者 485
　　支持 299
　　図 1018
　　知見 1056, 1078
　　著者 192
　　表 652
　　評論 248, 423
　　文献 187
　　方法論 1200
pseudonym 529
psychological 141, 1127
psychologist 76, 94
psychology 42, 461–463, 491
psychometric 661, 1196
psychotherapy 533
public 494
publish 338, 345, 348, 1074, 圜 annouce, issue, print
　［主語］
　　著者 1074
purchase 571, 572
purpose 386, 404, 414, 415, 529, 603, 766, 1023, 圜 aim, intention

◆ Q

qualitative 75, 圜 quantitative
quantitative 820, 圜 qualitative
question 94, 317, 318, 365, 395, 407, 408, 417, 457, 493, 528, 611, 649–651, 714, 1184–1186, 1189, 1190, 1197, 1238, 圜 answer

questionnaire 42–44, 484, 609, 612, 615, 634, 646, 647, 660, 749

◆ R

racial 479
radial 798
radiate 550
raise 315, 457, 圜 decline
random 520, 525, 729, 733, 756, 758, 771
randomize 737, 739, 975
　［主語］
　　順序 738, 744
randomly 570, 689–691, 694, 695
range (n) 149, 323, 527, 537, 635, 圜 area, limit, scope
range (v) 439, 475, 516, 546, 627, 631, 673, 943, 1238, 1239, 1245, 圜 extend, run, vary
　［主語］
　　効果量 55
　　コーエンの d 979
　　参加者 469, 473
　　被験体 544
　　負荷量 919
　　割合 800
rat 48, 411, 684, 699, 742, 761, 790, 795, 796, 798, 1254, 1257
rate (n) 516, 517, 617, 782, 1230, 1260
rate (v)
　［主語］
　　参加者 627, 647
　　評定者 760
rater 756, 759–762
rather 335
rating 763
ratio 785, 820, 1007
rationale 122, 443, 444
reach 595, 1181, 圜 contact, gain, make, touch
　［主語］
　　被験体 720
read 648
reader 1170
reanalyze 1037
reason 288, 371, 422, 1129, 1136, 1138, 圜 cause, intention, rationality
reasonable 1143, 1144
receive 591, 791, 794, 796, 1156, 圜 accept,

encounter, get, meet, suffer
　［主語］
　　参加者　499, 501, 502, 581
　　被験体　545
　　ラット　48, 742, 790
recent　137, 212–214, 231, 232, 257, 299, 327, 447, 1074, 1079
recently　113, 134, 215, 216, 278, 311, 圞 currently, lately
recommend　1192
record　599, 603, 817, 圞 document, note, tape
　［主語］
　　参加者　486
　　時間と回数　783
recording　557, 600, 圞 record, tape, video
recruit　489–491, 圞 engage, enrol, obtain
　［主語］
　　彼ら　488
　　参加者　460, 492, 513
reduce　299, 432, 圞 gain
　［主語］
　　理論　266
refer　98, 108, 576, 圞 apply, cite, direct, relate
　— to　95, 99, 106
reference　85, 86, 101, 529, 圞 citation, recommendation, relevance
reflect　174, 238, 1134
　［主語］
　　結果　1126
　　サイズ　524
refusal　506, 516
refuse　515
regard　20, 229, 305, 479, 715, 796, 1162, 1196, 1252, 圞 consider, mind, respect
region　480, 圞 area, part, place
regress　933, 1002
regression　808, 809, 951–953, 956, 958, 959, 965, 966
regulation　545
reinforcement　784
relate　250
　be —d to　389, 941
relation　967
relationship　50, 372, 410, 428, 882, 927, 929, 940, 942, 946, 947, 951, 965
relatively　346, 355, 471, 圞 comparatively

relevant　419
　be — to　1225
　［主語］
　　要因　1149
reliability　17, 662–664, 667, 669, 673, 757, 758
reliable　871
reliance　1166
rely (— on)　122, 1148
remain　48, 322, 1185
　it — to be　375
　it — unclear　1139
　［主語］
　　パターン　151
remainder　742, 圞 remains, rest
repeat　744, 812, 883
　［主語］
　　手続き　719
replace　512
replicate　1180, 1183, 1203
　［主語］
　　研究　1084
　　実験　1085
replication　1182
report　24, 206, 313, 332, 474, 476, 617, 626, 804, 815, 818, 870, 918, 1008, 1102, 1106, 圞 describe, tell
　it be —ed that　207
　［主語］
　　応用　156
　　研究　27, 181, 226
　　サンプル　836
　　実験　175
　　対数　1007
　　著者　146, 149, 310
　　内的整合性　666
　　パターン　183
　　表　1000, 1004
　　割合　331
represent　294, 629, 635, 1253, 1269, 圞 denote, describe, stand for, symbolize
　［主語］
　　研究　399, 1220
　　等式　283
representation　1253
representative　1254
　be — of　523, 525

reprint　1275
request (n)　653
request (v)　749
require　145, 517
　be —d to　125, 781
　［主語］
　　課題　574
　　限界　1168
　　日記　605
　　人　772
　　問題　373
requirement　504
research　8, 9, 24, 29, 33, 71, 75, 79, 92, 119, 136, 138, 140, 161, 163, 164, 180, 181, 185, 188, 189, 193, 194, 212, 214, 217, 219, 229, 235–237, 247, 250, 256, 261, 278, 296, 298, 307, 316, 317, 319, 321, 337, 339, 344, 345, 350, 352, 360–362, 367, 368, 374, 376, 381, 395, 401, 435, 447, 450, 461, 493, 497, 663, 666, 702, 703, 774, 915, 1035, 1036, 1071, 1081, 1084, 1088, 1110, 1144, 1151, 1158, 1160, 1167, 1179, 1180, 1184, 1186–1194, 1196, 1197, 1205, 類 analysis, examination, investigation
researcher　78, 84, 114, 169, 220, 330, 363, 582, 660, 1191
reservation　1171
resolution　554, 類 definition, 対 dullness
resolve　762, 類 answer, decide, determine, separate
resonance　553
respect　371, 761, 類 regard, relation
respective　523
respectively　885, 917, 978, 989, 1259
respond　837
　［主語］
　　学生　497
　　参加者　611, 628, 636
　　被験体　784
respondent　468, 626
response　126, 279, 483, 517, 528, 557, 601, 629, 641, 643, 650, 840, 842, 1258, 1264, 1267
restriction　699, 類 limitation
result (n)　63, 65, 67, 68, 151, 176, 224, 231, 244, 245, 262, 297, 455, 456, 633, 859, 945, 987, 995, 998, 999, 1003, 1006, 1011, 1012, 1016, 1059, 1060, 1066, 1071, 1074, 1079, 1083, 1086, 1089, 1096, 1097, 1102–1104, 1106, 1108, 1111–1113, 1125, 1126, 1150, 1153, 1157, 1161, 1165, 1170, 1176, 1179, 1183, 1195, 1203, 1213, 1214, 類 consequence, outcome
result (v) (— in)　32, 186, 193, 751, 855, 類 end in
retest　663, 664, 673
return　516, 783
　［主語］
　　電子メール　498
reveal
　［主語］
　　カイ二乗分析　861
　　結果　245, 1011
　　研究　159
　　事後検定　908
　　調べた結果　936
　　図　1019
　　相関分析　940
　　多変量分散分析　906
　　t 検定　864
　　分散分析　892, 895, 900
　　分析の結果　878
　　メタ分析　152
reversal　559
reverse (adj)　642, 742, 類 contrary, opposite
reverse (v)　類 invert
　［主語］
　　尺度　1242
　　随伴性　788
reverse-scored　643
reverse-scoring　644
review (n)　171, 202, 248, 420, 422, 423, 448, 775, 1079, 1208, 1210, 類 commentary, inspection, survey
review (v)　173, 184, 322, 775, 類 assess, inspect, reconsider
　［主語］
　　相関分析　946
　　著者　311
　　我々（著者）　419
revise　1265
right　1268, 対 left
risk　1149
RMSEA　923, 1233
robust　661, 1191
role　162, 315
room　542, 595, 類 chamber, space

root   923, 🔄 base, origin, stem
root-mean-square   1233
rotate   914, 916, 1001
rotation   914, 936
rout   715
rule (n)   1255
rule (v) (— out)   1034, 1132, 🔄 decide, judge
run   554, 555, 🔄 execute, operate

◆ S

s (単位)   546, 601, 747, 793
sagittal   1256
salary   475
salient   239
same   220, 224, 451, 646, 1146, 🔄 different, other
　be the — as   707
sample (n)   40, 331, 363, 472, 480, 481, 487, 491, 518–520, 523, 525, 652, 668, 756, 771, 800, 836, 864, 1072, 1162, 1239, 🔄 example, part
sample (v)   435, 520, 521, 🔄 test, try
say   333
scale   129, 135, 390, 439, 526, 608, 618, 626–631, 633, 636, 645, 665, 667, 822, 1007, 1008, 1242, 1248, 1251
scanner   553
scenario   560
schedule (n)   784, 786
schedule (v)   735
Scheffé comparison   912
schematic   1246, 1252, 1253
scheme   753, 🔄 diagram, strategy
scholar   1080, 🔄 savant, student
school   465, 466, 477, 494, 516, 523, 524
scope   1192, 🔄 range, reach
score (n)   149, 527, 633, 637, 644, 670, 699, 718, 821–824, 841, 842, 888, 893, 894, 917, 923, 939, 941, 970, 997, 1234, 🔄 point
score (v)   17, 526, 603, 644, 🔄 achieve, count
［主語］
　評定者   756
scree plot   936
screen (n)   547, 554, 566, 568, 569, 590, 🔄 monitor
screen (v)   509
search   🔄 explore, research, seek
［主語］
　著者   815

電子データベース   816
seat   595, 🔄 sit
［主語］
　参加者   592
second (ordinal)   280, 373, 404, 422, 443, 604, 681, 754, 756, 758, 817, 932, 954, 955, 961, 994, 1029, 1129, 1138, 1154, 1171, 1213, 🔄 first
second (単位)   840 (→ s (単位))
section   615, 715, 770, 1256
see   101, 174, 202, 375, 857, 996, 🔄 check, consult, determine, find information
seek   533
［主語］
　研究   392
seem
　it — to   1144
［主語］
　研究   257
　文献   243
　理論   277
select   679
［主語］
　課題   441
　反応   601
self-administered   438
self-report   613
semester   771
seminal   154
send   497, 🔄 direct
［主語］
　手紙   494
　電子メール   496
senior   464, 1237, 🔄 junior
seniority   468
separate (adj)   798
separate (v)   744, 790, 🔄 break, divide, isolate
separately   1260
sequence   687, 🔄 succession
sequentially   815
series   174, 175, 415, 578, 867, 953, 1028, 1041
serve (— as)   118, 467, 602, 677, 738, 763, 930, 957, 🔄 be used, function
service   277, 468
session   512, 678, 720, 732–736, 739, 742, 783, 790–792
set (n)   575, 611, 740, 🔄 collection, group

set (v)　276, 914
　— out to　384
　〔主語〕
　　有意水準　805
setting　1203
several　80, 158, 373, 423, 448, 544, 655, 1167, 1168, 1172, 1189, 1190
sex　611, 1134
shape　155, 対 form
share　1214, 対 have the same
shock　782, 対 impact
short　622, 対 concise, 対 long
show　141, 299, 601, 797, 932, 967, 1012, 1013, 1274, 対 demonstrate, present
　〔主語〕
　　概略図　1246
　　患者　329
　　研究　158, 163, 168, 217, 1039
　　交互作用　920
　　子供　577
　　参加者　728, 853
　　事後分析　907
　　尺度　135, 665
　　図　1016, 1017
　　知見　1040, 1042
　　著者　173, 174
　　テューキーの事後比較検定　909, 910
　　表　985, 1008
　　負荷量　914
　　文献　167, 226, 227
　　分散分析　891, 902
　　分類　717
significance　804, 986, 対 implication, importance
significant　56, 142, 201, 302, 312, 359, 813, 860, 862, 865, 871–875, 878, 880, 881, 892, 896, 898–901, 903, 905, 906, 911, 912, 940, 944, 946, 959, 964, 981, 982, 1012, 1044, 対 important, 対 nonsignificant
　〔主語〕
　　項　904
　　効果　877
　　差　894
　　統計量　982
　　偏相関　947
significantly　218, 220, 313, 863, 864, 866, 869, 870, 893, 907, 909, 938, 939, 941, 945, 960, 962, 963, 1013, 1020
similar　183, 218
　be —　to　621
similarities　1214
simple　913, 対 complex
simulation　999
site　597
sitting　736
situate　547, 対 locate
size　55, 245, 524, 820, 822, 823, 978, 980, 1008
slope　948, 973
small　245, 359, 899, 963, 980, 1162, 対 little, 対 large
social　1127
software　557, 921
solid　1269
solve　575, 1120, 対 answer, resolve
somewhat　1092
sophisticated　1204
sophomore　464, 1237
space　550
span (n)　748
span (v)　93
spatial　1249
speaker　547
special　14, 271
specific　271
specifically　208, 344, 対 generally
speculate　1142, 対 guess, hypothesize
speculative　1197
speech　752
spend　855, 対 pass
spite　1178
square　923, 1271
stability　390
stage　276, 280, 780, 998
stainless　539
stand-alone　554
standard　558, 632, 651, 868, 985, 986, 988–990, 対 criterion, measure
standardize　803, 919, 923, 1000, 1002, 1196, 1265
　〔主語〕
　　下位尺度　637
　　測度　632
standing　464, 1237
start (n)　585
start (v)　728, 対 begin

索　引　　*367*

State（州の名称）　2, 5–7, 26, 540, 550, 572,
　　🔲 country
state (n)　684, 🔲 condition
state (v)　255, 287, 🔲 say, tell
　［主語］
　仮説　287
statement　286
static　993
station　736
statistic　801, 820, 861–863, 865, 866, 876, 879, 880,
　　882, 891–893, 895–898, 900, 901, 903, 905, 909,
　　912, 920, 922, 923, 944, 981, 982, 984
statistical　13, 804, 868
statistically　872, 959, 1102
Statistics（統計量）　861–863, 865, 866, 876, 879,
　　880, 882, 891–893, 895–898, 900, 901, 903, 905,
　　909, 912, 920, 922, 944
status　528, 🔲 grade, position
steel　539
stem (— from)　298
step　932, 954–957, 959, 962, 1161, 1220, 1227
stimulus　126, 557, 564–566, 568, 601, 707, 708,
　　742, 781, 791, 1247, 1248, 1250, 1251
stopper　539
story　717, 🔲 narrative
strategy　304
stratify　700, 771
Street Address（所在地住所）　30, 31
strength　1172, 1175, 🔲 weakness
strengthen　179
　［主語］
　結果　1112
stringent　1200
strong　97, 170, 180, 259, 942, 1083
strongly　197, 200, 628, 943, 944, 🔲 weakly
structural　932, 933, 1004
structure　54
student　78, 461–463, 470, 477, 480, 497, 515, 524,
　　659, 690, 705, 771
study (n)　35–40, 57, 80, 81, 83, 84, 90, 123, 125,
　　131, 137, 142, 148, 150, 152, 156–160, 162, 166,
　　168, 174, 176, 178, 183, 188, 191, 213, 216, 218,
　　225, 226, 231, 232, 239, 248, 249, 257, 324, 327,
　　336, 340, 342, 345–349, 373, 377, 378, 383,
　　385–388, 390–392, 394, 395, 398, 399, 401, 404,
　　405, 407–410, 413, 414, 416, 428, 437, 446, 447,
　　449, 450, 461, 487, 493, 497, 504–506, 510, 511,
　　522, 538, 543, 580, 583, 597, 604, 620, 624, 662,
　　664, 671, 673, 703, 709, 722, 749–751, 774, 798,
　　804, 820, 976, 977, 982, 1007, 1008, 1023–1030,
　　1037, 1039, 1040, 1043, 1044, 1046, 1073, 1074,
　　1076, 1077, 1081, 1089, 1091, 1096, 1103, 1105,
　　1117, 1138, 1140, 1144, 1150, 1152–1155, 1159,
　　1166, 1167, 1169, 1172–1175, 1177, 1182, 1189,
　　1195, 1198, 1201, 1208, 1217, 1220, 1221, 1223,
　　1224, 1226, 1227, 🔲 examination, research
study (v)　139, 364, 366, 371, 412
　［主語］
　我々（著者）　389, 402
subcategory　845
subject (n)　540, 544, 548, 551, 588, 589, 684, 699,
　　720, 724, 748, 784, 787, 812, 886–888, 983,
　　🔲 participant, theme
　［主語］
　我々（著者）　936
subject (v)　936
subscale　135, 634, 636, 637
subset　758
subsidiary　381, 1026
substantial　165, 170, 189, 🔲 large, significant
substantive　1181
subtest　620
successfully　1218
succession　561, 🔲 sequence
successive　734
such　588, 637, 649, 1169, 1205
sufficiently　364, 507
suggest　90, 146, 187, 243, 245, 320, 374, 449, 453,
　　944, 966, 1052, 1075, 1081, 1082, 1098, 1100
　［主語］
　仮説　285
　結果　67, 244, 1089, 1096, 1097, 1102, 1195
　研究　214, 229, 235–237, 239, 327
　証拠　66, 87, 155, 238, 290, 322, 1099
　推計　326
　説明　1128
　知見　240, 1080
　著者　161, 242
　データ　234, 1094, 1142
　表　1010
　文献　233
　分析　1095, 1101

suggestion   19, 20, 🔀 indicaton, proposition
sum   636, 637, 1213, 1223, 🔀 summarize
summarize   765, 984, 1069, 🔀 sum
　［主語］
　　結果   1003
　　特徴   983
summary   996, 1022, 1115, 1208
support (n)   11, 123, 180, 246, 248–250, 259, 298,
　　299, 1054–1056, 1077, 1078, 1111, 1177, 1217,
　　1223, 🔀 foundation
support (v)   164, 349, 1072, 1119
　be —ed by   8
　［主語］
　　結果   65, 455, 1066, 1086
　　研究   161, 229, 247
　　知見   64, 1057
surprised   1065
surprising   1092
surprisingly   1062
survey   438, 496–499, 506, 515, 659, 771, 773,
　　🔀 examination, study
symptom   332, 411, 831
system   752, 🔀 scheme
systematic   350, 376
systematically   84, 🔀 carefully

◆ T

t-test   802, 814, 864, 865, 867
table   487, 592, 595, 651, 652, 669, 717, 914,
　　983–1013, 1228–1231
take   161, 238, 239, 326, 431, 463, 737, 1098, 1108,
　　1114, 🔀 accompany, assume, capture, carry, 🔀 give
　— a step toward   1227
　— place   594, 596
　［主語］
　　検査   745
　　実験   746
tale   717
tap   604, 🔀 take, use
target   126
task   45, 115, 126, 127, 228, 280, 414, 436, 441,
　　442, 446, 573, 574, 578–580, 585, 590, 737, 798,
　　1248
technical   12, 14
tell   586, 🔀 describe, distinguish, inform

［主語］
　参加者   582, 583, 585, 587
　被験者   589
temperature   536, 542
tend (— to)   205, 219, 236, 362, 1119, 🔀 be inclined
tendency   105, 🔀 inclination
term   98–100, 113, 399, 418, 815, 881, 904, 910,
　　1132
test   128, 222, 341, 390, 394, 446, 525, 562, 570,
　　579, 606, 621, 649, 654, 655, 663, 664, 673, 712,
　　713, 715, 720, 731–733, 743–745, 783, 803, 804,
　　814, 856, 860, 868, 869, 887, 909, 910, 921, 952,
　　956, 966, 986, 1016, 1024, 1029, 1195, 1200,
　　🔀 assessment, examination, trial
［主語］
　子供   466
　参加者   595, 736
　被験体   551, 748
　ラット   684
　我々（著者）   38, 397, 432, 433
testing   720, 731, 783, 1204
thank (n, pl)   14
thank (v)   11, 17–19, 21, 22
theme   307, 332, 🔀 idea, topic
then   318, 403, 415, 577, 637, 721, 817, 824
theoretical   258, 358, 1127, 1128, 🔀 applied,
　　empirical
theorist   276
theory   106, 123, 239, 241, 264–271, 273, 275, 277,
　　295, 296, 449, 1061, 1081, 1082, 1178, 1218
therapeutic   1199
therapy   342
therefore   194, 316, 321, 414, 415, 512, 878,
　　🔀 accordingly, consequently, thus
thesis   24, 250, 377
third   373, 404, 442, 833, 932, 954, 961, 994, 1154,
　　1171, 1173, 1213
threaten   1101
threesome   695
thus   233, 260, 337, 347, 498, 1111, 1145
tie (v)   296, 🔀 attach, draw, link, restrict
time   47, 76, 146, 490, 536, 656, 657, 660, 748,
　　783, 840, 855, 970, 1146, 🔀 duration, instance,
　　interval, occasion
timely   319
title   1275, 🔀 name

to date   77, 159, 340, 343, 356, 1111, 1160
together   161, 238, 239, 431, 1098, 1108, 1114
tolerance   950
too   122, 1137
tool   134
top   549, 1267, 対 bottom
topic   1206, 類 issue, subject
total   496, 515, 676, 680, 724, 729, 842, 917, 928
touch   547
toward   1220
tradition   119
train   1257, 1258, 1267, 類 direct, exercise, instruct
　be —ed to   116
trained (adj)   493
training (n)   47, 559, 585, 723, 729, 779, 783, 787, 790, 791, 856, 998, 類 exercise, instruction, preparation
trajectory   973, 999
transcribe
　〔主語〕
　　インタビュー   769
　　発言   752
transcription   16
transition   378
transplantation   798
treat   532
　be —ed as   507
treatment   304, 402, 545, 744, 802, 1148, 1262
trend   447, 882, 1053
triad   695
trial   565, 593, 646, 647, 685, 720, 723–730, 732, 733, 738, 740, 787–789, 816, 848, 849, 975, 1010, 1199, 類 experiment, test
trigger   289
trio   695, 類 threesome, triad
true   722
try   119, 類 attempt, test
turn (— on)   47, 783, 類 change, convert
two-tailed   1244
two-way   883
typical   126
typically   115, 1206

◆ U

unanswered   1185, 1190
unaware   760
unclear   322, 対 clear
　it be — why   1139
undeliverable   498
undergird   445
undergraduate   463
underlie   114, 444, 1032
underline   1107, 類 emphasize, underscore
underscore   1117, 類 emphasize, underline
　〔主語〕
　　論点   370
understand   409, 410, 1220, 類 believe, comprehend
understandable   1127
understanding   369, 412, 766, 1205, 1220, 1227
understudied (adj)   1206
unexpected   1064
unfortunately   339
unique   1152, 1226
unit   521, 1245
university   1, 3–5, 461–463, 480, 491, 660, 690, 771, 775, 776
unrelate (be —d to)   143
unresolved   395
upper   1266
use (n)   172, 304, 342, 555, 776
use (v)   45, 122, 123, 147, 220, 224, 446, 557, 576, 580, 607, 609, 610, 623, 631, 636, 660, 671, 706, 709, 722, 753, 798, 806, 814, 815, 819, 825, 827, 860, 911, 921, 930, 940, 1198, 1203, 1234, 1250, 1255, 1266, 類 apply, consume, employ, manipulate
　be —d as   129
〔主語〕
　階層的重回帰分析   952
　階層的なロジスティック回帰分析   965
　課題   127
　クリップ   559
　研究   522, 624
　研究者   114
　検定   804
　実験   459
　質問紙   484
　尺度   608
　重回帰モデル   958
　修正版   625
　成長曲線モデル   972
　総数   676

370　　　　　　　　　索　　引

　　短縮版　622
　　治療の方略　304
　　t 検定　803
　　データ　156
　　ビデオカメラ　603
　　標準化得点　923
　　分散分析　812
　　変数　680
　　ノンパラメトリック法　868
　　マッチドペア法　700
　　目録　616
　　我々（著者）　98, 966
useful　19, 133
　　it be ― to　1202
usefully　1187
utility　1157

◆ V

valid　515
validate　65, 関 confirm, corroborate
validation　664
validity　38, 135, 662–664, 671, 672
valuable　15, 316
　　it be ― to　1203
value　989, 1241
variable　138, 141, 669, 679, 680, 738, 806, 809, 814, 878, 885, 923, 950, 953, 956, 1038
variance　810–812, 814, 883–885, 890, 896, 902, 905, 906, 917, 936, 948, 949, 959
variant　459
variation　778, 関 deviation, diversity
vary　675, 715
　　― across　225
　　[主語]
　　拒否率　516
　　得点　893
　　我々（著者）　45
verify　817
version　22, 27, 275, 563, 616, 622–625, 743, 825, 827, 921, 関 account, variant
versus　802, 896
very　84, 439, 1113, 1156, 1197
via　548
video　603
view (n)　192, 240, 334, 335, 425, 736, 1051, 関 opinion, perspective
view (v)　568, 関 consider
volume　572, 793
voluntary　500
volunteer　491

◆ W

wall　549
want　1029, 関 need, require
warrant　1181
　　[主語]
　　関係　372
　　治療的作用，臨床的適応　1199
　　ポイント　1049
watch　760, 関 follow, observe, see, view
water　539–541
wave　490
way　604, 778, 1153, 1154, 関 manner, method, path
weakly　200
weakness　359, 対 strength
web-based　771
week　534, 734, 748
weigh　534, 795, 関 have a weight of
weight　537
well　182, 256, 900, 905, 922, 992, 1144, 1162, 関 satisfactorily, skilfully
well-validated　613
when　414
where　376
whereas　226, 559, 588, 708
which　376
while　226
why　376, 1209, 1210
wide　550, 1199
widely　139, 616, 623
willing (be ― to)　503
wish (― to)　15, 関 hope, want
within-participant(s)　885, 887
within-subject(s)　811
witness　306, 関 observe
woman　461, 468, 471, 480, 491, 650
word　209
wording　653
work　13, 23, 26, 27, 82, 221, 314, 396, 476, 1084, 1086, 1088, 1091, 1107, 関 function, labour, operate

索　引　　*371*

　[主語]
　　研究　1196
working　1031
worth　309
worthy　1184
would　1188
write　591, 605, 774, compose, record
　[主語]
　　ソフトウェア　557

◆ Y

year　130, 166, 468, 472–474, 476, 544, 692, 771
yen　497, 499, 500, 502, 503
yield　896, produce, submit

◆ あ

アーム　550, 798
アイデア　82
相反する　28
明らか　1169, 1182
明らかである (clear)　251, 366
明らかである (evident)　184, 881
明らかではない (remain unclear)　1139
明らかにする (clarify)　367, 1222
明らかにする (determine)　415, 797, 889, 905, 1140
明らかにする (indicate)　663
明らかにする (reveal)　152, 159, 245, 936, 1011, 1019
挙げられる (include)　70
値　989, 1241
値する (deserve)　1173
与えられる (receive)　48, 545, 794
与える (deliver)　782
与える (feed)　540
与える (give)　588, 589, 592, 646, 712, 715, 718
与える (lend)　1077
与える (offer)　281, 1070, 1226
与える (provide)　1056, 1078, 1111（→もたらす）
新しい　460
当たり　840
悪化させる (impair)　168
集める (collect)　124, 480, 602
宛名　660
当てはまり　924, 925
当てはめる (fit)　948
後に行われる (follow)　685

アプローチ　120–122, 429, 444, 703, 966
表す (denote)　284
表す (indicate)　1269, 1271, 1273
表す (present)　487
表す (represent)　283, 1253
ある (available)　343, 413
ある (find)　865
ある (have)　879
ある (show)　135, 920
ある程度の　1172
α　616, 639, 640, 642, 663–666, 668–670, 931
α 係数　667, 670
安定性　390

◆ い

言い回し　653
委員会　777
言うまでもない (it goes without saying)　333
意外である (surprise)　1092
いくつかの　158, 226, 1172, 1174
維持する (maintain)　537, 542, 786, 1263
異性　611
依存　1166
依存する (depend)　240
依存的　53
至らせる (prompt)　431
至るところ　86
位置　480, 558
一因　1135
一部である (form part of)　24
一歩前進させる (take a step toward)　1227
一連　174, 175, 415, 578, 867, 953, 1028, 1041
一貫して　141, 177–180, 229, 929
一貫していない (inconsistent)　223
一致　932
一致させる (match)　768
一致する (consistent)　57, 192, 203, 230, 297, 456, 1059, 1075, 1080, 1081, 1083, 1178
一致する (correspond)　1076
一致する (fit)　922
一致する (join)　1071
一致する (in line with)　240, 1074, 1079, 1082
一対比較　911
一定　1035, 1248, 1251
一般化　151
一般的　183, 186, 407, 1186

索　引

一方　230
意図　722
意味　70, 73, 74, 241, 1110, 1150, 1174
意味する (denote)　100
意味する (implicate)　1121
意味する (imply)　1103, 1113
意味する (indicate)　842
意味する (refer)　98, 99（→さす，のことである，呼ぶ）
意味をもつ (have…implications)　241, 1110, 1150, 1151
入れる (enter)　956
因果関係　1140
因果的　1204
因子　914, 916, 917, 936, 937
因子間　1004
因子負荷量　1000
因子分析　54, 633, 914, 915, 921, 922, 932, 1003, 1265
インターネット　497
インタビュー　751, 768, 769
インフォームドコンセント　497, 774
引用情報　1275
引用する (cite)　249

◆う

ウェブ　771
浮かび上がらせる (raise)　457
受け取る (receive)　499, 501, 502, 591
受ける (be funded)　9
受ける (be provided)　10
受ける (receive)　581, 791
後ろ　547
内　491, 536, 539, 542, 572, 739, 772, 811, 812, 885-888, 950, 1230, 1240

◆え

影響　76, 180, 778, 966, 1126, 1146
影響する (affect)　410, 1202
影響する (influence)　173, 203, 282, 1099
影響力　154
影響を及ぼす (affect)　167, 837
影響を及ぼす (have…effect on)　89, 856
描き出す (lead to a picture of —)　1207
描く (construct)　1015
描く (draw)　1248

選ぶ (choose)　543, 635
選ぶ (draw)　520
選ぶ (select)　441, 679
得られる (come)　188
得る (find)　224
得る (obtain)　123, 759, 944
得る (reach)　1181
円　1271
円（お金）　497, 499, 500, 502, 503
演繹的　802
援助　10-17

◆お

応用　156, 316
応用研究　79
終える (complete)　512
大きい　514, 518, 522, 963, 980
多くの　84, 160, 166-170, 183, 187, 215, 307, 891, 969, 1150, 1153, 1173, 1175, 1199, 1213
置く　547
送る (send)　494, 496
行う (administer)　606, 726
行う (carry)　579, 798
行う (complete)　578, 727
行う (conduct)　84, 416, 417, 538, 710, 751, 754, 757, 767, 792, 808, 809, 825, 827, 838, 883, 890, 905, 914, 921, 951, 1024
行う (investigate)　814
行う (make)　126, 802
行う (perform)　115, 553, 725, 739, 789, 858, 886, 887
行う (run)　554
行う (subject)　936
行われる (occur)　748
行われる (take place)　594, 596
起こる (occur)　195, 198
雄　538, 795
オッズ比　820
驚く (be surprised)　1065
同じである (identical)　706
思われる (appear)　260, 1141, 1212
思われる (seem)　243, 257, 277, 1144
恩恵を被る (benefit)　1206
温度　536
オンライン調査　496, 498, 773

◆か

回　490, 656, 657, 720, 724, 725, 727–729, 733, 735, 736, 782, 788, 790, 793, 796, 849
概観する (review)　184, 311, 322（→評論する）
回帰　959, 966
回帰する (regress)　933, 1002
開始　728
開始する (begin)　726
解釈する (interpret)　252, 256, 349, 1170
下位尺度　634, 636
回収する (collect)　438
回数　783
概説　822, 921
改善　57, 1225
階層化　700
階層的
　——重回帰分析　951–953, 956
　——重回帰モデル　958
　——多変量重回帰モデル　953
　——ロジスティック回帰モデル　965
解像度　554
改訂する (adapt)　614, 624
改訂する (modify)　624
改訂する (revise)　1265
改訂版　624
回転　914, 916, 936, 1001
回答　483, 528（→反応）
回答する (administer)　497
回答する (complete)　41, 44, 131, 499, 612, 634, 647, 658, 660, 709（→記入する，答える）
回答する (fill)　609（→記入する，答える）
回答する (respond)　636（→記入する，答える）
回答者　468, 626
回答率　517
カイ二乗検定　814, 860, 862
カイ二乗統計　923
カイ二乗分析　861, 862
カイ二乗分布　861
概念化する (conceptualize)　108, 215, 393, 399, 845
概念的　278
開発　664
開発する (develop)　42, 78, 127, 278, 279, 282, 391, 614, 619, 623, 752
改変　778
概略図　1246, 1252

カウンターバランスする (counterbalance)　740, 741, 743, 744
書く (complete)　716
書く (write)　557
学習　507, 1018
確証　1070, 1072
確証的因子分析　54, 921, 922, 932, 1003, 1265
確証を与える (corroborate)　1072
確信度　629
学生　42, 461, 463, 470, 480, 497, 515, 524, 690, 705, 771
拡大する (extend)　1088
拡張する (extend)　364, 395, 396, 459, 1086, 1087, 1218
確定する (determine)　1134
獲得　559, 579, 788
学内　491
確認する (confirm)　62, 63, 221, 811, 859, 873, 913, 1060, 1061, 1108, 1161
確認する (validate)　65, 613
隔年　26
学年　771
確率　161, 520
確率が高い (likely)　147
確立する (establish)　69, 354, 414, 1196
過去　66, 306, 320, 446
数少ない　697
仮説　38, 64, 285, 287, 299, 432–434, 455, 722, 802, 902, 1024, 1029, 1030, 1054–1058, 1063, 1066, 1195, 1200, 1217, 1252
仮説を立てる (hypothesize)　424, 426, 429, 430
家族　476
課題　45, 115, 126, 127, 228, 280, 321, 414, 436, 441, 442, 446, 573, 574, 578–580, 585, 737, 739, 1248
傾き　948, 973
偏りがある (bias)　1165
価値　15, 1203
学期　771
活性化させる (activate)　314
カッパ　914
過程　1121
仮定　292, 294, 361, 445, 1029, 1032
仮定する (assume)　269, 427
仮定する (hypothesize)　286
仮定する (posit)　293

仮定する (postulate) 291, 297
カテゴリー 641, 753, 845
カテゴリー変数 814
過渡期 378
かなり…（尺度における）631
かなりの 331
可能 151, 253, 546, 1122, 1123, 1200
可能性 1034, 1097, 1219
可能性がある (possible) 1124, 1139
可能性がある (potential) 506
可能性が高い (likely) 196, 478, 1098
壁 549
かまわない (willing) 503
画面 554, 590
代わり 418, 589, 1128, 1131, 1132
考え 1080, 1177, 1217
考え方 240, 1128
考える (believe) 288
考える (consider) 428, 1161（→考察する，考慮する）
考える (understand) 369
間隔をあける (intervene) 734
間隔をあける (separate) 744
環境 1203
関係 50, 79, 372, 410, 428, 927, 929, 942, 947, 951, 965
関係する (concern) 378, 442, 1138
関係する (relate) 250, 389
関係する (relevant) 1225
頑健 661, 1191
観察 178
観察する (observe) 218, 272, 411, 727, 899, 923, 1084
観察者 755, 757
感謝 14
感謝する (acknowledge) 12
感謝する (express) 16
感謝する (grateful) 13, 20
感謝する (thank) 11, 17–19, 21, 22
患者 130, 329
感情 830
関心 211, 380, 381
関心がある (interest) 379
関数 893, 948, 1229, 1230, 1249
完全 627, 722, 857, 991
観点 1127（→見方）

勧誘する (invite) 496–498, 771
関与 1121
関与する (play a role in) 315
完了する (complete) 498, 515, 724, 737, 773, 788
関連 140, 142, 419, 875, 972, 1114, 1222
関連する (associate) 32, 202, 231, 330, 358, 945, 1262
関連する (relevant) 1149

◆ き

キー 601, 711
期間 525, 602, 656, 748, 970
記述 546, 749, 784
基準 325, 511, 618, 720, 976
基準関連妥当性 664
機序 114, 192, 199, 301
帰する (attribute) 1137
帰される (due) 1133（→ためである，による）
帰せられる (be attributable to) 290
軌跡 973, 999
基礎 444, 1032, 1088（→基盤）
帰属 1275
規則的 729
基礎とする (build on) 1088
既存 237, 414, 1173
期待する (expect) 58, 435
拮抗する (compete) 1216
記入する (complete) 438（→回答する，答える）
基盤 905, 1144（→基礎）
基本的 294, 787
機密が保持される (confidential) 530
機密性 531
機密保持 529
決める (determine) 194
決める (shape) 155
疑問 94, 317, 365, 395, 1186
逆転 559, 644（→反対）
逆転項目 642, 643
逆転する (reverse) 788, 1242
客観的 341
Q 統計量 820, 981, 982
吸入する (inspire) 795
寄与 394, 1173
寄与する (add to) 1173
寄与する (contribute) 23, 40, 962, 1225
教育 474, 476

競合　398
強固にする (strengthen)　1112（→強める）
教示　46, 581, 588, 589, 591, 592
教示する (instruct)　584, 707, 711, 1033
強調　72, 271
強調する (emphasize)　268, 447
強調する (highlight)　422, 1209
強調する (place emphasis on)　72, 271
強調する (underline)　1107
強調する (underscore)　370, 1117
共通　136, 160, 292, 330, 332, 617, 831
共通因子分析　914
強度　850
共変量　930, 957, 1002
興味　90, 94（→関心）
興味深い　156, 1011, 1046, 1185
興味を引く (intrigue)　94
強力に　197（→強く）
拒否する (refuse)　515
拒否率　516
許容度　950
距離　568, 1249
記録　557, 600
記録する (record)　486, 599, 783, 817
議論　66, 1049
議論する (discuss)　1210（→論じる）
近似誤差平均平方根　923, 1233

◆く

偶然　1134
空白部分　1158
国　1–7, 26, 535, 550, 572
区別　1102
区別する (distinguish)　809, 829, 885
組み合わせる (combine)　645, 815
組み合わせる (cross)　46
比べて　1020, 1089, 1202（→よりも）
比べる (compare)　478, 879, 896, 909（→比較する）
繰り返しのある　812, 883
繰り返す (repeat)　719（→反復する）
クリック　601
クリップ　559
グループ　171–175, 192, 282, 514, 524, 541, 693, 736, 1033, 1072, 1077
黒い　1271, 1272
黒地　590

クロンバックの α　669（→α 係数）
詳しく　1010, 1019, 1206
群　228, 467, 522, 586, 697, 699, 798, 802, 828, 847, 862, 871, 879, 891, 909, 911, 912, 920, 1015, 1254, 1256, 1257, 1267
群間差　1134
訓練　47, 585, 723, 779, 783, 791, 856, 998
訓練する (train)　116, 493, 1257, 1258, 1267

◆け

系　204, 392
経過　76, 146, 284
経過観察　647
計画　445
計画する (design)　383, 398, 1025
計画する (plan)　838
経験　544
経験する (experience)　327, 626
経験する (receive)　742, 790
経験的　63, 71, 78, 165, 246, 259, 413, 1077, 1078, 1217
傾向　105, 1053
傾向がある (tend)　205, 219, 236, 362, 1119
傾向が強い (likely)　1062
警告　1170, 1171
掲載する (display)　1021（→掲示する）
掲載する (post)　492（→掲示する）
計算する (calculate)　602, 645, 807, 821, 822, 840, 1260
計算する (compute)　132, 820, 823, 841, 947, 1234
掲示する (post)　491（→掲載する）
形式　749
係数　667, 669, 673, 761, 806, 1002, 1231, 1265
形成する (form)　638, 644（→構成する）
計装　664
系統的　84, 350, 376
経由　548
ケージ　541, 542, 551
結果　32, 63, 65, 67, 68, 151, 176, 224, 244, 245, 249, 262, 297, 431, 455, 456, 559, 633, 679, 751, 762, 859, 865, 873, 878, 895, 906–908, 910, 922, 936, 945, 946, 969, 987, 995, 998, 999, 1003, 1006, 1011, 1012, 1055, 1059, 1060, 1071, 1074, 1079, 1083, 1086, 1089, 1097, 1102, 1106, 1108, 1111–1113, 1125, 1126, 1150, 1153, 1157, 1161, 1165, 1170, 1176, 1179, 1183, 1195, 1203, 1213,

1214
結果となる (result in) 32, 751, 855（→もたらす）
結果変数 136, 679
結婚する (marry) 476
欠損する (miss) 799
欠損値 511, 800, 1232
決定する (determine) 293, 386, 387, 528
決定する (resolve) 762
決定的 185, 261, 1181
月齢 535, 692
結論 1174, 1181, 1211, 1213, 1214, 1216–1219, 1224, 1225
結論する (conclude) 60, 172, 259, 263, 431, 1079, 1215, 1216
県 540, 572
原因 235
限界 213, 311, 1166–1169, 1172–1174, 1177–1179
限界がある (have limitations) 1169, 1172
研究 372, 493, 662, 709, 751, 774, 820, 976, 1074, 1096, 1167, 1177, 1179, 1196
研究する (examine) 76, 79, 363（→調べる，調査する，分析する）
研究する (explore) 370（→調べる，調査する，分析する）
研究する (investigate) 81, 451（→調べる，調査する，分析する）
研究する (study) 364（→調べる，調査する，分析する）
研究者 78, 84, 114, 169, 220, 330, 495, 582, 660, 817, 1080, 1191
言及 85, 86, 529, 1173
言及する (include references to) 85
言及する (note) 157, 1067（→述べる，報告する）
言及する (reference) 529（→参照する）
研究内容を説明する (debrief) 721, 722（→ディブリーフィング）
研究補助者 493
研究問題 1189, 1190
検査 128, 341, 390, 606, 620, 621, 655, 743, 745
検査する (examine) 43
検索エンジン 815
検索語 815
検索する (search) 815, 816
検証 222, 1200, 1204
　　検証する (test) 394, 397, 432, 433, 921, 1024, 1029

減少させる (decrease) 53, 163
減少させる (reduce) 299, 432
減少する (decrease) 160
減少する (lower) 517
現存 311, 361, 1178
顕著である (notable) 1053（→注目すべき）
限定する (limit) 345, 920, 1162, 1183
厳密 1200

◆こ

考案する (design) 612
効果 36, 37, 45, 137, 368, 379, 388, 402, 432, 683, 853, 877, 878, 880, 881, 883, 890, 891, 895, 900, 901, 905, 906, 920, 964, 986, 999, 1005, 1025, 1028, 1034, 1038, 1085, 1116, 1132, 1198, 1216
効果的 57, 244
効果量 55, 245, 820–824, 963, 978, 980, 1008
合計 680, 729
合計する (sum) 636, 637
貢献 1152
貢献する (contribute) 1153, 1154
広告 491, 492, 497
交互作用 881, 889, 895, 899, 900–905, 920, 956, 964, 970
考察する (consider) 1171, 1174（→考える，考慮する）
公式 819, 1234
後者 882
構成概念 931
構成される (consist) 565（→である，できている，成り立つ）
構成する (comprise) 1119（→形成する）
構成する (construct) 633（→形成する）
構成する (make up) 931（→形成する）
構造 54
構造方程式モデル 932, 933
構造モデル 1004
公的 474
行動 797, 939
行動研究 798
購入する (purchase) 571, 572
広範 261, 1199
広範囲 355
候補 356
候補者 496
後方支援 14

索　引

項目　562, 567, 570, 612, 616, 618, 619, 625, 628, 634, 635, 638, 640, 642, 645, 648, 670, 800, 844, 858, 861, 914, 919, 931, 936
交絡因子　971
考慮　1168
考慮する (consider)　1146, 1174, 1194
超える　476, 761, 843
心に留める (bear/with…in mind)　1170, 1171
個人　602, 1264, 1268
答え　1185
答える (answer)　493, 1189
答える (complete)　43, 749, 771（→記入する，回答する）
答える (report)　626
答える (respond)　611, 628（→記入する，回答する）
固定する (fix)　552
異なる　126, 237, 563, 674, 740, 743, 798, 878, 885, 987, 1191, 1254, 1267
異なる (differ)　218, 257, 699, 802, 910
異なる (vary)　225, 516, 715
子供　39, 204, 466, 468, 481, 495, 512, 577, 586, 593, 595, 692, 712, 727, 752, 847, 853
子供間　885（→参加者間，被験者間，被験体間）
子供内　885（→参加者内，被験者内，被験体内）
誤反応　849, 1230
個別に　466, 536, 540, 570
コミュニティ　491
コメント　13, 18, 20–22
固有値　936, 937
雇用する (employ)　437
根拠　122, 443, 444
根拠とする (undergird)　445
今後　1196
混合型（の分散分析）　811, 884, 885, 888
混合物　795
コンタクトをとる (contact)　503
混同する (confound)　1164
困難　329（→難しい，難しさ）
コンパイルする (compile)　557
コンピュータ　547, 554, 556, 568, 569, 736

◆さ

差　810, 814, 850, 860–862, 865, 871, 872, 874, 876, 879–882, 891, 892, 894, 896, 898, 899, 908, 911, 912, 980, 1009, 1134
差異　1133
歳　130, 468, 469, 472, 473, 544, 692（→年齢）
最近　113, 134, 137, 212-217, 231, 232, 257, 278, 299, 311, 327, 447, 1074, 1079
再掲　1275
再現　1182
再現する (replicate)　1084, 1085, 1180, 1183, 1203
最後　1208
最終　954
最終的　762, 770
採取する (tap)　604
最初　154, 280, 403, 577, 615, 731, 785, 795, 916, 1161
最初の…である (first)　1159, 1224
最小　735
最大　732, 735
最適　1201
再テスト信頼性　663, 664, 673
採点　644（→点数化）
再分析する (reanalyze)　1037
採用する (adopt)　620, 701
採用する (use)　122
材料　558
遮る　736
先払い　660
作成する (create)　563（→つくる）
捧げる (dedicate)　355
さす (refer)　108（→意味する，のことである，呼ぶ）
させる (cause)　335
させる (have)　222
させる (make)　287
査定する (assess)　758（→評価する）
査読　815
さらす (expose)　682, 787
さらなる　219, 367, 368, 372, 373, 1070, 1078, 1161, 1180, 1181
さらに　65, 217, 234, 299, 310, 374, 493, 503, 511, 604, 744, 956, 1154, 1192, 1193, 1197, 1204, 1205, 1213
参加　500, 503
参加する (participate)　461–463, 496–498, 583, 690
参加資格　493, 504, 505
参加者　41, 48, 115, 117, 126, 204, 222, 363, 439, 460, 465–467, 473, 477, 479, 482, 485–487, 491, 492, 499–503, 505–509, 511, 513–516, 526, 530,

558, 561, 563, 573, 574, 577, 578, 581–585, 587, 588, 592, 593, 595, 611, 612, 627–630, 633, 634, 636, 646, 647, 651, 658, 682, 685, 686, 689, 694, 705, 707, 709, 711, 712, 716, 722, 723, 725, 727, 728, 735, 736, 752, 753, 763–765, 768, 773, 799, 807, 828–830, 833, 835, 848, 853, 983, 1162, 1232, 1254, 1257, 1258, 1264
参加者間　886–888（→子供間，被験者間，被験体間）
参加者内　886, 888（→子供内，被験者内，被験体内）
参加者プール　491
算出する (calculate)　821
参照する (see)　174, 202, 857, 996（→言及する）
酸素　795
サンプル　40, 331, 363, 472, 480, 481, 487, 491, 518–520, 521, 523–525, 668, 756, 800, 836, 864, 1072, 1162, 1239

市　1–7, 26, 27, 535, 540, 550, 572
飼育する (house)　534, 536, 540–542
飼育地域　536
シェフェ法　912
支援　11
支援する (support)　8
四角　1271
視覚的　736
時間　76, 146, 536, 542, 660, 736, 745–747, 783, 790, 792, 840, 855
時間がかかる (take)　746（→要する）
刺激　126, 557, 564, 566, 568, 601, 707, 708, 742, 781, 791
刺激呈示　557
刺激配置　1247, 1248
刺激表示　565, 1250, 1251
志向　168
試行　565, 593, 646, 647, 685, 720, 723, 724–730, 732, 733, 738, 740, 787–789, 848, 849, 1010
事後比較　813, 909, 910, 912
示唆　19, 20
示唆する (suggest)　66, 67, 87, 90, 146, 155, 161, 187, 214, 229, 233–240, 242–245, 285, 290, 320, 322, 326, 327, 374, 449, 453, 944, 966, 1010, 1052, 1075, 1080–1082, 1089, 1094–1102, 1128, 1142, 1195

支持　123, 180, 190, 246, 248–250, 259, 298, 299, 1054–1056, 1072, 1077, 1078, 1111, 1177, 1217, 1223
支持する (affirm)　1118
支持する (lend support)　250, 1077
支持する (provide support)　180, 248, 299, 1056, 1078, 1177, 1217, 1223
支持する (support)　64, 65, 161, 164, 229, 247, 349, 455, 1057, 1066, 1086, 1119
支持を得る (find support)　1054
指針　776
指数　638, 923
事前にスクリーニングを行う (prescreen)　508
従う (follow)　545, 618, 702
したがって　448, 570, 752, 802, 822
実験　13, 46, 61, 62, 116, 175, 299, 415, 417, 418, 433, 442, 452–456, 458, 459, 501, 503, 534, 554, 555, 564, 565, 585, 594, 658, 688, 690, 706–708, 713, 722, 725, 726, 728, 731, 746, 760, 776, 794, 975, 1041, 1085, 1145, 1157, 1161, 1214, 1216, 1247, 1253, 1266
実験室　114, 658
実験者　570, 577, 593, 658, 758
実験的　343, 536, 537, 545
実験動物　776
実行　546, 555
実際に示す (demonstrate)　593
実施　13, 745, 1199
実施する (administer)　149, 556, 657, 715, 737, 743, 745（→行う）
実施する (conduct)　13, 17, 715（→行う）
実施順序　737
実質的　189, 1181
実証する (demonstrate)　1105, 1208
実証する (document)　204（→立証する）
実践　321
実践的　70
質的　75
湿度　536
質問　493, 611, 714, 1238
質問紙　42–44, 484, 612, 615, 634, 646, 647, 660, 749
質問セット　611
実用的　1150, 1151
指摘する (point)　171
しばしば　96, 206, 207, 329

索　引

379

自発的　500
支払う (pay)　497, 500, 503
指標　670, 676
示される (find)　312
示す (contain)　992
示す (demonstrate)　663 (→例証する)
示す (display)　668, 988, 991, 994, 995, 1001, 1002, 1014
示す (evidence)　635, 664
示す (give)　986, 1022
示す (have)　973, 1232
示す (illustrate)　1020 (→例証する)
示す (include)　992
示す (indicate)　52, 61, 153, 157, 162, 170, 179, 185, 211, 219, 439, 750, 867, 911, 922, 1012, 1140, 1197, 1241, 1270
示す (list)　652
示す (make)　849
示す (point)　68, 210
示す (present)　651, 669, 984, 987, 989, 990, 993, 997–999, 1005, 1006, 1240
示す (provide)　423, 652, 1018
示す (report)　1000, 1004, 1007
示す (reveal)　864, 892, 895, 940
示す (show)　141, 158, 163, 167, 168, 173, 174, 217, 227, 329, 665, 717, 853, 891, 902, 907, 909, 910, 914, 920, 967, 985, 1008, 1016, 1017, 1039, 1040, 1042, 1246
社会心理学的　1127
尺度　129, 135, 390, 439, 526, 608, 618, 619, 626–631, 633, 634, 636, 637, 645, 665, 667, 822, 1007, 1008, 1238, 1242 (→リッカート尺度)
斜交回転　914
州　540, 572
自由　783
自由時間　660
自由摂食　537
重回帰　808, 951–953, 956, 958
収集　14–16, 596, 597
収集する (collect)　656 (→集める, 回収する)
住所　660
修正　623–625, 911
修正版　623
収束　176
収束的妥当性　135, 664, 672
従属変数　678, 679, 738, 953

重大　359 (→重要)
縦断的　191, 522, 1204
集中する (center)　258
集中する (focus)　1187
十分　182, 195, 245, 256, 364, 613, 665, 668, 672
重要 (critical)　297
重要 (important)　138, 309, 320, 369, 394, 1045, 1147, 1148, 1160, 1164, 1206
重要 (primary)　357
重要である (salient)　239
重要性　68, 210, 268, 338, 1107, 1118
終了　501–503, 736
受講　463
主効果　880, 881, 891, 895, 901, 905, 913
主成分　937
主成分分析　936
主張　154, 286, 1036, 1077, 1078, 1111, 1119
主張する (argue)　169, 254, 262, 276, 308, 334, 357, 1106, 1129, 1130
主張する (contend)　425
出現　738
出現する (emerge)　164, 356, 875
出版する (publish)　338, 345, 348, 1074
主要　307, 358
遵守する (adhere)　777
遵守する (comply)　29
遵守する (follow)　776
順序　563, 570, 733, 737–739, 741, 743, 744
使用　172, 304, 342, 776
使用する (use)　522, 706, 804, 868, 958 (→使う, 用いる)
上記　589
消去　854
条件　440, 581, 587, 588, 591, 682, 683, 689, 690, 692, 694, 739, 744, 760, 854, 863, 866, 873, 895, 987, 1052, 1156, 1229, 1250, 1251, 1258, 1261, 1267
条件づけ　780, 1257
証拠　66, 87, 88, 123, 140, 144, 165, 177, 179, 187–195, 232, 238, 262, 290, 322, 1056, 1059, 1099, 1111, 1120, 1181, 1221
詳細　546, 1018, 1223
症例　323
生じさせる (bring)　177
焦点　420, 1188
焦点を当てる (focus)　77, 91, 241, 271, 277, 360,

362, 396, 408, 421, 1027
〜しようとする (try) 119
承認する (approve) 497, 774, 776, 777
静脈内 572
証明する (identify) 212
省略 854
除外された (not included) 643
除外する (drop) 511
除外する (eliminate) 697
除外する (exclude) 506, 514, 818, 843
除外する (omit) 510
除外する (rule out) 1132
除外する (screen out) 509
食物 541
食物カップ 539
女性 461, 463, 468, 470–473, 480, 491, 611, 650
所属する (affiliate) 6
所属する (be) 7, 31
書面 591, 774
知らされていない (blind) 754–756, 761
調べる (examine) 35, 39, 61, 83, 337, 346, 352, 385, 388, 390, 401, 410, 583, 837, 889, 951, 1023, 1035, 1036, 1088, 1156, 1159, 1202
調べる (explore) 242, 450, 1160
調べる (investigate) 36, 93, 137, 340, 347, 415, 809, 1027, 1192, 1207
調べる (study) 139, 364, 366, 371, 389, 402, 412
調べる (test) 38, 525, 649
調べること 936, 1206, 1207
印をつける (endorse) 834
事例 800（→症例）
事例研究 156
白い 1271
進行中である (continue) 305
人口統計（学） 484, 487, 523, 525, 615, 983, 1228
審査する (review) 775
信じる (believe) 273, 1176
診断 325, 341
診断基準 618
慎重 256
進展させる (advance) 1179（→発展させる）
真の 722, 1134
信頼性 17, 662–664, 667, 673, 757, 758
信頼性係数 669
心理学者 76, 94
心理学専攻学生 42

心理学的 141
心理学入門 461
心理学科 491
心理学科目 462, 463

◆す

推計 326
推計する (estimate) 325
推奨する (recommend) 1192
推測する (assume) 1143
推定 610
推定する (estimate) 475, 610, 806, 932, 933, 953, 972, 1261
推定値 323, 1261
随伴性 788
推論する (speculate) 1142
推論的 1197
少ない 346, 352, 1115, 1162
少なくとも 161, 744
スクリープロット 936
ステーション 736
ステップ 956, 957, 959, 962, 966, 1161
ステンレススチール 539
スピーカー 547
座らせる (seat) 592, 595

◆せ

正確 653
生起させる (instigate) 120
制御 536
制御する (control) 557, 674, 809, 813, 947, 968, 971, 1038, 1197
制限 699, 1171
性差 1134
精神測定学的 1196
生成 570
成績 715, 892
清掃 783
正答 720
正当化する (justify) 172
正当性 722, 817
正の 882, 940, 941, 1012
セクション 715
積極的 517
摂取 326, 539–541
接触する (have access to) 48

索　引　　*381*

セッション　512, 678, 720, 732–736, 739, 742, 783, 790–792
接続する (connect)　547, 554
設定　567, 729
設定する (schedule)　735
設定する (set)　805, 914
説得的　1120
説得力のある　164, 190, 193, 194, 371, 1111
切片　948, 973（→y切片）
説明　253, 356, 357, 400, 418, 1122, 1123, 1128, 1131–1133, 1138
説明する (account for)　917, 936, 948, 949
説明する (describe)　704, 839
説明する (explain)　54, 258, 593, 773, 959, 1125, 1128
説明力をもつ　245
世話　545, 776
栓　539
全域で　492
前訓練　559
線形　808, 948
宣言する (declare)　28
先行研究　33, 57, 236, 314, 363, 395, 450, 662, 666, 671, 702, 784, 915, 1084, 1089, 1112, 1144
潜在的　428, 931, 971, 1117
前述　238（→上記）
全体　515, 746, 833, 849, 949, 1100, 1226
全体的　185, 245, 270, 296, 517, 523, 524, 637, 841, 934
選択　849
選択する (select)　601
選択肢　650
前提とする (assume)　427
先入的な知識のない　757
洗練化された　1204

◆そ

増加　369, 855
増加させる (increase)　53, 163, 299, 432
増加する (increase)　158, 785
相関　141, 201, 807, 882, 926, 940, 942, 944, 946, 991–994, 1004, 1012, 1245
相関する (correlate)　200, 220, 938, 939, 1013
相関する (intercorrelate)　943
相関する (relate)　941
相関係数　761, 861, 1231

相関分析　940, 946
相互作用する (interact)　797（→交互作用）
造語する (coin)　113
操作　837, 858, 859, 896
操作する (manipulate)　433, 588, 674, 675, 713, 1033
操作チェック　763–765
操作的に定義される (operationalize)　96
増大　92（→増加）
相対的　471（→比較的）
装置　495, 546, 552, 708, 783, 1246
相反　28
増分妥当性　672
促進　278
測定　136, 744
測定する (measure)　129, 136, 347, 576, 598, 599, 604, 978
測定モデル　1004
測度　41, 45, 65, 69, 128, 132, 133, 220, 441, 613, 614, 623, 632, 639, 654, 640, 642–644, 652, 658, 672, 677, 678, 820, 872, 941
ソフトウェア　557, 921
それぞれ　245, 523, 646, 729, 754, 885, 917, 936, 953, 978, 989, 1235, 1259, 1260
それゆえ　194, 233, 260, 316, 321, 414, 512, 1145
存在　347, 1160
存在しない (lack)　336
存在する (exist)　341, 342
損傷する (lesion)　857

◆た

対応のあるt検定　865
対応関係　852
大会　26, 27
大学　1, 3–5, 461–463, 480, 491, 660, 690, 771, 775, 776
滞在　783, 855
体重　534, 536, 537, 795
対照的　227, 254, 355
対照的である (contrast)　1090
大体　456
大多数　476, 833
態度　41
対比させる (contrast)　400, 459
代表する (be representative of)　523, 525
代表的　1254

大部分　250, 359, 360, 363
タイムリーである (timely)　319
高い　313, 526, 635, 644, 663, 759, 842, 864, 869, 870, 879, 907
高い（尺度における）　630
互いに　736, 910, 943, 1164
多種多様な　141
多数　216, 330, 468
尋ねる (ask)　503, 651
畳む (collapse)　878
達成　507
達成する (accomplish)　406
タッチスクリーン　547
妥当　65
妥当性　38, 135, 613, 662–664, 671, 672
たびたび　85
多変量分散分析　890, 905, 906
ためである (due)　274, 879（→帰される，による）
頼る (rely)　122, 1148
単位得点　461–463
段階　280, 631, 706, 715, 731, 780, 932, 954, 955, 972, 998, 1235
段階的　785
探求する (explore)　114, 348
探索 (explore)　783
探索的　838, 1174
短縮版　622
男性　461, 463, 470–473, 480, 611

◆ ち

地域　466, 480, 516, 536
小さい　245, 899, 963, 980
チェック　17, 757, 763–765
近く　325（→ほぼ）
逐次的　815
知見　64, 69, 74, 160, 221, 223, 226, 240, 279, 307, 320, 429, 431, 452, 453, 457, 879, 1040–1044, 1046–1048, 1056, 1057, 1063, 1064, 1070, 1072, 1075, 1076, 1078, 1080–1083, 1086–1088, 1090, 1091, 1093, 1096, 1133, 1135, 1136, 1140, 1143, 1160, 1171, 1173, 1178, 1180, 1212, 1222
知識　351, 757
着手する (set out)　384
着席　736
チャンスレベル　869
注意　310

注意する (note)　1164, 1167, 1248
中央　47, 550, 569, 783
中央値　475, 477
注視　567
注射　793, 796
注射する (inject)　411, 572
抽出　520, 756, 771, 937
抽出する (draw)　363, 514, 518
抽出する (extract)　49, 817, 914
抽出する (sample)　435
中程度　200, 526, 665, 666, 668, 943, 963
注入　857
注入する (deliver)　793
注目　309, 1048, 1128, 1156
注目すべき (notable)　1128
注目する (note)　309, 313
調査　338, 496–499, 515, 771, 773
調査する (examine)　409
調査する (explore)　75
調査する (investigate)　364
調査票　438, 659
長所　1172, 1175
調整　956
調整する (adjust)　824
調整する (moderate)　964
調整変数　428, 956
調節する (modulate)　401, 797
直接　391, 928
直接的　50, 1198
治療　304, 402, 532, 744, 802, 1148, 1199, 1262

◆ つ

追加する (add)　954
追加的　1232
追跡調査　221, 374（→フォローアップ）
使う (use)　557, 623, 636, 660, 921, 1203（→使用する，用いる）
月　27, 534, 535, 663, 656, 692, 734, 748, 798
つくる (construct)　743
つくる (create)　639（→作成する）
つくる (model)　446
告げる (inform)　497, 530, 774
告げる (tell)　582, 583, 587, 589
伝える (tell)　585
続く (continue)　305, 339, 352, 720, 723, 1110
続く (last)　747

索　引

つながる (lead)　193, 317
強い　259, 942, 943
強く　97, 170, 180, 200, 628, 944, 1083（→強力に）
強まる (strengthen)　179

◆て

である
　宛先は…である (address)　30, 31
　意味は…である (represent)　1220
　時間は…である (last)　732, 792
　内容は…である (consist)　472, 491, 562, 564, 566（→構成される，できている，成り立つ）
　内容は…である (read)　648
　範囲は…である (range)　469, 544, 979
　役割は…である (serve)　118, 467, 763, 930
　…ようである (appear)　57, 372
提案　229, 357, 445, 1112
提案する (present)　82
提案する (propose)　264, 289, 314, 393, 1219
定義　96
定義する (define)　101–103, 105, 916
提起する (raise)　315（→浮かび上がらせる）
提供する (provide)　133, 189, 191, 194, 232, 262, 485, 615, 799, 1120, 1176, 1221
t 検定　802–804, 814, 864, 865, 867
呈示　729, 742
呈示される (turn on)　47, 783
呈示する (offer)　674
呈示する (present)　117, 280, 539, 546, 548, 558, 561, 567–570, 590, 601, 729, 733, 781
程度　300, 386, 454, 627, 1202
定比率　785
ディブリーフィング　773（→研究内容を説明する）
データ　14–16, 25, 26, 39, 156, 164, 191, 234, 413, 480, 511, 596, 799, 820, 826, 844, 884, 922, 924, 932, 948, 1007, 1008, 1017, 1037, 1070, 1094, 1142, 1204
データセット　522
テーブル　592, 595
適合　923, 1241
適合度　923, 934, 974, 1233
適合度指標　934, 935, 974, 1233
適切　601, 932
（～から）できている (consist)　549（→構成される，である，成り立つ）

できない (fail)　1091
できる (able)　144, 232, 505
デザイン　46, 459, 688, 694, 811, 1034, 1201
デジタル　769
テスト　562, 570, 579, 663, 664, 673, 712, 713, 715, 720, 731–733, 744, 783
テストする (test)　446, 466, 551, 595, 684, 736, 748, 856
テストバッテリー　654, 655
手続き　704, 706–708, 719, 776–778
出迎える (greet)　658
テューキーの事後比較検定　813, 909, 910
点　135, 149, 255, 458, 526, 527, 626, 628, 630, 636, 707, 708, 718, 763, 1051, 1153, 1154, 1162, 1271
天井効果　549
点数化する (score)　17, 603, 756
点線　1269
伝達する (convey)　169

◆と

問う (ask)　640
同意　186, 506, 516, 517
同意する (agree)　334, 772, 834
同意する（尺度における）　627, 628
同意しない（尺度における）　627, 628
同一である (identical)　458, 708, 709, 727
同一である (same)　224, 646, 707
統計的検定　868
統合する (integrate)　392
洞察　22, 281, 1109, 1226
洞察を深める (offer…insight into)　1204
同時　1146
同時投与する (coadminister)　797
統制　685, 802, 969
統制群　698, 802, 1257
統制条件　689
当然である (warrant)　372, 1199（→必要である）
同定する (identify)　49, 92, 493, 937, 975, 1193
導入する (obtain)　535（→入手する）
動物実験委員会　776
投与　684, 797
投与量　794, 796, 797
同様　273, 565
通して　800, 807, 816, 848, 1191, 1253
等質性　820

384　　　　　　　　　　　索　　引

溶かす (dissolve)　572
特徴　330, 411, 442, 525, 983, 1128
特徴づける (characterize)　110–112
得点　149, 527, 633, 636, 637, 644, 670, 699, 821–824, 841, 888, 893, 894, 923, 939, 941, 970, 997, 1234
特に　97, 208, 271, 281, 289, 344, 369, 370, 380, 1147–1149, 1185
匿名性　531
独立　754, 756, 758, 817, 864
独立型　554
とする (consider)　843
とする (posit)　267
土台　549
とても…（尺度における）　439
トピック　1206
伴う (accompany)　111
取り入れる (introduce)　134
取り組む (address)　71, 78, 80, 84, 364, 395, 407, 414, 417, 418, 991, 1026, 1158
努力　77, 258, 355
努力する (work)　1196
取る (obtain)　600
ドル　475–477, 497, 499, 500, 502, 503

◆ な

ない (lack)　245, 336
ナイーブ　536, 537
内的整合性　390, 616, 663–669
内的妥当性　672
内容　648
内容妥当性　664
なぜ　317, 354, 376, 422, 1139, 1186, 1209, 1210
名乗る (identify oneself)　482
成り立つ (be composed of)　481, 730, 845（→構成される，である，できている）
成り立つ (comprise)　687（→構成される，である，できている）
成り立つ (consist)　124, 642, 732, 733, 740, 770, 932, 1239（→構成される，である，できている）
なる (lead to)　1207

◆ に

にある (lie in)　321
2 値　820

日記　605
入手可能である (available)　653
入力する (enter)　955
による (due)　1133（→帰される，ためである）

◆ ね

年次　26, 27
年収　476
年俸　475
年齢　130, 469, 472, 473, 534, 544（→歳）

◆ の

濃度　795
能力　598
のことである (describe)　109
のことである (indicate)　101
のことである (refer)　95（→意味する，さす，呼ぶ）
述べる (describe)　716
述べる (express)　1080
述べる (note)　104, 259（→言及する，報告する）
述べる (observe)　274
述べる (represent)　399
述べる (state)　255, 287

◆ は

バージョン　275, 563, 743, 825–827, 921（→版）
媒介する (mediate)　51, 430, 927, 966, 967
媒介変数　933
媒介分析　966
媒介モデル　1004
排除する (rule out)　1034
配信不能　498
配達　536
配置　742, 1247–1249
配置する (assign)　692, 694
配布する (distribute)　659
入る　783
測る (measure)　616, 624（→測定する）
白色　590, 1271
橋渡し　1157
パスウェイ解析　429
外す (screen out)　509
パソコン　556
パターン　141, 151, 183, 934, 1001, 1011
働く (work)　476
発見する (find)　1065

索　　引

発症　315
発達　276
発達する (develop)　76, 146
発達心理学的　1127
発展させる (advance)　1155
発表する (present)　25, 26
幅広い　635
払う (pay)　310
版　616, 622–624, 625（→バージョン）
範囲　149, 323, 439, 1191, 1192
範囲である (range)　55, 473, 475, 516, 546, 673, 800, 919, 943, 979, 1238, 1239, 1245
反映する (reflect)　174, 238, 524, 1126, 1134
反して (contrary)　1063
半数　742（→半分）
反対　66, 231, 357, 742
範疇　483
判定する (determine)　454, 649, 755, 965, 1198
判定法　1196（→評価）
反応　126, 557, 601, 629, 641, 643, 650, 837, 840, 842, 1258, 1264, 1267（→回答）
反応する (respond)　784
反復する (repeat)　744
半分　48, 833（→半数）
番目　304, 761, 933, 961, 1027

◆ひ

日　579, 731, 734, 735, 748, 789, 796
比 (ratio)　820, 1007
比較　802
比較する (compare)　391, 398, 525, 778, 822, 1053
比較的　346, 352, 355
比較適合度指標　923, 1233
引き合わせる (introduce)　495
引き起こす (lead to)　94, 186, 307
引き起こす (result in)　186
引き起こす (trigger)　289
引き換え　461, 462
引き出す (draw)　1213
引く (intrigue)　94
低い　313, 665, 666, 668, 909
低い（尺度における）　630
被験者　588, 589, 983
被験者間　811, 884–888（→子供間，参加者間，被験体間）
被験者内　811, 886–888（→子供内，参加者内，被験体内）
被験体　540, 544, 548, 551, 684, 699, 720, 724, 748, 784, 787
被験体間　812（→子供間，参加者間，被験者間）
被験体内　812（→子供内，参加者内，被験者内）
非常に多くの　84, 166, 167, 170, 1199
必要　256, 310, 366, 505, 1191
必要性 (need)　370
必要である (necessary)　1034, 1161, 1182
必要である (need)　366–368, 376, 1180, 1183, 1193, 1198
必要である (warrant)　372, 1049, 1181（→当然である）
必要とする (require)　373, 1168
等しい　23, 471, 472, 771
一握りの　345, 349
批判　19
批判的　420
秒　546, 559, 601, 747, 793, 840
評価　714, 1196
評価する (assess)　45, 128, 130, 134, 459, 606–609, 611, 619, 622, 623, 625, 633, 639, 648, 713, 856, 858, 890, 892, 923, 934, 947, 1034
評価する (evaluate)　121, 343, 368, 411, 680, 934, 974, 1025, 1028
評価する (rate)　617
表現する (express)　830
表示　565, 566, 1250, 1251
表示域　554
表出　378
標準化 t 検定　803
標準化する (standardize)　632, 637, 919, 923, 1000, 1002, 1196, 1265
標準誤差　990, 1230
標準的　558, 651, 868
標準偏差　469, 472, 473, 476, 473, 632, 735, 985, 986, 988, 989
評定　763
評定する (rate)　617, 627, 630, 647, 760, 764
評定者 (rater)　756, 759–762
評論　174, 202, 248, 420, 422, 423, 448, 1079, 1208, 1210
評論する (review)　173, 419（→概観する）
比率　785
比例　266
広げる (expand)　1205

386 索　引

ヒントを得る　580, 703

◆ ふ

フィードバック　601, 751
フィールド　1203
封筒　660
プール　491
フォローアップ　493（→追跡調査）
不可欠である (critical)　303
不可欠である (essential)　374
賦活する (activate)　88
負荷量　914, 919, 1000
複合的　644
腹腔内　572
含む (contain)　619, 712
含む (include)　332, 612, 643, 654, 655, 714, 851, 918, 954
含む (involve)　199, 298
符号化　754, 761
符号化する (code)　752, 753, 758
符号化担当者　754, 761, 762
不十分　1206
蓋　539
負の　928, 940, 941, 1012
部分　615, 770, 959, 1214
部分集合　758
部分的　8, 25, 927, 1066, 1099, 1125
プラス　1241
フルタイム　476
プログラム　556
プログラムする (program)　555
プロマックス　914
分　47, 546, 659, 676, 732, 736, 737, 739, 745, 747, 782, 783, 793, 840
分解　1005
分割する (break)　844
文献　40, 85, 86, 89, 91, 167, 170, 184, 187, 226, 227, 233, 243, 311, 351, 357, 359, 369, 394, 419, 705, 1087, 1153, 1154–1157, 1173, 1178, 1179
分散　936, 948
分散分析　806, 810, 811, 812, 883–888, 891, 892, 894–896, 898, 900, 902
分析　16, 151, 249, 507, 636, 818, 838, 858, 873, 878, 915, 918, 932, 968, 995, 1066, 1095, 1101, 1104, 1158, 1204
分析する (analyze)　39, 696, 717, 810, 826, 839, 884, 885, 888
再分析する (reanalyze)　1037
分析する (examine)　418, 801, 803, 808, 860, 1191
分析する (investigate)　683, 814, 1197
分析する (explore)　40
分布　526, 862
文脈　255
分野　90, 307, 1154
分類　717, 1232
分類する (categorize)　483, 526
分類する (classify)　153, 800
分類する (group)　641

◆ へ

平均　149, 468, 469, 472–474, 476, 537, 632, 735, 822, 834, 846–848, 865, 874, 943, 973, 977, 985–990, 1230, 1257–1260, 1267
平均する (average)　841, 842, 894
平均的　468, 973
部屋　595
変化　401, 905, 970
変化させる (alter)　797, 856, 889
変化させる (vary)　45, 675
変化する (vary)　893
変形　459
返信する (respond)　497
変数　138, 141, 669, 680, 738, 806, 814, 878, 885, 923, 950, 953, 956, 991, 1038
弁別（的）妥当性　135, 672

◆ ほ

ポイント　569, 590, 1049
包括的　1207
包含　976
報告　307
報告する (describe)　406
報告する (note)　915（→言及する，述べる）
報告する (present)　1157
報告する (provide)　192
報告する (report)　24, 27, 146, 149, 156, 175, 181, 183, 206, 207, 226, 310, 313, 331, 332, 474, 476, 617, 666, 815, 836, 870, 918, 1007, 1008, 1102, 1106
報告する (show)　226
膨大　93, 140
方法　123, 604, 701, 778, 822, 839

索　引

方法論　1200
法律　29
募集する (recruit)　460, 488–492, 513
母集団　523, 524, 1183
保証する (ensure)　508
保証する (guarantee)　531
ボタン　601
ほとんど…ない　35, 343, 344, 350, 365, 413, 1156, 1185
ほとんどの　258
ボランティア　491
ボンフェローニの修正　911

◆ま

マイナス　1241
マウス　601, 783
麻酔する (anesthetize)　795
まったく違う（尺度における）　439
まったく…ない（尺度における）　631, 650
マッチさせる (match)　698, 768
まとめる (combine)　637, 670
ままである (remain)　151, 322, 375, 1139, 1185

◆み

見出す (find)　33, 140, 143, 147, 150, 200, 220, 228, 231, 249, 324, 330, 430, 673, 862, 880, 881, 898, 969, 977, 981, 1073, 1085, 1090, 1091
見出す (obtain)　905
見出す (reveal)　861, 906, 908, 946
見える (appear)　203
未解決　395, 1190
見方　192, 258, 334, 335, 1118（→観点）
水　539–541
見せる (show)　577, 728
満たす (meet)　976
満たす (reach)　720
導く (direct)　773
認める (acknowledge)　1163
みなす (treat)　507
見本　652
見舞われる (witness)　306
見られる (be seen)　101
見られる (find)　86, 881
見られる (indicate)　912
見られる (note)　912
見られる (observe)　882, 905

見られる (obtain)　897
見られる (reveal)　900, 906, 908
見られる (there be)　901, 929, 1009
見られる (yield)　896
見る (watch)　760

◆む

無関係である　143
無作為　520, 525, 570, 689–691, 694, 695, 729, 733, 756, 758, 771
無作為化する (randomize)　737–739, 744, 975
無視する (ignore)　365, 1093
無視する (neglect)　1215
矛盾　224, 226, 643
矛盾する (contradict)　1091
難しい (have difficulty)　288（→困難, 難しさ）
難しさ　715（→困難, 難しい）
結びつき　114, 806, 808
結びつく (be associate with)　963
結びつく (be connected to)　530
結びつく (be tied to)　296
結びつく (have…ties to)　97
結びつける (link)　927

◆め

明暗サイクル　534, 536, 542
明確　185
明確化する (clarify)　261
明確化する (delineate)　344
明瞭化する (illustrate)　272
迷路　550, 783, 798, 1018
メール　30, 31, 496, 498, 530
雌　538, 795

◆も

目的　270, 382, 386, 404–406, 413–415, 755, 766, 1023, 1027, 1029
目的とする (aim)　387, 394, 407, 417
目的とする (seek)　392
目録　613, 616
文字に書き起こす (transcribe)　752, 769
もたらされる (come from)　351
もたらす (produce)　915
もたらす (provide)　187, 190, 192, 193, 299, 1059, 1109, 1161, 1223（→与える）
もたらす (result in)　32, 193（→結果となる）

用いられる (serve)　602
用いる (apply)　100, 451
用いる (employ)　740
用いる (use)　45, 98, 114, 123, 127, 129, 147, 156, 220, 224, 446, 459, 484, 557, 559, 576, 580, 603, 608–610, 616, 622–624, 625, 631, 671, 676, 680, 700, 706, 709, 712, 798, 803, 812, 814, 815, 825, 827, 860, 911, 923, 930, 940, 952, 965, 966, 972, 1198, 1234, 1250, 1255, 1266
モデル　65, 118, 230, 242, 278–282, 291, 293, 295, 297, 298, 397–400, 921–926, 932–935, 949, 950, 953, 958–963, 971, 972, 974, 1002–1004, 1006, 1204, 1233, 1255, 1265
基づく (be based on)　25, 429, 435, 580, 610, 622, 823, 1014, 1063, 1212, 1245
基づく (be guided by)　449
基づく (draw from)　705
もとの　635
求める (ask)　130, 255, 575, 577, 586, 615, 617, 626, 630, 660, 685, 705, 764, 765（→要求する）
モニター　554
問題　78, 79, 302, 315, 318, 358, 361, 373, 381, 407, 408, 414, 417, 457, 575, 1026, 1148, 1184, 1185, 1190, 1197

◆や

役立つ (help)　1222
役立つ (serve)　118, 763
薬物　684, 797
役割を果たす (play a role)　162（→関与する）

◆ゆ

有意　56, 142, 201, 218, 220, 313, 860, 862–866, 869–875, 877, 878, 891–896, 898–901, 903–907, 909, 910–912, 928, 938–941, 943–947, 959, 960, 962–964, 981, 982, 986, 1012, 1013, 1020, 1272
有意差傾向　879, 881, 882
有意水準　804, 805, 868
有意性　804
有益　13, 18, 21, 89, 222, 1187
有効　515, 554, 859
有効性　858
誘発する (elicit)　873
有望　1151
有望性　1117
有用　19, 133, 1202

有用性　1157
床　549
行き先　715
由来する (stem from)　298

◆よ

よい　230, 924, 925
よく　54, 409, 412, 922, 1241
容易　595
要因　76, 87, 92, 185, 212, 312, 619, 694, 806, 810–812, 829, 883, 887, 888, 891, 892, 895, 900, 903, 905, 918, 928, 969, 978, 1002, 1149
要求　653
要求する (ask)　629（→求める）
要求する (require)　125, 145, 517, 574, 605, 772, 781
要件　504
用語　98–100, 113, 815
様式　119
要する (take)　737, 745（→時間がかかる）
ようである (appear)　57, 345, 372
要約　1022, 1208, 1213, 1223
要約する (summarize)　765, 983, 984, 1003, 1069
予想　1060
予想する (envision)　1201
予想する (expect)　275, 328, 1062, 1115
予想する (predict)　876
予想外　1064
予測　230, 248, 295, 761, 1059, 1061, 1063, 1083
予測する (be predictive of)　960
予測する (lead to the prediction)　295
予測する (predict)　197, 237, 296, 434, 953, 961, 970
予測変換　56, 809, 958
予備的　27, 751, 787, 1056, 1113
予備的研究　749, 750
呼ぶ (call)　107
呼ぶ (refer)　106（→意味する，さす，のことである）
よりも (compared)　925（→比べて）
弱く　200
弱める (attenuate)　1100
弱める (reduce)　266

◆ら

来訪する (come)　735

ラット　699, 742, 761, 795

◆り

利益相反　28
理解　412, 766, 1205, 1227
理解する (understand)　369, 409, 410, 1220
理解できる (gain an understanding)　412
理解できる (understandable)　1127
罹患　149, 205, 324
リスト　561, 563, 651, 991
リッカート型　631
リッカート尺度　636（→尺度）
立証する (document)　256, 355
立証する (establish)　182, 662, 1130
理にかなう　1143, 1144
理由　288, 371, 422, 1129, 1136, 1138, 1139
留意する (note)　1045, 1218
量　572, 793
料金別納　660
両親　493
利用する (draw on)　447
量的　820
理論　106, 123, 239, 241, 264–271, 273, 275, 277, 295, 296, 449, 1061, 1081, 1082, 1178, 1218
理論家　276
理論的　258, 358, 1127, 1128
理論的根拠　122, 443, 444
臨床心理学的　1127
臨床的　487, 1127
倫理委員会　774, 775

◆る

類似　621, 1214

累積する (accumulate)　166

◆れ

例　423, 851, 1250, 1251, 1254
例外　1093, 1238
例証する (demonstrate)　37, 54, 142, 145, 166, 176, 191, 375, 415, 671, 672, 1076, 1086, 1087, 1114, 1116, 1155, 1214, 1216（→示す）
例証する (illustrate)　213, 999, 1104, 1157（→示す）
例題　725, 728
レベル　45, 715, 846, 869, 870, 874
連続　561, 687, 720, 734, 814
連続変数　814
連絡を行う (contact)　493

◆ろ

録音する (audiotape)　769
ロジスティック回帰分析　809, 965
論じる (discuss)　73, 74, 255, 311, 1068
論点　272, 370
論評する (comment)　274
論文　815

◆わ

y 切片　948（→切片）
枠組み　203, 242, 393, 1207
分ける (block)　731
わずか　351, 359
割り当てる (assign)　563, 689–691, 693, 695, 699
割増　463
悪い　924

著者略歴

高橋 雅治(たかはし まさはる)
1986年 北海道大学大学院心理学専攻博士後期課程単位取得退学.
現 在 旭川医科大学医学部教授(文学博士).専門は学習心理学・認知神経科学.

デイビッド・W・シュワーブ(David W. Shwalb)
1985年 ミシガン大学発達心理学博士課程修了.
現 在 Southern Utah University 教授(Ph.D).専門は発達心理学・異文化間比較心理学.

バーバラ・J・シュワーブ(Barbara J. Shwalb)
1986年 ミシガン大学心理学および教育学博士課程修了.
現 在 Southern Utah University 講師(Ph.D).専門は発達心理学・異文化間比較心理学.

心理学英語[精選]文例集　　定価はカバーに表示

2019年3月15日 初版第1刷

著 者	高 橋 雅 治
	デイビッド・W・シュワーブ
	バーバラ・J・シュワーブ
発行者	朝 倉 誠 造
発行所	株式会社 朝 倉 書 店

東京都新宿区新小川町6-29
郵便番号　162-8707
電 話　03(3260)0141
Ｆ Ａ Ｘ　03(3260)0180
http://www.asakura.co.jp

〈検印省略〉

Ⓒ 2019〈無断複写・転載を禁ず〉　　真興社・渡辺製本

ISBN 978-4-254-52021-7　C3011　　Printed in Japan

JCOPY　＜出版者著作権管理機構 委託出版物＞
本書の無断複写は著作権法上での例外を除き禁じられています.複写される場合は,そのつど事前に,出版者著作権管理機構(電話 03-5244-5088, FAX 03-5244-5089, e-mail: info@jcopy.or.jp)の許諾を得てください.

旭川医大 髙橋雅治・
D.W.シュワーブ・B.J.シュワーブ著
心理学のための 英語論文の基本表現
52018-7 C3011　　　　A5判 208頁 本体3000円

実際の論文から集めた約400の例文を，文章パターンや解説，和訳とあわせて論文構成ごとに提示。アメリカ心理学会（APA）のマニュアルも解説。〔構成〕心理学英語論文の執筆法／著者注／要約／序文／方法／結果／考察／表／図

日大 羽生和紀著
心理学のための 英語論文の書き方・考え方
52019-4 C3011　　　　A5判 196頁 本体2800円

英語論文の発想や考え方からスタイル・投稿の心構えまでわかりやすく解説。〔内容〕構成・展開・文章のスタイル／文体・文法／単語の選び方／英語力／内容の法則／論文の構造分析／表と図／投稿・再投稿／Q&A／参考図書・引用文献

前広大 坂和正敏・名市大 坂和秀晃・
南山大 Marc Bremer著
自然・社会科学者のための 英文Eメールの書き方
10258-1 C3040　　　　A5判 200頁 本体2800円

海外の科学者・研究者との交流を深めるため，礼儀正しく，簡潔かつ正確で読みやすく，短時間で用件を伝える能力を養うためのEメールの実例集である。〔内容〕一般文例と表現／依頼と通知／訪問と受け入れ／海外留学／国際会議／学術論文／他

京大 青谷正妥著
英　語　学　習　論
—スピーキングと総合力—
10260-4 C3040　　　　A5判 180頁 本体2300円

応用言語学・脳科学の知見を踏まえ，大人のための英語学習法の理論と実践を解説する。英語学習者・英語教師必読の書。〔内容〕英語運用力の本質と学習戦略／結果を出した学習法／言語の進化と脳科学から見た「話す・聞く」の優位性

核融合科学研 廣岡慶彦著
理科系のための 入門英語プレゼンテーション
［CD付改訂版］
10250-5 C3040　　　　A5判 136頁 本体2600円

著者の体験に基づく豊富な実例を用いてプレゼン英語を初歩から解説する入門編。ネイティブスピーカー音読のCDを付してパワーアップ。〔内容〕予備知識／準備と実践／質疑応答／国際会議出席に関連した英語／付録（予備練習／重要表現他）

核融合科学研 廣岡慶彦著
理科系のための 実戦英語プレゼンテーション
［CD付改訂版］
10265-9 C3040　　　　A5判 136頁 本体2800円

豊富な実例を駆使してプレゼン英語を解説。質問に答えられないときの切り抜け方など，とっておきのコツも伝授。音読CD付〔内容〕心構え／発表のアウトライン／研究背景・動機の説明／研究方法の説明／結果と考察／質疑応答／重要表現

千葉大 斎藤恭一・千葉大 梅野太輔著
アブストラクトで学ぶ 理系英語 構造図解50
10276-5 C3040　　　　A5判 160頁 本体2300円

英語論文のアブストラクトで英文読解を練習。正確に解釈できるように文の構造を図にしてわかりやすく解説。強力動詞・コロケーションなど，理系なら押さえておきたい重要語句も丁寧に紹介した。研究室配属後にまず読みたい一冊。

前筑波大 海保博之監修　慶大 坂上貴之編
朝倉実践心理学講座1
意思決定と経済の心理学
52681-3 C3311　　　　A5判 224頁 本体3600円

心理学と経済学との共同領域である行動経済学と行動的意思決定理論を基盤とした研究を紹介，価値や不確実性について考察。〔内容〕第I部「価値を測る」／第II部「不確実性を測る」／第III部「不確実な状況での意思決定を考える」

日本基礎心理学会監修
坂上貴之・河原純一郎・木村英司・
三浦佳世・行場次朗・石金浩史責任編集
基礎心理学実験法ハンドブック
52023-1 C3011　　　　B5判 608頁 本体17000円

多岐にわたる実験心理学の研究法・実験手続きを1冊で総覧。各項目2ないし4頁で簡潔に解説。専門家・学生から関心のある多様な分野の研究者にも有用な中項目事典。〔内容〕基礎（刺激と反応，計測と精度，研究倫理，など）／感覚刺激の作成と較正（視覚，聴覚，触覚・体性など）／感覚・知覚・感性（心理物理学的測定法，評定法と尺度校正など）／認知・記憶・感情（注意，思考，言語など）／学習と行動（条件づけなど）／生理学的測定法（眼球運動，脳波など）／付録

上記価格（税別）は 2019年2月現在